The Crime of Aggression in International Criminal Law

Sergey Sayapin

The Crime of Aggression in International Criminal Law

Historical Development, Comparative Analysis and Present State

ASSER PRESS

Springer

Sergey Sayapin
Prevention and Communication Department
ICRC Regional Delegation in Central Asia
Tashkent
Uzbekistan

ISBN 978-90-6704-926-9 ISBN 978-90-6704-927-6 (eBook)
DOI 10.1007/978-90-6704-927-6

Library of Congress Control Number: 2013951246

Published by T.M.C. ASSER PRESS, The Hague, The Netherlands www.asserpress.nl

Produced and distributed for T.M.C. ASSER PRESS by Springer-Verlag Berlin Heidelberg

Printed on acid-free paper

Springer is part of Springer Science+Business Media (www.springer.com)

Foreword

The subject of this monograph is the act of aggression—a topic, which lies at the very heart of both public international law and international criminal law. Acts of aggression are, on the one hand, a State's internationally wrongful acts that violate the prohibition of the use of force, and, on the other hand, the conduct of leaders of a State for which they can be held individually criminally responsible. The talented young researcher comprehensively addresses these two concepts.

The first part of the book discusses the act of aggression as an internationally wrongful act by a State. The Author introduces this first part by reaching back far into the history of mankind, to that of Ancient Greece and China. The more detailed recent history benefits from the Author's Uzbek background in that he also analyses, for example, the Soviet Union's policies with respect to the act of aggression, and, as such, delves into a diversity of sources in the Russian language. When addressing the *ius ad bellum* as it stands today, the Author, in line with prevailing legal theory, gives the United Nations Charter, and especially the Security Council's powers under Chapter VII of this Charter, the central role in maintaining peace. He also refers to recent conflicts and analyses newly developed doctrines and concepts, such as the humanitarian intervention or the "pro-democratic intervention", which expose weaknesses in this system.

The main focus of this work lies in the second part, which is entitled "The Individual Crime". The Author recalls the crucial role that the judgment of the Nuremberg Military Tribunal played in the development of international criminal law in that it established that individuals may be criminally responsible for crimes that affect the international community as a whole. The Author also discusses the historically central role of "crimes against peace", which are a source of the present day "most serious crimes of concern to the international community as a whole", as expressed in Article 5 of the Rome Statute, and include crimes against humanity, genocide and war crimes.

The Author recalls and discusses the relevant aspects of this judgment and of that by the Tokyo Military Tribunal as well as of those delivered under the Control Council Law No. 10. On that basis, he carries out an insightful analysis of the codification of this crime in national systems and of the customary international law view on the crime of aggression.

The codification of the crime of aggression at the international level only took place in June 2010 at the First Review Conference of the Rome Statute. An amendment to the Rome Statute was adopted that endows the International Criminal Court with jurisdiction over this crime as of 2017 at the earliest. States have now started to ratify this amendment. The Author's analyses culminate in a discussion of the *actus reus* and the *mens rea* elements of the crime of aggression as laid down in Article 8*bis* of the Rome Statute, as well as in an explanation of the complex mechanism that will allow the International Criminal Court to exercise its jurisdiction.

This monograph is based on a thorough study of the available English, German and, in particular, Russian academic sources relevant to the crime of aggression and addresses in-depth all relevant aspects of the subject, while also demonstrating clarity of expression and quality of analysis. It is a highly commendable work, not only for academics and students in this area, but also for practitioners in this field of law. It is hoped that the Author will continue to contribute as a researcher to this field of law.

The Hague, Summer 2013

Anita Ušacka
Judge, Appeals Division, International Criminal Court
Professor, Dr. iur, LL.D (Lewis and Clark Law School)
Former Judge, Constitutional Court of Latvia

Preface

Since after the Second World War, the crime of aggression is – along with genocide, crimes against humanity and war crimes – a "core crime" under international law. However, despite a formal recognition of aggression as a matter of international criminal law and the reinforcement of the international legal regulation of the use of force by States, numerous international armed conflicts occurred but no one was ever prosecuted for aggression since 1949.

This book examines the evolution of aggression as an internationally wrongful act of State and a corresponding individual crime. After a cross-cultural historical introduction to the subject, it offers an overview of contemporary international law on the use of inter-State armed force, and makes an original proposal for the development of Draft Articles on the use of force by States. The book makes a case for a judicial review of the inter-State use of force – by the International Court of Justice or, as the case may be in the future, by the International Criminal Court. It further scrutinises in a detailed manner the relevant jurisprudence of the Nuremberg and Tokyo Tribunals as well as of the Nuremberg follow-up trials, and makes proposals for a more successful prosecution for aggression in the future. In identifying customary international law on the subject, the volume draws upon a wealth of applicable sources of national criminal law and puts forward a useful classification of States' legislative approaches towards the criminalisation of aggression at the national level. It also offers a detailed analysis of the current international legal regulation of the use of force and of the Rome Statute's substantive and procedural provisions pertaining to the exercise of the International Criminal Court's jurisdiction with respect to the crime of aggression, after 1 January 2017.

It is hoped that the book would be useful to both practitioners and students of international law and relations in that it brings together, in a comparative fashion, the normative experience of various States representing the major legal systems of the world, and of relevant international organs, and seeks to identify ways for reinforcing individual criminal responsibility for the use of inter-State force in contravention of international law.

Tashkent, December 2013 — Sergey Sayapin

Acknowledgments

I have carried out research for this book under the guidance of Professor Gerhard Werle at the Humboldt-Universität zu Berlin. I am very grateful to Professor Werle for his attention towards details, pedagogical wisdom and continued support throughout my research. Working with him has been a most remarkable academic experience. My sincere thanks are also due to Professor Florian Jessberger at the Universität Hamburg, and to Professor Martin Heger at the Humboldt-Universität zu Berlin. I was also most fortunate to benefit from the superior professionalism and human qualities of current and former staff members of Professor Werle's Chair: my work was greatly facilitated by Ms. Anja Schepke, Dr. Paul Christoph Bornkamm, Dr. Moritz Vormbaum, Dr. Gregoria Palomo Suárez and Mr. Aziz Epik. Ms. Elke Nuerck and Ms Petra Krause were most helpful in following the administrative aspects of my research.

I take this occasion to thank colleagues from whose expertise in law or linguistics I benefited while identifying and interpreting relevant pieces of national legislation: Associate Professor Gleb Bogush (Russia), Ms Irene Chang (USA), Professor Eric David (Belgium), Ms Clare Feikert (USA), Mr. Donald M. Ferencz (United Kingdom), Associate Professor Mykola Gnatovsky (Ukraine), Mr. Tahir Hanfi (Pakistan), Mr. Matthew D. Heaphy (USA), Mr. Piotr Kielic (Poland), Associate Professor Timur Korotkyy (Ukraine), Mr. Alpaslan Mamak (Turkey), Miss Polina Nevzorova (Uzbekistan), Dr. Yaël Ronen (Israel), Mr. Peter Roudik (USA), Associate Professor Vera Rusinova (Russia), Professor Yuval Shany (Israel), Mr. Kersi B. Shroff (USA), Mr. Issam M. Saliba (USA), Mr. Julio Pinheiro Faro Homem de Siqueira (Brazil), Mr. Eduardo Soares (USA), Dr. Hsien-Li Tan (Singapore) and Associate Professor Vladimir Vardanyan (Armenia).

Likewise, I am immensely grateful to my colleagues and friends at the Regional Delegation of the International Committee of the Red Cross (ICRC) in Central Asia who supported and encouraged me throughout the writing process: Mr. Yves Arnoldy, Mr. Rustam Atadjanov, Mr. Pierre-Emmanuel Ducruet, Mr. Sherzod Eraliev, Mr. Marsel Gabbazov, Mr. Yves Giovannoni, Mr. Abdukhalim Khukumov, Dr. Raffaello Müller, Ms Viktoriya Romanova, Ms Jennet Shihmuradova and Mr. Sergey Shorin. A special word of thanks is due to Dr. Maria Teresa Dutli, formerly ICRC Regional Legal Advisor for Eastern Europe and Central Asia.

I am exceptionally grateful to Judge Anita Ušacka of the International Criminal Court's Appeals Division for her having found the time, despite her very busy schedule, to read the manuscript and the endorsing Foreword.

The staff and reviewers at T. M. C. Asser Press and Springer have been extremely professional throughout the publication process. My special thanks are due to Mr. Philip van Tongeren for his support for the project since the very submission of the manuscript, and to Ms Marjolijn Bastiaans for her expert advice on the manuscript management.

My very special thanks are due to Professor Françoise Hampson (University of Essex, United Kingdom) for her having first shared with me the idea of this book's topic, and to Dr. Ravshan Khakimov, Chairman of the Uzbek Association of International Law and my first teacher of international law at Tashkent's University of World Economy and Diplomacy, for his having inspired my interest for what subsequently became my passion and profession.

Finally – but no less importantly – I thank my mother, Ms. Olga Sayapina, for her being a fantastic mom and friend. I would not have succeeded without her love, support, attention and smile.

Obviously, any omission in the book remains entirely my responsibility. I will be pleased to receive readers' comments and advice at: sergey.sayapin@yahoo.com.

Contents

Abbreviations

ACHPR	African Charter of Human and Peoples' Rights
ACHR	American Convention on Human Rights
AJCL	American Journal of Comparative Law
AJIL	American Journal of International Law
ALER	American Law and Economics Review
ASP	Assembly of States Parties
AUILR	American University International Law Review
AULR	American University Law Review
Asian JIL	Asian Journal of International Law
BCICLR	Boston College International and Comparative Law Review
BYIL	British Yearbook of International Law
Case Western Reserve JIL	Case Western Reserve Journal of International Law
Chinese JIL	Chinese Journal of International Law
CIS	Commonwealth of Independent States
Columbia JTL	Columbia Journal of Transnational Law
CLF	Criminal Law Forum
CSTO	Collective Security Treaty Organisation
Duke JCIL	Duke Journal of Comparative and International Law
Duke LJ	Duke Law Journal
ECHR	European Convention on Human Rights
EJCCLCJ	European Journal of Crime, Criminal Law and Criminal Justice
EJIL	European Journal of International Law
Fordham ILJ	Fordham International Law Journal
German YIL	German Yearbook of International Law
Harvard ILJ	Harvard International Law Journal
Hastings ICLR	Hastings International and Comparative Law Review
HuV-I	Humanitäres Völkerrecht—Informationsschriften
Indiana ICLR	Indiana ICLR
ICC	International Criminal Court
ICCPR	International Covenant on Civil and Political Rights
ICC Statute	Rome Statute of the International Criminal Court
ICJ	International Court of Justice
ICL	International Criminal Law

ICLQ	International and Comparative Law Quarterly
ICRC	International Committee of the Red Cross
ICTR	International Criminal Tribunal for Rwanda
ICTY	International Criminal Tribunal for the Former Yugoslavia
IHL	International Humanitarian Law
ILC	International Law Commission
ILP	International Law and Politics
ILQ	International Law Quarterly
IRPL	International Review of Penal Law
IRRC	International Review of the Red Cross
JCS	Journal of Church and State
JCSL	Journal of Conflict and Security Law
JICJ	Journal of International Criminal Justice
LCP	Law and Contemporary Problems
Leiden JIL	Leiden Journal of International Law
McGill LJ	McGill Law Journal
Michigan JIL	Michigan Journal of International Law
NATO	North Atlantic Treaty Organisation
NGO	Non-Governmental Organisation
Pace ILR	Pace International Law Review
RC	Review Conference
Rome Statute	Rome Statute of the International Criminal Court
SULR	Seattle University Law Review
UN	United Nations
UN GA	United Nations General Assembly
UNTS	United Nations Treaty Series
UPJIL	University of Pennsylvania Journal of International Law
US	United States
USA	United States of America
USSR	Union of the Soviet Socialist Republics
WGCA	Working Group on the Crime of Aggression
WUGSLR	Washington University Global Studies Law Review
Yale JIL	Yale Journal of International Law
YBILC	Yearbook of the International Law Commission
ZaöRV	Zeitschrift für ausländisches öffentliches Recht und Völkerrecht

Introduction

Wars have been plaguing humanity since time immemorial, and even now, at the beginning of the twenty-first century, a statement made in 1880 by the Institute of International Law appears to be an unfortunate truism: "War holds a great place in history, and it is not to be supposed that men will soon give it up—in spite of the protests which it arouses and the horror which it inspires [...]".[1] Throughout history, war has, over and over again, been condemned, rationalised and idealised. As John Keegan has commented so passionately, "[w]arfare is almost as old as man himself, and reaches into the most secret places of the human heart, places where self dissolves rational purpose, where pride reigns, where emotion is paramount, where instinct is king".[2] Having probably been among men's strongest passions, war has certainly been one of their most important occupations. According to Jean S. Pictet (1914–2002), of the past 3,400 years, no more than 250 years were entirely peaceful, and around 14,000 wars occurred during the past 5,000 years.[3] Over millennia, wars were waged for plunder and booty, to acquire new territories and subjects, for religious reasons or, more recently, out of a desire to implant particular political, ideological or economic systems on new grounds.[4] Historically, in some cultures, warfare was indeed part of the respective civilisations themselves.[5] Unlike in the past, when wars were almost always regarded as a natural business of States and their sovereigns and could be waged, with not too many formalities, as soon as a suitable *casus belli* presented (or invented) itself, today's wars do usually require rather sophisticated pretexts, and their conduct is increasingly formalised by the written *jus in bello*[6] and customary international humanitarian law.[7]

[1] Institute of International Law, Preface to the Manual on the Laws of War on Land 1880, quoted in: Neff (2005, p. vi).

[2] See Keegan (2004, p. 3).

[3] Pictet (2001, p. 91).

[4] Teichman (2006, p. 6).

[5] Such cultures include, for example, the Zulus in southern Africa, the Mamelukes (slave warriors) in the medieval Muslim Caliphates, or the Samurais in Japan. See Keegan (2004, pp. 24–46).

[6] According to some Authors, international humanitarian law has even become too detailed, "unreal" and "*too* humane"—and hence too complex to apply in practice. See Robertson (2002, p. 197) (emphasis in original).

[7] See, generally, Henckaerts, and Doswald-Beck (2005).

These juridical formalities do not, however, always succeed in making modern wars more just or less cruel.

Few issues of international law are as sensitive and problematic as that of aggression.[8] As Benjamin Ferencz put it, "[i]t is seemingly easier to evoke aggression than to dispel it, and easier to commit aggression than to define it".[9] The notion is highly sensitive in that it directly concerns State sovereignty,[10] and it is problematic, because no legally binding definition of potentially universal application could be produced, until just recently, either for the purpose of State responsibility or with a view to establishing individual criminal responsibility for directing acts of aggression committed by States. Despite some isolated attempts in the past,[11] the launching or waging of aggressive wars was not criminally punishable until after the Second World War. True, there were ideas and policies aimed at the prevention of wars throughout history. Already in the later part of the first millennium BC, some initial signs of perception of war as a pathological, unnatural state of affairs were recorded in civilisations as distant from each other, both geographically and culturally, as China and Rome.[12] In Ancient Rome, this tendency was subsequently reinforced by Christianity, which propounded a strong (although not complete)[13] rejection of war and quite quickly became a leading teaching throughout the Roman Empire.[14] During the Middle Ages, an important "peace programme" (Peace of God and Truce of God), which encouraged "kings and princes to take up the restoration of order in their own interests",[15] was implemented in Western Europe under the influence of the Catholic Church. Equally, Eastern European and non-European cultures continued offering philosophical and political initiatives to the same effect.[16]

---

[8] See Borchard (1933, pp. 114–117); Borchard (1941, pp. 618–625); Borchard (1942, 628–631); Borchard (1943, 46–57); Carlston (1966, pp. 728–734); Cherkes (2009, pp. 103–119); Eagleton (1951, pp. 719–721); generally, Franck (2002); Gorohovskaya (2009, 45–52); Inogamova-Hegay (2009, 139–156); generally, Karoubi (2004); Keegan (2004); Kelsen (1944); Koh (2011, 57–60); Steinberg and Zasloff (2006, pp. 64–87); generally, Stone (1958); Teichman (2006); Verdirame (2007, pp. 83–162); Wright (1925, 76–103); Wright (1953, pp. 365–376); Wright (1956, 514–532); Yasuaki (2003, pp. 105–139); generally, Walzer (1977); Weisburd (1997).

[9] Ferencz (1972, pp. 491).

[10] See Baumgarten (1931, pp. 305–334); Baumgarten (1933, pp. 192–207); Koskenniemi (2011, pp. 61–70); Lansing (1907a, pp. 105–128); Lansing (1907b, pp. 297–320); Lansing (1921, pp. 13–27); Loewenstein (1954, 222–244); McCarthy (2010, pp. 43–74); Schrijver (2000, 65–98); Wang (2004, pp. 473–484); generally, Levin (2003).

[11] See, for example, Maridakis (2006, pp. 847–852).

[12] See Neff (2005, p. 14).

[13] Apparently, even Jesus himself did not resent the occurrence of "just" wars: "Do not think that I have come to bring peace on earth; I have not come to bring peace, but a sword" (Gospel of Matthew 10:34).

[14] See Teichman (2006, p. 164).

[15] Contamine (1984, pp. 270–274).

[16] See Teichman (2006, pp. 153–161). For details, see infra Chap. 1, especially 1.1.1.1, 1.1.1.2, 1.1.1.4.

However, none of these policies could amount, at the time, to a decisive prohibition of resorting to armed force in inter-State relations, and still less could they warrant the individual criminal responsibility of authors of even most perilous aggressive wars. For instance, on 13 March 1815, by a declaration issued in reaction to Napoleon's escape from Elba, he was excluded "from civil and social relations" for his previous actions "as an Enemy and Disturber of the tranquillity of the World".[17] However, the practical decision to imprison him without trial "not only until Peace, but after Peace" was regarded by some leading international lawyers as an "Exception to general rules of the Law of Nations".[18] Just over a century later, the arraigned German Kaiser Wilhelm II escaped punishment in that he had found refuge in The Netherlands after Germany's defeat in the First World War, and the Allies' request for his extradition was refused. Moreover, the Commission on the Responsibility of the Authors of the War concluded that the "supreme offence against international morality and the sanctity of treaties" the Kaiser had committed was rather a "moral" one, and not one under international law of the time.[19] During the 1920s, the Draft Treaty of Mutual Assistance (1923) and the League of Nations Protocol for the Settlement of International Disputes (1924) referred to aggressive war as an international crime but none of these treaties was ever ratified (see infra1.1.6.3). The idea was also incorporated in relevant resolutions adopted by the League of Nations (1927) and the Pan American Conference (1928)[20] but those resolutions did not possess a binding force.

Even after the Second World War, it was not established, until after the Judgment of the Nuremberg Tribunal had been pronounced (see infra3.1.1) and subsequently reaffirmed by a United Nations General Assembly Resolution,[21] that the launching of an aggressive war was a crime. There exists evidence that "only one year before the London Conference three of the big four had gone on record that aggressive war was not in itself a crime".[22] During the Conference itself, there was substantial doubt as to whether there had existed a customary basis for charges of aggressive war.[23] Whilst the impact of the Nuremberg and Tokyo trials on the subsequent development of international law is now undisputed, details of their material law and procedure were criticised extensively both by contemporary commentators and during the decades that followed.[24] Some of the essential critique focused on the *ex post facto* character of the charge of aggressive war. The Nuremberg International Military Tribunal had to interpret the London Charter at

[17] Stewart (1951), at 573, especially note 8.

[18] *Ibid.*, p. 574.

[19] See Cryer (2005, pp. 33–34), especially note 196.

[20] International Military Tribunal (Nuremberg), Judgment of 1 October 1946, p. 446.

[21] See UN General Assembly Resolution 95(I), 11 December 1946.

[22] Minear (1971, p. 50).

[23] *Report of Robert H. Jackson 1949, pp. 65–67, 295, 327, 335.*

[24] For an overview of such critique, see Kelsen (1944, pp. 13–15); Kelsen (1947), 156 et seq.; Tomuschat (2006, 830–844). For details, see infra Chap. 1, especially 1.2.1 and 1.2.2.

length, in order to substantiate its compatibility with existing international law (see infra3.1.1). In turn, at the Tokyo trial (see infra3.1.2), where the majority of Judges concurred with their colleagues at Nuremberg in the interpretation of the rules on the crime of aggressive war, two dissenting (by Judges Pal and Röling) and one concurring (by Judge Bernard) opinion were nevertheless formulated, which cast doubt on the legal supportability of the charge of aggression.[25]

After 1948, the crime of aggression entered the national criminal laws of many States (see infra4.1) but it was not treated as a matter of binding *international* law for over half a century. The 1949 Geneva Conventions for the Protection of Victims of War set up an ambitious system for the penal repression of their grave breaches as war crimes[26] but, surprisingly enough, no similar mechanism was established to criminalise the "supreme international crime", as aggression was termed at the Nuremberg trial. The 1968 United Nations Convention on the Non-applicability of Statutory Limitations to War Crimes and Crimes against Humanity left the crime of aggression beyond its scope.[27] The Statute of the International Criminal Tribunal for the Former Yugoslavia did not mention the crime of aggression among the crimes within the Tribunal's jurisdiction, although it might have theoretically done so.[28] As a result of a lasting international political unwillingness to move forward decisively, the authors of some alleged crimes of aggression managed to evade justice.[29] As M. Cherif Bassiouni so rightly noted, "[t]he history of ICL is one driven by facts, characterised by practical experiences, dominated by pragmatism, and constantly gripped by the conflicting demands of *realpolitik* on the one hand, and those of justice on the other".[30] It appears that with regard to the crime of aggression the demands of *realpolitik* were, time and again, more successful than those of justice.

There existed hope that this political unwillingness would come to an end in 1998, with the adoption of the Rome Statute of the International Criminal Court.[31] However, due to pressure from some delegations at the Rome Conference and the absence of a general consensus on the applicable international law,[32] it was impossible to define the crime before the adoption of the Statute. The Court was given jurisdiction over the crime of aggression on the futuristic condition that it

---

[25] Cryer (2005, p. 243). See also Röling and Cassese (1992, p. 67).

[26] See Article 50 of the First Geneva Convention, Article 51 of the Second Geneva Convention, Article 130 of the Third Geneva Convention and Article 147 of the Fourth Geneva Convention.

[27] See UN General Assembly resolution 2391 (XXIII), annex, 23 UN GAOR Supp. (No. 18) at 40, U.N. Doc. A/7218 (1968), Article I.

[28] See Cryer (2005, 244); Zolo (2007, p. 804).

[29] As Cassese notes, "since 1946 there have been no national or international trials for alleged crimes of aggression, although undisputedly in many instances States have engaged in acts of aggression, and in few cases the Security Council has determined that such acts were committed by States". See Cassese (2003, p. 112).

[30] Bassiouni (2003, p. 18).

[31] See Akhavan (2001, pp. 7–31).

[32] Leanza (2004, pp. 12–15).

would be exercised "once a provision is adopted in accordance with articles 121 and 123 defining the crime and setting out the conditions under which the Court shall exercise jurisdiction with respect to this crime. Such a provision shall be consistent with the relevant provisions of the Charter of the United Nations".[33] The subsequent drafting process stretched itself over 12 years after the adoption of the Rome Statute and finally resulted in the adoption of relevant substantive and procedural provisions in 2010.[34]

Now as the 2010 Kampala amendments pertaining to the crime of aggression for the purpose of the International Criminal Court are accumulating ratifications required for their entry into force—and once they reach the requisite threshold of 30 ratifications and the ICC Assembly of States Parties activates the Court's jurisdiction with respect to the crime (see infra5.1.2 and 5.3.2.2), the prosecution of individuals for its planning, preparation, initiation or execution may take a qualitatively new turn—it is important to take stock of relevant developments in customary and conventional international law, to identify current challenges to the international legal regulation of the use of force in inter-State relations, and to suggest measures for enforcing—as efficiently as possible—individual criminal liability for the crime of aggression at the international and national levels. More particularly, I intended:

- to comprehensively consider the evolution of various cultures' attitudes towards war, and to single out key factors, which had contributed to the restraint of States' recourse to war as an instrument of national or international policy;
- to re-examine the current regulation of the inter-State use of force under conventional and customary international law, as well as under applicable *jus cogens*, and to offer a classification of uses of force by States in the light of applicable international law;
- with due regard to relevant twentieth century international jurisprudence, to demonstrate the functional relationship between aggressive State conduct and individual acts prompting such conduct, and accordingly to substantiate the criminality of individual acts leading to States' acts of aggression and other crimes against peace;
- to study, in a comparative fashion, the predominant legislative approaches towards the criminalisation of individual acts leading to States' acts of aggression and other crimes against peace;
- to critically reflect upon the substance of the 2010 Kampala amendments pertaining to the crime of aggression and their implications for the ensuing development of relevant international and national criminal law.

---

33 Rome Statute of the International Criminal Court, U.N. Doc. A/CONF.183/9, adopted on 17 July 1998 (hereinafter referred to as the Rome Statute, the ICC Statute, or the Statute), Article 5(2).

34 For an overview of the drafting process, see infra1.2.6. For a detailed analysis of the relevant provisions adopted at the First Review Conference of the States Parties to the Rome Statute (Kampala, 31 May–11 June 2010), see infra Chap. 5.

Accordingly, this book is organised into six chapters. Chapter 1 considers the historical origins of the legal restraints on the use of force in international relations and of the criminalisation of aggression. In providing a chronological overview of relevant international instruments and examples of State practice, the chapter follows, as much as possible, a multi-civilisation approach, in order to display the international dimensions of the issue and the awareness thereof that had existed in different cultures throughout history. The overall purpose of Chap. 1 is to provide a *historical* introduction into the subject matter of the volume, whereas *substantive* details are given more attention in subsequent chapters.

Chapter 2 dissects aggression as an internationally wrongful act of a State and characterises its definitional elements under applicable modern international law. It starts by analysing the nature of States' obligation under Article 2(4) of the UN Charter to refrain from the threat or use of force in their international relations, and subsequently examines the elements of the 1974 Definition of Aggression, which served as a basis for many—if not most—contemporary legal discussions on the matter. The chapter subsequently analyses the "Charter-based", "Charter-related" and "extra-Charter" exceptions—including, in particular, the protection of a State's own nationals abroad, and so-called "humanitarian" and "pro-democratic interventions"—to the prohibition of the use of force, in order to identify the limits of lawful (and, consequently, unlawful) uses of force by States under international law.

Chapter 3 explores the relationship between aggression as an internationally wrongful act of a State and the individual criminal responsibility of its authors. The foundations for the individual criminal responsibility for the crime of aggression under international law are examined in conjunction with the jurisprudence of the Nuremberg and Tokyo Tribunals and of relevant trials held under the Control Council Law № 10. Next, an overview of provisions on the crime of aggression and other crimes against peace contained in the International Law Commission's Draft Codes of Offences (1951) and of Crimes (1996) against the Peace and Security of Mankind—as vectors leading to the subsequent integration of such crimes in relevant sources of national and international criminal law—is offered.

Chapter 4 offers an overview of 42 national laws criminalising aggression and examines, in a comparative fashion, the *actus reus* and *mens rea* of the crime. With due regard to the applicable legislative models, the material, formal and truncated *corpus delicti* of the crime of aggression—a possible basis for the inference of customary international law on the matter—and the range of the crime's possible subjects are analysed. The chapter also reviews selected problematic issues related to the indirect enforcement of criminal responsibility for the crime of aggression. The propaganda for war is briefly examined as a separate crime.

Finally, Chap. 5 offers an in-depth analysis of the material and procedural provisions on the crime of aggression adopted for the purpose of the Rome Statute of the International Criminal Court. In particular, it analyses the definition of the crime of aggression for the purpose of the Statute, examines the applicability of general principles of criminal law to the crime, expounds the procedural aspects of the exercise of jurisdiction over the crime of aggression by the Court, and offers brief remarks on the Elements of the crime of aggression. Overall conclusions and recommendations are summarised in Chap. 6.

With due regard to the universal nature of the issue under discussion, I have attempted to make the volume as "internationally researched" as possible.[35] The text has primarily been written on the basis of normative and doctrinal sources originally published in English, German, French, Russian and Spanish. Unless indicated otherwise, all translations from the latter four languages into English are mine. I have endeavoured to make the text accurate as of 18 November 2012. Later updates were introduced in the text where possible.

References

Akhavan P (2001) Beyond impunity: can international criminal justice prevent future atrocities? AJIL 95:7–31
Bassiouni MC (2003) Introduction to international crime law. Transnational Publishers, Inc., New York,
Baumgarten A (1931) Souverenität und völkerrecht. ZaöRV 2:305–334
Baumgarten A (1933) Souverenität und völkerrecht. ZaöRV 3:192–207
Borchard E (1933) War and peace. AJIL 27:114–117
Borchard E (1941) War, neutrality and non-belligerency. AJIL 35:618–625
Borchard E (1942) The place of force in international law. AJIL 36:628–631
Borchard E (1943) The place of law and courts in international relations. AJIL 37:46–57
Carlston KS (1966) A framework for the legal analysis of war-peace issues. AJIL 60:728–734
Cassese A (2003) International crime law, Oxford University Press, New York
Cherkes ME (2009) Ispolzovanie sily v mejdunarodnyh otnosheniyah (The use of force in international Relations). Almanach of International Law 1:103–119
Contamine P (1984) War in the middle ages, translated by M. Jones. Basil Blackwell Publisher, Oxford
Cryer R (2005) Prosecuting international crimes: selectivity and the international criminal law regime. Cambridge University Press, Cambridge
Eagleton C (1951) International law or national interest. AJIL 45:719–721
Ferencz BB (1972) Defining aggression: where it stands and where it's going. AJIL 66:491–508
Franck TM (2002) Recourse to force: state action against threats and armed attacks. Cambridge University Press, Oxford
Gorohovskaya EV (2009) Agressiya kak mejdunarodnoe prestuplenie: genezis razvitiya ponyatiya (Aggression as an international crime: the genesis of the notion's development). Almanach of International Law 1:45–52
Henckaerts JM, Doswald-Beck L (eds) (2005) Customary international humanitarian law. Volume I: Rules. Cambridge University Press, Oxford
Inogamova-Hegay LV (2009) Voprosy prestupleniya agressii v mejdunarodnom ugolovnom prave [Issues of the crime of aggression in international criminal law]. In: Bogush GI and Trikoz EN (eds.), Международное уголовное правосудие: современные проблемы [International criminal justice: Contemporary issues], Moscow, p. 139–156
International Military Tribunal (1946). The trial of German major war criminals. In: Proceedings of the international military tribunal sitting at Nuremberg, Germany, Part 22, 22nd August 1946–1st October, 1946

[35] Cf. Petersen 2011, 149–163; Korotkyy 2010, 138–151.

Jackson RH (1949) United States representative to the international conference on military trials. U.S. Government Printing Office, Washington, DC (Report)
Karoubi MT (2004) Just or unjust wars: international law and unilateral use of armed force by states at the turn of the twentieth century. Ashgate, Burlington
Keegan J (2004) A history of warfare, 2nd edn. Norton, Pimlico
Kelsen H (1944) Peace through law. The University of North Carolina Press, Chapel Hill
Kelsen H (1947) Will the judgment in the nuremberg trial constitute a precedent in international law?. ILQ 1:153–171
Koh T (2011) International law and the peaceful resolution of disputes: Asian perspectives, contributions, and challenges. Asian JIL 1:57–60
Korotkyy TR (2010) Ot *jus inter gentes* k *jus inter civilisatione* (From *jus inter gentes* to *jus inter civilisatione*). Almanach of International Law 2:138–151
Koskenniemi M (2011) What use for sovereignty today? Asian JIL 1:61–70
Neff SC (2005) War and the law of nations: a general history. Cambridge University Press, Cambridge
Lansing R (1907a) Notes on sovereignty in a state. AJIL 1:105–128
Lansing R (1907b) Notes on sovereignty in a state. AJIL 1:297–320
Lansing R (1921) Notes on world sovereignty. AJIL 15:13–27
Leanza U (2004) The historical background. In: Politi M, Nesi G (eds) The international criminal court and the crime of aggression. Ashgate Publishing Limited, Aldershot, pp. 3–15
Levin ID (2003) Suverenitet (Sovereignty). Yuridicheskiy Centre Press, Moscow
Loewenstein K (1954) Sovereignty and international co-operation. AJIL 48:222–244
Maridakis GS (2006) An ancient precedent to Nuremberg. JICJ 4:847–852
McCarthy C (2010) The paradox of international law of military occupation: sovereignty and the reformation of Iraq. JCSL 10:43–74
Minear R (1971) Victor's justice: the Tokyo War Crimes Trial. Princeton University Press, Princeton
Petersen N (2011) International law, cultural diversity, and democratic rule: beyond the divide between universalism and relativism. Asian JIL 1:149–163
Pictet J (2001) Razvitie i printsipy mejdunarodnogo gumanitarnogo prava (Development and principles of international humanitarian law). ICRC, Moscow
Robertson G (2002) Crimes against humanity: struggle for global justice, 2nd edn. Penguin Books, Westminster
Röling BVA and Cassese A (1992) The Tokyo trial and beyond. Polity Press, oxford
Schrijver N (2000) The changing nature of state sovereignty. BYIL 71:65–98
Steinberg RH and Zasloff JM (2006) Power and international law. AJIL 100:64–87
Stewart JH (1951) The imprisonment of Napoleon: a legal opinion by Lord Eldon. AJIL 45:571–577
Stone J (1958) Aggression and World Order. University of California Press, Berkeley
Teichman J (2006) The philosophy of war and peace. Imprint Academic, Exeter
Tomuschat C (2006) The legacy of Nuremberg. JICJ 4:830–844
Verdirame G (2007) The 'sinews of peace': international law, strategy, and the prevention of war. BYIL 78:83–162
Walzer M (1977) Just and unjust wars: a moral argument with historical illustrations. Basic Books, New York
Wang G (2004) The impact of globalization on state sovereignty. Chinese JIL 3:473–484
Weisburd AM (1997) Use of force: the practice of states since world war II. The Pennsylvania State University Press, Philadelphia
Wright Q (1925) The outlawry of war. AJIL 19:76–103
Wright Q (1953) The outlawry of war and the law of war. AJIL 47:365–376
Wright Q (1956) The prevention of aggression. AJIL 50:514–532
Yasuaki O (2003) International law in and with international politics: the functions of international law in international society. EJIL 14:105–139
Zolo D (2007) Who is afraid of punishing aggressors? On the double-track approach to international criminal justice. JICJ 5:799–807

Part I
The Internationally Wrongful Act of State

Chapter 1
Historical Background of the Criminalization of Aggression

Abstract Aggression was not criminalized before 1945. Throughout centuries, and in all cultures, despite isolated efforts aimed at setting conditions for "lawful" uses of force, rulers and States felt at liberty to resort to force to enforce their political goals. It was only after the Second World War—more precisely, after the Nuremberg and Tokyo trials, followed by trials under the Control Council Law № 10—that aggression was recognized as a crime under international law. But even then, no more prosecutions for the crime occurred after 1949, for political reasons, despite numerous inter-State uses of force. A revival of the criminalization of aggression came with the adoption, on 17 July 1998, of the Rome Statute of the International Criminal Court where the crime of aggression was listed—along with genocide, crimes against humanity and war crimes—as one within the jurisdiction of the Court. Twelve more years had elapsed before the States Parties to the Statute agreed upon a definition of the crime of aggression for the purpose of the Statute, and upon the complex procedural conditions for the exercise of the Court's jurisdiction with respect to the crime. Generally, the chapter serves as a historical introduction to substantive matters dealt with in subsequent chapters of the book, and provides a background for almost any issue of relevant international law raised elsewhere in the volume.

Contents

S. Sayapin, *The Crime of Aggression in International Criminal Law*,
DOI: 10.1007/978-90-6704-927-6_1,

Human societies knew wars from prehistoric times.[1] Beyond all doubt, warfare had become a usual feature of human living much earlier than did law, State, and other sophisticated social institutions. It arguably is approximately as ancient as religion—another prominent factor in virtually all civilizations.[2] In fact, in the course of millennia, war became a legal and social institution of such a standing that its legitimacy was never disputed seriously until the first half of the past century[3]—a markedly immature age for as important a reform. With all the pain and destruction wars brought about, they were commonly seen as acceptable political practices, and sometimes even as noble endeavors uniting peoples in their human destiny and exclusively capable of displaying all human virtues and vices.[4] In a world where, throughout centuries, "there [was] no greater good than for a warrior to fight in a righteous war,"[5] there could obviously not be any place for declaring the phenomenon of war as "criminal." One's own war is always righteous—all the criminals were always on the other side.

This chapter examines, chronologically and cross-culturally, the evolution of attitudes toward war(fare), from antiquity to our days. The chapter's purpose is to show how the waging of war was transformed from a largely glorified and sometimes mystical concept to a legally restrained and, in appropriate circumstances, even a criminal enterprise. The primary focus of the chapter will be on the *jus ad bellum*, i.e., the "right" to wage war, as opposed to the *jus in bello*—the conventional or customary

---

1 On primeval warfare, see, generally, Davie 1929; Turney-High 1971.

2 See generally Hinnells 2007; Iles Johnston 2007; Scaglia 2011.

3 It is submitted that all major "just war" doctrines were essentially different from the landmark twentieth- and twenty-first-century developments in international law in that they actually sought to define "fair" conditions for the occurrence of wars (positive restriction), instead of banning the phenomenon of war as such, with a few strictly defined exceptions (negative restriction). See Neff 2005, pp. 54–68; Werle 2009b, p. 405. Also, see infra 1.1.2.3.

4 Coppieters et al. 2002, p. 25.

5 *The Bhavagad Gita* 1962, p. 51.

rules relative to the conduct of hostilities.[6] Yet, before turning to the particulars, it appears useful to recall some definitional features of war, so well summarized by Stephen Neff,[7] as each of them could be applicable to the contemporary understanding of aggression as an internationally wrongful act of State and an individual crime.

Firstly, war is a collective undertaking.[8] It is carried out by organized collectivities under the command of public authorities and is supposed to be aimed at the furtherance of shared interests of the community. The collective nature of war—as regards the conduct of hostilities—has been reflected in applicable regulations, policies, and even terminologies.[9] However, the decision to start a war, the direction of the war effort throughout its entire duration as well as the subsequent termination of hostilities and the making of peace arrangements is up to fairly limited circles of political, military, and some other superior decision-makers (see infra 3.2), subject to their States' relevant constitutional provisions. Since no one can exercise more rights than he or she actually has—i.e., no one can arrange the commission of an act of aggression but only those supreme officials who are capable of supervising and managing the war effort of a State—the range of possible subjects of a crime of aggression is automatically reduced to those narrow circles. While anyone in a State's military or political hierarchy may, in appropriate circumstances, be held accountable either for the direct commission of war crimes or crimes against humanity in the course of an armed conflict, or for tolerating such crimes and refraining from taking preventive, disciplinary or penal measures against their perpetrators in accordance with international legal rules on the responsibility of superiors, this would not apply to the crime of aggression. An order to start an international armed conflict is, *de lege lata*, not manifestly unlawful (see infra 5.2.12). It therefore makes sense that aggression has been conceived of as a "leadership crime" and excludes officials below the supreme decision-making level (see infra 4.2).

Secondly, until the twentieth century, most wars were fought against foreign enemies rather than against domestic adversaries.[10] The distinction between the two types of armed violence was so sharp that internal hostilities were almost never referred to as "wars" but rather as "revolts," "riots," "revolutions," or "policing." While the modern

---

[6] The scholarly literature on the *jus in bello* is abundant. See highlights on the subject in: Artsibasov and Yegorov 1989; Batyr 2006; Best 1994; David 2011; Deyra 2002; Dinstein 2004; Green 1993; Heintschel von Heinegg and Epping 2007; *International Dimensions of Humanitarian Law* 1988; Kalugin 2006; Kalugin and Akulov 2004; Kalugin et al. 1999; Khakimov 2007; Kotlyarov 2003; McCoubrey and White 1992; Rajabov 2006; Rusinova 2006; Sassóli and Bouvier 2006; Zemmali 1997.

[7] For an excellent cross-cultural summary of the definitional features of war, see Neff 2005, pp. 14–29.

[8] Ibid., pp. 15–18.

[9] Notably, many key categories of international humanitarian law have been devised in plural or denote collectivities—e.g., "the civilian population," "civilians," "combatants," "protected persons," "prisoners-of-war," etc.

[10] See Neff 2005, pp. 18–20.

law of armed conflicts also increasingly applies to non-international armed conflicts—another legal novelty which is just over 60 years old (or "new"?)—the concept of aggression remained restricted to the inter-State uses of the armed force, and it is hardly correct to refer to armed conflicts between, for example, a State's central and local authorities, where a region *de jure* belongs to the State in question, as "aggression."[11] In line with this intermediate conclusion, this text will not deal with situations of intra-State armed violence, because these cannot qualify as aggression by definition.

Thirdly, for the most part, wars have been seen as activities subordinated to more or less clearly defined rules.[12] It must be admitted that the codification of the *jus in bello*, i.e., of rules applicable to the conduct of hostilities, has been more comprehensive than that of the *jus ad bellum* and, at a later stage, of the *jus contra bellum*.[13] However, as will be shown below, the twentieth century has also seen an unparalleled development of the *jus contra bellum*, and the normative outcomes resulting from these crucial developments must be considered as replacing, for the most part, previous ones, for such must have been the intention of their drafters. Since public international law constitutes the *ratione materiae* of international crimes,[14] essential developments within the former must of necessity be taken into account for the interpretation of the latter. More particularly, it will be argued below (see infra 1.2, especially 1.2.1) that the adoption of the Charter of the United Nations in 1945 has influenced the subsequent development of international criminal law beyond the limited and specific scope of the Nuremberg and Tokyo Judgments (see infra 3.1.1 and 3.1.2). The concept and elements of the individual crime of aggression have traditionally been based upon these Judgments, without due regard to the fact that they had been pronounced on the basis of international law which had *predated* the Second World War, and the lack of State practice with regard to the crime of aggression—i.e., the limited number of trials on the charges of the crime of aggression after that war (see infra 3.1.3)—should not be taken as a valid reason to conclude that binding international law—international criminal law's *ratione materiae* foundation—did not develop with regard to the crime of aggression ever since. True, there have been no criminal trials where the new, post-1945, international law could have been applied. But the lack of such case law should not bring one to the deceptive conclusion that international law underlying the criminalization of aggression is still the same as it stood in 1945–1949. The absence of trials on the matter only means that *there have been no opportunities to apply and interpret the new international law* after 1949.

---

[11] For example, the launching of the armed conflict in South Ossetia (8–12 August 2008) was sometimes referred to as Georgia's "aggression". However, it is submitted that this terminology was inaccurate in the circumstances, since, at the time of the attack, South Ossetia did not *de jure* constitute a recognized State. See generally International Fact-Finding Mission on the Conflict in Georgia, Report, Volume I (September 2009).

[12] See Neff 2005, pp. 20–25.

[13] See Kemp 2010, pp. 47–48.

[14] Bassiouni 2003, p. 8.

After all, judicial decisions—even such authoritative ones as the Nuremberg and Tokyo Judgments—are not *sources* of international law. They are "subsidiary means for the determination of rules of law,"[15] which means that the respective Tribunals only *interpreted* international law, without actually *creating* any new law, and therefore, in the post 1945-world, relevant legally protected interests (international peace and security), the existence of acts of aggression, and the individual criminal responsibility for such acts must be inferred from the Charter of the United Nations and other pertinent sources of contemporary international law (for details, see infra Chap. 2).

And last but not least, it is important—for the sake of applying law appropriately—that there be some sort of a temporal and circumstantial boundary between peace and war.[16] This feature has a crucial meaning for the purpose of determining the existence of a crime of aggression, especially if one interprets it in a more contemporary way than "planning, preparation, initiation or waging of a war of aggression" (the definition accepted by the Nuremberg Tribunal, see infra 3.1.1). The chief problems about "wars of aggression" are (1) the precise location of their beginning in time, (2) their magnitude, and (3) duration. In the past, when it was common to declare wars, it was fairly easy to determine from which date a state of war was effective. Now that wars are hardly declared at all, it is less clear whether an armed conflict begins from firing a first shot, killing or wounding a first person or destroying a first material object (see infra 4.3.1.3). Further, it is fairly easy to say that aggression is there when it is of a scale comparable to that of Germany or Japan in the Second World War. But what about lesser but nonetheless significant uses of inter-State military force (e.g., Iraq's use of force against Kuwait in 1991 or the US-led invasion of Iraq in 2003)? Might their authors' responsibility not be invoked as a matter of international criminal law just because these armed conflicts have resulted in less than 50 million deaths? And, finally, is a war lasting less than 6 years, by definition, not one of aggression? It will be suggested in this book that some further criteria than purely quantitative should be involved when "measuring" aggression as an internationally wrongful act of a State and as an individual crime. Continuing to maintain the exceptionally high definitional threshold of aggression set by the Nuremberg and Tokyo Tribunals—and it is worth recalling that that level of the armed conflict's magnitude was recognized by those Tribunals simply *as a matter of fact* in the Second World War, which should not mean that *all* unlawful uses of inter-State military force below that level must mechanically be discarded as not reaching the legally relevant "bottom line" of aggression—would be a misinterpretation of current public international and international criminal law.

---

[15] Cf. Statute of the International Court of Justice, Article 38(1)(d).

[16] See Neff 2005, pp. 25–29.

1.1 An Overview of the *jus ad bellum* Before World War II

1.1.1 The Ancient World

In the ancient world, both international law (as we understand it now) and diplomacy as a tool for making international law stood, with rare exceptions, entirely at the service of war.[17] In most cultures where the waging of wars was common,[18] diplomatic means—in the form of treaties—were used either at the close of wars, in order for victors to impose their conditions of peace upon the vanquished (and in order for the latter to inescapably accept those conditions), or in anticipation of prospective conflicts, in order to secure alliances for the wartime future. The earliest recorded examples of treaties concluded between rulers of ancient States testify vividly to the prominence of war-making in the daily lives of their subjects and in their own external policies. The following sections will provide an overview of philosophical, political or legal—as far as they could have *then* been viewed as legal—attitudes toward war in the major ancient civilizations and cultures.[19] The following text cannot be regarded as a comprehensive historical account, for reasons of limited volume space, but rather aims at giving an idea of how the complex notions of war and peace were perceived, at the time, in the respective contexts.

1.1.1.1 Asian Civilizations

1.1.1.1.1 Egypt[20]

Probably due to its relative geographic isolation, Egypt was, at the dawn of its history, the most peaceful nation of the ancient world. It was only by the time of the New Kingdom (sixteenth–fourteenth centuries BC) that it had to learn defending itself against some of its powerful neighbors—such as Assyria, Babylon, the Hittite Kingdom, Nubia, and Syria—and established a professional army (which

---

[17] See Martens 2008, p. 27.

[18] See Neff 2005, pp. 25–29.

[19] According to F. F. Martens (1845–1909), "for theoretical, purely a priori reasons, one could not agree that barbarian and ancient peoples knew international law. It suffices to analyze concepts and feelings which prevailed among peoples who were just at the dawn of their histories, and about whom we have quite veritable information, to become convinced of an absolute impossibility to suppose [the existence of] any rational need for a law among these peoples, for a certain order in the sphere of [their] mutual relations." See Martens 2008, p. 31.

[20] Traditionally, Egypt was not regarded as an African civilization, despite its geographical location in Northern Africa, due to its culture's fundamentally distinctive features. See, for example, Vasilyev 2003, pp. 98–120.

consisted, to a large extent, of mercenaries).[21] According to the *Correspondence of Tell el-Amarna* (fifteenth to fourteenth centuries BC),[22] Pharaoh Amenophis III (1388–1353/1351 BC) concluded, through dynastic marriages, strategic alliances with Mitanni and Babylon. Both alliances were established in counterweight to growing threats from the Hittite Kingdom, Egypt's successful rival in the competition for the Sinai mines, the Lebanese forests and trade routes.[23] This rivalry, which continued throughout the fourteenth century BC, exhausted both parties and resulted in the conclusion, in about 1268 BC, of a peace and alliance treaty between the Hittite king Hattusili III (reigned in about 1275–1250 BC), and Pharaoh Ramses II (reigned in about 1289–1213 BC), which was long regarded as the most ancient known international treaty.[24] The treaty consisted of an introduction, a number of operative provisions and a solemn conclusion. The introduction emphasized previously good relations between the Egyptians and the Hittites and stated the parties' mutual desire to establish "a perpetual peace, friendship, and fraternity."[25] The operative provisions established a defensive and offensive alliance against external and internal enemies, and set up an "extradition" procedure, whereas the conclusion contained an oath to which the deities of both lands were witnesses.[26] This treaty subsequently served as a model for many similar agreements concluded in the ancient world, including in Greece and Rome.[27]

1.1.1.1.2 Middle East

As the might of Egypt and the Hittite Kingdom began gradually to decline, Assyria—with Ashur as its center located between the rivers Tigris and Euphrates—emerged as a new regional power. During the early period of its history, Assyria was part of the Babylonian Kingdom, and the king of Ashur was subordinated to the king of Babylon but this distinction faded away over time. The territory of Assyria started growing in about the fourteenth century BC; already at the time the *Correspondence of Tell el-Amarna* was being written, the Assyrian kings referred to themselves as "rulers of the universe" whom "gods [had called upon] to reign over the country lain between Tigris and Euphrates."[28] Assyria

---

[21] Ibid., pp. 121–135.

[22] Accidentally discovered in 1887 by a peasant woman in Tell el-Amarna, the *Correspondence* consists of some 360 cuneiform tablets with records of communications between Pharaohs of XVIII dynasty (1550–1292 BC) and rulers of neighboring kingdoms. The *Correspondence* is held at the British Museum in London and the Staatsmuseum in Berlin.

[23] Potemkin 1941, pp. 18–20.

[24] Ibid., p. 22.

[25] Ibid., p. 21.

[26] Ibid., p. 22.

[27] Ibid., pp. 21–22.

[28] Ibid., p. 23. See also Vasilyev 2003, pp. 124–127.

attained the supremacy of its might under the Sargonides (around 800–700 BC) who, having themselves come out of the military caste, conducted important reforms in Assyria's political and military order. *Inter alia*, they increased the numbers of the Assyrian army to a hitherto unprecedented maximum of 150,000 men and conducted sweeping conquests of neighboring territories. Assyria's authority was challenged by three strong coalitions—ones led by Egypt (in the south-west), by Elam (in the south-east) and Urartu (in the north). Their struggle lasted for several centuries and ultimately exhausted Assyria's might. In the sixth century BC, the Achaemenid Persia founded by Cyrus II ((ruled in 559–530 BC) absorbed all Middle Eastern States and became the strongest State of the ancient world.[29] His empire flourished until the defeat of Darius III (ruled in 336–330 BC) by Alexander the Great in 330 BC.

1.1.1.1.3 China

In China, the classical conceptions of war were being shaped along with classical schools of the philosophical and political thought.[30] Since the Era of Warring States (fifth to third centuries BC), it was accepted that war was natural to a person's life and state of mind. Indeed, Sun Bin's "Military Laws" (fourth century BC) suggested that war had origins similar to those of animals' instincts.[31] The so-called School of Legalists (*Fa Tzia*), supportive of China's emerging despotic Empire, was preoccupied with arranging for efficient ways of State administration, above all, for "enriching the State and strengthening the army."[32] According to legalists, a State could only have two useful occupations:

> [A State's] welfare can be attained through agriculture and war, just as a ruler can be honored only for [his positive attitude toward] agriculture and war. Indeed, if a people are not engaged in agriculture and warfare, it means that the ruler [of this people] likes empty speeches, and that there does not exist an established system of awarding official posts. If posts are awarded in accordance with an established system, a State is governed well. When efforts of a people are focused on one [and the same], a State is prosperous. A prosperous and well-governed State is a path toward dominance in the world [...] It is difficult to attack a State which likes power, and a State which is not likely to be attacked would certainly attain prosperity. It is easy to attack a country where eloquence is honored, and a State, which can easily be attacked, would necessarily find itself in danger.[33]

Although it proved impossible to implement all principles of "legalism" in practice, for the "human factor"—i.e., human feelings and private interests—could not be dispensed with altogether, many fundamentals of this doctrine (for example,

---

29 See Vasilyev 2003, pp. 136–153.

30 Malyavin 2002, p. 11. See also Li 2002, pp. 20–58; Vasilyev 2003, pp. 199–214.

31 See Malyavin 2002, p. 54.

32 Ibid., p. 45.

33 Ibid., pp. 45–46.

one of "strengthening the army") were implemented successfully in Chinese rulers' subsequent policies.

At the same time, views favoring the avoidance of military violence gradually took shape. The recognized founder of Chinese philosophy, Confucius (551–479 BC) and his followers were remarkably moralist in their attitudes toward warfare, and condemned it as a manifestation of barbarism and stupidity.[34] In the words of a fourteenth-century scholar Liu Yin, "one cannot conclude that Confucians did not [at all] reflect on war, but they were giving [continued] primacy to personal perfection, to the maintenance of family peace, the establishment of order in the State and the pacification of China."[35] The views of Mo Di (Mo Tzu), a fifth-century thinker who was in favor of attacking directly only mutineers and robbers, were similar.[36] Paradoxically, in so reasoning, China's most consistent pacifists have ideologically contributed to the development of defensive tactics and fortification techniques.[37]

An overview of ancient Chinese military doctrines would not be inclusive without a mention of Sun Tzu's classic "On the Art of War".[38] This book contained the most complete and systemic account of the main principles and methods of Chinese military strategy. Despite its obviously practical orientation, the book has always been appreciated by China's scribes as a superb piece of literature. Apparently, it is this exceptional combination of literary worth and strategic vision that turned this book into a canonical treatise. As many other ancient authors, Sun Tzu regarded warfare as a sad but inevitable phenomenon. However, he believed that war was "manageable", because it was a logical undertaking, a controlled human effort.[39] Sun Tzu's book reflected in a superb manner a distinctive feature of Chinese culture—that of strategic thinking. Not specific solely to the military domain, the phenomenon of *stratagems* developed, over centuries, into a behavioral ethos, which managed to reach into nearly all aspects of public life in Chinese society, and to embrace virtually all its members irrespective of their occupation and social status.[40] The classical canon of stratagems embraces thirty-six rules originating from tales and parables of ancient Chinese rulers, heroes, and folklore characters; each rule is formulated in a short moralistic phrase and is accompanied by a collection of suitable historic or legendary case studies. Although *stratagems*, being spiritual rather than material

34 Ibid., p. 18.

35 Ibid., pp. 18–19.

36 Ibid., p. 29.

37 Ibid.

38 See generally Sun Tzu 2005. Although it is widely believed that Sun Tzu (or Sun Wu) lived in the seventh century BC, there is no unity among scholars as to when the book attained its canonical shape. According to some historians, it dates back to the sixth–fifth centuries BC. According to others, the treatise was completed no earlier than in the second half of the fifth century. However, most of the contemporary scholars suggest that the text could have been completed around the first half of the fourth century BC.

39 See Malyavin 2002, p. 56.

40 The significance of "stratagems" for China's culture has been the subject of comprehensive dedicated research. See, for example, Von Senger 2004a, b.

accomplishments, are probably less well known among laymen as China's contributions to the world culture than are paper, compass and gunpowder, their influence upon the lives of non-Chinese societies was significant indeed, insofar as notable non-Chinese statesmen in Western and Eastern Europe and North America were reported to have applied them, on occasions, in their decision-making.[41]

1.1.1.1.4 India

The best-known and, at its time, ancient India's most influential code of conduct were the *Laws of Manu* ("Manu-smrti").[42] As reported by V. Potemkin, the original text of the *Laws*, which must have been shaped during the first millennium BC, was lost, and the Sanskrit version known today dates back to approximately the first century AD.[43] The text was discovered by a British expedition in the eighteenth century and translated into a number of European languages during the nineteenth and twentieth centuries.[44] The *Laws of Manu* were written "on behalf" of the first king, a "perfectly wise" man who considered the issues in question through the prism of his wisdom and other outstanding personal qualities.[45] According to Manu, a truly skilled diplomat's art consisted in his aptitude to prevent war and strengthen peace: "[P]eace and its counterpart [war] depend on ambassadors, for they alone make allies and [also can] make them quarrel [...] Affairs which make peace among kings or cause wars [among them] are within their power."[46] According to the *Laws*, the most important issues of international life should preferably have been resolved through pacific means—the use of force was plainly considered a secondary method.[47]

1.1.1.2 European Civilizations

1.1.1.2.1 Ancient Greece

Fyodor F. Martens (1845–1909) noted in his classic textbook that isolationism and the sense of supremacy over other peoples were the decisive features, which prevailed in and were shaping the internal and external policies of ancient Greek city States,[48] and that, in this sense, Greeks were not much different from most of their

41 Harro von Senger reports examples of Niccolo Machiavelli, Napoleon, Richard Nixon, Joseph Stalin, and other notable statesmen who were using stratagems in their decision-making.

42 See Potemkin 1941, p. 33. See also Vasilyev 2003, pp. 167–180.

43 See Potemkin 1941, p. 33.

44 Ibid.

45 Ibid.

46 Ibid.

47 Potemkin 1941, p. 34. See also Subedi 2003, pp. 339–361.

48 See Martens 2008, p. 32.

contemporaries.[49] Classic Greek philosophers—such as Fucidide (470 or 450—between 399 and 396 BC), Heraclites (544–483 BC), Plato (427–347 BC), Aristotle (384–322 BC), Dionisius (around 60–around 7 BC)—constantly emphasized in their works Greeks' unique standing as a people and their "divine" right to treat others with despise and superiority.[50] However small a city State, its population would look at non-Greeks (βαρβαροι)—who did not enjoy any civil rights in Greece—in a condescending way.[51] Demosphenes (384–322 BC) alleged in his discourses that "barbarians" were destined by nature to be slaves to Greeks—which meant that, in a political and legal sense, Greeks alone were considered eligible for rights inherent in the human person.[52] Clearly, such attitudes toward foreigners made impracticable the maintenance of peace in Greek polities' international—and even in intra-Hellenic—relations.

Over centuries, unity among Greek city States was lacking, despite their inhabitants' common ethnic origins, language, religious views, and other cultural bonds.[53] In such circumstances, wars, paradoxically, helped bring citizens of Greek polities closer to each other and end their pre-existing isolation.[54] Systemic preparations for wars also helped build two most powerful military alliances—the Lacedemon (headed by Sparta) and Delos (headed by Athens) unions. Their relations were tense from the outset, and these tensions resulted, in 431–404 BC, in a large-scale War of Peloponnesus. In 395–387, the Unions' major powers fought, again, in the so-called Corinth war, which resulted in Athens' temporary hegemony.[55] Under Philippe II (359–336 BC), Macedonia became an important regional power and started threatening Greek polities. Political tensions within Athens and Macedonia's skilful manoeuvers provoked a war between them, which resulted, in 338 BC, in Athens' and their allies' defeat and the subjugation of all Greek city States, except Sparta.[56]

According to F. Martens, Greeks' wars against other nations also served as a means for making peoples better known to each other, for the establishment of pacific relations after international wars served the purpose of implanting new

[49] O. Zhidkov thus comments on the organization of an ancient Greek polity: "From the point of view of its internal organization, an ancient polity was a closed State outside which there remained slaves, strangers and even natives of other Greek polities. To citizens themselves, [their own] polity was a kind of political microcosm with its proper [...] forms of political organization, traditions, customs, law, etc." See Zhidkov and Krasheninnikova 2001, p. 132.

[50] See Martens 2008, p. 38.

[51] Ibid.

[52] Ibid.

[53] F. Martens names among such factors the mutual recognition of at least some fundamental rights of each other's citizens, and a nationwide influence exercised by the Delphic Sibyl and the Olympic Games. See Martens 2008, p. 42.

[54] See ibid.

[55] Potemkin 1941, pp. 41–42, 49.

[56] Ibid., pp. 50–55.

cultural elements on foreign grounds.[57] Thus, for example, until the Macedonian wars against Persia (331–330 BC), Greeks only had a very limited knowledge of Persians, whereas after the conquest, "appropriate trade relations were established between them." Likewise, Alexander the Great (356–323 BC) and his successors and, later, Romans, made elements of antique European culture known in remote parts of Asia and Northern Africa.[58]

1.1.1.2.2 Ancient Rome

Whereas Greeks did not originally strive to unite themselves under a common authority and developed within the borders of their respective polities, Rome was consistent in implementing the idea of national unity in its internal and external policies, having brought most of the ancient States, which were in existence at the time, under a single political umbrella.[59]

During the Republican period (509–27 BC), the acquisition of territories through wars was a common feature of Rome's political life. For the purpose of preserving peace in the immediate vicinity of the capital city, the populations of the Italian peninsula were being granted certain privileges deriving from equality treaties (*foedera aequa*), whereas the residents of more distant lands had to accept more severe conditions (*foedera non aequa*), and their pre-existing independent status and rights were almost entirely destroyed.[60] As Rome's territory grew, its international relations—in the proper sense of the word—diminished accordingly, and previously concluded treaties were gradually replaced by the authority of the Roman civil law.[61] In turn, during the imperial phase of its history (27 BC–476 AD), Rome continued implanting its language, culture, political and legal views in provinces, with a view to further strengthening the State structure and making the population's social structure ever more homogenous.[62] The issuance of Emperor Caracalla's edict in 212 AD marked the formation of an internally firm political body, all parts of which were subordinated to uniform laws, administration and judicial system—in fact, the virtual end of Rome's international relations, for all political and legal processes within the Empire would henceforth occur between different peoples who were subjects of the same State.[63] However, social, political and religious tensions within the Empire eventually resulted in its division in the Western and Eastern parts (in 395 AD), and the Western part's dramatic downfall and ultimate military defeat in 476 AD.

---

57 See Martens 2008, p. 33.

58 See ibid.

59 See ibid., p. 48.

60 Ibid., pp. 52–53.

61 Ibid., p. 53.

62 Ibid., p. 56.

63 Ibid., p. 57.

1.1.2 The Middle Ages

The downfall of the Western Roman Empire entailed an extinction of antique political and legal systems—indeed, the demolition of civilizations, which had embodied the supreme cultural attainments of the ancient European world. In a political and legal sense, the Western European societies were thrown backwards for centuries to come, and had to make new—cultural and military—ways from primitive proto-States to larger "barbarian" kingdoms and, ultimately, to centralized nation-States.[64] In turn, in Asia, social evolutions were subordinated to determinants of another kind,[65] which makes reasonable their rather detailed consideration below.

1.1.2.1 Islamic Attitudes Toward War

Islam is a world religion, which is intrinsically and naturally related to a legal system that even now, more that thirteen centuries after its coming into being, continues to exercise a major influence upon followers of the "parent" religion. Indeed, the Sharia exercises an unparalleled degree of influence upon all spheres of Muslims' lives—it seems that not a single aspect, from one's birth to death, escapes regulation by law. The reason for this phenomenal success lies in the divine character of the Sharia: unlike other legal systems, which have been instituted by States and thus are prone to human vices and weaknesses, the Sharia is free, in a faithful Muslim's eyes, from any deficiency, because it was granted to humankind by Allah through the intermediary of His Prophet, and must hence be unconditionally followed as a manifestation of God's perfect will.

For reasons of space, general issues, such as the origins and sources of applicable Islamic law, will not be dwelt upon here, for they can be found in abundant scholarly literature,[66] but instead, more specific grounds for launching wars and repelling attacks under Islamic law will be named.[67] Generally speaking, no wars were allowed between Muslims as a matter of principle.[68] The Sharia only permit-

---

[64] Ibid., pp. 62, 64.

[65] See Vasilyev 2003, pp. 232–247.

[66] See generally Anderson 1976; Al-Azmeh 1988; Al-Qaradawi 1985; Behruz 2011, pp. 270–301; Calder 1993; Coulson 1964; Edge 1996; Hallaq 1997; Khadduri 1966; Legais 2009, pp. 246–264; Mallat 1993; Rahmanov and Rahmanov 2003; Rosen 1989; Ruthven 2006; Saidov 1994, 2000, pp. 296–310; Schacht 1964; Weeramantry 1999.

[67] See Davis 2011, pp. 59–72; Hashmi 2002, pp. 194–216; Ilesanmi 2011, pp. 27–36; Johnson 2011, pp. 37–49; Malekian 2011, pp. 30–32, 171–191; March and Modirzadeh 2013, pp. 367–389; Oba 2002, pp. 817–850; Oh 2011, pp. 50–58; Samad 2011, pp. 84–108; Sardar Ali and Rehman 2005, pp. 321–343; Shah 2013, pp. 343–365.

[68] See Malekian 2011, pp. 30–32.

ted wars between Muslims (*dar al islam*) and infidels (*dar al garb*) but these were subject to specific conditions regarding their commencement[69] and conduct.[70] Muslims were allowed to use military force against infidels both in offence and in defence.[71] According to Mahiudin Abu Zakaria Yahya Ibn Sharif en-Nawawi, during the first century of Islam, launching wars against infidels for the purpose of disseminating the Muslim faith was a duty for accomplishing which all adult and sane members of the *ummah* (Muslim community) bore a joint responsibility.[72] The issuance of an authorization by the Sovereign or his deputy was thereby essential.[73] In situations where territories inhabited by Muslims were invaded, they—including persons with limited legal personality, such as "poor, children, debtors, and slaves"—had a duty to resist enemies by all possible means, without prior authorization.[74] If an organized resistance was not feasible, each Muslim should have defended his life and property, or else allowed himself to be taken prisoner, if quarter was not denied.[75] In turn, the capture of a single Muslim combatant was itself a sufficient ground for attacking infidels, in order to release him, if there was any prospect for success.[76]

Given that the Sharia, by definition, possesses in our days the same divine authority for many Muslims as it did thirteen centuries ago—and, in any event, the weight of its authority is greater by far than are religious prescriptions in modern non-Muslim societies—and given the number of theocratic Islamic States in the world, a few conclusions of current relevance can be drawn from the above regulations of Islamic international law. Firstly, modern Muslim States are quite unlikely to wage large-scale wars against other Muslim States.[77] On the contrary, in the face of a common "threat" embodied in non-Islamic (chiefly, Western) values, policies, and institutions,[78] Islamic States should be expected to continue uniting themselves under the umbrella of

[69] Ibid., pp. 178–190.

[70] Ibid., pp. 193–223.

[71] Notably, Jews and Christians were not considered "infidels" but belonged to the category of *kitabi*—"people of the Book"—with whom Muslims were called upon to maintain a peaceful intercourse.

[72] En-Nawawi 1992, p. 457.

[73] Ibid, p. 458.

[74] Ibid.

[75] Ibid.

[76] Ibid.

[77] The 1980–1988 war between Iran and Iraq was a notable contemporary exception. On this war, see generally El Azhary 1984; Karsh 2002; Karsh 2009; Rajaee 1993; Willett 2004.

[78] On ideological tensions between Islam and Christianity, see generally Spencer 2005.

Islamic values and policies.[79] Secondly, in view of an ongoing proliferation of non-mainstream Islamic ideologies and institutions, of which sometimes even States hosting them are not, or not fully, in control, one may assume that, in some parts of the world, rules of Islamic international law—including rules governing the use of force against perceived enemies—would gain increasing significance, and indeed, might prevail over secular general international law.[80] It is submitted that awareness of relevant rules of Islamic law in non-Islamic States might help prevent, at least, some international armed conflicts between Islamic and non-Islamic States in the future.

1.1.2.2 Attitudes Toward War in Japan

According to L. Hearn, "almost the entire veritably known history of Japan consists of one lasting episode—the rise and fall of its military might".[81] Likewise, Oscar Ratti and Adele Westbrook suggested in their comprehensive treatise on Japan's military history that, throughout centuries, the entire social structure of the Japanese nation was "dominated by ideas, ethics and feelings of duty proper to the military caste".[82] Their references to testimonies made by some Western historians regarding the Japanese people's "inherent militancy" are telling. Thus, in an article presented to the Asiatic

---

[79] See Article 1 of the Charter of the Organisation of Islamic Conference: "The objectives of the Organisation of the Islamic Conference shall be: 1. To enhance and consolidate the bonds of fraternity and solidarity among the Member States; 2. To safeguard and protect the common interests and support the legitimate causes of the Member States and coordinate and unify the efforts of the Member States in view of the challenges faced by the Islamic world in particular and the international community in general; 3. To respect the right of self-determination and non-interference in the domestic affairs and to respect sovereignty, independence and territorial integrity of each Member State; 4. To support the restoration of complete sovereignty and territorial integrity of any Member State under occupation, as a result of aggression, on the basis of international law and cooperation with the relevant international and regional organisations; [...] 8. To support and empower the Palestinian people to exercise their right to self-determination and establish their sovereign State with Al-Quds Al-Sharif as its capital, while safeguarding its historic and Islamic character as well as the Holy places therein; [...] 11. To disseminate, promote and preserve the Islamic teachings and values based on moderation and tolerance, promote Islamic culture and safeguard Islamic heritage; 12. To protect and defend the true image of Islam, to combat defamation of Islam and encourage dialogue among civilizations and religions; [...] 14. To promote and to protect human rights and fundamental freedoms including the rights of women, children, youth, elderly and people with special needs as well as the preservation of Islamic family values; [...] 16. To safeguard the rights, dignity and religious and cultural identity of Muslim communities and minorities in non-Member States; 17. To promote and defend unified position on issues of common interest in the international fora; 18. To cooperate in combating terrorism in all its forms and manifestations, organized crime, illicit drug trafficking, corruption, money laundering, and human trafficking [...]."

[80] See Khadduri 1956, pp. 358–372.

[81] Quoted in Ratti and Westbrook 2006, p. 25. See also Vasilyev 2003, pp. 451–460 and infra 3.1.2.1.

[82] See Ratti and Westbrook 2006, p. 25.

Society of Japan in 1874, an American orientalist William Elliot Griffis (1843–1928) remarked upon the "normality" of hostilities among the Japanese clans.[83] The same author elsewhere pointed to telling names of streets and quarters in the Japanese capital Edo—"Helmet," "Arrow," "Bow," and the like.[84] In turn, in his account of the Japanese culture, an Irish scholar Francis Brinkley (1841–1912) wrote as follows:

> Behind a visible passion for all which is superior and fine, there is a strong hidden addiction to the pompousness of military parades and the speediness of mortal attacks; and just exactly as the shogun was trying to show to the citizens of his capital an enchanting picture of a trouble-free peace, although it was merely a decoration for extensive military preparations, so did the Japanese at all times like switching their attention between fencing schools and ikebana, between battlefields and gardens of stones, thereby gaining pleasure from dangers and struggle of the former and, at the same time, enjoying the finesse and calmness of the latter.[85]

An opinion voiced by Professor Edwin Oldfather Reischauer (1910–1990) in the twentieth century largely corresponded to the preceding observations:

> Two centuries of artificial peace under the Edo government's careful eye and strict control have made an irreversible impact upon the people. The militant, almost recklessly courageous Japanese of the sixteenth century turned, by the nineteenth century, into a submissive people who were expecting, obediently, guiding instructions from their governors and fulfilling, in unquestioning ways, any orders from the top [...]
>
> People got used to "instinctively" listening to edifications offered by the country's military leaders, assuming that, by virtue of their status, those leaders always were "sincere and honest" [...] Seven centuries of domination by the military caste [...] have shaped ways of thinking and behaving which could not be easily got rid of in the new time, and they have not been erased even today.[86]

Oscar Ratti and Adele Westbrook suggested that these behavioral patterns were preserved, in almost unaltered ways, until Japan's capitulation in the Second World War on 2 September 1945, when it became clear that the military defeat should also result in a change of traditional ethics.[87] The dissolution of the armed forces after the war and the subsequent constitutional ban on their re-establishment must have been yet another severe blow against the defeated nation's pride.[88] However, it must have been the same exceptional spirit of resolve and national

[83] Ibid., p. 27.

[84] Ibid.

[85] Quoted ibid., pp. 27–28.

[86] Quoted ibid., p. 28.

[87] Ibid., p. 32.

[88] See Article 9 of the Constitution of Japan (promulgated on 3 November 1946, came into force on 3 May 1947): "Aspiring sincerely to an international peace based on justice and order, the Japanese people forever renounce war as a sovereign right of the nation and the threat or use of force as means of settling international disputes. In order to accomplish the aim of the preceding paragraph, land, sea and air forces, as well as other war potential, will never be maintained. The right of belligerency of the state will not be recognized." The text is available at: http://www.kantei.go.jp/foreign/constitution_and_government_of_japan/constitution_e.html (last accessed 17 November 2012).

unity, which had been cultivated over centuries, that helped Japan in the remarkably successful reconstruction of its post-war life and in its ensuing establishment among the world's leading economic powers.

1.1.2.3 European "*Just War*" Doctrines[89]

Despite that many distinguished proponents of the medieval European just war doctrines were theologians, these doctrines did, as a matter of fact, contain a strong secular component related to the natural law theory.[90] As S. Neff put it, "[t]he ethos of just-war doctrine [...] was that of the lawyer rather than the priest, of the rationalist rather than the zealot".[91] The universal natural law was meant to apply, on equal terms, to all persons (and even animals), and its content could be understood through human reason, a capacity possessed by all people, irrespective of their religious affiliation.[92] It was precisely this universal and secular character of natural law that distinguished medieval European views on war—and international law generally—from those of the Islamic world (see supra 1.1.2.1).[93]

Nick Fotion, Bruno Coppieters and Ruben Apresyan trace the development of the European just war doctrine back to St. Augustine (354–430) who is commonly regarded as its founder.[94] According to St. Augustine, the doctrine's major principles are the *just cause* principle and the principle of *legitimate authority*.[95] The first principle means that a State must have a sufficient ground to start a war. As quoted by St. Thomas Aquinas (1225–1274), St. Augustine wrote: "A war is usually considered just, if it makes retribution for injustice, when a people or a State must be punished for their unwillingness to make good for the damage caused by their subjects, or to return what they had acquired illegally."[96] As the principle developed over centuries, its content gained new important elements. From Fransisco de Vitoria's (1492–1546) point of view, a *justa causa* would also be there where a people sought to overcome a violation of their rights. In Vitoria's opinion, such a violation would give a just cause not only to its immediate victim but to the community of States as a whole.[97] Francisco Suárez (1548–1617) went

---

[89] See generally Von Elbe 1939, pp. 665–688; Elshtain 2001, pp. 1–25; Hershey 1911, pp. 901–933; Kunz 1951a, pp. 528–534.

[90] See Neff 2005, p. 54.

[91] Ibid.

[92] See ibid., pp. 54–55.

[93] See ibid., p. 55.

[94] See Coppieters et al. 2002, p. 33.

[95] See ibid.

[96] Quoted ibid., p. 48.

[97] Ibid. See also Barthelemey 1904, p. 11. F. de Vitoria's opinion suggests an appealing parallel to the present-day understanding of States' inherent right to individual or collective self-defence.

even further and suggested that the just cause principle would allow the victim to punish those guilty of injustice. This right would emanate from the victim's assumed jurisdiction over the culprits.[98] In turn, in the opinion of Hugo Grotius (see infra 1.1.2.4) and Emer de Vattel (1714–1767), the just cause principle also comprised preventing the occurrence of possible injustice in the future. However, Vattel warned that one should not be misled by unfounded assumptions and should not himself become an aggressor.[99]

In turn, the principle of *legitimate authority* meant that only designated authorities, properly empowered to govern a people or a State, might involve their subjects in war. This structural principle reaffirmed a State's sovereign monopoly to use the military force and placed limits upon its private uses.[100] In its modern shape, the principle determines the competence of a limited range of national (mainly, the executive and legislative branches of power) and international bodies (United Nations Security Council, regional security arrangements) to act as authorized agents of this sovereign monopoly.[101] We will more than once come back to this principle's essential aspects throughout the volume.

Nick Fotion, Bruno Coppieters and Ruben Apresyan add to these original principles four other ones. The so-called principle of *good intentions* marked an intermediate momentum between St. Augustine's original just war doctrine and subsequent developments. In the past, in line with natural law ideals, it meant that soldiers fighting in a war should not have had their hearts filled with hatred for the enemy (although true intentions in a war often were far from good).[102] Today, the principle simply

---

98 Coppieters et al. 2002, p. 48.

99 Ibid. See also De Vattel 1863, p. 368.

100 See Weber 1990, p. 645.

101 See Coppieters et al. 2002, pp. 65–86.

102 Nick Fotion, Bruno Coppieters and Ruben Apresyan list 16 typical intentions, or motivations, which have been moving people to go to wars throughout history (see ibid., pp. 87–88):

- to kill and plunder (barbarian wars);
- to become famous in a war (knightly wars);
- to realise commercial interests (trade wars);
- to implement a colonial expansion (colonial wars);
- to conquer other States' territories and resources (wars of conquest);
- to attain goals of a religion (crusades and religious wars);
- to implement structural or political changes within a country (civil wars);
- to break off a State or to prevent secession (secessionist wars);
- to export revolution to other countries (revolutionary wars);
- to regain territories lost in previous wars (wars to restore the *status quo*);
- to take revenge for an injustice (retributive wars);
- to defend a country against aggression (wars of selfdefence);
- to prevent a possible aggression in the future (preventive wars);
- to make a pre-emptive strike (pre-emptive wars);
- to help a State which has become victim of an aggression (wars in defence of other States);
- to help a people who are threatened by genocide or other grave or mass human rights violations (humanitarian intervention).

means that a State should only seek to attain the goal it had declared before the start of the war, and may not use the war for any other, selfish purpose.[103] Thus, if a State repels an aggression, it should limit its effort to fighting the enemy back and, possibly, holding the individual authors of the aggression criminally liable (for an overview of indirect and direct enforcement mechanisms, see infra 4.6.1 and 4.6.2) but not use its action in self-defence as a pretext for a consequent annexation of the enemy State's territory, placing it under an unlimited political control, or otherwise unduly limiting the defeated enemy's right to self-determination (cf. infra 2.4.3.1–2.4.3.3).

The fourth principle—the principle of the *likelihood of success*—is linked in substance to that of *proportionality*. The principle of the likelihood of success means that a State should refrain from using force, if doing so would entail critical consequences, especially if the potential adversary is obviously stronger in military terms.[104] In turn, the principle of proportionality suggests that the degree of (human, ethical, military, political, financial, etc.) losses during a prospective military campaign should not exceed that of expected benefits.[105] As explained by Nick Fotion, Bruno Coppieters and Ruben Apresyan, this principle would have been violated, for example, if NATO had decided, in 1968, to use nuclear weapons (or other weapons of mass destruction) to support the Czecho-Slovak resistance against the Soviet occupation, or to commence the Third World War for the same purpose. Thus, even if the just cause principle might theoretically have authorized NATO to take an action, the principle of proportionality should have necessarily prevented the decision.[106]

The sixth, and final, principle in the classification offered by Nick Fotion, Bruno Coppieters and Ruben Apresyan is that of *last resort*. The principle is usually interpreted as an encouragement, or permission, for a State to go to war, after recourse was had to all other means of settling a dispute.[107] The authors of the classification warn, though, that the principle should be read in a sensible and practical way, on the one hand, because the range of pacific means available to parties to a dispute could be virtually indefinite, and, on the other hand, because any given pacific means may or may not lead to desired results, depending on the circumstances.[108] It should therefore be interpreted as a last *reasonable* resort—before starting a military campaign, one should make oneself convinced that all further diplomatic efforts would be meaningless.[109]

The just war doctrine survived to our day and probably is the most solid ethical foundation of the modern *jus ad bellum*. The doctrine has been criticized by militarists and pacifists alike—for its alleged softness and opportunism, respectively—and yet it appears to represent the mankind's best "invention" on the subject

[103] Ibid., pp. 87–112.

[104] Ibid., pp. 113–128.

[105] Ibid., pp. 129–140.

[106] Ibid., p. 37.

[107] Ibid., pp. 141–167.

[108] Ibid., pp. 142–143.

[109] Ibid.

matter. In fact, it may be contended that modern provisions of international law pertaining to the use of force derive from the just war doctrine, and we shall revert to its essential aspects in Chap. 2.

1.1.2.4 Impact of Hugo Grotius' *De jure belli ac pacis*

In 1625, at the peak of the Thirty Years' War in Europe (1618–1648), a Dutch lawyer Hugo de Groot (1583–1645)—who is probably better known under the Latin version of his name, Hugo Grotius and is generally regarded as the "father" of modern international law—published a treatise, which was destined to exercise a profound impact upon the subsequent development of international law in Europe and, later, throughout the world.[110] The volume was entitled *De jure belli ac pacis libri tres* ("Three Books of the Law of War and Peace")[111] and principally devoted to the laws Christian peoples should obey in time of war. A study of history and literature of the ancient (mostly, European) world and the Middle Ages, the book contained an extensive set of facts and authoritative opinions on whose basis the author concluded that Christian peoples, if they chose to go to wars, would indeed be obliged to limit belligerent violence by compliance with certain inalienable rights emanating from the very human nature.[112] However, in the first place, a faithful Christian should strive to maintain peace:

> If therefore a peace sufficiently safe can be had, it is not ill secured by the condonation of offenses, and damages, and expenses: especially among Christians, to whom the Lord has given his peace as his legacy. And so St. Paul, his best interpreter, exhorts us to live in peace with all men. As Sallust says: "A good man takes up the beginning of war reluctantly, and does not follow its extremes willingly."[113]

According to Hugo Grotius, the overriding laws obliging Christian peoples to behave in such a controlled manner were of a natural (*jus naturale*) and positive (*jus voluntarium*) character. The latter was subdivided in human law (*jus humanum*) and divine law (*jus divinum*). In turn, human law was constituted of civil law (*jus civile*) and international law (*jus gentium*).[114] While civil law was there to regulate everyday intercourse between individuals, the purpose of international law was to set common standards of intercourse between entire peoples.[115] The great Dutch lawyer had not lived to see the end of the Thirty Years' War, but the fruits of his labors in international law were soon acknowledged as they

---

[110] See Murphy 1982, pp. 477–498, Sandifer 1940, pp. 459–472; Scott 1925, pp. 461–468; Wilson 1941, pp. 205–226; generally, Tuck 1999.

[111] For an English translation of the book, see Grotius 1853.

[112] See ibid., pp. 1–8.

[113] Ibid., p. 453.

[114] For brief illustrations of this classification, see ibid., pp. xxv–xxvii. The details of those various types of law are offered throughout H. Grotius' book.

[115] Martens 2008, p. 138.

shaped some key decisions taken at the Congress of Westphalia (see infra 1.1.2.5), and, more generally, all subsequent development of international law would be marked by the spirit of his outstanding contribution.

1.1.2.5 Impact of the 1648 Peace of Westphalia

In the sixteenth century, the emerging Reformation movement shattered the Central, Western and Northern Europe,[116] which ultimately resulted in more far-reaching social changes than ones of a purely religious nature. The enduring and brutal struggle between Catholics and Protestants culminated in the Thirty Years' War (1618–1648) whose conclusion, on 15 May and 24 October 1648, respectively, produced a fundamentally novel European political order.[117] As Professor Fyodor F. Martens pointed out, the 1648 Peace of Westphalia was essential for the future of European politics in at least four interrelated respects.[118] Firstly, the European States' interdependence and benefits of solidarity were confirmed. Secondly, the spiritual schism, which had already *de facto* existed between the Western European peoples, was formalized, and the independent standing of Protestantism was acknowledged. Thirdly, European powers were henceforth practically enabled to maintain lasting tensions in the heart of Europe by interfering, time and again, in the German Empire's internal affairs. Fourthly, and finally, France's authority became unchallenged, and, Sweden established itself as a new considerable player in European affairs whose influence would become exceptionally strong, especially in Northern Europe, in the decades to come—until its authority was successfully challenged by Russia under Peter the Great (1672–1725), during the first quarter of the eighteenth century.

1.1.3 Impact of the Napoleonic Wars and of the 1814–1815 Vienna Congress

On 1 (13) November 1814, an international Congress opened in Vienna, with a view to defining new political foundations for Europe, after the previous, Westphalian, system had been destroyed by the 1789 French Revolution and the devastating Napoleonic wars.[119] The Congress was attended by the Austrian, Russian and Prussian monarchs as well as by representatives of almost all other European States (except the Ottoman Empire). As Henry Kissinger observed, the negotiators "achieved what they had set out to do,"[120] for after the Vienna Congress, Europe

[116] See generally Collinson 2006; MacCulloch 2004; Oberman 2004.

[117] See Gross 1948, pp. 20–41; Hershey 1912, pp. 30–69.

[118] Martens 2008, pp. 78–82.

[119] See Baldwin 1907, pp. 565–578; Stewart 1951, pp. 571–577; Stockder 1916, pp. 492–508.

[120] Kissinger 1994, p. 79.

experienced the longest period of international peace in its history: no war occurred between the Great Powers for 40 years, and after the 1853–1856 Crimean War, there was no general war for nearly another 60 years, until the start of the First World War.[121] This probably makes the Vienna Congress the most successful peace-making mechanism ever.

1.1.4 Carl von Clausewitz's "On War"

L. Willmot most certainly allowed for no exaggeration in characterizing the place of Carl von Clausewitz's "On War" among writings on military theory as "unique".[122] A successful graduate of the Berlin *Kriegsakademie*, Carl von Clausewitz (1790–1831) held a number of posts in the Prussian and Russian armies before he was promoted, in 1818, to the rank of Major General and appointed Director of the Prussian War College (*Allgemeine Kriegsschule*). It was over the subsequent 12 years that he wrote the book of his life where he expressed his views on the nature of war and the means and methods of waging it. Carl von Clausewitz died from cholera in 1831, not having been able to complete the manuscript. It was edited and first published as a book by his widow Marie von Clausewitz in 1832.[123]

Carl von Clausewitz defined the key concept of his book—war—as "an act of violence intended to compel our opponent to fulfil our will".[124] According to von Clausewitz, in theory, there are two types of wars—"absolute" wars, which are waged until a complete victory of one side over the other, and "limited" wars, which are constrained by a variety of factors—but in reality, only the latter type is possible,[125] for an absolute war would threaten to undermine its political goal, and would therefore be "an absurdity."[126] In practice, the conduct of wars is always limited by a variety of factors—first of all, those of politics.

In fact, "politics" is probably the most important keyword of Clausewitz's book. Widely known are his assertions that "the source of war is politics", and that war is "simply the continuation of policy by other means."[127] Clausewitz's critics have continuously been misinterpreting this view as a suggestion that, in

---

[121] Ibid.

[122] L. Willmot, "Introduction", in Von Clausewitz 1997, p. ix.

[123] See: «Iz predisloviya Marii fon Klauzevits k pervomu izdaniyu» [«From Maria von Clausewitz's Preface to the First Edition»], in: Von Clausewitz 2002a, volume I, pp. 5–9. See also: Von Clausewitz 2002b, volume II.

[124] See Von Clausewitz 2002a, b, volume I, 2.

[125] Ibid., pp. 333–336.

[126] Ibid., p. 3.

[127] Ibid., p. 24. See also Werle 2009b, p. 405.

his "militarist" view, war is but a usual and permissible component of a State's international politics. It seems, though, that his genuine view—and this is where the real value of the book is—consisted in a conviction that functions of policy-makers and military servicemen should be *divided*, so that the sight of the political goal of a conflict would never be lost. Clausewitz went even further in this argument: he asserted that governments should always be in control of military developments and arms carriers, and that it would be irrational to allow the military to take over the political direction of war.[128] This suggestion will be essential to our further argumentation with regard to the range of possible subjects of a crime of aggression (see infra 4.2).

1.1.5 Impact of the 1899 and 1907 Hague Peace Conferences

According to Irina Rybachenok, by 1898, the peace-time armies of the leading European powers totalled 4,250,000 persons, and worldwide there were around 5,250,000 active servicemen.[129] In the case of a worldwide war, up to 44,250,000 persons could participate in combat, and if this army had received an order to exterminate the planet's entire population, each soldier should have killed no more than 32 other persons.[130] The European armies' maintenance costs were colossal: Russia was spending on its army annually 772.5 million francs, Germany—675 million, France—650 million, Great Britain—450 million, Austria—432.5 million, Italy—267.25 million.[131] It was thus amidst a pan-European arms race that Russia suggested,[132] on 12 (24) August 1898, to hold an international conference, which "could become a good sign for the coming century" and result in "a joint

---

[128] Ibid.

[129] See Rybachenok 2005, p. 16.

[130] Ibid.

[131] Ibid.

[132] It is not clear who exactly was the author of the idea to convene the First Peace Conference. According to some sources, it originated from a report by Russia's War Minister Alexey N. Kuropatkin to Emperor Nicholas II (1868–1918) of 28 February (12 March) 1898, on the expedience of concluding a treaty with Austria regarding a mutual limitation of armaments. According to others, it was the Finance Minister Sergey Y. Witte (1849–1915) who discussed with the Foreign Minister M. N. Muraviev the harmful effects of ever-increasing armaments. According to Professor F. F. Martens, it was a counsellor to the Russian Embassy to Hungary A. K. Basil and his secretary, M. G. Priklonsky, who had addressed a memo on the principles of international arbitration to Russia's Foreign Ministry, and this memo attracted the attention of a senior Foreign Ministry advisor V. N. Lamsdorf who authored an according policy proposal, which was presented to the Emperor's attention on 31 March (12 April) 1898. See Rybachenok 2005, pp. 17–30.

recognition of the fundamentals of law and justice, on which the security of States and the welfare of peoples are founded".[133]

The Russian initiative met with an outstanding success,[134] and the First Peace Conference opened in The Hague on 6 (18) May 1899. An unprecedented event, it was attended by 110 delegates representing 26 States.[135] The work was organized in 3 commissions, whereby the First Commission was in charge of agenda items 1–4, the Second Commission dealt with items 5–7, and the Third Commission was entrusted with agenda item 8.[136] The conference lasted 10 weeks and concluded its work on 17 (29) July 1899.[137] As the Head of the Russian Delegation and the Conference Chairman Baron Egor E. Staal (1822–1907) put it, "the achievements [of the Conference were] imperfect but practical."[138] These achievements were

[133] Ibid., p. 35.

[134] Ibid., pp. 53–54.

[135] The conference was attended by delegations of Austro-Hungary, Belgium, Bulgaria, China, Denmark, France, Germany, Greece, Italy, Japan, Luxembourg, Mexico, The Netherlands, Norway, Persia, Portugal, Romania, Russia, Serbia, Siam, Sweden, Spain, Switzerland, Turkey, the United Kingdom, and the United States. See Rybachenok 2005, pp. 131–132.

[136] The conference agenda followed the structure of a circular note dispatched by Russia's Foreign Minister to Ambassadors accredited in Saint-Petersburg on 30 December 1898, which suggested, in particular, the following items:
(1) the freezing of current numbers of servicemen in the land and marine armed forces and of military budgets, and a preliminary consideration of means for reducing the said armed forces and budgets in the future;
(2) the prohibition to introduce in armies and fleets of new types of firearms and explosives, as well as of stronger types of gunpowder than ones currently in use;
(3) the limitation of using in wars on land of destructive explosives currently in existence, as well as the prohibition of dropping explosives from balloons or of using them in other similar manners;
(4) the prohibition of using in wars at sea of submarines carrying mines or of other similar devices; the obligation not to construct, in the future, warships equipped with rams;
(5) the application of the 1864 Geneva Convention, as supplemented in 1868, to wars at sea;
(6) the recognition of neutrality, on the same grounds, of ships and boats involved in rescuing the shipwrecked during or after battles at sea;
(7) the revision of the 1874 Brussels Declaration on the laws and customs of war, which was not yet ratified;
(8) the adoption of rules for an appropriate application of good offices, mediation and voluntary arbitration, for the purpose of preventing armed confrontations between States, as well as reaching an agreement on ways of using these means and establishing uniform practices thereof. See Rybachenok 2005, pp. 299–302.

[137] For reasons of space, the progress of the conference is not discussed here. For an overview, see Rybachenok 2005, pp. 126–163.

[138] Baron Staal's concluding speech was published in the "Birzhevye vedomosti" ["The Stock Exchange Newsletter"] newspaper of 23 July (4 August) 1899.

embodied in three Conventions[139] and three Declarations.[140] The Final Act was signed by representatives of all 26 participating Powers, whereas the Conventions and Declarations were signed, at the closure of the Conference, by delegates who had received full powers from their respective Governments. Ultimately, all attending Powers had all the documents signed, with some reservations, by the agreed date of 31 December 1900.[141]

Without a doubt, the legal and institutional mechanisms established by the Conference were of a major importance (cf., however, infra 1.1.6.2). States had recourse to some of those procedures already before the First World War[142]—which, nevertheless, could not prevent the very occurrence and many horrors of that war. Supplanted, in 1907,[143] by a number of successor conventions and declarations,[144] the so-called "Hague Law" was held, in mid-twentieth century, by the Nuremberg and Tokyo Tribunals (see infra 1.2.2, 1.2.3, 3.1.1 and 3.1.2)—at least, as far as the law of armed conflicts was concerned—to constitute customary international law.

---

[139] See Convention (I) for the Pacific Settlement of International Disputes (29 July 1899); Convention (II) with Respect to the Laws and Customs of War on Land (29 July 1899); and Convention (III) for the Adaptation to Maritime Warfare of the Geneva Convention of 22 August 1864 (29 July 1899).

[140] See on the Prohibiting Launching of Projectiles and Explosives from Balloons (29 July 1899); Declaration on the Use of Projectiles the Object of Which is the Diffusion of Asphyxiating or Deleterious Gases (29 July 1899); and Declaration on the Use of Bullets Which Expand or Flatten Easily in the Human Body (29 July 1899).

[141] See Rybachenok 2005, p. 164.

[142] See Clarke 1907, pp. 342–408; De Sillac 1911, pp. 968–986; Hershey 1908, pp. 29–49; Penfield 1907, pp. 330–341; Ralston 1907, pp. 321–329; Scott 1908b, pp. 815–822; Scott 1912, pp. 316–358; Scott 1908c, pp. 772–810.

[143] See American Society of International Law 1907a, pp. 431–440; American Society of International Law 1907b, pp. 945–954; De Bustamante 1908, pp. 95–120; Hill 1907, pp. 671–691; Hull 1908, pp. 731–742; Malanczuk 1997, pp. 22–23; Scott 1908a, pp. 78–94; Scott 1908d, pp. 1–28; Stowell 1908, pp. 50–62; Werle 2009b, p. 405.

[144] See Convention (I) for the Pacific Settlement of International Disputes (18 October 1907); Convention (II) Respecting the Limitation of the Employment of Force for the Recovery of Contract Debts (18 October 1907); Convention (III) Relative to the Opening of Hostilities (18 October 1907); Convention (IV) Respecting the Laws and Customs of War on Land (18 October 1907); Convention (V) Respecting the Rights and Duties of Neutral Powers and Persons in Case of War on Land (18 October 1907); Convention (VI) Relating to the Status of Enemy Merchant Ships at the Outbreak of Hostilities (18 October 1907); Convention (VII) Relating to the Conversion of Merchant Ships into War-ships (18 October 1907); Convention (VIII) Relative to the Laying of Automatic Submarine Contact Mines (18 October 1907); Convention (IX) Concerning Bombardment by Naval Forces in Time of War (18 October 1907); Convention (X) for the Adaptation to Maritime War of the Principles of the Geneva Convention (18 October 1907); Convention (XI) Relative to Certain Restrictions with Regard to the Exercise of the Right of Capture in Naval War (18 October 1907); Convention (XII) Relative to the Creation of an International Prize Court (18 October 1907, not ratified); Convention (XIII) Concerning the Rights and Duties of Neutral Powers in Naval War (18 October 1907). The Conference also adopted a Declaration Extending Declaration II from the 1899 Conference to Other Types of Aircraft and a Declaration on Obligatory Arbitration.

1.1.6 *Evolution of International Legal Attitudes Toward War Under the Aegis of the League of Nations*

1.1.6.1 Impact of US President W. Wilson's "Fourteen Points"

At the end of the First World War (1914–1918),[145] Germany—unlike one would expect a vanquished country to be—was still very powerful,[146] both in terms of population[147] and in economic terms.[148] In Henry Kissinger's opinion, Germany remained strong enough, after the war, to prevail over any one of its major rivals individually, and probably even over a grouping of two of them.[149] It was in these complex circumstances[150] that the twenty-eighth President of the United States Woodrow Wilson (1856–1924) made public, on 8 January 1918, a proposal of a post-war settlement, which entered history under the title of "Fourteen Points".[151] For the purpose of this research, the proposal was revolutionary inasmuch as it sought to replace the pre-existing system of the Great Powers' alliances by one of universal collective security, and to replace the "balance [...] determined by the sword," as President Wilson put it in a speech at London's Guildhall on 28 December 1918, by a consistent rule of law:

> They [the Allied soldiers] fought to do away with an old order and to establish a new one, and the center and characteristic of the old order was that unstable thing which we used to call the "balance of power"—a thing in which the balance was determined by the sword which was thrown in the one side or the other; a balance which was determined by the unstable equilibrium of the competitive interests [...] The men who have fought in this war have been the men from free nations who were determined that that sort of thing should end now and forever.[152]

---

[145] For international legal views on some aspects of the First World War, see a series of articles: Garner 1915a, pp. 72–112; Garner 1915b, pp. 372–401; Garner 1915c, pp. 594–626; Garner 1915d, pp. 818–857; Garner 1916a, pp. 12–41; Garner 1916b, pp. 238–269; Renault 1915, pp. 1–16.

[146] See American Society of International Law 1914, pp. 881–886; Fenwick 1929, pp. 812–815; Willoughby 1918a, pp. 266–282; Willoughby 1918b, pp. 251–265.

[147] According to statistics provided by Henry Kissinger, in 1920, France had a population of 41 million, while Germany's was 65 million, which statistics made the French statesman Aristide Briand (1862–1932) to answer critics of his appeasing policy toward Germany with the argument that he was pursuing the foreign policy of France's birth rate. See Kissinger 1994, p. 228.

[148] Again, according to H. Kissinger, Germany's economy was boosting: in 1913, France produced 41 million tonnes of coal compared with Germany's 279 million tonnes; by the late 1930s, the disparity grew to 47 million tonnes produced by France against Germany's total of 351 million tonnes. See Kissinger 1994, p. 228. See also Adamthwaite 1977, p. 4.

[149] Kissinger 1994, p. 229.

[150] For a contemporaneous view of international affairs at the time, see Kocourek 1918, pp. 498–518.

[151] See Avalon Project: http://avalon.law.yale.edu/20th_century/wilson14.asp (last accessed 13 November 2012).

[152] W. Wilson, "An Address at Guildhall, 28 December 1918", in Link (ed.) (1966–), volume 53, p. 532.

President Wilson must have been contemplating the post-war collective security system already during the Great War, as in a speech delivered to the Senate in January 1917, he dwelled upon the recognition of nations' equal rights as a more reliable foundation for the maintenance of international peace, irrespective of each nation's individual strength:

> Right must be based upon the common strength, not upon the individual strength, of the nations upon whose concert peace will depend. Equality of territory or of resources there of course cannot be; nor any other sort of equality not gained in the ordinary peaceful and legitimate development of the peoples themselves. But no one asks or expects anything more than an equality of rights. Mankind is looking now for freedom of life, not for equipoises of power.[153]

As will be seen below, the League of Nations, which was soon to be established, made possible some of Woodrow Wilson's initiatives. Incapable, in the circumstances prevailing at the time, to "end all wars",[154] the new international organization has nonetheless created an environment for further developing regional and potentially universal antiwar ideas and mechanisms, a forum without which the United Nations' more sophisticated mechanisms would probably not have been feasible at a later stage. Besides, some of the international legal instruments created by the League of Nations were referred to in the 1946 Nuremberg Judgment as evidence of prohibition of aggressive wars under customary international law (see infra 3.1.1).

1.1.6.2 Impact of the 1919 Treaty of Versailles (Including the Covenant of the League of Nations)

According to William Schabas, the real history of prosecutions for international crimes began after the First World War.[155] The Treaty of Versailles of 26 June 1919 laid down the conditions of Germany's capitulation in the First World War and provided, *inter alia*, for the arraignment of Kaiser Wilhelm II (1859–1941)[156] and the prosecution of German combatants charged with violations of the laws and

[153] W. Wilson, "An Address to the Senate, 22 January 1917", in Link (ed.) (1966–), volume 40, p. 539.

[154] On 11 November 1918, British Prime Minister David Lloyd George (1863–1945) thus heralded the conclusion of an armistice between Germany and the Allied Powers: "I hope that we may say that thus, this fateful morning, come to an end all wars". Quoted in Taylor 1965, p. 114.

[155] Schabas 2004, pp. 19–22. M. Cherif Bassiouni points to much earlier examples, such as the trial of Conradin von Hohenstaufen in 1268 and Peter von Hagenbach in 1474, although he acknowledges that links between these experiences and modern developments are rather difficult to establish. See Bassiouni 2003, pp. 23–24.

[156] Treaty of Versailles, Article 227: "The Allied and Associated Powers publicly arraign William II of Hohenzollern, formerly German Emperor, for a supreme offence against international morality and the sanctity of treaties." See also Werle 2009b, p. 406; Safferling 2012, p. 9.

customs of war before Allied military tribunals.[157] While the latter provision was not much contended, the arraigned Kaiser's indictment was more controversial as a matter of international law. Even the Allies themselves, in response to Germany's protest against Article 227, acknowledged that the indictment did not have "a juridical character as regards its substance, but only in its form. The ex-Emperor is arraigned as a matter of high international policy".[158] It is therefore not by chance or omission that Article 227 did not refer to either "aggression" or, more generally, "crimes against peace": in 1919, international law knew no such notions.[159] As is known, the arraigned Kaiser found refuge in The Netherlands who refused his extradition on the ground of the Allied extradition request's non-compliance with the principle of double criminality: "The supreme offence against international morality and the authority of treaties [...] does not appear in the provisions on penal infractions contained in the laws of Holland or in the treaties she has concluded."[160] Thus, a potentially prominent attempt of an international criminal prosecution for aggression failed on both substantive and procedural grounds.

Otherwise, as Stephen Neff noted, the Treaty of Versailles and the Covenant of the League of Nations,[161] which was part of the former (Articles 1–26), did exercise a profound influence on international law's attitude toward war in that war ceased to be a legitimate institution of international law in the nineteenth-century sense.[162] The Covenant sought, for the first time in history, to inculcate the principle of international law, albeit in a restrictive manner, that the normal state of international affairs was that of peace, and war required strict and specific validations.[163] Yet, the Covenant's chief deficiency consisted in that it focused on the prevention of *wars* but left out other, lesser forms of inter-State armed coercion short of war, such as interventions, forcible reprisals, and acts of necessity.[164] Besides, it did not *outlaw* wars resolutely but sought to *limit* the League's Member States' right to resort to wars for the purpose of settling disputes. The Covenant set up two procedures of international dispute settlement: the political mechanism consisted in an inquiry by the League of Nations' Council, and judicial inter-State disputes could be submitted to arbitration.[165] However, once 3 months would have

---

[157] The so-called Leipzig trials, which ensued in 1919–1921, did not deal with the crime of aggression but only with war crimes and therefore will be left beyond the scope of this chapter. For an overview of the trials, see Köchler 2003, pp. 54–58. See also Safferling 2012, pp. 9–11.

[158] *Reply of the Allied and Associated Powers to the Observations of the German Delegation and the Conditions of Peace*, Paris, 16 June 1919, HMSO, Misc. No 4 (1919).

[159] See Sellars 2012, pp. 7–40; Wright 1924, pp. 755–767; Wright 1935, pp. 373–395.

[160] The French original of this response is quoted in Schabas 2004, p. 21.

[161] See Malanczuk 1997, pp. 23–26; Von Tabouillot 1937, pp. 15–37.

[162] See Neff 2005, pp. 279, 293.

[163] See ibid., p. 285.

[164] Ibid.

[165] See Goodrich 1938, pp. 738–758; Hedges 1928, pp. 560–565.

elapsed after the pronouncement of either the Council's or the arbitrators' decision, a party to the dispute, which disagreed with the decision, might resort to the use of armed force.[166]

It appears that, for the sake of objectivity, the historical impact of the Treaty of Versailles and of the Covenant of the League of Nations—the former's constitutive part—should be assessed separately. Whereas the Treaty was, overall, a tool for imposing political conditions upon the defeated Germany, which soon would be regarded by some political forces within Germany as humiliating,[167] and for extracting reparations worth 132 billion gold francs[168] (it is, *inter alia*, these factors that would bring about a new World War in 1939), the Covenant was an unprecedented breakthrough, an attempt of previously unseen authority to secure lasting peace among the world's nations. It would be overly unjust to criticize the Covenant's faults without acknowledging its historic attainments at the given time,[169] for international law is incapable of anticipating future developments beyond the degree of its authors' agreed intentions.

1.1.6.3 Impact of the 1923 Draft Treaty of Mutual Assistance and the 1924 League of Nations Protocol for the Pacific Settlement of International Disputes

Throughout the 1920s and 1930s, the League of Nations accomplished important drafting work aimed at limiting recourse to armed force by international law. A first notable example of such work was the Draft Treaty of Mutual Assistance communicated to Members of the League on 27 September 1923.[170] Article I of the Treaty stated "that aggressive war [was] an international crime," and that the parties would "undertake that no one of them will be guilty of its commission." The draft text was submitted to 29 states,[171] about half of whom were in favor of accepting it. The principal objection to the Treaty appeared to consist in the

---

[166] Covenant of the League of Nations, Article 12: "1. The Members of the League agree that if there should arise between them any dispute likely to lead to a rupture, they will submit the matter either to arbitration or to inquiry by the Council, and they agree in no case to resort to war until three months after the award by the arbitrators or the report by the Council. 2. In any case under this Article the award of the arbitrators shall be made within a reasonable time, and the report of the Council shall be made within six months after the submission of the dispute."

[167] Germany was virtually excluded from Europe's political life until the conclusion of the 1925 Locarno Treaties (see infra 1.1.6.4).

[168] On Germany's reparations after the First World War, see Temperley 1920, pp. 40–91.

[169] For a critique of the Covenant, see Israelyan 1990, pp. 18–21; Khakimov 2012, p. 30.

[170] Cf. Williamson 2009, p. 83.

[171] In 1923, the League of Nations comprised 54 States. See National Membership of the League of Nations: http://www.indiana.edu/~league/nationalmember.htm (last accessed 13 November 2012).

difficulty of defining the acts which would constitute "aggression," rather than any doubt as to the criminality of aggressive war.[172]

Next year, Great Britain and France jointly proposed to the League of Nations' Members a draft Protocol for the Pacific Settlement of International Disputes, with a view to "[a]sserting that a war of aggression constitutes a violation of this solidarity and an international crime,"[173] and to making possible "the reduction of national armaments to the lowest point consistent with national safety and the enforcement by common action of international obligations."[174] Following its initiators' rigorous discussions on which types of armaments—land or maritime—the Protocol should precisely relate to, it was adopted by the League Assembly on 2 October 1924.[175]

The Protocol's Article 2 contained the Parties' mutual obligation "in no case to resort to war either with one another or against a State which, if the occasion arises, accepts all the obligations hereinafter set out, *except in case of resistance to acts of aggression*" (emphasis added).[176] Since a more comprehensive prohibition of the use of force was not yet possible at the time (see infra 1.1.6.5), the mutual character of the rule, i.e., one allowing for exceptions as a matter of principle, was the Protocol's chief weakness. Further, the Parties undertook, under Article 11, "to come to the assistance of the State attacked or threatened, and to give each other mutual support by means of facilities and reciprocal exchanges as regards the provision of raw materials and supplies of every kind, openings of credits, transport and transit, and for this purpose to take all measures in their power to preserve the safety of communications by land and by sea of the attacked or threatened State". This key obligation was, however, practically limited by another clause contained in the same Article to the effect that each State Party should contribute to the peace maintenance effort "in the degree which its geographical position and its particular situation as regards armaments allow." Obviously, this clause allowed for evasions, if a State wished to avoid participating in a specific collective security action.[177] Ultimately, the Protocol did not attain the required level of support—even one of its initiators, Great Britain, refrained from ratifying it in the end—and never entered into force.[178] On the other hand, as the Nuremberg Tribunal noted in its Judgment, "[a]lthough the Protocol was never ratified, it was signed by the leading statesmen of the world, representing the vast majority of the

---

[172] See *Commentary on the Definition of a Case of Aggression*, Records of the Fourth Assembly (1923), Meetings of Committees, Minutes of the Third Committee, pp. 206–208, referred to in Williamson 2009, p. 83.

[173] League of Nations, *Protocol for the Pacific Settlement of International Disputes*, 2 October 1924. Online. UNHCR Refworld, available at: http://www.unhcr.org/refworld/docid/40421a204.html (accessed 15 May 2012), 3rd preambular paragraph.

[174] Ibid., 5th preambular paragraph.

[175] See Potemkin 1945, pp. 311–312.

[176] See ibid., p. 313.

[177] See ibid.

[178] Ibid. See also Bassiouni and Ferencz 2008, p. 210.

civilized states and peoples, and may be regarded as strong evidence of the intention to brand aggressive war as an international crime."[179]

1.1.6.4 Impact of the 1925 Locarno Treaties

In late September 1925, German Ambassadors accredited in Paris, Brussels, London and Rome conveyed through verbal notes addressed to the respective Governments Germany's willingness to convene a conference to negotiate guarantee pacts between herself and the addressees of the notes.[180] The Ambassadors accompanied the transmission of the notes by oral proposals to the effect of revising at the conference the "Guilt Clause"—Article 231 of the Versailles Treaty (see supra 1.1.6.2) whereby Germany and her allies had been declared as being solely responsible for unleashing the First World War.[181] The German official position—expressed in the verbal notes—was as follows:

> The demand of the German people to be released from the burden of this false accusation is quite fair. As long as this has not been done, and as long as a member of the community of nations is branded as a criminal before all mankind, no true mutual understanding and conciliation among peoples shall be possible.[182]

Despite that the Allies had not agreed to formally revise their assessment of the past events, they confirmed their participation in the proposed conference, which opened on 5 October 1925 at Locarno (Switzerland) and lasted until 16 October 1925.[183]

As Britain's Foreign Secretary Sir Joseph Austen Chamberlain (1863–1937) said, "without a doubt, the Locarno Conference [was] more important than all conferences convened since the conclusion of the Versailles Treaty."[184] Unlike at the conclusion of the latter, Germany enjoyed at Locarno a status equal to that of other participants—five treaties out of seven concluded at the conference were with the participation of Germany,[185] and soon after the conference (in 1926), she was admitted to the League of Nations and granted a permanent seat in the League Council, alongside France, Great Britain, Japan, and Italy.[186] The conference resulted in the conclusion of the so-called "Rhineland Pact," i.e., a multilateral guarantee treaty between Germany,

---

179 International Military Tribunal (Nuremberg), Judgment of 1 October 1946, p. 446.

180 See Potemkin 1945, p. 327.

181 Article 231 of the Versailles Treaty read as follows: "The Allied and Associated Governments affirm and Germany accepts the responsibility of Germany and her allies for causing all the loss and damage to which the Allied and Associated Governments and their nationals have been subjected as a consequence of the war imposed upon them by the aggression of Germany and her allies."

182 Quoted in Potemkin 1945, p. 328.

183 See ibid., pp. 328–332.

184 Ibid., p. 328.

185 Ibid., p. 331.

186 See National Membership of the League of Nations, supra note 171. See also Potemkin 1945, p. 333.

Belgium, France, Great Britain, and Italy,[187] four bilateral arbitration agreements—respectively, between Germany and Belgium (see infra 3.1.1.4 on Germany's attack against Belgium in the Second World War), Czechoslovakia (see infra 3.1.1.1), France,[188] and Poland (see infra 3.1.1.2), and two bilateral guarantee agreements—respectively, between France and Poland and between France and Czechoslovakia.[189] All treaties were signed in London on 1 December 1925 and ratified soon thereafter.[190]

It is worth recalling that, after the 1925 Locarno Conference, one important country—the Soviet Union—still remained uninvolved in the European security framework. V. Potemkin assumed candidly that, in the post-Locarno regime, both sides—Europe and the Soviet Union—must have been equally alarmed about a possible confrontation, and it must have been in anticipation of a future conflict that, on 24 April 1926, a Soviet-German Treaty of Friendship and Neutrality was signed.[191] The treaty stipulated that, if an attack occurred against a State Party, the other State Party would have to maintain neutrality (Article 2), and that none of the States Parties might join coalitions for the purpose of boycotting the other State Party economically or financially (Article 3). This bilateral treaty was succeeded to, in August 1939, by the Molotov-Ribbentrop Pact.[192]

1.1.6.5 Impact of the 1928 General Treaty for the Renunciation of War as an Instrument of National Policy

The General Treaty for the Renunciation of War as an Instrument of National Policy was adopted in Paris on 27 August 1928.[193] Also known as the Kellogg-Briand Pact, after its two major sponsors—the US Secretary of State Frank Kellogg (1856–1937)

---

[187] The "Rhineland Pact" obliged its States Parties to respect the territorial *status quo* set out in the Versailles Treaty, more specifically—the inviolability of frontiers laid down in that Treaty between, respectively, Germany and Belgium and Germany and France (Article 1), and required them not to use military force against each other, except in cases of legitimate self-defence or collective measures under Article 16 of the Covenant of the League of Nations (Article 2). All matters of dispute were to be settled by means of arbitration or in the framework of truce commissions. In Articles 4 and 5, sanctions against violator States were outlined. See Potemkin 1945, pp. 331–332.

[188] Interestingly enough, the Judgment of the Nuremberg Tribunal (see infra 3.1.1) did not deal separately with Germany's war against France unlike it did with her aggression against some other European States, the USSR and the USA.

[189] See Potemkin 1945, p. 331.

[190] Ibid., p. 333. See also Werle 2009b, p. 406.

[191] See Potemkin 1945, pp. 334–338.

[192] On Germany's aggression against the USSR, see infra 3.1.1.6. In this context, a remarkable statement by Charles de Gaulle (1890–1970) is worth recalling: "Treaties are like roses and young girls: they are preserved as long as they are preserved". Quoted in Lukashuk 2008, p. 121. Cf. Fenwick 1952, pp. 296–298.

[193] For text, see the Avalon Project: http://www.yale.edu/lawweb/avalon/imt/kbpact.htm (last accessed 13 November 2012).

and France's Minister for Foreign Affairs Aristide Briand (1862–1932)—the treaty was a momentous step in the progressive development of international law in that it introduced a comprehensive ban on the unilateral waging of war in pursuit of national policy.[194] The Pact's drafting history was usefully summarized in an article by Frank Kellogg.[195] The treaty was initially conceived of as a bilateral instrument to be concluded between France and the United States, in a series of bilateral and regional treaties on the pacific settlement of international disputes concluded between some European powers, the United States and Japan, during the 1920s.[196] In a note addressed to Frank Kellogg on 27 June 1927, Aristide Briand proposed the following wording of the envisaged treaty's key provisions:

> The high contracting parties solemnly declare, in the name of the French people and the people of the United States of America, that they condemn recourse to war and renounce it respectively as an instrument of their national policy toward each other [...]
>
> The settlement or the solution of all disputes or conflicts, of whatever nature or of whatever origin they may be, which may arise between France and the United States of America, shall never be sought by either side except by pacific means.[197]

In response to a subsequent French proposal dated 28 December 1927, the United States agreed to the substance of the initiative but suggested to conclude, instead, a multilateral treaty open to adherence by all States, thus extending the benefits of a treaty originally envisaged as between two nations alone.[198] France replied in the positive, indicating, however, that the multilateral treaty might only provide for the renunciation of *wars of aggression* alone, because France was bound by contractual obligations under the Covenant of the League of Nations, the 1925 Treaties of Locarno and other similar guarantee arrangements, whereas a bilateral treaty with the United States could constitute a comprehensive and unqualified ban on the mutual use of force.[199] The US Secretary of State disagreed with this reasoning. In his communication of 27 February 1928, he wrote that it was not obvious how obligations under the proposed multilateral instrument could be incompatible with those under the Covenant of the League of Nations (see supra 1.1.6.2), given their common goal of preventing international wars.[200] He stressed that the US Government desired to "see the institution of war abolished" and stood ready "to conclude [...] a single multilateral treaty open to [...] adherence by any and all [...] governments binding the parties thereto not to resort to war with one another."[201]

---

[194] In this context, the term *unilateral* is used to denote a use of force by a State (or a group of States united by the same war aims) against another State or group of States outside the collective guarantee regime set up under Article 10 of the Covenant of the League of Nations.

[195] See generally Kellogg 1928, pp. 253–261.

[196] Ibid., pp. 254–256, 258.

[197] Ibid., p. 258.

[198] Ibid., pp. 258–259.

[199] Ibid., p. 259.

[200] Ibid., pp. 259–260.

[201] Ibid., p. 260.

Eventually, the Kellogg-Briand Pact was adopted in the restrictive format proposed by France—probably because the League Member States did not wish to further limit their already restricted capacity to employ military force.[202] The adoption of the Pact was regarded by some scholars as a landmark event that should have made the future occurrence of wars altogether *impossible*—although it would have probably been more correct to consider it, instead, as a means to make, at least, some wars *unlawful*.[203] Regrettably, neither the Covenant of the League of Nations nor the Kellogg-Briand Pact were able to prevent the eruption of the Second World War, despite their near-universality at the time.[204] It seems the Pact's chief weakness was in the absence of a definition of aggression, despite a formal prohibition of "recourse to war" in the sense of Article I—a challenge to which the world's politicians all too easily and too willingly submitted. As will be recalled below, the repercussions of this severe omission would be felt over the decades to come.

1.1.6.6 Impact of the 1933 Soviet Union's Draft Definition of Aggression

In February 1933, the Soviet Union had made a proposal of a definition of aggression, which was later somewhat pompously characterized as a major "contribution toward confirming and developing the principle of banning the wars of aggression".[205] The proposal was presented to the attention of the Assembly of the League of Nations' Committee on Security Questions and read as follows:

> 1. The aggressor in an international conflict shall be considered that state which is the first to take any of the following actions:
>
>   a. Declaration of war against another state.
>   b. The invasion by its armed forces of the territory of another state without declaration of war.
>   c. Bombarding the territory of another state by land, naval, or air forces.
>   d. The landing in, or introduction within the frontiers of another state, of land, naval, or air forces without the permission of the government of such a state, or

---

[202] See Article I of the Kellogg-Briand Pact: "The High Contracting Parties solemly declare in the names of their respective peoples that they condemn recourse to war for the solution of international controversies, and renounce it, as an instrument of national policy in their relations with one another."

[203] See Borchard 1929a, pp. 126–131; Borchard 1929b, pp. 116–120; Cryer 2005, p. 242; Fenwick 1932, pp. 787–789; Kunz 1951b, pp. 46–48; Finch 1933, pp. 725–732; Hill 1928, pp. 823–826; Hyde 1928, pp. 262–269; Hyde 1941, pp. 117–118; Von Mandelsloh 1933, pp. 617–627; Schlüter 1942, pp. 24–32; Werle 2009b, pp. 406–407; Wilson 1932, pp. 327–328; Wilson 1936, pp. 80–83; Wright 1932, pp. 362–368; Wright 1933, pp. 39–61.

[204] Gerhard Werle notes that the Kellogg-Briand Pact was adhered to by 63 of 67 States which existed at the time (except Argentina, Bolivia, El Salvador and Uruguay). See Werle 2009a, p. 479, especially note 27. See also Bilfinger 1940, pp. 1–23; Boye 1930, pp. 766–770; Clark 1917, pp. 790–793; Myers 1948, pp. 320–354.

[205] Nasinovsky 1968, quoted in Bassiouni and Ferencz 2008, p. 211.

the infringement of the condition of such permission, particularly as regards the sojourn or extension of area.

e. The establishment of a naval blockade of the coasts or ports of another state.

2. No consideration whatsoever of a political, strategic or economic nature, including the desire to exploit natural riches or to obtain any sort of advantages or privileges on the territory of another state, to references to considerable capital investments or other special interest in a given state, or to the alleged absence of certain attributes of state organization in the case of a given country, shall be accepted as justification of aggression as defined in Clause 1.[206]

Notably, no attack might be justified by:

1. The internal situation in a given state, as for instance:

   a. Political, economic or cultural backwardness of a given country.
   b. Alleged maladministration.
   c. Possible danger to life or property of foreign residents.
   d. Revolutionary or counterrevolutionary movements, civil war, disorders, or strikes.
   e. The establishment or maintenance in any state of any political, economic, or social order.

2. Any acts, laws, or violations of a given state, as for instance:

   a. The infringement of international agreements.
   b. The infringement of the commercial, concessional or other economic rights or interests of a given state or its citizens.
   c. The rupture or diplomatic or economic relations.
   d. Economic or financial boycott.
   e. Repudiation of debts.
   f. Non-admission or limitation of immigration, or restriction of rights or privileges of foreign students.
   g. The infringement of the privileges of official representatives of other states.
   h. The refusal to allow armed forces transit to the territory of a third state.
   i. Religious or antireligious measures.
   j. Frontier incidents.

3. In the case of mobilization or concentration of armed forces to a considerable extent in the vicinity of its frontiers, the state which such activities threaten may have recourse to diplomatic or other means for the peaceful solution of international controversies. It may at the same time take steps of a military nature, analogous to those described above, without, however, crossing the frontier.[207]

The draft definition was worded in quite strong terms and might have embodied—if it had been adopted—an important international legal development[208]: it presumed the existence of an act of aggression at the instance of a first use of armed force, allowed for no political, strategic or economic justification of

[206] Quoted ibid.

[207] Quoted ibid., at p. 212.

[208] As the 1933 draft definition noticeably resembles, both in its structure and content, the 1974 Definition of Aggression adopted by the United Nations General Assembly (see infra 2.3), one might assume that the latter document's drafters must have been inspired by the earlier text.

aggression, declared military interventions in other States—notably, even in the cases of serious violations of those States' domestic laws or of international law—as inadmissible, and expressly prohibited the crossing of international frontiers.[209] Yet, the draft definition's chief weakness must have consisted in its incompatibility with political and military realities at the time: Japan seized Manchuria in 1932 (see infra 3.1.2.1), Germany initiated the Second World War in 1939 (see infra 3.1.1),[210] and even the Soviet Union—the initiator of the draft definition—did not refrain, in 1939, from participating in the division of Poland and, in 1940, from the annexation of the Baltic States, the painful consequences of which actions can be felt even today.

1.2 Evolution of the Concept of Aggression After World War II

After the Second World War (1939–1945), the international and national legal developments pertaining to the criminalization of aggression entered a qualitatively new phase. With the consecutive establishment of the Nuremberg and Tokyo Tribunals and the parallel constitution of the United Nations, the international legal order at last did away with the legality of the use of military force in international relations, except in limited and precisely defined circumstances (see infra Chap. 2). The next sections will outline a chronology of relevant developments since 1945.

1.2.1 Work Accomplished by the United Nations War Crimes Commission

The United Nations War Crimes Commission was set up at a Diplomatic Conference in London, on 20 October 1943.[211] Its task was to undertake preparatory investigative work for the future prosecution of the Axis major war criminals and to make initial arrangements for the trials' legal aspects.[212] According to the Official History of the Commission, among its most important tasks was to determine

[209] On the draft definition, see generally Bilfinger 1937, pp. 483–496; Brown 1934, pp. 733–736; Chakste 1949, pp. 21–36; Wright 1935, pp. 373–395.

[210] Cf. Bassiouni and Ferencz 2008, p. 212.

[211] On the activities of the Commission, see generally Bathurst 1945, pp. 565–570. See also Safferling 2012, p. 12.

[212] See Bathurst 1945, p. 568.

"whether aggressive war amounts to a criminal act"[213]—an uneasy task in light of the pre-existing international law which, at best, concerned itself with attempting to impose some limitations on States' previously unqualified right to resort to the use of force in international relations (see supra 1.1.6). It appears that a successful argumentation in favor of the criminalization of aggression was first offered, within the Commission's Legal Committee, by Dr. Bohuslav Ečer (1893–1954) of Czechoslovakia, in March 1944. He is quoted by A. J. Kochavi to have stated that the Axis powers' aims in the Second World War were "to enslave foreign nations, to destroy the civilization of those nations, and physically to annihilate a considerable section of their populations on racial, political or religious grounds," and that the "launching and waging of the war" was the Axis powers' "paramount crime".[214] His vision was innovative—indeed visionary of the future progressive development of international law with respect to aggression (see infra 3.1.1 and 3.1.2)—in that he wrote in a proposal:

> Aggressive war is a crime, and by its character an international crime, because it aims against peace and international order. The total aggressive war started by Germany and her allies in 1939 is additionally an international crime in its territorial extent and the number of victims of the aggression.
>
> Not only the aggressor States as such, but also their rulers and military leaders are personally responsible in the eyes of the law for the gigantic chain of crimes which compose this war and which are punishable under the criminal laws of the countries affected.
>
> The penalty according to all these laws is death.[215]

William Schabas notes that Dr. Ečer's proposal gave rise to an intensive debate, which resulted in two reports on the subject, authored by Arnold McNair (1885–1975) of the United Kingdom and Bohuslav Ečer, respectively.[216] The McNair report—supported by a majority of the Commission—concluded that "acts committed by individuals merely for the purpose of preparing and launching aggressive war, are, lege lata, not 'war crimes.'"[217] In turn, Ečer's report suggested that the other offences within the Commission's competence should be dealt with as secondary to the offence of the criminal war.[218] Ultimately, the Commission was not able to come to an agreement, and the appropriateness of "crimes against peace" as part of the Nuremberg tribunal's *ratione materiae* jurisdiction remained uncertain until the 1945 London Conference (see infra 1.2.2).[219]

---

213 United Nations War Crimes Commission 1948, p. 180. See also Cryer 2005, p. 242.

214 Kochavi 1998, p. 97.

215 United Nations War Crimes Commission 1948, pp. 100–101.

216 Schabas 2004, 24.

217 See "Report of the Sub-Committee appointed to consider whether the preparation and launching of the present war should be considered 'war crimes'", Doc. C55, 27 September 1944.

218 See "Minority Report presented by Dr. B. Ecer on the question whether the preparation and launching of the present war should be considered as crimes being within the scope of the United Nations War Crimes Commission", Doc. C56, 27 September 1944.

219 Schabas 2004, p. 26.

1.2.2 London Agreement of 8 August 1945 and the Charter of the Nuremberg International Military Tribunal

While the United Nations War Crimes Commission (see supra 1.2.1) was preparing a practical ground for the future trials and collecting evidence, the Allied leaders were planning the post-war political organization of the world and formulating policies for the criminal prosecutions of the Axis major war criminals.[220] Notably, the Allies' early approaches to the prosecution were quite divergent. As Telford Taylor (1908–1998) recalled, the United Kingdom had initially favored their summary execution, because "their guilt was so black" that it was "beyond the scope of any judicial process".[221] It seems the true reason for this reluctance lay in the United Kingdom's concern that the accused would use the trial as a forum for propaganda and self-justification—a concern which ultimately proved true.[222] The United States and France intended the prospective tribunal to help document the history of the Second World War, inform the world and serve as a future deterrent.[223] The Soviet Union, which advocated for the International Military Tribunal from, at least, as early as 1943, for it had undoubtedly borne the heaviest human and economic burden of the war,[224] did not, at the same time, miss the opportunity to use it to cover up some advantages it had taken of the non-aggression pact it had concluded with Germany in 1939, such as the invasion of Eastern Poland, Finland, and the Baltic States.

The International Military Tribunal at Nuremberg was established pursuant to the Agreement for the Prosecution and Punishment of the Major War Criminals of the European Axis, which the Allied Powers had concluded in London on 8 August 1945, with the Charter of the Tribunal annexed to it.[225] The Tribunal's procedure combined elements from the British and American common law procedures, the French civil law procedure, and the Soviet criminal procedure.[226] The crimes within the Tribunal's jurisdiction were listed in Article 6 of its Charter.[227]

---

[220] See Aufricht 1944, pp. 119–124; Borchard 1944, pp. 284–289; Eagleton 1942, pp. 229–241; Eagleton 1943a, pp. 495–499; Eagleton 1943b, pp. 642–644; Jessup 1941, pp. 329–331; Korovin 1946, pp. 742–755; Kuhn 1941, pp. 114–117; Kunz 1952a, pp. 114–119; Stowell 1944, pp. 106–108; Wright 1943, pp. 97–103.

[221] Taylor 1992, p. 29. See also Safferling 2012, pp. 12–13.

[222] See Taylor 1992, p. 319. See also Bassiouni 2003, pp. 406–407.

[223] See generally Fenby 2006.

[224] See Zelinskaya 2006, pp. 416–418.

[225] See Ehard 1949, pp. 223–245; Finch 1947, pp. 20–37; Kemp 2010, pp. 81–94; Schick 1947, pp. 770–794; Tomuschat 1994, pp. 237–247; Wright 1947, pp. 38–72; Wright 1945, pp. 257–285.

[226] Bassiouni 2003, p. 408; Safferling 2012, pp. 14–15.

[227] Charter of the International Military Tribunal, Article 6(a): "Crimes against peace: namely, planning, preparation, initiation or waging of a war of aggression, or a war in violation of international treaties, agreements or assurances, or participation in a Common Plan or Conspiracy for the accomplishment of any of the foregoing".

As M. Cherif Bassiouni reports, a general agreement existed during the London negotiations that the major legal validation for "crimes against peace" was the 1928 Kellogg-Briand Pact (see supra 1.1.6.5), the applicability of which the Soviet Union nevertheless wished to limit by adding the phrase "by the European Axis" to Article 6(a).[228] This limitation was reportedly avoided owing to Justice Robert Houghwout Jackson's (1892–1954) successful argumentation to the effect that the universal prohibition of aggression was binding upon all States, including the United States of America.[229]

As M. Cherif Bassiouni and Benjamin Ferencz note, it was not quite clear in 1945 what exactly was meant by "aggression".[230] It follows from Article 6(a) that individual acts (planning, preparation, initiation or waging) leading to a *war of aggression* were just one of three types of crimes against peace within the jurisdiction of the Tribunal. In other words, a literal interpretation of the Charter suggests that a war of aggression was not the same as a war in violation of international treaties, nor was it equal to participation in a Common Plan or Conspiracy for launching either of the two types of inter-State wars.[231] However, as such, the "war of aggression" was not clearly defined anywhere in the Tribunal's Charter or Judgment. In the Judgment, though, there were some interpretative indications as to what had constituted practical examples of aggression in the course of the Second World War: aggression consisted, *inter alia*, in Germany's attack against the Soviet Union "without warning of any kind, and without the shadow of legal excuse".[232] In other words, in the opinion of the Tribunal, a war of aggression should have been characterized by the absence of a declaration and of a sufficient legal justification. However, this conclusion is only partially correct.[233] It appears from Article 6(a) that a war of aggression's another distinctive feature from the other type of war criminalized under the Charter should have been the absence of

---

228 Bassiouni 2003, p. 409.

229 *Report of Robert H. Jackson* (1949), pp. vii–viii.

230 Bassiouni and Ferencz 2008, p. 319. See also Cryer 2005, p. 243; Sayapin 2009, p. 157.

231 Both the Indictment and the Judgment of the Tribunal confirm this distinction between the elements of three crimes and explain that "[t]he "Common Plan or Conspiracy" charged in the Indictment covers twenty-five years, from the formation of the Nazi Party in 1919 to the end of the war in 1945", while planning and waging the wars in question constituted separate undertakings. See International Military Tribunal (Nuremberg), Judgment of 1 October 1946, p. 447.

232 Ibid., p. 441.

233 One may legitimately ask here, in somewhat surprised a manner, whether a war of the Second World War's magnitude and cruelty could not have formally been characterized as one of aggression, if it had been "properly" (in the sense of applicable Hague Conventions) declared and legally motivated, and would therefore have been excluded from the Charter's scope of *ratione materiae* applicability. Since the answer obviously is in the negative, one should conclude that a definition of aggression, should one have been produced for the purpose of the Nuremberg Tribunal, must have included other—or further—definitional elements.

"international treaties, agreements or assurances" between the attacking and attacked States, because the existence of such arrangements would have automatically placed the war in question within the second category of the crimes against peace.[234] As the Tribunal noted in its Judgment, the principal treaties in question included the relevant Hague Conventions (see supra 1.1.5), the Versailles Treaty (see supra 1.1.6.2), treaties of mutual guarantee, arbitration and non-aggression (see supra 1.1.6.4) and the Kellogg-Briand Pact (see supra 1.1.6.5). Given that the majority of States which existed at the time, including, at any rate, the European nations which Germany attacked in the Second World War (see infra 3.1.1), were parties to either (or several) of the above treaties, the Charter's formal distinction between "wars of aggression" and "wars in violation of international treaties, agreements or assurances" appears even odder. If, in the language of the Tribunal, a war of aggression was one "without the shadow of legal excuse," any reasonable "justification" of a war against any of the targeted nations should logically have been founded upon either of those treaties. But since no such reasonable justification could have been produced by Germany, because it would have automatically violated an applicable treaty in question, it follows that either the distinction introduced in Article 6(a) was largely artificial and should therefore not have been made, or that a "war of aggression" was, in fact, at the same time one "in violation of applicable international treaties, agreements or assurances," and the said distinction in law made no sense in practice. The two definitional elements would thus have made more sense, if they had been applied conjointly rather than as alternatives.

Apparently, the creators of the Tribunal were not uninformed of the substantive and procedural weaknesses of its legal basis,[235] for they only allowed trials of German nationals to be held in Nuremberg in 1945–1946, to the exclusion of the possibility of having Allied nationals indicted for the crimes within the Tribunal's *ratione materiae* jurisdiction. However, criticisms against the organization and functioning of the Nuremberg Tribunal went even further than that. In addition to the Tribunal's discriminatory nature,[236] the victorious Powers' inequitable post-war treatment of German minorities in Eastern Europe and the Soviet Union's double standards of law and morality were also pointed to as indicia of the Allied Powers' inconsistent policies of applying the law they had themselves created at the

[234] The Tribunal refrained from considering which of the aggressive wars against 12 nations were at the same time wars in violation of international treaties, agreements or assurances, for it satisfied itself with the conclusion that "certain of the defendants planned and waged aggressive wars [...] and were therefore guilty of this series of crimes." See International Military Tribunal (Nuremberg), Judgment of 1 October 1946, p. 442.

[235] See Burchard 2006, pp. 800–829; Safferling 2012, pp. 15–18; Tomuschat 2006, p. 832.

[236] Dahm 1961, p. 292.

London Conference.[237] To conclude, with all indisputable impact the Nuremberg Tribunal exercised upon the subsequent development of international (especially, criminal) law, it was not free from a few—probably, inescapable—flaws, which make possible its critique even today.

1.2.3 International Military Tribunal for the Far East

While the *ratione materiae* jurisdiction of the International Military Tribunal for the Far East (the Tokyo Tribunal) was by and large modeled after that of the Nuremberg Tribunal (see infra 3.1.2), the Tokyo Tribunal was even more exposed to critique, as far as its procedural side was concerned, than was its European counterpart. The Tokyo Tribunal's Charter[238] was drafted by Joseph Berry Keenan (1888–1954)—formerly Assistant to the US Attorney General—who was subsequently appointed Chief Prosecutor of the Tribunal.[239] The Charter was approved on 19 January 1946 by General Douglas MacArthur's (1880–1964) administrative proclamation in his capacity of Commander in Chief of the United States Forces in the Pacific—not even by a treaty akin to the 1945 London Agreement (see supra 1.2.2).[240] The Commander in Chief was entitled to exercising a substantial control over the structure and performance of the Tribunal. Under Article 2 of the Charter, General MacArthur appointed Judges from among nominated nationals of Australia, Canada, China, France, Great Britain, India, The Netherlands, New Zealand, the Philippines, the Soviet Union, and the United States. Moreover, under Article 3(a), the President of the Tribunal was also appointed by the Commander in Chief.[241] The selection of defence counsels could be "subject to disapproval [...] at any time by the Tribunal" (Article 9). More predictably than not, the Tokyo trial ended with the conviction of all defendants: seven death

---

[237] Tomuschat 2006, p. 834.

[238] Charter of the International Military Tribunal for the Far East, Article 5(a): "Crimes against peace: namely, the planning, preparation, initiation or waging of a declared or undeclared war of aggression, or a war in violation of international law, treaties, agreements or assurances, or participation in a common plan or conspiracy for the accomplishment of any of the foregoing." See Brown 1939, pp. 538–541; Fenwick 1937, pp. 694–696; Kemp 2010, pp. 94–98.

[239] See Hisakazu 2011, p. 7.

[240] The proclamation laid down that "the constitution, jurisdiction and functions of this Tribunal are those set forth in the Charter of the International Military Tribunal for the Far East, approved by me today". See *Special Proclamation by the Supreme Commander for the Allied Powers*, 19 January 1946, quoted in Werle 2009a, p. 12, note 52. See also Safferling 2012, pp. 18–19.

[241] For a critical assessment of the Tribunal, see Köchler 2003, pp. 68, 157–161; generally Minear 1971.

sentences and sixteen life sentences were imposed, one defendant was sentenced to 20 years of imprisonment, and one defendant received a 7-year prison term. The Emperor himself was not indicted for political reasons (cf. infra 3.1.2.7).[242]

Unlike the Nuremberg Tribunal, the Tokyo trial has been strongly criticized even *from within*. In his dissenting opinion, Judge Radhabinod Pal (1886–1967) of India openly characterized the Tribunal as a dangerous manifestation of "victors' justice",[243] and its legal basis (both procedural and material) as being incompatible with international law:

> In prescribing the rules of evidence for this trial[244] the Charter practically discarded all the procedural rules devised by the various national systems of law, based on litigious experience and tradition, to guard the tribunal against erroneous persuasion, and thus left us, in the matter of proof, to guide ourselves independently of any artificial rules of procedure [...][245] As a judicial tribunal, we cannot behave in any manner which may justify the feeling that the setting up of the tribunal was only for the attainment of an objective which was essentially political, though cloaked by a juridical appearance.[246]

As far as charges under Article 5(a) of the Charter were specifically concerned (see infra 3.1.2), Judge Pal questioned their legitimacy too, "keeping in view the generally prevalent behavior of the powers in international life".[247] As Hans Köchler recalls, Judge Pal was the only member of the Tribunal who raised the issue of the nuclear bombing of Hiroshima and Nagasaki in August 1945[248] as a violation of the laws and customs of war by the Allies.[249] Naturally, Judge Pal's dissenting opinion was not read out at the trial, not published with the Judgment in Tokyo and was not quoted frequently ever since.[250]

---

242 See generally Hata and Jansen 2007; Hoyt 1992; Manning 1989; Otomo 2011, pp. 63–78.

243 For the sake of objectivity, it may be noted that Judge Radhabinod Pal's dissenting opinion might not have been without a political bias, for he was known as a sympathiser of the Indian National Army (INA), an Indian faction which collaborated with Japan with a view to liberating India from British colonization. See Takeshi 2011, pp. 127–144, and Cryer 2005, p. 243.

244 Article 13(a) of the Tokyo Charter read: "All purported admissions or statements of the accused are admissible".

245 See "Judgment of Mr Justice Pal, Member from India," reprinted in Röling and Rüter 1977, at p. 629.

246 Ibid., p. 1037.

247 Ibid., p. 1035.

248 On the use of nuclear weapons, see Akande 1998a, pp. 165–217; Borchard 1946, pp. 161–165; Brown Firmage 1969, pp. 711–746; D'Amato 1967, pp. 66–77; Falk 1965, pp. 759–793; Falk 1997, pp. 64–75; Garvey 2008, pp. 339–357; Matheson 1997, pp. 417–435; Skordas 2001, pp. 191–224; Thomas 1945, pp. 736–744; Turlington 1946, pp. 165–167.

249 See Henderson 2011, pp. 311–321; Tanaka 2011, pp. 293–310.

250 See Simpson 2011, at p. 27; Köchler 2003, pp. 159–161.

1.2.4 Allied Control Council Law № 10

The Allied Control Council was a collective governing body of the Allied Occupation Zones in Germany after the Second World War.[251] The Control Council was established by the Potsdam Agreement of 2 August 1945 and operated from August 1945 to March 1948 with the Soviet Union, the United Kingdom, the United States and France as its members.[252] The Council enacted an important number of laws, directives, and other acts, which dealt with political, legal, and institutional matters—such as demilitarisation and denazification—but also with everyday ones such as telephone tariffs and combating venereal diseases.[253] For the purpose of this book, the Control Council Law № 10 ("Punishment of Persons Guilty of War Crimes, Crimes Against Peace, and Against Humanity"), issued on 20 December 1945, is of particular relevance. The substantive part of the Law (Article II) was largely—albeit not entirely[254]—based on the Charter of the Nuremberg Tribunal, and the crimes against peace were specifically defined as:

> [i]nitiation of invasions of other countries and wars of aggression in violation of international laws and treaties, including but not limited to planning, preparation, initiation or waging a war of aggression, or a war in violation of international treaties, agreements or assurances, or participation in a common plan or conspiracy for the accomplishment of any of the foregoing.[255]

Each of the so-called follow-up trials under the Control Council Law № 10 involved a specific professional category of defendants, including some high-ranking officials in Germany's armed forces, industry, economy, judiciary, healthcare, as well as the Nazi party and State.[256] On trials of defendants charged with crimes against peace under the Control Council Law № 10,[257] see infra 3.1.3.

---

[251] See Nobleman 1947, pp. 650–655; Plischke 1947, pp. 807–827.

[252] The initial members of the Control Council were Marshal Georgy Zhukov (1896–1974) for the Soviet Union, Field Marshal Bernard Montgomery (1887–1976) for the United Kingdom, General Dwight Eisenhower (1890–1969) for the United States, and General Jean de Lattre de Tassigny (1889–1962) for France.

[253] For an account of the Control Council's activity, see generally Ziemke 1990.

[254] For example, as far as the definition of crimes against humanity were concerned, there was no more requirement in Article 2 of the Law for a link between crimes against humanity and crimes against peace, or war crimes.

[255] Control Council Law № 10, *Official Gazette Control Council for Germany*, No. 3, 31 January 1946, pp. 50 et seq., Article II(1)(a).

[256] See Cowles 1948, pp. 299–319; Kemp 2010, pp. 98–101; Nobleman 1946, pp. 803–811; Rie 1954, pp. 470–474; Safferling 2012, pp. 19–20.

[257] For an overview of trials with respect to crimes against peace, see Heller 2011, pp. 179–202.

1.2.5 Attitudes Within the United Nations System

The establishment of the United Nations in 1945 was a development of a paramount importance for the purpose of regulating the resort to force by international law.[258] For the first time in history, the drafters of an international treaty—the Charter of the United Nations—sought to ban *all* resort to force, with only two expressly defined exceptions.[259] Although the United Nations was incapable of preventing the proliferation of non-international armed conflicts after the Second World War,[260] it seems to have succeeded, overall, in reinforcing the principle that the right of States to go to war with one another was no longer unlimited (cf. supra 1.1.6.2).[261] After 1945, States have almost always endeavored to explain their international uses of force, in one way or another, by way of interpreting the relevant provisions of the Charter or of other international instruments (see infra 2.4). Moreover, as it will be maintained further in this volume, the adoption of the Charter should be regarded as a foundation to post-Nuremberg developments pertaining to the criminalization of aggression.

1.2.5.1 Charter of the United Nations

The fundamental prohibition of resort to military force in contravention of the Purposes of the United Nations was laid down in Article 2(4) of the Charter (see infra Chap. 2).[262] In the opinion of Stephen Neff, it was a pragmatic rule, which embodied "an urgent response to local and immediate demands and conditions rather than an expression of eternal verities".[263] Over the following decades, the provision was recognized as one of customary international law and a peremptory norm of general international law from which no derogation is allowed (see infra 2.1.2, 2.1.3, 2.2). While the content of Article 2(4) will be examined more carefully in Chap. 2, a few of its key implications merit a mention here. As Stephen Neff notes, the first three legal effects were already known from the interwar

[258] See Aust 2005, pp. 223–232; Briggs 1947, pp. 433–435; Briggs 1957, pp. 517–529; Chakste 1948, pp. 590–600; Clark 2011, pp. 337–342; Eagleton 1945, pp. 751–754; Falk 2003, pp. 590–598; Finch 1945, pp. 541–546; Frowein 1976, pp. 147–167; Kelsen 1945, pp. 45–83; Kemp 2010, pp. 104–108; Köchler 2006, pp. 323–340; Kunz 1952b, pp. 504–508; Lim 2007, pp. 307–328; Pellet 1995, pp. 401–425; Ratner 1995, pp. 426–444; Schachter 1994, pp. 1–23; Shaw 2008, pp. 1204–1281; Wilson 1970, pp. 139–143.

[259] For an analysis of the Charter-based exceptions to the prohibition of the use of force, see infra 2.4.1.

[260] According to M. Cherif Bassiouni, no less than 250 armed conflicts took place since 1945, which have claimed an estimated 170 million lives. See Bassiouni 2003, pp. 91–92, note 142.

[261] See generally Hoffmann 1995.

[262] UN Charter, Article 2(4): "All Members shall refrain in their international relations from the threat or use of force against the territorial integrity or political independence of any state, or in any other manner inconsistent with the Purposes of the United Nations".

[263] See Neff 2005, p. 317.

period, i.e., already from the League of Nations' Covenant regime, while the latter one was specific to the world order established by the UN Charter.[264]

Firstly, States, which used force in violation of Article 2(4), were liable to pay compensation for all damage resulting from an internationally wrongful act.[265] However, according to S. Neff, the quality of such compensations was different from, for instance, that of reparations imposed after the First World War, when Germany was originally required to bear the entire financial burden of the war but, in the end, the amount of reparations was limited to damages she had caused to civilian persons and property during the war.[266] The post-World War II compensation regimes were explicitly limited to the actual material damages incurred as a result of the conflicts.[267] Secondly, when a violation of Article 2(4) occurred, third States were no longer obliged to apply the law of neutrality but, conversely, they might legitimately assist the victim(s) of the unlawful use of force, for example, by placing at their disposal armaments or funding.[268] Thirdly, in line with the 1932 Stimson Doctrine,[269] such uses of force should produce no entitlement to the recognition of territorial or other material acquisitions,[270] and to no other international legal rights or obligations, including the recognition of governments.[271] This provision was reaffirmed in the General Assembly's Friendly Relations Declaration (see infra 1.2.5.3).

---

[264] Neff 2005, pp. 319–322. Actually, Stephen Neff singled out five legal implications of Article 2(4), the fifth one being the possibility of criminal prosecutions for aggression by the International Military Tribunals at Nuremberg and Tokyo as well as the subsequent trials under Control Council Law № 10. Yet, this conclusion seems somewhat questionable, because all of those trials occurred parallel to and relatively independently of the UN Charter. The Charter did not serve as these Tribunals' legal basis, their respective Judgments were not interpretative of the Charter but only of the pre-existing international law, and, last but not least, the Charter did not concern itself with the legal standing of individuals under international law and with issues of individual criminal responsibility. It was rather an instrument for the regulation of the conduct of States as Members of a (newly established, at the time) universal international organization. Another sort of conclusion would have probably been more accurate—that the Charter has substantially modified the *ratione materiae* source of the law of crimes against peace, i.e., public international law's provisions on the use force, and that any future criminal prosecutions for the crime of aggression (if there had been any) should of necessity have taken account of the Charter's relevant provisions. This proposition will be argued further in this volume.

[265] See Neff 2005, p. 319. See also Wright 1953, at pp. 372–373.

[266] See supra 1.1.6.2, especially note 165 and accompanying text.

[267] See Neff 2005, pp. 319–320.

[268] Ibid., p. 320. See also Lauterpacht 1968, pp. 58–68.

[269] See Meiertöns 2010, pp. 83 et seq.

[270] See Neff 2005, p. 321. See also Orakelashvili 2006, pp. 218–219.

[271] See Neff 2005, p. 321. See also Dugard 1987, pp. 27–35.

Finally, according to Stephen Neff, a novel implication of the Charter's prohibition of the use of force consisted in that the UN Security Council might now enforce international peace through collective actions of a non-military (see infra 2.4.1.5.1) or military (see infra 2.4.1.5.2) nature, without that a *state* of war in the technical legal sense would thereby be created.[272] The legal nature of peace enforcement under the aegis of the United Nations will be dealt with infra at 2.4.1.5. We will now turn to useful—indeed, indirectly indicative of customary international law—examples of attitudes toward the use of inter-State armed force on the part of relevant main organs of the United Nations.

1.2.5.2 Attitudes of the UN Security Council

Under Article 39 of the Charter, the Security Council has been given the primary responsibility for the maintenance of international peace and security, including the power to "determine the existence of any [...] act of aggression".[273] Yet, according to some commentators, the Security Council was largely biased in the exercise of that power, for until the adoption of the General Assembly resolution 3314, on 14 December 1974 (see infra 1.2.5.3 and 2.3), the Council did not have any normative guidance as to what should (or might) constitute aggression. From 1946 to 1986—when dozens of international armed conflicts took place—the Council passed only two decisions under Article 39 that there was a "breach of the peace" (with respect to Korea in 1950[274] and to the Falkland Islands in 1982).[275] During the same period, the Security Council referred to "aggression" only in the instances of Israel (see infra 2.1.3) and South Africa, and determined no more than seven cases of "threat to international peace and security".[276] The Security Council did not classify the Soviet invasion in Afghanistan on 25 December 1979 as an act of aggression,[277] and even the Iraqi invasion in Kuwait on 2 August 1990 was characterized as a breach of international peace and security.[278] Given the

272 See Neff 2005, pp. 322–325.

273 On the powers of the Security Council, see Alvarez 1996, pp. 1–39; Blokker 2005, pp. 1–29; Bowett 1994, pp. 89–101; Eagleton 1946, pp. 513–533; Hulsroj 2002, pp. 59–93; Österdahl 2005, pp. 1–20; Saul 2005, pp. 141–146; Schachter 1964, pp. 960–965; Schrijver 2007, pp. 127–138; Ward 2003, pp. 289–305; Wellens 2003, pp. 15–70.

274 See Young and Kent 2004, pp. 146–152.

275 Ibid., p. 573.

276 Koskenniemi 1996, at p. 458. See also Bertrand 1995, pp. 349–359.

277 Young and Kent note that even friends of the USSR, such as India, were critical over the invasion. In the absence of a negative qualification by the Security Council, it was condemned by the UN General Assembly by 104 to 18 votes. See Young and Kent 2004, p. 493.

278 See Security Council Resolution 660 (1990).

recurrent use of vetoes[279] in the Council between 1945 and 1992,[280] it is not surprising that acts of aggression were determined only exceptionally rarely.[281]

We will more than once come back to the Security Council's role in the determination of acts of aggression, including in conjunction with the International Criminal Court's jurisdiction over the respective individual crime. It suffices to mention here that, since States' obligations under the Charter of the United Nations prevail over their obligations under any other international agreement,[282] including the Rome Statute, and three permanent Members of the Council having the veto power (China, Russia and the United States) are not (currently) Parties to the Statute, the purportedly independent[283] International Criminal Court *would*, in fact, considerably depend on the Security Council in the exercise of jurisdiction over the individual crime of aggression. The modes of procedural interaction between the ICC and the Security Council will be dealt with below, at 5.3.2.7–5.3.2.9, 5.3.3.

1.2.5.3 Attitudes of the UN General Assembly

As Christine Gray notes, almost since the establishment of the United Nations, some of its Members felt a need to have the Charter's provisions on the use of force clarified in the General Assembly resolutions.[284] She suggests that the first essential resolution on the subject was the 1949 Resolution on the Essentials of Peace,[285] followed in 1950 by the momentous "Uniting for Peace" resolution (see infra 2.4.2.1).[286] In 1986, the International Court of Justice recalled in its Nicaragua Judgment (see infra 1.2.5.4, 2.1.1–2.1.3) the 1970 Friendly Relations

[279] Cf. UN Charter, Article 27(3): "Decisions of the Security Council on all other matters shall be made by an affirmative vote of nine members including the concurring votes of the permanent members; provided that, in decisions under Chapter VI, and under para 3 of Article 52, a party to a dispute shall abstain from voting".

[280] During the said period, the Soviet Union used its veto right 114 times; USA sixty-nine; United Kingdom thirty; France eighteen; China three. See Roberts and Kingsbury 1993, p. 10. See also Potter 1945, pp. 318–322; Reisman 1980, pp. 904–907; Rudzinski 1951, pp. 443–461.

[281] As Christine Gray notes, condemnations by the Security Council and the General Assembly occurred mostly with respect to States which were, in some sense, seen as "outlaws" under international law—for example, Portugal, Southern Rhodesia, Israel, South Africa, and Indonesia. See Gray 2008, p. 21.

[282] UN Charter, Article 103: "In the event of a conflict between the obligations of the Members of the United Nations under the present Charter and their obligations under any other international agreement, their obligations under the present Charter shall prevail".

[283] See ICC Statute, 9th preambular paragraph.

[284] See Gray 2008, p. 9.

[285] UN General Assembly Resolution 290 (IV), 1 December 1949.

[286] See Gray 2008, p. 9. On the resolution, see generally Andrassy 1956, pp. 563–582; Kemp 2010, pp. 21–24.

Declaration[287] and the 1974 Definition of Aggression (see infra 2.3) as authoritative evidence of customary international law on the prohibition of the use of force.[288] In 1987, the Declaration on the Enhancement of the Effectiveness of the Principle of Refraining from the Threat or Use of Force in International Relations (Declaration on the Non-Use of Force) was added to their number.[289] Even then, argues C. Gray, although these resolutions were adopted unanimously or by consensus and might be regarded as a reflection of customary international law,[290] they did leave a few key questions unanswered—such as the scope of the right to self-defence (see infra 2.4.1), the meaning of "force" (see infra 2.1.1.2), colonial peoples' right to use force in furtherance of self-determination (see infra 2.4.2.2), or a State's entitlement to reclaim territory seized forcibly by another State (see infra 2.1.3).[291] On other occasions, where the UN General Assembly did, as a matter of fact, condemn specific uses of force in its resolutions,[292] it did not necessarily name the violator States. It is submitted that the General Assembly might, in the future, usefully task the International Law Commission with clarifying the content of the aforesaid issues and promulgate the Commission's findings (issued for example, in the format of "Draft Articles" on the use of force by States), as it did, in December 2001, with respect to the Draft Articles on the responsibility of States for internationally wrongful acts (see infra 1.2.5.6). Alternatively, the "Draft Articles" on the use of force by States might be promulgated by the UN Secretary-General, by analogy with the 1999 Bulletin "Observance by United Nations forces of international humanitarian law".[293]

1.2.5.4 Attitudes of the International Court of Justice

After the Cold War, the role of the International Court of Justice in the progressive development of international law on the use of force and the practicability of judicial review of the Security Council's resolutions on the subject has been increasingly

---

[287] See Houben 1967, pp. 703–736.

[288] See *Case Concerning Military and Paramilitary Activities in and against Nicaragua (Nicaragua case),* ICJ Reports (1986), para 188; *Legality of the Threat or Use of Nuclear Weapons (Nuclear Weapons Advisory Opinion),* ICJ Reports (1996), para 70.

[289] UN General Assembly Resolution A/RES/42/22, 18 November 1987.

[290] See Gray 2008, p. 9.

[291] Ibid., pp. 9–10.

[292] See, for example, UN General Assembly Resolution 38/10, 11 November 1983; UN General Assembly Resolution A/RES/3212 (XXIX), 1 November 1974; UN General Assembly Resolution A/RES/38/7, 2 November 1983.

[293] See document ST/SGB/1999/13, 6 August 1999.

debated.[294] From Christine Gray's viewpoint, the principal questions here—about which, in line with the Court's (so far) neutral position on the issue, there is no recognizable unity among publicists[295]—are whether a judicial review should be feasible as a matter of principle, and whether such a potentially disagreeing review would be (in-)consistent with the Security Council's primary responsibility for the maintenance of international peace and security, "in order to ensure prompt and effective action by the United Nations" in the sense of Article 24 of the United Nations Charter.[296] Significantly, in its examination of admissibility in the *Nicaragua* case (see infra 2.1.1–2.1.3)—historically, the first leading case on the use of force the International Court of Justice had to deal with—the International Court of Justice was unambiguous in asserting its general competence to treat *any* questions of international law[297]—thus, also issues pertaining to the legality of the use of force.[298] In the same decision, the Court opined that the Security Council's authority under Article 24 of the UN Charter was indeed primary but not exclusive[299]—and hence allowing for alternative legitimate means for restoring international peace and security, including referral to the International Court of Justice. As C. Gray so rightly concluded, the Court wisely justified its competence to adjudicate the case, without overriding the Security Council's authority under the Charter[300]:

> [I]f in the present proceedings it becomes necessary for the Court to judge in this respect between the Parties [...] it cannot be debarred from doing so by the existence of a procedure for the States concerned to report to the Security Council in this connection.[301]

Following the *Nicaragua* case, States brought to the International Court of Justice's attention no less than seventeen cases on the use of armed force in

---

294 On the role of the International Court of Justice, see generally: Alexandrov 2006, pp. 29–38; Andrassy 1958, pp. 1–23; Bedjaoui 2006, pp. 1–27; Briggs 1959, pp. 301–318; Brown 1959, pp. 195–244; Brownlie 1998, pp. 703–730; Carlston 1950, pp. 728–737; Condorelli 1995, pp. 388–400; Golsong 1971, pp. 673–696; Gordon 1965, pp. 794–833; Gross 1971, pp. 253–326; Gross 1972, pp. 479–490; Harris 2004, pp. 50–53, 1027–1088; Hudson 1948, pp. 630–632; Hudson 1957, pp. 569–573; Jennings 1987, pp. 3–16; Lawson 1952, pp. 219–238; Malanczuk 1997, pp. 281–293; McWhinney 2006, pp. 3–13; Münch 1961, pp. 221–248; Reisman 1969, pp. 1–27; Schachter 1960, pp. 1–24; Schwelb 1972, pp. 337–351; Shaw 2008, pp. 1057–1117; Tanzi 1995, pp. 539–572; Thirlway 2005, pp. 15–28; Yee 2005, pp. 393–416.

295 See, for example, Akande 1998b, pp. 437–467; Hargrove 1987, pp. 135–143; Payandeh 2006, pp. 41–71; Lopes Pegna 1998, pp. 724–736; generally, Schweigman 2001.

296 See Gray 2008, p. 14.

297 *Nicaragua* case (Jurisdiction and Admissibility), ICJ Reports (1984), para 94.

298 See Gray 2008, p. 15.

299 See ibid., p. 16. See also *Nicaragua* case (Jurisdiction and Admissibility), supra note 297, paras 90, 95.

300 See Gray 2008, p. 16.

301 *Nicaragua* case (Jurisdiction and Admissibility), supra note 297, para 98, quoted in Gray 2008, p. 16.

international relations,[302] which involved disputes between Cameroon and Nigeria,[303] Iran and the USA,[304, 305] Serbia and Montenegro and ten NATO Member States,[306] Pakistan and India,[307] the Democratic Republic of the Congo and, respectively, Burundi,[308] Rwanda[309] and Uganda.[310] In August 2008, one more case—formally related to the application of the International Convention on the Elimination of All Forms of Racial Discrimination but in substance dealing, *inter alia*, with the use of force—was instituted by Georgia against the Russian Federation.[311] It is submitted that these notable developments do speak in favor of the Court's competence and increasingly important role in the interpretation of international law applicable to the use of armed force in inter-State relations, and that its growing jurisprudence on the subject may—as a subsidiary means for the determination of rules of international law (cf. Article 38(1)(d) of the ICJ

---

302 See Gray 2008, p. 16. For an overview of the Court's jurisprudence on the subject, see Gray 2003, pp. 867–905.

303 See *Land and Maritime Boundary between Cameroon and Nigeria (Cameroon v. Nigeria: Equatorial Guinea intervening)*, Judgment of 11 June 1998, ICJ Reports (1998), Judgment on the merits of 10 October 2002, ICJ Reports (2002).

304 See *Oil Platforms (Islamic Republic of Iran v. United States of America)*, Judgment of 12 December 1996, ICJ Reports (1996), Judgment on the merits of 6 November 2003, ICJ Reports (2003).

305 See *Aerial Incident of 3 July 1988 (Islamic Republic of' Iran v. United States of America)*, Order of 22 February 1996, ICJ Reports (1996), p. 9.

306 See *Legality of the U*se of Force (Serbia and Montenegro v. Belgium), Judgment of 15 December 2004, ICJ Reports (2004); *Legality of Use of Force (Serbia and Montenegro v. Canada)*, Judgment of 15 December 2004, ICJ Reports (2004); *Legality of Use of Force (Serbia and Montenegro v. France)*, Judgment of 15 December 2004, ICJ Reports (2004); *Legality of Use of Force (Serbia and Montenegro v. Germany)*, Judgment of 15 December 2004, ICJ Reports (2004); *Legality of Use of Force (Serbia and Montenegro v. Italy)*, Judgment of 15 December 2004, ICJ Reports (2004); *Legality of Use of Force (Serbia and Montenegro v. Netherlands)*, Judgment of 15 December 2004, ICJ Reports (2004); *Legality of Use of Force (Serbia and Montenegro v. Portugal)*, Judgment of 15 December 2004, ICJ Reports (2004); *Legality of Use of Force (Serbia and Montenegro v. Spain) (Provisional Measures)*, Order of 2 June 1999, ICJ Reports (2004); *Legality of Use of Force (Serbia and Montenegro v. United Kingdom)*, Judgment of 15 December 2004, ICJ Reports (2004); *Legality of Use of Force (Yugoslavia v. United States of America), (Provisional Measures)*, Order of 2 June 1999, ICJ Reports (1999).

307 See *Aerial Incident of 10 August 1999 (Pakistan v. India)*, ICJ Reports (2000).

308 See *Armed Activities on the Territory of the Congo (Democratic Republic of the Congo v. Burundi)*, Application of 23 June 1999.

309 See *Armed Activities on the Territory of the Congo (Democratic Republic of the Congo v. Rwanda)*, Application of 23 June 1999.

310 See *Armed Activities on the Territory of the Congo (Democratic Republic of the Congo v. Uganda)*, Judgment of 19 December 2005, ICJ Reports (2005).

311 See Case Concerning Application of the International Convention on the Elimination of All Forms of Racial Discrimination (Georgia v. Russian Federation), Preliminary Objections, Judgment of 1 April 2011, ICJ Reports (2011).

Statute)—also be useful for the purpose of criminalizing aggression, at the national level (see infra 4.1) or through the medium of the International Criminal Court (see infra Chap. 5).

1.2.5.5 Attitudes of the Secretary-General

The role of the Secretary-General in the institutional performance of the United Nations evolved noticeably over the decades of the organization's operation.[312] Strictly speaking, under Chapter XV of the Charter, the Secretary-General's functional competence is quite limited. Pursuant to Article 97 (second sentence), the Secretary-General "shall be the chief administrative officer of the Organization". Article 98 further provides that the Secretary-General should "act in that capacity in all meetings of the General Assembly, of the Security Council, of the Economic and Social Council, and of the Trusteeship Council", and should perform "such other functions as are entrusted to him by these organs." Under the same Article, the Secretary-General is required to provide annual reports on the work of the United Nations to the General Assembly. It must have been this very tool that enabled the Secretary-General to share his views and concerns with the other principal organs of the United Nations and with external publics—along with his right, under Article 99, to "bring to the attention of the Security Council any matter which in his opinion may threaten the maintenance of international peace and security"—and made his role increasingly important, especially since the end of the Cold War.

As the United Nations was challenged, throughout its existence, by the obvious need to make its various principal organs' efforts aimed at the maintenance of international peace and security more coherent, the sixth Secretary-General Boutros Boutros-Ghali produced, in 1992, a detailed report on the subject matter,[313] in which those efforts were categorized under the headings of preventive diplomacy, peace-keeping, peace-making and peace-building, depending on the actual state of affairs in the development of a conflict.[314] The report suggested that

---

312 See Franck 1995, pp. 360–387; Kunz 1946, pp. 786–792; Mammen 2006, pp. 293–296.

313 An amended edition of the report was issued in 1995. See, generally, Boutros-Ghali 1995.

314 Ibid., para 15: "Our aims must be:

- To seek to identify at the earliest possible stage situations that could produce conflict, and to try through diplomacy to remove the sources of danger before violence results;
- Where conflict erupts, to engage in peacemaking aimed at resolving the issues that have led to conflict;
- Through peace-keeping, to work to preserve peace, however fragile, where fighting has been halted and to assist in implementing agreements achieved by the peacemakers;
- To stand ready to assist in peace-building in its differing contexts: rebuilding the institutions and infrastructures of nations torn by civil war and strife; and building bonds of peaceful mutual benefit among nations formerly at war;
- And in the largest sense, to address the deepest causes of conflict: economic despair, social injustice, and political oppression. It is possible to discern an increasingly common moral perception that spans the world's nations and peoples, and which is finding expression in international laws, many owing their genesis to the work of this Organization."

most principal organs of the United Nations must practically be involved in the settlement of disputes as these arise and develop,[315] whereby the Secretary-General and other senior staff members of the Secretariat were to be accorded special roles in the exercise of "preventive diplomacy," i.e., in the taking of early political and diplomatic action for the purpose of preventing conflicts from arising, escalating or spreading:

> The most desirable and efficient employment of diplomacy is to ease tensions before they result in conflict—or, if conflict breaks out, to act swiftly to contain it and resolve its underlying causes. Preventive diplomacy may be performed by the Secretary-General personally or through senior staff or specialized agencies and programmes, by the Security Council or the General Assembly, and by regional organizations in cooperation with the United Nations. Preventive diplomacy requires measures to create confidence; it needs early warning based on information gathering and informal or formal fact-finding; it may also involve preventive deployment and, in some situations, demilitarized zones.[316]

Without a doubt, the report was a momentous development in the United Nations' institutional doctrine. However, given that many of the substantive measures recommended in the report (for example, a more universal acceptance of general jurisdiction of the International Court of Justice, as a mechanism for resolving international disputes, by the turn of the millennium (para 39(a)), the formation of the permanent United Nations armed forces under Article 43 of the Charter (para 43), or a better cooperation with regional arrangements (paras 60–65), which quite noticeably failed, at least, in Kosovo and Iraq) were not enforced ever since, one feels inclined to conclude, regretfully, that Boutros Boutros-Ghali's constructive proposals were, for practical reasons, not realistic—at least, at the present stage of international relations—despite their formal compatibility with international law.

1.2.5.6 Attitudes of the International Law Commission

The International Law Commission (ILC) was set up by the United Nations General Assembly resolution 174 (II) of 21 November 1947 as a subsidiary expert body of the General Assembly, with a view to promoting the progressive development of (primarily, public) international law and its codification.[317] Since its establishment, the Commission dealt with many important areas of international law, including, for example, diplomatic and consular law, the law of treaties, the responsibility of States (see infra 2.2) and, more recently, also of international organizations for internationally wrongful acts, the fragmentation of international law, and

---

[315] Ibid., para 23.

[316] Ibid. For details, see paras 24–33.

[317] Cf. Statute of the International Law Commission, adopted by the General Assembly in resolution 174 (II) of 21 November 1947, as amended by resolutions 485 (V) of 12 December 1950, 984 (X) of 3 December 1955, 985 (X) of 3 December 1955 and 36/39 of 18 November 1981, Article 1. The Statute is available at the official ILC website: http://untreaty.un.org/ilc/texts/instruments/english/statute/statute_e.pdf (last accessed 13 November 2012).

other areas.[318] Some of the key substantive and procedural issues of international criminal law—such as the codification of international crimes or the establishment of an international criminal court—have also been on the Commission's agenda.[319]

As far as (the crime of) aggression is specifically concerned, it was already incorporated in the International Law Commission's 1951 Draft Code of Offences against the Peace and Security of Mankind.[320] It was stipulated in Article 1 of the Draft Code, in line with the 1946 Nuremberg Principles,[321] that the offences listed therein were "crimes under international law, for which the responsible individuals [should] be punished," and Article 2(1) characterized any act of "aggression" as an offence within the meaning of Article 1 (see infra 3.1.4).[322] Soon thereafter, the work on the Draft Code was suspended and resumed in the early 1980s, after the adoption of a definition of aggression, in 1974 (see supra 1.2.5.3 and infra 2.3). The ILC produced the first edition of the Draft Code of Crimes against the Peace and Security of Mankind in 1991,[323] and its final edition (with commentaries) was adopted in 1996 (see infra 3.1.5), with the following understanding:

> [W]ith a view to reaching consensus, the Commission has considerably reduced the scope of the Code. On first reading in 1991, the draft Code comprised a list of 12 categories of crimes. Some members have expressed their regrets at the reduced scope of coverage of the Code. The Commission acted in response to the interest of adoption of the Code and of obtaining support by Governments. It is understood that the inclusion of certain crimes in the Code does not affect the status of other crimes under international law, and that the adoption of the Code does not in any way preclude the further development of this important area of law.[324]

Unlike some other crimes, which had featured in the 1991 edition of the Draft Code of Crimes against the Peace and Security of Mankind but were eliminated from the 1996

---

[318] For texts, instruments and final reports issued by the Commission, see the official ILC website: http://www.un.org/law/ilc/ (last accessed 13 November 2012). Interestingly enough, the Commission did not consider it appropriate, in late 1940s, to deal with international humanitarian law, allegedly because the Commission believed that that branch of law would no longer be topical, in view of the United Nations Charter's prohibition of the threat or use of force in international relations. See Best 1994, pp. 210–211. It seems to this author, though, that the Commission must have been pragmatic in declining to work on matters of IHL, because the ICRC—the guardian of humanitarian law—possessed a sufficient expertise in the area, and the Commission did not wish to duplicate its functions.

[319] See Crawford 1994, pp. 140–152; Safferling 2012, pp. 20–22.

[320] For a detailed overview of the Commission's work on the Draft Code, including this and subsequent developments, see the official ILC website: http://untreaty.un.org/ilc//summaries/7_3.htm (last accessed 12 November 2012). See also Kemp 2010, pp. 108–116.

[321] General Assembly Resolution 95(I), 11 December 1946.

[322] Report of the International Law Commission, 6th Session (1954), II *ILC Yearbook*, pp. 140, 151.

[323] See the official ILC website: http://untreaty.un.org/ilc//summaries/7_4.htm (last accessed 12 November 2012).

[324] *Yearbook of the International Law Commission, 1996*, vol. II (Part Two), para 46.

one,[325] the crime of aggression was naturally maintained in the final text. As an essential source pertaining to the interpretation of the crime of aggression, Article 16 of the 1996 Draft Code will be considered in greater detail below, at 3.1.5. Likewise, a concise overview of Chapter III of Part Two of the 2001 Draft Articles on the responsibility of States for internationally wrongful acts ("Serious breaches of obligations under peremptory norms of general international law")—although they are less directly concerned with the subject matter of this research—will be offered below, at 2.2.

1.2.6 Rome Statute of the International Criminal Court

1.2.6.1 Initial Reference to the Crime in Article 5 of the Rome Statute

Two years after the adoption of the 1996 Draft Code of Crimes against the Peace and Security of Mankind by the International Law Commission (see supra 1.2.5.6), the Rome Statute of the International Criminal Court was adopted by the United Nations Diplomatic Conference of Plenipotentiaries on the Establishment of an International Criminal Court,[326] with a view to establishing a permanent international criminal jurisdiction with respect to the most serious crimes of international concern.[327] The Statute entered into force on 1 July 2002, in accordance with Article 126(1).[328] The crime of aggression was among the most difficult

---

[325] The 1991 edition of the Draft Code included "aggression", "threat of aggression", "intervention," as well as "colonial domination and other forms of alien domination", along with ten other types of crimes. See infra 3.1.5.

[326] For the text of the Conference's Final Act, see: http://untreaty.un.org/cod/icc/prepcomm/prepfra.htm (last visited 15 November 2012).

[327] ICC Statute, Article 1 ("The Court"): "An International Criminal Court ('the Court') is hereby established. It shall be a permanent institution and shall have the power to exercise its jurisdiction over persons for the most serious crimes of international concern, as referred to in this Statute, and shall be complementary to national criminal jurisdictions. The jurisdiction and functioning of the Court shall be governed by the provisions of this Statute". See generally Ambos 1996, pp. 519–544; Arsanjani 1999, pp. 22–43; Arsanjani and Reisman 2005, pp. 385–403; Aust 2005, pp. 277–282; Bassiouni 2006, pp. 421–427; Blumenson 2006, pp. 797–867; Boister 2003, pp. 953–976; Bottini 2004, pp. 503–562; Cassese 1999, pp. 144–171; Cryer 2005, pp. 57–59, 142–167; Evered 1994, pp. 121–158; Gomaa 2004, pp. 55–77; Graefrath 1990, pp. 67–88; Grover 2010, pp. 543–583; Kirsch 2007, pp. 539–547; Kirsch and Holmes 1999, pp. 2–12; Kirsch and Oosterveld 2001, pp. 1141–1160; Kivalov 2009, pp. 5–18; Leanza 2004, pp. 3–15; Leigh 2001, pp. 124–131; Meron 1998, pp. 18–31; Natarajan and Kukaj 2011, pp. 357–365; Neubacher 2006, pp. 787–799; Safferling 2012, pp. 47–52; Scarf 1994, pp. 103–119; Sunga 1998, pp. 61–83; Tomuschat 1998, pp. 335–347; Tomuschat 2012, pp. 673–681; Wedgwood 1999, pp. 93–107; Zimmermann 1998, pp. 47–108.

[328] Ibid., Article 126(1) ("Entry into force"): "This Statute shall enter into force on the first day of the month after the sixtieth day following the date of the deposit of the sixtieth instrument of ratification, acceptance, approval or accession with the Secretary-General of the United Nations". See Lijun 2003, pp. 599–622.

issues the Rome Conference had to face.[329] A majority of States represented at the Rome Conference were of the opinion that the individual crime of aggression *should* be among crimes within the jurisdiction of the Court. However, there were considerable differences regarding the applicable substantive (i.e., the definition of the crime) and procedural (i.e., the exercise of jurisdiction over the crime) law.[330] The draft Statute submitted to the Conference contained three definitional alternatives, ranging from a general definition with no specific examples of acts of aggression in its structure to a rather detailed one inspired by the 1974 Definition of Aggression (see infra 2.3).[331] As none of these represented an obvious preference,[332] the delegates prudently agreed upon a temporary compromise, which was reflected in the final edition of Article 5 of the Rome Statute ("Crimes within the jurisdiction of the Court"):

> 1. The jurisdiction of the Court shall be limited to the most serious crimes of concern to the international community as a whole. The Court has jurisdiction in accordance with this Statute with respect to the following crimes:
>
> (a) The crime of genocide;
> (b) Crimes against humanity;
> (c) War crimes;
> (d) The crime of aggression.
>
> 2. The Court shall exercise jurisdiction over the crime of aggression once a provision is adopted in accordance with articles 121 and 123 defining the crime and setting out the conditions under which the Court shall exercise jurisdiction with respect to this crime. Such a provision shall be consistent with the relevant provisions of the Charter of the United Nations.

Further work on the definition of the crime of aggression for the purpose of the Statute and on relevant jurisdictional issues was entrusted to the Preparatory Commission for the International Criminal Court.

1.2.6.2 Work Accomplished by the Preparatory Commission for the Establishment of an International Criminal Court

The Preparatory Commission for the Establishment of an International Criminal Court was established by Resolution F of the Final Act of the United Nations Diplomatic Conference of Plenipotentiaries on the Establishment of an International Criminal Court.[333] In accordance with para 7 of the Resolution, the

---

329 See Schabas 2004; Gomaa 2004, especially at p. 55, note 4; Stancu 2004, pp. 87–91; Yáñez-Barnuevo 2004, pp. 109–117.

330 See Ferencz 2007, pp. 551–566.

331 For an overview of the three options, see Leanza 2004, at p. 13.

332 Ibid.

333 See U.N. Doc. A/CONF.183/10, Annex I(F). The text of the Final Act is accessible at: http://untreaty.un.org/cod/icc/prepcomm/prepfra.htm (last visited 15 May 2012).

work on the definition of the crime of aggression was among the Commission's principal tasks:

> The Commission shall prepare proposals for a provision on aggression, including the definition and Elements of Crimes of aggression and the conditions under which the International Criminal Court shall exercise its jurisdiction with regard to this crime. The Commission shall submit such proposals to the Assembly of States Parties at a Review Conference, with a view to arriving at an acceptable provision on the crime of aggression for inclusion in this Statute. The provisions relating to the crime of aggression shall enter into force for the States Parties in accordance with the relevant provisions of this Statute.

According to Mauro Politi, the first phase (February–August 1999) of the Commission's work was not very fruitful.[334] He notes that especially the permanent members of the Security Council—unlike representatives of developing countries who were in favor of having a broader definition and wanted to limit, as far as possible, the influence of the Security Council upon the future adjudication of the crime of aggression[335]—did not seem to consider the definition of the crime of aggression as a priority and suggested to define it in a restrictive manner, i.e., in the spirit of the Nuremberg and Tokyo Judgments (see infra 4.1.1 and 5.1.1.1). During the second phase (December 1999–June 2000), the Preparatory Commission put together a consolidated text of various drafting proposals (both regarding the definition of the crime and the Court's relationship with the Security Council), and compiled a list of guiding questions to be answered. According to Mauro Politi, this more constructive approach did have an overall positive impact on the substance.[336] The third phase (concluded in March 2001) was quite productive, as the debate on the crime of aggression took advantage of the completion of the Rules of Procedure and the Elements of Crimes, and might henceforth focus on quite specific definitional issues.[337]

1.2.6.3 Work Accomplished by the Special Working Group on the Crime of Aggression of the Assembly of States Parties to the Rome Statute of the International Criminal Court

The Special Working Group on the Crime of Aggression of the Assembly of States Parties to the Rome Statute of the International Criminal Court was established in 2003. It was open to all States, irrespective of whether they have signed or ratified the Rome Statute, and to a limited number of civil society representatives and

---

[334] See Politi 2004, at pp. 44–46; Kemp 2010, pp. 207–208.

[335] See Politi 2004, p. 45.

[336] Ibid.

[337] Ibid. See also Clark 2002, pp. 859–890.

legal experts. The Working Group held a number of meetings in 2004–2008[338] and submitted its final report to the Assembly of States Parties on 13 February 2009. The final report contained the following wording of the draft Article 8 bis of the Rome Statute ("Crime of aggression")[339]:

1. For the purpose of this Statute, "crime of aggression" means the planning, preparation, initiation or execution, by a person in a position effectively to exercise control over or to direct the political or military action of a State, of an act of aggression which, by its character, gravity, and scale, constitutes a manifest violation of the Charter of the United Nations.
2. For the purpose of paragraph 1, "act of aggression" means the use of armed force by a State against the sovereignty, territorial integrity or political independence of another State, or in any other manner inconsistent with the Charter of the United Nations. Any of the following acts, regardless of a declaration of war, shall, in accordance with United Nations General Assembly resolution 3314 (XXIX) of 14 December 1974, qualify as an act of aggression:

   (a) The invasion or attack by the armed forces of a State of the territory of another State, or any military occupation, however temporary, resulting from such invasion or attack, or any annexation by the use of force of the territory of another State or part thereof;
   (b) Bombardment by the armed forces of a State against the territory of another State or the use of any weapons by a State against the territory of another State;
   (c) The blockade of the ports or coasts of a State by the armed forces of another State;
   (d) An attack by the armed forces of a State on the land, sea or air forces, or marine and air fleets of another State;
   (e) The use of armed forces of one State which are within the territory of another State with the agreement of the receiving State, in contravention of the conditions provided for in the agreement or any extension of their presence in such territory beyond the termination of the agreement;
   (f) The action of a State in allowing its territory, which it has placed at the disposal of another State, to be used by that other State for perpetrating an act of aggression against a third State;
   (g) The sending by or on behalf of a State of armed bands, groups, irregulars, or mercenaries, which carry out acts of armed force against another State of such gravity as to amount to the acts listed above, or its substantial involvement therein.

This draft combined the elements of three principal approaches toward the criminalization of aggression (for details, see infra 4.1). Paragraph 1, which listed four modes of criminal conduct (planning, preparation, initiation or execution of an act of aggression, cf. infra 5.1.1.1.2), was reflective of the so-called "Nuremberg and Tokyo model" (see infra 4.1.1). However, the last phrase in the same paragraph constituted a noticeable departure from the Nuremberg Charter and Judgment in

---

338 See the calendar of the Special Working Group on the Crime of Aggression at: http://www.icc-cpi.int/menus/asp/asp%20events/previous%20calendar/calendar%20of%20the%20special%20working%20group%20on%20the%20crime%20of%20aggression?lan=en-GB (last accessed 15 November 2012).

339 Cf. document ICC-ASP/7/SWGCA/2 (20 February 2009), pp. 11–12. See also Cassese 2007, pp. 841–849; Clark 2009, pp. 1103–1115; Kemp 2010, pp. 208–237; Kress 2007, pp. 851–865; Kress 2009, pp. 1129–1146; Murphy 2009, pp. 1147–1156; Paulus 2009, pp. 1117–1128; Sayapin 2009, pp. 157–173; Weisbord 2008, pp. 161–220; Weisbord 2009, pp. 1–68.

that it did not limit the phenomenon of aggression to "wars of aggression" but rather criminalized the concerned individuals' personal participation in "manifest violation[s] of the Charter of the United Nations". Thus, a substantive connection to Article 2(4) of the Charter of the United Nations (see infra 2.1) was set up, and the provision's center of gravity was shifted from the Nuremberg and Tokyo model to the more contemporary legal foundation rooted in the Charter (see infra 4.1.2 and 4.1.3). Finally, para 2 made an explicit reference to the United Nations General Assembly resolution 3314 (XXIX) of 14 December 1974 (see supra 1.2.5.3 and infra 2.3) and restated the content of its Article 3 as a matter of its own substance. It thus sought to elevate the General Assembly resolution's "soft law" provisions, of which only the last paragraph had been recognized by the International Court of Justice as reflective of customary international law,[340] to the level of binding international law. The Special Working Group's proposal was adopted by the Assembly of States Parties on 26 November 2009 by consensus[341] and submitted to the First Review Conference of the States Parties to the Rome Statute of the International Criminal Court as a *Conference Room Paper on the Crime of Aggression*.[342] The Conference adopted this provision by consensus (for a detailed analysis, see infra 5.1).[343]

1.2.6.4 Work Accomplished by the First Review Conference of the States Parties to the Rome Statute of the International Criminal Court

The First Review Conference of the States Parties to the Rome Statute of the International Criminal Court (Kampala, 31 May–11 June 2010) was tasked, *inter alia*, with appraising the draft amendments to the Rome Statute to the effect of introducing a definition of the crime of aggression for the purpose of the Statute and laying down the conditions under which the Court might, in the future, exercise its jurisdiction with respect to the crime.[344] While the substance of a draft definition of the crime of aggression had been generally agreed upon in February 2009 (see supra 1.2.6.3), in the opinion of Kai Ambos, "jurisdictional issues almost led to the failure of the entire endeavour".[345] Obviously, the most controversial issues were the role of the UN Security Council in triggering an ICC investigation into an alleged crime of

[340] See *Nicaragua* Judgment, supra note 288, paras 106 et seq. Also, see infra 2.3.2.

[341] Cf. document ICC-ASP/8/Res. 6, 1 (26 November 2009).

[342] Cf. document RC/WGCA/1/Rev. 2 (7 June 2010).

[343] This is not to say that the draft definition of the crime did not raise any contentions at all during the Conference. See Ambos 2010, at p. 469.

[344] See Jacobs 2010, pp. 131–152; Kress and Von Holtzendorff 2010, pp. 1179–1217; Politi 2012, pp. 267–288; Triffterer 2010, pp. 9–64.

[345] Ambos 2010, p. 464.

aggression,[346] and the consent on the part of an alleged aggressor State to the adjudication of an purported crime of aggression.[347] The draft texts ultimately submitted to the Review Conference combined those approaches with alternatives providing for a more independent action on the part of the Prosecutor[348]:

Article 15 *bis*
Exercise of jurisdiction over the crime of aggression
(State referral, proprio motu)

1. The Court may exercise jurisdiction over the crime of aggression in accordance with article 13 (a) and (c), subject to the provisions of this article.
2. Where the Prosecutor concludes that there is a reasonable basis to proceed with an investigation in respect of a crime of aggression, he or she shall first ascertain whether the Security Council has made a determination of an act of aggression committed by the State concerned. The Prosecutor shall notify the Secretary-General of the United Nations of the situation before the Court, including any relevant information and documents.
3. Where the Security Council has made such a determination, the Prosecutor may proceed with the investigation in respect of a crime of aggression.
4. **(Alternative 1)** In the absence of such a determination, the Prosecutor may not proceed with the investigation in respect of a crime of aggression.
4. **(Alternative 2)** Where no such determination is made within [6] months after the date of notification, the Prosecutor may proceed with the investigation in respect of a crime of aggression, provided that the Pre-Trial Chamber has authorized the commencement of the investigation in respect of a crime of aggression in accordance with the procedure contained in article 15;
5. A determination of an act of aggression by an organ outside the Court shall be without prejudice to the Court's own findings under this Statute.
6. This article is without prejudice to the provisions relating to the exercise of jurisdiction with respect to other crimes referred to in article 5.

Article 15 *ter*
Exercise of jurisdiction over the crime of aggression
(Security Council referral)

1. The Court may exercise jurisdiction over the crime of aggression in accordance with article 13 (b), subject to the provisions of this article.
2. Where the Prosecutor concludes that there is a reasonable basis to proceed with an investigation in respect of a crime of aggression, he or she shall first ascertain whether the Security Council has made a determination of an act of aggression committed by the State concerned. The Prosecutor shall notify the Secretary-General of the United Nations of the situation before the Court, including any relevant information and documents.
3. Where the Security Council has made such a determination, the Prosecutor may proceed with the investigation in respect of a crime of aggression.
4. In the absence of such a determination, the Prosecutor may not proceed with the investigation in respect of a crime of aggression.
5. A determination of an act of aggression by an organ outside the Court shall be without prejudice to the Court's own findings under this Statute.
6. This article is without prejudice to the provisions relating to the exercise of jurisdiction with respect to other crimes referred to in article 5.

---

346 Ibid.

347 Ambos 2010, p. 471.

348 Cf. document RC/WGCA/1/Rev. 2, Annex I, No. 3 (footnotes omitted).

As Kai Ambos reports, in the course of heated negotiations, a compromise solution was shaped, whereby a larger freedom of action was accorded to the Prosecutor under Article 15 bis (for an analysis of its final edition, see infra 5.3.2), and an effective role of the Security Council was specified both in Articles 15 bis and 15 ter (for an analysis, see infra 5.3.3).[349] Importantly, none of the permanent members of the Security Council who also are Parties to the Rome Statute objected to the final texts of the provisions.[350]

References

Adamthwaite A (1977) France and the Coming of the Second World War, 1936–1939. Frank Cass, London

Akande D (1998a) Nuclear weapons, unclear law? Deciphering the nuclear weapons advisory opinion of the International Court. BYIL 69:165–217

Akande D (1998b) The competence of International Organizations and the advisory jurisdiction of the International Court of Justice. EJIL 9:437–467

Al-Azmeh A (ed) (1988) Islamic law: social and historical contexts. Routledge, London

Alexandrov S (2006) The compulsory jurisdiction of the International Court of Justice: how compulsory is it? Chinese JIL 5:29–38

Al-Qaradawi Y (1985) The lawful and the prohibited in Islam. American Trust Publication, Indianapolis

Alvarez JE (1996) Judging the security council. AJIL 90:1–39

Ambos K (1996) Establishing an International Criminal Court and an International Criminal Code: observations from an International Criminal Law viewpoint. EJIL 7:519–544

Ambos K (2010) The crime of aggression after Kampala. German YIL 53:463–509

American Society of International Law (1907a) The second peace conference of the Hague, Editorial Comment. AJIL 1:431–440

American Society of International Law (1907b) The second peace conference of the Hague, Editorial Comment. AJIL 1:945–954

American Society of International Law (1914) Germany and international peace, Editorial Comment. AJIL 8:881–886

Anderson N (1976) Law reform in the Muslim world. The Athlone Press, London

Andrassy J (1956) Uniting for peace. AJIL 50:563–582

Andrassy J (1958) Betrachtungen über die Zuständigkeit des Internationalen Gerichtshofes. ZaöRV 19:1–23

Arsanjani MH (1999) The Rome Statute of the International Criminal Court. AJIL 93:22–43

Arsanjani MH, Reisman WM (2005) The law-in-action of the International Criminal Court. AJIL 99:385–403

Artsibasov IN, Yegorov SA (1989) Voorujennyy konflikt: pravo, politika, diplomatiya [Armed Conflict: Law, Politics, Diplomacy]. Moscow, International Relations

Aufricht H (1944) Post-war planning and limitation of sovereignty. AJIL 38:119–124

Aust A (2005) Handbook of International Law. Cambridge University Press, Cambridge

Baldwin SE (1907) The international congresses and conferences of the last century as forces working toward the solidarity of the world. AJIL 1:565–578

Barthelemey J (1904) The founding fathers of International Law. Paris, V. Giard & E. Brière, Paris

[349] Ambos 2010, pp. 473–475.

[350] Ibid., pp. 475–476.

Bassiouni MC (2003) Introduction to International Criminal Law. Transnational Publishers, Inc., Ardsley

Bassiouni MC (2006) The ICC – Quo Vadis? JICJ 4:421–427

Bassiouni MC, Ferencz B (2008) The crime against peace and aggression: from its origins to the ICC. In: Bassiouni MC (ed) International Criminal Law, vol I, 3rd edn. Martinus Nijhoff Publishers, Leiden, pp 207–242

Bathurst ME (1945) The United Nations War Crimes Commission. AJIL 39:565–570

Batyr VA (2006) Mejdunarodnoe gumanitarnoe pravo [International Humanitarian Law]. Yustitsinform, Moscow

Behruz H (2011) Sravnitelnoe pravovedenie [Comparative Jurisprudence]. Phoenix, TransLit

Bertrand M (1995) The UN as an Organization: a critique of its functioning. EJIL 6:349–359

Best G (1994) War and law since 1945. Clarendon Press, Oxford

Bilfinger C (1937) Die russische Definition des Angreifers. ZaöRV 7:483–496

Bilfinger C (1940) Die Kriegserklärungen der Westmächte und der Kelloggpakt. ZaöRV 10:1–23

Blokker N (2005) The security council and the use of force—on recent practice. In: Blokker N, Schrijver N (eds) The security council and the use of force: theory and reality—a need for change? Martinus Nijhoff Publishers, Boston, pp 1–29

Blumenson E (2006) The challenge of a global standard of justice: peace, pluralism and punishment at the International Criminal Court. Columbia JTL 44:797–867

Boister N (2003) Transnational Criminal Law? EJIL 14:953–976

Borchard E (1929a) The Kellogg Treaties Sanction War. ZaöRV 1:126–131

Borchard E (1929b) The multilateral treaty for the renunciation of war. AJIL 23:116–120

Borchard E (1944) Flaws in post-war peace plans. AJIL 38:284–289

Borchard E (1946) The atomic bomb. AJIL 40:161–165

Bottini G (2004) Universal jurisdiction after the creation of the International Criminal Court. ILP 36:503–562

Boutros-Ghali B (1995) An agenda for peace. United Nations, New York

Bowett D (1994) The impact of security council decisions on dispute settlement procedures. EJIL 5:89–101

Boye T (1930)Shall a state which goes to war in violation of the Kellogg-Briand Pact have a belligerent's rights in respect of neutrals? AJIL 24:766–770

Briggs HW (1947) The United Nations and International Legislation. AJIL 41:433–435

Briggs HW (1957) Towards the rule of law? AJIL 51:517–529

Briggs HW (1959) The United States and the International Court of Justice: a re-examination. AJIL 53:301–318

Brown PM (1934) The Russian Soviet Union and the Law of Nations. AJIL 28:733–736

Brown PM (1939) Undeclared wars. AJIL 33:538–541

Brown C (2006) The inherent powers of International Courts and Tribunals. BYIL 77:195–244

Brown Firmage E (1969) The treaty on the non-proliferation of nuclear weapons. AJIL 63:711–746

Brownlie I (1998) Principles of Public International Law, 5th edn. Clarendon Press, Oxford

Burchard C (2006) The Nuremberg trial and its impact on Germany. JICJ 4:800–829

Calder N (1993) Studies in early Muslim jurisprudence. Clarendon Press, Oxford

Carlston KS (1950) Interpretation of peace treaties with Bulgaria, Hungary, and Rumania, advisory opinions of the International Court of Justice. AJIL 44:728–737

Cassese A (1999) The Statute of the International Criminal Court: some preliminary reflections. EJIL 10:144–171

Cassese A (2007) On some problematical aspects of the crime of aggression. Leiden JIL 20:841–849

Chakste M (1948) Justice and Law in the Charter of the United Nations. AJIL 42:590–600

Chakste M (1949) Soviet concepts of the State: International Law and Sovereignty. AJIL 43:21–36

Clark JB (1917) Shall there be war after the war? AJIL 11:790–793

Clark RS (2002) Rethinking aggression as a crime and formulating its elements: the final work-product of the preparatory commission for the International Criminal Court. Leiden JIL 15:859–890

Clark RS (2009) Negotiating provisions defining the crime of aggression, its elements and the conditions for icc exercise of jurisdiction over it. EJIL 20:1103–1115
Clark RS (2011) The role of the United Nations. In: Natarajan M (ed) International Crime and Justice. Cambridge University Press, Cambridge, pp 337–342
Clarke RF (1907) A permanent tribunal of international arbitration: its necessity and value. AJIL 1:342–408
Collinson P (2006) The reformation: a history. Random House Publishing Group, New York
Condorelli L (1995) La Cour Internationale de Justice: 50 ans et (pour l'heure) pas une ride. EJIL 6:388–400
Coppieters B, Fotion N, Apresyan R (eds) (2002) Nravstvennye ogranicheniya voyny: problemy i primery [Moral Restraints on War: Issues and Examples]. Gardariki, Moscow
Coulson NJ (1964) A history of Islamic Law. Edinburgh University Press, Edinburgh
Cowles WB (1948) Trials of war criminals (Non-Nuremberg). AJIL 42:299–319
Crawford J (1994) The ILC's Draft Statute for an International Criminal Tribunal. AJIL 88:140–152
Cryer R (2005) Prosecuting international crimes: selectivity and the international criminal law regime. Cambridge University Press, Cambridge
D'Amato A (1967) Legal aspects of the French nuclear tests. AJIL 61:66–77
Dahm G (1961) Völkerrecht, Band III. Kohlhammer, Stuttgart
David E (2011) Printsipy prava voorujennyh konfliktov [Principles of the Law of Armed Conflicts], 2nd edn. ICRC, Moscow
Davie MR (1929) The evolution of war: a study on its role in early societies. Kennikat Press, New Haven
Davis GS (2011) Sharia reasoning and the pursuit of democracy: John Kelsay's arguing the just war in Islam. JCS 53:59–72
De Bustamante AS (1908) The Hague Convention concerning the rights and duties of neutral powers and persons in land warfare. AJIL 2:95–120
De Sillac MJ (1911) Periodical peace conferences. AJIL 5:968–986
De Vattel E (1863) The Law of Nations or the principles of natural law, Book III. Guillaumin, Paris
Deyra M (2002) L'essentiel du droit des conflits armés. Guliano éditeur
Dinstein Y (2004) The conduct of hostilities under the Law of International Armed Conflict. Cambridge University Press, Cambridge
Dugard J (1987) Recognition and the United Nations. Grotius, Cambridge
Eagleton C (1942) Organization of the community of nations. AJIL 36:229–241
Eagleton C (1943a) Punishment of war criminals by the United Nations. AJIL 37:495–499
Eagleton C (1943b) Some questions as to the place of the individual in the International Law of the Future. AJIL 37:642–644
Eagleton C (1945) International law and the charter of the United Nations. AJIL 39:751–754
Eagleton C (1946) The jurisdiction of the Security Council over disputes. AJIL 40:513–533
Edge I (ed) (1996) Islamic Law and legal theory. Dartmouth, Aldershot
Ehard H (1949) The Nuremberg Trial against the major war criminals and international law. AJIL 43:223–245
El Azhary MS (ed) (1984) The Iran–Iraq War: an historical: economic and political analysis. Croom Helm Ltd, New York
Elshtain JB (2001) The third annual Grotius Lecture: just war and humanitarian intervention. AUILR 17:1–25
En-Nawawi M (1992) A manual of Muhammadan Law according to the school of Shafii. Navrang, New Delhi
Evered TC (1994) An International Criminal Court: recent proposals and American concerns. Pace ILR 6:121–158
Falk RA (1965) The *Shimoda* Case: a legal appraisal of the atomic attacks upon Hiroshima and Nagasaki. AJIL 59:759–793

Falk RA (1997) Nuclear weapons, International law and the World Court: a historic encounter. AJIL 91:64–75
Falk RA (2003) What future for the UN Charter System of war prevention? AJIL 97:590–598
Fenby J (2006) Alliance: the inside story of how Roosevelt, Stalin and Churchill won one war and began another. Pocket Books, San Francisco
Fenwick CG (1929) Germany and the Crime of the World War. AJIL 23:812–815
Fenwick CG (1932) The implication of consultation in the Pact of Paris. AJIL 26:787–789
Fenwick CG (1937) War without a declaration. AJIL 31:694–696
Fenwick CG (1952) When is a treaty not a treaty? AJIL 46:296–298
Ferencz BB (2007) Enabling the International Criminal Court to punish aggression. WUGSLR 6:551–566
Finch GA (1933) A pact of non-aggression. AJIL 27:725–732
Finch GA (1945) The United Nations Charter. AJIL 39:541–546
Finch GA (1947) The Nuremberg Trial and international law. AJIL 41:20–37
Franck TM (1995) The Secretary-General's role in conflict resolution: past, present and pure conjecture. EJIL 6:360–387
Frowein JA (1976) Der Beitrag der internationalen Organisationen zur Entwicklung des Völkerrechts. ZaöRV 36:147–167
Garner JW (1915a) Some questions of International Law in the European War. AJIL 9:72–112
Garner JW (1915b) Some questions of International Law in the European War. AJIL 9:372–401
Garner JW (1915c) Some questions of International Law in the European War. AJIL 9:594–626
Garner JW (1915d) Some questions of International Law in the European War. AJIL 9:818–857
Garner JW (1916a) Some questions of International Law in the European War. AJIL 10:12–41
Garner JW (1916b) Some questions of International Law in the European War. AJIL 10:238–269
Garvey JI (2008) A new architecture for the non-proliferation of nuclear weapons. JCSL 12:339–357
Golsong H (1971) Role and functioning of the International Court of Justice: proposals recently made on the subject. ZaöRV 31:673–696
Gomaa MM (2004) The definition of the crime of aggression and the ICC jurisdiction over that crime. In: Politi M, Nesi G (eds) The International Criminal Court and the crime of aggression. Ashgate Publishing Limited, Burlington, pp 55–77
Goodrich LM (1938) The nature of the advisory opinions of the Permanent Court of International Justice. AJIL 32:738–758
Gordon E (1965) The World Court and the interpretation of constitutive treaties: some observations on the development of an International Constitutional Law. AJIL 59:794–833
Graefrath B (1990) Universal criminal jurisdiction and an International Criminal Court. EJIL 1:67–88
Gray C (2003) The use and abuse of the International Court of Justice: cases concerning the use of force after Nicaragua. EJIL 14:867–905
Gray C (2008) International law and the use of force, 3rd edn. Oxford University Press, Oxford
Green LC (1993) The contemporary law of armed conflict. Manchester University Press, Manchester
Gross L (1948) The peace of Westphalia, 1648–1948. AJIL 42:20–41
Gross L (1971) The International Court of Justice: consideration of requirements for enhancing its role in the international legal order. AJIL 65:253–326
Gross L (1972) Review of the role of the International Court of Justice. AJIL 66:479–490
Grotius H (1853) On the rights of war and peace. Cambridge University Press, Cambridge
Grover L (2010) A call to arms: fundamental dilemmas confronting the interpretation of crimes of the Rome Statute of the International Criminal Court. EJIL 21:543–583
Hallaq WB (1997) A history of Islamic legal theories—an introduction to Sunni Usal al-Fiqh. Cambridge University Press, Cambridge
Hargrove JL (1987) The Nicaragua Judgment and the future of the law of force and self-defense. AJIL 81:135–143

Harris DJ (2004) Cases and materials on International Law, 6th edn. Sweet & Maxwell, London
Hashmi SH (2002) Interpreting the Islamic ethics of war and peace. In: Hashmi SH (ed) Islamic political ethics: civil society, pluralism and conflict. Princeton University Press, Princeton, pp 194–216
Hata I, Jansen MB (2007) Hirohito: the Shōwa emperor in war and peace. Global Oriental, Folkestone
Hedges RY (1928) Justiciable disputes. AJIL 22:560–565
Heintschel von Heinegg W, Epping V (eds) (2007) International humanitarian law facing new challenges: symposium in honour of Knut Ipsen. Springer, Berlin
Heller KJ (2011) The Nuremberg military tribunals and the origins of international criminal law. Oxford University Press, Oxford
Henderson I (2011) The Firebombing of Tokyo and other Japanese cities. In: Tanaka Y, McCormack T, Simpson G (eds) Beyond victors' justice? The Tokyo War Crimes Trial revisited. Martinus Nijhoff Publishers, Leiden, pp 311–321
Hershey AS (1908) Convention for the peaceful adjustment of international differences. AJIL 2:29–49
Hershey AS (1911) The history of international relations during antiquity and the middle ages. AJIL 5:901–933
Hershey AS (1912) History of international law since the peace of Westphalia. AJIL 6:30–69
Hill DJ (1907) The second peace conference at The Hague. AJIL 1:671–691
Hill DJ (1928) The multilateral treaty for the renunciation of war. AJIL 22:823–826
Hinnells JR (ed) (2007) A handbook of ancient religions. Cambridge University Press, Cambridge
Hisakazu F (2011) The Tokyo Trial: humanity's justice v victors' justice. In: Tanaka Y, McCormack T, Simpson G (eds) Beyond victors' justice? The Tokyo War Crimes trial Revisited. Martinus Nijhoff Publishers, Leiden, pp 3–21
Hoffmann S (1995) Thoughts on the UN at fifty. EJIL 6:317–324
Houben PH (1967) Principles of international law concerning friendly relations and co-operation among states. AJIL 61:703–736
Hoyt EP (1992) Hirohito: the emperor and the man. Praeger, New York
Hudson MO (1948) The effect of advisory opinions of the World Court. AJIL 42:630–632
Hudson MO (1957) The succession of the International Court of Justice to the Permanent Court of International Justice. AJIL 51:569–573
Hull WI (1908) Obligatory arbitration and the Hague conferences. AJIL 2:731–742
Hulsroj P (2002) The legal function of the Security Council. Chinese JIL 1:59–93
Hyde CC (1928) Safeguarding peace—a constructive suggestion. AJIL 22:262–269
Hyde CC (1941) Secretary Hull on the Kellogg-Briand Pact. AJIL 35:117–118
Iles Johnston S (ed) (2007) Ancient religions. Harvard University Press, Cambridge
Ilesanmi SO (2011) Sharia reasoning, political legitimacy, and democratic visions. JCS 53:27–36
International Dimensions of Humanitarian Law (1988) Henry Dunant Institute, UNESCO, Martinus Nijhoff Publishers, Dordrecht
International Military Tribunal (Nuremberg), Judgment of 1 October 1946. In: The trial of German major war criminals. Proceedings of the International Military Tribunal sitting at Nuremberg, Germany, Part 22 (22 Aug–1 Oct 1946)
Israelyan VL (1990) Diplomaty litsom k litsu [Diplomats Face to Face]. Moscow «Iz predisloviya Marii fon Klauzevits k pervomu izdaniyu» [«From Maria von Clausewitz's Preface to the First Edition»] (2002). In: Von Clausewitz C, O voyne [On War], Moscow, Terra Fantastica, volume I, pp 5–9
Jacobs D (2010) The sheep in the box: the definition of the crime of aggression at the International Criminal Court. In: Burchard C, Triffterer O, Vogel J (eds) The review conference and the future of the International Criminal Court: proceedings of the first AIDP symposium for young penalists in Tübingen, Germany, co-organized by the AIDP YP Committee. Wolters Kluwer Law & Business, Carl Heymanns Verlag, Cologne, pp 131–152
Jessup PC (1941) International law and totalitarian war. AJIL 35:329–331

Johnson JT (2011) Tracing the contours of the *Jihad* of individual duty. JCS 53:37–49

Kalugin VY (2006) Kurs mejdunarodnogo gumanitarnogo prava [Treatise on international humanitarian law]. Tessey, Minsk

Kalugin VY, Akulov DV (2004) Presechenie narusheniy v mehanizme implementatsii mejdunarodnogo gumanitarnogo prava [The Repression of Violations in the Mechanism of Implementation of International Humanitarian Law]. Tessey, Minsk

Kalugin VY, Pavlova LV, Fisenko IV (1999) Mejdunarodnoe gumanitarnoe pravo [international humanitarian law]. Tessey, Minsk

Karsh E (2002) The Iran–Iraq War 1980–1988. Osprey Publishing, London

Karsh E (2009) The Iran–Iraq War. The Rosen Publishing Group, Inc., New York

Kellogg FB (1928) The war prevention policy of the United States. AJIL 22:253–261

Kelsen H (1945) The old and the new league: The Covenant and the Dumbarton Oaks proposals. AJIL 39:45–83

Kemp G (2010) Individual criminal liability for the international crime of aggression. Intersentia, Oxford

Khadduri M (1956) Islam and the modern law of nations. AJIL 50:358–372

Khadduri M (1966) The Islamic law of nations: Shaybani's Siyar. The Johns Hopkins Press, Baltimore

Khakimov R (2007) Mejdunarodnoe gumanitarnoe pravo [International Humanitarian Law], 2nd edn. Tashkent

Khakimov R (2012) Mejdunarodnaya pravosubyektnost: voprosy istorii, teorii i praktiki [International Legal Personality: Issues of History, Theory and Practice]. Tashkent

Kirsch P (2007) The role of the International Criminal Court in enforcing international criminal law. AULR 22:539–547

Kirsch P, Holmes JT (1999) The Rome Conference on an International Criminal Court: the negotiating process. AJIL 93:2–12

Kirsch P, Oosterveld V (2001) Negotiating an institution for the twenty-first century: multilateral diplomacy and the International Criminal Court. McGill LJ 46:1141–1160

Kissinger H (1994) Diplomacy. Simon & Schuster Paperbacks, New York

Kivalov SV (2009) Mijnarodne kriminalne pravosuddya: vid Nyurberzskogo viyskovogo tribunalu do Mijnarodnogo kriminalnogo sudu [International Criminal Justice: from the Nuremberg Military Tribunal to the International Criminal Court]. Almanac Int Law 1:5–18

Kochavi AJ (1998) Prelude to Nuremberg, allied war crimes policy and the questions of punishment. University of North Carolina Press, Chapel Hill

Köchler H (2003) Global justice or global revenge? International criminal justice at the crossroads. Springer, New York

Köchler H (2006) The United Nations Organization and global power politics: the antagonism between power and law and the future of world order. Chinese JIL 5:323–340

Kocourek A (1918) Some reflections on the problem of a society of nations. AJIL 12:498–518

Korovin EA (1946) The Second World War and international law. AJIL 40:742–755

Koskenniemi M (1996) The place of law in collective security. Michigan JIL 17:455–490

Kotlyarov II (2003) Mejdunarodnoe pravo i voorujennye konflikty. Moscow

Kress C (2007) The crime of aggression before the first review of the ICC Statute. Leiden JIL 20:851–865

Kress C (2009) Time for decision: some thoughts on the immediate future of the crime of aggression: a reply to Andreas Paulus. EJIL 20:1129–1146

Kress C, Von Holtzendorff L (2010) The Kampala compromise on the crime of aggression. JICJ 8:1179–1217

Kuhn AK (1941) The organization of peace. AJIL 35:114–117

Kunz JL (1946) The legal position of the Secretary General of the United Nations. AJIL 40:786–792

Kunz JL (1951a) Bellum Justum and Bellum Legale. AJIL 45:528–534

Kunz JL (1951b) The chaotic status of the laws of war and the urgent necessity for their revision. AJIL 45:37–61

Kunz JL (1952a) Ending the war with Germany. AJIL 46:114–119
Kunz JL (1952b) The United Nations and the rule of law. AJIL 46:504–508
Lauterpacht E (1968) The legal irrelevance of the "State of War. Proc Am Soc Int Law 62:58–68
Lawson RC (1952) The problem of the compulsory jurisdiction of the World Court. AJIL 46:219–238
Leanza U (2004) The historical background. In: Politi M, Nesi G (eds) The International Criminal Court and the crime of aggression. Ashgate Publishing Limited, Aldershot, pp 3–15
Legais R (2009) Velikie pravovye sistemy sovremennosti [The great contemporary legal systems]. Wolters Kluwer, New York
Leigh M (2001) The United States and the Statute of Rome. AJIL 95:124–131
Li Z (2002) Traditional Chinese World Order. Chinese JIL 1:20–58
Lijun Y (2003) Some critical remarks on the Rome Statute of the International Criminal Court. Chinese JIL 2:599–622
Lim SL (2007) The great power balance, the United Nations and what the framers intended: in partial response to Hans Köchler. Chinese JIL 6:307–328
Link AS (ed) (1966–) The papers of Woodrow Wilson. Princeton University Press, Princeton
Lopes Pegna O (1998) Counter-claims and obligations *Erga Omnes* before the International Court of Justice. EJIL 9:724–736
Lukashuk II (2008) Mejdunarodnoe pravo: Obshchaya chast [International Law: General Part], 3rd edn. Wolters Kluwer, New York
MacCulloch D (2004) The reformation. Viking, New York
Malanczuk P (1997) Akehurst's modern introduction to international law, 7th revised edn. Routledge, London
Malekian F (2011) Principles of Islamic international criminal law: a comparative study, 2nd edn. Brill, London
Mallat C (1993) The renewal of Islamic law. Cambridge University Press, Cambridge
Malyavin VV (2002) Kitayskaya voennaya strategiya [Chinese Military Strategy]. Astrel, Moscow
Mammen L (2006) Auf dem Weg zu einer umfassenden Strategie im weltweiten Vorgehen gegen den Terrorismus – Eine Analyse des Berichts des Generalsekretärs der Vereinten Nationen zur Anti-Terrorismusstrategie. HuV-I 19:293–296
Manning P (1989) Hirohito: the war years. Bantam Books, New York
March AF, Modirzadeh NK (2013) Ambivalent universalism? *Jus ad Bellum* in modern islamic legal discourse. EJIL 24:367–389
Martens FF (2008) Sovremennoe mejdunarodnoe pravo tsivilizovannyh narodov [Contemporary International Law of Civilised Peoples], vol I. Zertsalo, Moscow
Matheson MJ (1997) The opinions of the International Court of Justice on the threat or use of nuclear weapons. AJIL 91:417–435
McCoubrey H, White N (1992) International law and armed conflict. Dartmouth, Aldershot
McWhinney E (2006) The International Court of Justice and international law-making: the judicial activism/self-restraint antinomy. Chinese JIL 5:3–13
Meiertöns H (2010) The doctrines of US security policy: an evaluation under international law. Cambridge University Press, Cambridge
Meron T (1998) Is international law moving towards criminalization? EJIL 9:18–31
Minear R (1971) Victor's justice: The Tokyo War Crimes Trial. Princeton University Press, Princeton
Münch F (1961) Zum Stand der internationalen obligatorischen Gerichtsbarkeit. ZaöRV 21:221–248
Murphy CF Jr (1982) The Grotian vision of world order. AJIL 76:477–498
Murphy SD (2009) Aggression, legitimacy and the International Criminal Court. EJIL 20:1147–1156
Myers DP (1948) Liquidation of league of nations functions. AJIL 42:320–354

Nasinovsky E (1968) The impact of 50 years of Soviet theory and practice on international law. Proceedings of the annual meeting of the American Society of International Law. AJIL 62:189
Natarajan M, Kukaj A (2011) The International Criminal Court. In: Natarajan M (ed) international crime and justice. Cambridge University Press, Cambridge, pp 357–365
Neff SC (2005) War and the law of nations: a general history. Cambridge University Press, Cambridge
Neubacher F (2006) How can it happen that horrendous state crimes are perpetrated? An overview of criminological theories. JICJ 4:787–799
Nobleman EE (1946) American military government courts in Germany. AJIL 40:803–811
Nobleman EE (1947) Quadripartite military government organization and operations in Germany. AJIL 41:650–655
Oba AA (2002) Islamic Law as customary law: the changing perspective in Nigeria. ICLQ 51:817–850
Oberman HA (2004) The reformation: roots and ramifications. T&T Clark International, Edinburgh
Oh I (2011) On democracy, violence, and the promise of Islam. JCS 53:50–58
Orakelashvili A (2006) Peremptory norms in international law. Oxford University Press, Oxford
Österdahl I (2005) The exception as the rule: lawmaking on force and human rights by the UN Security Council. JCSL 10:1–20
Otomo Y (2011) The decision not to prosecute the emperor. In: Tanaka Y, McCormack T, Simpson G (eds) Beyond Victors' justice? The Tokyo war crimes trial revisited. Martinus Nijhoff Publishers, Leiden, pp 63–78
Paulus A (2009) Second thoughts on the crime of aggression. EJIL 20:1117–1128
Payandeh M (2006) Rechtskontrolle des UN-Sicherheitsrates durch staatliche und überstaatliche Gerichte. ZaöRV 66:41–71
Pellet A (1995) La formation du droit international dans le cadre des Nations Unies. EJIL 6:401–425
Penfield WL (1907) International arbitration. AJIL 1:330–341
Plischke E (1947) Denazification law and procedure. AJIL 41:807–827
Politi M (2004) The debate within the preparatory commission for the International Criminal Court. In: Politi M, Nesi G (eds) The International Criminal Court and the crime of aggression. Ashgate Publishing Limited, Aldershot, pp 43–51
Politi M (2012) The ICC and the crime of aggression: a dream that came through and the reality ahead. JICJ 10:267–288
Potemkin VP (ed) (1941) Istoriya diplomatii [History of Diplomacy], vol I. OGIZ, Moscow
Potemkin VP (ed) (1945) Istoriya diplomatii [History of Diplomacy], vol III. OGIZ, Moscow
Potter PB (1945) Voting procedure in the Security Council. AJIL 39:318–322
Rahmanov A, Rahmanov A (2003) Islamskoe pravo [Islamic Law]. Tashkent
Rajabov SA (2006) Implementatsiya norm mejdunarodnogo gumanitarnogo prava v Respublike Tadjikistan: problemy teorii i praktiki [The Implementation of International Humanitarian Law in the Republic of Tajikistan: Issues of Theory and Practice]. Dushanbe
Rajaee F (ed) (1993) The Iran–Iraq War: the politics of aggression. University Press of Florida, Gainesville
Ralston JH (1907) Some suggestions as to the Permanent Court of Arbitration. AJIL 1:321–329
Ratner SR (1995) Image and reality in the UN's peaceful settlement of disputes. EJIL 6:426–444
Ratti O, Westbrook A (2006) Samurai: istoriya, traditsii, voinskoe iskusstvo [The Samurais: History, Traditions, Military Art]. Eksmo, Moscow
Reisman WM (1969) The enforcement of international judgments. AJIL 63:1–27
Reisman WM (1980) The legal effect of vetoed resolutions. AJIL 74:904–907
Renault L (1915) War and the law of nations in the twentieth century. AJIL 9:1–16
Report of Robert H. Jackson, United States Representative to the International Conference on Military Trials (1949). U.S. Government Printing Office

Rie R (1954) The war crimes trials. AJIL 48:470–474
Roberts A, Kingsbury B (eds) (1993) United Nations, divided world: The UN's roles in international relations, 2nd edn. Oxford University Press, Oxford
Röling BVA, Rüter CF (eds) (1977) The Tokyo Judgment. The International Military Tribunal for the Far East (I.M.T.F.E.), 29 April 1946–12 Nov 1948, vol II. APA—University Press, Amsterdam BV
Rosen L (1989) The anthropology of justice—law as culture in Islamic society. Cambridge University Press, Cambridge
Rudzinski AW (1951) The so-called double veto. AJIL 45:443–461
Rusinova VN (2006) Narusheniya mejdunarodnogo gumanitarnogo prava: individualnaya ugolovnaya otvetstvennost i sudebnoe presledovanie [Violations of International Humanitarian Law: Individual Criminal Responsibility and Prosecution]. Yurlitinform, Moscow
Ruthven M (2006) Islam in the world, 3rd edn. Granta Books, London
Rybachenok IS (2005) Россия и Первая конференция мира 1899 года в Гааге [Russia and the First Hague Peace Conference of 1899]. ROSSPEN, Moscow
Safferling C (2012) International criminal procedure. Oxford University Press, Oxford
Saidov AH (ed) (1994) Hidoya: kommentarii musulmanskogo prava [The Hidoyah: a commentary of Muslim Law], vol I. Tashkent
Saidov AH (2000) Sravnitelnoe pravovedenie [Comparative jurisprudence]. Yurist, Moscow
Samad J (2011) John Locke and Muslim Liberalism. JCS 53:84–108
Sandifer DV (1940) Rereading Grotius in the Year 1940. AJIL 34:459–472
Sardar Ali S, Rehman J (2005) The concept of Jihad in Islamic international law. JCSL 10:321–343
Sassóli M, Bouvier AA (2006) How does law protect in war? vols I and II , 2nd edn. ICRC, Geneva
Saul B (2005) Definition of "Terrorism" in the UN Security Council: 1985–2004. Chinese JIL 4:141–146
Sayapin S (2009) K voprosu ob opredelinii prestupleniya agressii: promejutochnaya otsenka raboty Spetsialnoy rabochey gruppy Assamblei gosudarstv-uchastnikov Rimskogo statuta [The definition of the crime of aggression revisited: a preliminary appraisal of the performance of the special working group of the state parties to the Rome Statute]. In: Bogush GI, Trikoz EN (eds) Mejdunarodnoe ugolovnoe pravosudie: sovremennye problemy [International Criminal Justice: contemporary issues]. Moscow, pp 157–173
Scaglia B (2011) Ancient religions: a history (Prehistoric, Ancient Greece and Rome, Vedic, Egyptian, and More). Webster's Digital Services
Scarf MP (1994) Getting serious about an International Criminal Court. Pace ILR 6:103–119
Schabas WA (2004) Origins of the criminalisation of aggression: how crimes against peace became the "Supreme International Crime". In: Politi M, Nesi G (eds) The International Criminal Court and the crime of aggression. Ashgate Publishing Limited, Aldershot, pp 17–32
Schacht J (1964) An introduction to Islamic law. Clarendon Press , Oxford
Schachter O (1960) The enforcement of international judicial and arbitral decisions. AJIL 54:1–24
Schachter O (1964) The Quasi-judicial role of the Security Council and the general assembly. AJIL 58:960–965
Schachter O (1994) United Nations Law. AJIL 88:1–23
Schick FB (1947) The Nuremberg trial and the international law of the future. AJIL 41:770–794
Schlüter F (1942) Kelloggpakt und Neutralitätsrecht. ZaöRV 11:24–32
Schrijver N (2007) Reforming the UN Security Council in pursuance of collective security. JCSL 12:127–138
Schweigman D (2001) The authority of the Security Council under chapter VII of the UN Charter: legal limits and the role of the International Court of Justice. Kluwer Law International, Boston

Schwelb E (1972) The International Court of Justice and the Human Rights Clauses of the Charter. AJIL 66:337–351

Scott GW (1908a) Hague Convention restricting the use of force to recover on contract claims. AJIL 2:78–94

Scott JB (1908b) Recommendation for a third peace conference at The Hague. AJIL 2:815–822

Scott JB (1908c) The proposed court of arbitral justice. AJIL 2:772–810

Scott JB (1908d) The work of the second Hague peace conference. AJIL 2:1–28

Scott JB (1912) The evolution of a permanent international judiciary. AJIL 6:316–358

Scott JB (1925) Grotius' De Jure Belli ac Pacis Libri Tres: The work of a lawyer, statesman and theologian. AJIL 19:461–468

Sellars K (2012) Delegitimizing aggression: first steps and false starts after the First World War. JICJ 10:7–40

Shah NA (2013) The use of force under Islamic law. EJIL 24:343–365

Shaw M (2008) International law, 6th edn. Cambridge University Press, Cambridge

Simpson G (2011) Writing the Tokyo Trial. In: Tanaka Y, McCormack T, Simpson G (eds) Beyond victors' justice? The Tokyo war crimes trial revisited. Martinus Nijhoff Publishers, Leiden, pp 23–33

Jennings R Sir (1987) The judicial enforcement of international obligations. ZaöRV 47:3–16

Skordas A (2001) Epilegomena to a silence: nuclear weapons, terrorism and the moment of concern. JCSL 6:191–224

Spencer R (ed) (2005) The myth of Islamic tolerance: how Islamic law treats non-Muslims. Prometheus Books, Amherst

Stancu IG (2004) Defining the crime of aggression or redefining aggression? In: Politi M, Nesi G (eds) The International Criminal Court and the crime of aggression. Ashgate Publishing Limited, Aldershot, pp 87–91

Stewart JH (1951) The imprisonment of Napoleon: a legal opinion by Lord Eldon. AJIL 45:571–577

Stockder AH (1916) The legality of the blockades instituted by Napoleon's Decrees, and the British Orders in Council, 1806–1813. AJIL 10:492–508

Stowell EC (1908) Convention relative to the opening of hostilities. AJIL 2:50–62

Stowell EC (1944) The juridical significance of World War II. AJIL 38:106–108

Subedi SP (2003) The concept in Hinduism of 'Just War'. JCSL 8:339–361

Sun Tzu (2005) The art of war. Nuvision Pubn

Sunga LS (1998) The crimes within the jurisdiction of the International Criminal Court (Part II, Articles 5–10). EJCCLCJ 6:61–83

Takeshi N (2011) Justice Pal (India). In: Tanaka Y, McCormack T, Simpson G (eds) Beyond victors' justice? The Tokyo War Crimes Trial revisited. Martinus Nijhoff Publishers, Leiden, pp 127–144

Tanaka Y (2011) The atomic bombing, the Tokyo Tribunal and the Shimoda Case: lessons for anti-nuclear legal movements. In: Tanaka Y, McCormack T, Simpson G (eds) Beyond victors' justice? The Tokyo War Crimes Trial revisited. Martinus Nijhoff Publishers, Leiden, pp 293–310

Tanzi A (1995) Problems of enforcement of decisions of the International Court of Justice and the law of the United Nations. EJIL 6:539–572

Taylor AJP (1965) British History 1914–1915. Clarendon Press, Oxford

Taylor T (1992) The anatomy of the Nuremberg Trials: a personal memoir. Little, Brown, Boston

Temperley HWV (ed) (1920) A history of the peace conference of Paris: a settlement with Germany. Henry Frowde and Hodder and Stoughton, London

The Bhavagad Gita (1962) trans: J. Mascaró. Penguin Books, London

Thirlway H (2005) The drafting of ICJ decisions: some personal recollections and observations. Chinese JIL 4:15–28

Thomas ED (1945) Atomic bombs in international society. AJIL 39:736–744

Tomuschat C (1994) International criminal prosecution: the precedent of Nuremberg confirmed. CLF 5:237–247

Tomuschat C (1998) Das Statut von Rom für den internationalen Strafgerichtshof. Die Friedens-Warte 73:335–347
Tomuschat C (2006) The legacy of Nuremberg. JICJ 4:830–844
Tomuschat C (2012) Zehn Jahre Internationaler Strafgerichtshof. Europäische Grundrechte Zeitschrift 39:673–681
Triffterer O (2010) The court in danger? Future perspectives for international criminal law and its enforcement mechanisms. In: Burchard C, Triffterer O, Vogel J (eds) The review conference and the future of the International Criminal Court: Proceedings of the first AIDP symposium for young penalists in Tübingen, Germany, co-organized by the AIDP YP Committee, Wolters Kluwer Law & Business, Carl Heymanns Verlag, pp 9–64
Tuck R (1999) The rights of war and peace: political thought and the international order from Grotius to Kant. Oxford University Press, Oxford
Turlington E (1946) International control of the atomic bomb. AJIL 40:165–167
Turney-High HH (1971) Primitive war: its practices and concepts, 2nd edn. University of South Carolina Press, Columbia
United Nations War Crimes Commission (1948) History of the United Nations War Crimes Commission and the Development of the Laws of War. H. M. Stationery Office, London
Vasilyev LS (2003) Istoriya Vostoka [History of the orient], vol 1. Vysshaya Shkola, Moscow
Von Clausewitz C (1997) On war. Wordsworth Editions Limited, Hertfortshire
Von Clausewitz C (2002a) O voyne [On war], vol I. Terra Fantastica, Moscow
Von Clausewitz C (2002b) O voyne [On war], vol II. Terra Fantastica, Moscow
Von Elbe J (1939) The evolution of the concept of the just war in international law. AJIL 33:665–688
Von Mandelsloh AG (1933) Die Auslegung des Kelloggpaktes durch den amerikanischen Staatssekretär Stimson. ZaöRV 3:617–627
Von Senger H (2004a) Stratagemy: o kitayskom iskusstve jit i vyjivat, tom 1: stratagemy 1–18 [Stratagems: on the Chinese Art of Living and Surviving, volume 1: stratagems 1–18]. Eksmo, Moscow
Von Senger H (2004b) Stratagemy: o kitayskom iskusstve jit i vyjivat, tom 2: stratagemy 19–36 [Stratagems: on the Chinese art of living and surviving, volume 2: stratagems 19–36]. Eksmo, Moscow
Von Tabouillot W (1937) Die Aufnahme der Völkerbundssatzung in den Versailler Vertrag. ZaöRV 7:15–37
Ward CA (2003) Building capacity to combat international terrorism: the role of the United Nations Security Council. JCSL 8:289–305
Weber M (1990) «Politika kak prizvanie i professiya» [«Politics as a Vocation and Profession»]. In: Weber M, Izbrannye proizvedeniya, Moscow, Progress
Wedgwood R (1999) The International Criminal Court: an American view. EJIL 10:93–107
Weeramantry CG (1999) Islamic jurisprudence: an international perspective. Sarvodaya Vishva Lekha, Ratmalana
Weisbord N (2008) Prosecuting aggression. Harvard ILJ 49:161–220
Weisbord N (2009) Conceptualising aggression. Duke JCIL 20:1–68
Wellens K (2003) The UN Security Council and new threats to the peace: back to the future. JCSL 8:15–70
Werle G (2009a) Principles of international criminal law, 2nd edn. T. M. C. Asser Press, The Hague
Werle G (2009b) The crime of aggression between international and domestic criminal law. In: Manacorda S, Nieto A (eds) Criminal law between war and peace. Ediciones de la Universidad de Castilla-La Mancha, Cuenca, pp 405–421
Willett E (2004) The Iran–Iraq war. The Rosen Publishing Group, Inc., New York
Williamson M (2009) Terrorism, war and international law: the legality of the use of force against Afghanistan in 2001. Ashgate Publishing Limited, Aldershot
Willoughby WW (1918a) The Prussian theory of government. AJIL 12:266–282

Willoughby WW (1918b) The Prussian theory of the state. AJIL 12:251–265
Wilson GG (1932) Use of force and war. AJIL 26:327–328
Wilson GG (1936) When does war begin? AJIL 30:80–83
Wilson GG (1941) Grotius: law of war and peace. AJIL 35:205–226
Wilson RR (1970) The United Nations as symbol and as instrument. AJIL 64:139–143
Wright Q (1924) Changes in the conception of war. AJIL 18:755–767
Wright Q (1932) When does war exist? AJIL 26:362–368
Wright Q (1933) The meaning of the pact of Paris. AJIL 27:39–61
Wright Q (1935) The concept of aggression in International Law. AJIL 29:373–395
Wright Q (1943) International law and the balance of power. AJIL 37:97–103
Wright Q (1945) War criminals. AJIL 39:257–285
Wright Q (1947) The law of the Nuremberg Trial. AJIL 41:38–72
Wright Q (1953) The outlawry of war and the law of war. AJIL 47:365–376
Yáñez-Barnuevo A (2004) The exercise of the International Criminal Court's Jurisdiction over the crime of aggression: short term and long term perspectives. In: Politi M, Nesi G (eds) The International Criminal Court and the crime of aggression. Ashgate Publishing Limited, Aldershot, pp 109–117
Yee S (2005) A proposal for formalizing the "No Case Exists" objections procedure at the International Court of Justice. Chinese JIL 4:393–416
Young J, Kent J (2004) International relations since 1945: a global history. Oxford University Press, Oxford
Zelinskaya NA (2006) Mejdunarodnye prestupleniya i mejdunarodnaya prestupnost [International Crimes and International Criminality]. Yuridichna literatura
Zemmali A (1997) Combattants et prisonniers de guerre en droit islamique et en droit international humanitaire. Editions A. Pedone, Paris
Zhidkov OA, Krasheninnikova NA (eds) (2001) Istoriya gosudarstva i prava [History of state and law], vol I. Norma, Moscow
Ziemke EF (1990) The U.S. Army in the occupation of Germany 1944–1946. Center of Military History United States Army, Washington, D.C.
Zimmermann A (1998) Die Schaffung eines ständigen internationalen Strafgerichtshofes: Perspektiven und Probleme vor der Staatenkonferenz in Rom. ZaöRV 58:47–108

Chapter 2
Elements of an Act of Aggression: An Overview of Modern International Law and Practice

Abstract The Charter of the United Nations is the principal source of contemporary international law for the regulation of the use of force in inter-State relations. It sets out the interrelated competences of the main bodies of the United Nations—first of all, of the Security Council, the General Assembly and the International Court of Justice—in the area of maintaining international peace and security, and confirms States' inherent right of self-defence as a matter of applicable customary international law. The Charter's main provision pertaining to the prohibition of the use of force—Article 2(4)—is at the heart of the in-depth legal analysis, as a rule of conventional and customary international law as well as one of *jus cogens*. The chapter suggests that any use of force not falling within one of three categories—Charter-based exceptions, Charter-related exceptions and extra-Charter exceptions to the prohibition of the use of force—might potentially qualify as aggression and entail consequences provided for under international law, including the individual criminal responsibility of its authors.

Contents

S. Sayapin, *The Crime of Aggression in International Criminal Law*,
DOI: 10.1007/978-90-6704-927-6_2, © T.M.C. ASSER PRESS and the author 2014

As was discussed above (see supra 1.2.5), a major objective of the modern international legal order, which is founded upon the Charter of the United Nations, consists in the maintenance of international peace and security. Contrary to a widespread opinion, the Charter contains more than just a few articles relating to the use of armed force[1]—there are, in effect, many more, from which circumstance it must be inferred that the conditions under which force can be used under current international law are more strictly defined than some scholars have suggested.[2] Article 2(4) of the Charter laid down a fundamental restriction on the use of force in international relations (see infra 2.1.1)—an obligation which was, from its inception, designed to be of a superior legal nature[3] and is now recognized to have acquired the character of customary international law (see infra 2.1.2) and even that of *jus cogens* (see infra 2.1.3). Notably, Peter Malanczuk suggests that this norm is now binding even for the few States which are not Members of the United Nations.[4]

Permitted uses of force are regulated by a sequence of the Charter's provisions, which is opened with the seventh preambular paragraph: "[T]o ensure [...] that armed force shall not be used, *save in the common interest* [...]" (emphasis added). Although the Preamble does not *per se* possess a legally binding force,[5] it does provide an indication as to the spirit of the subsequent articles. In line with the Preamble's "common interest" clause, Article 1(1) lists among the purposes of the United Nations "effective *collective* measures for the prevention and removal of threats to peace, and for the suppression of acts of aggression or other breaches of

[1] Some treatises on public international law essentially limit themselves to the analysis of Articles 2(4), 24, 41, 42 and 51 of the Charter. See, for example, Adilkariev 2003, pp. 272–276; Kalamkaryan and Migachev 2005, pp. 381–384; Kolosov and Kuznetsov 1998, pp. 310–323; Kovalev and Chernichenko 2008, pp. 761–765; Kuznetsov 2001, pp. 490–497. However, a more comprehensive overview of applicable law, involving more provisions of the UN Charter relating to the use of force and relevant customary international law, shall be required for our purpose.

[2] See Franck 1970, pp. 809–837; Franck 2003, pp. 607–620; Henkin 1971, pp. 544–548; Wood 2005, pp. 75–90.

[3] Cf. Charter of the United Nations, Article 103: "In the event of a conflict between the obligations of the Members of the United Nations under the present Charter and their obligations under any other international agreement, their obligations under the present Charter shall prevail".

[4] Malanczuk 1997, p. 309. In turn, A. Randelzhofer specifies that States which are not members of the United Nations "are protected, though not bound" by Article 2(4). See A. Randelzhofer, "Article 2(4)," in Simma 1994, p. 115.

[5] See Lukashuk 2004b, p. 585.

peace" (emphasis added, see infra 2.4.1.5).[6] At least, two of the United Nations main organs, the General Assembly (Article 12, cf. supra 1.2.5.3 and infra 2.4.2.1) and the Security Council (Articles 24(1) and 39, cf. supra 1.2.5.2 and infra 2.4.1.5), were given powers to react, albeit in different manners, to threats to peace, breaches of peace, and acts of aggression.[7] Chapters VII ("Action with Respect to Threats to the Peace, Breaches of the Peace, and Acts of Aggression") and VIII ("Regional Arrangements") are devoted in their entirety, correspondingly, to the maintenance of international peace and security through collective action under the auspices of the United Nations or of regional arrangements. More specifically, Article 42 endows the Security Council with the authority to "take such action by air, sea or land forces as may be necessary to maintain or restore international peace and security." Article 43 was intended to set a framework for the conclusion of agreements between the Security Council and the United Nations Member States who would participate in the maintenance of international peace and security, and Article 44 is devoted to specific relations between the Security Council and Member States who, not being members of the Security Council, would participate in such operations (for a discussion, see infra 2.4.1.5.2). The fundamental Article 51 recognizes the Member States' "inherent right to self-defence" against armed attacks (see infra 2.4.1.1–2.4.1.4). Finally, already outdated Articles 53 and 107 of the Charter address the use of force, where necessary, against former enemies in the Second World War. [8]

During the period since the 1999 NATO operation in Kosovo,[9] and especially in connection with the US-led *Operation Enduring Freedom* (Afghanistan)[10] and, subsequently, *Operation Iraqi Freedom* (Iraq), a number of novel doctrines have been put forward with a view to justifying these uses of force (cf. supra 1.1.2.3)—potentially an important development in a field of international law as conservative as the post-1945 *jus ad bellum*,[11] for, at times, these doctrines claimed to be as far-reaching

6 UN Charter, Article 1(1), emphasis added.

7 On the role of the International Court of Justice in this domain, see supra 1.2.5.4.

8 With the admission of Italy (1955), Japan (1956) and Germany (1973) as "peace-loving States" (in the language of Article 4 of the Charter) to the United Nations, these provisions became obsolete and were recommended for deletion from the Charter. See: "A More Secure World: Our Shared Responsibility, Report of the High-level Panel on Threats, Challenges and Change," UN Doc. A/59/565 (2004), para 298, published at: http://www.un.org/secureworld/ (last accessed 15 November 2012); In Larger Freedom: Towards Development, Security and Human Rights for All, Report of the Secretary-General, UN Doc. A/59/2005 (2005), para 217, published at: http://www.un.org/largerfreedom/ (last accessed 15 November 2012). See also Odello 2005, pp. 231–262.

9 Cf. Badescu 2011, p. 1: "In March 1999, the North Atlantic Treaty Organization (NATO) started a bombing campaign against the Former Federal Republic of Yugoslavia to protect the Albanian population in Kosovo frombeing ethnically cleansed [...] NATO's actions were morally justified yet violated international law, as the UN Security Council had not authorized the military intervention"

10 See Schmidt-Radefeldt 2005, pp. 245–253.

11 As Rein Müllerson so candidly noted, "the legal texts concerning use of force have indeed undergone little, if any, change since the adoption of the UN Charter in 1945. Even General Assembly resolutions on the issue have not contained anything that could be even remotely defined as 'progressive development of international law.'" See Müllerson 2002, pp. 150–151.

as to be able to modify the Charter's provisions on the use of force. By contrast, it is argued in this chapter that Article 2(4) and relevant customary international law should not be interpreted in too broad a manner,[12] and that any use of force in inter-State relations, which would not be compatible with the overarching prohibition contained in Article 2(4), would accordingly constitute a breach of the Charter.[13] Then again, since not all unlawful uses of inter-State armed force constitute acts of aggression (see infra 2.3 and 5.1.1.2–5.1.1.3),[14] and hence entail individual criminal liability under customary international law (see infra 4.1–4.2) and the Rome Statute of the International Criminal Court (see infra Chap. 5), it will be an aim of this chapter to distinguish between distinctively aggressive and other, less grave, unlawful uses of inter-State armed force which, though breaching Article 2(4), would not (necessarily) entail individual criminal responsibility.

2.1 Nature of States' Obligation to Refrain from the Threat or Use of Force in International Relations (Article 2(4) of the UN Charter)

As the Covenant of the League of Nations (see supra 1.1.6.2) and the Kellogg-Briand Pact (see supra 1.1.6.5) were unable to prevent the Second World War, it was an aim of the drafters of the Charter of the United Nations to remedy the deficiencies of both instruments (see supra 1.2.5).[15] The ambitious reform which they undertook to accomplish was without a precedent in that it sought to transform the traditional *jus ad bellum*, which had not excluded States' right to use force in furtherance of their foreign policies, into a novel *jus contra bellum*, which not only outlawed war as a legitimate means of settlement of international disputes but also banned most uses of military force short of war and even threats to use force in international relations.[16] This section examines the relevant rule contained in the Charter as a conventional one (see infra 2.1.1), as one of customary international law (see infra 2.1.2) and of *jus cogens* (see infra 2.1.3).

---

[12] Again, in the words of Rein Müllerson, "[i]n the domain of use of force, which is so central to international law that novelties in it may affect the very foundations of this legal system as a whole, significant changes have occurred only after most terrible conflicts, which, using today's formula, have shocked the conscience of humankind. In such cases, changes in the political configuration of the world, in international law generally and in *jus ad bellum* in particular, have not only coincided in time and space, but have all been caused by the same set of factors and reflect different facets of the same process." See Müllerson 2002, p. 151.

[13] See Schrijver 2005, pp. 36–37.

[14] The UN Charter distinguishes, in Article 39, between threats to international peace and security, breaches of peace and aggression but does not define either of the terms. Cf. infra note 30.

[15] See Dinstein 2001, p. 80.

[16] See Simma 1994, p. 111.

2.1.1 Treaty Obligation Under Article 2(4)

A provision of paramount importance, Article 2(4) has been referred to as "the cornerstone of peace in the Charter," "the heart of the United Nations Charter" or the "basic rule of contemporary public international law."[17] Undoubtedly, Article 2(4) is by far better worded than was Article 1 of the Kellogg-Briand Pact (cf. supra 1.1.6.5), for it prohibits the use of force in general and not only war, and covers even threats of force. Besides, this rule of international law, in conjunction with related ones (see supra introductory note to this chapter), creates—in the words of Albrecht Randelzhofer, at least in theory—an institutional United Nations system of collective sanctions against *any* offender (Articles 39–51).[18] However, as will be seen, even this major provision is not without ambiguities. As adopted at the San Francisco Conference, Article 2(4) reads:

> All Members shall refrain in their international relations from the threat or use of force against the territorial integrity or political independence of any state, or in any other manner inconsistent with the Purposes of the United Nations.

2.1.1.1 Protected States and Values

The content of Article 2(4) raises a number of legal and technical issues. First, whilst formally creating legal obligations only for the United Nations Members, the provision in fact protects Members and non-Members ("any State") alike.[19] Second, it singles out two groups of objects which are protected against unlawful threats or use of force under the Charter: on the one hand, States' territorial integrity and political independence are mentioned as specific examples of protected values; on the other hand, it is also forbidden to issue threats or use force "in any other manner inconsistent with the Purposes of the United Nations." These two groups of protected values, although equated in one provision, are not quite of the same nature (because Article 2 technically lists the institutional Principles—not the Purposes—of the United Nations). Whereas the territorial integrity and political independence are referred to in Article 2(4) expressly and in a self-contained manner, the purposes of the United Nations are listed separately in Article 1 of the Charter and include:

- the maintenance of "international peace and security" and related undertakings to that end (Article 1(1));
- developing "friendly relations among nations based on respect for the principle of equal rights and self-determination of peoples," and taking "other appropriate measures to strengthen universal peace" (Article 1(2));

---

17 Ibid.

18 Ibid. See also Waxman 2013, pp. 151–189; Werle 2009, p. 407.

19 See Malanczuk 1997, p. 309.

- developing "international co-operation in solving international problems of an economic, social, cultural, or humanitarian character, and in promoting and encouraging respect for human rights and for fundamental freedoms for all without distinction as to race, sex, language, or religion" (Article 1(3));
- and being "a centre for harmonizing the actions of nations in the attainment of these common ends" (Article 1(4)).

Nonetheless, since both parts of the phrase are to be read in conjunction, one may conclude that the purposes of the United Nations are, as objects protected under Article 2(4) of the Charter, of an equal value with the territorial integrity and political independence of States. Importantly, an inverse interpretation of Article 2(4) appears to suggest that (Members of) the United Nations *might* lawfully threaten to use force in their international relations, or use it, in order to preserve the territorial integrity or political independence of theirs or, in appropriate circumstances, also of (an)other State(s), or in another manner, which would be consistent with the Purposes of the United Nations. The foremost exceptions to the prohibition contained in Article 2(4) will be considered below at 2.4.

2.1.1.2 The Meaning of "Force"

The meaning of the notion "force" referred to in Article 2(4) is essential. It is generally agreed among scholars that this provision covers, in the first place, the threat or use of *armed* or *military* force—i.e., the employment by a State of its regular armed forces[20] (in a broad sense currently accepted in international law[21]), or of irregular armed groups.[22] and of means[23] and methods of warfare (in the sense of applicable international humanitarian law) against another State, its nationals, public or private property. Although Article 2(4) contains no qualification of the term "force," one may derive this conclusion from the Charter's related provisions (for example, from Articles 41 and 46 where this explicit qualification is found), the 1970 Friendly Relations Declarations and from the Charter's *travaux préparatoires*: it is known, for instance, that the proposal Brazil made on 6 May 1945 at the San Francisco Conference with a view to extending the prohibition of force to economic coercion, was explicitly—and quite correctly—rejected.[24] As Albert Randelzhofer notes, an extension of Article 2(4) to other forms of force would

[20] Christine Gray refers to "an invasion by the regular armed forces of one state into the territory of another state" as "[t]he paradigm case" of an armed attack. See Gray 2008, p. 128.

[21] For a current definition of armed forces under international law, cf. Article 43 of the First Additional Protocol to the 1949 Geneva Conventions, of 8 June 1977.

[22] It is understood that the activities of those groups should be attributable to the State in question in accordance with international law. See Gray 2008, pp. 132–140.

[23] See ibid., at 128, especially notes 57 and 58, respectively, regarding the use of missiles and naval mines as particular types of armed attacks, and at 129, especially, note 59, regarding the regulation of cyber-attacks.

[24] See Simma 1994, p. 112.

result in leaving States virtually with no internationally lawful means of exerting pressure upon States that violate international law.[25] Correspondingly, the first Principle in the 1970 Declaration on Principles of International Law Concerning Friendly Relations and Cooperation among States in Accordance with the Charter of the United Nations, which interpreted Article 2(4), dealt solely with the military force,[26] and the prohibition of economic, political and other types of coercion was covered under the heading of non-intervention.[27]

The following sections will briefly examine the use of two particular types of force—the so-called "physical" and "indirect" force—which, while being distinct from the use of armed force, may, in some circumstances, entail the effects of the latter (first and foremost, the exercise by a State of its right to self-defence (cf. infra 2.4.1.1–2.4.1.4).

2.1.1.2.1 Physical (Non-military) Force

It is submitted that in situations where a State does not resort to its armed forces, irregulars or means and methods of warfare (cf. supra 2.1.1.2) against another State, its nationals, public or private property, there is no use of military force in the sense of Article 2(4) of the UN Charter. Even so, States can be affected by forcible measures of a social, natural or technical kind not involving the use of military force in a proper sense of the word—i.e. by manifestations of the so-called "physical" force—whose effects at times can be just as critical as those of military force.[28] It appears that a contemporary—and most relevant—example of physical non-military force, which, as a matter of fact, did produce the effects of an armed attack, were the terrorist attacks of 11 September 2001 in New York, Washington, D.C. and Pennsylvania.[29] They

---

[25] Ibid.

[26] Cf. the General Assembly Resolution 2625 (XXV) of 24 October 1970, Annex, Principle 1, for text see: http://daccess-dds-ny.un.org/doc/RESOLUTION/GEN/NR0/348/90/IMG/NR034890.pdf?OpenElement (accessed 9 October 2012).

[27] Ibid., Principle 3, para 2.

[28] See Simma 1994, p. 112. Cf. Kulagin 2006, pp. 79–103; Sayapin 2009, pp. 8–13

[29] For insightful comments on the impact of the 9/11 attacks on international law, see Abi-Saab 2002, pp. 305–313; Arnold 2006, pp. 297–319; Bianchi 2006, pp. 881–919; Branche 2007, pp. 543–560; Cassese 2001, pp. 993–1001; Droege 2007, pp. 515–541; Fitzpatrick 2003, pp. 241–264; Franck 2001, pp. 839–843; Hudson 2009, pp. 702–717; Kemp 2010, pp. 59–63; McWhinney 2002a, pp. 280–286; Murphy 2003a, pp. 347–364; Neuman 2003, pp. 283–298; Neuman 2004, pp. 1019–1029; Newman and Clarke 2011, pp. 290–296; Pejic 2005, pp. 71–100; Pellet and Tzankov 2004, pp. 68–72; Ratner 2002, pp. 905–921; Reisman 2003, pp. 82–90; Roberts 2004, pp. 721–749; Ross 2007, pp. 561–590; Ruys and Verhoeven 2005, pp. 289–320; Sassóli 2006, pp. 959–981; Shaw 2008, pp. 1159–1166; Tams 2009, pp. 359–397; Vagts 2003, pp. 313–326; Von Schorlemer 2003, pp. 265–282; Warbrick 2004, pp. 989–1018; Wellens 2003, pp. 15–70; Yee 2002, pp. 287–293; Zwitter 2008, pp. 24–33.

were of such an unparalleled magnitude that the UN Security Council pronounced in its resolution 1368 (2001)[30] that "such acts, like any act of international terrorism, [were] a *threat* to international peace and security" (emphasis added), and emphasized "that those responsible for aiding, supporting or harboring the perpetrators, organizers and sponsors of these acts [should] be held accountable."[31] These provisions necessitate at least two observations for the purpose of our argument. First, the Security Council held "any act of international terrorism"—including the specific ones, which occurred on 11 September 2001—to be a threat to international peace and security considerable enough to be commensurate with the invocation by a victim State of its "inherent right of individual or collective self-defence in accordance with the Charter,"[32] i.e., one comparable to an "armed attack" in the sense of Article 51 of the Charter (cf. infra 2.4.1.1). Yet, in this author's view, the attacks of 11 September 2001 were, *stricto sensu*, not "armed," unless the hijacked civilian airplanes were to be regarded, by analogy, as "military weapons." True, the airplanes have been *used* to perform the destruction they did but they were not meant, by their primary function, to be used for killing people and destroying property, and should therefore not be regarded as "military weapons" or "means of warfare" in the sense of applicable international law. The Security Council's reference to Article 51 was entirely appropriate in the light of the 9/11 terrorist attack's *effects* comparable to those of an armed attack but not because of the attack's armed or military *nature*.

Second, the attack of 11 September 2001 was carried out not by a State, or on behalf of a State, but by a non-State actor on its own behalf. That an act of aggression can, in accordance with current theory, only be committed by a State (see infra 3.1.5), might be yet another reason for not having termed the attack an act of aggression. As a matter of fact, Article 51 of the UN Charter does not specify that an armed attack in respect of which a State's right of individual or collective self-defence may be invoked must of necessity be committed by a State. It states that "[n]othing in the present Charter shall impair the inherent right of individual or collective self-defence, *if an armed attack occurs* against a Member of the United Nations" (emphasis added), without specifying the origin of the armed attack. Accordingly, a literal interpretation of Article 51 suggests that every Member of the United Nations has an inherent right to individual or collective self-defence against *any kind* of armed attack, be it carried

---

[30] In so doing, the Security Council acted in accordance with Article 39 of the Charter: "The Security Council shall determine the existence of any threat to the peace, breach of the peace, or act of aggression and shall make recommendations, or decide what measures shall be taken in accordance with Articles 41 and 42, to maintain or restore international peace and security." Notably, neither this Article nor any other Article in the Charter defines these terms, and the practical distinction between the three types of situations is left up to the Security Council.

[31] Resolution 1368, adopted by the Security Council at its 4370th meeting, on 12 September 2001, paras 1 and 3.

[32] Ibid., 3rd preambular paragraph.

out by another State or a non-State entity. The decisive issue is therefore that of accommodating Article 51's requirement that the attack in question be armed, whereas the attack of 11 September 2001 was, as was discussed above, of an extremely violent but still non-military nature; it was the *effect* of the attack that placed it on an equal footing with an armed one. To conclude, the United States, befallen by an international terrorist attack, was right in invoking Article 51 but that invocation should have been founded on the quasi-military effects of the physical attack rather than on its ostensibly military nature. More generally, a State finding itself under an international terrorist attack is certainly entitled to repel it, including by military means, individually or collectively, without thereby violating Article 2(4) of the Charter, but the precise justification of an invocation of the right to self-defence under Article 51 should depend on the circumstances in each case.

2.1.1.2.2 "Indirect Force"

As was discussed above at 2.1.1.2, the scope of Article 2(4) is indeed limited to the proscription of armed force but, notably, this proscription also embraces the concept of "indirect force." This notion generally stands for a State's technical or organizational involvement in an international armed conflict ongoing between other States (cf. infra 5.1.1.3.6), or else in a non-international armed conflict occurring in another State[33]—for example, by sending to that State armed bands, groups, irregulars or mercenaries (cf. infra 5.1.1.3.7). The UN General Assembly interpreted the prohibition of indirect force in the 1970 Friendly Relations Declaration (cf. supra 1.2.5.3) as follows:

> Every State has the duty to refrain from organising or encouraging the organization of irregular forces or armed bands, including mercenaries, for incursion into the territory of another State.
>
> Every State has the duty to refrain from organizing, instigating, assisting or participating in arts of civil strife or terrorist acts in another State or acquiescing in organized activities within its territory directed towards the commission of such acts, when the acts referred to in the present paragraph involve a threat or use of force.[34]

Obviously, as Albrecht Randelzhofer notes, both prohibited modes of action—the organization or encouragement of irregular forces or armed bands, on the one hand, and the prohibition of participation in acts of civil strife or terrorist acts, on the other hand—are worded in such a broad manner that virtually every act of technical or organizational support rendered by a State would be covered by "organizing," "encouraging," "instigating," "assisting" or "participating," and the meaning of "armed force" under international law would thereby almost inevitably be blurred.[35]

---

[33] See Gray 2008, pp. 105–110.

[34] See the Friendly Relations Declaration, supra note 26, paras 8 and 9.

[35] See Simma 1994, p. 113.

With a view to avoiding this effect, the International Court of Justice made a proper observation in the *Nicaragua* Judgment that not every act of assistance should be regarded as a use of force.[36] However, the Court did not suggest any definitive criteria for determining which acts of assistance, and in which circumstances were to be viewed as an internationally wrongful threat or use of force in the sense of Article 2(4) of the Charter.[37] It appears that such a criterion might consist in the legal evaluation of the threat or use of force itself, and the employment of "indirect force" in its furtherance would derive its (il)legality from that of the main effort. In other words, providing assistance in the circumstances of an internationally lawful use of force should be regarded as lawful, whereas employing "indirect force" in support of a threat or use of force in breach of Article 2(4) of the Charter would itself constitute a breach thereof. Should the International Law Commission be tasked with producing the "Draft Articles" on the use of force by States (see supra 1.2.5.3), its expert opinion on the issue of "indirect force" might hopefully contribute to resolving the normative ambiguity left unanswered by the International Court of Justice in the *Nicaragua* Judgment.

2.1.2 Obligation Under Customary International Law[38]

In addition to its conventional nature (see supra 2.1.1), some publicists deem Article 2(4) of the Charter to also be part of customary international law.[39] Yet, this point of view is only partially accurate. In the *Nicaragua* Judgment, the International Court of Justice held that the use of force was also—in addition to its being subject to the Charter's conventional provisions—regulated by customary

[36] See *Case Concerning Military and Paramilitary Activities in and against Nicaragua (Nicaragua case),* ICJ Reports (1986), para 116.

[37] Ibid., paras 95, 97, 107, 110.

[38] See Baker 2010, pp. 173–204; Bernhardt 1976, pp. 50–76; Bing 2010, pp. 81–109; Brownlie 1998, pp. 4–11; D'Amato 1969, pp. 211–223; D'Amato 1987, pp. 101–105; Harris 2004, pp. 20–42; Kunz 1953, pp. 662–669; Norman and Trachtman 2005, pp. 541–580; Roberts 2001, pp. 757–791; Skubiszewski 1971, pp. 810–854; Strebel 1976, pp. 301–346.

[39] The International Law Commission held the view that "the great majority of international lawyers today unhesitatingly hold that Article 2, paragraph 4, together with other provisions of the Charter, authoritatively declares the modern customary law regarding the threat or use of force." See *ILC Yearbook* 1966, vol. II, p. 247. The view expressed by T. Gazzini may also be noted: "[T]he norms on the use of force embodied in the Charter and those existing under international law are substantially identical because of the interaction between the Charter and customary international law, on the one hand, and the virtual universality of the UN, on the other hand." See Gazzini 2006, at 320. See also Doehring 1976, pp. 77–95.

rules of international law, the content of which was not necessarily identical to that of the treaty provisions:

> As regards the suggestion that the areas covered by the two sources of law are identical, the Court observes that the United Nations Charter [...] by no means covers the whole area of the regulation of the use of force in international relations.[40]

The ICJ held explicitly that the operation of the Charter did not either "subsume" or "supervene" applicable customary international law,[41] and that "the areas governed by the two sources of law [did] not exactly overlap, and the substantive rules in which they are framed [were] not identical in content."[42] Moreover, the Court ruled that nothing should impair the parallel applicability of a relevant customary norm, even if a conventional norm and a customary norm were to have exactly the same content.[43] This leads us to a discussion of the International Court of Justice's view of customary international law on the prohibition of the use of force between States, as it was reflected in the *Nicaragua* Judgment, with a view to reconciling it with Article 2(4).

2.1.2.1 Article 2(4) of the UN Charter Versus Customary International Law

This distinguished Judgment has, in fact, been somewhat inconsistent on a few essential points. Having, on the one hand, acknowledged the primacy of the Charter of the United Nations in the legal regulation of the use of force in international relations, the ICJ nonetheless considered it apposite to "supplant" the Charter's relevant rules by customary international law applicable to a given case.[44] Having further claimed to embark on the determination of such rules, the Court, in fact, limited itself to concluding that the practice of States must "in general, be consistent" with the rules in question,[45] without considering the idiosyncratic particulars of such

---

[40] See *Nicaragua* Judgment, supra note 35, para 176. For a contrary position, see *The Legality of United States Participation in the Defense of Viet-Nam*, 4 March 1966, where the United States affirmed that "it should be recognized that much of the substantive law of the Charter has become part of the general law of nations through a very wide acceptance by nations the world over. This is particularly true of the Charter provisions on the use of force", quoted in Falk 1968, p. 585. See also Constantinou 2000, p. 204.

[41] *Nicaragua* Judgment, para 174.

[42] Ibid., para 175.

[43] Ibid.

[44] In the words of Tarcisio Gazzini, the Court concluded "that the rules on the use of force cannot be construed on the basis of postulates established through the inclusion of these rules in the Charter and their reiteration in subsequent documents. Rather, it has to be determined through the analysis of the practice regarding the interpretation and application of these norms by the subjects to which these are addressed." See Gazzini 2006, at 321.

[45] See *Nicaragua* Judgment, para 186.

practice in a more comprehensive fashion. And, finally, when assessing the *opinio juris* on the subject, the ICJ regarded, quite inaccurately, a few non-binding ("soft law") sources as constituting evidence of States' *opinio juris* on the prohibition of the use of force.[46]

As was noted above at 2.1.2, the Court's starting point was that the legal regulation of the use of force in international relations was not limited to the United Nations Charter and also included rules of customary international law.[47] The Court referred, by way of providing an example of continued application of customary international law alongside the Charter, to its Article 51—a State's inherent right to individual or collective self-defence.[48] Having restated the Charter text that "nothing [in the present Charter] shall impair" the realization of this inherent right in the event of an armed attack, the Court concluded that Article 51 would only be meaningful on the assumption that the right in question were of a customary nature—even if its present content was indeed confirmed and influenced by the Charter[49] (for a detailed discussion of States' right to self-defence, see infra 2.4.1.1–2.4.1.4). Nor did the Charter regulate all aspects of the right's content and ways of implementation: for example, it did not contain any rule to the effect that individual or collective self-defence would warrant only measures which are proportionate to the armed attack and necessary to respond to it efficiently—a rule well established in customary international law.[50] The ICJ observed likewise that the notion of "armed attack," which triggers the exercise of the right of self-defence by the State(s) affected by the attack, was not defined in the Charter, and was not part of either general or particular treaty law either.[51] In the absence of detailed conventional regulations on such issues, the Court could not plausibly conclude that Article 51 of the UN Charter "subsume[d] and supervene[d]" applicable customary international law. Instead, the ICJ concluded that, with regard to the use of force in inter-State relations, customary law continued to apply alongside treaty law, and that the areas governed by the two sources of international law did not "overlap exactly."[52]

---

[46] Ibid., paras 191–192.

[47] A passage in the Separate Opinion of the Court's President, Judge Singh, on the interrelation between the rules of customary and conventional law on the use of force is remarkable: "If an issue was raised whether the concepts of the principle of non-use of force and the exception to it in the form of use of force for self-defence are to be characterized as either part of customary international law or that of conventional law, the answer would appear to be that both concepts are inherently based in customary international law in their origins, but have been developed further by treaty-law. In any search to determine whether these concepts belong to customary or conventional international law it would appear to be a fallacy to try to split any concept to ascertain what part or percentage of it belongs to customary law and what fraction belongs to conventional law. There is no need to try to separate the inseparable [...]" See Separate Opinion of President Nagendra Singh, 152.

[48] See *Nicaragua* Judgment, para 24.

[49] Ibid., para 176.

[50] Ibid.

[51] Ibid.

[52] Ibid.

2.1.2.2 Customary International Law on the Use of Force: The State Practice

Substantial problems started emerging when the Court attempted to identify the gist of rules of customary international law governing the use of force in inter-State relations. Having noted that there existed a substantial degree of accord between Nicaragua and the United State as to the applicable rules of customary law,[53] the Court nevertheless declared its willingness to deal with the matter:

> This concurrence of their [the Parties'] views does not however dispense the Court from having itself to ascertain what rules of customary international law are applicable. The mere fact that States declare their recognition of certain rules is not sufficient for the Court to consider these as being part of customary international law, and as applicable as such to those States. Bound as it is by Article 38 of its Statute to apply, *inter alia,* international custom "as evidence of a general practice accepted as law", the Court may not disregard the essential role played by general practice. Where two States agree to incorporate a particular rule in a treaty, their agreement suffices to make that rule a legal one, binding upon them; but in the field of customary international law, the shared view of the Parties as to the content of what they regard as the rule is not enough. The Court must satisfy itself that the existence of the rule in the *opinio juris* of States is confirmed by practice.[54]

The Court did not thereby require "that in the practice of States the application of the rules in question should have been perfect, in the sense that States should have refrained, with complete consistency, from the use of force or from intervention in each other's internal affairs."[55] In other words, the Court was not of the view that, in order for Article 2(4) and other relevant rules of the UN Charter to be recognized as customary, the corresponding State practice must be in exact conformity with those rules. Instead, the ICJ deemed it sufficient that the State practice[56] be in *general* consistency with such rules, and that instances of State conduct inconsistent with a given rule should generally be treated as breaches of that rule, and not as indications of the recognition of a new rule:

> If a State acts in a way *prima facie* incompatible with a recognised rule, but defends its conduct by appealing to exceptions or justifications contained within the rule itself, then

---

[53] Ibid., para 187.

[54] Ibid., para 184.

[55] Ibid., para 186.

[56] It has been suggested that "[b]oth physical and verbal acts of States constitute practice that contributes to the creation of customary international law. Physical acts include, for example, battlefield behavior, the use of certain weapons and the treatment provided to different categories of persons. Verbal acts include military manuals, national legislation, national case-law, instructions to armed and security forces, military communiqués during war, diplomatic protests, opinions of official legal advisers, comments by governments on draft treaties, executive decisions and regulations, pleadings before international tribunals, statements in international organizations and at international conferences and government positions taken with respect to resolutions of international organizations." See Henckaerts and Doswald-Beck 2005, p. xxxii.

> whether or not the State's conduct is in fact justifiable on that basis, the significance of that attitude is to confirm rather than to weaken the rule.[57]

In the opinion of Nicholas Tsagourias, the ICJ allowed for a methodological inaccuracy in that it focused predominantly on the *opinio juris*, from which it deduced, almost mechanically, the conformity of State practice and refused to test the actual practice of States with respect to the prohibition of the use of inter-State force.[58] It appears that the issue of State practice in an area as crucial and delicate as this should have been treated with more attention, for at present it is not sufficiently measurable. Michael J. Glennon observes that, according to the 2004 Report of the High-Level Panel on Threats, Challenges and Change,[59] "from 1945 to 1989, states used military force numerous times in interstate disputes. By one count, force was employed 200 times, and by another count, 680 times."[60] In other words, he goes on, "the panel does not tell us who is right; indeed, it does not seem to care who is right. Apparently, it would not matter whether the rules had been violated 200 or 680 or 6800 times—the panel seems to suppose the number of violations is irrelevant."[61] However, he continues, the actual number of violations of a rule is important, for at least two reasons:

> First [...] the report rejects humanitarian intervention by states. The reason, the report says, is that humanitarian intervention by states would pose a fatal risk to the stability of the global order. Yet, how can we know how great the threat would be to the stability of the global order unless we know how stable that order really is—unless we know how effective the current rules actually have been in preventing the use of force?
>
> Second, after the number of violations exceeds a certain point, it is reasonable to conclude that states no longer consent to the rule and that the rule is no longer binding—that it has fallen into desuetude. Without examining the extent of non-compliance, however, it is impossible to know whether the rule is still a good law. Why does the panel assume that the law is what it believes the law *should be*?[62]

---

[57] *Nicaragua* Judgment, para 186.

[58] As N. Tsagourias point out, it would have been more accurate to derive the *opinio juris*, as evidence of States' conviction that their behavior is in conformity with binding rules of international law, from their practice (in the first place, physical but also verbal acts), whereas the inverse methodology is not as convincing. See Tsagourias 1996, p. 85. Besides, in practices contrary to established rules of customary international law there is, in fact, an inherent risk that these contrary practices can, over time, "shake" the rules and weaken them. T. Gazzini thus explained the technicality of reforming a rule of customary international law: "The process of change is ignited by the proposal for a new legal regulation put forward by some States. These States develop and manifest an *opinio necessitatis* to the effect that a norm ought to be changed. When the generality of the States composing the international community express their acceptance, or at least acquiesce, to such a proposal, conscious of its potential binding effect, the norm changes." Importantly, there may be periods when the content of customary rules would not be clear: "Given the incremental nature of this process, rules may occasionally be in a state of flux or legal incertitude. This is physiological in a horizontal system such as the international legal system." See Gazzini 2006, p. 321.

[59] See supra note 8.

[60] Quoted in Glennon 2006, p. 310. See also Bleckmann 1976, pp. 374–406; Bleckmann 1977, pp. 107–121.

[61] Glennon 2006, p. 311.

[62] Ibid.

2.1.2.3 Customary International Law on the Use of Force: The *opinio juris*

As concerns the *opinio juris*, the Court did not produce any more clarity on the matter either, for it followed from the Parties' submissions to the Court that they regarded Article 2(4) as being generally reflective of customary international law on the issue in question, and that they did not challenge the obligation emanating from that Article "to refrain in their international relations from the threat or use of force against the territorial integrity or political independence of any State, or in any other manner inconsistent with the purposes of the United Nations."[63] The Court nonetheless felt that it had to go beyond the submissions of the States involved in the dispute, and to satisfy itself as to the existence in customary international law of a more universal *opinio juris* of the mandatory character of this rule. According to the Court, an adequate *opinio juris* might be inferred from, *inter alia*, the attitude of the parties to the dispute and of other Members of the United Nations towards relevant General Assembly resolutions, especially towards the 1970 Friendly Relations Declaration (see supra 1.2.5.3):

> The effect of consent to the text of such resolutions cannot be understood as merely that of a "reiteration or elucidation" of the treaty commitment undertaken in the Charter. On the contrary, it may be understood as an acceptance of the validity of the rule or set of rules declared by the resolution by themselves. The principle of non-use of force, for example, may thus be regarded as a principle of customary international law [...][64]

As regards the United States in particular, an expression of its stance towards the prohibition of the use of force was alleged to be found in some of its earlier verbal acts, such as its approval of a resolution condemning aggression adopted at the Sixth International Conference of American States (18 February 1928),[65] or its ratification of the Montevideo Convention on Rights and Duties of States (26 December 1933) whose Article 11 obliged States Parties not to recognize territorial acquisitions or special advantages which have been obtained by force.[66] In the same spirit, the acceptance by the US of the principle of the prohibition of the use of force, which was integrated in the 1975 CSCE Final Act's Declaration of principles whereby the participating States had undertaken to "refrain in their mutual

63 *Nicaragua* Judgment, para 188.

64 Ibid.

65 Ibid., para 189.

66 See Article 11 of the Montevideo Convention on the Rights and Duties of States, 26 December 1933: "The contracting states definitely establish as the rule of their conduct the precise obligation not to recognize territorial acquisitions or special advantages which have been obtained by force whether this consists in the employment of arms, in threatening diplomatic representations, or in any other effective coercive measure. The territory of a state is inviolable and may not be the object of military occupation nor of other measures of force imposed by another state directly or indirectly or for any motive whatever even temporarily," text available at: http://www.jus.uio.no/english/services/library/treaties/01/1-02/rights-duties-states.xml (last accessed 15 November 2012).

relations, as well as in their international relations in general" from the threat or use of force, was considered to constitute an evidence of its official position towards the legal prohibition of the inter-State use of force.[67] Thus, without examining actual State practice, the International Court of Justice held that the acceptance of the above non-binding declarations and resolutions, most of which had been worded in political—not even legal—terms, proved to a sufficient degree the existence of an *opinio juris* prohibiting the use of force in international relations.[68]

This conclusion could not have been more dubious, for instead of reflecting upon appropriate State practice, the Court merely acknowledged the Parties' verbal acts as evidence of customary international law. As a matter of fact, the provisions of General Assembly resolutions are not necessarily endowed with *opinio juris*—the psychological conviction that their rules do indeed reflect binding international law. As Nicholas Tsagourias recalled—by reference to H. Hart—States sometimes consent to rules either because they face popular "criticism and pressure," or because the rules at issue are "not mandatory."[69] In N. Tsagourias' view, the General Assembly resolutions, in addition to their non-mandatory legal status under the UN Charter,[70] always are products of policy deals, concessions and political wrestling over the United Nations Member States' national interests.[71] He also recalled, quite properly, H. W. A. Thirlway's suggestion to the effect that, in order for a UN General Assembly resolution to be regarded as evidence of *opinio juris,* there should be "a sufficient body of state practice for the usage element of the alleged custom to be established without reference to the resolution."[72] However, the confusing statistics offered in the High Panel Report (see supra 2.1.2.2) lead one to conclude that the State practice with regard to the legal prohibition of the use of force is not either coherent or uniform. Besides, as N. Tsagourias suggested, the fact that States at times behave inconsistently with the General Assembly resolutions they consented to allows assuming that States sometimes vote in the General Assembly for what they believe international law "*ought* to be"—or *might* be in the future—and not for what it "actually is" at the present stage.[73] The legal justifications for some of States' modern practices in the area of the use of force are examined below, at 2.4.

---

[67] See Conference on Security and Co-operation in Europe, Final Act, 1 August 1975, Principle II ("Refraining from the threat or use of force"), text available at: http://www.osce.org/mc/39501 (last accessed 15 November 2012).

[68] See *Nicaragua* Judgment, paras 186 and 189.

[69] Quoted in Tsagourias 1996, at 86 and 92, note 42.

[70] UN Charter, Article 14: "Subject to the provisions of Article 12, the General Assembly may recommend measures for the peaceful adjustment of any situation, regardless of origin, which it deems likely to impair the general welfare or friendly relations among nations, including situations resulting from a violation of the provisions of the present Charter setting forth the Purposes and Principles of the United Nations"

[71] See Tsagourias 1996, at 86.

[72] Quoted in Tsagourias 1996, at 87 and 93, note 45.

[73] See Tsagourias 1996, at 87.

2.1.3 Jus cogens *Obligation*

Whereas the treaty-based and customary nature of Article 2(4) has been considered above (see supra 2.1.1–2.1.2), it may also be useful to reflect on whether this provision—or at least some of its elements—also constitutes a *jus cogens* norm, a peremptory norm of general international law.[74] If this indeed is the case, the legal consequences of its breach should be more far-reaching than those of a breach of an "ordinary" conventional or customary rule of international law.[75] The *jus cogens* rules give rise to *erga omnes* obligations,[76] that is to say, their breaches affect the interests of larger groups of States—indeed, those of the international community of States as a whole[77]—which suggests that international law should provide States with more compelling tools for reacting to such breaches, commensurate with their particular gravity.

The International Law Commission's Articles on Responsibility of States for Internationally Wrongful Acts[78] (cf. supra 1.2.5.6) suggest, in Articles 40[79] and

[74] See the Vienna Convention on the Law of Treaties, Article 53 ("Treaties conflicting with a peremptory norm of general international law ("jus cogens")): "[...] For the purposes of the present Convention, a peremptory norm of general international law is a norm accepted and recognized by the international community of States as a whole as a norm from which no derogation is permitted and which can be modified only by a subsequent norm of general international law having the same character." See Scheuner 1967, pp. 520–532; Scheuner 1969, pp. 28–38.

[75] See Abashidze 2009, pp. 505–510; Bassiouni 1996, pp. 63–74; Brownlie 1998, pp. 511–519; Christakis 2006, pp. 127–166; Kadelbach 2006, pp. 21–40; Klein 2002, pp. 1241–1255; Malanczuk 1997, pp. 57–59; Orakhelashvili 2005, pp. 59–88; Riesenfeld 1966, pp. 511–515; Salcedo 1997, pp. 583–595; Schwelb 1967, pp. 946–975; Scobbie 2002, pp. 1201–1220; Shelton 2006, pp. 291–323; Sicilianos 2002, pp. 1127–1145; Talmon 2006, pp. 99–126; Tomuschat 2006, pp. 425–436; Von Verdross 1966, pp. 55–63; Vranes 2005, pp. 391–405; Vranes 2006, pp. 395–418; Weiler and Paulus 1997, pp. 545–565; Wyler 2002, pp. 1147–1160.

[76] See Lukashuk 2004a, p. 252.

[77] See ibid.

[78] See UN General Assembly resolution A/RES/56/589, 12 December 2001. On the Articles, see: Aust 2005, pp. 407–429; Bowett 1999, pp. 163–173; Brown Weiss 2002, pp. 798–816; Caron 2002, pp. 857–873; Condorelli 1994, pp. 106–115; Crawford 1999a, pp. 435–460; Crawford 2002, pp. 874–890; Crawford et al. 2001, pp. 963–991; Dominicé 1999, pp. 353–363; Dupuy 1992, pp. 139–148; Dupuy 2002, pp. 1053–1081; Gaja 1999, pp. 365–370; Gaja 2010, pp. 11–14; Garcia-Amador 1955, pp. 339–346; Gattini 1999, pp. 397–404; Gibney 2007, pp. 1–14; Harris 2004, pp. 504–654; Kunz 1960, pp. 324–347; Malanczuk 1997, pp. 254–272; Murphy 2001, pp. 626–628; Nollkaemper 2003, pp. 615–640; Nolte 2002, pp. 1083–1098; O'Connell 2002, pp. 63–79; Pellet 1999, pp. 425–434; Posner and Sykes 2007, pp. 1–63; Rosenstock 2002, pp. 792–797; Spinedi 2002, pp. 895–899; Tams 2002, pp. 1161–1180; Wilmshurst 2004, pp. 93–96; Wyler 2002, pp. 1147–1160.

[79] See Articles on Responsibility of States for Internationally Wrongful Acts, Article 40 ("Application of this chapter"):
1. This chapter applies to the international responsibility which is entailed by a serious breach by a State of an obligation arising under a peremptory norm of general international law.
2. A breach of such an obligation is serious if it involves a gross or systematic failure by the responsible State to fulfil the obligation.

41,[80] a number of important implications, if a State's use of force in violation of Article 2(4) of the Charter were to be regarded as a breach of a peremptory norm of general international law, and not "merely" of treaty law or customary international law.[81] First, it follows from Article 40 of Articles on Responsibility of States that a breach by a State of an obligation arising under a peremptory norm of general international law can be "serious"—if it involves "a gross or systematic failure by the responsible State to fulfil the obligation"—and "less-than-serious," logically, if the obligation in question is breached to a minor degree or not systematically.[82] The UN Charter makes a formal distinction, in Article 39, between three types of breaches of obligations arising under Article 2(4): threats to the peace, breaches of the peace and acts of aggression—but does not contain any more specific normative or practical criteria for distinguishing between them. It appears that acts of aggression, as the most serious type of breaches in this classification, should of necessity fall within the ambit of Article 40 of the 2001 Articles,[83] whereas threats to the peace or breaches of the peace, although breaching Article 2(4), might not necessarily reach this threshold of gravity. We will not tackle threats to the peace or breaches of the peace in much detail, for the sake of volume space, as they do not fall within the scope of this research. The definitional particulars of acts of aggression are dealt with below, at 2.3 and 5.1.1.2–5.1.1.3.

Second, States are required ("*shall* cooperate")—not merely allowed or encouraged—to bring an end, by joint efforts, to any serious breach within the meaning of Article 40. Under current international law, such "lawful means" for suppressing acts of aggression—as the most serious breaches of the obligation arising under Article 2(4) of the UN Charter—include the suspension of rights and privileges under the Charter of the United Nations (Article 5), expulsion from the UN membership (Article 6), individual or collective self-defence (Article 51, see infra 2.4.1.1–2.4.1.4), collective enforcement action under the auspices of the Security

[80] See ibid., Article 41 ("Particular consequences of a serious breach of an obligation under this chapter"): 1. States shall cooperate to bring to an end through lawful means any serious breach within the meaning of Article 40. 2. No State shall recognize as lawful a situation created by a serious breach within the meaning of Article 40, nor render aid or assistance in maintaining that situation. 3. This article is without prejudice to the other consequences referred to in this Part and to such further consequences that a breach to which this chapter applies may entail under international law.

[81] The legal consequences of internationally wrongful acts of a lesser gravity than those of serious breaches of peremptory norms of general international law are outlined in Chapters 1("General principles") and 2 ("Reparation for injury") of the Articles' Part II, and consist in the continued duty of performing the obligation breached (Article 29), of ceasing and not repeating the internationally wrongful act in question (Article 30), and of making full reparation for the injury caused by the internationally wrongful act (Article 31). In turn, full reparation for the injury caused may take the form of restitution, compensation and satisfaction, either singly or in combination, in accordance with the provisions of Chapter II.

[82] In the latter situation, only general rules on the implementation of the international responsibility of States laid down in the Articles (Part II, Chapters I and II) would apply.

[83] See Lukashuk 2008a, p. 287.

Council (Chapter VII, see infra 2.4.1.5), or having recourse to regional security arrangements (Chapter VIII). The victim of a serious breach of an obligation arising under Article 2(4) of the UN Charter should not be left alone vis-à-vis the aggressor State(s). Instead, lawful means must be used to put an end to such an aggression as soon as possible.[84]

Third, States are required to refrain from recognizing as lawful situations created by serious breaches of *jus cogens*, and from rendering aid or assistance in maintaining such situations. Acts of aggression can lead to a variety of unlawful results (see infra 4.1 and 4.5.1–4.5.4) most of which are, in one way or another, related to the victim State's territorial integrity or political independence (cf. supra 2.1.1.1). As will be shown below at 2.1.3.2, States and relevant international bodies have, as a rule, indeed refrained from recognizing the legal validity of circumstances resulting from unlawful uses of force or from violations of the principle of self-determination of peoples (cf. infra 2.4.2.2), which most probably testifies to the respective rules' status of *jus cogens*.

And last but not least, Article 41(3) mentions that serious breaches of obligations arising under *jus cogens* norms may also entail "further consequences" under international law. Assuming that Article 2(4) indeed constitutes *jus cogens*, one should think, among such further consequences, of a direct (see infra Chap. 5) or indirect (see infra 4.6.1 and Chap. 4) enforcement of individual criminal responsibility (see especially infra 5.2.4) of natural persons who would have contributed to the planning, preparation, initiation or execution of an act of aggression by a State (see infra 2.3 and 5.1.1.2–5.1.1.3). As will be discussed below (at 5.3.2.7 and 5.3.3), a determination by the Security Council that an act of aggression—a serious breach of an obligation arising under the hypothetical *jus cogens* provision contained in the Charter's Article 2(4)—has been committed should predictably lead to the identification of individuals who caused that act to happen, and to the determination of their criminal responsibility for the act. Likewise, the ICC Prosecutor's substantiated assumption about a State's having committed an act of aggression—even without a plain determination to the effect by the Security Council—may, in appropriate circumstances, lead to the same consequences (see infra 5.3.2.8–5.3.2.9).

Having outlined the specific consequences that the most serious type of breach of Article 2(4) of the Charter of the United Nations—an act of aggression—would necessitate, if this Article were confirmed to constitute *jus cogens*, the suitability of attributing this status to Article 2(4) should now be examined. This analysis should help in the assessment of a lasting discrepancy between the Charter's strongly worded prohibition of the use of inter-State force (see supra 2.1.1) and the actual, deplorably frequent, practice of its use (see supra 2.1.2.2). In other words, should State practices diverging, in serious ways, from Article 2(4) of the Charter be regarded as testifying to the emergence of new customary rules of international law on the inter-State use of force, or should they, instead, be viewed as serious breaches of obligations arising under a peremptory norm of general international law?

[84] See Okimoto 2011b, p. 35.

The 1969 Vienna Convention's definition of a peremptory norm of general international law (*jus cogens*, see supra note 74) includes a number of elements whose consideration should be useful for the purpose of this research: (1) a norm in question must be accepted and recognized by the international community of States as a whole; (2) due to its overarching character, such a norm allows for no derogation in any circumstances; and (3) it is a norm of a lasting, system-building nature, for it can be modified only by a subsequent norm of general international law having the same character. To which extent does the prohibition of the use of force embodied in Article 2(4) of the Charter of the United Nations meet these criteria?

2.1.3.1 Acceptance and Recognition by the International Community of States as a Whole

Article 2(4) is, by and large, accepted and recognized by the international community of States as a whole. As a Principle of the United Nations, it is binding upon all United Nations Member States and, as was pointed out above (see supra note 4), Article 2(4) also provides protection to non-Members, without being formally binding upon them. It was relied upon in numerous acts adopted by international bodies—such as the United Nations General Assembly (see supra 1.2.5.3) or the CSCE/OSCE—and in decisions of the International Court of Justice (cf. supra 2.1.2.2–2.1.2.3). Yet, as was noted above at 2.1.2.2, the practice of applying Article 2(4) since 1945 has not always been consistent with such formal recognitions. States were breaching the prohibition, directly or indirectly, on a variety of grounds but most frequently invoking the right to individual or collective self-defence, which is referred to in the Charter's Article 51 as a plain exception to the prohibition of the use of force (see infra 2.4.1.1–2.4.1.4). As was noted above (see supra 2.1.2.1), Article 51 does not itself regulate the implementation of this inherent right and necessitates further regulation by rules of customary international law—which creates space for (possibly selfish) interpretations of the provision. It may thus be concluded, somewhat paradoxically, that Article 2(4) is not contested by States verbally but is in fact breached, more often than could reasonably be expected from a Principle of the United Nations, as a matter of their practice.

2.1.3.2 Non-derogable Character

Now turning to the second criterion, one should ask whether there exist any specific (normative or practical) standards on whose basis one could differentiate between legitimate uses of force and "derogations" from Article 2(4)—which are not allowed, if that rule indeed constitutes one of *jus cogens*.[85] Clearly, the assertion of

[85] Article 2(4) itself contains only one such criterion—against which all relevant State practice, as inconsistent as it is—must be measured: no threat or use of force is to be applied by a State "against the territorial integrity or political independence of any state, or in any other manner inconsistent with the Purposes of the United Nations" (cf. supra 2.1.1.1).

a legal title over territory by (armed) force (cf. supra 2.1.1.2 and infra 4.1.2, 5.2.2–5.2.3) is among such specific standards. According to Alexander Orakhelashvili—a recognized authority on *jus cogens*—since 1945, the prohibition of deriving legal title from illegal uses of force and breaches of the principle of self-determination did acquire the status of a peremptory norm of general international law.[86] In his important treatise on the subject, A. Orakhelashvili recalled the opinions of Sir Robert Yewdall Jennings (1913–2004) to the effect that a use of force might not result in the acquisition of title if it has been condemned as illegal,[87] and of Charles de Visscher (1884–1973)—that international law could not regard as lawful the benefits ensuing from the use of force, if it outlaws the use of force in an absolute way.[88] A. Orakhelashvili evoked further that several territorial changes had been regarded as null and void due to their conflict with the *jus cogens* norms: for instance, "Jordan's occupation of East Jerusalem since 1948 was a violation of Article 2(4) of the UN Charter, and consequently Jordan was unable to acquire the sovereignty over that area,"[89] and "[t]he Israeli Occupation of the West Bank and East Jerusalem was similarly void for an identical reason."[90] Consequently, he concluded that the corollaries of the said occupations[91] had not merely been denoted as "illegal"—they had been deemed null and void, that is to say, no legal effect could be derived from them ab initio.[92] Therefore, despite the lapse of time, these territories are still referred to as occupied territories, and Israel as an occupying power.[93] A. Orakhelashvili recalled that these unequivocal characteristics had been confirmed by the UN Security Council in Resolution 672 (1990) and by the ICJ in the 2004 *Wall* Advisory Opinion.[94] A. Cassese (1937–2011) explained these opinions of the key bodies of the United Nations in the following manner:

> [A]t present general international law has departed markedly from the principle of effectiveness: de facto situations brought about by force of arms are no longer automatically endorsed

---

[86] Orakhelashvili 2006b, pp. 218–219.

[87] See R. Jennings, *The Acquisition of Territory in International Law* (1967), p. 54, referred to in Orakhelashvili 2006b, p. 218.

[88] C. de Visscher, *Les effectivités du droit international public* (1967), pp. 115–116, referred to in Orakhelashvili 2006b, p. 218.

[89] See Orakhelashvili 2006b, p. 220.

[90] Ibid.

[91] In accordance with Article 2 common to the 1949 Geneva Conventions on the Protection of Victims of War, the Conventions apply, in addition to any international armed conflicts, "to all cases of partial or total occupation [...] even if the said occupation meets with no armed resistance." Consequently, Israel was expected to comply fully with the Fourth Geneva Convention since its entry into force for Israel on 6 July 1951. Cf. the ICRC database on international humanitarian law: http://www.icrc.org/ihl (last accessed 14 November 2012).

[92] See Orakhelashvili 2006b, p. 220.

[93] Ibid.

[94] See *Legal Consequences of the Construction of a Wall in the Occupied Palestinian Territory*, Advisory Opinion of 9 July 2004, ICJ Reports (2004), especially paras 19, 20, 31, 73, 74, 77 and others, referred to in Orakhelashvili 2006b, p. 220. See also Orakhelashvili 2006a, pp. 119–139.

> and sanctioned by international legal standards. At present the principle of legality is overriding—at least at the normative level—and effectiveness must yield to it.[95]

A. Orakhelashvili further stressed that the voidness of a forcible acquisition of territory should result in the nullity of juridical acts emanating from the unlawful exercise of sovereign powers in furtherance of that acquisition.[96] Thus, the International Court of Justice recalled in the *Wall* Advisory Opinion resolution 298 (1971) adopted by the Security Council on 25 September 1971 to the effect that "all legislative and administrative actions taken by Israel to change the status of the City of Jerusalem, including expropriation of land and properties, transfer of populations and legislation aimed at the incorporation oî the occupied section, are totally invalid and cannot change that status."[97] The Court further recalled the Security Council Resolution 478 (1980) by which a provision in Israel's Basic Law on the status of Jerusalem as the "complete and united" capital of Israel,[98] along with all measures "which have altered or purport to alter the character and status of the Holy City of Jerusalem," were declared null and void.[99] The ICJ also recalled the UN Security Council's attitude—expressed in resolution 446 (1979) of 22 March 1979—towards "the policy and practices of Israel in establishing settlements in the Palestinian and other Arab territories occupied since 1967" as being in flagrant violation of the provisions of the Fourth Geneva Convention relative to the Occupying Power's rights and responsibilities,[100] especially Article 49.[101] The Court ruled that

---

[95] Quoted in Orakhelashvili 2006b, p. 221.

[96] Articles 42–56 of the 1907 Hague Regulations lay down the legal framework for the administration of occupied territories by an Occupying Power. In line with those provisions, recalls A. Orakhelashvili, the Security Council pronounced in its Resolution 497 (1981) that Israel's policies of imposing "its laws, regulations and jurisdiction over the occupied Golan Heights [were] null and void." See Orakhelashvili 2006b, p. 221.

[97] See *Legal Consequences*, para 75, quoted in Orakhelashvili 2006b, p. 221.

[98] Cf. Article 1 of the Basic Law of Israel, text available at: http://www.knesset.gov.il/laws/special/eng/basic10_eng.htm (last accessed 16 November 2012), quoted in Orakhelashvili 2006b, p. 221.

[99] See *Legal Consequences*, paras 74–75, quoted in Orakhelashvili 2006b, p. 221.

[100] See *Legal Consequences*, para 99, quoted in Orakhelashvili 2006b, p. 221.

[101] Cf. Geneva Convention IV, Article 49: "Individual or mass forcible transfers, as well as deportations of protected persons from occupied territory to the territory of the Occupying Power or to that of any other country, occupied or not, are prohibited, regardless of their motive. Nevertheless, the Occupying Power may undertake total or partial evacuation of a given area if the security of the population or imperative military reasons so demand. Such evacuations may not involve the displacement of protected persons outside the bounds of the occupied territory except when for material reasons it is impossible to avoid such displacement. Persons thus evacuated shall be transferred back to their homes as soon as hostiltities in the area in questions have ceased. The Occupying Power undertaking such transfers or evacuations shall ensure, to the greatest practicable extent, that proper accommodation is provided to receive the protected persons, that the removals are effected in satisfactory conditions of hygiene, health, safety and nutrition, and that members of the same family are not separated. The protecting Power shall be informed of any transfers and evacuations as soon as they have taken place. The Occupying Power shall not detain protected persons in an area particularly exposed to the dangers of war unless the security of the population or imperative military reasons so demand. The Occupying Power shall not deport or transfer parts of its own civilian population into the territory it occupies."

those measures were "without legal effect" and could not alter the status of these territories (including of East Jerusalem) as occupied territories, and the continued status of Israel as an Occupying Power was confirmed accordingly.[102] In A. Orakhelashvili's opinion, the peremptory prohibition of the use of force under international law was also relevant in the cases of East Timor[103] and Northern Cyprus[104]: "[I]n all these cases the invalidity of titles as confirmed by the United Nations organs [was] implementing and declaratory of the *jus cogens* nullity, not just a discretionary action."[105]

To wrap up on the second criterion, one may suggest, by way of analogy, that, if the prohibition of the use of armed force against the territorial integrity or political independence of States and the principle of self-determination of peoples were found, both by the International Court of Justice and leading publicists, to constitute a peremptory norm of general international law (*jus cogens*), there should be little reason to oppose why the other fundamental values protected by Article 2(4)—such as "international co-operation in solving international problems of an economic, social, cultural, or humanitarian character, and in promoting and encouraging respect for human rights and for fundamental freedoms for all without distinction as to race, sex, language, or religion" (cf. Article 1(3) of the UN Charter)—as well as the other Purposes of the United Nations (cf. supra 2.1.1.1) might not be protected in a similar manner. If that were indeed so, the case for the legitimacy of "humanitarian intervention"—an international military tool to stop large-scale violations of fundamental human rights—could become a good deal stronger (see infra 2.4.3.2).[106]

2.1.3.3 Normative Stability

As for the last criterion—that a *jus cogens* norm can be modified only by a subsequent norm of general international law having the same character—it seems to evoke no particular difficulty. It has been observed above (see note 11) that the conservative law regulating the use of force in international relations has experienced virtually no changes since the adoption of the Charter of the United Nations (cf. supra 1.2.5.1)—and no considerable revision of its text is to be expected in a foreseeable future, due to the complex technicalities of revising a treaty as

---

[102] See Orakhelashvili 2006b, p. 222. See also *Legal Consequences*, para 78.

[103] See *Case Concerning East Timor (Portugal v. Australia)*, Judgment of 30 June 1995, ICJ Reports (1995).

[104] On this case, see Harris, O'Boyle and Warbrick 1995, pp. 7, 520, 643–644, 646, 652–653, 655, 674.

[105] Orakhelashvili 2006b, p. 222.

[106] Igor Lukashuk seems to share this supposition. See Lukashuk 2004a, pp. 249–250.

system-building as the Charter.[107] For sure, Article 2(4) shall not be formally replaced by an alternative provision having the same status for decades to come—which means that States should have to adapt their conduct to its requirements, or else learn better interpreting its content—as a matter of putting the principle of legality into practice, to borrow from Antonio Cassese's statement quoted above (at 2.1.3.2)—in their favor, in light of their conflicting practices. Whereas rules of customary international law can indeed be altered by the practice of States (cf. supra 2.1.2.2), a peremptory norm of general international law (*jus cogens*) cannot be modified by any contrary practice of States, for any contrary practice would itself constitute a breach of the norm in question. As the foregoing analysis suggests, there are sufficient grounds to believe that Article 2(4) of the UN Charter does constitute a peremptory norm of general international law, and aggression should be regarded as a serious breach thereof and entail both the responsibility of a delinquent State and the individual criminal responsibility of its authors, in the sense of Article 41(3) of the 2001 Articles on Responsibility of States for Internationally Wrongful Acts. A more detailed analysis of this assumption will now be offered.

2.2 Aggression as a Serious Breach of a Peremptory Norm of General International Law

As the Articles on Responsibility of States for Internationally Wrongful Acts were being drafted (cf. supra 1.2.5.6), there was an important debate within the International Law Commission as to whether and how the Articles should reflect the existence of a "hierarchy" of obligations arising under international law and, accordingly, one of breaches of those obligations (cf. supra 2.1.3).[108] The learned debate involved such contentious issues as the legal nature of international responsibility, the feasibility of imposing responsibility on sovereign States and of enforcing a collective "criminal liability" of States, the appropriateness of classifying States' infractions as international delicts and international crimes, and the like.[109] A vast majority of the International Law Commission's members favored

---

[107] Cf. Article 109 of the UN Charter: "1. A General Conference of the Members of the United Nations for the purpose of reviewing the present Charter may be held at a date and place to be fixed by a two-thirds vote of the members of the General Assembly and by a vote of any nine members of the Security Council. Each Member of the United Nations shall have one vote in the conference. 2. Any alteration of the present Charter recommended by a two-thirds vote of the conference shall take effect when ratified in accordance with their respective constitutional process by two-thirds of the Members of the United Nations including all the permanent members of the Security Council.

[108] Lukashuk 2004a, pp. 262–266.

[109] Ibid., pp. 260–261.

the adoption of this two-level classification.[110] Hence, the Commission's Special Rapporteur on International Responsibility, Roberto Ago (1907–1995), suggested, in 1976, a categorization of breaches of States' international obligations under the headings of international crimes and international delicts:

1. An act of a State which constitutes a breach of an international obligation is an internationally wrongful act, regardless of the subject matter of the obligation breached.
2. An internationally wrongful act which results from the breach by a State of an international obligation so essential for the protection of fundamental interests of the international community that its breach is recognized as a crime by that community as a whole.
3. Subject to paragraph 2, and on the basis of the rules of international law in force, an international crime may result, *inter alia*, from:

   (a) A serious breach of an international obligation of essential importance for the maintenance of international peace and security, such as that prohibiting aggression;

   [...]

4. Any internationally wrongful act which is not an international crime in accordance with paragraph 2 constitutes an international delict.[111]

This proposal took into account post-War developments in international criminal law (see supra 1.2) inasmuch as it referred to aggression, in an explicit manner, among serious breaches of international obligations of essential importance for the maintenance of international peace and security (Article 19(3)(a)) and characterized these as international crimes (Article 19(2)). Even so, as the International Law Commission's attitude towards the "criminal responsibility of the State" evolved over time, the final version of the Articles contained no reference to international crimes but dealt with less controversially worded "internationally wrongful acts" (Article 2) and "serious breaches of peremptory norms of general international law" (Article 40, cf. supra 2.1.3). Notably, the final edition of the Articles, unlike R. Ago's earlier proposal, made no more specific mention of aggression and offered no other samples of serious breaches of international obligations. The effects of this omission are twofold: on the one hand, the formulation

---

[110] For instance, T. Elias was in favor of the notion "international crime," E. Hambro used the concept "international criminal acts," and J. Castañeda underscored that breaches of *erga omnes* obligations—such as acts of genocide—should be regarded as international crimes. See *Ejegodnik Komissii mejdunarodnogo prava* 1973, volume I, session 1203, para 26. However, it should be noted that the sensitive term "international crime" was to be used, for the purpose of the draft Articles, in the words of D. Levin of the Soviet Union, "in the sense of international law, and not in the sense of criminal law, that is to say, the abovementioned conduct of a State [serious breach of an obligation emanating from a fundamental rule of international law] should entail a more severe political condemnation on the part of other States, as well as more severe international sanctions, including collective sanctions from an international organization or a number of States." See Levin 1966, p. 29. In the International Law Commission's opinion, the issue of individuals' criminal responsibility for their role in the commission of international crimes was to be dealt with essentially separately from—although in a functional conjunction with—the responsibility of States, which approach was duly reflected in the 2001 edition of the Articles. See Lukashuk 2004a, pp. 262–263.

[111] *Ejegodnik Komissii mejdunarodnogo prava* 1976, volume II (Part Two), p. 110.

included in the Articles' final edition is comprehensive enough to allow States to react, by lawful means, to a serious breach of any peremptory norm of general international law; on the other hand, the range of these norms has not been determined in a clear-cut manner and is capable of further development over time.[112] Although the prohibition of aggression is, under modern international law, among the least dubious of such norms, it does merit a supplementary test.

2.2.1 *Aggression as a Serious Breach of an Obligation Arising Under Article 2(4) of the Charter of the United Nations*

Comprehensive opinions favoring the qualification of the prohibition of the use of force under Article 2(4) of the UN Charter as a *jus cogens* norm are to be found in the official proceedings of international judicial and expert bodies, in States' statements at international conferences,[113] and in the international legal doctrine (cf. supra 2.1.3).

2.2.1.1 Attitude of the International Court of Justice

The International Court of Justice observed in para 190 of the *Nicaragua* Judgment that Article 2(4) "is frequently referred to in statements by State representatives as being not only a principle of customary international law but also a fundamental or cardinal principle of such law."[114] This affirmative opinion took account of the official positions of both Nicaragua and the United States in the case:

> Nicaragua in its Memorial on the Merits submitted in the present case states that the principle prohibiting the use of force embodied in Article 2, paragraph 4, of the Charter of the United Nations "has come to be recognized as *jus cogens*". The United States, in its

---

[112] As the International Law Commission put it in its Commentary on Article 40, "[i]t is not appropriate to set out examples of the peremptory norms referred to in the text of article 40 itself, any more than it was in the text of article 53 of the 1969 Vienna Convention. The obligations referred to in article 40 arise from those substantive rules of conduct that prohibit what has come to be seen as intolerable because of the threat it presents to the survival of States and their peoples and the most basic human values." See Draft articles on Responsibility of States for Internationally Wrongful Acts with commentaries, *Yearbook of the International Law Commission* 2001, volume II (Part Two), p. 112.

[113] At the 1968–1969 United Nations Conference on the Law of Treaties, a number of Governments characterized the prohibition of aggression as peremptory: see *Official Records of the United Nations Conference on the Law of Treaties* 1968, 52nd meeting, paras 3, 31 and 43; 53rd meeting, paras 4, 9, 15, 16, 35, 48, 59 and 69; 54th meeting, paras 9, 41, 46 and 55; 55th meeting, paras 31 and 42; and 56th meeting, paras 6, 20, 29 and 51.

[114] *Nicaragua* Judgment, para 190. See also Christenson 1987, 93–101.

Counter-Memorial on the questions of jurisdiction and admissibility, found it material to quote the views of scholars that this principle is a "universal norm", a "universal international law", a "universally recognized principle of international law", and a "principle of *jus cogens*".[115]

The Court's observation was echoed, in an even more assertive way, in the Separate Opinion of the President of the Court, Judge Nagendra Singh (1914–1988), who stated that "the principle of non-use of force belongs to the realm of *jus cogens*, and is the very cornerstone of the human effort to promote peace in a world torn by strife."[116]

2.2.1.2 Attitude of the International Law Commission

The International Law Commission also dealt with the legal implications of the characterization of the prohibition of aggressive use of force as a *jus cogens* norm, especially in the course of the codification work on the Vienna Convention on the Law of Treaties. The Commission held that a peremptory norm of general international law forbidding aggressive use of force had already come into existence in 1945,[117] which meant that any treaty designed to instigate aggression against another State made after the entry into force of the Charter would be invalid ab initio, and that any acts performed in reliance on such a treaty would be illegal. In its Commentary on Article 50 of its draft Articles on the Law of Treaties, the Commission reiterated its view that "the law of the Charter concerning the prohibition of the use of force in itself constitutes a conspicuous example of a rule in international law having the character of *jus cogens.*"[118] The specific discussions on issues arising from the effects of aggression on treaties were concerned, *inter alia*, with the effects of the determination of an act of aggression on the treaty relations of an aggressor State,[119] and the nature and validity of treaties concluded between the victorious States and vanquished aggressors ("case of an aggressor State").[120]

---

[115] *Nicaragua* Judgment, para 190.

[116] Separate Opinion of President Nagendra Singh, 153.

[117] *Yearbook of the International Law Commission* 1963, volume II, pp. 198–199.

[118] *Yearbook of the International Law Commission* 1966, volume II, p. 247.

[119] In this regard, the Commission discussed "[q]uite apart from any questions of *jus cogens,* the problem [...] of an aggressor being obliged to terminate or withdraw from certain treaties." See ibid., pp. 181, 186.

[120] A draft article on the "case of an aggressor State" read as follows: "Nothing in the present articles may be invoked by an aggressor State as precluding it from being bound by a treaty or any provision in a treaty which in conformity with the Charter of the United Nations it has been required to accept in consequence of its aggression." See ibid. p. 197. A rephrased version of this article read: "The present articles are without prejudice to any obligation in relation to a treaty which may arise for an aggressor State in consequence of measures taken in conformity with the Charter of the United Nations with reference to that State's aggression." See ibid., p. 222.

In its Commentary on the 2001 Articles on Responsibility of States for Internationally Wrongful Acts, the International Law Commission has been even more assertive in pointing out the *jus cogens* character of the prohibition of aggression. Although not having provided any examples of peremptory norms of general international law in the Articles' final text, the Commission did give such examples in its official Commentary on Article 40 (see supra 2.1.3). Having recalled that such practices as "slavery and the slave trade, genocide, and racial discrimination and apartheid [...] have been prohibited in widely ratified international treaties and conventions admitting of no exception,"[121] the ILC reminded further the ICJ's conclusions to the effect that the fundamental rules of international humanitarian law applicable in armed conflict were "intransgressible" in character and hence peremptory,[122] and that "[t]he principle of self-determination [was] one of the essential principles of contemporary international law," which gave rise to "an obligation to the international community as a whole to permit and respect its exercise." [123] In the International Law Commission's view, the prohibition of aggression under international law was likewise generally agreed to be regarded as peremptory, for a few reasons: it is consistent with every State's "legal interest in the protection of certain basic rights and the fulfilment of certain essential obligations,"[124] constitutes an obligation *erga omnes*,[125] and serves the purpose of protecting "the survival of each State and the security of its people."[126] As Article 40 of the 2001 Articles does not itself lay down any procedure for determining whether or not a serious breach of an obligation arising under a peremptory norm of general international law has been committed,[127] it is useful to look into the rules for attributing an act of aggression to a delinquent State.

---

[121] See Draft articles on Responsibility of States for Internationally Wrongful Acts with commentaries, supra note 112, at 112.

[122] *Legality of the Threat or Use of Nuclear Weapons*, Advisory Opinion of 8 July 1996 (ICJ Reports 1996), para 79, quoted ibid, at 113.

[123] In the *East Timor* case, the International Court of Justice stated that "Portugal's assertion that the right of peoples to self-determination, as it evolved from the Charter and from United Nations practice, has an *erga omnes* character, is irreproachable." See *East Timor (Portugal* v. *Australia), Judgment,* ICJ Reports (1995), para 29, quoted ibid, at 113.

[124] See ibid., p. 33.

[125] See ibid, p. 127.

[126] See ibid.

[127] Paragraph 9 of the Commentary on Article 40 reads that "[i]t is not the function of the articles to establish new institutional procedures for dealing with individual cases, whether they arise under chapter III of Part Two or otherwise. Moreover, the serious breaches dealt with in this chapter are likely to be addressed by the competent international organizations, including the Security Council and the General Assembly. In the case of aggression, the Security Council is given a specific role by the Charter of the United Nations." See Draft articles on Responsibility of States for Internationally Wrongful Acts with commentaries, supra note 112, at 127.

2.2.2 *Attribution of Aggression to a State Under International Law*

The conduct of an organ of a State, or of a person or entity directed, instigated or controlled by a State, is usually attributed to that State.[128] This rule has acquired the character of a customary norm of international law.[129] In conformity with this recognized rule, Article 4 ("Conduct of organs of a State") of the 2001 Articles reads:

1. The conduct of any State organ shall be considered an act of that State under international law, whether the organ exercises legislative, executive, judicial or any other functions, whatever position it holds in the organization of the State, and whatever its character as an organ of the central Government or of a territorial unit of the State.
2. An organ includes any person or entity which has that status in accordance with the internal law of the State.

As the International Law Commission pointed out, "[a]s a normative operation, attribution must be clearly distinguished from the characterization of [a State's] conduct as internationally wrongful."[130] The distinctive task of attribution is to establish whether an act in question is an act of the State for the purpose of responsibility, and this can be done by showing that an internationally wrongful act—or, for the purpose of this research, an alleged act of aggression in the quality of a serious breach of an obligation arising under a *jus cogens* norm, Article 2(4) of the Charter—committed by a State derived from an act performed by an organ of that State.[131] Since international law does not, as a rule, govern the internal organization of States and the functions of their organs, the domestic law and practice of each State are crucial in determining what constitutes an organ for the purposes of responsibility. In particular, the power to declare a war or, more generally, to engage a State in an international armed conflict is usually possessed by the executive or the legislature, or else is divided between these branches—hence the potential authors of a hypothetical act of aggression are to be sought, first and foremost, among officials belonging to these categories (cf. infra 4.2.1–4.2.3). However, whereas each State certainly determines its internal structure and functions through its own laws and practices, international law does have a role to play, as far as States' war-making functions (in both *jus ad bellum* and *jus in bello*) are concerned: it should be recalled that "the characterization of an act of a State as internationally wrongful is governed by international law," and that "such characterization is not

[128] Lukashuk 2004a, p. 109. See also Kramer and Michalowski 2005, pp. 446–469; Nollkaemper 2005, pp. 133–171.

[129] Lukashuk 2004a, pp. 109–147.

[130] See Draft articles on Responsibility of States for Internationally Wrongful Acts with commentaries, supra note 112, p. 39.

[131] Ibid.

affected by the characterization of the same act as lawful by internal law."[132] Consequently, any decision to use military force against another State, even if has been taken in accordance with an initiator State's appropriate domestic laws and procedures, must be tested in light of applicable international law, with due regard to the *jus cogens* character of Article 2(4) of the UN Charter. Applicable thematic sources, such as the 1974 Definition of Aggression, may be helpful for this purpose, as interpretative tools.

2.3 Elements of an Act of Aggression Under the 1974 Definition of Aggression

The General Assembly resolution 3314 (XXIX) was adopted on 14 December 1974, as an interpretation of Article 2(4) of the UN Charter, with a Definition of Aggression annexed to it[133] (cf. supra 1.2.5.3). Constructed, to a substantial extent, upon the draft definition of aggression proposed by the Soviet Union in 1933 (see supra 1.1.6.6) and upon alternative drafts suggested by the USSR and groups of Western and developing States during the 1950s and 1960s,[134] the new definition was adopted, almost thirty years after the entry into force of the UN Charter, as a guideline for the Security Council's determination of the existence of an act of aggression[135] and was generally (albeit not universally) recognized.[136] A useful interpretative instrument, the Definition—as a General Assembly resolution—was not legally binding and allegedly had "no visible impact" on the subsequent practice of the Security Council,[137] probably, due to the two major blocks' political confrontation in the Cold War.[138] Yet, although the Definition had lacked a binding force and suffered from a number of structural and substantial deficiencies, it is worth considering here in some detail, as it did exercise a considerable impact on the drafting of the Rome Statute's definition of the crime of aggression (see infra 5.1.1.3).

---

132 See 2001 Articles on State Responsibility, Article 3 ("Characterization of an act of a State as internationally wrongful").

133 UN GA Res. 3314 (XXIX), *GAOR* 29th Sess., Supp. No. 31 (1974). See generally Kemp 2010, pp. 116–124; Werle 2009, p. 407.

134 Ferencz 1972, at 495.

135 Garvey (1976–1977), pp. 193–194.

136 Stone 1977, pp. 224–246; Hazard 1968, pp. 701–710.

137 See Bassiouni and Ferencz 1999, at 313, 334. On some contemporary aspects of the Definition's impact, see Sayapin 2009, pp. 3–42.

138 See McWhinney 1962, pp. 951–970; McWhinney 1965, pp. 1–15; Reisman 1990, pp. 859–866.

2.3.1 "Chapeau" of the Definition

The 1974 Definition contains a general part followed by an incomplete list of examples of acts of aggression. The general part of the Definition (Article 1) reads as follows:

> Aggression is the use of armed force by a State against the sovereignty, territorial integrity or political independence of another State, or in any other manner inconsistent with the Charter of the United Nations, as set out in this Definition.

Yoram Dinstein singled out six essential distinctions between this formula and the primary rule articulated in Article 2(4) of the Charter of the United Nations (cf. supra 2.1.1): "(i) the mere threat of force is excluded; (ii) the adjective 'armed' is interposed before the noun 'force'; (iii) 'sovereignty' is mentioned together with the territorial integrity and the political independence of the victim State; (iv) the victim is described as 'another' (rather than 'any') State; (v) the use of force is proscribed whenever it is inconsistent with the UN Charter as a whole, and not only with the Purposes of the United Nations; (vi) a linkage is created with the rest of the Definition."[139] It has been suggested that the adding of a number of elements to the definition of aggression was just intended to raise the assessment threshold and accordingly to do away with the possibility of invoking shooting "a few stray bullets across a boundary" as the commission of an act of aggression by a State.[140] Yet, the normative and practical influence of this major—indeed, progressive—development in international law could have been more far-reaching. Its more precise wording, in comparison with Article 2(4) of the Charter, could have made the Definition a workable tool for the protection of sovereign interests of individual States and for the maintenance of international peace and security, and so would have reinforced the impact of Article 2(4) itself. The chief problem with the Definition was its recommendatory status of an annex to a General Assembly resolution.[141] If the Definition had been bestowed with a proper adequate legal force—for instance, by way of approval by

---

[139] Dinstein 2001, p. 116.

[140] Article 2 of the Definition provided that alleged acts of aggression or their consequences should be of "sufficient gravity" and that minor incidents of the use of armed force might therefore not constitute aggression, subject to appreciation by the Security Council in accordance with the Charter. Cf. B. Broms, "The Definition of Aggression," 154 *Recueil des Cours de l'Academie de Droit International* (1977), p. 346, referred to in Dinstein 2001, p. 116.

[141] UN Charter, Article 11: "1. The General Assembly may consider the general principles of co-operation in the maintenance of international peace and security, including the principles governing disarmament and the regulation of armaments, and may *make recommendations* with regard to such principles to the Members or to the Security Council or to both. 2. The General Assembly may discuss any questions relating to the maintenance of international peace and security brought before it by any Member of the United Nations, or by the Security Council, or by a state which is not a Member of the United Nations in accordance with Article 35, paragraph 2, and, except provided in Article 12, may *make recommendations* with regard to any such questions to the state or states concerned or to Security Council or to both. Any such question on which action is necessary shall be referred to the Security Council by the General Assembly either before or after discussion [...]."

the Security Council whose decisions are mandatory for all Members of the United Nations[142] and the carrying out of whose foremost function[143] the Definition was intended to facilitate—it would have become a "harder" source of international law and should have been complied with by States in a more consistent manner.

2.3.2 *Examples of Acts of Aggression*

In furtherance of the general part, Article 3 of the Definition lists possible examples of acts of aggression, regardless of their being accompanied by a declaration of war:

> (a) The invasion or attack by the armed forces of a State of the territory of another State, or any military occupation, however temporary, resulting from such invasion or attack, or any annexation by the use of force of the territory of another State or part thereof;
> (b) Bombardment by the armed forces of a State against the territory of another State or the use of any weapons by a State against the territory of another State;
> (c) The blockade of the ports or coasts of a State by the armed forces of another State;
> (d) An attack by the armed forces of a State on the land, sea or air forces, or marine and air fleets of another State;
> (e) The use of armed forces of one State which are within the territory of another State with the agreement of the receiving State, in contravention of the conditions provided for in the agreement or any extension of their presence in such territory beyond the termination of the agreement;
> (f) The action of a State in allowing its territory, which it has placed at the disposal of another State, to be used by that other State for perpetrating an act of aggression against a third State;
> (g) The sending by or on behalf of a State of armed hands, groups, irregulars or mercenaries, which carry out acts of armed force against another State of such gravity as to amount to the acts listed above, or its substantial involvement therein.

Notably, each subparagraph of Article 3 refers to an action performed *by or on behalf of a State*, thereby confirming that aggression is an internationally unlawful act of State committed against another State. The list is quite comprehensive (cf., however, infra 5.1.1.3.8), probably with one exception consisting in that subparagraphs (a) and (b) seem to be somewhat repetitive, for it is difficult to imagine how an "attack by the armed forces of a State of the territory of another State" (subparagraph (a), cf. infra 5.1.1.3.1) can be carried out without "the use of any weapons" referred to in subparagraph (b) (cf. infra 5.1.1.3.2),—as was discussed above (under 2.1), the word "attack" implies its military character and, consequently, the use of weapons.[144] On the other hand, the "[b]ombardment by the armed forces of a State against the territory of

[142] Ibid., Article 25: "The Members of the United Nations agree to accept and carry out the decisions of the Security Council in accordance with the present Charter"

[143] Cf. Article 24 of the UN Charter.

[144] Cf. also Article 51 of the UN Charter: "Nothing in the present Charter shall impair the inherent right of individual or collective self-defence if an *armed* attack occurs against a Member of the United Nations [...]" (emphasis added).

another State or the use of any weapons by a State against the territory of another State" is well possible without "the invasion or attack by the armed forces of a State" prohibited under subparagraph (a), and the singling out of bombardment or the use of weapons as a separate type of aggression is therefore justified.

Out of these, only the last subparagraph was explicitly pronounced by the International Court of Justice to be declaratory of customary international law (cf. infra 5.1.1.3.7).[145] Yoram Dinstein maintains, however, that, possibly, the other portions of the 1974 Definition's Article 3 may too be regarded as being indicative of "harder" rules of international law than the General Assembly resolutions are as a rule.[146] As a matter of fact, the *Nicaragua* case is not an apposite source to look for the attitude of the ICJ towards the issue in question, for in that case, the Court could not practically examine whether subparagraphs (a)–(f) of Article 3 were reflective of customary international law, because the factual basis of the case was limited to subparagraph (g).[147] The absence of the Court's jurisprudence on subparagraphs (a)–(f) of the 1974 Definition's Article 3 should therefore not be interpreted as the ICJ's unambiguously disapproving or doubtful attitude towards their substance but simply as a matter of fact that the Court did not yet have an opportunity of scrutinize their legal force in light of customary international law.

2.3.3 Non-Exhaustive Character of the List

Another problem about the international legal value of the 1974 Definition is that its Article 3 is not exhaustive, and the Security Council may itself determine what other international uses of force may amount to aggression.[148] This autonomy of political appraisal accorded to the Council is indeed warranted in the light of its required operational flexibility as an international organ primarily charged with the maintenance of international peace and security (see supra note 143). Yet, the *legal* qualification of uses of force as acts of aggression, in order for them to necessitate specific consequences for States and individuals under applicable international law (see supra 2.2.1.2), should involve more strictly defined assessment criteria and a less politicized procedure than the Security Council's is. As the Rome Statute's definition of an individual crime of aggression contains a direct reference to the 1974 Definition (see infra 5.1.1.2–5.1.1.3), one must note that the ICC Statute's

[145] *Nicaragua* Judgment, paras 106 et seq. As was discussed above (under 2.1.3), in the 2004 *Wall* Advisory Opinion, the Court found that the lasting occupation by Israel of adjacent Palestinian territories and related administrative measures were in violation of international law. See Burgis 2008, pp. 33–63. It may be recalled in this regard that "any military occupation, however temporary, resulting from such invasion or attack, or any annexation by the use of force of the territory of another State or part thereof" is too characterized as aggression under subparagraph (a) of the 1974 Definition's Article 3.

[146] Dinstein 2001, p. 118.

[147] Ibid.

[148] UN GA Res. 3314 (XXIX), supra note 121, Annex, Article 4.

Article 8 bis (2)—unlike its "parent provision"—is exhaustive, in accordance with the principle of legality (*nullum crimen sine lege*) established in ICL. Whilst the Security Council may indeed "determine that other acts [than only those listed in Article 3 of the 1974 Definition may] constitute aggression under the provisions of the Charter,"[149] the ICC Statute does not allow for such an extensive interpretation of elements of individual crimes within its jurisdiction (see infra 5.2.1).

2.3.4 The Problem of the "First Use" of Force

In accordance with Article 2 of the 1974 Definition, the first use of armed force by a State in contravention of the Charter of the United Nations constitutes *prima facie* evidence of an act of aggression, although the Security Council may, in conformity with the Charter, conclude that a determination that an act of aggression has been committed would not be justified in the light of other relevant circumstances, including the fact that the acts concerned or their consequences are not of sufficient gravity.[150] It appears that the reference to the first use of armed force should be read in connection with the essential circumstance that follows, namely, that such first use of armed force must be "in contravention of the Charter." It is conceivable that a State uses minor force against another State in the first instance but the target State responds to the trivial incident in a disproportionately forceful fashion and thus—in overreaction—itself violates the Charter. In such a case, the target State might itself probably be found guilty of committing aggression[151] (cf. infra 4.3.1.1.2). It must have been for this reason that the first use of force is not as such referred to in the Rome Statute's Article 8 bis but the major qualification of the potentially aggressive use of armed force—namely, its use in manifest violation of the Charter of the United Nations—is integrated in the provision (cf. infra 5.1.1.1.5). It would then be up to appropriate international organs to assess on a case-by-case basis (cf. infra 5.3.2.7–5.3.2.9, 5.3.3) whether it was the first actual use of force or a forceful response thereto that would have been in manifest violation of the Charter and hence would have constituted an act of aggression.

2.3.5 The Discretionary Power of the UN Security Council

In accordance with the Charter, the primary power to determine acts of aggression rests with the Security Council.[152] Yet, in many instances, even the manifestly hostile behavior of States was not qualified as acts of aggression (see supra 1.2.5.2).

---

[149] Ibid.

[150] Ibid., Article 2 (first sentence): "The first use of armed force by a State in contravention of the Charter shall constitute *prima facie* evidence of an act of aggression [...]."

[151] Dinstein 2001, p. 117.

[152] Cf. supra note 143.

The motivation behind such a restrictive application of the concept of aggression must have been far from purely legal: the Security Council is an international political body in whose action interests of its members—especially of permanent members—prevail,[153] and it may not be expected to apply rules of international law in the same impartial way as a judicial body—such as the International Court of Justice or the International Criminal Court—should have to.[154] It may be asserted with a good degree of certainty that the normative standards for the determination of aggression listed in Article 3 of the 1974 Definition were not often used by the Security Council due to political and procedural circumstances, and not necessarily due to that Article's inherent substantive deficiencies.

By contrast, these provisions should, hopefully, become more workable in the future practice of the International Criminal Court. Although the content of Article 8 bis (2) of the Rome Statute was drawn literally from Article 3 of the 1974 Definition of Aggression (see infra 5.1.1.3), and Article 8 bis (2)—probably, unnecessarily—made an explicit mention of the General Assembly resolution 3314 (XXIX) (see infra 5.1.1.2), the verbatim integration of these provisions in the Rome Statute as a matter of its own content should elevate them from the rank of "soft law" to the level of treaty law binding upon an increasing number of States Parties to the Statute, once Article 8 bis enters into force (see infra 5.1.2), and the Security Council might not ignore this development (see infra 5.3.2.7–5.3.2.9, 5.3.3).

2.4 Exceptions to the Prohibition of the Use of Force

It may be inferred from the foregoing analysis (cf. supra 2.1–2.3) that any use of force in inter-State relations not expressly authorized by international law would constitute a breach of Article 2(4) of the Charter of the United Nations, and the most serious breaches of an obligation arising under this *jus cogens* provision may be found to constitute aggression. Hence, an examination of lawful exceptions to the imperative prohibition of the use of force is required, to help identify acts, which do not, as a matter of current or emerging international law, qualify as aggression and, consequently, cannot entail States' responsibility under international law and individuals' liability under international or national criminal law. On the other hand, it may be assumed that any inter-State use of force, which cannot be justified by one of the lawful exceptions analyzed below, might constitute an act of aggression and should be subjected to an appropriate judicial scrutiny. This section will examine three categories of exceptions to Article 2(4): the Charter-based exceptions, i.e. ones explicitly mentioned in the UN Charter; the Charter-related exceptions, which are not explicitly mentioned in the UN Charter but have been inferred from its pertinent

---

[153] Cf. Link 1998, p. 120; Chauprade 2003, p. 767.

[154] See Higgins 1970, pp. 1–18; Johnstone 2003, pp. 437–480.

provisions by international organs; and, last but not least, extra-Charter exceptions, which derive from extra-Charter sources of international law.

2.4.1 Charter-Based Exceptions

The Charter of the United Nations allows explicitly only for two exceptions to the prohibition of the use of force—States' "inherent" right of individual or collective self-defence (Article 51) and collective security measures under Chapter VII (Articles 39–50).[155] Both legal regimes will be considered in turn.

2.4.1.1 Individual or Collective Self-Defence: General Observations

As was noted by Oscar Schachter, at the origin of States' inherent right of self-defence[156] there stood two principal schools of thought—the natural law school represented, *inter alia*, by Hugo Grotius (cf. supra 1.1.2.4), and the *realpolitik* school represented by practitioners such as the US Secretary of State Dean Gooderham Acheson (1893–1971).[157] According to the natural law school, States' right of self-defence is intrinsic in their nature and may be invoked in a variety of circumstances—ranging from "an extreme circumstance of self-defence"[158] to routine situations below the threshold of life-or-death existential emergencies. In other words, in the opinion of the natural law scholars, the exercise by a State's of its right of self-defence should be regarded as its regular and legitimate function, among such other functions—such as the maintenance of law and order, the regulation of its internal and external affairs, the emission of currency, and the like.[159] At the same time, as a technique of self-help—which, according to Yoram Dinstein, is typical to all primitive legal systems, including international law[160]—individual or collective self-defence was quite beyond the confines of law.[161]

---

[155] See generally Kelsen 1948, pp. 783–796.

[156] On the right of self-defence, see generally: Dinstein 2001, pp. 157–245; Gill 2006, pp. 361–369; Harris 2004, pp. 886–971; Kemp 2010, pp. 57–59; Kretzmer 2013, pp. 235–282; Kunz 1947, pp. 872–879; Okimoto 2011a, pp. 45–75; Shah 2007, pp. 95–126; Shaw 2008, pp. 1131–1146.

[157] See generally Schachter 1989, at 259–260. Dean Acheson shared his views in 1963—in connection with the Cuban missile crisis—and, according to Louis Henkin, "received no support from the audience." For details, see L. Henkin, *How Nations Behave: Law and Foreign Policy* (Council on Foreign Relations, 1968), pp. 265–267, referred to in Schachter 1989, at 260, note 8.

[158] *Legality of the Threat or Use of Nuclear Weapons*, para 97.

[159] On functions of the State, see Korelsky and Perevalov 1998, pp. 142–153; Marchenko 2002, pp. 336–353.

[160] See Y. Dinstein, "International Law as a Primitive Legal System," in 19 *New York University Journal of International Law and Politics* (1986–1987), p. 12, quoted in Dinstein 2001, p. 159.

[161] Dinstein 2001, p. 160.

Since—especially before the First World War but also between two World Wars (see supra 1.1)—any State might, in principle, resort to war against any other State, the quality of self-defence as a legal concept was rather limited. In the words of Eduardo Jiménez de Aréchaga (1918–1994), self-defence essentially "was not a legal concept but merely a political excuse for the use of force."[162] This actual state of affairs allowed representatives of the *realpolitik* school, in their turn, to conceive of States' right of self-defence in terms of "power,"[163] not of law—a view that might prevail until the entry into force of the Charter of the United Nations, with due regard to its Articles 2(4) (see supra 2.1) and 51 (see infra 2.4.1.1.1–2.4.1.1.5). It appears that, already in the inter-war period, a decisive argument in favor of the legal nature of the right of self-defence—suitably recalled by O. Schachter—was put forward by Sir Hersch Lauterpacht (1897–1960) in his seminal treatise *The Function of Law in the International Community*: "It [the right of self-defence] is regulated to the extent that it is the business of the courts to determine whether, how far, and for how long, there was a necessity to have recourse to it."[164] In point of fact, it would make no sense to refer to self-defence as a State's *right* under international law, if a State using armed force, allegedly, in self-defence were not willing or prepared to justify its military action in terms of such international law as may be applicable. H. Lauterpacht's opinion was recalled in the Nuremberg Tribunal's Judgment (for details, see infra 3.1.1),[165] and the Tribunal itself confirmed that "whether action taken under the claim of self-defence was in fact aggressive or defensive must ultimately be subject to investigation or adjudication if International Law is ever to be enforced."[166]

2.4.1.1.1 Article 51 of the Charter of the United Nations

As a matter of conventional international law, the general conditions under which States may resort to force in self-defence are specified in Article 51 of the Charter of the United Nations:

> Nothing in the present Charter shall impair the inherent right of individual or collective self-defence if an armed attack occurs against a Member of the United Nations, until the Security Council has taken measures necessary to maintain international peace and security.

Whereas it may be agreed that Article 51 does not indeed represent an exhaustive regulation of States' right of self-defence under modern international law (cf. supra 2.1.2.1), it is submitted that it does constitute a suitable and overarching

---

[162] E. Jiménez de Aréchaga, "International Law in the Past Third of a Century," in 159 *Recueil des Cours de l'Académie de Droit International* (1978), p. 96, quoted in Dinstein 2001, p. 160.

[163] On the role of power in modern international politics, see Kissinger 1994, pp. 804–836.

[164] H. Lauterpacht, *The Function of Law in the International Community* (1933), p. 180, quoted in Schachter 1989, p. 261.

[165] See Schachter 1989, pp. 261–262.

[166] International Military Tribunal (Nuremberg), Judgment of 1 October 1946, p. 436.

conventional framework for the exercise of this right's customary elements, which "fill" and complement the framework but do not replace it as such.[167] An outline of the main elements of Article 51 is offered below.

2.4.1.1.2 "Nothing in the present Charter shall impair the inherent right [...]"

The opening language of Article 51 confirms the inviolability of a State's right of self-defence as a matter of principle. The right of self-defence is referred to as "inherent"—in line with the natural law theory recalled above—and is placed in a relatively superior position with respect to the other provisions of the Charter ("Nothing in the present Charter shall impair [...]), i.e. the right of self-defence, if exercised by a State in good faith, appears to stand above any other rule of the Charter.[168] The exercise of the right, though, is subject to two cumulative conditions (see infra 2.4.1.1.4–2.4.1.1.5).

2.4.1.1.3 "[... O]f individual or collective self-defence [...]

It is presumed that the term "self-defence" means recourse to armed or military force (cf. supra 2.1.1.2.1–2.1.1.2.2 and infra 2.4.1.1.4),[169] and does not, for the purpose of Article 51, directly cover non-military (e.g. diplomatic, economic, etc.) measures, which of course may too be used—as subsidiary tools[170]—in order to restore the security of a State or States under attack. A State may exercise its right of self-defence individually or collectively with other States, whereby the collective exercise of the right may be more or less formalized—respectively, under the auspices of regional security organizations (e.g. NATO, CSTO, etc.) or else in the format of temporary international coalitions formed for the purpose of specific operations.[171]

2.4.1.1.4 "[I]f an armed attack occurs against a Member of the United Nations [...]"

It formally appears from this formula that Article 51 protects only Members of the United Nations. However, the "inherent" nature of States' right of self-defence (see supra 2.4.1.1.2) as well as the applicability of the UN Charter's more general regulations on the use of force to all States, including non-Members (see supra 2.1.1.1) lets

[167] See generally Skakunov 1973 *Samooborona v mejdunarodnom prave* [Self-Defence in International Law]. Moscow, referred to in Lukashuk 2008b p. 289.

[168] According to Igor Lukashuk, "[s]uch a right is an indispensable institution of any legal system." See Lukashuk 2008b, p. 290.

[169] See ibid., p. 289.

[170] See ibid., pp. 407–410.

[171] See ibid., pp. 296–297.

one conclude that the Charter recognizes, as a matter of fact, any State's right of self-defence, on the condition that the State is subjected to an armed attack. Two key issues are worthy of noting in this regard. First, the right of self-defence must be understood as a lawful reaction only to an *armed attack*—i.e. the employment by a State of its regular armed forces (in a broad sense currently accepted in international law), or of irregular armed groups (cf. supra 2.1.1.2.1), and of means and methods of warfare (in the sense of applicable international humanitarian law) against another State, its nationals, public or private property (cf. supra 2.1.1.2), or the employment of such physical force by a non-State actor as would result in *effects* comparable to those of an armed attack (cf. supra 2.1.1.2.2). In the sense of Article 51, no other factor may justify the use of armed force in self-defence.[172] Second, there exists a substantial controversy among scholars regarding the admissibility of anticipatory (preventive, pre-emptive or interceptive) self-defence in the case of an imminent danger of an armed attack. For the purpose of this research, the issue will be dealt with below, at 2.4.1.2–2.4.1.4, in more detail. It suffices to mention here that competent international courts—in the first place, the International Court of Justice—did not yet pronounce themselves on the matter,[173] although it was maintained in at least one dissenting opinion that Article 51 should not confine States' right of self-defence to cases "if, and only if an armed attack occurs."[174]

2.4.1.1.5 "[U]ntil the Security Council has taken measures necessary to maintain international peace and security"

It follows from the concluding clause of Article 51 that the Security Council must take measures to maintain international peace and security, if an armed attack occurs against a Member of the United Nations. The nature of these measures is considered below, at 2.4.1.5. It may appear from the language that the right of self-defence ceases, once the Security Council has taken the required measures.[175] It is submitted, though, that in practice a State may continue exercising its right of self-defence until the full restoration of international peace and security, with due regard to its "inherent" (cf. supra 2.4.1.1.2) and, consequently, inalienable nature.

2.4.1.2 Preventive Self-Defence

Since the end of the Second World War (cf. supra 1.2 and infra 3.1.1–3.1.3), there has only been a limited State practice favoring the legitimacy of preventive

[172] See ibid., p. 290.

[173] Cf. *Nicaragua* Judgment, para 194: "[T]he issue of the lawfulness of a response to the imminent threat of an armed attack has not been raised. Accordingly the Court expresses no view on that issue"

[174] Judge Schwebel, ibid., para 190.

[175] See Lukashuk 2008b, p. 290.

self-defence.[176] A notable case—appropriately recalled by M. Kinacioglu[177]—was Israel's attack, in 1981, against an Iraqi nuclear reactor under construction, on the purported ground that it would be used for producing material for nuclear weapons, which Iraq would employ for attacking Israel. The circumstances of the case were considered by the Security Council,[178] and the Israeli action was unanimously condemned: "[T]he military attack by Israel [was] in clear violation of the Charter of the United Nations and the norms of international conduct."[179] The Security Council members' views about the legitimacy of preventive self-defence as such were thereby divided.[180]

Dieter Wiefelspütz suggested defining preventive self-defence as "repelling an attack, which is not immediately challenging or threatening, or repelling a danger, which is not at hand."[181] This author shares D. Wiefelspütz's opinion to the effect that the absence of an identifiable threat or danger should render preventive self-defence internationally unlawful, unlike pre-emptive self-defence (see infra 2.4.1.3) whose legitimacy under international law—although not completely undisputed—is more well-founded.[182] With due regard to the "Webster formula,"[183] it appears that the preventive self-defence theory does not indeed meet the normative criteria laid down in Article 51 of the Charter of the United Nations (see supra 2.4.1.1.1–2.4.1.1.5) and should be discarded.

2.4.1.3 Pre-emptive Self-Defence

Especially after 11 September 2001 (cf. supra 2.1.1.2.1), the United States has been the world's foremost promoter of the concept of pre-emptive self-defence.[184]

---

176 On the notion of preventive self-defence, see Fischer 2003, pp. 4–7; Kröning 2003, pp. 82–87; Luban 2004, pp. 207–248; Potter 1951, pp. 142–145; Wiefelspütz 2006, pp. 103–111.

177 Kinacioglu 2008, at 39.

178 See ibid., with references to documents UN Doc. S/PV. 2280 (1981), at 16; UN Doc. S/PV.2283 (1981), at 56; UN Doc. S/PV.2282 (1981), at 42; UN Doc. S/PV.2288 (1981), at 14.

179 Security Council Resolution 487 (1981), quoted in Kinacioglu 2008, at 39.

180 Kinacioglu 2008, at 39.

181 Wiefelspütz 2006, at 103.

182 Ibid.

183 In the words of former US Secretary of State Daniel Webster (1782–1852), in order for anticipatory self-defence to be lawful, the threat to be countered ("the necessity") must be "instant, overwhelming and leaving no choice of means, and no moment for deliberation," quoted in Wiefelspütz 2006, at 108.

184 As such, the claim was not a novelty in the United States' foreign policy. Over 15 years before the issuance of the "Bush Doctrine" cited in the body of the text, President Ronald Reagan declared in his *Address to the Nation on the Air Strikes against Libya*, 14 April 1986, *Public Papers of the United States Presidents*, 1986, volume I, 468–469: "We believe that this pre-emptive action against the terrorist installations will not only diminish Colonel Qadhafi's capacity to export terror, it will provide him with incentives and reasons to alter his criminal behavior." See also "*Testimony of the Legal Adviser of the Department of State*" (1986) AJIL 80, at 641.

In the 2002 *National Security Strategy to Combat Weapons of Mass Destruction*, President George W. Bush declared as follows:

> United States military force and appropriate civilian agencies must have the capability to defend against weapons of mass destruction-armed adversary, including in appropriate cases through pre-emptive measures. This requires capabilities to detect and destroy an adversary's weapons of mass destruction assets before their weapons are used [...] The primary objective of a response is to disrupt an imminent attack or an attack in progress, and eliminate the threat of future attacks.[185]

This statement only received a limited support among international lawyers, not least because in its concluding sentence, three essentially different legal regimes (interceptive self-defence, pre-emptive self-defence and preventive self-defence) had been put together in a manner, which is inappropriate from the point of view of applicable international law, under the same umbrella. Notably, even the closest ally of the United States in the "global war against terror"—the United Kingdom—expressed reservations about the notion of pre-emptive self-defence. The British Foreign Secretary commented on the issue as follows:

> The issue of pre or post–pre-emption in respect of Iraq, I do not quite see the relevance. The issue is that here you have a regime which is in clear breach of an endless number of Security Council Resolutions requiring them to do certain things under Chapter VII [...][186]

Pre-emptive self-defence stands for a State's military action against potential adversary (usually, another State) in expectation of a hypothetical armed attack.[187] Pre-emptive self-defence differs both from preventive (see supra 2.4.1.2) and interceptive (see infra 2.4.1.4) self-defence in that its political constituent is indeed oriented towards a more or less defined potential threat, but the relevant military action is devoid, in a strict sense, of a *prima facie* defensive quality. The main justification the supporters of pre-emptive self-defence put forward is the imperfection of the Security Council's decision-making procedure (cf. supra 1.2.5.2 and 2.3.5), whereby the Council's permanent members

[185] United States President, *National Security Strategy to Combat Weapons of Mass Destruction*, 17 September 2002, 3.

[186] United Kingdom, House of Commons, Foreign Affairs Committee, 2nd Report, Session 2002–2003, para 150.

[187] M.-E. O'Connell, "The Myth of Preemptive Self-Defense" 2002, *American Society of International Law* 2: footnote 10, defines pre-emptive self-defence as "use of force to quell any possibility of future attack by another State, even where there is no reason to believe that an attack is planned and where no prior attack has occurred." According to Reisman (2003, at 87), pre-emptive self-defence is concerned with "conjectural and contingent threat of *possible* attack" (italics in the original). See also Bothe 2003, pp. 227–240; Ching 2013, pp. 1–8; Farer 2003, pp. 621–628; Gazzini 2008, pp. 25–32; Gray 2002b, pp. 437–448; Gray 2005, pp. 555–578; Gray 2011, pp. 35–53; Guiora 2008, pp. 3–24; Henderson 2004, pp. 3–24; Johnstone 2004, pp. 813–838; Kinacioglu 2008, pp. 33–48; Von Lepel Frhr. 2003, pp. 77–81; Lukashuk and Boklan 2003, pp. 587–597; McWhinney 2002b, pp. 421–436; Reisman and Armstrong 2006, pp. 525–550; Sapiro 2003, pp. 599–607; Sofaer 2003, pp. 209–226; Tuzmukhamedov 2006, pp. 374–384; Wedgwood 2003, pp. 576–585; Zagaynov 2006, pp. 29–45.

and their allies are protected against any possible enforcement action (see infra 2.4.1.5). However, this is not completely true. As the example of the Security Council resolution 487 (1981) shows (see supra 2.4.1.2, especially note 179), even the closest allies of permanent Security Council members are not entirely immune from condemnation under the UN Charter (whereas the permanent members themselves indeed are). Furthermore, however flawed the Council's procedure may be, the Charter's rule to the effect that non-defensive uses of military force are only allowed for the purpose of enforcing relevant Security Council decisions (see infra 2.4.1.5), which have been taken on behalf of all Members of the United Nations,[188] remains valid—and, in that sense, the United States-led coalition's invasion of Iraq in 2003 was clearly unlawful. In the aftermath of the invasion, an overwhelming majority of States opposed the United States' conduct decisively, asserting, on the one hand, that the eradication of the Security Council's primary authority in dealing with situations threatening international peace and security[189] would denote the end of collective supervision over the international use of force and, eventually, of multilateralism in the post-World War II international relations[190] (cf. supra 1.2), and, on the other hand, that a reintroduction of States' liberty to resort to military action unilaterally would be unwarranted under modern international law.[191] In other words, such a reintroduction would put an end to the entire contemporary normative and institutional system of maintaining international peace and security. As Christopher Greenwood correctly observed, there must be a point beyond which self-defence ceases to be an exception to the prohibition of the use of force under international law and itself becomes plainly inconsistent with this prohibition.[192]

2.4.1.4 Interceptive Self-Defence

Unlike in the context of anticipatory self-defence (see supra 2.4.1.2–2.4.1.3), interceptive self-defence is resorted to when the danger of an armed attack against a

[188] UN Charter, Article 24(1): "In order to ensure prompt and effective action by the United Nations, its Members confer on the Security Council primary responsibility for the maintenance of international peace and security, *and agree that in carrying out its duties under this responsibility the Security Council acts on their behalf*" (emphasis added).

[189] Greenwood emphasizes that "no State is entrusted under the Charter [of the United Nations] with the power to take military action to preserve or restore international peace and security without such a [Security Council] decision," Greenwood 2003, at 20.

[190] Cf. Delbrück 2001, at 19; Corten and Dubuisson 2002, at 76; Farer 2002, pp. 99–100.

[191] The UK Foreign Affairs Committee, supra note 186, para 154, pointed out "that should the United States, British and other governments seek to justify military action against Iraq for example, on an expanded doctrine of "pre-emptive self-defence," there is a serious risk that this will be taken as legitimising the aggressive use of force by other, less law-abiding States."

[192] Greenwood 2003, at 36, confirms that "[t]here is [...] no right to take military action against a threat that is not imminent."

State is grave, imminent and unmistakable. The nature of interceptive self-defence was illustratively explained by Yoram Dinstein:

> Let us assume hypothetically that the Japanese carrier striking force, *en route* to the point from which it mounted the notorious attack on Pearl Harbor in December 1941, had been intercepted and sunk by the US Pacific Fleet prior to reaching its destination and before a single Japanese naval aircraft got anywhere near Hawaii. If that were to have happened, and the Americans had succeeded in aborting an onslaught which in one fell swoop managed to change the balance of military power in the Pacific, it would have been preposterous to look upon the United States as answerable for inflicting an armed attack upon Japan [...]
>
> Had the Japanese striking force been destroyed on its way to Pearl Harbor, this would have constituted not an act of preventive war but a miraculously early use of counter-force. To put it in another way, the self-defence exercised by the United States (in response to an incipient armed attack) would have been not anticipatory but interceptive in nature. Interceptive, unlike anticipatory, self-defence takes place after the other side has committed itself to an armed attack in an ostensibly irrevocable way. Whereas a preventive strike anticipates an armed attack that is merely 'foreseeable' (or even just 'conceivable'), an interceptive strike counters an armed attack which is 'imminent' and practically 'unavoidable'. It is the opinion of the present writer that interceptive, as distinct from anticipatory, self-defence is legitimate even under Article 51 of the Charter.[193]

It is only possible to agree with Yoram Dinstein's conclusion. Indeed, it would be unwise on the part of a potential victim State to wait for a fatal blow ("armed attack" in the sense of Article 51 of the UN Charter), which would incapacitate or severely harm that State's defensive potential. If the aggregate of circumstances at a given time[194] leaves no doubt as to the impending attack, the potential victim State(s) should be entitled—by virtue of Article 51 of the Charter—to intercepting the attack by offering a targeted and proportionate military reaction. As was discussed above (at 2.4.1.1), though, a State exercising its right to self-defence in an interceptive manner must be prepared to justify its conduct in a court of law. Importantly, "[t]he invocation of the right to self-defence must be weighed on the ground of the information available (and reasonably interpreted) at the moment of action, without the benefit of *post factum* wisdom."[195]

---

[193] See Dinstein 2001, pp. 171–172 (italics in original, footnotes omitted).

[194] Yoram Dinstein gave the following practical example of a comprehensive assessment of circumstances prompting interceptive self-defence: "[I]n the 'Six Days War' of June 1967, Israel was the first to open fire. Nevertheless, a careful analysis of the events surrounding the actual outbreak of the hostilities (assuming that the factual examination was conducted, in good faith, at the time of action) would lead to the conclusion that the Israeli campaign amounted to an interceptive self-defence, in response to an incipient armed attack by Egypt (joined by Jordan and Syria). True, no single Egyptian step, evaluated alone, may have qualified as an armed attack. But when all of the measures taken by Egypt (especially the peremptory ejection of the United Nations Emergency Force from the Gaza Strip and the Sinai Peninsula; the closure of the Straits of Tiran; the unprecedented build-up of Egyptian forces along Israel's borders; and constant sabre-rattling statements about the impending fighting) were assessed in the aggregate, it seemed to be crystal clear that Egypt was bent on an armed attack, and the sole question was not whether war would materialize but when." See ibid., p. 173.

[195] Ibid (italics in original).

2.4.1.5 Collective Security Measures Under Chapter VII

Unlike the mechanism of individual or collective self-defence examined above at 2.4.1.1–2.4.1.4, which is designed against "outside" aggression, the collective security mechanism is—in the words of Y. Dinstein—"introverted" in the sense that it is there to employ force against aggressors from within the system.[196] The principal difference between these mechanisms is that self-defence is exercised at the discretion of a State or States, against which (armed or physical) force has been employed (cf. supra 2.1.1.2), and collective security is founded upon the centralized authority of an organ of the international community—the Security Council of the United Nations (cf. supra 1.2.5.2).[197]

The United Nations' collective security system is set out in Chapter VII of its Charter (Articles 39–51). It follows from Article 39[198] that the Security Council's functions in this domain are both preventive and restorative. As Yoram Dinstein put it:

> The notion of maintaining international peace and security has a preemptive thrust. The purpose is to ensure, before it is too late, that no breach of the peace will in fact occur. Measures taken by the Council to forestall a breach of international peace and security have deterrence and prevention as their goals. Once a breach of international peace and security occurs (notwithstanding any prophylactic measures that may have been taken), the situation changes dramatically. At this point, the Council's mission is to restore the peace. It has to take steps calculated to re-establish international law and order.[199]

Pursuant to Article 39, the Security Council can make non-mandatory recommendations or take binding decisions, in order to propel action by the Member States of the United Nations. A grammatical interpretation of Article 39 suggests that measures of a non-military and military nature—listed, respectively, in Articles 41 and 42—are associated with mandatory decisions rather than with recommendations.[200] Let us succinctly consider non-military and military measures provided for in Chapter VII.

2.4.1.5.1 Non-military Measures

Article 41 of the Charter deals with non-military measures and reads as follows:

> The Security Council may decide what measures not involving the use of armed force are to be employed to give effect to its decisions, and it may call upon the Members of the

---

[196] Ibid., p. 246.

[197] Ibid. See also Caron 1993, pp. 552–588.

[198] UN Charter, Article 39: "The Security Council shall determine the existence of any threat to the peace, breach of the peace, or act of aggression and shall make recommendations, or decide what measures shall be taken in accordance with Articles 41 and 42, to maintain or restore international peace and security"

[199] See Dinstein 2001, p. 248.

[200] Ibid.

> United Nations to apply such measures. These may include complete or partial interruption of economic relations and of rail, sea, air, postal, telegraphic, radio, and other means of communication, and the severance of diplomatic relations.

Notably, this list is not exhaustive ("[the measures] *may* include [...]"), and the Security Council may itself decide which other measures not involving the use of force may be employed.[201]

2.4.1.5.2 Military Measures

As was discussed above (at 1.2.5.2), the Security Council became noticeably more functional in matters of maintaining international peace and security after the end of the "Cold War." Chapter VII of the Charter was invoked, as a whole, in a number of resolutions adopted by the Security Council, as were some of its specific Articles.[202] Nevertheless, as was observed in the UN Secretary-General's report entitled *An Agenda for Peace* (cf. supra 1.2.5.5), the key provision in Chapter VII, Article 42,[203] was not used, due to the absence of special agreements required by Article 43, and alternative means had to be sought. The same discord among the permanent Security Council members that rendered impossible the conclusion of special agreements under Article 43 did also cause the invalidity of Article 106 of the Charter and the ineptitude of the Military Staff Committee provided for under Article 47. Therefore, over time, two principal alternative mechanisms have developed—peacekeeping and non-Article 42 peace-enforcement.

The functional modalities of both mechanisms have been well summarized in Yoram Dinstein's classic monograph.[204] To borrow from his terminology, the principal function of a peacekeeping force is that of a "*cordon sanitaire*"—to physically separate parties to a conflict and to prevent further clashes.[205] All peacekeeping forces—unlike forces set up for peace-enforcement—are established and maintained with the consent of all States concerned and are normally not authorized to employ military force, except in self-defence.[206] Peacekeeping forces are usually—although not always—associated with the United Nations and

---

[201] See ibid., p. 249. See also Conforti 1991, pp. 110–113; Coppieters et al. 2002, pp. 165–167.

[202] See Dinstein 2001, pp. 256–263.

[203] See UN Charter, Article 42: "Should the Security Council consider that measures provided for in Article 41 would be inadequate or have proved to be inadequate, it may take such action by air, sea, or land forces as may be necessary to maintain or restore international peace and security. Such action may include demonstrations, blockade, and other operations by air, sea, or land forces of Members of the United Nations"

[204] See Dinstein 2001, pp. 263–273.

[205] Ibid., p. 263. See also generally *Report of the Panel on UN Peacekeeping Operations*, UN, 23 August 2000 (*Brahimi Report*), document A/55/305–S/2000/809. See also Breau 2006, pp. 429–464; Gaja 1995, pp. 39–58; Gray 2001, pp. 267–288; Kühne 1995, pp. 91–112; Murphy 2003b, pp. 71–99; White 2001, pp. 127–146; Bilostkiy 2010, pp. 333–372.

[206] See Dinstein 2001, p. 263. See also Garvey 1970, pp. 241–269.

are made up of national contingents supplied by the UN Member States.[207] Thus, as an aggregate of representatives of national armed forces with an international mandate, peacekeeping forces have a dual legal status:

> [T]he commander of the United Nations force is head in the chain of command and is answerable to the United Nations. The functions of the force as a whole are international. But its individual component forces have their own national duty and discipline and remain in their own national service.[208]

It must also be noted that members of the UN peacekeeping forces are bound to comply with the fundamental principles and rules of international humanitarian law when they use force in self-defence.[209]

In turn, as Yoram Dinstein put it, peace-enforcement is a practical way for getting round Article 42 of the Charter in the absence of special agreements provided for in Article 43.[210] Since the 1990s, the Security Council has been *authorizing* individual or collective military actions by the UN Member States (instead of *imposing* a duty upon them to engage in such actions), in order to enforce its resolutions.[211] The *Operation Desert Storm* (1990) is broadly regarded as a "revolutionary development" and "the catalyst for fundamental change in the international regulation of the use of force."[212] The ensuing operations in Somalia (1992), Rwanda (1994), the former Yugoslavia (1994–1995),[213] Haiti (1994[214] and 2004), Albania (1997),[215] the Central African Republic (1997), East Timor (1999),[216] Liberia, the Democratic Republic of the Congo,[217] and Côte d'Ivoire (2003), Kosovo (1999), Afghanistan (2001–2014), Iraq (2003–2011),[218] Chad (2007) and other actions followed in the novel trend. In carrying out the peace enforcement operations, the Security Council largely relied upon

207 See Dinstein 2001, p. 268.

208 *Attorney-General v. Nissan* (1969), [1970] *A.C.* 179, 223, quoted in Dinstein 2001, p. 268.

209 See document ST/SGB/1999/13 (Secretary-General's Bulletin "Observance by United Nations forces of international humanitarian law"). See also Abrisketa 2009, pp. 85–93; Okimoto 2011b, pp. 164–238; Tsagourias 2006, pp. 465–482.

210 See Dinstein 2001, p. 268.

211 See Byers 2002, pp. 21–41; Frowein 1987, pp. 67–79; Harris 2004, pp. 972–1023; Stein 1987, pp. 56–66; Van Walsum 2005, pp. 65–74.

212 See Gray 2008, p. 327. See also Dominicé 1991, pp. 85–109; Reisman 1994, pp. 120–133; Tavernier 1990, pp. 278–285.

213 See Cox 1999, pp. 201–244; Gray 1997, pp. 155–197; Figà-Talamanca 1996, pp. 164–175; Gaeta 1996, pp. 147–163; Gazzini 2001, pp. 391–435.

214 See Corten 1995, pp. 116–133.

215 See Kreß 1997, pp. 329–362.

216 See Chinkin 1993, pp. 206–222; Drew 2001, pp. 651–684; Maffei 1993, pp. 223–238.

217 See Okowa 2007, pp. 203–255.

218 See Buchan 2007, pp. 37–64; Dörr 2003, pp. 181–188; Fassbender 2002, pp. 273–303; Franck 2003, pp. 607–620; Gray 2002a, pp. 1–19; Heintze 2003, pp. 16–21; Howse 2002, pp. 89–92; Lowe 2003, pp. 859–871; McWhinney 2003, pp. 571–585; Stahn 2003, pp. 804–823; Stromseth 2003, pp. 628–642; Taft IV and Buchwald 2003, pp. 557–563; Wedgwood 2003, pp. 576–585; Wheatley 2006, pp. 531–551; Yoo 2003, pp. 563–576; Zedalis 1999, pp. 37–50.

regional arrangements dealt with in Chapter VIII of the Charter (Articles 52–54).[219] The level of success in those operations has not been consistent. Besides, as Christine Gray observed, the policy of involving regional arrangements[220] might not be free from ulterior motives (cf. the principle of good intentions dealt with above at 1.1.2.3):

> There is [...] a danger that interested states operating under UN authorization would gain legitimacy to further their own interests. The early tradition of not using the forces of permanent members of the Security Council or of those states with geographical or historical interests in the state concerned has been further circumvented through this type of operation. Thus it was the USA that led the 1994 and 2004 operations in Haiti, France in Rwanda and the Central African Republic (1997), Italy in Albania, and Australia in East Timor. There was some suspicion of the motives of these states. In Rwanda *Operation Turquoise* was criticized for providing a safe haven for the perpetrators of genocide. These were, however, all temporary, limited forces operating with the consent of the host states even where this was not expressly indicated in the relevant resolutions. It is not clear that the use of the EU to lead an operation instead of a single member state will necessarily meet this concern as to ulterior motives. There were newspaper reports that the use of the EU in the DRC was interpreted by some as evidence of foreign state support for the incumbent President in the elections. And Chad seems to have regarded an EU force led by its former colonial power and current supporter, France, as more acceptable than a UN force.[221]

It is obvious that, at the present stage of affairs, "[c]lear divisions have emerged between those states claiming to act on behalf of the international community and those who reject such claims in the absence of express Security Council authorization of force"[222] The latter group of States suggests that the United States, the United Kingdom and some other States have gone too far in their interpretation of "implied authorisations by the Security Council" for them to use force,[223] and stricter compliance with the UN Charter would be required in the future. Notably, even a former Secretary-General of the United Nations supported this opinion of a majority of States within the international community, by having stated, at a press conference on 10 March 2003, in rather direct a manner: "If the US and others were to go outside the [Security] Council and take military action, it would not be in conformity with the Charter [of the United Nations]."[224]

---

[219] See Dinstein 2001, p. 269.

[220] See Abass 2000, pp. 211–229; Al-Qahtani 2006, pp. 129–147; Bebr 1955, pp. 166–184; Dolzer 1987, pp. 113–133; Gazzini 2003, pp. 231–263; Khadduri 1946, pp. 756–777; Van Kleffens 1949, pp. 666–678; Leeds 2003, pp. 427–439; Levitt 2005, pp. 213–251; Mandel 2001, pp. 95–128; Ofosu-Amaah 1987, pp. 80–94; Schreuer 1995, pp. 477–499; Simma 1999, pp. 1–22; Stein 1987, pp. 5–112; Wills 2004, pp. 387–418; Wolfrum 1993, pp. 576–602; Zöckler 1995, pp. 274–286; Zwanenburg 2005, pp. 189–211; Zwanenburg 2006, pp. 483–508.

[221] See Gray 2008, p. 334 (footnotes omitted).

[222] Ibid., p. 368. See also Benvenisti 2004, pp. 677–700; Glennon 2000, pp. 3–25; Hathaway 2000, pp. 121–134; Krisch 2005, pp. 369–408; Wedgwood 2000, pp. 349–359; Zemanek 1987, pp. 32–43.

[223] See Chinkin 2000, pp. 31–41; Gowlland-Debbas 2000, pp. 361–383; Koskenniemi 2005, pp. 113–124; Koskenniemi 2004, pp. 305–314; Lehman 2000, pp. 1–2; Licková 2008, pp. 463–490; Neuhold 2004, pp. 263–279; Pellet 2000, pp. 385–392; Wolfrum 2004, pp. 255–262.

[224] See document Off-the-cuff: Secretary-General's press conference (unofficial transcript), available at: http://www.un.org/sg/offthecuff/?nid=394 (last visited 15 May 2012).

2.4.2 *Charter-Related Exceptions*

The second group of exceptions to the prohibition of the use of force (cf. supra 2.1) is not to be found in the Charter of the United Nations explicitly but is still related to it and can be inferred, more or less credibly, from some of its programmatic and operative provisions. The UN General Assembly resolution 377 A (V) ("Uniting for Peace") of 3 November 1950 (see infra 2.4.2.1) and the use of force in pursuance of peoples' right to self-determination (see infra 2.4.2.2) are the principal examples.

2.4.2.1 "Uniting for Peace"

As the draft resolution "Uniting for Peace"[225] was being discussed in the UN General Assembly, numerous arguments deriving from both positive international law and legal scholarship were suggested for and against it.[226] It was noticeable already at the time that the Security Council's procedure for the maintenance of international peace and security lacked perfection, and it was sought to remedy this flaw through the medium of the General Assembly (cf. supra 1.2.5.3). The first operative paragraph of the resolution read as follows:

> The General Assembly [...]
>
> 1. *Resolves* that if the Security Council, because of lack of unanimity of the permanent members, fails to exercise its primary responsibility for the maintenance of international peace and security in any case where there appears to be a threat to the peace, breach of the peace, or act of aggression, the General Assembly shall consider the matter immediately with a view to making appropriate recommendations to Members for collective measures, including in the case of a breach of the peace or act of aggression the use of armed force when necessary, to maintain or restore international peace and security. If not in session at the time, the General Assembly may meet in emergency special session within twenty-four hours of the request therefor. Such emergency special session shall be called if requested by the Security Council on the vote of any seven members, or by a majority of the Members of the United Nations.

Since 1956, ten emergency special sessions were convened under the resolution.[227]

The principal argument put forward against the resolution consisted in that it would constitute a violation of the UN Charter inasmuch as it would bequeath the General Assembly with a role, which is in fact the Security Council's, and thereby ignore a fundamental working principle of the United Nations, i.e. the unanimity of all permanent members of the Security Council as a requisite condition for an

---

225 See UN General Assembly resolution 377 (V), 3 November 1950.

226 For a comprehensive analysis of the resolution, see generally Andrassy 1956, pp. 563–582; Kemp 2010, pp. 21–24; Tomuschat 2001, pp. 289–303; Woolsey 1951, pp. 129–137.

227 See official website of the United Nations: http://www.un.org/en/ga/sessions/emergency.shtml (last visited 10 November 2012).

effective maintenance of international peace and security.[228] In turn, according to the resolution's opponents, it was inconsistent with the UN Charter and constituted, technically, an illicit amendment thereof, contrary to Articles 108 and 109.[229]

However, although a strict division of tasks between the General Assembly and the Security Council was indeed intended by the Charter's drafters, it was accomplished only to an extent.[230] Under Article 24(1) of the Charter, the Security Council bears the "primary responsibility" for the maintenance of international peace and security. [231] Yet, as Juraj Andrassy noted, a literal reading of this expression suggests the existence of another—"subsidiary" or "supplementary"—responsibility, which, according to the resolution's proponents, should have been conferred upon the General Assembly.[232] Under Article 10 of the Charter,[233] the General Assembly is authorized to discuss any questions or matters within the competence of the United Nations—and thus also matters of maintaining international peace and security, although they are under the "primary responsibility" of the Security Council.[234] In Article 11(2),[235] three types of possible reactions by the General Assembly with respect to such matters are distinguished: (1) a mere discussion of a question, (2) the adoption of a recommendation, and (3) the necessity of (enforcement) action.[236] The General Assembly's authority to discuss questions and matters within the scope of the UN Charter is not restricted. With respect to "action," it is commonly acknowledged that it means an "enforcement action" or a "military action."[237] Since, in accordance with the second sentence of Article 11(2), the General Assembly may not itself take substantive decisions with respect to such questions and is obliged to refer them to the Security Council,[238] paragraph 1 of resolution 377 (V) limits the

---

[228] See Andrassy 1956, p. 563.

[229] Ibid.

[230] See ibid., pp. 563–564. See also Greenwood Onuf 1970, pp. 349–355.

[231] See Brunnée 2005, pp. 107–132.

[232] Doc. A/C.1/SR. 360, p. 101, referred to in Andrassy 1956, p. 564.

[233] UN Charter, Article 10: "The General Assembly may discuss *any questions or any matters* within the scope of the present Charter or relating to the powers and functions of any organs provided for in the present Charter, and, except as provided in Article 12, may make recommendations to the Members of the United Nations or to the Security Council or to both on any such questions or matters" (emphasis added).

[234] Cf. Andrassy 1956, p. 565.

[235] Ibid., Article 11(2): "The General Assembly may discuss any questions relating to the maintenance of international peace and security brought before it by any Member of the United Nations, or by the Security Council, or by a state which is not a Member of the United Nations in accordance with Article 35, paragraph 2, and, except as provided in Article 12, may make recommendations with regard to any such questions to the state or states concerned or to the Security Council or to both. Any such question on which action is necessary shall be referred to the Security Council by the General Assembly either before or after discussion".

[236] For a discussion of these types of reaction, see Andrassy 1956, p. 566.

[237] See ibid., pp. 566–567. See also Bentwich and Martin 1950, p. 40; Goodrich and Hambro 1946, p. 99; Kelsen 2008, pp. 204–205.

[238] See Andrassy 1956, pp. 567–568.

Assembly's competence to "making [...] recommendations." In the case of such a referral, the Security Council might not remain inactive (otherwise it would not act in accordance with the Purposes of the United Nations, cf. the Charter's Article 1(1)), and would be duty-bound to take substantive decisions. It appears that the potential of the UN General Assembly resolution 377 (V) has not been sufficiently exploited, and its operative mechanism might help suppress at least some acts of aggression in the future. The capacity of the General Assembly as an international forum for exchange among nations and peoples with different political, economic and religious backgrounds, including in the area of maintaining international peace and security, is quite sizeable, and the Security Council—whose function consists in putting into action, promptly and effectively (cf. the first sentence of Article 24(1) of the UN Charter), the legitimate collective ambitions of all nations represented in the General Assembly—might not ignore the Assembly's recommendations made under resolution 377 (V).

2.4.2.2 The Use of Force in Pursuance of Peoples' Right to Self-Determination

The question whether national liberation movements might use force in pursuit of peoples' right to self-determination[239]—and whether like-minded States might assist them in this pursuit[240]—has been on international lawyers' agenda since after the Second World War (cf. supra 1.2 and infra 3.1.1–3.1.3). As the Charter of the United Nations (see specifically supra 1.2.5.1) whose Articles 73 and 74 dealt with the status of non-self-governing territories had entered into force, many of the former colonies started progressively claiming independence from their "mother countries," including by military force. As Christine Gray recalls, this tendency started out by violent independence movements in Tunisia, Morocco and Algeria against France, in Malaya, Kenya and Cyprus against the UK, in Indonesia against The Netherlands, and in India against Portuguese authority in Goa.[241] Especially the latter case caused a heated debate in the Security Council where some States maintained that the issue should be regarded as one of colonialism (for Portugal sought to preserve its authority in Goa), and another group of States argued that it was about India's allegedly unlawful use of force breaching Article 2(4)[242] (cf. supra 2.1–2.2). As decolonization progressed, some ex-colonies and socialist States increasingly asserted the right for national liberation movements to use force—and for third States to support them—a claim that was

[239] See Brownlie 1998, pp. 599–602; Tomuschat 1993, pp. 8–11; Van Boven 1995, pp. 461–476; Weller 2009, pp. 111–165.

[240] See Malanczuk 1997, pp. 326–337.

[241] See Gray 2008, p. 59.

[242] Ibid., p. 60.

resolutely resisted by Western States.[243] In the General Assembly (cf. supra 1.2.5.3), compromise solutions were found at the expense of ambiguity; Christine Gray identified at least three relevant examples. The key document on decolonization—the 1960 Declaration on the Granting of Independence to Colonial Countries and Peoples[244]—made no direct reference to the use of force but some of the subsequent resolutions on the subject did use expressions, which could be interpreted as endorsing the use of force in certain circumstances.[245] Thus, resolution A/RES/2105 (XX) "recognise[d] the legitimacy of the *struggle* by the peoples under colonial rule to exercise their right to self-determination and independence and invite[d] all states to provide material and moral assistance to the national liberation movements in colonial territories" (emphasis added).[246] Christine Gray notes that the meaning of "struggle"—whether it meant in this specific context "armed struggle" or "peaceful struggle"—remained unclear[247]; it appears to this author that the word's usual literary meaning does imply the permissibility of a use of force. In a similar way, the 1970 Friendly Relations Declaration did not plainly allow for the use of force by national liberation movements but it called upon States

> [t]o refrain from any forcible action which deprives peoples [...] of their right to self-determination and freedom and independence. In their actions against, and resistance to, such forcible action in pursuit of the exercise of the right to self-determination, such peoples are entitled to seek and to receive support in accordance with the purposes and principles of the Charter.[248]

A comparable approach was used in Article 7 of the General Assembly resolution 3314 (XXIX) (cf. supra 2.3):

> Nothing in this Definition [...] could in any way prejudice the right to self-determination, freedom and independence, as derived from the Charter, of peoples forcibly deprived of that right and referred to in the Declaration on Principles of International Law concerning Friendly Relations and Co-operation among States in accordance with the Charter of the United Nations, particularly peoples under colonial and racist regimes or other forms of

---

243 Ibid. Cf. also Article 1(4) of the First Additional Protocol to the 1949 Geneva Conventions ("General principles and scope of application"): "The situations referred to in the preceding paragraph include armed conflicts which peoples are fighting against colonial domination and alien occupation and against racist regimes in the exercise of their right of self-determination, as enshrined in the Charter of the United Nations and the Declaration on Principles of International Law concerning Friendly Relations and Co-operation among States in accordance with the Charter of the United Nations."

244 See UN General Assembly resolution 1514 (XV) of 14 December 1960, available at: http://www.un.org/ga/search/view_doc.asp?symbol=A/RES/1514(XV) (last accessed 15 November 2012).

245 See Gray 2008, p. 60.

246 See UN General Assembly resolution A/RES/2105 (XX), 20 December 1965, quoted in Gray 2008, p. 60.

247 See Gray 2008, p. 60.

248 See the Friendly Relations Declaration, supra note 26, Principle 5, para 5, quoted in Gray 2008, p. 61.

> alien domination; nor the right of these peoples to struggle to that end and to seek and receive support, in accordance with the principles of the Charter and in conformity with the abovementioned Declaration.[249]

As the issue of the use of force in the context of self-determination currently remains pertinent—principally, if not exclusively—only in the context of Palestine[250] and the continued occupation of the West Bank and Gaza by Israel (cf. supra 2.1.3.2),[251] it may for the most part be regarded as one of the past. Ethnic groups' claims to secession from existing States based on the right to self-determination are typically not supported by States.[252] In the few remaining contexts where self-determination remains on the agenda, the United Nations must take all necessary measures to ensure, to the maximum extent possible, its progressive and peaceful implementation, with due regard to the interests of and in association with all parties involved, for the risks inherent in the lasting inter-ethnic and interreligious conflict in the area—if not managed aptly—may result in dramatic effects to the Middle East and the world at large.

2.4.3 *Extra-Charter Exceptions*

The extra-Charter exceptions to the prohibition of the use of force are the most problematic in the sense that they have no express or implicit foundations in the Charter of the United Nations and derive, in the quality of emerging norms of customary international law, from extra-Charter sources of international law. As these rules are not yet codified in written sources, their content remains vague, and the quality of international recognition is not undisputed. In this sense, they may be termed "purported"—or, in the best of cases, "emerging"—exceptions to the prohibition of the use of force (cf. supra 2.1). The three most notable examples we will focus upon are the protection of nationals abroad (see infra 2.4.3.1), the so-called "humanitarian intervention" (see infra 2.4.3.2), and the "pro-democratic intervention" (see infra 2.4.3.3).

2.4.3.1 Forcible Protection of Nationals Abroad

The political and scholarly discussion on the legitimacy of the so-called "forcible protection of nationals abroad" has been ongoing for decades now. The substantive basis for this important debate consisted in military interventions

---

249 Quoted in Gray 2008, p. 62.

250 See Boyle 1990, pp. 301–306; Cassese 1993, pp. 564–571; Crawford 1990, pp. 307–313; Husain 2003, pp. 207–225; Malanczuk 1996, pp. 485–500; Vidmar 2013, pp. 19–41.

251 See Gray 2008, p. 64.

252 Ibid. See also Aust 2005, p. 23; Crawford 1999b, pp. 85–117; Heintze 2008, pp. 238–246; Werner 2001, pp. 171–190.

carried out by a few States in other States, without the Security Council authorizations, for the purpose of rescuing and/or evacuating their nationals who were menaced by a collapse of law and order or by other life-threatening dangers in the respective target States.[253] As Christine Gray notes, there is currently no unity of opinion among policy-makers as to the legality of such military actions: throughout numerous debates within the Security Council and the General Assembly,[254] many of these claims were regarded as pretexts to intervene in States' domestic affairs, in violation of a respective Principle of the United Nations,[255] and as a modern type of the nineteenth century "gunboat diplomacy."[256] Consultations on the issue of diplomatic protection, which were held in the General Assembly in 2000, contributed to this important debate.[257] It appears that customary international law on the "forcible protection of nationals abroad," as it currently stands, does not spell out either the range of exceptional circumstances where States might have recourse to military force to protect or rescue their nationals abroad or the extent of such force, which could be used to this end.

Among scholars, the supporters and antagonists of the concept have fashioned more than a few mutually exclusive views based, chiefly, on the Charter of the United Nations and its relevant *travaux préparatoires*.[258] Both opposing groups included outstanding authorities in international law, and many scholars have at times claimed to represent the prevalent views, but it seems very difficult to establish which group is, as a matter of fact, more representative[259]; it is probably more accurate to say that, to date, the legal scholarship has been largely incapable of bringing contradictory State practices to a common denominator.

At times, the military operations under discussion are regarded as a sub-type of "humanitarian intervention" (see infra 2.4.3.2), as both types of operations (1) take place outside the territory of the intervening State, (2) involve the use of inter-State military force in the sense of Article 2(4) of the Charter (cf. supra 2.1), and (3) aim at preventing the infliction of physical harm on identifiable persons or groups in the territory of the target State.[260] Still, there exists common agreement that, from the point of view of international law, the two types of operations must

---

253 See, for example, Gazzini 2005, pp. 170–171; Gray 2008, p. 156.

254 See Gray 2008, p. 158.

255 See UN Charter, Article 2(7): "Nothing contained in the present Charter shall authorize the United Nations to intervene in matters which are essentially within the domestic jurisdiction of any state or shall require the Members to submit such matters to settlement under the present Charter; but this principle shall not prejudice the application of enforcement measures under Chapter VII"

256 On this concept, see generally Cable 1994, Hood 1983.

257 For an overview of these consultations, see Corten 2008, pp. 774–777.

258 See Gray 2008, pp. 157–158.

259 See ibid., pp. 156–157, especially note 184.

260 See Eichensehr 2008, p. 462. See more generally Beyerlin 1977, pp. 213–243; Ruys 2008, pp. 233–271; Shaw 2008, pp. 1143–1145.

be kept distinct.[261] The principal reason for that distinction is in those operations' different *ratione personae* fields of application: whereas the purpose of "humanitarian intervention" is to protect the target State's population against massive and/or grave violations of human rights, military operations for the protection of nationals seek to defend the intervening States' own nationals whose lives or physical integrity are under an imminent threat in the to-be-attacked State.

As a rule, States and publicists justify the "forcible protection of nationals" by a combination of three cumulative conditions: (1) there has to exist an impending threat of physical injury being caused to a State's nationals; (2) the territorial sovereign must be unwilling or unable to protect them, and (3) the military action of the intervening State may not extend beyond the purpose of protecting its nationals against the identified impending threats.[262] It is not doubted that States' right to such interventions was undisputed before 1945.[263] Likewise, it is agreed that they are fully consistent with the Charter of the United Nations where the host State grants its consent to an intervention. On the other hand, whether States' military operations aimed at protecting their nationals by force where no such sovereign consent is granted, or where its authority is dubious—for example, where there is a high intensity non-international armed conflict ongoing within the to-be-attacked State—are compatible with relevant international law (cf. supra 2.1) is one of the principal issues of present-day *jus ad bellum*.[264]

Scholars who favor the "forcible protection of nationals" doctrine give a number of reasons.[265] One group of publicists suggests, quite plausibly, that such military operations do not breach the prohibition of the use of force contained in the Charter's Article 2(4), because they do not affect the "territorial integrity or political independence" of a State; their only aim is to rescue foreign nationals from an imminent threat, which the host State is unable or unwilling to remove.[266] According to another mainstream approach, military operations aimed at providing protection to a State's nationals abroad represent a form of self-defence under Article 51 of the Charter of the United Nations [267] (cf. supra 2.4.1.1). A two-level argument is often offered to substantiate this claim. First, it is asserted that the Charter recognized the *inherent* right of States to self-defence (cf. supra 2.4.1.1.2), which implies this right's rather broad interpretation in the context of the relevant pre-existing customary international law, which had encompassed, *inter alia*, the right of each State to protect its nationals abroad. Second, it is suggested that a State's nationals who are temporarily abroad do still constitute a part of that State's

[261] See Eichensehr 2008, pp. 461–463.

[262] Cf. Waldock 1952, at 467.

[263] See Brownlie 1968, p. 289.

[264] For a discussion, see Doswald-Beck 1985, pp. 189–252; Ronzitti 1985, pp. 1–88.

[265] For an overview of the relevant argumentation, see Zedalis 1990, pp. 221–244.

[266] Similar views have been expressed, for instance, in Paust 1978, at 89–90; Higgins 1994, pp. 220–221.

[267] This group of scholars includes, for example, Gerard 1967, at 254–255; Schachter 1986, at 139; Lillich 1993a, at 216.

population and thus embody its basic attribute[268]; hence, a deliberate attack against that State's nationals abroad may be taken for an attack against the State itself, and the State might, on this basis, exercise its right to self-defence on the basis of Article 51. Occasionally, some other justifications have been offered but they did not become as common as these two; they included references to the existence of a "state of necessity"[269] or to "humanitarian considerations" and fundamental human rights.[270] Another group of publicists have maintained, probably most accurately, that the right of State to protect its national abroad should be considered as a novel, essentially customary in nature and self-sufficient exception to Article 2(4), as it cannot be easily placed into the current framework of international law.[271] This author tends to agree to the permissibility of the mechanism under discussion, on the condition that it be resorted to as a matter of exceptional legitimacy where a host State is manifestly unable or unwilling to remove the threat, especially where the level of violence against individuals requiring protection reaches that of a widespread or systematic attack in the sense of Article 7(1) of the Rome Statute. Of course, it is understood that a State so intervening in another State must immediately withdraw, together with its rescued nationals, once the operation is over, and must be prepared to subsequently justify its good intention in a court of law.

2.4.3.2 "Humanitarian Intervention"

Likewise, the legal regulation of the so-called "humanitarian intervention" is among the most complex issues of modern *jus ad bellum*.[272] Sean Murphy defined "humanitarian intervention" as "the threat or use of force by a State, group of States, or international organization primarily for the purpose of protecting the nationals of the target state from widespread deprivations of internationally recognized human rights."[273] The key issue here is exceptionally difficult: should States be permitted as

---

[268] See Lukashuk 2008a, p. 25.

[269] Raby 1988, pp. 253–272.

[270] See, for instance, Gordon 1977, at 132; Schweisfurth 1980, at 161.

[271] This opinion has been expressed, for example, by Ronzitti 2006, at 354.

[272] See the United Nations Secretary-General's Press Release SG/SM/7136 (20 September 1999) where Kofi Annan stated that humanitarian intervention would constitute a "core challenge to the Security Council and the United Nations as a whole in the next century"; see also Bederman 2001, at 717; Abashidze 2006, pp. 360–373; Berman 2006, pp. 743–769; Cassese 1999a, pp. 791–799; Cassese 1999b, pp. 23–30; generally Chesterman 2001; Craven 2002, pp. 43–61; Dekker 2001, pp. 115–126; Dias 2011, pp. 48–62; Dreist 2002, pp. 68–77; Glanville 2012, pp. 1–32; Hilpold 2001, pp. 437–467; Kemp 2010, pp. 64–69; Lietzau 2004, pp. 281–304; Lillich 1993b, pp. 557–575; McClean 2008, pp. 123–152; Nardin 2013, pp. 67–82; Reisman 2000, pp. 3–18; Shaw 2008, pp. 1155–1158; Stowell 1939, pp. 733–736; generally Tesón 2005; Thakur 2011, pp. 32–47; Werle 2009, at 413; Zwitter 2007, pp. 231–236.

[273] See Murphy 1996, pp. 11–12. Badescu's definition is quite similar: "The definition of humanitarian intervention used in this study is the use of armed force by either a state, a group of states, or an international organization to address widespread suffering or death among civilians in another state affected by grave violations of human rights," see Badescu 2001, at 8 (footnotes omitted).

a matter of international law to intervene militarily, without a Security Council authorization, in other States, in order to stop genocide or other atrocities of a comparable magnitude?[274]

During the past decade, the issue became particularly important in connection with international coalitions' interventions in Kosovo (1999)[275] and Iraq (2003) as well as with the community of States' failure to do so in the Sudan.[276] The principal apprehension related to the legitimacy of "humanitarian intervention" is that, if it is once legalized, States would exploit it as a pretext for waging wars to attain their selfish national interests.[277] This policy problem was well known since the time of Grotius and the medieval European classics of international law that followed him (see supra 1.1.2.4). The doctrine of "humanitarian intervention" had been quite influential at the beginning of the twentieth century,[278] before the League of Nations erected initial legal barriers to the inter-State use of force after the end of the First World War (see supra 1.1.6.1–1.1.6.2). After the entry into force of the Charter of the United Nations' (cf. supra 1.2.5.1), the center of gravity in the international political[279] and scholarly[280] debate determinedly shifted towards opposing "humanitarian intervention." Notably, even States that have themselves been involved in "humanitarian interventions" without Security Council authorizations, tended not to justify their conduct in terms of a legal *right* to practise such interventions, and explained it as *ad hoc* solutions.[281]

---

[274] C.G. Badescu summarized the essence of current scholarly debate about the concept of "humanitarian intervention" as follows: "Lawyers, international relations theorists, philosophers, and policy makers alike have addressed the dilemmas of humanitarian intervention from a variety of approaches. Discussions on whether there is a legal right of humanitarian intervention, on how to address ethical considerations and what morality requires, and on the practical dilemmas related to the politics of intervention abound in the relevant literature," see Badescu 2001, at 2 (footnotes omitted).

[275] See Charney 1999, pp. 834–841; Chinkin 1999, pp. 841–847; Henkin 1999, pp. 824–828; Joyner 2002, pp. 597–619; Milano 2003, pp. 999–1022; Orford 1999, pp. 679–711; Wheatley 2000, pp. 261–273; White 2000, pp. 27–43.

[276] See "Warum hat der Sicherheitsrat keine humanitäre Intervention in dem Fall "Sudankonflikt" gestartet? Eine Erklärung anhand der Konstruktivismus-Theorie," available at: http://www.e-polis.cz/evropska-unie/571-warum-hat-der-sicherheitsrat-keine-humanitare-intervention-in-dem-fall-sudankonflikt-gestartet-eine-erklarung-anhand-der-konstruktivismus-theorie.html (last accessed 15 November 2012).

[277] See Goodman 2006, pp. 107–141.

[278] See Brownlie 1968, p. 338.

[279] Within five years since the 1999 intervention in Kosovo, more than 130 States representing about 80 per cent of the world's population have issued policy statements to the effect of rejecting the legality of humanitarian intervention. See, for example, UN Doc. S/PV.4011 (10 June 1999) documenting China's opinion that humanitarian intervention "promote[s] hegemonism under the pretext of human rights"

[280] See, for example, Bilder 1999, at 153, 161; Schachter 1984, at 1620, 1629.

[281] See, for example, United Kingdom Foreign Office, Policy Document No. 148, reprinted in *BYIL* (1986), at 614, 619.

Although some publicists have suggested otherwise,[282] it is widely agreed that international law forbids States to use force unilaterally even for the purpose of rescuing victims of humanitarian catastrophes.[283] The chief treaty regulating the use of force, the Charter of the United Nations does not name "humanitarian interventions" among lawful exceptions to Article 2(4) (cf. supra 2.4.1–2.4.2), and relevant General Assembly resolutions confirm this overarching rule[284] (cf. supra 1.2.5.3). It was also confirmed by the International Court of Justice[285] and recognized in leading treatises that "humanitarian intervention" was prohibited under both the relevant treaty law and customary international law, some inconsistent State practices over the past decade or so notwithstanding.[286]

In light of the issue's undoubted importance, one may assume, though, that the legal regulation of humanitarian intervention might develop, to some extent, in a foreseeable future. Following ECOWAS interventions in Liberia (1990) and Sierra Leone (1997) and NATO's intervention in Kosovo (1999), some authors appeared to suggest that new rules allowing for an exception to the prohibition of the use of force under Article 2(4) of the Charter might be emerging.[287] Some time ago, even a codification of the law of "humanitarian intervention" was suggested in the doctrine.[288] It remains to be seen whether and to which extent States—whose majority expressed themselves against the legitimisation of humanitarian intervention some time ago (cf. supra note 279)—might allow their practices and *opinio juris* to take an alternative direction.

2.4.3.3 "Pro-democratic Intervention"

Whereas the US-led coalition's intervention in Iraq in March 2003 divided opinions within the international community,[289] the declared aim of introducing democracy in that country after the establishment of a military occupation regime

---

[282] For a persuasive discussion in favor of the lawfulness of humanitarian intervention, see Greenwood 1999, at 141.

[283] Cf. Badescu 2001, pp. 48–73.

[284] Cf., for example, Definition of Aggression, GA Res. 3314 (XXIX) (14 December 1974); Declaration on Principles of International Law Concerning Friendly Relations and Cooperation Among States in Accordance with the Charter of the United Nations, GA Res. 2625 (XXV) (24 October 1970); Declaration on the Inadmissibility of Intervention and Interference in the Internal Affairs of States, GA Res. 36/103 (9 December 1981).

[285] See *Nicaragua* Judgment, para 268: "[W]hile the United States might form its own appraisal of the situation as to respect for human rights in Nicaragua, the use of force could not be the appropriate method to monitor or ensure such respect [...] The Court concludes that the argument derived from the preservation of human rights in Nicaragua cannot afford a legal justification for the conduct of the United States [...]"

[286] Cf., for example, Cassese 2005, pp. 373–374; Brownlie 1998, pp. 710–712; Shaw 2008, p. 1046; Malanczuk 1997, p. 221.

[287] See, for instance, Gray 2008, p. 99.

[288] See Henke 2009, pp. 15–21.

[289] See S/PV.4726, 26 March 2003, and S/PV.4726 (Resumption 1), 27 March 2003.

was not practically contested. The change of Iraq's political regime from dictatorial to democratic was an official political end of *Operation Iraqi Freedom*,[290] in line with the dual ambition of President George W. Bush's administration, on the one hand, to remove threats emanating from "rogue" States and, on the other hand, to proliferate democracy—the Middle East and, more generally, the Muslim world being a special focus of this aspect of the United States' foreign policy.[291]

It seems that this ambition, however inconsistent with the pre-existing international law in force it might have been, did manage to influence the practice of the Security Council to a sizeable extent, at least for the duration of President Bush's terms of office. As W. H. Taft IV and T. F. Buchwald argued, *Operation Iraqi Freedom* had found its legal basis in a specific reading of the Security Council resolutions 678 (1991), 687 (1991), and 1441 (2002), whereby the purported "material breach" of Iraq's disarmament obligations under resolution 687 (1991) recovered the right to use armed force provided under resolution 678 (1991).[292] For our purpose, the question is to which extent the Security Council resolutions 1483 (2003), 1511 (2003), and 1546 (2004)—which were adopted in the aftermath of the intervention with a view to giving legal effect to the reality of a forcible regime change—might be regarded as reflections of the Security Council's *legitimate* political authority in accordance with the Charter of the United Nations.

It may appear that Iraq's "forced democratization" is not coherent with current international law: in accordance with Article 43 of the Regulations annexed to the 1907 Hague Convention (IV) with respect to the Laws and Customs of War on Land, an intervening State, which establishes a military occupation regime, is obliged to respect "unless absolutely prevented, the laws in force in the [occupied] country." Article 43 embodies customary international law,[293] and the forced democratization of occupied territories must consequently be disallowed. Yet, this conclusion is somewhat incomplete in view of Articles 24(1) and 103 of the Charter of the United Nations: if the UN Members' obligations under the Charter prevail over those under other international treaties, including the 1907 Hague Convention (IV), and the Members agree that, in carrying out its duties for the purpose of maintaining international peace and security, the Security Council acts on their behalf, one may conclude that resolutions of the Security Council may, in certain cases, deviate from written international law, even if relevant provisions also amount to customary law (as the 1907 Hague Regulations do). As a matter of practice, there is little use in some Council members' *ex post facto* critique of the US-led coalition's intervention in and occupation of Iraq and the subsequent regime change, if they themselves allowed for the adoption of relevant Security Council resolutions, by not having

[290] See Agence France Presse, "The leaders' two declarations: "We uphold a vision of international security," *New York Times*, 17 March 2003.

[291] Cf., for example, President Bush´s address to the General Assembly of the United Nations, of 12 September 2002, and relevant paragraphs in the US *National Security Strategy* (2002).

[292] Taft IV and Buchwald 2003, at 557. See also Bennoune 2002, pp. 243–262; Werle 2009, at 413.

[293] See *Legal consequences*, para 89.

vetoed them. To conclude on this issue, the Security Council's indecisive behavior with respect to developments in Iraq—and, later, also in Libya—established critical precedents whose future implications remain to be seen.[294]

References

Abashidze AH (2006) Mejdunarodno-pravovye problemy vmeshatelstva ["International Legal Issues of Intervention"]. Moscow J Int Law 61:360–373

Abashidze AH (2009) Uchastie gosudarstv v Rimskom statute Mejdunarodnogo ugolovnogo suda kak novyy vid obyazatelstv *erga omnes* ["The Participation of States in the Rome Statute of the International Criminal Court as a New Type of *Erga Omnes* Obligations"]. In: Bogush GI, Trikoz EN (eds), *Mejdunarodnoe ugolovnoe pravosudie: sovremennye problemy* [International Criminal Justice: Contemporary Issues], Moscow, pp 505–510

Abass A (2000) The new collective security mechanism of ECOWAS: innovations and problems. JCSL 5:211–229

Abi-Saab G (2002) The proper role of international law in combating terrorism. Chinese JIL 1:305–313

Abrisketa J (2009) Blue helmets and international humanitarian law: how they come together. HuV-I 22:85–93

Adilkariev HT (ed) (2003) *Mejdunarodnoe pravo* [International Law], Tashkent

Al-Qahtani M (2006) The Shanghai cooperation organization and the law of international organizations. Chinese JIL 5:129–147

Andrassy J (1956) Uniting for peace. AJIL 50:563–582

Arnold R (2006) Human rights in times of terrorism. ZaöRV 66:297–319

Aust A (2005) Handbook of international law. Cambridge University Press, Cambridge

Badescu CG (2001) Humanitarian intervention and the responsibility to protect: Security and human rights. Routledge

Baker RB (2010) Customary international law in the 21st century: old challenges and new debates. EJIL 21:173–204

Bassiouni MC (1996) International crimes: Jus cogens and obligatio erga omnes. Law Contemp Probl 59:63–74

Bassiouni MC, Ferencz BB (1999) The crime against peace. In: Bassiouni MC (ed.), International criminal law, 2nd ed, Transnational Publishers vol. I, pp 313–347

Bebr G (1955) Regional organizations: a United Nations problem. AJIL 49:166–184

Bederman DJ (2001) Globalization, international law and United States foreign policy. Emory Law J 50:717–742

Bennoune K (2002) 'Sovereignty vs. Suffering'? Re-examining sovereignty and human rights through the lens of Iraq. EJIL 13:243–262

Bentwich N, Martin A (1950) A commentary on the charter of the United Nations. New York

Benvenisti E (2004) The US and the use of force: double-edged hegemony and the management of global emergencies. EJIL 15:677–700

Berman N (2006) Intervention in a 'Divided World': axes of legitimacy. EJIL 17:743–769

Bernhardt R (1976) Ungeschriebenes Völkerrecht. ZaöRV 36:50–76

Beyerlin U (1977) Die israelische Befreiungsaktion in Entebbe in völkerrechtlicher Sicht. ZaöRV 37:213–243

Bianchi A (2006) Assessing the effectiveness of the UN Security Council's anti-terrorism measures: the quest for legitimacy and cohesion. EJIL 17:881–919

Bilder R (1999) Kosovo and the "New Interventionism": promise or peril? J Trans Law Policy 9:153–182

[294] See Müllerson 2008, pp. 1–31.

Bilotskiy S (2010) Mijnarodne pravo ta mirotvorcha diyalnist na suchasnom etapi ["International Law and Peacepeeking Action at the Present Stage"]. In: *Oleksandru Zadorojnyomu—50: Statti ta esse uchniv i koleg* [Alexander Zadorozhny at 50—Articles and Essays by Students and Colleagues]. Odessa, Phoenix, pp 333–372
Bing JB (2010) The relations between treaties and custom. Chinese JIL 9:81–109
Bleckmann A (1976) Völkergewohnheitsrecht trotz widersprüchlicher Praxis? ZaöRV 36:374–406
Bleckmann A (1977) Zur Verbindlichkeit des allgemeinen Völkerrechts für internationale Organisationen. ZaöRV 37:107–121
Bothe M (2003) Terrorism and the legality of pre-emptive force. EJIL 14:227–240
Bowett D (1999) Crimes of state and the 1996 report of the international law commission on state responsibility. EJIL 9:163–173
Boyle FA (1990) The creation of the state of Palestine. EJIL 1:301–306
Branche R (2007) Torture of terrorists? Use of torture in a "war against terrorism": justifications, methods and effects: the case of France in Algeria, 1954–1962. IRRC 89:543–560
Breau SC (2006) The impact of the responsibility to protect on peacekeeping. JCSL 11:429–464
Brownlie I (1968) International law and the use of force by states. Clarendon Press, Oxford
Brownlie I (1998) Principles of public international law, 5th edn. Clarendon Press, Oxford
Brown Weiss E (2002) Invoking state responsibility in the twenty-first century. AJIL 96:798–816
Brunnée J (2005) The Security Council and self-defence: which way to global security?". In: Blokker N, Schrijver N (eds), The Security Council and the use of force: theory and reality—a need for change? Martinus Nijhoff Publishers, pp 107–132
Buchan R (2007) International community and the occupation of Iraq. JCSL 12:37–64
Burgis M (2008) Discourses of division: law, politics and the ICJ advisory opinion on the legal consequences of the construction of a wall in the occupied Palestinian territory. Chin JIL 7:33–63
Byers M (2002) The shifting foundations of international law: A decade of forceful measures against Iraq. EJIL 13:21–41
Cable J (1994) Gunboat diplomacy 1919–1991: Political applications of limited naval force. St. Martin's Press, New York
Caron DD (1993) The legitimacy of the collective authority of the Security Council. AJIL 87:552–588
Caron DD (2002) The ILC articles on state responsibility: the paradoxical relationship between form and authority. AJIL 96:857–873
Cassese A (1993) The Israel—PLO agreement and self-determination. EJIL 4:564–571
Cassese A (1999a) A follow-up: Forcible humanitarian countermeasures and *Opinio Necessitatis*. EJIL 10:791–799
Cassese A (1999b) *Ex iniuria ius oritur*: are we moving towards international legitimation of forcible humanitarian countermeasures in the world community? EJIL 10:23–30
Cassese A (2001) Terrorism is also disrupting some crucial legal categories of international law. EJIL 12:993–1001
Cassese A (2005) International law, 2nd edn. Oxford University Press, Oxford
Charney JI (1999) Anticipatory humanitarian intervention in Kosovo. AJIL 93:834–841
Chauprade A (2003) Géopolitique: constantes et changements dans l'histoire. Ellipses, Paris
Chesterman S (2001) Just war or just peace? Humanitarian intervention and international law. Oxford University Press, Oxford
Ching B (2013) Pre-emptive or similar type of self-defense in the territory of foreign states. Chin JIL 12:1–8
Chinkin CM (1993) East Timor moves into the world court. EJIL 4:206–222
Chinkin CM (1999) Kosovo: a "Good" or "Bad" war? AJIL 93:841–847
Chinkin CM (2000) The state that acts alone: bully, Good Samaritan or iconoclast? EJIL 11:31–41
Christakis T (2006) L'obligation de non-reconnaissance des situations créées par le recours illicite à la force ou d'atres actes enfreignant des règles fondamentales. In: Tomuschat C,

Thouvenin JM (eds), The Fundamental Rules of the International Legal Order: Jus Cogens and Obligations Erga Omnes, Martinus Nijhoff Publishers, pp 127–166

Christenson GA (1987) The World Court and Jus Cogens. AJIL 81:93–101

Condorelli L (1994) Le règlement des différends en matière de responsabilité internationale des Etats: quelques remarques candides sur le débat á la C.D.I. EJIL 5:106–115

Conforti B (1991) Non-coercive sanctions in the United Nations charter: some lessons from the Gulf War. EJIL 2:110–113

Constantinou A (2000) The right of self-defence under customary law and article 51 of the charter. Ant N, Sakkoulas

Coppieters B, Fotion N, Apresyan R (eds) (2002) Nravstvennye ogranicheniya voyny: problemy i primery [Moral Restraints on War: Issues and Examples]. Moscow, Gardariki

Corten O (2008) Le droit contre la guerre; l'interdiction du recours á la force en droit international contemporain. Pedone, Paris

Corten O (1995) La résolution 940 du Conseil de sécurité autorisant une intervention militaire en Haíti: L'émergence d'un principe de légitimité démocratique en droit international? EJIL 6:116–133

Corten O, Dubuisson F (2002) Liberté immuable": une extension abusive du concept de légitime defense. RGDIP 106:51–77

Cox M (1999) The Dayton agreement in Bosnia and Herzegovina: a study of implementation strategies. BYIL 70:201–244

Craven MCR (2002) Humanitarianism and the quest for smarter sanctions. EJIL 13:43–61

Crawford J (1990) The creation of the state of Palestine: too much too soon? EJIL 1:307–313

Crawford J (1999a) Revisiting the draft articles on state responsibility. EJIL 10:435–460

Crawford J (1999b) State practice and international law in relation to secession. BYIL 70:85–117

Crawford J (2002) The ILC's articles on responsibility of states for internationally wrongful acts: a retrospect. AJIL 96:874–890

Crawford J, Peel J, Olleson S (2001) The ILC's articles on responsibility of states for internationally wrongful acts: completion of the second reading. EJIL 12:963–991

D'Amato A (1969) The concept of special custom in international law. AJIL 63:211–223

D'Amato A (1987) Trashing customary international law. AJIL 81:101–105

Dekker IF (2001) Illegality and legitimacy of humanitarian intervention: synopsis of and comments on a Dutch report. JCSL 6:115–126

Delbrück (2001) The fight against global terrorism: self-defense or collective security as international police action? Some comments on the international legal implications of the War Against Terrorism. Ger YIL 44:9–23

Dias GM (2011) Responsibility to protect: new perspectives to an old dilemma. In: Silverburg SR (ed) International law: contemporary issues and future developments, Westview Press, pp 48–62

Dinstein Y (2001) War, aggression and self-defence, 3rd edn. Cambridge University Press, Cambridge

Doehring K (1976) Gewohnheitsrecht aus Verträgen. ZaöRV 36:77–95

Dolzer R (1987) Enforcement of international obligations through regional arrangements: structures and experience of the oaS. ZaöRV 47:113–133

Dominicé C (1991) La sécurité collective et la crise du Golfe. EJIL 2:85–109

Dominicé C (1999) The international responsibility of states for breach of multilateral obligations. EJIL 10:353–363

Dörr O (2003) Staats- und völkerrechtliche Aspekte des Irak-Krieges 2003. HuV-I 16:181–188

Doswald-Beck L (1985) The legal validity of military intervention by invitation of the government. BYIL 56:189–252

Dreist P (2002) Humanitäre Intervention—Zur Rechtmäßigkeit der NATO-Operation ALLIED FORCE. HuV-I 15:68–77

Drew C (2001) The east Timor story: international law on trial. EJIL 12:651–684

Droege C (2007) "In truth the leitmotiv": the prohibition of torture and other forms of ill-treatment in international humanitarian law. IRRC 89:515–541

Dupuy PM (1992) Dionisio Anzilotti and the law of international responsibility of states. EJIL 2:139–148
Dupuy PM (2002) A general stocktaking of the connections between the multilateral dimension of obligations and codification of the law of responsibility. EJIL 13:1053–1081
Ejegonik Komissii mejdunarodnogo prava [Yearbook of the International Law Commission] (1973), vol. I
Ejegodnik Komissii mejdunarodnogo prava [Yearbook of the Commission of International Law] (1976), vol. II
Eichensehr KE (2008) Defending nationals abroad: assessing the lawfulness of forcible hostage rescues. Va J Int Law 48:451–484
Falk R (ed) (1968) The Vietnam War and international law. Princeton University Press, Princeton
Farer T (2002) The Bush doctrine and the United Nations Charter frame. IS 37:91–100
Farer TJ (2003) The prospect for international law and order in the wake of Iraq. AJIL 97:621–628
Fassbender B (2002) Uncertain steps into a post-cold war world: the role and functioning of the un security council after a decade of measures against Iraq. EJIL 13:273–303
Ferencz BB (1972) Defining aggression: where it stands and where it's going. AJIL 66:491–508
Figà-Talamanca N (1996) The role of NATO in the peace agreement for Bosnia and Herzegovina. EJIL 7:164–175
Fischer H (2003) Zwischen autorisierter Gewaltanwendung und Präventivkrieg: Der völkerrechtliche Kern der Debatte um ein militärisches Eingreifen gegen den Irak. HuV-I 16:4–7
Fitzpatrick J (2003) Speaking law to power: the war against terrorism and human rights. EJIL 14:241–264
Franck TM (1970) Who killed article 2(4)? or: changing norms governing the use of force by states. AJIL 64:809–837
Franck TM (2001) Terrorism and the right of self-defense. AJIL 95:839–843
Franck TM (2003) What happens now? The United Nations after Iraq. AJIL 97:607–620
Frowein JA (1987) Collective enforcement of international obligations. ZaöRV 47:67–79
Gaeta P (1996) The Dayton Agreements and international law. EJIL 7:147–163
Gaja G (1995) Use of force made or authorized by the United Nations. In: Tomuschat C (ed), The United Nations at age fifty: a legal perspective. Kluwer Law International, pp 39–58
Gaja G (1999) Should all references to international crimes disappear from the ILC draft articles on state responsibility? EJIL 10:365–370
Gaja G (2010) The position of individuals in international law: an ILC perspective. EJIL 21:11–14
Garcia-Amador FV (1955) State responsibility in the light of the new trends of international law. AJIL 49:339–346
Garvey JI (1970) United Nations peacekeeping and host state consent. AJIL 64:241–269
Garvey JI (1976–1977) The UN definition of "Aggression": law and illusion in the context of collective security. Va J Int Law 17:177–194
Gattini A (1999) Smoking/no smoking: some remarks on the current place of fault in the ILC draft articles on state responsibility. EJIL 10:397–404
Gazzini T (2001) NATO coercive military activities in the Yugoslav crisis (1992–1999). EJIL 12:391–435
Gazzini T (2003) NATO's role in the collective security system. JCSL 8:231–263
Gazzini T (2005) The changing rules on the use of force in international law. Manchester University Press, Manchester
Gazzini T (2006) The rules on the use of force at the beginning of the XXI century. JCSL 11:319–342
Gazzini T (2008) A response to Amos Guiora: Pre-emptive self-defence against non-state actors? JCSL 13:25–32
Gerard A (1967) L'opération Stanleyville-Paulis devant le Parlement belge et les Nations Unies. Revue belge de droit international 3:242–269
Gibney M (2007) Genocide and state responsibility. Hum Rights Law Rev 7:1–14

Gill TD (2006) The temporal dimension of self-defence: anticipation, pre-emption, prevention and immediacy. JCSL 11:361–369
Glanville L (2012) The responsibility to protect beyond borders. Hum Rights Law Rev 12:1–32
Glennon MJ (2000) American hegemony in an unplanned world order. JCSL 5:3–25
Glennon MJ (2006) The emerging use-of-force paradigm. JCSL 11:309–317
Gowlland-Debbas V (2000) The limits of unilateral enforcement of community objectives in the framework of UN peace maintenance. EJIL 11:361–383
Goodman R (2006) Humanitarian intervention and pretexts for war. AJIL 100:107–141
Goodrich LM, Hambro E (1946) Charter of the United Nations: commentary and documents. World Peace Foundation, Boston
Gordon DJ (1977) Use of force for the protection of nationals abroad: the Entebbe incident. Case West Res J Int Law 9:117–134
Gray C (1997) Bosnia and Herzegovina: civil war or inter-state conflict? Characterization and consequences. BYIL 68:155–197
Gray C (2001) Peacekeeping after the Brahimi report: is there a crisis of credibility for the UN? JCSL 6:267–288
Gray C (2002a) From unity to polarization: international law and the use of force against Iraq. EJIL 13:1–19
Gray C (2002b) The US national security strategy and the new "Bush Doctrine" on preemptive self-defense. Chin JIL 1:437–448
Gray C (2005) The Bush Doctrine revisited: the 2006 national security strategy of the USA. Chin JIL 4:555–578
Gray C (2008) International law and the use of force, 3rd edn. Oxford University Press, Oxford
Gray C (2011) President Obama's 2010 United States national security strategy and international law on the use of force. Chin JIL 10:35–53
Greenwood C (1999) Humanitarian intervention: the case of Kosovo. Finnish Yearb Int Law 10:141–175
Greenwood C (2003) International law and the pre-emptive use of force: Afghanistan, Al-Qaida, and Iraq. San Diego Int Law J 4:7–37
Greenwood Onuf N (1970) Professor Falk on the quasi-legislative competence of the General Assembly. AJIL 64:349–355
Guiora AN (2008) Anticipatory self-defence and international law—a re-evaluation. JCSL 13:3–24
Harris DJ (2004) Cases and materials on international law, 6th edn. Sweet & Maxwell
Harris DJ, O'Boyle M, Warbrick C (1995) Law of the European convention on human rights. Butterworths
Hathaway JC (2000) America, defender of democratic legitimacy. EJIL 11:121–134
Hazard JN (1968) Why try again to define aggression? AJIL 62:701–710
Heintze HJ (2003) Zerfällt der Irak unter amerikanischen Bomben? HuV-I 16:16–21
Heintze HJ (2008) Indigenous peoples and the right of self-determination—is the claim to self-determination a trap? HuV-I 21:238–246
Henckaerts JM, Doswald-Beck L (eds) (2005) Customary international humanitarian law volume I Rules. Cambridge University Press, Cambridge
Henderson C (2004) The Bush Doctrine: from theory to practice. JCSL 9:3–24
Henke C (2009) Vorschlag für ein Übereinkommen über die Regelung der völkerrechtlichen Voraussetzungen einer humanitären Intervention. HuV-I 22:15–21
Henkin L (1971) The reports of the death of article 2(4) are greatly exaggerated. AJIL 65:544–548
Henkin L (1999) Kosovo and the law of humanitarian intervention. AJIL 93:824–828
Higgins R (1994) Problems and process: international law and how we use it. Oxford University Press, Oxford
Higgins R (1970) The place of international law in the settlement of disputes by the Security Council. AJIL 64:1–18
Hilpold P (2001) Humanitarian intervention: is there a need for a legal reappraisal? EJIL 12:437–467

Hood M (1983) Gunboat diplomacy 1895–1905: great power pressure in Venezuela. Allen & Unwin, Boston
Howse R (2002) The road to Baghdad is paved with good intentions. EJIL 13:89–92
Hudson B (2009) Justice in a time of terror. Br J Crim 49:702–717
Husain AM (2003) Who is the legitimate representative of the Palestinian people? Chin JIL 2:207–225
International Military Tribunal (Nuremberg), Judgment of 1 October (1946) The trial of German major war criminals. In: Proceedings of the International Military Tribunal sitting at Nuremberg, Germany, Part 22 (22nd August, 1946 to 1st October, 1946)
Johnstone I (2003) Security Council deliberations: the power of the better argument. EJIL 14:437–480
Johnstone I (2004) US–UN relations after Iraq: the end of the world (order) as we know it? EJIL 15:813–838
Joyner DH (2002) The Kosovo intervention: legal analysis and a more persuasive paradigm. EJIL 13:597–619
Kadelbach S (2006) Jus cogens, obligations erga omnes and other rules—the identification of fundamental norms. In: Tomuschat C, Thouvenin JM (eds), The fundamental rules of the international legal order: Jus Cogens and Obligations Erga Omnes, Martinus Nijhoff Publishers, pp 21–40
Kalamkaryan A, Migachev YI (2005) Mejdunarodnoe pravo [International Law]. Eksmo Education, Moscow
Kelsen H (1948) Collective security and collective self-defense under the charter of the United Nations. AJIL 42:783–796
Kelsen H (2008) The law of the United Nations: a critical analysis of its fundamental problems, 7th printing. The Lawbook Exchange Ltd, New York
Kemp G (2010) Individual criminal liability for the international crime of aggression. Intersentia
Khadduri M (1946) The Arab league as a regional arrangement. AJIL 40:756–777
Kinacioglu M (2008) A response to Amos Guiora: reassessing the parameters of use of force in the age of terrorism. JCSL 13:33–48
Kissinger H (1994) Diplomacy. Simon & Schuster Paperbacks
Klein P (2002) Responsibility for serious breaches of obligations deriving from peremptory norms of international law and United Nations law. EJIL 13:1241–1255
Kolosov YM, Kuzbetsov VI (eds) (1998) Mejdunarodnoe pravo [International Law]. Moscow
Korelsky VM, Perevalov VD (eds) (1998) Teoriya gosudarstva i prava [The Theory of State and Law]. Norma—Infra-M, Moscow
Koskenniemi M (2004) Perceptions of justice: walls and bridges between Europe and the United States. ZaöRV 64:305–314
Koskenniemi M (2005) International law in Europe: between tradition and renewal. EJIL 16:113–124
Kovalev AA, Chernichenko SV (eds) (2008) Mejdunarodnoe pravo [International Law]. Omega-L, Moscow
Kramer RC, Michalowski RJ (2005) War, aggression and state crime. Br J Crim 45:446–469
Kreß C (1997) Die Rettungsoperation der Bundeswehr in Albanien am 14. März 1997 aus völker- und verfassungsrechtlicher Sicht. ZaöRV 57:329–362
Kretzmer D (2013) The inherent right to self-defence and proportionality in jus ad bellum. EJIL 24:235–282
Krisch N (2005) International law in times of hegemony: unequal power and the shaping of the international legal order. EJIL 16:369–408
Kröning V (2003) Prävention oder Präemption? HuV-I 16:82–87
Kühne W (1995) The United Nations, fragmenting states, and the need for enlarged peacekeeping. In: Tomuschat (ed) The United Nations at age FIFTY: a legal perspective, Kluwer Law International, pp 91–112
Kulagin VM (2006) Mejdunarodnaya bezopasnost [International Security]. Aspect Press, Moscow

Kunz JL (1947) Individual and collective self-defense in article 51 of the Charter of the United Nations. AJIL 41:872–879
Kunz JL (1953) The nature of customary international law. AJIL 47:662–669
Kunz JL (1960) Sanctions in international law. AJIL 54:324–347
Kuznetsov VI (ed) (2001) Mejdunarodnoe pravo [International Law]. Moscow, Yurist
Leeds BA (2003) Do alliances deter aggression? The influence of military alliances on the initiation of militarized interstate disputes. Am J Polit Sci 47:427–439
Lehman JS (2000) Unilateralism in international law: a United States—European symposium. EJIL 11:1–2
Levin DB (1966) Otvetstvennost gosudarstv v sovremennom mejdunarodnom prave [The Responsibility of States in the Contemporary International Law]. Moscow
Levitt J (2005) The peace and Security Council of the african union, the use of force and the united nations security council: the case of sudan. In: Blokker N Schrijver N (eds.) The Security Council and the use of force: theory and reality—a need for change? Martinus Nijhoff Publishers, pp 213–251
Licková M (2008) European exceptionalism in international law. EJIL 19:463–490
Lietzau WK (2004) The role of military force in foreign relations, humanitarian intervention and the Security Council. ZaöRV 64:281–304
Lillich R (1993a) Forcible protection of nationals abroad: the Liberian incident of 1990. German YIL 35:2105 et seq
Lillich R (1993b) Humanitarian intervention through the United Nations: towards the development of criteria. ZaöRV 53:557–575
Link W (1998) Die Neuordnung der Weltpolitik an der Schwelle zum 21. Jahrhundert. Verlag C. H, Beck OHG
Lowe V (2003) The Iraq crisis: what now? The ICLQ 52:859–871
Luban D (2004) Preventive war. Philos Public Aff 32:207–248
Lukashuk I (2004a) Pravo mejdunarodnoy otvetstvennosti [The Law of International Responsibility]. Wolters Kluwer, Moscow
Lukashuk I (2004b) Sovremennoe pravo mejdunarodnyh dogovorov [Contemporary Law of Treaties], volume I. Wolters Kluwer, Moscow
Lukashuk I (2008a) Mejdunarodnoe pravo: Obshchaya chast [International Law: General Part], 3rd edn. Wolters Kluwer, Moscow
Lukashuk I (2008b) Mejdunarodnoe pravo: Osobennaya chast [International Law: Specific Part], 3rd edn. Wolters Kluwer, Moscow
Lukashuk I, Boklan D (2003) The concept of the US national security and international law: a view from Moscow. Chin JIL 2:587–597
Maffei MC (1993) The case of east Timor before the International Court of Justice—some tentative comments. EJIL 4:223–238
Malanczuk P (1996) Some basic aspects of the agreements between Israel and the PLO from the perspective of international law. EJIL 7:485–500
Malanczuk P (1997) Akehurst's modern introduction to international law, 7th revised edn. Routledge
Mandel M (2001) Politics and human rights in international criminal law: our case against NATO and the lessons to be learned from it. Fordham Int Law J 25:95–128
Marchenko MN (2002) Obshchaya teoriya gosudarstva i prava [The General Theory of State and Law], vol 1. Zertsalo-M, Moscow
McClean E (2008) The responsibility to protect: the role of international human rights law. JCSL 13:123–152
McWhinney E (1962) Peaceful co-existence" and soviet-western international law. AJIL 56:951–970
McWhinney E (1965) Changing international law method and objectives in the era of the soviet-western detente. AJIL 59:1–15
McWhinney E (2002a) International law-based responses to the September 11 international terrorist attacks. Chin JIL 1:280–286

McWhinney E (2002b) President Bush and the new U.S. national security strategy: the continuing relevance of the legal adviser and international law. Chin JIL 1:421–436
McWhinney E (2003) The US/British invasion of Iraq and the United Nations Charter prohibition of the use of force: the paradox of unintended consequences. Chin JIL 2:571–585
Milano E (2003) Security Council action in the balkans: reviewing the legality of Kosovo's territorial status. EJIL 14:999–1022
Müllerson R (2002) Jus ad bellum: plus ça change (le monde) plus c'est la même chose (le droit). JCSL 7:149–189
Müllerson R (2008) Promoting democracy without starting a new cold war? Chin JIL 7:1–31
Murphy R (2003a) United Nations peacekeeping in Lebanon and Somalia, and the use of force. JCSL 8:71–99
Murphy SD (1996) Humanitarian intervention: the United Nations in an evolving world order. University of Pennsylvania Press, Philadelphia
Murphy SD (2001) U.S. comments on ILC draft articles on state responsibility. AJIL 95:626–628
Murphy SD (2003b) International Law, the United States, and the non-military 'War' against terrorism. EJIL 14:347–364
Nardin T (2013) From right to intervene to duty to PROTECT: Michael Walzer on humanitarian intervention. EJIL 24:67–82
Neuhold H (2004) Law and force in international relations—European and American positions. ZaöRV 64:263–279
Neuman GL (2003) Humanitarian law and counterterrorist force. EJIL 14:283–298
Neuman GL (2004) Comment, counter-terrorist operations and the rule of law. EJIL 15:1019–1029
Newman GR, Clarke RV (2011) "Terrorism". In: Natarajan M (ed), International Crime and Justice, Cambridge University Press, pp 290–296
Nollkaemper A (2003) Concurrence between individual responsibility and state responsibility in international law. ICLQ 52:615–640
Nollkaemper A (2005) Attribution of forcible acts to states: connections between the law on the use of force and the law of state responsibility. In: Blokker N, Schrijver N (eds), The security council and the use of force: theory and reality—a need for change? Martinus Nijhoff Publishers, pp 133–171
Nolte G (2002) From Dionisio Anzilotti to Robert Ago: the classical law of state responsibility and the traditional primacy of a bilateral conception of inter-state relations. EJIL 13:1083–1098
Norman G, Trachtman JP (2005) The customary international law game. AJIL 99:541–580
O'Connell ME (2002) Debating the law of sanctions. EJIL 13:63–79
Odello M (2005) Commentary on the United Nations' high-level panel on threats, challenges and change. JCSL 10:231–262
Official Records of the United Nations Conference on the Law of Treaties, First Session, Vienna, 26 March to 24 May (1968) Summary records of the plenary meeting and of the meetings of the Committee of the Whole (United Nations publication, Sales No. E.68.V.7)
Ofosu-Amaah GKA (1987) Regional enforcement of international obligations: Africa. ZaöRV 47:80–94
Okimoto K (2011a) The cumulative requirements of *Jus ad Bellum* and *Jus in Bello* in the context of self-defense. Chin JIL 10:45–75
Okimoto K (2011b) The distinction and relationship between Jus ad Bellum and Jus in Bello. Hart Publishing
Okowa PN (2007) Congo's War: the legal dimension of a protracted conflict. BYIL 78:203–255
Orakhelashvili A (2005) The impact of peremptory norms on the interpretation and application of United Nations Security Council resolutions. EJIL 16:59–88
Orakhelashvili A (2006a) Legal consequences of the construction of a wall in the occupied palestinian territory: opinion and reaction. JCSL 11:119–139
Orakhelashvili A (2006b) Peremptory norms in international law. Oxford University Press, Oxford
Orford A (1999) Muscular humanitarianism: reading the narratives of new interventionism. EJIL 10:679–711
Paust JJ (1978) Entebbe and self-help: the Israeli response to terrorism. Fletcher Forum 2:86–91

Pejic J (2005) Terrorist acts and groups: a role for international law? BYIL 76:71–100

Pellet A (1999) Can a state commit a crime? Definitely, yes! EJIL 10:425–434

Pellet A (2000) Brief remarks on the unilateral use of force. EJIL 11:385–392

Pellet A, Tzankov V (2004) Can a state victim of a terror act have recourse to armed force? HuV-I 17:68–72

Posner EA, Sykes AO (2007) An economic analysis of state and individual responsibility under international law. Am Law Eco Rev 9:1–63

Potter PB (1951) Preventive war critically considered. AJIL 45:142–145

Raby J (1988) The state of necessity and the use of force to protect nationals. Can Yearb Int Law 26:253–272

Ratner SR (2002) *Jus ad Bellum* and *Jus in Bello* after September 11. AJIL 96:905–921

Reisman WM (1990) International law after the Cold War. AJIL 84:859–866

Reisman WM (1994) The raid on Baghdad: some reflections on its lawfulness and implications. EJIL 5:120–133

Reisman WM (2000) Unilateral action and the transformations of the world constitutive process: the special problem of humanitarian intervention. EJIL 11:3–18

Reisman WM (2003) Assessing claims to revise the laws of war. AJIL 97:82–90

Reisman WM, Armstrong A (2006) The past and future of the claim of preemptive self-defense. AJIL 100:525–550

Riesenfeld SA (1966) *Jus Dispositivum* and *Jus Cogens* in international law: In the light of a recent decision of the German Supreme Constitutional Court. AJIL 60:511–515

Roberts AE (2001) Traditional and modern approaches to customary international law: a reconciliation. AJIL 95:757–791

Roberts AE (2004) Righting wrongs or wronging rights? The United States and human rights post-september 11. EJIL 15:721–749

Ronzitti N (1985) Rescuing nationals abroad through military coercion and intervention on grounds of humanity. Martinus Nijhoff Publishers, Dordrecht

Ronzitti N (2006) The expanding law of self-defence. JCSL 11:343–359

Rosenstock R (2002) The ILC and state responsibility. AJIL 96:792–797

Ross J (2007) Black letter abuse: the US legal response to torture since 9/11. IRRC 89:561–590

Ruys T (2008) The 'Protection of Nationals' doctrine revisited. JCSL 13:233–271

Ruys T, Verhoeven S (2005) Attacks by private actors and the right of self-defence. JCSL 19:289–320

Salcedo JAC (1997) Reflections on the existence of a hierarchy of norms in international law. EJIL 8:583–595

Sapiro M (2003) Iraq: the shifting sands of preemptive self-defense. AJIL 97:599–607

Sassóli M (2006) Terrorism and war. JICJ 4:959–981

Sayapin S (2009) International law and the use of force: from the charter of the united nations to the Rome statute of the international criminal court. Asian Yearb Int Law 15:3–42

Schachter O (1984) The right of states to use armed force. Mich Law Rev 82:1620–1646

Schachter O (1986) In defense of international rules on the use of force. Univ Chicago Law Rev 53:113–146

Schachter O (1989) Self-defense and the rule of law. AJIL 83:259–277

Schmidt-Radefeldt R (2005) Enduring Freedom—Antiterrorkrieg für immer?—Ein Beitrag zum *Jus Post Bellum* in Afghanistan. HuV-I 18:245–253

Scheuner U (1969) Conflict of treaty provisions with a peremptory norm of general international law. ZaöRV 29:28–38

Scheuner U (1967) Conflict of treaty provisions with a peremptory norm of general international law and its consequences: comments on articles 50, 61 and 67 of the ILC's 1966 draft articles on the law of treaties. ZaöRV 27:520–532

Schrijver N (2005) Challenges to the prohibition to use force: Does the straitjacket of article 2(4) UN Charter begin to gall too much?". In: Blokker N, Schrijver N (eds), The Security Council and the use of force: theory and reality—a need for change? Martinus Nijhoff Publishers, pp 31–45

Schreuer C (1995) Regionalism v. universalism. EJIL 6:477–499
Schwelb E (1967) Some aspects of international *Jus Cogens* as formulated by the International Law Commission. AJIL 61:946–975
Schweisfurth T (1980) Operations to rescue nationals in third states involving the use of force in relation to the protection of human rights. 23 German YIL 23:159 et seq
Scobbie I (2002) The invocation of responsibility for the breach of 'obligations under peremptory norms of general international law. EJIL 13:1201–1220
Shah NA (2007) Self-defence, anticipatory self-defence and pre-emption: international law's response to terrorism. JCSL 12:95–126
Shaw M (2008) International law, 6th edn. Cambridge University Press, Cambridge
Shelton D (2006) Normative hierarchy in international law. AJIL 100:291–323
Sicilianos LA (2002) The classification of obligations and the multilateral dimension of the relations of international responsibility. EJIL 13:1127–1145
Simma B (ed) (1994) The Charter of the United Nations: a commentary. Oxford University Press, Oxford
Simma B (1999) NATO, the UN and the use of force: legal aspects. EJIL 10:1–22
Skubiszewski K (1971) Elements of custom and the Hague court. ZaöRV 31:810–854
Sofaer AD (2003) On the necessity of pre-emption. EJIL 14:209–226
Spinedi M (2002) State responsibility v. individual responsibility for international crimes: *Tertium Non Datur*? EJIL 13:895–899
Stahn C (2003) Enforcement of the collective will after Iraq. AJIL 97:804–823
Stein E (1987a) Collective enforcement of international obligations. ZaöRV 47:56–66
Stein T (1987b) Die regionale Durchsetzung völkerrechtlicher Verpflichtungen: Europa. ZaöRV 47:95–112
Stone J (1977) Hopes and loopholes in the 1974 definition of aggression. AJIL 71:224–246
Stowell EC (1939) Humanitarian intervention. AJIL 33:733–736
Strebel H (1976) Quellen des Völkerrechts als Rechtsordnung. ZaöRV 36:301–346
Stromseth JE (2003) Law and force after Iraq: A transitional moment. AJIL 97:628–642
Taft WH IV, Buchwald TF (2003) Preemption, Iraq, and international law. AJIL 97:557–563
Talmon S (2006) The duty not to 'Recognize as Lawful' a situation created by the illegal use of force or other serious breaches of a *Jus Cogens* obligation: an obligation without real substance?". In: Tomuschat C, Thouvenin JM (eds), The fundamental rules of the international legal order: Jus Cogens and Obligations Erga Omnes, Martinus Nijhoff Publishers, pp 99–126
Tams CJ (2002) Do serious breaches give rise to any specific obligations of the responsible state? EJIL 13:1161–1180
Tams CJ (2009) The use of force against terrorists. EJIL 20:359–397
Tavernier P (1990) Le caractère obligatoire de la résolution 598 (1987) du conseil de sécurité relative à la guerre du golfe. EJIL 1:278–285
Tesón F (2005) Humanitarian intervention: and inquiry into law and morality, 3rd edn. Transnational Publishers
Thakur R (2011) The Responsibility to protect and the North-South divide. In: Silverburg SR (ed.) International law: contemporary issues and future developments, Westview Press, pp 32–47
Tomuschat C (2006) Reconceptualizing the debate on *Jus Cogens* and obligations *Erga Omnes* – Concluding Observations. In: Tomuschat C, Thouvenin JM (eds), The fundamental rules of the international legal order: Jus Cogens and obligations Erga Omnes, Martinus Nijhoff Publishers, pp 425–436
Tomuschat C (1993) Self-determination in a post-colonial world. In: Tomuschat C (ed), Modern law of self-determination, Kluwer Academic Publishers, pp 1–20
Tomuschat C (2001) "Uniting for Peace"—Ein Rückblick nach 50 Jahren. Die Friedens-Warte 76:289–303
Tsagourias N (2006) Consent, neutrality/impartiality and the use of force in peacekeeping: their constitutional dimension. JCSL 11:465–482

Tsagourias N (1996) The Nicaragua case and the use of force: the theoretical construction of the decision and its deconstruction. JCSL 1:81–93
Tuzmukhamedov BR (2006) K voprosu ob uprejdenii siloy ["Pre-emption by Force Revisited"]. Moscow J Int Law 61:374–384
Vagts DF (2003) Which courts should try persons accused of terrorism? EJIL 14:313–326
Van Boven T (1995) Human rights and rights of peoples. EJIL 6:461–476
Van Kleffens EN (1949) Regionalism and political pacts. AJIL 43:666–678
Van Walsum P (2005) The Security Council and the use of force: Kosovo, east Timor and Iraq. In: Blokker N, Schrijver N (eds), The Security Council and the use of force: theory and reality—a need for change? Martinus Nijhoff Publishers, pp 65–74
Vidmar J (2013) Palestine and the conceptual problem of implicit statehood. Chin JIL 12:19–41
Von Lepel Frhr OM (2003) Die präemptive Selbstverteidigung im Lichte des Völkerrechts. HuV-I 16:77–81
Von Schorlemer S (2003) Human rights: substantive and institutional implications of the war against terrorism. EJIL 14:265–282
Von Verdross A (1966) Jus Dispositivum and Jus Cogens in international law. AJIL 60:55–63
Vranes E (2005) Lex Superior, Lex Specialis, Lex Posterior—Zur Rechtsnatur der "Konfliktlösungsregeln. ZaöRV 65:391–405
Vranes E (2006) The definition of 'Norm Conflict' in international law and legal theory. EJIL 17:395–418
Waldock CHM (1952) The regulation of the use of force by individual states in international law. Receuil des Cours 81:451–517
Warbrick C (2004) The European response to terrorism in an age of human rights. EJIL 15:989–1018
Waxman MC (2013) Regulating resort to force: form and substance of the UN charter regime. EJIL 24:151–189
Wedgwood R (2003) The fall of Saddam Hussein: Security Council mandates and preemptive self-defense. AJIL 97:576–585
Wedgwood R (2000) Unilateral action in the UN system. EJIL 11:349–359
Weiler JHH, Paulus AL (1997) The structure of change in international law or is there a hierarchy of norms in international law? EJIL 8:545–565
Wellens K (2003) The UN Security Council and new threats to the peace: back to the future. JCSL 8:15–70
Weller M (2009) Settling self-determination conflicts: recent developments. EJIL 20:111–165
Werle G (2009) The crime of aggression between international and domestic criminal law. In: Manacorda S, Nieto A (eds), Criminal law between war and peace. Cuena, pp 405–421
Werner WG (2001) Self-determination and civil war. JCSL 6:171–190
Wheatley S (2000) The foreign affairs select committee report on Kosovo: NATO action and humanitarian intervention. JCSL 5:261–273
Wheatley S (2006) The Security Council, democratic legitimacy and regime change in Iraq. EJIL 17:531–551
White ND (2001) Commentary on the report of the panel on United Nations peace operations (The Brahimi Report). JCSL 6:127–146
White ND (2000) The legality of bombing in the name of humanity. JCSL 5:27–43
Wiefelspütz D (2006) Die Zulässigkeit präemptiver oder präventiver Anwendung militärischer Gewalt. HuV-I 19:103–111
Wilmshurst E (2004) Definition of the crime of aggression: state responsibility or individual criminal responsibility?. In: Politi M, Nesi G (eds), The International Criminal Court and the crime of aggression, Ashgate Publishing Limited, pp 93–96
Wills S (2004) Military interventions on behalf of vulnerable populations: the legal responsibilities of States and international organizations engaged in peace support operations. JCSL 9:387–418
Wolfrum R (2004) American-European dialogue: perceptions of international law—introduction. ZaöRV 64:255–262

Wolfrum R (1993) Der Beitrag regionaler Abmachumgen zur Friedenssicherung: Möglichkeiten und Grenzen. ZaöRV 52:576–602
Wood M (2005) Towards new circumstances in which the use of force may be authorized?. In: Blokker N, Schrijver N (eds), The Security Council and the use of force: theory and reality—a need for change? Martinus Nijhoff Publishers, pp 75–90
Woolsey LH (1951) The "Uniting for Peace" resolution of the United Nations. AJIL 45:129–137
Wyler E (2002) From 'State Crime' to responsibility for 'serious breaches of obligations under peremptory norms of general international law'. EJIL 13:1147–1160
Yearbook of the International Law Commission (1963), volume II
Yearbook of the International Law Commission (1966), volume II
Yearbook of the International Law Commission (2001), volume II
Yee S (2002) The potential impact of the possible US responses to the 9–11 atrocities on the law regarding the use of force and self-defence. Chin JIL 1:287–293
Yoo J (2003) International law and the war in Iraq. AJIL 97:563–576
Zagaynov ET (2006) Uprejdayushchaya samooborona v zapadnoy doktrine mejdunarodnogo prava ["Pre-emptive Self-Defence in the Western Doctrine of International Law"]. Moscow J Int Law 62:29–45
Zedalis RJ (1990) Protection of nationals abroad: is consent the basis of legal obligation? Texas J Int Law 25:221–244
Zedalis RJ (1999) Dealing with the weapons inspections crisis in Iraq. ZaöRV 59:37–50
Zemanek K (1987) The unilateral enforcement of international obligations. ZaöRV 47:32–43
Zöckler M (1995) Germany in collective security systems—anything goes? EJIL 6:274–286
Zwanenburg M (2005) NATO, its member states and the security council. In: Blokker N, Schrijver N (eds), The Security Council and the use of force: theory and reality—a need for change? Martinus Nijhoff Publishers, pp 189–211
Zwanenburg M (2006) Regional organisations and the maintenance of international peace and security: three recent regional African peace operations. JCSL 11:483–508
Zwitter A (2007) Menschliche Sicherheit, Humanitäre Intervention und ihre völkerrechtlichen Perspektiven. HuV-I 20:231–236
Zwitter A (2008) An international law perspective on the long-term prevention of terrorism. HuV-I 21:24–33

Part II
The Individual Crime

Chapter 3
International Legal Foundations of the Individual Criminal Responsibility for the Crime of Aggression

Abstract This chapter analyzes, in a detailed manner, the legacy of the Nuremberg and Tokyo trials, as well as of trials under the Control Council Law № 10, with respect to the criminalization of aggression under international law, and delineates the contours of a legal framework for an indirect and direct enforcement of individual liability for the crime. The International Law Commission's expert work on the subject—as a matter covered in the Draft Code of Offences against the Peace and Security of Mankind and the Draft Code of Crimes against the Peace and Security of Mankind—is recalled at some length. Finally, the legislative developments within a number of national legal systems (for details, see Chap. 4) and the adoption of a definition of the crime of aggression for the purpose of the Rome Statute of the International Criminal Court (for details, see Chap. 5) are alluded to as key consequences of the post-World War II international jurisprudence on the crime of aggression.

Contents

S. Sayapin, *The Crime of Aggression in International Criminal Law*,
DOI: 10.1007/978-90-6704-927-6_3, © T.M.C. ASSER PRESS and the author 2014

"Crimes against International Law are committed by men, not by abstract entities, and only by punishing individuals who commit such crimes can the provisions of International Law be enforced".[1] This pioneering formula divided international law into "before" and "after", because "after" Nuremberg it became clear that individuals committing crimes of international concern—even the most high-ranking officials of States—might not be shielded from prosecution by the armor of State sovereignty.[2] The Nuremberg Judgment was ground-breaking in that it introduced in international law a number of legal notions and institutions, which had hitherto been unknown to this legal system. The criminal prosecution of individuals directly under international law—including for acts, which had been legal under their State's national laws—was the foremost among such novelties.[3] It was recognised, for the first time in history, that the "act of State" doctrine was not relevant in the context of such heinous crimes, because a systemic commission of crimes was not a normal function of the State.[4] Further, these individuals—holders of high-ranking posts in the Third Reich's political and military structures—were stripped of their immunity, because it too was considered immaterial in view of the gravity of the crimes committed. As specifically concerns wars of aggression—and other crimes against peace within the jurisdiction of the Tribunal (see supra 1.2.2)—the Nuremberg Tribunal was the first court of law in history to have indicted individuals with such crimes, and this too signaled the beginning of a new era in international law—in fact, the true beginning of international criminal law.[5] Soon after that, the charges of crimes against peace were brought against individuals by the Tokyo Tribunal and under the Control Council Law No. 10. The historical background of those trials was outlined above, at 1.2.2–1.2.4, and in this

---

[1] International Military Tribunal (Nuremberg), Judgment of 1 October 1946, p. 447.

[2] Although no State official has yet been prosecuted for a crime against peace since the conclusion of the Nuremberg follow-up trials (see infra 3.1.3), "no fewer than sixty-seven heads of state or government from around the globe have been, at a minimum, criminally charged for their misconduct while in office" since 1990, see Lutz and Reiger 2009, at p. 2. See also List of Prosecutions of Heads of State or Government, January 1990 to June 2008, Lutz and Reiger 2009, pp. 295–305.

[3] See Korowicz 1956, pp. 533–562; Manner 1952, pp. 428–449; Mosler 1962, pp. 1–48; Müllerson 1990, pp. 33–43. See also Justice R. Jackson's important statement on the significance of the Nuremberg Tribunal for the future development of international and national law: "We are able to do away with domestic tyranny and violence and aggression by those in power against the rights of their own people only when we make all men answerable to the law. This trial represents mankind's desperate effort to apply the discipline of the law to statesmen who have used their powers of state to attack the foundations of the world's peace and to commit aggressions against the rights of their neighbors", quoted in Safferling 2012, p. 66.

[4] See Andrews 1975, pp. 41–50; Delson 1972, pp. 82–93; Kingsbury 1910, pp. 359–372; Malanczuk 1997, pp. 121–123; Perreau-Saussine 2008, pp. 176–254; Sucharitkul 2005, pp. 1–43; Zander 1959, pp. 826–852.

[5] Unlike many commentators, Larry May considers that crimes against peace were the *principal* charge brought against the defendants at Nuremberg, and crimes against humanity and war crimes were secondary. See May 2008, p. 250. See also Clark 2007, pp. 527–550; Kelsen 1947, pp. 153–171; Weigend 2012, pp. 41–58.

chapter their contributions to the criminalization of aggression are summarized and examined. Their jurisprudence is crucial, because, to date, it constitutes the entirety of case law pertaining to the crime of aggression.[6]

This case law laid the foundation to subsequent normative developments whose international dimension is considered below in this chapter (3.1.4–3.1.7) and in Chap. 5. These consist, first and foremost, in the International Law Commission's definitions of the crime of aggression included in the 1951 Draft Code of Offences against the Peace and Security of Mankind and the 1996 Draft Code of Crimes against the Peace and Security of Mankind, as well as in relevant amendments to the Rome Statute of the International Criminal Court. These developments confirmed the status of aggression as a "leadership crime"—a feature, which is examined in 4.2. The relevant normative developments at the national level are analyzed in Chap. 4.

3.1 Individual Criminal Responsibility for Aggression Committed by a State

The challenge that all post-World War II courts faced with respect to the crimes against peace was twofold. First, it was about proving the criminality of aggression as such, which had not hitherto been an acknowledged issue in international law (see supra 1.2.1–1.2.3). Second, it was about establishing links between the aggressive behavior of States and individual acts—at the level of their *actus reus* and *mens rea*—for which natural persons could be held criminally liable. These two issues will be in the center of attention throughout this chapter.

3.1.1 Nuremberg Judgment

The Nuremberg Tribunal dealt with crimes against peace on two counts: Count One of the Indictment charged the defendants with "the formulation or execution of a Common Plan Or Conspiracy to commit" crimes against peace, whereas Count Two charged them with "the planning, preparation, initiation and waging of wars of aggression, which were also wars in violation of international treaties, agreements and assurances", against a number of States.[7] The Tribunal found it "convenient to consider the question of the existence of a common plan and the

[6] See Antonopoulos 2001, pp. 33–62; Kress 2004, pp. 347–352.

[7] International Military Tribunal (Nuremberg), Judgment of 1 October 1946, p. 411. See also at p. 421 and Article 6(a) of the Nuremberg Tribunal's Charter: "Crimes against peace: namely, planning, preparation, initiation or waging of a war of aggression, or a war in violation of international treaties, agreements or assurances, or participation in a common plan or conspiracy for the accomplishment of any of the foregoing".

question of aggressive war together" (because they represented two consecutive stages of the same criminal enterprise), and subsequently to determine the defendants' individual criminal liability.[8]

The starting point of the Tribunal's reasoning—which was afterwards widely recognised and quoted in the international legal doctrine—was as follows:

> The charges in the Indictment that the defendants planned and waged aggressive wars are charges of the utmost gravity. War is essentially an evil thing. Its consequences are not confined to the belligerent States alone, but affect the whole world.
>
> To initiate a war of aggression, therefore, is not only an international crime; it is the supreme international crime differing only from other war crimes in that it contains within itself the accumulated evil of the whole.[9]

In the Tribunal's opinion, Germany's wars of aggression charged in the Indictment "did not come suddenly out of an otherwise clear sky".[10] The Judges came to the conclusion that these wars of aggression were "premeditated and carefully prepared", and that they were undertaken when "the moment was thought opportune for [them] to be carried through as a definite part of the pre-ordained scheme and plan".[11] This plan provided for two main goals: (1) "the disruption of the European order as it had existed since the Treaty of Versailles" (see supra 1.1.6.2–1.1.6.5), and (2) "the creation of a Greater Germany beyond the frontiers of 1914".[12] Since the conquest of foreign territories was a necessary component in the realisation of those ambitions, the Tribunal held that Germany's new "[w]ar was seen to be inevitable, or at the very least, highly probable" in Europe's immediate political process at the time.[13]

The Tribunal found an official expression of the foundations of Nazi Germany's aggressive policy in Hitler's *Mein Kampf*—even though this policy had not been "inflexible" or "incapable of modification".[14] In the Tribunal's view, the importance of Hitler's book consisted "in the unmistakable attitude of aggression revealed throughout its pages".[15] Surprisingly enough, the significance of *Mein Kampf* is introduced in the Judgment under the heading of "Preparation for Aggression", and not in the following section ("The Planning of Aggression"). It

---

[8] See International Military Tribunal (Nuremberg), Judgment of 1 October 1946, pp. 421 and ff.

[9] Ibid., p. 421.

[10] Ibid., p. 422.

[11] Ibid.

[12] Ibid.

[13] Ibid.

[14] Ibid., p. 423.

[15] Ibid. At the same page of the Judgment, a telling excerpt from *Mein Kampf* is quoted: "Therefore we National Socialists have purposely drawn a line through the line of conduct followed by pre-war Germany in foreign policy. We put an end to the perpetual Germanic march towards the South and West of Europe, and turn our eyes towards the lands of the East. We finally put a stop to the colonial and trade policy of the pre-war times, and pass over to the territorial policy of the future. But when we speak of new territory in Europe today, we must think principally of Russia and the border States subject to her".

will be argued below (see infra 4.3.1.1.1–4.3.1.1.2, and 5.1.1.1.2) that the concept of planning includes for the most part conceptual measures, while preparation essentially means taking practical and organizational measures for carrying out the planned aggression. Hence it would have made sense to reverse the titles of the sections in the Judgment. Be that as it may, the Tribunal did assess the role of Hitler's book in Germany's aggressive effort properly enough, as it was a major tool in the propaganda for war and institutionalized cultivation of inter-ethnic hatred.[16]

The development of conspiracy to commit aggression was analyzed under the heading "The Planning of Aggression" (pp. 423–425 of the Judgment). The exposition began by reference to four secret meetings held by Hitler, respectively, on 5 November 1937, 23 May 1939, 22 August 1939, and 23 November 1939, where Hitler made "important declarations" (in the language of the Tribunal) of his aggressive purposes.[17] Despite the defence's efforts to disprove the veracity of these meetings' records, the Tribunal acknowledged their authenticity—by virtue of their careful preservation in the archives of the German Government—and quoted them extensively as evidence of Hitler's aggressive design. His recorded programmatic statement on the intended "reinforcement of the Reich" was quite plain:

> One year later, Austria came; this step also was considered doubtful. It brought about a considerable reinforcement of the Reich. The next step was Bohemia, Moravia, and Poland. This step also was not possible to accomplish in one campaign. First of all, the western fortification had to be finished. It was not possible to reach the goal in one effort. It was clear to me from the first moment that I could not be satisfied with the Sudeten German territory. That was only a partial solution. The decision to march into Bohemia was made. Then followed the erection of the Protectorate and with that the basis for the action against Poland was laid, but I was not quite clear at that time whether I should start first against the East and then in the West or vice versa [...] Basically I did not organize the armed forces in order not to strike. The decision to strike was always in me. Earlier or later I wanted to solve the problem. Under pressure it was decided that the East was to be attacked first.[18]

3.1.1.1 Annexation of Austria and Czechoslovakia

The following pages of the Judgment contain extracts from records of earlier meetings where plans to attack individual countries were discussed. The invasion of Austria on 12 March 1938 (for further details, see infra 3.1.3.1.2) was characterized as a "premeditated aggressive step in furthering the plan to wage aggressive wars against other countries. As a result Germany's flank was protected, that of Czechoslovakia being greatly weakened".[19] This course of action, which met no

[16] See also Gott 1938, pp. 704–718; Vagts 1990, pp. 661–704.

[17] See International Military Tribunal (Nuremberg), Judgment of 1 October 1946, p. 423.

[18] Meeting of 23 November 1939, record reproduced at p. 423 of the Judgment. See also Tomuschat 1996, pp. 1–69.

[19] Meeting of 23 November 1939, record reproduced at p. 425 of the Judgment.

armed resistance, was deemed to have been an annexation, despite the existence, at the time, of "the strong desire expressed in many quarters for the union of Austria and Germany".[20] The Tribunal held that "[t]hese matters, even if true, are really immaterial, for the facts plainly prove that the methods employed to achieve the object were those of an aggressor".[21]

The next step was the planned subjugation of Czechoslovakia:

> On 28th May, 1938, Hitler ordered that preparations should be made for military action against Czechoslovakia by the 2nd October, and from then onwards the plan to invade Czechoslovakia was constantly under review. On 30th May, 1938, a directive signed by Hitler declared his "unalterable decision to smash Czechoslovakia by military action in the near future".[22]

Preparations for the use of force against Czechoslovakia continued throughout the year, and on 14 March 1939, Czechoslovakia's third President Emil Hácha (1872–1945) and Minister for Foreign Affairs František Chvalkovský (1885–1945) were "compelled to sign an agreement consenting to the incorporation of the Czech people in the German Reich", so that Bohemia and Moravia could be "saved from destruction".[23] In view of the issued threat, Hacha and Chvalkovsky consented to the agreement, which was signed on behalf of Germany by Adolf Hitler (1889–1945) and Joachim von Ribbentrop (1893–1946).[24] On 15 March 1939, Bohemia and Moravia were occupied, and on 16 March 1939, Germany issued a decree to the effect of "incorporating them into the Reich as a protectorate".[25] The decree was signed by Joachim von Ribbentrop and Wilhelm Frick (1877–1946).[26]

3.1.1.2 Attack Against Poland (Fall Weiss)

Germany's next declared aim was the Free City of Danzig.[27] The decision to occupy it was taken despite the applicability of an arbitration treaty signed between Germany and Poland in 1925 (see supra 1.1.6.4) and of a bilateral treaty of non-aggression of 26 January 1934,[28] and contrary to a number of Hitler's pub-

---

[20] Ibid., p. 427. See also Garner 1938, pp. 421–438; Wright 1944, pp. 621–635.

[21] International Military Tribunal (Nuremberg), Judgment of 1 October 1946, p. 427.

[22] Ibid., p. 428.

[23] Ibid., p. 429.

[24] Ibid.

[25] Ibid. See also Decree of the Führer and Reich Chancellor concerning the Protectorate of Bohemia and Moravia, 16 March 1939, Document No. 2119-PS, 1939 Reichsgesetzblatt, Part I, p. 485, also available at: http://avalon.law.yale.edu/imt/2119-ps.asp (last accessed 15 November 2012).

[26] International Military Tribunal (Nuremberg), Judgment of 1 October 1946, p. 429.

[27] See generally Giannini 1932.

[28] See International Military Tribunal (Nuremberg), Judgment of 1 October 1946, p. 429. See also the German-Polish Agreement of 26 January 1934, available at: http://avalon.law.yale.edu/wwii/blbk01.asp (last accessed 15 November 2012).

lic assurances to the effect of maintaining pacific relations between Germany and Poland.[29] After the occupation of Bohemia and Moravia—as if in anticipation of further developments—Great Britain and France gave an assurance to Poland, on 31 March 1939, that in the event of any threat or use of force, which would plainly jeopardise Poland's independence, both States would lend Poland "all the support in [their] power".[30] Soon after that, Germany's armed forces received a directive regarding *Fall Weiss* (as the German invasion of Poland was codenamed):

> The Führer has added the following directions to Fall Weiss.
>
> (1) Preparations must be made in such a way that the operation can be carried out at any time from 1st September 1939 onwards.
> (2) The High Command of the Armed Forces has been directed to draw up a precise time-table for Fall Weiss and to arrange by conferences the synchronized timings between the three branches of the armed forces.[31]

On 11 April 1939, Hitler signed a further directive to the armed forces, one of whose annexes read as follows:

> Quarrels with Poland should be avoided. Should Poland, however, adopt a threatening attitude towards Germany, 'a final settlement' will be necessary, notwithstanding the pact with Poland. The aim is then to destroy Polish military strength, and to create in the East a situation which satisfies the requirements of defence. The Free State of Danzig will be incorporated into Germany at the outbreak of the conflict at the latest. Policy aims at limiting the war to Poland, and this is considered possible in view of the internal crisis in France, and British restraint as a result of this.[32]

On 23 May 1939, a conference was held where Hitler exposed his vision of the current political situation and immediate aims, and admitted that the reason for attacking Poland consisted not so much in the Danzig problem but in the need to expand the "Lebensraum":

> The solution of the problem demands courage. The principle by which one evades solving the problem by adapting oneself to circumstances is inadmissible. Circumstances must rather be adapted. This is impossible without invasion of foreign States or attacks upon foreign property [...]
>
> There is therefore no question of sparing Poland, and we are left with the decision to attack Poland at the first suitable opportunity. We cannot expect a repetition of the Czech

---

[29] At p. 430 of the Judgment, the following statement made by Hitler on 20 February 1938 during his address to the Reichstag is quoted: "And so the way to a friendly understanding has been successfully paved, an understanding which, beginning with Danzig, has today, in spite of the attempts of certain mischief-makers, succeeded in finally taking the poison out of the relations between Germany and Poland and transforming them into a sincere, friendly co-operation. Relying on her friendships, Germany will not leave a stone unturned to save that ideal which provides the foundation for the task which is ahead of us – peace". Also, on 30 January 1939, Hitler stated to the Reichstag: "During the troubled months of the past year, the friendship between Germany and Poland has been one of the most reassuring factors in the political life of Europe".

[30] Ibid.

[31] Ibid.

[32] Ibid., pp. 430–431.

> affair. There will be war. Our task is to isolate Poland. The success of the isolation will be decisive [...] The isolation of Poland is a matter of skilful politics.[33]

Hitler was a realist—he understood that Great Britain and France might render military support to Poland. He therefore did not exclude the carrying out of a military campaign in the West of Europe before attacking Poland,[34] and tasked his Foreign Minister Joachim von Ribbentrop with negotiating a non-aggression pact with the Soviet Union (see supra 1.1.6.4). As is evinced by Hitler's recorded statements, his decision to attack Poland ripened by 22 August 1939,[35] and the initial date of the planned attack was 26 August 1939.[36] However, on 25 August, Great Britain signed a mutual assistance pact with Poland, whereby its earlier assurance given to Poland was reinforced.[37] Hitler decided to postpone the immediate invasion of Poland and engaged in a diplomatic game with Great Britain, for the purpose of isolating Poland.[38] As it became apparent that Great Britain and France would enforce their assurances issued to Poland, Hitler ordered, on 31 August 1939, to attack Poland.[39] The Second World War began.

3.1.1.3 Attack Against Denmark and Norway (Operation Weserübung)

On 31 May 1939, Germany signed a non-aggression treaty with Denmark.[40] Despite that the treaty provided that the parties were "firmly resolved to maintain peace between Denmark and Germany under all circumstances",[41] Germany invaded Denmark on 9 April 1940, and the latter surrendered after barely 2 h of attempted resistance. The occupation of Denmark lasted until the withdrawal of the German armed forces following their surrender to the Allies on 5 May 1945.

On the same day, 9 April 1940, Germany also invaded Norway. Hitler's directive of 1 March 1940 ordering the attack against Denmark and Norway

---

[33] Meeting of 23 May 1939, record reproduced at p. 431 of the Judgment.

[34] This is made clear by his statement of 22 August 1939: "It was clear to me that a conflict with Poland had to come sooner or later. I had already made this decision in the spring, but I thought that I would first turn against the West in a few years, and only afterwards against the East [...] I wanted to establish an acceptable relationship with Poland in order to fight first against the West. But this plan, which was agreeable to me, could not be executed since essential points have changed. It became clear to me that Poland would attack us in case of a conflict with the West". Meeting of 22 August 1939, record reproduced at p. 432 of the Judgment.

[35] Ibid., p. 432.

[36] Ibid., p. 433.

[37] Ibid.

[38] Ibid.

[39] Ibid.

[40] For text, see *League of Nations Treaty Series*, volume 197, p. 38.

[41] Quoted in: International Military Tribunal (Nuremberg), Judgment of 1 October 1946, p. 434.

stated that the operation "should prevent British encroachment on Scandinavia and the Baltic".[42] The defence used this very argument during the trial but the Tribunal rejected it, because it regarded preventive action in foreign territory as justified only in case of "an instant and overwhelming necessity for self-defence, leaving no choice of means, and no moment of deliberation".[43] The Tribunal's point of view was sponsored by the content of two memoranda—signed, respectively, by Erich Raeder (1876–1960) on 3 October 1939, and by Karl Dönitz (1891–1980) on 9 October 1939. The first of these memoranda, entitled "Gaining of Bases in Norway", spelled out "the aim of improving [Germany's] strategic and operational position",[44] and it—coupled with records made by Alfred Jodl (1890–1946) in his diary on 13, 14 and 21 March 1939, and with entries in the diary of the Naval Operations Staff on 23 and 26 March 1939[45]—left the Tribunal with no doubt as to the true purpose of the Norwegian operation:

> From all this it is clear that when the plans for an attack on Norway were being made, they were not made for the purpose of forestalling an imminent Allied landing, but, at the most, that they might prevent an Allied occupation at some future date.[46]

3.1.1.4 Attack Against Belgium, The Netherlands and Luxemburg

The plan of attack against Belgium and the Netherlands was crafted in August 1938, at the same time as the Czech operation was being planned (see supra 3.1.1.1).[47] Hitler contemplated the possibility of a future war with Great Britain and France, and Belgium and the Netherlands were considered useful as air bases in the war against the former.[48] Throughout the second half of 1939, Belgium, the Netherlands and Luxemburg were repeatedly assured that Germany would respect their neutrality[49] but military plans were adjusted as the situation was developing. On 23 November 1939, Hitler stated:

> We have an Achilles heel: The Ruhr. The progress of the war depends on the possession of the Ruhr. If England and France push through Belgium and Holland into the Ruhr, we shall be in the greatest danger [...] In Belgium and Holland the sympathies are all for France and England [...] If the French Army marches into Belgium in order to attack us, it will be too late for us. We must anticipate them [...] My decision is unchangeable; I shall attack France and England at the most favourable and earliest moment. Breach of the neutrality of Belgium and Holland is meaningless. No one will question that when we have

42 Quoted ibid., p. 435.

43 Ibid. See also supra 2.4.1.2.

44 Ibid., p. 436.

45 Ibid., pp. 435–436.

46 Ibid., p. 436.

47 Ibid., p. 437.

48 Ibid.

49 Ibid.

> won. We shall not bring about the breach of neutrality as idiotically as in 1914. If we do not break the neutrality, then England and France will. Without attack, the war is not to be ended victoriously.[50]

In line with this reasoning, on 10 May 1940, Germany's armed forces invaded the Netherlands, Belgium, and Luxemburg, and their governments received analogous memoranda whereby they were informed of the alleged reason for invasion, i.e., that the armed forces of Great Britain and France were intending to use their territories for transiting into the Ruhr—an argument that was not accepted by the Tribunal, in view of recorded evidence before it.[51] The Tribunal took note of the assurance given to all three countries to the effect that "their integrity and their possessions would be respected".[52]

3.1.1.5 Attack Against Yugoslavia and Greece (Operation Marita)

On 12 August 1939, Hitler had a meeting with Italian Foreign Minister (and Benito Mussolini's son-in-law) Galeazzo Ciano (1903–1944) at Obersalzberg, during which he said:

> Generally speaking, the best thing to happen would be for the neutrals to be liquidated one after the other. This process could be carried out more easily if on every occasion one partner of the Axis covered the other while it was dealing with the uncertain neutral. Italy might well regard Yugoslavia as a neutral of this kind.[53]

However, Germany's proposal did not immediately meet with Italy's support, and Hitler had to assure Yugoslavia of the inviolability of its frontiers in October 1939—one of many assurances, which were broken as soon as opportune circumstances were ripe.[54] On 28 October 1940, Italy attacked Greece, and next month, Hitler wrote to Benito Mussolini (1883–1945), urging him that no extension of military operations in the Balkans could be envisaged before March 1941.[55] On 18 March 1941, Hitler confirmed his intention to attain the "complete occupation [of Greece as] a prerequisite of any settlement",[56] and on 6 April 1941—the day of Germany's invasion of Greece and Yugoslavia—Hitler declared that the attack against Greece was a reaction to the arrival of Great Britain's armed forces there on 3 March.[57] Yet, the Tribunal concluded—in view of the evidence presented to its attention—that aggressive war against Greece and Yugoslavia had been in the

---

50 Ibid.

51 Ibid., p. 438.

52 Ibid.

53 Ibid.

54 Ibid.

55 Ibid.

56 Quoted ibid., p. 438.

57 Ibid., p. 439.

planning since at least August 1939, and the landing of British troops in Greece in early March 1941 was used as an occasion for the occupation of both countries.[58]

3.1.1.6 Attack Against the USSR (Case Barbarossa)

Undoubtedly, Germany's campaign against the USSR was the most sizeable and costliest—in terms of human and material resources invested on both sides—part of the Second World War.[59] The Nuremberg Tribunal held Germany's war against the Soviet Union to have been one of aggression[60]—which it certainly was—but there exist some serious reasons to believe (which were naturally not examined at Nuremberg) that the Soviet Union itself was preparing carefully for an offensive (not defensive!) war against Germany,[61] and would perhaps have committed an act of aggression, if Germany had not struck first on 22 June 1941. According to an unorthodox opinion—which is not recognised by official historical scholarship, at least, in Russia—the date of the Soviet attack was set for 6 July 1941, and Hitler's strike against the Soviet Union was pre-emptive.[62] This theory does explain exceptionally heavy losses—both human and material—during the first months of the campaign: if the Soviet Union was indeed preparing for offensive military operations, and its defensive facilities had indeed been weakened to the extent alleged by the unconventional historian,[63] then a temporal interval for restoring the country's defensive potential seemed only natural. However unacceptable this theory may appear to a majority of official Soviet and post-Soviet historians, it is not entirely unfounded. The Soviet Union was, in effect, not a pacifist State (cf. supra 1.1.6.6), and it was Germany's only significant military rival in continental Europe—which circumstances allow Germany's allegations of a pre-emptive use of force against the Soviet Union (unlike with regard to smaller and less powerful European nations, which fell victims to Germany's earlier attacks) to look somewhat better corroborated (see supra 3.1.3.1–3.1.3.5).[64] While it remains as a fact that Germany did first attack the Soviet Union on 22 June 1941, and the latter was thus automatically placed in a defensive position, before that, the Soviet Union had annexed Eastern Poland and the Baltic States, in line with the Soviet-German non-aggression pact of 23 August 1939,[65] and was expelled from the League of

---

[58] Ibid.

[59] See Henderson 2011, at p. 321.

[60] See International Military Tribunal (Nuremberg), Judgment of 1 October 1946, pp. 440–441.

[61] See generally Suvorov 2004.

[62] Ibid., pp. 363–364.

[63] Ibid., pp. 95–115.

[64] See International Military Tribunal (Nuremberg), Judgment of 1 October 1946, p. 441. See also Ginsburgs 1958, pp. 69–84; Makarov 1935, pp. 34–60; Makarov 1936, pp. 479–495.

[65] See the Treaty of Non-aggression between Germany and the Soviet Union, 23 August 1939, available at: http://www.fordham.edu/halsall/mod/1939pact.html (last accessed 15 November 2012).

Nations.[66] Germany must—quite rightly—have regarded those developments as a serious menace to herself, and was confirmed to have been making—at least, since 1940—practical arrangements for commencing hostilities against the Soviet Union, in spite of the non-aggression pact.[67]

Notably, Hitler devoted substantial thinking to the attack against the Soviet Union already at the time of writing *Mein Kampf*. A passage in the book is telling:

> If new territory were to be acquired in Europe, it must have been mainly at Russia's cost, and once again the new German Empire should have set out on its march along the same road as was formerly trodden by the Teutonic Knights, this time to acquire soil for the German plough by means of the German sword and thus provide the nation with its daily bread.[68]

The conceptual planning for *Case Barbarossa* was completed in November 1940, and requisite practical preparations must have been completed by 15 May 1941.[69] Hitler's Directive 21 of 18 December 1940 instructed as follows:

> The German armed forces must be prepared to crush Soviet Russia in a quick campaign before the end of the war against England [...] Great caution has to be exercised that the intention of an attack will not be recognized.[70]

The Tribunal acknowledged the individual roles of defendants Alfred Rosenberg (1893–1946), Wilhelm Keitel, Alfred Jodl, Erich Raeder, Walther Funk (1890–1960), Hermann Göring (1893–1946), Joachim von Ribbentrop, and Wilhelm Frick and their associates in devising the political and economic architecture of the occupied Soviet territories—more particularly, in their economic exploitation, mass deportations of the population, murders of political and social leaders, and, ultimately, in the Soviet Union's contemplated partition and annihilation of its statehood.[71] At the conference of 16 July 1941, in which H. Göring, W. Keitel, A. Rosenberg, and Martin Bormann (1900–1945?) participated, Hitler stated:

> There can be no talk of the creation of a military power west of the Urals, even if we should have to fight 100 years to achieve this [...] All the Baltic regions must become part of the Reich. The Crimea and adjoining regions (north of the Crimea) must likewise be incorporated into the Reich. The region of the Volga as well as the Baku district must likewise be incorporated into the Reich. The Finns want Eastern Karelia. However, in view of the large deposits of nickel, the Kola penninsula must be ceded to Germany.[72]

The Nuremberg Tribunal's conclusion with regard to Germany's attack against the Soviet Union was unique in that it comprised a working definition of aggression—

---

[66] See Gross 1945, pp. 35–44.

[67] See International Military Tribunal (Nuremberg), Judgment of 1 October 1946, p. 440.

[68] Quoted ibid., p. 441.

[69] Ibid., p. 440.

[70] Quoted ibid.

[71] Ibid.

[72] Quoted ibid., p. 441.

a keyword of the Tribunal's Charter, which, however, had not been defined either in the Charter or anywhere else in the text of the Judgment. It qualified the attack as "plain aggression" and described it—in the preceding sentence—as a "carefully prepared scheme launched [...] without warning of any kind, and without the shadow of legal excuse".[73] For a note on this "working definition" of aggression, cf. supra 1.2.2.

3.1.1.7 War Against the United States

Germany's declaration of war against the United States on 11 December 1941 was a particular case.[74] As a matter of fact, Germany's hostile acts against the United States did not constitute, either "planning, preparation, initiation or waging of a war of aggression", or "a war in violation of international treaties, agreements or assurances" in the acute sense that was relevant to her other enemies in the Second World War. First, Germany's armed forces did not confront those of the United States until the summer of 1944—that is, until the Allies' landing in Normandy,[75] when the war in Europe has long been at the stage of "waging" (and hence there was a lengthy temporal gap between the "initiation" of Germany's war against the United States and its actual "waging"; this allegedly corresponded to Germany's plans "of the prosecution of the war against America at a later date"[76]). Second, whereas Germany's declaration of war indeed violated one category of applicable "international treaties, agreements or assurances"—such as the Kellogg-Briand Pact (see supra 1.1.6.5)—it did comply with the tripartite pact, concluded by Germany, Italy, and Japan on 27 September 1940, whereby Germany was obliged to give military support to her allies.[77] Hence, the central point of the Judgment with respect to Germany's war against the United States was not about their direct confrontation but about her "encouragement [given to Japan] to adopt a policy which would almost certainly bring the United States into the war".[78] This conclusion is supported by the final sentence in the Judgment's relevant section: "[W]hen Japan attacked the United States fleet in Pearl Harbor and thus made aggressive war against the United States, the Nazi Government caused Germany to enter that war at once on the side of Japan by declaring war themselves on the United States".[79] For a detailed overview of Japan's aggressions in the Second World War, see infra 3.1.2.

---

[73] Ibid.

[74] Ibid., pp. 441–442.

[75] See generally Baxter 1992; Doherty 2004; Neillands 2004.

[76] Quoted in: International Military Tribunal (Nuremberg), Judgment of 1 October 1946, p. 441.

[77] Ibid.

[78] Ibid., p. 442.

[79] Ibid.

3.1.1.8 Observations

The Nuremberg Tribunal's historic achievement was unprecedented: it established the individual criminal responsibility of persons who had been involved in the perpetration of crimes under international law—crimes against peace, war crimes, and crimes against humanity—in the capacity of State organs. In effect, they contributed to the commission of those appalling crimes in the course of accurately performing their official functions—and the Tribunal therefore had to prove that the perpetration of crimes under international law was not a normal function of a State (see supra introductory note to this chapter). Likewise, it was an historic challenge for the Tribunal to condemn wars of aggression not merely as a matter of "wrongfulness" or "illegality" but as one of *criminality*. In other words, the Tribunal confirmed in its Judgment the validity of (then quite recent) treaty-based rules prohibiting an aggressive use of force by one State against another, and bestowed those international legal prohibitions addressed to States with individual criminal sanctions addressed to officials acting as organs of States. In that sense, the Nuremberg Tribunal testified to the formation of an "instant custom"[80] on the subject.

A substantial limitation of the Nuremberg Judgment with respect to aggression consisted in that it only confirmed the criminality of full-scale *wars* of aggression but left out aggressive uses of force of lesser gravity, and this restrictive interpretation of international law would impact upon a number of national legal systems (see infra 4.1.1). However, it must be borne in mind that the Nuremberg Tribunal dealt with the circumstances of a specific armed conflict, and it would be erroneous to regard as "aggression" only armed conflicts of the Second World War's scale and duration. After the Second World War, new rules for maintaining international peace took roots in international law (see supra Chap. 2), which the Nuremberg Tribunal could not have taken into account, and the contemporary legal qualification of aggression must be based upon more recent and progressive standards than ones, which were valid in 1945–1946. In this sense, the development of alternative theories for the criminalization of aggression after the Second World War (see infra 4.1.2–4.1.4) is worthy of approval.

At Nuremberg, all 22 defendants were charged under Article 6(a) of the Tribunal's Charter, and 12 were found guilty of this type of crimes—namely, Hermann Göring,[81] Rudolf Hess,[82] Joachim von Ribbentrop,[83] Wilhelm Keitel,[84]

[80] On "instant custom", see Lukashuk 2008, p. 166.

[81] See Werle 2009b, at p. 408. For an overview of H. Göring's views of the Second World War and his role in it, see Goldensohn 2004, pp. 101–134.

[82] Ibid., pp. 135–136.

[83] Ibid., pp. 182–196.

[84] Ibid., pp. 157–168.

Alfred Rosenberg,[85] Wilhelm Frick,[86] Walther Funk,[87] Karl Dönitz,[88] Erich Raeder, Alfred Jodl,[89] Arthur Seyss-Inquart, and Constantin von Neurath.[90] A few lower-ranking German officials were subsequently charged with crimes against peace under the Control Council Law No. 10 (see infra 3.1.3). It can only be regretted that some figures who would have deserved being in the dock at Nuremberg—such as Adolf Hitler, Benito Mussolini, Joseph Stalin, and their close associates—were missing there, for different reasons. Despite its substantive and procedural deficiencies (see supra 1.2.2), the Nuremberg Tribunal did succeed in punishing, as a minimum, a part of "the accumulated evil" of the Second World War.[91] The German co-authors of this war must have been prepared to accept the liability and punishment for their part in it, for Hitler himself said: "[T]he Right lies in Victory".[92]

3.1.2 Tokyo Judgment

Despite its scholarly critique—some of which might be quite legitimate (see supra 1.2.3)—the Judgment of the International Military Tribunal for the Far East is an exceptionally valuable source of interpretation of aggression as a crime under international law.[93] Itself more than three times as voluminous as the Nuremberg Judgment, the Tokyo Judgment devoted 1079 pages to crimes against peace alone,[94] whereas the Nuremberg Judgment allotted to crimes against peace only 21 pages. This section reproduces—in a fairly succinct manner suitable for the purpose of this book—the Tribunal's interpretation of crimes against peace, and offers some concluding observations.

3.1.2.1 Growing Role of the Military in Japan Before the Second World War

The Tribunal's starting point in the analysis of Japan's aggressive policy before and during the Second World War was the purportedly inherent militarist character of the Japanese nation (cf. supra 1.1.2.2) and the supremacy of the military in the

[85] Ibid., pp. 197–203.

[86] Ibid., pp. 40–46.

[87] Ibid., pp. 76–100.

[88] Ibid., pp. 3–17.

[89] Ibid., pp. 137–138.

[90] Ibid., pp. 169–173.

[91] Cf. International Military Tribunal (Nuremberg), Judgment of 1 October 1946, p. 421.

[92] Quoted ibid., p. 432.

[93] See International Military Tribunal for the Far East, Judgment of 12 November 1948.

[94] Ibid., pp. 48512–49591.

nation's politics ultimately attained by the first half of the twentieth century.[95] It was alleged in the Judgment that Japan's ambition to bring together "the corners of the world under one roof" dated back to as early as 660 BC when the Empire of Japan was founded, and over time, this ambition became ever stronger.[96] In the twentieth century, this idea was developed by Dr. Shūmei Ōkawa (1886–1957) who had originally been among the accused at the Tokyo trial but later the case against him was dropped, due to his purported mental instability.[97] The Judgment summarized Dr. Okawa's views as follows:

> He stated that since Japan was the first state to be created, it was therefore Japan's divine mission to rule all nations. He advocated the Japanese occupation of Siberia and the South Sea Islands. In 1925 and thereafter, he predicted a war between East and West, in which Japan would be the champion of the East. He said, in 1926, that Japan should endeavor to fulfil that sublime mission by developing a strong spirit of nationalism. He had organized a patriotic society which advocated the liberation of the colored races and the moral unification of the world. He had often, at the invitation of the Army General Staff, lectured to them along these lines.[98]

Such views provided an ideological foundation to the Japanese expansion, and the practical role of the military started growing noticeably in 1927–1929, during Giichi Tanaka's (1864–1929) term of office as Prime Minister.[99] This tendency was slowed down under Tanaka's successor, Osachi Hamaguchi (1870–1931)[100] but the military had already largely absorbed Dr. Ōkawa's ideas of establishing, by

---

[95] Cf. ibid., pp. 48513–48514: "The outstanding feature of the period under review [from 1928 onwards] is the gradual rise of the military and their supporters to such a predominance in the government of Japan that no other organ of government, neither the elected representatives of the people, nor the civilian ministers in the Cabinet, nor the civilian advisers of the Emperor in the Privy Council and in his entourage, latterly imposed any effective check on the ambitions of the military. The supremacy of the influence of the military and their supporters in Japanese civilian administration and foreign affairs as well as in purely military concerns was not achieved at once nor without the occurrence of events which threatened its accomplishment, but it was ultimately achieved. The varying fortunes of the protagonists in the political struggle which culminated in the supremacy of the military will be found to provide the explanation of many of the events abroad. Japanese warlike adventures and the preparations therefor ebbed and flowed with the varying fortunes of the political struggle in the Japanese homeland".

[96] Ibid., p. 48514.

[97] See Britannica Online Encyclopedia: http://www.britannica.com/EBchecked/topic/426437/Okawa-Shumei (last accessed 13 November 2012).

[98] International Military Tribunal for the Far East, Judgment of 12 November 1948, pp. 48515–48516.

[99] Ibid., pp. 48516–48517.

[100] The Judgment described these reforms as follows: "Throughout the year 1930 the Hamaguchi Cabinet followed a policy of retrenchment which sharpened the antagonism of the military faction. Smaller budgets were voted for the Army and Navy. The standing Army was reduced in size. The Treaty for Naval Disarmament was ratified in the face of strong opposition. Among young naval officers and in the patriotic societies there was considerable indignation", see p. 48519.

military force, a new State in Manchuria[101] and of "the liberation of the Asiatic peoples",[102] and became so powerful as to actually shape the nation's politics:

> Liberalism had [...] become the chief target of the Army's resentment, and in January 1931 a plot was hatched to overthrow it [...] Although [it] failed, it had set the precedent for later developments. The Army had aroused great public resentment against the advocates of disarmament and liberalism. One such malcontent had assassinated the liberal Premier, Hamaguchi. In some quarters the naval and military reduction program was regarded as an unwarranted interference by the Cabinet with the affairs of the armed forces. The militarists had in a measure succeeded in diverting to their own ends the patriotic sentiment of loyalty to the Emperor.[103]

Observably, that period was marked by unceasing tension between Japan's civilian and military authorities, and the turnover of Prime Ministers was a frequent feature of Japanese politics. Osachi Hamaguchi's successor, Reijiro Wakatsuki (1866–1949) reportedly "expressed concern at the Army's failure to carry out thoroughly the policy of the government".[104] Indeed, it was during his term of office that "[t]he Army had achieved its goal of a war of conquest in Manchuria, and had shown itself to be more powerful than the Japanese Cabinet".[105] The succeeding Prime Minister, Tsuyoshi Inukai (1855–1932)[106] who "extolled democracy and condemned fascism" was murdered in his official residence only after a week in office.[107] This murder effectively marked the end of civilian political control over governmental decisions until after the Second World War. Under the next Prime Minister, Makoto Saitō (1858–1936), the Japanese armed forces were already preparing for war against the Soviet Union (in an official rhetoric at the time, Japan's "absolute enemy" who, according to the Military Affairs Bureau, "aimed to destroy the national structure of Japan"),[108] and for further military operations in China.[109]

---

[101] For a very detailed account of Japan's aggression against China, see pp. 49007–49405 of the Judgment. See also Lauterpacht 1934, pp. 43–60.

[102] International Military Tribunal for the Far East, Judgment of 12 November 1948, pp. 48518–48519.

[103] Ibid., p. 48519.

[104] Ibid., p. 48525.

[105] Ibid., p. 48527.

[106] Ibid., pp. 48528–48529.

[107] Ibid., p. 48531.

[108] Ibid., p. 48536.

[109] Ibid., p. 48532. It was also observed, at p. 48535, as follows: "Soon after the Saito Cabinet had taken office, War Minister ARAKI had announced that, in view of the establishment of Manchukuo, the resolutions of the League of Nations and statements previously made by Japan could no longer be considered binding upon her. The League of Nations in 1931 appointed the Lytton Commission to investigate the circumstances of Japan's intervention in Manchuria. After the report of the Lytton Commission had been received, the League had voiced strong disapprobation of Japanese activities in Manchuria, and in fostering new incidents elsewhere in China. In view of this opposition to her plans, the Saito Cabinet decided, on 17 March 1933, to give notice of Japan's intention to withdraw from the League of Nations; and, 10 days later, that action was taken. Simultaneously steps were taken to exclude foreigners from Japan's mandated Pacific islands. Preparations for war in the Pacific could therefore be made in breach of treaty obligations, and freed from foreign surveillance".

3.1.2.2 Consolidation of "Imperial Way" as Japan's Official Policy

Parallel to the aforesaid events, measures were taken to influence the public opinion within the country, so as to secure, as far as possible, popular support for the war effort[110]:

> In June 1933 War Minister A[raki] made a speech of the utmost significance. In form it was an emotional appeal to the patriotism of the Japanese people, exhorting them to support the Army in a time of crisis. But in it was clearly revealed a settled intention to achieve the armed conquest of East Asia, which A[raki] identified with the traditional goal of Hakko Ichiu.[111]

> In fostering a sentiment for war, he drew liberally upon the political philosophy which Okawa and H[ashimoto] had popularised. Japan, said A[raki], was eternal, and was destined to expand [...]
>
> The path for the people to follow, said A[raki], was the "way of the Emperor", and the Army of Japan was the Emperor's Army. It would therefore fight against anyone who opposed it in its task of spreading the "Imperial Way".
>
> A[raki] also discussed the term "national defence", which was later to become the basic principle of Japanese preparations for war. It was, he said, not limited to the defence of Japan itself, but included also the defence of the "way of the country" [...] He therefore showed clearly that by "national defence" was meant the conquest of other countries through force of arms. In his writings of the same period A[raki ...] reaffirmed once more his country's determination to crush any country which turned against the "Imperial Way".

During the second half of 1933, Sadao Araki's (1877–1966) policy gained an extensive popular support and official recognition in the Cabinet,[112] and continued during the term of office of the next Prime Minister—Keisuke Okada (1868–1952).[113] Next year—parallel to Foreign Minister Kōki Hirota's (1878–1948) efforts to uphold a semblance of friendly relations with the United States[114]—Japan showed that it had a "special position in China"[115]; the Tribunal summarized it as follows:

> It was this divergence of opinion which had necessitated Japan's withdrawal from the League of Nations. Although she desired friendly relations with other countries, Japan would act on her own responsibility in keeping peace and order in East Asia. This responsibility was one which she could not evade; nor could she share it with countries other

[110] Ibid., pp. 48536–48538. See also Williams 1933, pp. 428–439.

[111] The term derives from a statement by Japan's legendary first Emperor Jimmu (seventh century BC): 八紘を掩うて宇と為さん ("Hakkō wo ooute ie to nasan"), meaning: "I shall cover the eight directions and make them my abode".

[112] International Military Tribunal for the Far East, Judgment of 12 November 1948, p. 48538.

[113] Ibid., pp. 48547–48548.

[114] For an analysis of coordination between foreign policy with army planning, see pp. 48545–48547 of the Judgment.

[115] Ibid., p. 48540.

> than China herself. Therefore any attempt by China to avail herself of foreign support in resisting Japan would be opposed.[116]

While Hirota was denying the existence of aggressive intentions against the United States on the part of Japan, the Japanese forces continued operations in the north of China, and in June 1935, China's armed forces had to retreat from the area.[117] In October 1935, it became known that a "virtually autonomous State" should be established there, for the purpose of furthering Japan's "national defence".[118]

The Tribunal summarized the militarist developments in mid-1930s as follows:

> During Okada's period of office many steps had been taken to place the Japanese nation in a state of preparation for war. H[irota], as Foreign Minister, and Nagano, as Japanese delegate to the London Naval Conference, played a major part in the policy which led Japan, in December 1934, to declare her intention of abrogating the Washington Treaty for Limitation of Naval Armaments, and to secede from the London Naval Conference in December of the following year. In the Mandated Islands during the same period, air bases and storage facilities were under construction at various points, and elaborate precautions were being taken to prevent foreign travellers from entering the area.
>
> During the year 1935 also, a strict censorship of news had been instituted under the immediate supervision of the Home Ministry; and newspapers had become little more than vehicles for the dissemination of government-approved propaganda. The police had exerted a large measure of censorship and control over all media of expression of public opinion. In August 1935 the War Ministry had issued regulations designed to investigate the conditions of military training in schools and universities, contribute to its developments and to ensure that the potential military value of the qualifications of graduating students was assessed. Despite repeated protests from the United States, an oil monopoly had been established in Manchuria by the Japanese; and machinery for the exploitation of the natural resources of that country had been provided.
>
> Since October 1935 at the latest the Army had taken an active and independent part in Japanese, foreign policy; for in that month the defendant O[shima], then Military Attache in Berlin, had begun negotiations for a Japanese-German Pact, and had expressed to Von Ribbentrop the desire of the Japanese Army General Staff for a general treaty between the two countries.[119]

On 9 March 1936, Koki Hirota became the country's next Prime Minister, after 30 months in office as Foreign Minister. As the Tribunal noted, "[u]nder this Cabinet the Army's scheme for a new order in East Asia became the settled policy of the Japanese government".[120] On 18 May 1936, the new government enacted an ordinance under which the Navy and War Ministers must be serving officers in the rank not below Lieutenant-General.[121] This reform finally secured the army's influence upon the government, and its outcomes were to be seen in the years to come.

---

116 Ibid.

117 Ibid., p. 48544.

118 Ibid.

119 Ibid., pp. 48549–48551.

120 Ibid., pp. 48553.

121 Ibid.

3.1.2.3 Conference of 11 August 1936

On 11 August 1936, Prime Minister Koki Hirota held a conference with Foreign Minister Hachirō Arita (1884–1965), War Minister Hisaichi Terauchi (1879–1946), and Navy Minister Osami Nagano (1880–1947), at which the framework of Japan's policy for the following years was agreed upon.[122] The key principle of Japan's national policy was to let the country "develop into the stabilisation power, nominal and virtual, in East Asia, secure peace in the Orient and contribute to the peace and welfare of mankind throughout the world".[123] In turn, the principal aim of Japan's foreign policy would consist "in securing a steady footing of [the] empire in the Eastern Continent as well as developing in the South Seas, under the joint efforts of diplomatic still and national defence".[124] This would certainly require extensive economic resources, which were to be acquired largely at the expense of the economic exploitation of North China.[125] The second principle concerned the future military planning: "In order to secure the stability of our Empire and to safeguard its development so as to acquire the position of the real stabilisation power in East Asia, nominally and virtually, we are to complete our defensive armament".[126] Under the third principle, Japan "should [have] strive[d] to eradicate the Russian menace on the North, in order to realise a steadfast development of Manchuria, and for the solid defence of both Japan and Manchuria",[127] and "should also [have] be[en] prepared for Britain and America, attempting at the same time an economic development by the close cooperation of Japan, China and Manchuria".[128] The last principle was phrased with noticeable caution: "For the furtherance of our plan to achieve the social and economic development of our Empire toward the South Seas, especially in the outer South Seas Islands Areas, we should take a gradual and peaceful measure, always avoiding to stimulate other nations, and try to fulfil our national strength correlative with the completion of Manchuria".[129] In the opinion of the Tribunal[130]:

> The statement of basic national policy which the Five Ministers adopted on 11 August 1936 expressed Japan's determination, not only to achieve the domination of East Asia, but also to extend her influence southwards. This expansion [...] would, if possible, be achieved peacefully; but the threat of military strength would be used to ensure diplomatic victories [...]
>
> It was frankly acknowledged that this policy could succeed only if backed by a vast plan of mobilization for war. It was agreed that the goal of naval expansion should be a force large

---

[122] Ibid., p. 48554.

[123] Quoted ibid.

[124] Quoted ibid., p. 48555.

[125] Ibid., p. 48556.

[126] Quoted ibid.

[127] Quoted ibid., p. 48557.

[128] Quoted ibid.

[129] Quoted ibid.

[130] Ibid., pp. 48559–48560.

> enough to secure to Japan the command of the Western Pacific against the United States Navy[131]; and that the goal of military expansion must be the creation of a fighting machine strong enough to inflict a crushing blow upon the strongest force which the Soviet Union could deploy upon its Eastern borders. It was recognized that these objectives in turn demanded the institution of a comprehensive programme for industrial development and self-sufficiency[132]; and that every phase of the lives of the Japanese people must be so directed and controlled[133] as best to prepare them to play their parts in a period of expected national emergency.[134]

In the following months, the influence of the military upon Japan's national and foreign policies continued growing.[135] In July 1937, Japan started a war against China,[136] and 1938–1939 saw intensive preparations for war with the Soviet Union.[137]

3.1.2.4 National General Mobilization Law

On 5 May 1938, a National General Mobilisation Law was enacted by an Imperial Ordinance.[138] An emergency law, in the words of the Tribunal, it:

> [...] could be extended to cover any and every type of product, raw material and enterprise. It gave the Cabinet virtually unlimited powers to conscript materials, and to control industry and companies. Under its provisions the government might expropriate lands and buildings; authorize the payment of subsidies and compensation; enforce stabilization measures; prevent the publication of information; and direct the occupational training and education of the Japanese people. Above all, it might direct and conscript the manpower of the nation [...]
>
> The provisions of the mobilization law serve to emphasize the many-sidedness and all-embracing nature of Japanese preparations for war [...] Every aspect of the national life was to be so ordered and controlled as to produce the maximum pitch of warlike efficiency. The entire strength of the Japanese nation was to be harnessed and developed with this single end in view [...][139]

On 19 May 1938, 2 weeks after the enactment of the National General Mobilization Law, a commentary with respect to its aims was published.[140] The commentary's careful wording (as summarized in the Judgment) addressed various

---

[131] For an overview of naval expansion under Prime Minister Hirota, see pp. 48578–48579 of the Judgment.

[132] For an overview of economic and industrial preparations for war, see pp. 48563–48565 of the Judgment.

[133] For a note on plans to control public opinion during the war, see p. 48566 of the Judgment. For an overview of censorship and the dissemination of propaganda, see pp. 48589–48592 of the Judgment.

[134] For an overview of military training at schools and universities, see pp. 48587–48589 of the Judgment.

[135] See pp. 48593 ff. of the Judgment, especially pp. 48607–48614, 48618–48620.

[136] Ibid., pp. 48629–48638.

[137] Ibid., pp. 48668–48671.

[138] Ibid., p. 48701.

[139] Ibid., pp. 48701–48703.

[140] Ibid., p. 48703.

aspects of public life, now to be restructured, and, in the opinion of the Tribunal, left no doubts as to future developments:

> Japan [...] was a country small in area and lacking in natural resources. She faced not only the determined resistance of Generalissimo Chiang Kai-shek in China but also Soviet armies, fully mobilized and bent upon aggression in the north. Moreover, she was surrounded by the powerful navies of the United States and of Great Britain [...]
>
> Nothing less than complete mobilization of all resources of material and manpower would suffice. Military success would depend chiefly upon the systematic and effective mobilization of the "synthetic national strength". This the National General Mobilization Law was designed to achieve [...]
>
> Manpower would be mobilised in order to adjust the demand and supply of labour; so that, as young men were called to the colours, their places in industry would be filled [...]
>
> Production of war materials at home would be increased at the expense of peacetime industries. Therefore, all producing enterprises, as well as import and export businesses, would be unified under government direction.
>
> The government [...] would unify and develop all transportation facilities. It would mobilise science so that the pitch of efficiency might be raised. It would assume responsibility for the collection of information and the dissemination of propaganda at home and abroad, seeking to foster morale and to unify opinion in Japan, while creating a favourable impression in other countries.
>
> The government would also equip itself with long-range flexible plans to meet the varying needs of a general mobilisation, so that the Army and Navy would always be adequately supplied [...] Private enterprises would be required to conform to the plans prepared [...] A National General Mobilisation Research Commission and various semi-official bodies would be created to administer the law. These, and some self-governing bodies, would assist the government both in the formulation and in, the execution of Cabinet policy.[141]

In the Tribunal's opinion, the enactment of the National General Mobilisation Law testified to the reality that "the Army had made itself the master of Japan's destiny",[142] and the Japanese nation was now ready for "aggrandisement through expansion of military power",[143] in spite of a severe economic and financial crisis, which struck the country's economy in May 1938.[144] In this light, Japan had to revise its plans of attacking the Soviet Union,[145] and took measures for reinforcing alliances with Germany and Italy.[146] Although those alliances were chiefly

[141] Ibid., pp. 48703–48706.

[142] Ibid., p. 48706.

[143] Ibid., p. 48707.

[144] Ibid., pp. 48711–48718.

[145] Ibid., pp. 48730–48734.

[146] Ibid., pp. 48742–48745, 48772–48783, 48832–48852, 48857–48860, 48863a–48865. On 4 May 1939, Prime Minister Kiichiro Hiranuma sent a personal note ("Hiranuma Declaration") to Hitler, in which he "expressed his admiration for Hitler's work in Germany, and advised that he was similarly engaged in the work of maintaining Japan's "New Order in East Asia". H[iranuma] expressed his satisfaction with the effect of the Anti-Comintern Pact in making possible the execution of the tasks which Germany and Japan had before them. He said that he now had in view the conclusion of an agreement which would strengthen the Anti-Comintern Pact and make closer the cooperation of Germany, Italy and Japan". See p. 48843 of the Judgment.

directed against the Soviet Union,[147] they also had an adverse effect upon Japan's relations with Western States,[148] which continued deteriorating throughout 1938.[149] At the same time, Japan severed her remaining relations with the League of Nations.[150] However, the conclusion of a Soviet-German non-aggression pact (see supra 1.1.6.4) in August 1939 brought about the end of the Hiranuma Cabinet,[151] which made possible—for a while—"the pursuit of a *modus vivendi* with the Western Powers".[152]

3.1.2.5 Japan Before the Pacific War

On 30 August 1939, General Nobuyuki Abe (1875–1953) was appointed as Prime Minister, and his Cabinet did not contain any single member of the previous administration.[153] The Tribunal observed that "[t]he foreign policy of the new Cabinet was to be that of cooperation with Great Britain and the United States",[154] and yet "the desire for better relations with the Western Powers implied no abandonment of the good of Japanese domination of China. This was the basic tenet of Japanese national policy. The Abe Cabinet desired the acceptance by the Western Powers of the "new order" in East Asia which Japan had created".[155] This inconsistency in foreign policy created new tensions between Japan and the West. Only 4 months later, in January 1940, the Abe Cabinet stepped down, and "with its resignation, the policy of fostering more friendly relations with the Western Powers was abandoned".[156]

The new Prime Minister was Admiral Mitsumasa Yonai (1880–1948) whose Cabinet adhered, during the first half of 1940, "to the policy of non-intervention in the European War, so that the full strength of the nation might be directed to the task of securing Japan's position in China, and of completing Japan's measures for

147 Ibid., pp. 48735–48738.

148 Ibid., pp. 48784–48786.

149 Ibid., pp. 48786–48792.

150 Ibid., pp. 48794–48797.

151 Ibid., pp. 48865–48868. The Tribunal summarized this development as follows: "The Cabinet's policy [...] had been completely discredited. Cabinet and nation had looked to Germany as an ally against the U.S.S.R. The Cabinet had from its very inception been pledged to achieving a more intimate relationship between Japan and the Axis powers. After meeting on 28 August 1939 and acknowledging the failure of their policy, the H[iranuma] Cabinet resigned en bloc". See pp. 48867–48868 of the Judgment.

152 Ibid., p. 48868.

153 Ibid.

154 Ibid., p. 48869.

155 Ibid., p. 48870.

156 Ibid., p. 48885.

war".[157] On 28 March 1940, War Minister Shunroku Hata (1879–1962) made a statement at the Budget Committee meeting to the effect that:

> [T]he Army was determined to uphold the policy of non-intervention in Europe, until Japan's own position had been consolidated [...] In order that the war in China might be settled there would be no change in Japan's policy, which was to concentrate her whole strength upon excluding any third power which interfered persistently with the establishment of Japan's "new order" in East Asia. H[ata] also made it clear that the Army regarded the policy of non-intervention purely as a matter of expediency.[158]

At the same time, Japan recognised her acute need for raw materials:

> The very reasons which led Japan to seek new sources of essential raw materials restrained her from provoking an immediate breach with the Western Powers from whose territories she was deriving important supplies of these materials [...]
>
> On 3 March 1940 there was formulated a policy which, taking cognisance of Japan's dependence upon the United States, set out measures through which Japan could eliminate her reliance upon that country [...] This secret Foreign Ministry document discloses an intention to revise the whole programme of economic and industrial expansion in order to achieve self-sufficiency in the essential materials of war and in order to establish an economic system which would make Japan independent of the goodwill of the United States. The new plan called for a vast expansion in the manufacture of machine tools, for experimentation with substitute materials for the production of "special steel", and for alternative sources for the supply of scrap iron, petroleum and other war materials [...][159]

In line with the abovementioned policy, on 17 March 1940, plans for southward expansion were discussed at a session of the Budget Committee. A member of the Committee (unnamed in the Judgment) "pointed out that Japan could find a treasure-chest of raw materials in the south, and took as instances the island of Mindanao in the Philippines and Celebes in the Netherlands East Indies. He advocated the seizure of these areas, though recognizing that this step could not at present be taken. Nevertheless he urged a fundamental change in national policy, saying that Japan must have both the North and the South as her objectives, and that her greatest exertions should be directed towards the south".[160] This view was backed by the Overseas Ministry,[161] and on 15 April 1940, Japan's intention to maintain "economic bonds" with "the regions of the South Seas, and especially with the Netherlands East Indies" was officially voiced by Foreign Minister Arita at a press conference.[162] Although phrased in diplomatic terms, this statement appeared to imply Japan's readiness to employ force, if need be, to preserve those "economic bonds".[163]

---

157 Ibid., p. 48892.

158 Ibid., p. 48896.

159 Ibid., pp. 48898–48902.

160 Ibid., pp. 48903–48904.

161 Ibid., p. 48904.

162 Ibid., p. 48905.

163 Ibid. Arita's statement prompted the Netherlands, the United States, Great Britain, France and Germany to assure Japan of their intention not to intervene in the Netherlands East Indies. See pp. 48913–48915, 48916–48919 of the Judgment.

As Japan's principal European ally, Germany, was putting into practice its aggressive policies in Europe (see supra 3.1.1), and Japan was contemplating equivalent developments in the Far East, the United States became concerned about the sphere of its own influence in that part of the world:

> Ambassador Grew was instructed to suggest to Arita that Japan and the United States should exchange notes declaring their common desire to maintain the status quo in regard to the Pacific possessions of the belligerent European Powers, except in as far as that status might be changed by peaceful means [...]
>
> On 24 June 1940 Grew made this proposal to Arita in strict confidence, making it clear, however, that the United States had not retreated from the stand taken upon other specific issues [...]
>
> Arita, being uncertain of Germany's attitude towards Japan, regarded this United States proposal as an extremely delicate matter [...]
>
> He referred to the pro-German trend of public opinion in Japan, and said that, although he was himself in favour of a rapprochement with the United States, that view had exposed him to severe criticism. Nevertheless he undertook to give the proposal careful consideration.
>
> On 28 June 1940 Foreign Minister Arita made Japan's reply to the United States proposal. He told Ambassador Grew that, in view of the existing international situation, he doubted whether consideration could be given to a formal exchange of notes on the basis which the United States had suggested. Japan [...] was greatly concerned with the effect which the European War would have upon the status of the Pacific possessions of the European belligerents [and therefore] did not consider it desirable to conclude any sort of agreement during the present transitionary period.[164]

It was soon to become clear why Foreign Minister Arita responded to Ambassador Joseph Grew (1880–1965) as he did. On 29 June 1940, the next day after turning down the United States' proposal, Arita delivered a speech, well summarized in the Judgment, in which he explained the importance of acting in accord with Germany:

> [Arita] made it apparent that the two nations shared a common philosophy, saying that Japan's ideal since the founding of the Empire had been that all nations should be able to find their proper places in the world. Japan's foreign policy [...] had been based upon this ideal, for which she had not hesitated to fight, even by staking her national existence [...]
>
> The conflict in Europe [...] had shown that war was usually due to failure to remedy the injustices of the existing order. It was for this reason that Japan had undertaken the task of constructing a "new order" in East Asia [...]
>
> Arita concluded his speech by admonishing the Western Powers against interference in his country's schemes [...] He stated that Japan [...] was paying serious attention [...] to the repercussions of the European War in the various regions of East Asia and the South Seas. The destiny of these regions was [...] a matter of grave concern to Japan "in view of her mission and responsibility as the stabilizing power in East Asia".[165]

Soon after this speech, Japan approached Germany with a proposal for a closer cooperation. On 8 July 1940, special envoy Naotake Satō (1882–1971), together with Japan's Ambassador to Berlin Saburō Kurusu (1886–1954), met Germany's

---

[164] Ibid., pp. 48930–48932.

[165] Ibid., pp. 48932–48934.

Foreign Minister Joachim von Ribbentrop, in order to secure German support for the incumbent Cabinet.[166] Von Ribbentrop—being, on the one hand, confident of German successes in Europe and, on the other hand, indubitably being aware of political instability within Japan—replied vigilantly:

> [Von Ribbentrop] welcomed Japan's desire for co-operation with Germany, but gave the impression that Germany, being now confident of victory in Europe, no longer attached great importance to assistance from Japan. He declared that new opportunities for co-operation would arise in the future, but declined to say anything more definite upon the grounds that he was unfamiliar with Japan's political aims.[167]

Following this meeting, on 12 July 1940, Japan's Foreign Ministry presented the first draft of a new plan whose principles should govern Japan's policy until her more direct confrontation with the Western Powers:

> Japan on the one hand and Germany and Italy upon the other would act in concert and in close co-operation within their respective spheres of influence. It would be agreed among the Axis countries that in South East Asia and in the South Pacific area Japan should enjoy the same freedom of action which Germany and Italy had arrogated to themselves in Europe [...]
>
> The coalition between [Japan and Germany] would provide each with added security against Soviet interference with their aggressive schemes. German economic assistance would enable Japan to reduce her dependency upon the United States, and Japan would ensure that Germany received from East Asia those raw materials of which she stood most urgently in need.[168]

This was the last essential governmental decision taken under Prime Minister Yonai, because on 16 July 1940, after 6 months in office, his Cabinet resigned, and Fumimaro Konoye (1891–1945) who had already held the office in 1937–1939 became the next Prime Minister. On 26 July 1940, 4 days after its formation, the new Cabinet announced its policy, which basically continued the line of the national policy decision of 11 August 1936 (see supra 3.1.2.3),[169] and sought to complete the domination of the military within Japan:

> It was stated that the world was now on the threshold of an historic change, and that new political, economic and cultural orders were in process of creation [...]
>
> It was declared that, if Japan were to act in accordance with the great ideal of Hakko Ichiu, the system of government must be fundamentally revised and the "national defence" structure of the state completed [...] For that purpose she would increase her armaments and would mobilize the entire strength of the nation. Japan would first concentrate upon a successful settlement of the war in China.
>
> By adopting a flexible policy she would plan and prepare to take advantage of changes in the world situation in order to advance her own national fortunes.[170]

[166] Ibid., p. 48946.

[167] Ibid., p. 48948.

[168] Ibid., pp. 48950–48951.

[169] See pp. 48977–48979 of the Judgment.

[170] Ibid., p. 48964.

On 27 July 1940, the practical arrangements for implementing this policy were discussed at the Liaison Conference—a new body, which permitted the military to directly participate in the Cabinet's decision-making.[171] The authority of the new body was superlative, as its composition included the army, navy and five key Ministers of the Cabinet, and practically surpassed that of the Imperial Conference, which would henceforth do "little more than accord formal approval to decisions already reached by the Liaison Conference".[172]

The new Konoye Cabinet's next success was that, on 9–11 September 1940, Germany's special envoy Heinrich Georg Stahmer (1892–1978) negotiated with Japan the terms of her alliance with Germany and Italy. At last, consultations, which lasted over years, materialised in concrete assurances:

> Germany, declared Stahmer, recognized and respected Japan's political leadership in East Asia. All that Germany required in that area was of an economic nature. She would collaborate with Japan, and would expect Japan to meet her economic needs [...]
>
> On [...] 27 September 1940, the Tripartite Alliance was concluded [...] The preamble to the Tripartite Alliance recited the resolve of the contracting powers to establish "new orders" in Europe and in Asia respectively; and their determination to assist one another in so doing. The instrument provided that Germany and Italy would respect Japanese leadership in Asia, and that Japan would respect German and Italian leadership in Europe. The three countries pledged their mutual cooperation, the details of which were to be settled by a specialized joint commission appointed for the purpose. If any contracting power should be attacked by any country not presently engaged in the European War or in the war in China, the other parties to the alliance would render political, economic and military assistance.
>
> Germany and Italy would confirm that the alliance would have no effect upon the present relations between the Soviet Union and any signatory power. The alliance would remain in force for 10 years, and provision was made for its renewal.[173]

The Tribunal was unequivocal in its assessment of the Tripartite Alliance as a manifestation of its authors' aggressive state of mind (on the crime of aggression's *mens rea* under customary international law, see infra 4.5):

> In summary, the Tripartite Pact was a compact made between aggressor nations for the furtherance of their aggressive purposes. Its true character was well revealed when one Privy Councillor asked how the statement contained in the Preamble of the Pact that each nation should have its proper place in the world could be reconciled with Hitler's principle that only the strongest should survive. Prime Minister Konoye, Foreign Minister Matsuoka, and War Minister T[ojo] answered jointly that only the strong nations were worthy of survival [...]
>
> The decisions of the leaders of Japan, which followed the downfall of the Yonai Cabinet, are of outstanding importance [...] They show that the conspirators were determined to extend the domination of Japan over a huge area and population and to use force, if necessary, to accomplish their aims. They show by plain admission that the purpose of the conspirators in entering into the Tripartite Pact was to secure support for the accomplishment of these illegal aims. They show that notwithstanding the seeming defensive

[171] See pp. 48980–48981 of the Judgment. On the significance of the Liaison Conferences, see also pp. 49434–49435 of the Judgment.

[172] Ibid., p. 48968.

[173] Ibid., pp. 48995–49001.

> terms of the Tripartite Pact, which were designed for publication, the obligations of the parties to support one another were expected to come into force if one of the parties became engaged in war whether defensive or aggressive. They wholly refute the contention of the defence that the purpose of the Tripartite Pact was to promote the cause of peace.[174]

In a subsequent chapter of the Judgment, the Tribunal was even more explicit in submitting that the conclusion of the Pact was an important step, which "contributed directly to the launching of the Pacific War on 8th December 1941".[175]

3.1.2.6 War in the Pacific

Less than a month after the conclusion of the Tripartite Pact, on 4 October 1940, Prime Minister Konoye made a press statement to the effect that "if the United States refused to understand the real intentions of Japan, Germany and Italy and continued its challenging attitude and acts, both the United States and Great Britain would be forced into war with Japan, meaning that Japan would be compelled to go to war with them [...] Japan was manoeuvering, diplomatically to induce the U.S.S.R., Great Britain and the United States to suspend aid to China".[176]

This statement was sufficient for the United States to reinforce its embargo upon exports of raw materials, which could be used for war purposes:

> A Presidential Proclamation was issued extending to all iron and steel scrap, except to the Western Hemisphere and Great Britain, the embargoes imposed in 1938 and 1939 in protest against Japan's disregard of treaties [...] The embargo was extended and placed under a licensing system on 10th December 1940. Copper, brass, zinc, bronze, nickel, and potash were added to the embargo list on 3rd February 1941. Scrap rubber was added on 5th May 1941. By 20th June 1941 the situation had so deteriorated that all petroleum exports from the United States were banned, except to Great Britain and South America.[177]

In the following months, organizational measures were taken to strengthen the nation's military preparedness. A series of appeals for popular support of the war policy were issued, and, on 30 September 1940, the Total War Research Institute was established by Imperial Ordinance as an official governmental body[178]:

> The ordinance provided that the Institute should be under the Prime Minister and control basic study and research in connection with national total war as well as with the education and training of officials and others to wage total war [...] Each Ministry of the Government was represented in the Institute [...] Students were selected from every branch and department of the country's activities. Lectures were delivered, studies or exercises were conducted. The Institute complied research reports on important subjects which were useful in planning total war.[179]

---

[174] Ibid., pp. 49005–49006.

[175] Ibid., p. 49410.

[176] Ibid., p. 49412.

[177] Ibid., pp. 49412–49413.

[178] Ibid., pp. 49417–49422.

[179] Ibid., pp. 49422–49423.

By early 1941, the Total War Research Institute was in active operation and compiled reports on such subjects as "The Estimate of the Domestic and Foreign Situation from the Total War Viewpoint", "Study of Total War Pertaining to the National Strength of Imperial Japan and the Foreign Powers", "Draft of the Plan for the Establishment of Greater East Asia", and "First Phase in the Total War Plan".[180]

At the time, Japan was already contemplating her attack against Singapore and the use of the territories of the French Indo-China and Thailand to that end.[181] In accordance with an armistice between Thailand and France, signed on 31 January 1941, Japan was authorized to supervise its implementation, until the conclusion of a formal peace treaty.[182] The treaty was made on 9 May 1941, significantly to the benefit of Japan, because it provided for the cessation of a territory to Thailand and for the establishment of the border along the Mekong River—an outcome that was anticipated in Japan since at least November 1940.[183] On 1 August 1941, Foreign Minister Yōsuke Matsuoka (1880–1946) summoned the French Ambassador and declared "that France should allow Japanese troops to be stationed in Northern French Indo-China and the right to establish air bases there for action against the National Government of China".[184] On 25 August, France agreed to Japan's demand, and the so-called Matsuoka-Henri Agreement, consisting of an exchange of letters, was signed on 30 August 1940:

> According to the Matsuoka-Henri Agreement, the occupation of French Indo-China was to be temporary as it was stated to be solely for action against China and would be limited to Tonkin Province [...]
>
> The arrangements for the establishment of air bases and the passage of Japanese troops into Tonkin Province were left for negotiation between the head of the Japanese Military Mission at Hanoi and the Governor-General of French Indo-China.[185]

Meanwhile, preparations for the attack against Singapore continued intensively:

> Aerial photography was undertaken in January 1941 to collect data for the landing operations at Kota Bharu. Additional mapping of that area was completed by the Japanese Hydrographic Office in July 1941. The maps were completed and printed by the Naval General Staff in early October 1941.
>
> The War Ministry, in conjunction with the Finance Ministry, as early as January 1941 commenced preparing military currency for use in the areas which they expected the Japanese troops to occupy in the advance to the South [...] The military currency thus prepared consisted of dollars which were suitable for use in Malaya, Borneo and Thailand; guilders for use in the Netherlands East Indies; and pésos for the Philippines [...]
>
> Military topographical data was being assembled for military operations in various parts of the world. Espionage activities in the Netherlands East Indies were being carried out

[180] Ibid., p. 49442.

[181] Ibid., pp. 49431–49434.

[182] On the conflict between the French Indo-China and Thailand, see pp. 49428–49431 of the Judgment.

[183] See p. 49434 of the Judgment.

[184] Ibid., p. 49448.

[185] Ibid., p. 49449.

> increasingly. Operations were being planned against Java, Sumatra, Bali and other places as well as Singapore. Mandated Islands were being fortified and plans were being completed for operations in the South Seas. Data were being assembled for use in Burma and Malaya. The work of printing military script for use in the occupation of southern areas continued.[186]

Initially, an attack against Singapore had been planned for the spring of 1941[187] but then Japan took a practical decision to conclude a non-aggression pact with the USSR, before proceeding any further. This move caused a wave of discontent in Germany but Japan followed its line:

> An important question was the time for the attack upon Singapore. The Germans urged its immediate commencement, but the Konoye Cabinet's policy from the beginning [...] had contemplated a Non-Aggression Pact with the U.S.S.R. to protect the Japanese rear during the attack upon Singapore and the Netherlands East Indies. Hitler insisted in his conversation with Matsuoka on 27 March 1941 [...] that a better opportunity to begin the attack than the present would newer occur again. Matsuoka replied that it was only a matter of time before Japan would attack as the Japanese had the feeling that otherwise she would lose a chance which might only return after a thousand years [...] The next day Ribbentrop tried to discourage Matsuoka from concluding the Pact with the U.S.S.R., stating that Japan should attack Singapore immediately and that if the U.S.S.R. interfered, Germany would attack the U.S.S.R. immediately. Ribbentrop repeated that assurance the following day. Matsuoka maintained his intention to visit Moscow on his return from Berlin and he concluded the Pact with the U.S.S.R. on the 13th of April 1941.[188]

In fact, Japan did not invade Singapore until February 1942, when the war in the Pacific already was well in progress.[189]

From early 1941, Japan was attempting to eliminate the threat of the United States Pacific Fleet by means of concluding a non-aggression pact with the United States:

> The suggestion was that [...] Japan should guarantee the security of the Philippines and Guam and the United States of America should recognize the Co-Prosperity Sphere. Preparation for an attack upon the United States forces was to proceed during the negotiations, so that in case the negotiations should fail, a surprise attack might be launched.
>
> A plan to destroy the United States Pacific Fleet while it lay at anchor in Pearl Harbor by a surprise attack to be launched while the United States was at peace with Japan was conceived and submitted to the Commander of the Combined Fleets for study. He approved the plan and transmitted it to the Imperial General Headquarters as early as January 1941. The plan called for the organization of a task force to deliver an aerial attack upon the United States Pacific Fleet at Pearl Harbor. To avoid detection and make the surprise complete, this force was to use a northern route little used by commercial shipping. In conjunction with the aerial attack, it was planned to use submarines to destroy any ships that might attempt to escape the [...] attack [...] The Japanese leaders considered that if the attack upon Pearl Harbor should be successful and result in the

---

[186] Ibid., pp. 49441–49442, 49445.

[187] Ibid., p. 49442.

[188] Ibid., pp. 49446–49447.

[189] Cf. pp. 49476–49477 of the Judgment: "It was feared by many of the Japanese leaders that this fleet might be used to reinforce Singapore, and they advocated an immediate attack upon Singapore to prevent this. The Japanese Navy, however, was demanding that more oil and other vital supplies be accumulated and that adequate preparations be made for replenishing those supplies before launching the attack upon Singapore".

> destruction of the United States Fleet, they would be able to seize all the important points in the Pacific and Indian Oceans [...] It was hoped then that the United States would weary of a prolonged and costly war and negotiate a peace which would recognize Japan's supremacy in the territories it would have seized.[190]

Negotiations between Japan and the United States continued throughout 1941.[191] Meanwhile, already in May 1941, the Japanese navy began training for the attack on Pearl Harbor:

> Dive bombing was practiced at Kagoshima, Japan, where the terrain resembled that at Pearl Harbor. The development of a shallow water torpedo had been started early in 1941 as the waters in Pearl Harbor were shallow [...] Refueling at sea was made a matter of special training in order to permit the use of the more secure northern route of approach to Pearl Harbor.[192]

In July and August 1941, it became apparent that Japan had difficulties with supplies of oil and other war materials, and there arose differences between Japan's army and navy regarding how to better remedy the deficit:

> The Navy had expected to obtain oil from Sakhalin and the Netherlands East Indies to replenish its supply in case the war should be prolonged. Now there was a possibility that the U.S.S.R. would become allied with the United States thus preventing the acquisition of oil from Sakhalin [...] The Army did not agree with the Navy and maintained that the accumulated supply of oil would be sufficient to ensure victory. [Prime Minister] Konoye [...] agreed that the situation was serious and that it was necessary to have an agreement between the Army and Navy without loss of time.[193]

The progressing disagreements within the Cabinet, though, led to its resignation on 16 October 1941:

> Konoye collected the letters of resignation of his Ministers on the morning of the 16th October 1941 and adding his own delivered them to the Emperor [...]
>
> Konoye's letter of resignation gives a vivid explanation of the situation. He explained that, when he organized the Third Konoye Cabinet to prosecute the expansion to the South, it was his firm conviction that his Cabinet's objective would be obtained through negotiations with the United States Government [...] Konoye said that T[ojo] had been demanding that war be commenced with the United States on 15th October in accordance with the decision of the Imperial Conference of 6th September and had given as his reason that the situation had come to a point when no other means could be found to obtain the Japanese demands. Konoye declared that it was impossible for him to accept the responsibility for plunging the Nation again into a titanic war the outcome of which could not be forecast.[194]

The next Prime Minister—who was to remain in office throughout the major part of the Second World War—war Hideki Tojo (1884–1948). He was promoted to General on 18 October 1941 and remained on active duty during his term of office

---

190 Ibid., pp. 49477–49479.

191 Ibid., pp. 49475–49498, 49508–49511, 49513–49522, 49525–49529, 49542–49548, 49550–49564, 49567–49569.

192 Ibid., p. 49498.

193 Ibid., pp. 49512–49513.

194 Ibid., pp. 49534–49535.

as Prime Minister and, simultaneously, as War Minister. He held both offices during the entire term of his Cabinet.[195]

On 5 November 1941, the Chief of the Naval General Staff ordered Admiral Isoroku Yamamoto (1884–1943), the Commander of Japan's Combined Fleet, to issue a Combined Fleet Operation Order, which provided for advancing southwards by attacking Singapore and the Philippines.[196] An attack upon Pearl Harbor was to cover those attacks.[197] The order read:

> The Empire is expecting war to break out with the United States, Great Britain and the Netherlands […] The time for outbreak of war (X-Day) will be given in an Imperial General Headquarters Order. This order will be given several days in advance. After 0000 h, X-Day, a state of war will exist. Each force will commence operations according to plan.[198]

Combined Fleet Operation Order No. 3 of 10 November 1941 fixed 8 December as "X-Day".[199] On 30 November, the Liaison Conference discussed the planned attack on Pearl Harbor and decided that there would be no declaration of war.[200] The Conference also agreed upon the form and substance of a verbal note regarding the rupture of negotiations with the United States, and discussed the terms of its delivery.[201] The Imperial Conference convened on 1 December 1941 to endorse the decisions taken in favour of war at the Liaison Conference the day before.[202] On 7 December 1941, the note addressed to the United States began arriving in Washington. It was transmitted in several parts.[203] President Franklin Delano Roosevelt (1882–1945) immediately sent a personal message to Emperor Hirohito (1901–1989), but this ultimate effort failed, as the message did not reach the Emperor before 00:00 of 8 December.[204] Japan's attack upon Kota Bharu began at 1:25 am and upon Pearl Harbor at 3:20 am (Tokyo time).[205] It was the beginning of Japan's war against the United States and its allies.[206]

---

[195] Ibid., p. 49536.

[196] Ibid., p. 49548.

[197] Ibid.

[198] Ibid., pp. 49548–49549.

[199] Ibid., p. 49550.

[200] Ibid., p. 49564.

[201] It was agreed that the delivery of the note should not be permitted to destroy the element of surprise in the attack. See ibid. See also Hill 1948, pp. 355–367.

[202] International Military Tribunal for the Far East, Judgment of 12 November 1948, pp. 49565–49566.

[203] Ibid., pp. 49567–49568.

[204] Ibid., p. 49568.

[205] Ibid., pp. 49568–49569.

[206] On 10 November 1941 Britain's Prime Minister Winston Churchill stated in a speech he gave in London: "We do not know whether the efforts of the United States to preserve peace in the Pacific will be successful. But, if they fail, I take this occasion to say—and it is my duty to say—that should the United States be involved in a war with Japan, a British declaration will follow within an hour". See pp. 49550–49551 of the Judgment. See also Stowell 1942, pp. 87–89; Woolsey 1942, pp. 77–83.

3.1.2.7 Observations

The International Military Tribunal for the Far East was by far more meticulous in documenting and analyzing the aggressive policies of the Japanese authors of the Second World War than had been its Nuremberg predecessor with respect to those of their German counterparts (see supra 3.1.1). In effect, about 70 % of the entire Judgment was allotted to crimes against peace alone, and war crimes and crimes against humanity were dealt with in the remaining part of the text (see pp. 49592–49762 of the Judgment). This percentage appears to corroborate the Tokyo tribunal's firmer attitude toward crimes against peace, as a "primary" crime under its Charter, than was the Nuremberg Tribunal's. Besides, the very fact of a second consecutive conviction of a group of individuals of this category of crimes under international law within 2 years (1946–1948) might as such be regarded as an indication of the emergence of customary international law on the subject (cf. infra 4.1.1).

The Tokyo tribunal analyzed an immense mass of documentary evidence, which left no doubt with respect to the individual roles of 23 defendants who were eventually found guilty of crimes against peace in pursuance of Japan's aggressive policies in the Far East,[207] in the sense of Article 5(a) of the Tokyo Charter. The Tokyo trial followed the precedent of Nuremberg in that it involved only the supreme functionaries of the Japanese Empire but a major difference was that the Allies decided not to prosecute Emperor Hirohito, for his role in Japan's politics had been more symbolic rather than genuine.[208] There is no doubt that Adolf Hitler *would* have been in the dock at Nuremberg, had he not committed suicide on 30 April 1945.

The frequent rotation of Japan's Cabinets in the years preceding the Second World War suggests the existence of severe frictions in Japanese politics and society at the time. Powerful militarist ambitions were resisted by actors who opposed the use of force but ultimately were incapable of preventing Japan's aggressions in the Far East. The individual criminal liability of the authors of these aggressions (and of related war crimes and crimes against humanity) was therefore quite deserved. It is regrettable indeed that the Tribunal did not determine the liability of perpetrators of crimes, which were within its subject matter jurisdiction but had been committed by the Allies—such as the nuclear bombardment of Hiroshima and Nagasaki—but this question is beyond the scope of this volume.

Despite sound objections to the legitimacy of the Tribunal (see supra 1.2.3), its setting up and performance were major historic developments. The criminalization

[207] The Tribunal convicted of crimes against peace Sadao Araki, Kenji Dohihara, Kingoro Hashimoto, Shunroko Hata, Kiichiro Hiranuma, Koki Hirota, Naoki Hoshino, Seishiro Itagaki, Okinori Kaya, Koichi Kido, Heitaro Kimura, Kuniaki Koiso, Jiro Minami, Akira Muto, Takasumi Oka, Hiroshi Oshima, Kenryo Sato, Shigetaro Shimada, Toshio Shiratori, Teiichi Suzuki, Shigenori Togo, Hideki Tojo, and Yoshijiro Umezu. Iwane Matsui and Mamoru Shigemitsu were found not guilty of crimes against peace. See pp. 49774–49851 of the Judgment. See also Werle 2009b, p. 408.

[208] See Otomo 2011, pp. 63–78.

of individual acts, which had led to Japan's involvement in the Second World War, was a prerequisite for its post-war demilitarization, and the latter, in turn, was a ground-breaking reform in a country, where, for the most part of its history, a culture of war was consistently being implanted in the hearts and minds of its nationals (cf. supra 1.1.2.2 and 3.1.2.1).

3.1.3 Trials Under the Control Council Law № 10

The trials held at Nuremberg under the Control Council Law № 10 (see supra 1.2.4) involved, *inter alia*, the issue of criminal liability for crimes against peace of a number of lower-ranking German political and military officials, as well as of individuals who had rendered support to Germany's war effort in their capacities of managers of industry and finance.[209] The following paragraphs will offer summaries of the relevant Judgments and some concluding observations. An emphasis will thereby be placed upon the Judgment in the *Ministries* trial—the only follow-up trial where some of the defendants have been convicted of crimes against peace. With respect to the other trials, the most essential points will be highlighted.

3.1.3.1 The Ministries Trial (The United States of America vs. Ernst von Weizsäcker et al.)

In the *Ministries* case, "[t]he defendants von Weizsaecker, Keppler, Bohle, Woermann, Ritter, von Erdmannsdorff, Veesenmayer, Lammers, Stuckart, Darré, Meissner, Dietrich, Berger, Schellenberg, Schwerin von Krosigk, Koerner, and Pleiger [were] charged with having participated in the initiation of invasions of other countries and wars of aggression [mostly in Europe but also against the United States], including but not limited to planning, preparation, initiation, and waging of wars of aggression in violation of international treaties, agreements, and assurances".[210]

At the outset, the Tribunal re-examined the defence of "newly discovered evidence [revealing] that Germany was not the aggressor" (cf. supra 3.1.1.6), which had been put forward by some—but not all—defendants,[211] and concluded that this defence was invalid because:

> [w]hen Hitler solemnly informed the world that so far as territorial questions were concerned Germany had no claims, and by means of solemn treaty assured Austria, France, Czechoslovakia, and Poland that he had no territorial demands to be made upon them, and

---

[209] For a contemporary scholarly overview of relevant trials held under Control Council Law № 10, see Heller 2011, pp. 179–202. See also Werle 2009b, p. 409.

[210] The *Ministries* Trial, 322. See also K. J. Heller, supra note 208, pp. 180–183.

[211] The *Ministries* Trial, p. 322.

> when he entered into treaties of peace and nonaggression with them, the status of repose and fixation was reached. These assurances were given and these treaties entered into when there could be no claim of existing compulsion. Thereafter aggressive acts against the territories of these nations became breaches of international law, prohibited by the provisions of the Kellogg-Briand Treaty to which Germany had become a voluntary signatory.[212]

The chronology of Germany's policies with respect to invasions of European countries will not be repeated here,[213] as it has been dealt with at some length above, at 3.1.1. Having recalled the sequence of events in question, the Tribunal concluded that "invasions and wars [...] against Austria, Czechoslovakia, Poland, the United Kingdom and France, Denmark and Norway, Belgium, the Netherlands, and Luxembourg, Yugoslavia and Greece, the Union of Soviet Socialist Republics, and the United States of America were unlawful and aggressive, violated international law, and were crimes within the definition of the London Charter and Control Council Law No. 10", and moved on to "to determine which, if any, of the defendants, knowing there was an intent to so initiate and wage aggressive war, consciously participated in either plans, preparations, initiations of those wars, or so knowing, participated or aided in carrying them on".[214]

3.1.3.1.1 Von Weizsäcker

The Tribunal characterized Ernst von Weizsäcker's (1882–1951) standing and role in the pursuance of the Reich policies as follows:

> The defendant Ernst von Weizsaecker entered the Foreign Office in 1920 and [...] was appointed Ministerial Director of the Political Division in 1937, and State Secretary in April 1938, serving in that capacity until the spring of 1943, when he was appointed German Ambassador to the Vatican.
>
> As State Secretary he was second only to the Foreign Minister, von Ribbentrop. All divisions of the Foreign Office were subordinate to him [...] Through him and his office all the activities of the Foreign Office were channeled, and all divisions were bound to report to him and in theory and generally in practice received instructions from him [...]
>
> His defense is that, although appearing to collaborate [with the Nazi State], he [...] was an active member of the resistance movement; that he never sympathized with, or approved of, the Party movement or of the Hitler program, and that when it became clear to him that the foreign policy of Hitler and von Ribbentrop entailed the danger of war, and that when he became informed that Hitler intended to use aggressive wars and invasions as a means to carry out his political plans, he became active in plots and plans to remove him from power by means of a Putsch to be engineered and executed by those chiefs of the army who held the same convictions as did he [...] that he was convinced that the policies of Hitler and von Ribbentrop entailed, as they did in fact, death, disaster, and destruction to the German people and the ruin of his Fatherland; and that his loyalty to both required him to use these methods for the salvation of all that he felt dear.[215]

---

[212] Ibid., p. 323.

[213] See pp. 324–335 of the Judgment.

[214] Ibid., pp. 335–336.

[215] Ibid., pp. 339–340.

The Tribunal, however, was of the opinion that "good intentions [do not] render innocent that which is otherwise criminal", and that "general benevolence toward individuals [should not be] a [...] justification for participation in crimes against the unknown many. Planning, preparing, initiating, or waging aggressive war with its attendant horror, suffering, and loss is a crime which stands at the pinnacle of criminality. For it there is no justification or excuse".[216] Despite this generally rigorous introduction, the Tribunal examined the evidence of von Weizsäcker's performance in the capacity of a senior Foreign Office official,[217] and held that he was not guilty of crimes against peace against Austria, the Sudetenland, Poland, Denmark, Norway, The Netherlands, Greece, Yugoslavia, the Soviet Union, and the United States of America, and established his guilt only with respect to Czechoslovakia. As written evidence examined at the trial showed, von Weizsäcker did actually manifest resistance to the implementation of many of the Third Reich's aggressive policies, which ultimately resulted in his loss of Ribbentrop's trust. A skilled political analyst, von Weizsäcker was able to phrase his concerns with regard to the Reich's policies in diplomatic terms, which allowed him to retain his position within the Foreign Office, but he was not able to change the course of events. Von Weizsäcker was sentenced to 7 years' imprisonment. The sentence was reduced to 5 years on 12 December 1949, and he was released in October 1950.

3.1.3.1.2 Keppler

Wilhelm Keppler (1882–1960) was acquainted with Hitler since 1927 and was his economic advisor. Since 1936, he was responsible for the Nazi Party's activities in Austria. It was "[n]o secret" that the Anschluss of Austria (see supra 3.1.1.1) was a key element in those policies.[218] In 1937, Keppler and his assistant Edmund Veesenmayer (1904–1977)—who was also among the defendants in the *Ministries* case—traveled to Austria several times, for consultations with local Nazi Party leaders. As a result of Germany's pressure, on 12 February 1938, Arthur Seyss-Inquart was appointed Austria's Minister of the Interior and head of the Security Police.[219] Next, on 10 March, Keppler delivered an ultimatum to the Austrian President Wilhelm Miklas (1872–1956) to the effect that Prime Minister Kurt Alois Josef Johann Edler von Schuschnigg (1897–1977) must be replaced by A. Seyss-Inquart, or else Germany would invade.[220] The Tribunal's conclusion with regard to Keppler's role in the annexation of Austria was as follows:

> The defendant would have us believe that he [...] had neither knowledge of nor activity in the unwarranted interference in Austrian affairs. His story, however, is quite incredible.

[216] Ibid., pp. 340–341.

[217] See pp. 341–384 of the Judgment.

[218] Ibid., p. 385.

[219] Ibid.

[220] Ibid., p. 386.

> He returned to Berlin to report, and after that, as he was ordered, he flew back to Vienna. He was there during the crucial hours. He admits conferring with Miklas and in fact the record of his telephone conversation with Goering so states. Keppler was in Vienna to do Hitler's will, and it is beyond the realm of possibility that he was not informed before he left Berlin precisely what was to occur and what part he was to play.
>
> Neither Hitler nor the Third Reich had the slightest justification or excuse to interfere in Austrian affairs [...] Hitler's actions became aggressive as soon as he felt that it was safe to do so and as soon as it became clear that there might be a plebiscite which possibly would upset his plans. Resistance by Austria was useless and hopeless, and therefore none was offered when the Wehrmacht poured over the borders and took possession of the Austrian state. But before the army marched in, armed bands of the SS and other Nazi organizations under German direction took possession of the government, arrested its leading officers, and patrolled the streets. In the unlawful invasion of Austria Keppler played an important part, and we find him guilty under count one.[221]

The tribunal also found Keppler guilty with respect to Czechoslovakia (for an overview of the annexation of Czechoslovakia, see supra 3.1.1.1):

> The defendant professes to have known nothing about Hitler's plan, although in one of his statements he admits that he thought something of that nature might occur. We are unable to believe him. He played an important part in this matter. The separation of Slovakia from the Czechoslovakian state was an important and an integral part of Hitler's plan of aggression.
>
> Nor did he go to Czechoslovakia merely as an observer. In his own affidavit he admitted that he was assigned in March 1939 to negotiate and conclude a treaty of friendship and defense with Slovakia. We find that the defendant had knowledge of Hitler's plan for aggression against Czechoslovakia, knew that it was indefensible, and that he willingly participated in it. We find him guilty under count one in connection with the aggression against Czechoslovakia.[222]

Wilhelm Keppler was sentenced to 10 years' imprisonment and released in 1951.

3.1.3.1.3 Wörmann

In April 1938–April 1943, Ernst Wörmann (1888–1979) was Ministerial Director in charge of the Foreign Office's Political Division. It was specifically alleged that Wörmann and some other defendants named "as high officials of the German Foreign Office played dominant roles in the diplomatic plans and preparations for invasions and wars of aggression, and later participated in the diplomatic phases of the waging of these wars".[223] It was alleged, in particular, that:

> [T]he defendant Woermann [...] participated in a series of diplomatic and political moves against Poland whereby, in disregard of recent assurances and agreements, the return of Danzig and the Polish Corridor was demanded as a pretext for aggression. Polish counterproposals for the peaceful settlement of German claims were rejected, and an energetic

---

[221] Ibid.

[222] Ibid., p. 388.

[223] Ibid.

> program to mobilize potential allies in the German cause of aggression and to neutralize France and Great Britain as possible opponents was undertaken [...]
>
> It is [...] asserted that defendant Woermann [...] also participated in the preparation of the aggressions against Norway, Denmark, the Netherlands, Belgium, and Luxembourg, and it is further asserted that defendant Woermann [...] participated in the preparation and planning of the attack against the Union of Soviet Socialist Republics on 22 June 1941. It is asserted that Woermann and others, through diplomatic efforts, secured the military support of Rumania and Hungary for such venture. It is further alleged that Woermann [...] from early 1941, made continuous diplomatic efforts to induce Japan to attack British possessions in the Far East. It is further alleged that Woermann [...] participated in the political development and direction of the occupied territories, particularly those territories wherein puppet governments under the domination of the German Foreign Office had been installed. By the maintenance of continuous diplomatic pressure, intimidation, and coercion, the puppet and satellite governments were compelled to support Germany in the course of its wars of aggression. Further, [Woermann and others] participated in the partitioning of certain of the occupied territories, including Yugoslavia, and in the evolution of plans for the final integration of the occupied countries into the orbit of the German Reich after the cessation of hostilities.[224]

The charges against E. Wörmann were confirmed with respect to Poland[225] but he was acquitted with respect to Czechoslovakia,[226] Denmark, Norway,[227] the Netherlands, Belgium, Luxemburg,[228] Greece,[229] Yugoslavia,[230] and the Soviet Union.[231] The Tribunal held that Wörmann—as a senior Foreign Office official—was definitely informed about developments with respect to all countries mentioned but did not play a personal decision-making role in the implementation of Germany's aggressive policies against them, except against Poland. Ernst Wörmann was sentenced to 7 years' imprisonment. The sentence was revised on 12 December 1949, and the term of imprisonment was reduced to 5 years. Wörmann was released in 1951.

3.1.3.1.4 Lammers

The charges under count one against Reich Minister and Chief of the Reich Chancellery Hans Heinrich Lammers (1879–1962) were numerous:

> These are to the effect that Lammers [...] was an active participant in Hitler's seizure of power, in that [he and other defendants] marshaled the financial, political, psychological, and propaganda support necessary for its success; that Lammers [...] cloaked the

[224] Ibid., pp. 388–389.

[225] Ibid., pp. 392–395.

[226] Ibid., pp. 391–392.

[227] With respect to Denmark and Norway, evidence against Wörmann was "meagre and unimpressive". See p. 395 of the Judgment.

[228] Ibid., pp. 395–396.

[229] Ibid., p. 397.

[230] Ibid.

[231] Ibid.

criminal activities of the NSDAP with a semblance of legality; that the defendant Lammers [...] coordinated a series of laws and decrees completely centralizing the control of the machinery of the German Government in the hands of the Third Reich; that he participated in the incorporation of conquered territories into the German Reich and in the administration of the incorporated and occupied territories; that he, in the furtherance of the planning and preparation for aggressive war, coordinated at the highest level the total mobilization of the economic, financial, administrative, and military resources of the Third Reich; that he signed laws and decrees including, among others, the Reich Defense Law,[232] decrees creating the Secret Cabinet Council and establishing the Ministerial Council for the Defense of the Reich, and the decree whereby Hitler assumed personal command of the Wehrmacht; that he further effected total mobilization by participation in meetings of the Reich Defense Council, the Reich Defense Committee,[233] the General Council for the Four Year Plan,[234] and the Ministerial Council for the Defense of the Reich whereby the military, economic, financial, agricultural, and rearmament phases of mobilization were accomplished; that he resolved jurisdictional problems and conflicts as to the respective spheres of competence in mobilization schemes of various supreme Reich authorities, and received reports regularly from the Plenipotentiary General for Economy, from the Plenipotentiary General for Administration, and the Plenipotentiary General for the Four Year Plan; that by virtue of the aforesaid activities and otherwise, the defendant Lammers synchronized the economic, financial, military, and administrative preparations with the general program of aggression; that Lammers [...] accompanied Hitler to Prague when German troops marched into Bohemia and Moravia; that the defendant Lammers [...] participated in the secret preparation for aggression against Norway; that a Fuehrer decree was signed by the defendant Lammers appointing Reichsleiter Rosenberg commissioner for the centralized control of problems relating to the Soviet Union and other eastern territories; that Lammers signed, among others, the laws uniting Austria, the Free State of Danzig, Memel, Eupen, Malmedy, and Moresnet with the German Reich, the decree appointing the Reich Commissioner for Austria, and legislation extending German civil administration to Austria, the Sudetenland, and the eastern territories (West Prussia and Poznan); that he was responsible for the overall coordination of the incorporation of these territories and participated in the appointment of administrators for the performance of the administrative tasks involved. He participated in the formulation of the law of 13 March 1938 which united Austria with the Reich; that in setting up German administration in Austria, he drafted and signed decrees which introduced German law and its enforcement by the Gestapo and SD, the Nuernberg Racial Decrees, and the Military Service Law[235]; that he participated in the formulation of the laws incorporating into the Reich the Sudetenland, Memel, Danzig, the eastern territories (West Prussia and Poznan), and Eupen, Malmedy, and Moresnet, and in plans for the incorporation of French territory; that the defendant Lammers signed the legislation establishing the Protectorate of Bohemia and Moravia and the authority of the German Reich to legislate in the Protectorate; that he also signed laws extending German administration to the Government General and to the occupied eastern territories, and signed legislation appointing administrators in the Protectorate, the Government General and other occupied territories, including the appointment of Goering as Plenipotentiary of the Four Year Plan in charge of the economic exploitation of the U.S.S.R.; that he was further responsible for coordinating with the supreme

[232] See pp. 401–403 of the Judgment.

[233] Ibid.

[234] See pp. 400–401 of the Judgment.

[235] Ibid., p. 405.

> authorities policies initiated in the occupied territories; and that he was actively engaged in the direction and administration of these territories.[236]

Upon examination of the documentary evidence at its disposal, the Tribunal confirmed that H. Lammers' position indeed allowed him to exercise "influence and authority" in the "formulation and furtherance of Nazi plans and acts of criminal aggression".[237] His participation in important planning and legislating exercises was confirmed, as numerous documents issued in furtherance of Germany's aggressions bore his signatures. He was convicted of crimes against peace against Czechoslovakia,[238] Poland,[239] Norway,[240] Belgium, the Netherlands, Luxemburg,[241] and the Soviet Union,[242] and acquitted of such charges with respect to Austria[243] and Denmark.[244] Lammers was sentenced to 20 years' imprisonment but the sentence was reduced to 10 years in January 1951, and he was released in December 1951.

3.1.3.1.5 Körner

Paul Körner (1893–1957)—permanent deputy to Hermann Göring since 22 October 1936—was charged with the following under count one:

> [Having] played a leading role in the planning, coordination, and execution of an economic program to prepare the German Reich for the waging of aggressive war [...] he was further responsible for coordinating the economic exploitation of the occupied territories in furtherance of the waging of aggressive war. It is further specifically charged that he [...] participated in the establishment of the Four Year Plan in 1936, and that thereafter he, as Goering's deputy, directed the office of the Four Year Plan which was charged with control over the essential economic activities of the German agencies preparing for war, exercised supreme authority in economic matters, was responsible for the development and stockpiling of critical war material [...] It is specifically alleged that Koerner [...] participated [...] in the creation of the Hermann Goering works in 1937, and that Koerner, as chairman of the Aufsichtsrat of said organization and holder of other high offices therein was influential in determining the policies of this huge organization which was founded in furtherance of the planning, preparation, and waging of wars of aggression. It is further specifically alleged that as early as November 1940 [...] Koerner was informed by Goering of the coming attack against the Soviet Union, and that thereafter Koerner

236 Ibid., pp. 398–400.

237 Ibid., p. 400.

238 Ibid., pp. 406–407.

239 Ibid., pp. 407–408.

240 Ibid., pp. 409–411.

241 Ibid., pp. 411–413.

242 Ibid., pp. 413–415.

243 Ibid., p. 405.

244 Ibid., p. 411.

> attended and advised the conferences which were convened to consider the scope and method of German exploitation of the eastern economies.[245]

As deputy to Göring in the latter's capacity of Plenipotentiary in charge of the Four Year Plan, as deputy chairman of the General Council, and as member of the Central Planning Board, Paul Körner had a privileged relationship with his superior in that the latter discussed with him "many things" that he did not discuss with others, because he "had confidence" in Körner,[246] and Körner had knowledge of documents indicative of the aggressive aims of Germany's policies.[247] As far as the Four Year Plan is specifically concerned, its importance for the German war effort was immense:

> One can evaluate correctly what the Four Year Plan means for the economic preparation of war, only when one considers that the Four Year Plan does not include only the food and raw material economy, only the entire industrial economic life, but that it also includes foreign commerce, money, and foreign exchange economy and finance, so that the entire economic life and production in Germany is authoritatively determined and executed by this plan.[248]

The Tribunal confirmed Körner's effective authority and administrative power in the designated areas of his competence.[249] His awareness of the plans to annex Austria was proved—although he might not have known the exact date of the planned invasion[250]—and he also knew of the plans to invade Czechoslovakia,[251] and to attack Poland[252] and the Soviet Union.[253] It was also established that he was involved in the acceleration of the production of war materials.[254] Paul Körner was sentenced to 15 years' imprisonment but the sentence was reduced to 10 years in 1951. He was released the same year.

3.1.3.1.6 Other Defendants

The other defendants in the *Ministries* case were acquitted under count one, as there existed no evidence of their awareness of or direct contribution to the planning, preparation, initiation or waging or Germany's aggressive wars.[255] Likewise, all defendants in the case were acquitted of participation "in a common plan and

[245] Ibid., pp. 417–418.

[246] Ibid., p. 419.

[247] Ibid., p. 421.

[248] Ibid., p. 420.

[249] Ibid., pp. 424–425.

[250] Ibid., p. 426.

[251] Ibid., p. 428.

[252] Ibid., p. 429.

[253] Ibid., pp. 430–434.

[254] Ibid., p. 426.

[255] See pp. 397–398, 415–417, 434 of the Judgment. See also Heller 2011, pp. 194–198.

conspiracy to commit [...] crimes against peace, including war crimes and crimes against humanity".[256]

3.1.3.2 The High Command Trial (The United States of America vs. Wilhelm von Leeb et al.)

The records of the *High Command* trial on crimes against peace are quite succinct[257] but their modest volume should not prejudge their quality. At the outset, the Tribunal chose to follow a Clausewitzian approach towards war (see supra 1.1.4) by defining it as "the exerting of violence by one state or politically organized body against another",[258] and proceeded to comment upon it as a means for the implementation of a predetermined national policy.[259] It held that "[i]f the policy under which [a war] is initiated is criminal in its intent and purpose it is so because the individuals at the policy-making level had a criminal intent and purpose in determining the policy",[260] and concluded accordingly that only individuals holding posts at the policy-making level can plausibly be charged with crimes against peace (cf., however, infra 4.2).[261] Besides, even among such individuals not everyone is automatically responsible:

> If a defendant did not know that the planning and preparation for invasions and wars in which he was involved were concrete plans and preparations for aggressive wars and for wars otherwise in violation of international laws and treaties, then he cannot be guilty of an offense. If, however, after the policy to initiate and wage aggressive wars was formulated, a defendant came into possession of knowledge that the invasions and wars to be waged, were aggressive and unlawful, then he will be criminally responsible if he, being on the policy level, could have influenced such policy and failed to do so.[262]

We will revert to the *mens rea* of crimes against peace below, at 4.5. It suffices to mention here that, in the Tribunal's opinion, "[t]he acts of commanders and staff officers below the policy level, in planning campaigns, preparing means for carrying them out, moving against a country on orders and fighting a war after it has been instituted, do not constitute the planning, preparation, initiation, and waging of war or the initiation of invasion that international law denounces as criminal".[263] Hence the Tribunal acquitted all defendants in the case of charges with respect to crimes against peace.[264]

---

[256] See pp. 434–435 of the Judgment. See also Heller 2011, pp. 198–201.

[257] The *High Command* Trial, pp. 484–490.

[258] Ibid., p. 484.

[259] Ibid., pp. 484–485.

[260] Ibid., p. 485.

[261] Ibid.

[262] Ibid., pp. 487–488.

[263] Ibid., p. 490. See also Heller 2011, pp. 194–198.

[264] The *High Command* Trial, p. 490.

3.1.3.3 The IG Farben Trial (The United States of America vs. Carl Krauch et al.)

The *IG Farben* trial involved a number of industrialists who had played important roles in Germany's war effort,[265] allegedly including in the commission of crimes against peace.[266] The value of this particular trial consists in the attention the Tribunal paid to the mental element of crimes against peace; it will consequently be dealt with at more length below, at 4.5. It suffices to observe here that the Tribunal did not establish the existence of a general awareness of Hitler's aggressive plans among Germany's population,[267] "either with respect to a general plan to wage aggressive war, or with respect to specific plans to attack individual countries, beginning with the invasion of Poland on 1 September 1939".[268] Neither did it establish the existence on the part of Carl Krauch (1887–1968) or other defendants in the case of "knowledge of the existence of a plan on the part of the leaders of the German Reich to start an aggressive war against either a definite or a probable enemy",[269] although in Krauch's view, the German Reich was, at the time, "being encircled and threatened by strong foreign powers, and that this situation might and probably would at some time result in war".[270] Likewise, the defendants' guilt of waging wars of aggression lacked evidence.[271] Thus, all defendants in the case were acquitted of charges with respect to crimes against peace.

3.1.3.4 The Krupp Trial (The United States of America vs. Krupp et al.)

In this case, Alfried Felix Alwyn Krupp von Bohlen und Halbach (1907–1967) and eleven other defendants—all industrialists in Germany's war effort—were acquitted of charges under counts pertaining to crimes against peace. Unlike in the cases

---

[265] The *IG Farben* trial, pp. 1080–1324.

[266] The relevant count of the Indictment read as follows: "All of the defendants, acting through the instrumentality of Farben and otherwise, with divers other persons during a period of years preceding 8 May 1945, participated in the planning, preparation, initiation, and waging of wars of aggression and invasions of other countries, which wars of aggression and invasions were also in violation of international laws and treaties. All of the defendants held high positions in the financial, industrial and economic life of Germany and committed these crimes against peace, as defined by Article II of Control Council Law No. 10, in that they were principals in, accessories to, ordered, abetted, took a consenting part in, were connected with plans and enterprises involving, and were members of organizations or groups, including Farben, which were connected with the commission of said crimes". See pp. 1095–1096 of the Judgment.

[267] Ibid., pp. 1101–1106.

[268] Ibid., p. 1106.

[269] Ibid., p. 1115.

[270] Ibid.

[271] Ibid., pp. 1123–1126. See also Heller 2011, pp. 194–198.

summarized above, the Tribunal did not even go into the particulars of the charges, having confined itself to a brief statement to the effect of the defendants' acquittal.[272]

3.1.3.5 Observations

The follow-up trials under the Control Council Law № 10 indeed represented a progressive development in substantive and procedural international criminal law, for a number of reasons. They probably were the first "internationalised" trials in contemporary history where essentially national courts construed their Judgments on the basis of a piece of legislation implementing international law.[273] Their predecessors—the Nuremberg and Tokyo tribunals (see supra 3.1.1 and 3.1.2, respectively)—were international in their origins and composition, and it was only natural for them to apply international law, whereas the application of international law by essentially national courts was a novelty in itself. Next, in rendering Judgments, the Tribunals did not simply repeat the conclusions of the Nuremberg or Tokyo but developed their own reasoning—in quite detailed a manner—applicable to the cases in question. In effect, they went much further—at least, than did their Nuremberg predecessor—in developing the theory of the mental element of aggression and other crimes against peace (for details, see infra 4.5). The conclusion that an individual may not be held responsible for crimes against peace without that he or she would have had an unmistakable knowledge of the aggressive nature of the war in question was subsequently anchored in the customary international law on the matter.

The follow-up trials under the Control Council Law № 10 also went beyond the confines of the Nuremberg and Tokyo tribunals' jurisprudence in reasonably broadening the range of subjects of crimes against peace. In view of the remarkable Judgment in the *Ministries* case, it should henceforth be accepted that such crimes could also be perpetrated by other decision-makers than only those belonging to the very highest policy-making circles. This important development in international law will be discussed below, at 4.2–4.3.

---

[272] See The *Krupp* trial, p. 1328: "On March 12 [1948], the defendants filed a joint motion for an acquittal on the charges of crimes against the peace [...] After a careful consideration of this motion, the prosecution's reply thereto, and the briefs and the evidence, we have come to the conclusion that the competent and relevant evidence in the case fails to show beyond a reasonable doubt that any of the defendants is guilty of the offenses charged in counts one [planning, preparation, initiation, and waging aggressive war] and four [participation in a common plan or conspiracy to commit crimes against peace]. The motion accordingly is granted and for the reasons stated the defendants are acquitted and adjudged not guilty on Counts one and four of the indictment".

[273] On modern internationalized courts, see Werle 2009a, pp. 101–106.

3.1.4 Draft Code of Offences Against the Peace and Security of Mankind

The International Law Commission submitted the first edition of the Draft Code of Offences against the Peace and Security of Mankind to the attention of the UN General Assembly already in 1951 (see supra 1.2.5.6).[274] The Draft Code contained five Articles, whereby Article 1 qualified offences against the peace and security of mankind as crimes under international law,[275] Article 3 dealt with the criminal liability of Heads of States and responsible government officials,[276] Article 4 was devoted to superior orders,[277] and Article 5 defined penalties.[278] The definitions of offences were contained in twelve paragraphs of Article 2, whereby aggression was defined as follows:

> Any act of aggression, including the employment by the authorities of a State of armed force against another State for any purpose other than national or collective self-defence or in pursuance of a decision or recommendation by a competent organ of the United Nations.

This definition fully corresponded to the letter of the Charter of the United Nations inasmuch as it described as an act of aggression the employment of armed force for any purpose other than in accordance with the Charter's Articles 51 and 42. In other words, it provided only for "Charter-based" exceptions to the prohibition of the use of force embodied in Article 2(4) of the Charter (see supra 2.4.1), and did not allow for the "Charter-related" (see supra 2.4.2) or "extra-Charter" ones (see supra 2.4.3).

It is expressly noted in the Commentary to the Draft Code that "no attempt is made to enumerate [acts of aggression] exhaustively. It is expressly provided that the employment of armed force in the circumstances specified in the paragraph is an act of aggression. It is, however, possible that aggression can be committed also by other acts, including some of those referred to in other paragraphs of

274 See Draft Code of Offences against the Peace and Security of Mankind with commentaries 1951, pp. 133–137. See also Fenwick 1952, pp. 98–100; Potter 1952, pp. 101–102.

275 1951 Draft Code, Article 1: "Offences against the peace and security of mankind, as defined in this Code, are crimes under international law, for which the responsible individuals shall be punishable".

276 Ibid., Article 3: "The fact that a person acted as Head of State or as responsible government official does not relieve him from responsibility for committing any of the offences defined in this Code".

277 Ibid., Article 4: "The fact that a person charged with an offence defined in this Code acted pursuant to order of his government or of a superior does not relieve him from responsibility, provided a moral choice was in fact possible to him".

278 Ibid., Article 5: "The penalty for any offence defined in this Code shall be determined by the tribunal exercising jurisdiction over the individual accused, taking into account the gravity of the offence".

article 2".[279] The Draft Code suggested that other internationally wrongful forms of employment of force by States might comprise, at least, the following acts:

- Threats by the authorities of a State to resort to an act of aggression against another State (Article 2(2))[280];
- The preparation by the authorities of a State for the employment of armed force against another State for any purpose other than national or collective self-defence or in pursuance of a decision or recommendation by a competent organ of the United Nations (Article 2(3))[281]:
- The incursion into the territory of a State from the territory of another State by armed bands acting for a political purpose (Article 2(4))[282];
- The undertaking or encouragement by the authorities of a State of activities calculated to foment civil strife in another State, or the toleration by the authorities of a State of organized activities calculated to foment civil strife in another State (Article 2(5))[283];
- The undertaking or encouragement by the authorities of a State of terrorist activities in another State, or the toleration by the authorities of a State of organized activities calculated to carry out terrorist acts in another State (Article 2(6))[284];
- Acts by the authorities of a State in violation of its obligations under a treaty which is designed to ensure international peace and security by means of restrictions or limitations on armaments, or on military training, or on fortifications, or of other restrictions of the same character (Article 2(7))[285];
- Acts by the authorities of a State resulting in the annexation, contrary to international law, of territory belonging to another State or of territory under an international regime (Article 2(8)).[286]

The doctrinal value of the 1951 Draft Code consists in that it restated the reasoning of relevant trials with respect to aggression and other crimes against peace (see supra 3.1.1–3.1.3) and laid foundations for subsequent developments in international criminal law as regards these crimes. The Draft Code did not acquire a binding force but its adoption did testify to a progressing integration of crimes against peace in the professional conscience of international lawyers from all major legal systems represented in the International Law Commission. Henceforth, work on integrating these crimes in binding (treaty-based and customary) sources would be an important tendency in international criminal law.

[279] Draft Code of Offences against the Peace and Security of Mankind with commentaries 1951, p. 135.

[280] Ibid.

[281] Ibid.

[282] Ibid.

[283] Ibid.

[284] Ibid., pp. 135–136.

[285] Ibid., p. 136.

[286] Ibid.

3.1.5 Draft Code of Crimes Against the Peace and Security of Mankind

The 1996 Draft Code of Crimes against the Peace and Security of Mankind was significantly more detailed than its 1951 predecessor (for an overview of the 1996 Draft Code's drafting history, see supra 1.2.5.6).[287] Article 16 of the 1996 Draft Code was a major novelty, indeed one indicative of the progressive development of international law, in that it connected in a succinct formulation the proscribed conduct of an aggressor State (internationally wrongful act) to the criminal behavior of individuals at that State's policy-making level (individual crime):

> An individual who, as leader or organizer, actively participates in or orders the planning, preparation, initiation or waging of aggression committed by a State shall be responsible for a crime of aggression.

The International Law commission addressed in this compact definition six important facets of the crime of aggression. Firstly, the phrase "[a]n individual [...] shall be responsible for a crime of aggression" implies that the Article relates to the crime of aggression only for the purpose of individual criminal responsibility, and the Draft Code does not regulate the State responsibility (on the latter point, see supra 2.1.3, 2.2.1, 2.2.2).[288] Secondly, the ILC reiterated that the range of subjects of a crime of aggression was restricted to "leaders" or "organizers"—in the opinion of the Commission, these must include government officials, senior military officers, diplomats, members of political parties and industrialists (cf. infra 4.2),[289] with due regard to the Judgments rendered by the Nuremberg and Tokyo tribunals and pursuant to the Control Council Law № 10 (see supra 3.1.1–3.1.3). Thirdly, their individual contributions to an aggressive war effort must be intentional (see supra 3.1.3.2, 3.1.3.5 and infra 4.5)–in this regard, the ILC recalled the acquittal of defendants Hjalmar Schacht, Karl Doenitz and Martin Bormann of some charges of crimes against peace, because they had been lacking a requisite *mens rea* (cf. supra 3.1.1.8).[290] Fourthly, Article 16 of the 1996 Draft Code invokes "aggression committed by a State"—that is to say, in the words of the Commission:

> The rule of international law which prohibits aggression [i.e., Article 2(4) of the UN Charter] applies to the conduct of a State in relation to another State. Therefore, only a State is capable of committing aggression by violating this rule of international law which

---

[287] See Draft Code of Crimes against the Peace and Security of Mankind with commentaries 1996, pp. 17–56. Part One of the Draft Code summarizes, in 15 Articles, the general part of international criminal law (cf infra 5.2), whereas Part Two contains the definitions of aggression (Article 16), genocide (Article 17), crimes against humanity (Article 18), crimes against United Nations and associated personnel (Article 19), and war crimes (Article 20).

[288] See Draft Code of Crimes against the Peace and Security of Mankind with commentaries 1996, p. 43.

[289] Ibid.

[290] Ibid., especially note 112.

> prohibits such conduct. At the same time, a State is an abstract entity which is incapable of acting on its own. A State can commit aggression only with the active participation of the individuals who have the necessary authority or power to plan, prepare, initiate or wage aggression [...] Thus, the violation by a State of the rule of international law prohibiting aggression gives rise to the criminal responsibility of the individuals who played a decisive role in planning, preparing, initiating or waging aggression. Individual responsibility for such a crime is intrinsically and inextricably linked to the commission of aggression by a State. The words "aggression committed by a State" clearly indicate that such a violation of the law by a State is a *sine qua non* condition for the possible attribution to an individual of responsibility for a crime of aggression.[291]

Fifthly, the ILC points out that an individual action amounts to a crime of aggression only if the conduct of the State in question is a grave violation of Article 2(4) of the Charter of the United Nations (see supra 2.1–2.3).[292] Here, a competent judicial authority—an appropriate national court or the International Criminal Court[293]—would have to examine two interrelated issues, i.e., whether a State conduct constitutes a breach of Article 2(4) (see supra 2.2), and whether the breach is of a sufficient gravity to qualify as an act of aggression entailing individual criminal responsibility (see infra Chaps. 4 and 5).[294] And finally, the ILC notes that the phases of the individual crime listed in Article 16—participating in or ordering the planning, preparation, initiation or waging of aggression may not be clearly separable (cf. infra 4.3),[295] and that contributing to "a single phase of aggression is enough to give rise to [individual] criminal responsibility".[296] This conclusion is reflective of customary international law on the matter (cf. infra 4.1.1).

As comprehensive as it is, the International Law Commission's Commentary to Article 16 of the 1996 Draft Code did not shed light—unlike its Commentary to Article 2 of the 1951 Draft Code where examples of acts of aggression were offered (see supra 3.1.4)—on the notion of an "act of aggression". In the light of the principle of legality (cf. infra 5.2.1–5.2.2), it was imperative to determine the range of "criminalisable" acts of aggression for the purpose of the individual criminal responsibility—but the ILC must have preferred leaving this task up to the drafters of Articles 5 and 8 bis of the Rome Statute of the International Criminal Court (see supra 1.2.6 and infra 5.1.1.2–5.1.1.3). It is assumed that the ILC might revert to the matter, if it is once tasked with developing Draft Articles on the use of force by States (cf. supra 1.2.5.3)—a document, which appears essential given the absence of the ILC's comprehensive opinion on the matter.

---

291 Ibid.

292 Ibid.

293 Cf. Article 8 of the 1996 Draft Code ("Establishment of jurisdiction"): "[...] Jurisdiction over the crime set out in article 16 shall rest with an international criminal court. However, a State referred to in article 16 is not precluded from trying its nationals for the crime set out in that article". Also, see Chaps. 4 and 5.

294 See Draft Code of Crimes against the Peace and Security of Mankind with commentaries 1996, p. 43.

295 Ibid.

296 Ibid.

3.1.6 *The Crime of Aggression in the Rome Statute of the International Criminal Court*

As the criminalisation of aggression under the Rome Statute of the International Criminal Court was reviewed supra at 1.2.6 and will be discussed in detail below in Chap. 5, it suffices to note here that the Rome Statute does establish an institutional mechanism for directly enforcing individual criminal responsibility for crimes under international law[297]—including for the crime of aggression.[298]

3.1.7 *Individual Criminal Responsibility for the Crime of Aggression: Towards the Revival of a Legal Regime?*

Geoffrey Robertson seems to have been somewhat inaccurate in his suggestion to the effect that, in the *Pinochet case*, sovereign immunity was not, for the first time, allowed to become sovereign impunity.[299] As was discussed supra at 3.1.1–3.1.3, there had been precedents of holding senior State officials liable for crimes under international law already in the first half of the twentieth century but it is true that there was a considerable time span between the late 1940s and the 1990s, during which period international criminal law was largely dormant.[300]

There have been no prosecutions for crimes against peace—including the crime of aggression—during the "Cold war", despite numerous occasions of international armed conflicts (see supra 1.2.5.2, especially note 274), and it was not until the end of confrontation between the Western and Socialist blocs that it became possible to move beyond the limits of declaratory General Assembly resolutions (see supra 1.2.5.3) and theoretically sound but non-binding documents of the International Law Commission with respect to aggression (see supra 1.2.5.6, 3.1.4–3.1.5). As will be seen in Chap. 4, there have also been some legislative developments at the national level but they were quite limited and did not yet result in any convictions. It is hoped that the adoption of a definition of the crime of aggression for the purpose of the International Criminal Court (see infra 5.1) might give an

---

[297] ICC Statute, Article 25(1): "The Court shall have jurisdiction over natural persons pursuant to this Statute".

[298] Ibid., Article 5: "1. The jurisdiction of the Court shall be limited to the most serious crimes of concern to the international community as a whole. The Court has jurisdiction in accordance with this Statute with respect to the following crimes: (a) The crime of genocide; (b) Crimes against humanity; (c) War crimes; (d) The crime of aggression. 2. The Court shall exercise jurisdiction over the crime of aggression once a provision is adopted in accordance with articles 121 and 123 defining the crime and setting out the conditions under which the Court shall exercise jurisdiction with respect to this crime. Such a provision shall be consistent with the relevant provisions of the Charter of the United Nations".

[299] Robertson 2002, p. 399.

[300] See Werle 2009a, p. 15.

impetus to further developments—both at the international and national levels—but this remains to be seen. It is clear that if "the peoples of the United Nations" are really "determined" to "save succeeding generations from the scourge of war",[301] they would have to take urgent, consistent and persevering measures, through their respective States, for the indirect and—in accordance with the principle of complementarity (see infra 5.3.1)—direct enforcement of criminal liability regimes applicable to individual authors of crimes of aggression. Without such tangible practical measures, declarations of enforcing the provisions of international law would remain no more than reflective of good intentions. In the 1940s, the international and internationalized tribunals did their share of enforcing individual criminal responsibility for crimes against peace (see supra 3.1.1–3.1.3). Would national and international courts now be able to do the job in the twenty-first century?

References

Andrews DR (1975) Act of state—executive determination. ZaöRV 35:41–50
Antonopoulos C (2001) Whatever happened to crimes against peace? JCSL 6:33–62
Baxter CF (1992) The Normandy Campaign, 1944: a selected bibliography. Greenwood Press, New York
Clark RS (2007) Nuremberg and the crime against peace. Washington Univ Global Stud Law Rev 6:527–550
Delson R (1972) The Act of State Doctrine—judicial deference or abstention? AJIL 66:82–93
Doherty R (2004) Normandy 1944: the road to victory. Spellmount, Staplehurst
Draft Code of Crimes against the Peace and Security of Mankind with commentaries (1996) Yearbook of the international law commission, vol II (Part Two), pp 17–56
Draft Code of Offences against the Peace and Security of Mankind with commentaries (1951) Yearbook of the International Law Commission, vol II, pp 133–137
Fenwick CG (1952) Draft code of offenses against the peace and security of mankind. AJIL 46:98–100
Garner JW (1938) Questions of state succession raised by the German annexation of Austria. AJIL 32:421–438
Giannini A (1932) The problem of Danzig, 2nd edn. Istituto per l'Europa orientale, Roma
Ginsburgs G (1958) A case study in the Soviet use of international law: Eastern Poland in 1939. AJIL 52:69–84
Goldensohn L (2004) Nuremberg interviews: an American psychiatrist's conversations with the defendants and witnesses. Vintage Books, New York
Gott VL (1938) The National Socialist theory of international law. AJIL 32:704–718
Gross L (1945) Was the Soviet Union expelled from the League of Nations? AJIL 39:35–44
Heller KJ (2011) The Nuremberg Military Tribunals and the origins of international criminal law. Oxford University Press, Oxford
Henderson I (2011) The firebombing of Tokyo and other Japanese cities. In: Tanaka Y, McCormack T, Simpson G (eds) Beyond victors' justice? The Tokyo War Crimes Trial revisited. Martinus Nijhoff Publishers, Leiden, pp 311–321
Hill N (1948) Was there an ultimatum before Pearl Harbor? AJIL 42:355–367

[301] See the Charter of the United Nations, 1st and 2nd preambular paragraphs.

International Military Tribunal (Nuremberg), Judgment of 1 October (1946) In: The trial of German major war criminals. Proceedings of the International Military Tribunal sitting at Nuremberg, Germany, Part 22 (22 Aug–1 Oct 1946)

International Military Tribunal for the Far East, Judgment of 12 November (1948) In: Pritchard J, Zaide SM (eds) The Tokyo War Crimes Trial, vol 22

Kelsen H (1947) Will the judgment in the Nuremberg Trial constitute a precedent in international law? ILQ 1:153–171

Kingsbury HT (1910) The "Act of State" doctrine. AJIL 4:359–372

Korowicz MS (1956) The problem of the international personality of individuals. AJIL 50:533–562

Kress C (2004) The Iraqi Special Tribunal and the crime of aggression. JICJ 2:347–352

Lauterpacht H (1934) Resort to war and the interpretation of the covenant during the Manchurian dispute. AJIL 28:43–60

Lukashuk II (2008) Mejdunarodnoe pravo: Obshchaya chast (International Law: General Part), 3rd edn. Wolters Kluwer, Moscow

Lutz EL, Reiger C (2009) Introduction. In: Lutz EL, Reiger C (eds) Prosecuting heads of state. Cambridge University Press, Cambridge, pp 1–24

Makarov AN (1935) Sowjet-Union und Völkerbund. ZaöRV 5:34–60

Makarov AN (1936) Die Völkerrechtswissenschaft in Sowjetrußland. ZaöRV 6:479–495

Malanczuk P (1997) Akehurst's modern introduction to international law, 7th revised edn. Routledge, London

Manner G (1952) The object theory of the individual in international law. AJIL 46:428–449

May L (2008) Aggression and crimes against peace. Cambridge University Press, Cambridge

Mosler H (1962) Die Erweiterung des Kreises der Völkerrechtssubjekte. ZaöRV 22:1–48

Müllerson RA (1990) Human rights and the individual as subject of international law: a Soviet view. EJIL 1:33–43

Neillands R (2004) The Battle of Normandy 1944. Cassell Military, London

Otomo Y (2011) The decision not to prosecute the emperor. In: Tanaka Y, McCormack T, Simpson G (eds) Beyond victors' justice? The Tokyo War Crimes Trial revisited. Martinus Nijhoff Publishers, Leiden, pp 63–78

Perreau-Saussine A (2008) British acts of state in English courts. BYIL 79:176–254

Potter PB (1952) Offenses against the peace and security of mankind. AJIL 46:101–102

Robertson G (2002) Crimes against humanity: struggle for global justice, 2nd edn. Penguin Books, London

Safferling C (2012) International criminal procedure. Oxford University Press, Oxford

Stowell EC (1942) Japan attacks the United States. AJIL 36:87–89

Sucharitkul S (2005) Jurisdictional immunities in contemporary international law from Asian perspectives. Chinese JIL 4:1–43

Suvorov V (2004) *Ledokol* [The Ice-Breaker]. Ast, Moscow

The High Command Trial (The United States of America vs. Wilhelm von Leeb et al.), US Military Tribunal Nuremberg, Judgment of 27 October (1948). In: Trials of war criminals before the Nuremberg Military Tribunals, vol IX

The IG Farben Trial (The United States of America vs. Carl Krauch et al.), US Military Tribunal Nuremberg, Judgment of 30 July (1948) In: Trials of war criminals before the Nuremberg Military Tribunals, vol VIII

The Krupp Trial (The United States of America vs. Krupp et al.), US Military Tribunal Nuremberg, Judgment of 31 July (1948) In: Trials of war criminals before the Nuremberg Military Tribunals, vol IX

The Ministries Trial (The United States of America vs. Ernst von Weizsäcker et al.), US Military Tribunal Nuremberg, Judgment of 11 April (1949) In: Trials of war criminals before the Nuremberg Military Tribunals, vol XIV

Tomuschat C (1996) Die Vertreibung der Sudetedeutschen. Zur Frage des Bestehens von Rechtsansprüchen nach Völkerrecht und deutschem Recht. ZaöRV 56:1–69

Vagts DF (1990) International law in the Third Reich. AJIL 84:661–704

Weigend T (2012) 'In General a Principle of Justice': the debate on the 'Crime against Peace' in the wake of the Nuremberg judgement. JICJ 10:41–58
Werle G (2009a) Principles of international criminal law, 2nd edn. T. M. C. Asser Press, The Hague
Werle G (2009b) The crime of aggression between international and domestic criminal law. In: Manacorda S, Nieto A (eds) Criminal law between war and peace. Cuena, pp 405–421
Williams ET (1933) Japan's mandate in the Pacific. AJIL 27:428–439
Woolsey LH (1942) War between the United States and the Axis powers. AJIL 36:77–83
Wright H (1944) The legality of the annexation of Austria by Germany. AJIL 38:621–635
Zander M (1959) The Act of State doctrine. AJIL 53:826–852

Chapter 4
The Principal Approaches Towards the Criminalisation of Aggression at the National Level

Abstract At least forty-two States have enacted legislation for the criminal repression of aggression and other crimes against peace. Useful as they are, these penal provisions are not uniform, though, and the diversity of States' approaches probably testifies to the absence of customary international law on the subject to date. This chapter examines those provisions in the framework of four main "legislative models", and extracts from them substantive and mental elements, which are essential for devising an inclusive *corpus delicti* of the crime of aggression. The "leadership requirement" is dealt with as a key element of the crime, and the propaganda for war is briefly considered as a separate crime against peace. The chapter concludes with an overview of key substantive and procedural matters of inter-State cooperation, if prosecutions for the crime of aggression are ever to take place within national legal systems.

Contents

Most of the national criminal law provisions quoted in Chapter 4 were retrieved from: http://legislationline.org/documents/section/criminal-codes (last accessed 15 November 2012). Where no English texts were available, unofficial translations were made by the author.

S. Sayapin, *The Crime of Aggression in International Criminal Law*,
DOI: 10.1007/978-90-6704-927-6_4, © T.M.C. ASSER PRESS and the author 2014

There have been no national or international prosecutions for the crime of aggression since the conclusion of the Nuremberg follow-up trials (see supra 3.1.3).[1] However, the Charters and Judgments of the Nuremberg and Tokyo Tribunals (see supra 3.1.1–3.1.2) as well as relevant Judgments rendered in accordance with the Control Council Law No 10 did, gradually, influence subsequent legislative developments with respect to aggression and other crimes against peace in a significant number of countries. These developments, it is assumed, might testify to a gradual emergence of customary international law[2] on the subject.

As will be seen below, the criminalisation of aggression at the national level is not yet universal. After the Second World War, the crime in question was a novelty in international law—as much as the idea of individual criminal responsibility under international law was itself a novelty (see supra 1.2.1–1.2.4)—and its progressing recognition in national legal systems was a matter of time.[3] At the time of writing, there exists no uniformity of opinion among States as to the *corpus delicti* of the crime (see infra 4.3 and 4.5).[4] Some States prefer to maintain in their national legislations the somewhat outdated—in this writer's opinion—definition of the crime of aggression as it was verbalised and interpreted by the Nuremberg and Tokyo Tribunals as well as in the course of the Nuremberg follow-up trials (see infra 4.1.1); others infer the criminality of aggression from the values protected by Article 2(4) of the Charter of the United Nations (see supra 2.1)—such as territorial integrity and political independence (see infra 4.1.2); other States criminalise war and hostilities as objective phenomena, with a view to establishing

[1] Notably, E. L. Lutz and C. Reiger suggest that Saddam Hussein "might have been put on trial for waging aggressive wars against Iran and Kuwait", see Lutz and Reiger 2009, at 1–2.

[2] See Marochkin 2006, pp. 329–344; O'Keefe 2002, pp. 293–335; Strebel 1976, pp. 168–189; Wildhaber and Breitenmoser 1988, pp. 163–207.

[3] On the implementation of international crimes in national legal systems, see Cryer 2005, pp. 117–122.

[4] See Reisinger Coracini 2009, pp. 725–754; Sayapin 2010a, pp. 294–316; Sayapin 2010b, pp. 165–187.

the individual criminal liability of persons who would have contributed to those States' involvement in almost any international armed conflict (see infra 4.1.3). Such a diversity of legislative approaches is quite explicable at a theoretical level—by virtue of legal traditions and cultures prevailing in a given State—but it may pose certain difficulties of a practical nature (see infra 4.6.1.2.2).

With the adoption, in June 2010, and prospective entry into force of an international definition of the crime of aggression for the purpose of the Rome Statute of the International Criminal Court (see infra 5.1), States Parties to the Statute may be required, in a foreseeable future, to carry out criminal prosecutions of persons allegedly involved in the commission of the crime. As the principle of complementarity (see infra 5.3.1) shall apply to the crime of aggression as much as it now does to other crimes within the jurisdiction of the ICC, the formal compatibility between relevant national criminal laws and the international definition of the crime would matter as much as would the goodwill of the States concerned.

The attitudes of States, which are not Parties to the Statute, towards the crime of aggression also represent an essential factor. In the first place, the very *fact* of criminalisation of aggression in those States is important—the more widespread the criminal prohibition, the stronger the restraint of the criminal occurrence. Second, such States might—or might not, for more or less formal reasons (see infra 4.6.1.2.2)—cooperate with other States in the criminal prosecution of individuals for aggression, and the compatibility of their national laws criminalising aggression with those of other States would play a decisive role.

This chapter considers, in a comparative fashion, a selection of national provisions relative to the crime of aggression—and to other similar crimes, because its elements may feature in national criminal laws under alternative titles—which apply in forty-two States representing all geographical regions of the world,[5] including twenty-four States Parties to the Rome Statute,[6] with a view to deducing patterns of legislative attitudes towards the crime of aggression ("legislative models"), which prevail in those States. Such an analysis should be helpful in at least two respects: (1) it should help identify the degree of substantive compatibility between the various national legislative models for the purpose of horizontal cooperation between States (Parties and non-Parties to the Rome Statute alike) in prosecuting individuals for the crime of aggression (see infra 4.6.1.2.2)—theoretically, even before the entry into force of the international definition of the crime (see infra 5.1.2) and quite independently of this factor—and (2) it should help identify implications for prospective cooperation between States (Parties and non-parties to the Rome Statute), where a given legislative model applies, and the International Criminal Court.

[5] By contrast, Gerhard Kemp listed only twelve States, which "provide[d] for the crime of aggression in one way or another as part of their penal codes" (see Kemp 2010, p. 129), and Stefan Barriga took note in his analysis of no more than "some two dozen countries worldwide", see Barriga 2011, at 330.

[6] See an up-to-date overview of States parties to the Rome Statute at: http://www.icc-cpi.int/Menus/ASP/states+parties/ (last accessed 24 April 2013). As of 1 May 2013, the ICC Statute has 122 States Parties.

Whereas forty-two States do not in fact constitute a majority within the international community—as much as twenty-four selected States Parties to the Rome Statute do not constitute a majority within the International Criminal Court's Assembly of States Parties—it is suggested that they indeed are a group representative enough, in order for conclusions sought after to be drawn. Within each legislative model, the international legal sources of criminalisation are recalled, and excerpts from relevant national laws are provided, separately for States Parties and non-parties to the Rome Statute. Such analysis of each model is followed by brief observations where the model's idiosyncratic aspects are highlighted and intermediary conclusions are offered. It is then attempted to deduce the essential material and mental elements of the *corpus delicti* of the crime of aggression as a possible basis for the inference of customary international law on the matter (see infra 4.3 and 4.5),[7] and a brief observation on the separate crime of propaganda for war is offered at 4.4. Section 4.2 examines critically the crime of aggression's customary "leadership element", and Sect. 4.6 offers an overview of selected issues related to the indirect enforcement of criminal responsibility.

4.1 Overview of National Criminal Laws Proscribing the Crime of Aggression

4.1.1 The "Nuremberg and Tokyo Model"

This legislative model is based upon the pertinent provisions of the Charters of the Nuremberg (see supra 1.2.2 and 3.1.1) and Tokyo (see supra 1.2.3 and 3.1.2) Tribunals and their Judgments as well as on the relevant jurisprudence under the Control Council Law № 10 (see supra 1.2.4 and 3.1.3). Those trials were designed

---

[7] It appears that the very existence of divergent national approaches towards defining the crime of aggression ("legislative models") examined infra at 4.1 might testify to the *absence* of customary international law on the matter, if the latter is to be defined as a "unitary, universal and exogenous" combination of State practice and *opinio juris*, cf. Goldsmith and Posner 2005, pp. 23–26. Contrary to the "traditional paradigm" suggesting that customary international law represents a stable normative framework voluntarily shared by many (or even most) members of the community of States, Jack L. Goldsmith and Eric A. Posner allege that State practices evolve over time (in other words, are subject to change and therefore not stable), depend, first and foremost, on States' national interests (and much less on external regulatory factors), and materialise in one of four principal models of interaction between States (or in combinations thereof): coincidence of interest, coercion, cooperation, and coordination, see idem 26–35. If we accept this less stringent approach towards customary international law, then inferences infra at 4.3 and 4.5—although comprehensive and systematic—might be regarded not as a restatement of customary international law on the crime of aggression (because there simply might be none *de lege lata*) but rather as a coherent summary of divergent normative models examined at 4.1, with a view to usefully reducing those models to a reasonable common denominator. On customary international law pertaining specifically to the crime of aggression, see Kemp 2010, pp. 137–148.

for the specific purpose of prosecuting high-ranking civilian and military officials and important industrialists who had contributed to the outbreak of the Second World War in Europe and the Far East, and the definitions of the crimes against peace were constructed accordingly. They were made to suit the realities of a massive war, which lasted for about six years, involved—as combatants and workers of the military economy—hundreds of millions of people, affected dozens of countries and entailed unmatched political, economic, legal and humanitarian effects. Given such degree of gravity of the Second World War's consequences, its prompt criminalisation was but an equitable development. The lessons of Nuremberg and Tokyo—and the efforts of the United Nations (see supra 1.2.5), which was being established concurrently—were all expected to prevent the occurrence of such wars in the future, and (so far) succeeded in attaining that aim. However, the problem with the "Nuremberg and Tokyo model" was that it did not cover international wars of a lesser gravity, and more than a few such international wars did occur after 1945. No trials—either international or national—took place for the prosecution of individuals who had contributed to the initiation of those wars. The subject matter jurisdiction of the International Criminal Tribunal for the Former Yugoslavia—the only international criminal tribunal established after 1945, which might have theoretically dealt with crimes against peace, if the drafters of its Statute had endowed it with an according jurisdiction—was limited to war crimes, genocide and crimes against humanity, and the causes of the violent international armed conflict remained beyond the Tribunal's attention.[8]

4.1.1.1 States Parties to the Rome Statute

Despite its substantive deficiencies—such as the restriction of criminalisation only to large-scale wars of aggression, the absence of a clear-cut definition of what constitutes a war of aggression in relevant provisions, and an insufficient distinction between the notions "wars of aggression" and "wars in violation of international treaties, agreements or assurances" in the Judgment of the Nuremberg Tribunal (see supra 1.2.2)—the Nuremberg and Tokyo model of the definition of the crime of aggression (and of other crimes against peace) did exercise a significant influence upon national criminal laws in quite many States Parties to the Rome Statute. Of twenty-four national criminal laws surveyed, seven—somewhat less than a third—may be attributed to this category. The basis for this classification is the explicit use of the term "war of aggression" in the definition of the crime and the reference to one or more modes of criminal contribution to a war of aggression. Thus, in accordance with the "parent" provisions contained in the Nuremberg and Tokyo Charters (see supra 1.2.2 and 1.2.3), Article 404 of the

[8] See ICTY Statute, Articles 1–5, available at: http://www.icty.org/x/file/Legal%20Library/Statute/statute_sept09_en.pdf (last accessed 16 November 2012).

Criminal Code of Georgia criminalises all four stages of the commission of the crime,[9] as does Article 395 of the Criminal Code of Tajikistan.[10]

Section 72 of Latvia's Criminal Code refers to the planning, preparation and waging of a war of aggression and mentions, in addition, instigation to a military aggression,[11] which constitutes a separate crime in many legal systems (see infra 4.4). Article 117 of the Criminal Code of Poland also encompasses three elements of the Nuremberg and Tokyo model (preparation, initiation and waging a war of aggression) as well as public incitement to a war of aggression.[12]

In turn, Article 442 of the Criminal Code of Montenegro[13] and Article 386 of Serbia's Criminal Code[14] explicitly cover only two types of criminal conduct (instigating to and ordering an aggressive war), only the latter of which can be strictly related to the Nuremberg and Tokyo model. Although neither the Nuremberg nor the Tokyo Charters refer to "ordering", it seems that this term may reasonably be equated to "initiation".

Although Section 80 of Germany's Criminal Code only mentions the preparation for a war of aggression,[15] it may be supposed that it also covers, at least, the

---

[9] Cf. the Criminal Code of Georgia, Article 404 ("Preparations for and waging of aggressive War"): "1. Planning of or preparing for the war of aggression shall be punishable by prison sentences ranging from seven to fifteen years in length. 2. Unleashing or waging of the war of aggression shall be punishable by imprisonment extending from ten to twenty years in length or by life imprisonment".

[10] Cf. Article 395 of the Criminal Code of Tajikistan ("Aggressive war"): "1. Planning or preparation of an aggressive war is punishable by imprisonment for 12–20 years with the confiscation of property. (2) Unleashing or conducting an aggressive war is punishable by imprisonment for 15–20 years with the simultaneous confiscation of property, or by the death penalty".

[11] Cf. the Criminal Code of Latvia, Section 72 ("Crimes against peace"): "For a person who commits crimes against peace, that is, commits planning, preparation or instigation to, or participation in, military aggression, or wages a war of aggression in violation of international agreements binding upon the Republic of Latvia, or commits participation in a conspiracy for the purpose of committing crimes mentioned in this Section, the applicable sentence is life imprisonment or deprivation of liberty for a term of not less than three and not exceeding twenty years".

[12] Cf. the Criminal Code of Poland, Article 117: "1. Who starts or leads a war of aggression shall be deprived of their liberty for no less than 12 years, for 25 years, or for the duration of their life. 2. Who prepares to commit the crime described in § 1, shall be deprived of their liberty for no less than 3 years. 3. Who publicly calls for starting a war of aggression, shall be deprived of their liberty for a period between 3 months and 5 years".

[13] Cf. the Criminal Code of Montenegro, Article 442 ("Aggressive war"): "1. Anyone who calls to or instigates aggressive war, shall be punished by imprisonment for a term of two to twelve years. 2. Anyone who orders waging aggressive war, shall be liable to imprisonment for a minimum term of ten years or a prison sentence of thirty years".

[14] Cf. Article 386 of the Criminal Code of Serbia ("War of aggression"): "1. Whoever calls for or instigates a war of aggression, shall be punished by imprisonment of two to twelve years. 2. Whoever orders waging a war of aggression, shall be punished by imprisonment of minimum ten years or imprisonment of thirty to forty years".

[15] Cf. the Criminal Code of Germany, Section 80 ("Preparation of a war of aggression"): "Whoever prepares a war of aggression (Article 26 subsection (1), of the Basic Law) in which the Federal Republic of Germany is supposed to participate and thereby creates a danger of war for the Federal Republic of Germany, shall be punished with imprisonment for life or for not less than ten years". See also Haumer and Marschner 2010, pp. 188–196; Kress 2004, pp. 245–264; Sayapin 2010b, pp. 169–173.

planning of such a war—although this earlier stage in the process is not mentioned explicitly—for preparation is hardly possible without prior or parallel planning.

4.1.1.2 Other States

The "Nuremberg and Tokyo model" is a well-established legal standard in the Commonwealth of Independent States (CIS) as regards the crime of aggression. Objectively, this is due to the crime's common origin in the Model Criminal Code, which was adopted on 17 February 1996 by the CIS Inter-parliamentary Assembly, and more subjectively, to the continuing influence of the Nuremberg and Tokyo trials' legacy in the post-Soviet theory of international criminal law.[16] In most CIS States, all four stages of the crime are covered by relevant norms. It seems, though, that there is some vagueness—even at the level of theory—regarding the legal qualification of the initiation of a war of aggression. Thus, for example, in the Criminal Codes of Azerbaijan,[17] Kazakhstan,[18] Moldova,[19] the Russian Federation[20] and Ukraine,[21] the initiation of an aggressive war is joined with its planning and preparation, as a stage, which is essentially related to and "concluding" the two preceding ones. In other words, in these Criminal Codes, the initiation of a war is regarded as an act, which is substantively distinct from waging a war—itself a more dangerous criminal manifestation, for it is punished with more severe

16 See Zelinskaya 2006, pp. 409–460.

17 Cf. the Criminal Code of Azerbaijan, Article 100 ("Planning, preparation, initiation or conducting an aggressive war"): "1. Planning, preparation or initiation of an aggressive war—shall be punished by imprisonment for a term from eight up to ten years. 2. Conducting an aggressive war—shall be punished by imprisonment for a term from ten up to fifteen years or life imprisonment".

18 Cf. the Criminal Code of Kazakhstan, Article 156 ("Planning, preparation, starting, or waging an aggressive war"): "1. Planning, preparation, or starting an aggressive war,—shall be punished by imprisonment for a period from seven to twelve years. 2. Waging an aggressive war shall be punished by imprisonment for a period from ten up to twenty years, or by capital punishment, or by life-time imprisonment".

19 Cf. the Criminal Code of Moldova, Article 139 ("Planning, preparing, unleashing or waging a war"): "1. Planning, preparing, unleashing a war—shall be punished with deprivation of liberty for a term between 12 and 20 years. 2. Waging a war—shall be punished with deprivation of liberty for a term between 16 and 25 years or imprisonment for life".

20 Cf. the Criminal Code of the Russian Federation, Article 353 ("Planning, preparing, unleashing, or waging an aggressive war"): "1. Planning, preparing or unleashing an aggressive war—shall be punishable by deprivation of liberty for a term of seven to fifteen years. 2. Waging an aggressive war—shall be punishable by deprivation of liberty for a term of 10 to 20 years".

21 Cf. the Criminal Code of Ukraine, Article 437 ("Planning, preparation and waging of an aggressive war"): "1. Planning, preparation or unleashing an aggressive war or armed conflict, or conspiring for any such purposes—shall be punishable by imprisonment for a term of seven to twelve years 2. Waging an aggressive war or aggressive military operations—shall be punishable by imprisonment for a term of ten to fifteen years".

penalties. By contrast, in the Criminal Codes of Armenia,[22] Belarus[23] and Uzbekistan[24]—as well as in the Criminal Codes of Georgia and Tajikistan referred to supra at 4.1.1.1—the initiation of a war is considered as the beginning of its waging, and more severe penalties are provided for initiating and waging a war than are for its planning and preparation. This latter approach seems to be more accurate, for the term "initiation" means the issuance of a formal order to commence hostilities (for the notion of the "moment of aggression", see infra 4.3.1.2)—in contradistinction to planning and preparation for a war,[25]—which will constitute the essence of the ensuing war until its conclusion.

4.1.1.3 Observations

Overall, the "Nuremberg and Tokyo model" appears to be among the most influential national approaches towards the crime of aggression. The attitude of States in whose national penal laws this model applies is based on a narrow construction of the term "war of aggression", which is limited to large-scale (and, probably, rather protracted) international armed conflicts. At least, this interpretation may reasonably be inferred from the case law of the Nuremberg and Tokyo Tribunals (see supra 3.1.1–3.1.2) as well as from the relevant jurisprudence of the Nuremberg follow-up trials (see supra 3.1.3) upon which this legislative model is based. Although the States concerned would probably tend to interpret any large-scale use of force against themselves as a war of aggression, irrespective of its duration (as was the case, for example, in August 2008,

---

[22] Cf. the Criminal Code of Armenia, Article 384 ("Aggressive war"): "1. Planning or preparing an aggressive war is punished with imprisonment for the term from 5 to 10 years. 2. Starting or conducting an aggressive war is punished with imprisonment for the term from 8 to 15 years".

[23] Cf. the Criminal Code of Belarus, Article 122 ("Preparation for or waging and aggressive war"): "1. Planning or preparing for an aggressive war—shall be punished with deprivation of liberty for a term between five and fifteen years. 2. Unleashing or waging an aggressive war – shall be punished with deprivation of liberty for a term between seven and twenty-five years, or with imprisonment for life, or with death penalty with a confiscation of property or without confiscation".

[24] Cf. the Criminal Code of Uzbekistan, Article 151 ("Aggression"): "Planning or preparing for an aggressive war or engagement in conspiracy in order to execute the said actions – shall be punished with imprisonment from ten to fifteen years. Initiating or waging of aggressive war – shall be punished with imprisonment from fifteen to twenty years".

[25] A leading Russian criminal law textbook explains this interrelation in the following manner: "Planning is, essentially, an element in the preparation for war. Besides, preparation for war includes building up volumes of offensive weapons and munitions, relocation and concentration of troops for attack, the mobilisation of economic capacities for the war, establishing economic reserves, carrying out propaganda campaigns, etc. Unleashing a war means starting hostilities, be these a large-scale attack or a local operation, which grows into an armed conflict. The waging of a war is its continuation until the end of hostilities". See Kudryavtsev et al. 2005b, p. 535. In this writer's view, the substance of and relationship between these consecutive stages of an aggressive enterprise are somewhat different and will be discussed below in this chapter, at 4.3.

when Georgia and Russia regarded each other's use of force in South Ossetia as aggression, cf. supra Chap. 1, note 11), one should assume that the "Nuremberg and Tokyo model" covers, first of all, large-scale and protracted wars of aggression. As this model applies both in Georgia and Russia, the given—rather quick—international armed conflict between them should probably not be termed a war of aggression for the purpose of criminal prosecution under the "Nuremberg and Tokyo model".

This model necessitates two more observations. First, there is—and cannot be—any standard, objective "minimum threshold" of magnitude—for example, in terms of military personnel or equipment involved, numbers of victims or duration—above and beyond which a neutrally termed "international armed conflict" becomes an emotionally stirring "war of aggression" worthy of criminalisation. In the absence of relevant clauses in national laws, it is also unclear whose authority to determine, in objective terms, the existence of a war of aggression the State or States in question should recognise as dependable—their own, the United Nations Security Council's or another international body's—before a national criminal prosecution could be initiated.

Second, therefore, if this legislative model is to remain workable in the contemporary world, the term "aggression" should be interpreted as a subjective rather than objective characteristic—as *animus aggressionis* (see infra 4.5), a specific form of *mens rea* incompatible, in the language of Article 8 bis of the Rome Statute (see infra 5.1), with the Charter of the United Nations. Thereby, the "measurable" aspects of a given international armed conflict (i.e. numbers of military personnel or victims or the conflict's duration) would be less decisive for the purpose of initiating a criminal prosecution, as any war waged with an *animus aggressionis* would constitute a "war of aggression" in the sense of the "Nuremberg and Tokyo model". Without a doubt, proving an aggressive intent may be quite difficult. However, a subjective interpretation of "aggression" should make possible national criminal prosecutions for the commission of "act[s] of aggression which, by [their] character, gravity and scale, [constitute] manifest violation[s] of the Charter of the United Nations" (see infra 5.1.1.1.4–5.1.1.1.5) but are "instantaneous", such as ones criminalised in subparagraphs (a)—invasion or attack by the armed forces of a State of the territory of another State (see infra 5.1.1.3.1), (b)—bombardment by the armed forces of a State against the territory of another State or the use of any weapons by a State against the territory of another State (see infra 5.1.1.3.2), or (d)—attack by the armed forces of a State on the land, sea or air forces, or marine and air fleets of another State—of Article 8 bis of the Rome Statute (see infra 5.1.1.3.4).

4.1.2 The "Territorial Integrity or Political Independence Model"

This national legislative approach towards the criminalisation of the use of force in inter-State relations derives from Article 2(4) of the Charter of the United Nations (see supra 2.1). Article 2(4) expressly mentions the "territorial integrity or political independence of any State" among the protected interests and refers, in addition, to "the Purposes of the United Nations" from which further protected interests may derive. This model seems to be no less authoritative than the "Nuremberg and Tokyo" one, for it rests upon a peremptory norm of international law from which no derogation is allowed (see supra 2.1.3). Whereas the "Nuremberg and Tokyo model" is largely based upon international law, which pre-dated the Second World War, this national criminal law model is founded upon a Principle of the Charter of the United Nations and is therefore more progressive.

The norms of national criminal laws which conform to this model contain no direct references to "aggression" and are typically phrased in terms of protecting "independence" and "integrity" of the State concerned from "subjugation", "war", "dependency", "foreign rule" and other similar threats or consequences. Here, the scope of the criminalised individual conduct is considerably broader than that which is required by the "Nuremberg and Tokyo model": the perpetrator needs not bring about a "war of aggression", in order for the criminal liability and punishment to occur, for it suffices if an individual contributes to the commission of a hostile act ("use of force") against the protected interests of a State, or even simply attempts or threatens to do so. In some national criminal laws, even economic pressure is qualified as a manifestation of criminal hostility. The range of potential perpetrators of the crime often comprises both a State's own nationals and foreign citizens.

4.1.2.1 States Parties to the Rome Statute

Out of twenty-four national criminal laws under consideration, five are covered by this model. Article 214 of Argentina's Criminal Code describes the possible perpetrator of the crime in question as "[a]ny Argentinean or person obliged to serve the Nation by virtue of [his or her] public function"[26]; both the civilian and military officials are covered by this provision (cf. infra 4.2.2–4.2.5). More specifically, Article 215 criminalises acts "directed at a total or partial submission of the Nation to a foreign domination or threatening its independence or integrity" as well as "inducing or permitting a foreign power to wage a war against the Republic".[27]

---

[26] Cf. the Criminal Code of Argentina, Article 214: "Any Argentinean or person obliged to serve the Nation by virtue of [his or her] public function who directs weapons against [the Nation], joins efforts with its enemies or provides them with any assistance shall be punished with deprivation of liberty for a term between ten and twenty-five years, or with a lifelong imprisonment, and, in any event, with a lifelong disqualification, unless other provisions of the present Code provide otherwise".

[27] Cf. the Criminal Code of Argentina, Article 215: "A person who commits the crime provided for the in preceding Article shall be punished with a lifelong imprisonment in the following cases: 1) when [he or she] commits an act aimed at a full or partial subjugation of the Nation to foreign domination or [an act] creating a danger to its independence or inviolability; 2) when [he or she] enables a foreign Power to wage a war against the Republic".

In turn, Article 150[28] of Bosnia and Herzegovina's Criminal Code criminalises that country's own and foreign nationals' attempts to violate the territorial integrity of the Federation. Article 150 does not refer explicitly to political independence—another protected interest mentioned in Article 2(4) of the Charter of the United Nations—but it seems to nevertheless be covered by Article 150, for it is hard to imagine the detachment of a part of the territory or its conjoining with another Entity without affecting the political independence of the given territory. Further, Article 151[29] criminalises attempts by Bosnia and Herzegovina's nationals to place the State in a position of subjugation or dependency in relation to another State—acts, which essentially are internal in nature but may be related to forcible external attempts to affect the State sovereignty (cf. infra 4.1.4).

Section 1 of chapter 12 of Finland's Criminal Code[30] also reflects Article 2(4) of the Charter of the United Nations, for its paras (1) and (2) are intended to protect Finland's territorial integrity, and para (3)—which criminalises "restricting the sovereignty of Finland in a comparably serious manner"—covers political independence as a constituent element of sovereignty.[31] Notably, in addition to military means, the Section also lists "economic pressure" among the criminal methods of compromising the sovereignty of Finland, which constitutes a departure from the prevailing interpretation of the term "force" used in Article 2(4) of the Charter (see supra 2.1.1).

Paragraph 83 of the Criminal Code of Norway[32] defines the crime in question in quite similar a manner. It does, however, specifically qualify the examples of methods by which the crime can be committed as "unlawful" and provides for two alternative measures of punishment, which are considerably more severe than the ones provided for in the corresponding provision of Finland's Criminal Code.

---

[28] Cf. the Criminal Code of Bosnia and Herzegovina, Article 150 ("Endangering the territorial integrity of the Federation"): "Whoever, by use of force or by threat of force, attempts to detach a part of the territory of the Federation, or to conjoin a part of its territory with another Entity, shall be punished by imprisonment for a term not less than five years".

[29] Cf. the Criminal Code of Bosnia and Herzegovina, Article 151 ("Getting the Federation in the Position of Subjugation or Dependency"): "A citizen of the Federation, who attempts to get the Federation in the position of subjugation or dependency in relation to another country, shall be punished by imprisonment for a term not less than five years".

[30] Cf. the Criminal Code of Finland, chapter 12 ("Treasonable offences"), Section 1 ("Compromising the sovereignty of Finland"): A person who by violence or the threat of violence or the military or economic pressure or support by a foreign state, for the purpose of: (1) rendering Finland or a part of Finland subject to the authority of a foreign state; (2) separating a part of Finland from the rest of the territory; or (3) otherwise restricting the sovereignty of Finland in a comparably serious manner, commits an act which causes the danger of said purpose being attained shall be sentenced for compromising the sovereignty of Finland to imprisonment for at least one and at most ten years.

[31] See Levin 2003, p. 91.

[32] Cf. the Criminal Code of Norway, para 83: "Any person who unlawfully attempts to cause or to be accessory to causing Norway or any part of the realm to be brought under foreign rule or incorporated into another State, or any part of the realm to be detached, shall be liable to detention for a term of not less than eight years or to imprisonment for a term of not less than eight years and not exceeding 21 years".

Finally, Article 266(1) of the Criminal Code of Switzerland[33] refers solely to the infringement or endangering of the independence of the Confederation. This choice of (and emphasis on) such an exclusively protected value as independence probably derives from Switzerland's permanent neutrality. The provision appears to criminalise internal acts against (cf. infra 4.1.4) as well as external interferences with the Confederation's independence. The second part of Article 266[34] criminalises entering into a relationship with a foreign government or its agents for the purpose of bringing about a war against the Confederation and, in this sense, almost exactly mirrors the approach reflected in Article 215(2) of Argentina's Criminal Code.

4.1.2.2 Other States

Notably, in the criminal legislations of a number of States, the "territorial integrity or political independence model" coexists with other legislative approaches towards protecting those States against unlawful uses of force. Thus, Article 246 of Ethiopia's Criminal Code[35] unambiguously mentions, in subparagraph (a), independence as a protected value but subparagraphs (b) and (c), respectively, refer to "intervention" and "hostile acts", which calls to mind the "objective war model" (see infra 4.1.3). In addition, Article 248 criminalises betrayals of Ethiopia's national interests, which lead to the involvement of the country in hostilities or aggravate its condition, if already at war (cf. infra 4.1.4.2).

Paragraph 156 of Iraq's Criminal Code[36] directly mentions the independence of the country and describes territorial integrity by reference to "its unity or the security

[33] Cf. the Criminal Code of Switzerland, Article 266(1): "Whoever undertakes an action aimed at encroaching upon or endangering the independence of the Confederation, [or at] bringing about a foreign Power's interference in the affairs of the Confederation—shall be punished with a deprivation of liberty of at least one year".

[34] Cf. the Criminal Code of Switzerland, Article 266(2): "Whoever enters in a relationship with the government of a foreign State or its agents, in order to bring about a war against the Confederation—shall be punished with a deprivation of liberty of at least three years. In grave cases, a lifelong deprivation of liberty may be assigned". See also Sayapin 2010b, pp. 175–178.

[35] Cf. the Criminal Code of Ethiopia, Article 246 ("Attacks on the independence of the State"): "Whoever commits an act intended to: (a) jeopardise or destroy the independence of the State; or (b) provoke intervention by a foreign State in the national affair, calculated to endanger its in dependence; or (c) initiate hostile acts by a foreign State against the Nation, or to involve it in a foreign war, hostilities, a blockade or occupation, is punishable with rigorous imprisonment from five years to twenty-five years, or, in cases of exceptional gravity, with life imprisonment or death".

[36] Cf. the Criminal Code of Iraq, para 156: "Any person who wilfully commits an act with intent to violate the independence of the country or its unity or the security of its territory and that act, by its nature, leads to such violation is punishable by death". It should be noted that, in accordance with Section 3(1) of the Coalition Provisional Authority Order No. 7 of 9 June 2003, the death penalty was suspended: "Capital punishment is suspended. In each case where the death penalty is the only available penalty prescribed for an offence, the court may substitute the lesser penalty of life imprisonment, or such other lesser penalty as provided for in the Penal Code".

of its territory". Besides, paras 158 and 159 criminalise individual acts, which lead to the commission of "hostile acts" against the country (see infra 4.1.3.2).

Finally, Article 300(1) of Turkey's Criminal Code[37] criminalises adverse acts aimed against the "territorial land", "National Unity", "certain portion of the territory under the sovereignty and administration of the State" and the "independence of the State", and Article 300(2) points to the substantive interrelation between the "territorial integrity or political independence model" and other related provisions. Article 302, which reflects the "war model", is especially relevant in this context (see infra 4.1.3.2).

4.1.2.3 Observations

The noticeable advantage of the "territorial integrity or political independence model"—in comparison with the "Nuremberg and Tokyo model" (see supra 4.1.1)—is that it derives from a current norm of *jus cogens*, Article 2(4) of the Charter of the United Nations. As the regulation of the use of force under Article 2(4) is capable of evolving in the course of time (see supra Chap. 2, especially notes 10 and 11), the relevant provisions of national criminal laws can retain their protective value, in the course of this evolution, even without formal amendments. As far as the States Parties to the Rome Statute are specifically concerned, this legislative model is also quite compatible with Article 8 bis of the Rome Statute (see infra 5.1), for Article 8 bis was itself constructed in substantive compatibility with the Charter of the United Nations (see infra 5.1.1.1.5).

Yet, by virtue of the same close link to the Charter, this legislative model appears to be lacking a degree of precision required by criminal law provisions (cf. infra 5.2.1–5.2.2). In particular, criminalisation of non-military means of exercising influence upon States—such as economic pressure—along with the use of armed force raises some doubts. Also, equating threats of force to the use of force for the purpose of criminalisation—as is done, for example, in the Criminal Codes of Bosnia and Herzegovina and Finland—contradicts the interpretation of the notion of aggression in resolution 3314 (XXIX) of 14 December 1974, where "threats of force" are no longer mentioned (see supra 2.3 and infra 5.1.1.3.1–5.1.1.3.8). It is therefore suggested that it would be more suitable to criminalise "threats of force" under the heading of "propaganda for war" (see infra

[37] Cf. the Criminal Code of Turkey, Article 300 ("Breach of national unity and territorial integrity"): "1. Any person who causes partition of the country by allowing another country to rule part or whole of territorial land, or breaches National Unity, or shows consent to separation of certain portion of the territory under the sovereignty and administration of the State and executes acts aimed to weaken the independence of the State, is punished with heavy life imprisonment. 2. In case of commission of another office along with this offence, the offender is additionally punished according to the provisions relating to this offence. 3. Security precautions specific to legal entities are imposed in case of commission of the offences defined in this article by corporation".

4.4), and to limit the practical application of the "territorial integrity or political independence model" to cases of actual inter-State uses of military force.

4.1.3 The "Objective War Model"

The distinctive feature of this legislative model consists in shifting the centre of gravity from more or less subjective value judgments—for such qualifications as "the war of aggression" or "the use of force against the territorial integrity or political independence" do contain elements of political and legal value judgments—towards criminalising "war" (in its material sense[38]), "declarations of war"[39] or "hostilities" and other equivalent phenomena, as these represent more objective and therefore, more measurable, occurrences. This legislative model derives from the same source as the previous one (see supra 4.1.2)—the international legal prohibition of the use of force under Article 2(4) of the Charter of the United Nations (see supra 2.1)—but it focuses, instead, on objective manifestations rather than subjective purposes of inter-State uses of force. While the "territorial integrity or political independence model" emphasises the mental element of the crime (cf. infra 4.5), the "objective war model" is about the objective criminality of an international use of force, from the actual commencement of hostilities (cf. infra 4.3.1.2) until the conclusion of the armed conflict in question.

As was also noted above with regard to the "Nuremberg and Tokyo model" (see supra 4.1.1.3), an essential problem with the "objective war model" consists in the absence in international law of a uniform definition of international armed conflict. With the entry into force of the Charter of the United Nations in 1945 (see supra 1.2.5.1), it was no longer lawful to formally declare wars, by virtue of the Charter's Article 2(4), and a more neutral notion—"armed conflict" was introduced in the 1949 Geneva Conventions for the Protection of Victims of War.[40] Yet, the Geneva Conventions did not contain any explanation of the new term, and the ICRC's official Commentary to the First Convention offered too broad a definition thereof.[41] Hence, the key question—when does an armed conflict begin? from the moment a first shot is fired? from the moment there is a first wounded person or a first prisoner of war is taken?—remained largely unresolved in international law. It would therefore be up to each State where the "objective model" applies to determine the

[38] See Dinstein 2001, p. 9.

[39] See Eagleton 1938, pp. 19–35.

[40] In accordance with Article 2 common to the 1949 Geneva Conventions, they apply "to all cases of declared war or of *any other armed conflict* which may arise between two or more of the High Contracting Parties, even if the state of war is not recognised by one of them" (emphasis added) as well as "to all cases of partial or total occupation of the territory of a High Contracting Party, even if the said occupation meets with no armed resistance".

[41] According to the commentary to the First Geneva Convention of 1949, '[a]ny difference arising between two states and leading to the intervention of armed forces is an armed conflict [...] even if one of the Parties denies the existence of a state of war [...]'. See Pictet 1952, p. 32.

starting moment of its participation in a "war" ("international armed conflict", "hostilities", etc.), in accordance with its national legislation. The problem was partially resolved with the adoption of the United Nations General Assembly resolution 3314 (XXIX) of 14 December 1974 (see supra 2.3) in whose Article 3 a number of acts were cited as examples of acts of aggression. However, as there have been no national criminal prosecutions for the crime of aggression, or for other related crimes, since 1974, it remains unknown whether the content of the resolution 3314 (XXIX) would have been useful, at a national level, for determining the starting moment of an armed conflict. By contrast, as the substance of the Resolution's Article 3 was integrated in Article 8 bis (2) of the Rome Statute (see infra 5.1.1.3), Article 8 bis should, with its entry of into force (see infra 5.1.2), constitute binding international law with respect to States Parties to the Rome Statute that would have ratified or accepted it, and, as such, provide a relatively objective framework for determining the moment of launching—presumably, unlawful—hostilities.

4.1.3.1 States Parties to the Rome Statute

No less than six national criminal laws under review are covered by this model. Article 211 of Albania's Criminal Code criminalises the provocation of war or of a military intervention.[42] This Article seems to address both Albanian and foreign nationals and to criminalise the provocation of war on behalf of as well as against Albania. Article 212 also provides for a specific crime of entering into an agreement for an armed intervention against Albania.[43] A similar provision, which also protects the interests of Norway's wartime allies, is contained in para 84 of the Criminal Code of Norway.[44]

Article 98 of Bulgaria's Criminal Code criminalises providing assistance to a foreign power at war with Bulgaria (para 1) and instigating war or other hostile acts against the country (para 2, cf. also infra 4.4).[45] Notably, Bulgaria criminalises in para 1 hostile acts committed not only by "a foreign country" but also by "a public group"—such as, for example, Al Qaeda. The definition covers any group engaging in a crime against Bulgaria, irrespective of its size, structure, motivation, ideology, etc.

---

[42] Cf. the Criminal Code of Albania, Article 211 ("Provocation of war"): "Committing acts with the intent to provoke a war or make the Republic of Albania face the danger of a [military] intervention by foreign powers, is punishable by no less than fifteen years of imprisonment".

[43] Cf. the Criminal Code of Albania, Article 212 ("Agreement for armed intervention"): "An agreement settled with foreign powers or states to cause an armed intervention against the territory of the Republic of Albania, is punishable by ten to fifteen years of imprisonment".

[44] Cf. the Criminal Code of Norway, para 84: "Any person who unlawfully causes or is accessory to causing an outbreak of war or hostilities against Norway or any State allied with Norway in time of war shall be liable to detention for a term of not less than five years or to imprisonment for a term of not less than five years and not exceeding 21 years".

[45] Cf. the Criminal Code of Bulgaria, Article 98: "1. Who abets a foreign country or a public group abroad in a war or other hostile act against the republic shall be punished by imprisonment from five to fifteen years. 2. The same punishment shall be imposed to those who commits an act with the purpose of instigating war or other hostile act against the republic".

The relevant provisions of the Criminal Codes of Guinea,[46] Niger[47] and Senegal[48] are practically identical, both as regards the elements of the crime and the penalty provided for its commission. All of them refer to "a declaration of war" as a point of reference at which the crime in question is regarded as accomplished. It may be inferred from the texts that the punishable "hostile acts" not authorised by the respective Governments include both military and non-military measures causing military reactions. One may assume that the meaning of the phrase "declaration of war" is not limited to its technical sense but also covers a physical outbreak of hostilities against a given State, without a formal declaration of war.[49]

In Article 279 of the Criminal Code of Romania,[50] a virtually universal approach towards the criminalisation of war is reflected, whereby the commission of hostile acts against one of the Member States of the North Atlantic Treaty Organisation, or of the European Union or of the Council of Europe is criminalised in the first place, and the security of any other State which is not at war with Romania is protected as well. As penal action is to be initiated upon request from a foreign State concerned, it may be assumed that the requesting foreign State would, in so doing, rely upon its own interpretation of "aggression" or "hostile act" under international law.

4.1.3.2 Other States

The "objective war model" has also earned a good degree of recognition in States, which are not Parties to the Rome Statute. Thus, in India, not only waging a war, or attempting to wage a war or abetting it, are criminalised,[51] but also conspiracy

---

[46] Cf. the Criminal Code of Guinea, Article 80: "He shall be punished with criminal detention [for a term] between ten and twenty years, who: 1) exposes the Republic of Guinea to a declaration of war by hostile acts not authorised by the Government [...]".

[47] Cf. the Criminal Code of Niger, Article 72: "He shall be punished with imprisonment [for a term] between ten and twenty years, who: 1) exposes Niger to a declaration of war by hostile acts not authorised by the Government [...]".

[48] Cf. the Criminal Code of Senegal, Article 66: "He shall be punished with criminal detention [for a term] between ten and twenty years, who: 1) exposes Senegal to a declaration of war by hostile acts not authorised by the Government [...]".

[49] See Lauterpacht 1968, pp. 58–68; Mégret 2002, pp. 361–399.

[50] Cf. the Criminal Code of Romania, Article 279 ("Hostile acts against a foreign State"): "1. The commission on Romanian territory of hostile acts against one of the Member States of the North Atlantic Treaty Organisation, or of the European Union or of the Council of Europe shall be punished by strict imprisonment from 7 to 10 years and the prohibition of certain rights. 2. The same penalty shall also sanction hostile acts against the security of States, others than those in paragraph 1, and which are not at war with Romania. 3. Penal action is initiated upon request expressed by the foreign State". See also Sayapin 2010b, pp. 178–181.

[51] Cf. the Criminal Code of India, Section 121 ("Waging, or attempting to wage war, or abetting waging of war, against the Government of India"): "Whoever wages war against the Government of India, or attempts to wage such war, or abets the waging of such war, shall be punished with death, or imprisonment for life, and shall also be liable to fine".

for the aforementioned purposes,[52] collecting arms with intention of waging a war,[53] as well as concealing a design to wage a war.[54] Almost identical provisions relating to waging a war,[55] conspiring for the purpose of waging a war,[56] and concealing a design to wage a war[57] are contained in the Criminal Code of Pakistan. The Criminal Code of the Republic of Korea contains an entire chapter entitled "Crimes concerning foreign aggression", which criminalises, *inter alia*, foreign aggression,[58] attempts to commit the crime,[59] as well as preparation, conspiracy

[52] Cf. the Criminal Code of India, Section 121A ("Conspiracy to commit offences punishable by section 121"): "Whoever within or without India conspires to commit any of the offences punishable by section 121, or conspires to overawe, by means of criminal force or the show of criminal force, the Central Government or any State Government, shall be punished with imprisonment for life, or with imprisonment of either description which may extend to ten years, and shall also be liable to fine".

[53] Cf. the Criminal Code of India, Section 122 ("Collecting arms, etc., with intention of waging war against the Government of India"): "Whoever collects men, arms or ammunition or otherwise prepares to wage war with the intention of either waging or being prepared to wage war against the Government of India, shall be punished with imprisonment for life or imprisonment of either description for a term not exceeding ten years, and shall also be liable to fine".

[54] Cf. the Criminal Code of India, Section 123 ("Concealing with intent to facilitate design to wage war"): "Whoever by any act, or by any illegal omission, conceals the existence of a design to wage war against the Government of India, intending by such concealment to facilitate, or knowing it to be likely that such concealment will facilitate, the waging of such war, shall be punished with imprisonment of either description for a term which may extend to ten years, and shall also be liable to fine".

[55] Cf. the Criminal Code of Pakistan, Section 121 ("Waging or attempting to wage war or abetting waging of war against Pakistan"): "Whoever wages war against Pakistan, or attempts to wage such war, or abets the waging of such war, shall be punished with death, or imprisonment for life and shall also be liable to fine".

[56] Cf. the Criminal Code of Pakistan, Section 121A ("Conspiracy to commit offences punishable by Section 121"): "Whoever within or without Pakistan conspires to commit any of the offences punishable by Section 121, or to deprive Pakistan of the sovereignty of her territories or of any part thereof, or conspires to overawe, by means of criminal force or the show of criminal force, the Federal Government or any Provincial Government, shall be punished with imprisonment for life, or with imprisonment of either description which may extend to ten years, and shall also be liable to fine".

[57] Cf. the Criminal Code of Pakistan, Section 123 ("Concealing with intent to facilitate design to wage war"): "Whoever, by any act, or by any illegal omission, conceals the existence of a design to wage war against Pakistan, intending by such concealment to facilitate or knowing it to be likely that such concealment will facilitate the waging of such war, shall be punished with imprisonment of either description for a term which may extend to ten years, and shall also be liable to fine".

[58] Cf. the Criminal Code of the Republic of Korea, Article 92 ("Inducement of foreign aggression"): "A person who, in conspiracy with a foreign country, causes to commence hostilities against the Republic of Korea, or who, in conspiracy with foreigners, fight against the Republic of Korea, shall be punished by death or imprisonment for life".

[59] Cf. the Criminal Code of the Republic of Korea, Article 100 ("Attempts"): "Attempts of the crimes provided in the preceding eight Articles shall be punished".

and propaganda for aggression (cf. also infra 4.4).[60] Notably, these provisions protect the interests of both the Republic of Korea and its allies.[61]

The Criminal Codes of another four States under consideration contain less detailed regulations. Paragraph 158[62] and 159[63] of Iraq's Criminal Code criminalise, respectively, the commission of hostile acts against the country, which may lead to the outbreak of war or the severing of diplomatic relations, and providing assistance in hostile operations against Iraq. Article 118[64] of the Criminal Code of the Philippines criminalises incitement to war or exposing Filipino nationals to reprisals. An additional Article refers to the crime of treason (see infra 4.1.4.2). Article 61 of Tunisia's Criminal Code lists five crimes relating to the waging of war.[65] Finally,

---

[60] Cf. the Criminal Code of the Republic of Korea, Article 101 ("Preparations, conspiracies, agitation or propaganda"): "1. A person who prepares or conspires with intent to commit any of the crimes of Articles 92 through 99 shall be sentenced to imprisonment for a limited term of not less than two years; provided that he denounces himself before carrying out the commission of the intended crimes, the punishment shall be mitigated or remitted. 2. The preceding paragraph shall apply to a person who agitates or propagates any of the crimes specified in Articles 92 through 99".

[61] Cf. the Criminal Code of the Republic of Korea, Article 104 ("Allied power"): "The provisions of this chapter shall apply to the act committed against an allied power".

[62] Cf. the Criminal Code of Iraq, para 158: "Any person who, in a foreign country or in association with it or with a person who is working on its behalf, attempts to commit hostile acts against Iraq that may lead to the outbreak of war or the severing of diplomatic relations or who provides it with the means to that end is punishable by death or life imprisonment". Please note the legal abolition of the death penalty in Iraq in accordance with the Coalition Provisional Authority Order No. 7 of 9 June 2003, see supra note 36.

[63] Cf. the Criminal Code of Iraq, para 159: "Any person who, in a hostile foreign country or in association with it or with a person who is working on its behalf, attempts to assist it in its hostile operations against Iraq or impede the military operations of the Republic of Iraq and any person who provides that country with the means to that end or assists it in any way to succeed in its hostile operations is punishable by death". Please note the legal abolition of the death penalty in Iraq in accordance with the Coalition Provisional Authority Order No. 7 of 9 June 2003, see supra note 36.

[64] Cf. the Criminal Code of the Philippines, Article 118 ("Inciting to war or giving motives for reprisals"): "The penalty of reclusion temporal shall be imposed upon any public officer or employee, and that of prison mayor upon any private individual, who, by unlawful or unauthorised acts provokes or gives occasion for a war involving or liable to involve the Philippine Islands or exposes Filipino citizens to reprisals on their persons or property".

[65] Cf. the Criminal Code of Tunisia, Article 61: "Any Tunisian or any foreigner shall be guilty of an attempt against the external security of the State and punished with sanctions indicated in article 62: 1) [if he or she] exposes Tunisia to a declaration of war by acts not authorised by the government; 2) [if he or she] exposes Tunisians to reprisals, by acts not authorised by the government; 3) [if he or she] enrols soldiers, in time of peace, in the Tunisian territory on the account of a foreign Power; 4) [if he or she] maintains, in time of war, without an authorisation from the government, correspondence or relations with subjects or agents of an enemy Power; 5) [if he or she] carries out, in time of war, in contravention of enacted prohibitions, directly or through an intermediary, acts of commerce with subjects or agents of an enemy Power".

Turkey criminalises, in addition to assaults upon its territorial integrity and political independence (see supra 4.1.2.2), provocations of war and cooperation with the authorities of foreign countries to serve this purpose.[66]

4.1.3.3 Observations

The "objective war model" is quite practical, as it focuses upon measurable manifestations of States' hostile conduct brought about by proscribed individual acts. The logic of this legislative model is plain: any act of military hostility against a given country is unlawful, and committing such an act is a crime. Markedly, this model usually does not require "full-scale" wars (cf. supra 4.1.1) to occur, in order for the crime to be completed. The commission of a single "hostile act" is sufficient, and war—if it results from such an act—is regarded as a circumstance aggravating criminal liability. The "objective war model" is apparently quite compatible with Article 8 bis of the Rome Statute (see infra 5.1), as examples of acts of aggression—an essential element of Article 8 bis (see infra 5.1.1.3)—could be helpful for the purpose of interpreting the national criminal laws of States Parties to the Rome Statute, which would have ratified or accepted the new provision (see infra 5.1.2), as to be criminalised "hostile acts".

4.1.4 The "Treason Model"

Unlike all foregoing legislative models, which for the most part deal with external, international manifestations of a State's aggressive behaviour, this model has to do with the domestic crime of treason, which is closely related to nationality as a stable link between a sovereign State and its citizens.[67] Hence, this legislative model is almost entirely regulated by domestic provisions of criminal law and—unlike the former ones (see supra 4.1.1–4.1.3)—has no source in international law. This

[66] Cf. the Criminal Code of Turkey, Article 302 ("Provocation of war against the State"): "1. Any person who provokes authorities of a foreign country to start war or to take hostile action against Turkish Republic, or cooperates with the authorities of a foreign country to serve this purpose, is punished with imprisonment from ten years to twenty years. The punishment to be imposed is increased by one-third in case of execution of provocation act through press or broadcast organs. 2. In practice of this article, direct and indirect encouragement or support of the organisations that are formed to commit crime against the security of Turkish Republic, is considered as a hostile action. 3. Precautions specific to legal entities are imposed in case of commission of the offences defined in this article by corporation".

[67] On the regulation of nationality in international law, see, for example Adilkariev 2003, pp. 147–154; Bekyashev 1999, pp. 183–186; Kalamkaryan and Migachev 2005, pp. 404–411; Kolosov and Kuznetsov 1998, pp. 110–122; Kovalev and Chernichenko 2008, pp. 182–195; Lukashuk 2008, pp. 371–386.

model is fundamentally concerned with "internal" hostile relations between a State and its nationals, which ultimately lead to the involvement of that State in an international war (armed conflict), or aggravate the situation of that State, if it already is at war with another State. In that sense, the relevant provisions criminalise the superlative degree of betrayal of a State's interests, which results—in an extreme case—in a military threat to the integrity of the State.

4.1.4.1 States Parties to the Rome Statute

It appears that this model is quite popular at the domestic level, as it covers about seven national criminal laws under review. Thus, in the absence of legislation on the crime of aggression, Part 5, section 80(1), of Australia's Criminal Code states:

> A person commits an offence, called treason, if the person: [...] (d) levies war, or does any act preparatory to levying war, against the Commonwealth; or (e) engages in conduct that assists by any means whatever, with intent to assist, an enemy: (i) at war with the Commonwealth, whether or not the existence of a state of war has been declared; and (ii) specified by Proclamation made for the purpose of this paragraph to be an enemy at war with the Commonwealth; or (f) engages in conduct that assists by any means whatever, with intent to assist: (i) another country; or (ii) an organisation; that is engaged in armed hostilities against the Australian Defence Force; or (g) instigates a person who is not an Australian citizen to make an armed invasion of the Commonwealth or a Territory of the Commonwealth; or (h) forms an intention to do any act referred to in a preceding paragraph and manifests that intention by an overt act.

Pursuant to section 80(1), the penalty for this crime is life imprisonment.

Similarly, Article 8 of Brazil's National Security Law of 14 December 1983[68] punishes with up to fifteen years in prison whoever enters into an understanding or negotiation with a foreign government, group, or their agents to provoke war or hostile acts against the country (cf. supra 4.1.3). If the war does occur or hostile acts break out, the punishment shall be doubled. Under Article 9, attempting to submit the national territory, or part of it, to the control or sovereignty of another country (cf. supra 4.1.2) shall be punished with 4–20 years in prison. If during the attempt a serious injury to a person occurs, the punishment shall be increased by one-third. If death occurs, the punishment shall be doubled. In accordance with Article 10 of the Law, he who entices foreigners to invade the national territory (cf. infra 4.3) shall be liable to punishment by deprivation of liberty for a term between three and ten years in prison, and if an invasion occurs, the punishment shall be doubled.

[68] The text of the law is available at the website of Brazil's Presidency: http://www.planalto.gov.br/ccivil/LEIS/L7170.htm#art35 (last visited on 15 May 2012).

Similarly, Sections 1 and 2 of Chapter 19 of Sweden's Criminal Code[69] and Article 271 of Romania's Criminal Code[70] contain formulas, which, if the Articles were not explicitly entitled "Treason", might justify categorising them under the earlier heading of the "territorial integrity or political independence model" (see supra 4.1.2): noticeably, Article 271 of Romania's Criminal Code protects Romania's State unity, indivisibility, sovereignty and independence, the State's immunity from foreign military occupation, economic or political undermining, and its capacity for defence. Coupled with Article 279 ("Hostile acts against a foreign State", see supra 4.1.3.1), Article 271 seeks to minimise the risk of the country's involvement in any international armed conflict, except in cases of compliance with its relevant obligations under international law.

Article 411(4) of France's Criminal Code[71] enumerates quite a broad range of foreign juridical or natural persons entering in hostile agreement with whom against France would cause the criminal liability of a French national. This illustrative range of subjects includes "foreign powers, foreign undertakings or organisations or enterprises or organisations under foreign control, or their agents". On the other hand, Article 81 of Japan's Criminal Code[72] is formally more restrictive and only refers to "foreign States", not including any other subjects. At a practical level, it seems, though, that Article 81 of Japan's Criminal Code would encompass a range of subjects somewhat comparable to that contained in Article 411(4) of the

---

[69] Cf. the Criminal Code of Sweden, Chapter 19 ("On Crimes against the Security of the Realm"): "Section 1: A person who with the intent that the Realm or a part thereof, by violent or otherwise illegal means or with foreign aid, be placed under foreign domination or made dependent on a foreign power, or that a part of the Realm be thus torn loose, takes action which involves danger that such intent be realised, shall be sentenced for high treason to imprisonment for ten years or for life or, if the danger was slight, for at least four and at most ten years... Section 2: A person who by violent means or foreign aid causes a danger of the Realm being involved in war or other hostilities, shall, unless it is high treason, be sentenced for instigating war to imprisonment for at least two and at most eight years".

[70] Cf. the Criminal Code of Romania, Article 271 ("Treason"): "The act of a Romanian citizen, of a person with no citizenship domiciling in Romania or of a foreigner working for the Romanian State of establishing connections with a foreign power or organisation or with its agents, in order to suppress or undermine the State unity, indivisibility, sovereignty or independence, by actions instigating a war against the country or facilitating foreign military occupation, or economic or political undermining, or undermining the State's capacity for defence, or submission to a foreign power, shall be punished by life detention or severe detention from 15 to 25 years and the prohibition of certain rights".

[71] Cf. the Criminal Code of France, Article 411(4): "Intelligence with a foreign power, a foreign undertaking or organisation or an enterprise or organisation under foreign control, or their agents, with a view to fomenting hostilities or acts of aggression against France, is punished by thirty years" criminal detention and a fine of € 450,000. The same penalties apply to furnishing a foreign power, a foreign undertaking or organisation, or an undertaking or organisation under foreign control, or their agents, with the means to start hostilities or commit acts of aggression against France".

[72] Cf. the Criminal Code of Japan, Article 81 ("Instigation of Foreign Aggression"): "A person who agrees with a foreign state and thereby causes the state to exercise armed force against Japan shall be punished by the death penalty".

French Criminal Code, as an abstract "foreign State" would not be able to cause any detriment to the national interests of Japan, without the involvement of its agents or relevant organisations. It seems that, in practice, this provision would cover natural and juridical persons representing, acting on behalf of, with support or approval of a foreign State, including persons who formally are non-State actors, if a link between their action and a foreign State is established.

A notable catalogue of treasonable acts leading to or otherwise related to war is contained in Chap. 6 of Nigeria's Criminal Code.[73] The provisions are all-embracing in that they generally criminalise the preparation for "any" war or warlike undertaking (Article 42), and single out specifically, as punishable by death, wars levied against the State for the purpose of intimidating or overawing the President or the Governor of a State (Article 37(1)). All relevant Articles in this chapter commence by referring to "any person", which makes explicit Nigeria's intention to protect itself against virtually any warlike assault from within or without the State (this condition is specifically mentioned in Article 37(2)). In this sense, Nigeria's defensive stance is almost absolute and elevates all attempts to involve Nigeria, "without lawful authority", in an international armed conflict to the level of the supreme crime against the State.

4.1.4.2 Other States

Article 102 of the People's Republic of China's Criminal Code appears to stand between the "treason model" and the "territorial integrity or political independence model" (cf. supra 4.1.2).[74] It lists among protected interests "the motherland's sovereignty, territorial integrity and security" but criminalises, as a specific mode

---

[73] Cf. the Criminal Code of Nigeria, Chap. 6 ("Treason and certain other offences"): "37. (1) Any person who levies war against the State, in order to intimidate or overawe the President or the Governor of a State, is guilty of treason, and is liable to the punishment of death. (2) Any person conspiring with any person, either within or without Nigeria, to levy war against the State with intent to cause such levying of war as would be treason if committed by a citizen of Nigeria, is guilty of treason and is liable to the punishment of death: (3) Provided that nothing in this section shall prevent any act from being treason which is so by the law of England as in form in Nigeria. 38. Any person who instigates any foreigner to invade Nigeria with an armed force is guilty of treason, and is liable to the punishment of death [...] 42. Any person who, without lawful authority, carries on, or makes preparation for carrying on, or aids in or advises the carrying on of, or preparation for, any war or warlike undertaking with, for, by, or against, any traditional chief, or with, for, by, or against any band of citizens, is guilty of a felony, and is liable to imprisonment for life. 43. A person cannot be tried for treason, or for any of the felonies defined in the three last preceding sections, unless the prosecution is commenced within two years after the offence is committed". See also Sayapin 2010b, pp. 182–185

[74] Cf. the Criminal Code of China, Article 102: "Whoever colludes with foreign states in plotting to harm the motherlan's sovereignty, territorial integrity and security is to be sentenced to life imprisonment or not less than ten years of fixed-term imprisonment. Whoever commits the crimes in the preceding paragraph in collusion with institutions, organisations, or individuals outside the country shall be punished according to the stipulations in the preceding paragraph".

of criminal conduct, "colluding" with foreign States, institutions, organisations or individuals outside the country, which brings the entire provision closer to the "treason model". Further, Ethiopia's Criminal Code criminalises, in Article 248,[75] taking up arms or engaging in hostile acts against Ethiopia as high treason, provided that the act is committed by an Ethiopian national or someone entrusted with the protection of Ethiopian national interests—whereby a norm, which is overall reflective of the "treason model" also reveals elements of the "war model" (see supra 4.1.3.2). Likewise, in the Philippines, treason leading to war is also criminalised,[76] in addition to incitement to war (see supra 4.1.3.2). Finally, Article 222[77] of Togo's Criminal Code criminalises, as treason, six types of activities directed against national defence.

4.1.4.3 Observations

The "treason model" has an indirect relationship to the crime of aggression, inasmuch as certain manifestations of treason are capable of involving the country of which a person committing the crime is a national, or against which his or her actions are directed, in an international armed conflict. It is a crime under national law, not one under international law, but this model is pertinent for the purpose of

---

[75] Cf. the Criminal Code of Ethiopia, Article 248 ("High treason"): "Whoever, enjoying Ethiopian nationality or being officially entrusted with the protection of Ethiopian national interests: (a) takes up arms or engages in hostile acts against Ethiopia; or (b) has dealings with or keeps up a secret correspondence with a power at war with Ethiopia, or with a person or body acting on behalf of such power, for the purpose of ensuring or promoting the enemy's success in any manner whatsoever; or (c) delivers to the enemy, whether directly or indirectly, an object, armament, plan, document or resources of any kind used for the national defence, or aids the enemy by rendering services or delivering supplies to him, is punishable with rigorous imprisonment from five to twenty-five years, or, in cases of exceptional gravity, with life imprisonment or death".

[76] Cf. the Criminal Code of the Philippines, Article 114 ("Treason"): "Any person who, owing allegiance to (the United States or) the Government of the Philippine Islands, not being a foreigner, levies war against them or adheres to their enemies, giving them aid or comfort within the Philippine Islands or elsewhere, shall be punished by reclusion temporal to death and shall pay a fine not to exceed P20,000 pesos. No person shall be convicted of treason unless on the testimony of two witnesses at least to the same overt act or on confession of the accused in open court. Likewise, an alien, residing in the Philippine Islands, who commits acts of treason as defined in paragraph 1 of this Article shall be punished by prision mayor to death and shall pay a fine not to exceed P20,000 pesos".

[77] Cf. the Criminal Code of Togo, Article 222: "Any national of Togo shall be punished by death for treason: 1) [if he or she] delivers to a foreign Power or its agents the territories, places, installations, supplies, vessels, aircraft or war material, which belong to Togo; 2) [if he or she] delivers intelligence to a foreign Power with a view to preparing hostilities against Togo, or facilitating the success of military operations orchestrated against Togo; 3) [if he or she] takes arms against Togo; 4) [if he or she] provokes [members of] Togo's military or Togo's allies to disobedience and treason in favour of a foreign Power; 5) [if he or she] voluntarily destroys a vessel, aircraft, weapon, war material or any other installation employed for national defence; 6) [if he or she] delivers a secret [related to] national defence to a foreign Power or assures [himself or herself] of the possession of such a secret with a view to delivering it to a foreign Power".

this research by virtue of its aim—that of preventing the occurrence of international wars and establishing the individual criminal liability of persons who would have contributed to their occurrence. As is apparent, provisions, which are covered by this legislative model, quite often contain elements of other ones considered above (see supra, especially, 4.1.2–4.1.3)—which is quite explicable, for all these models share a common object of regulation. Due to the specific nature of the "treason model", it will not frequently be recalled in the subsequent analysis. It was useful to outline it here, for the sake of having a comprehensive picture.

4.2 Aggression as a "Leadership Crime"

Although most of the national criminal laws referred to in this chapter are formulated in general terms and hence appear to apply to an indefinite range of persons ("whoever", "any national", "any person", etc.), in practice, their application should involve—primarily, if not exclusively—national leaders capable of directing their States' military efforts.[78] It is therefore useful to devote a section to the range of the crime of aggression's potential subjects where their key characteristics would be summarised. In a way, this section could be considered as a prelude to— and a constitutive part of— the crime of aggression's *corpus delicti* whose material and mental elements are examined below, respectively, at 4.3 and 4.5.

4.2.1 Exclusion of Lower Ranking State Agents

It generally follows from the jurisprudence of the Nuremberg and Tokyo tribunals (see supra 3.1.1–3.1.2), as well as from that of the follow-up Nuremberg trials (see supra 3.1.3), that lower ranking State agents should not, in most cases, be held liable for aggression, because they may not be aware, by virtue of their position or function, of aggressive plans and intentions of their superiors. Correct as this conclusion may be, it does not, however, answer the question: is there the "lowest hierarchical level" in a State's structure below which the subjects of the crime of aggression cannot plausibly be found?

There probably is not a single answer to this question. In the follow-up trials under the Control Council Law № 10, most defendants were acquitted of crimes against peace—mostly due to the lack of a requisite mental element (cf. infra 4.5)—but indictments against them had contained relevant charges, which means that they could theoretically have been convicted of crimes against peace (as five of

[78] On distinctive features of criminality among political and ruling élites, see Luneev 2005, pp. 661–705. In V. Luneev's opinion, the most dangerous forms of élites' criminality are "political corruption" and "political terrorism", which possess the following common features: (1) political leaders' crimes are intrinsically related to their status; (2) as a rule, there are no direct witnesses to such crimes who would be interested in having them prosecuted; (3) these crimes are committed through "highly intellectual" means; and (4) by virtue of their status, the subjects of these crimes are relatively better equipped for evading criminal liability and punishment than are ordinary citizens, see ibid., pp. 664–665. See also Dubber 2007, pp. 977–1001.

them were, see supra 3.1.3.1.1–3.1.3.1.5), had the requisite mental element been in place. Among the defendants, there have been quite senior individuals in the Third Reich's politics and economy, and the absence or existence of the mental element had to be established on a case by case basis. Hence, a more accurate way to phrase the question probably is as follows: if an act of aggression occurs, what could be the guiding principle for identifying its possible authors, in order of priority?

A workable way to proceed would be to analyse an alleged aggressor State's national legislation (including its Constitution, relevant laws and subsidiary normative acts such as decrees, regulations, directives, instructions, etc.) and practices (as far as these may deviate from the legislation), which regulate the authorisation of the use of force by that State, and to consider indicting individuals who occupy the posts in question accordingly. It goes without saying that, during the trial, the degree of individual guilt should be determined as objectively as possible, for partiality in cases where the political element is central by definition would inescapably have an adverse effect both upon the image of the trial and, more broadly, upon the quality of the administration of justice. In most cases, the range of persons involved would encompass the Heads of States and governments, ministers in charge of the armed and security forces, foreign relations, economy and finance, officials in charge of telecommunications and information, chiefs of ruling parties, members of the national legislatures, and holders of other major posts. Individuals within each of these categories can have a role to play in the commission of the crime of aggression, with due regard to the functional indispensability test (see infra 4.3.1.1.2).

4.2.2 Role of Political Leaders

If politics is to be understood as relations between various subjects in their exercise of political power,[79] then political leaders (predominantly civilian but also military, if a State is ruled by a military government) *always* stand at the origin of a State's aggressive behaviour and must, in every case, have a place among individuals charged with an alleged crime of aggression. They determine the overall course of their country's development, define its official ideology (as long as one is allowed[80]), shape its legislation and oversee the latter's implementation, decide upon the order of shaping the country's armed forces, arrange for the collection of taxes to support the functioning of the State machinery, conclude military alliances, and perform an array of other functions, which are essential to the country's military (defensive or offensive) effort. The guiding role of political leaders is critical at all stages of the crime of aggression—planning, preparation, initiation and waging (for details, see infra 4.3)—and the tribunals whose Judgments with respect to crimes against peace have been considered above (see supra 3.1.1–3.1.3)

[79] See Marchenko 2003, p. 67.

[80] Cf., for example, Article 12 of the Constitution of the Republic of Uzbekistan: "In the Republic of Uzbekistan, public life shall develop on the basis of a diversity of political institutions, ideologies, and opinions. No ideology shall be granted the status of state ideology".

took due account of that role. Among the defendants, there were former officials of the German and Japanese Foreign Offices, of Germany's Reich Chancellery, a number of its civilian ministries and agencies and the Nazi party, and their guilt was proved by the records of officials meetings, in which they had participated and where future aggressions had been discussed, by the content of official documents they had signed, by their public (oral and written) statements, and by other appropriate evidence. As the political constituent is decisive in the military—and specifically aggressive—behaviour of a State (cf. supra 1.1.4), individuals in charge of shaping aggressive policies are to be held criminally liable in the first place.

4.2.3 Role of Military Leaders

The role of military leaders in a State's aggressive effort is fundamental, irrespective of whether they are commanded over by civilian authorities (as was the case in Germany, see supra 3.1.1 and 3.1.3), or whether they actually dominate a country's politics (as was the case in Japan, see supra 3.1.2).[81] It is the task of military leaders to develop and arrange for the implementation of practical measures for ensuring the success of military operations necessary for the achievement of preconceived aggressive political goals. This includes developing military strategies and tactics, designing operational plans, organising intelligence, arranging movements of troops and equipment, calculating the armed forces' needs for weapons and munitions, issuing operational orders and instructions, and carrying out other specifically military functions, which contribute to a State's aggressive effort. The indictment and conviction of Germany's and Japan's senior military leaders of crimes against peace by post-World War II tribunals was for that reason fully warranted, and analogous indictments would certainly be issued in future trials with respect to the crime of aggression, if and when such trials were ever to take place.

4.2.4 Role of Economic Leaders

The possibility of holding German economic leaders criminally liable for crimes against peace had not been excluded in the post-World War II trials (see supra 3.1.3.3–3.1.3.4) but, in fact, no defendants who represented the industrial or financial circles were convicted of those crimes. It was held that none of the defendants had been aware of the aggressive aims of Germany's political and military leaders, and therefore could not be held liable for aggression. Conceivably, economic leaders could play a (supporting) role in the *preparation* for and *executing* (waging) an aggression but they would be less involved in its *planning* (much of which is

[81] It must be noted that, for our purpose, the expression "military leaders" is used in its generic sense so as to include officials in charge of a State's armed and security forces, such as the army, police, security services and other units, which may be called upon to perform military functions in an international armed conflict.

secret) and could not *initiate* it, because the "moment of aggression"—for the notion, see infra 4.3.1.2—essentially is a political and military phenomenon. Their role in a country's war effort would consist in producing materials (equipment, munitions, fuel, military software, etc.) and managing financial resources required for it. However, as they would usually perform those functions in defensive and offensive wars alike, it is imperative that their acts′ aggressive mental element be proven accordingly, if they are to be held criminally liable for aggression.[82]

4.2.5 Role of Other (Religious, Social) Leaders

There was no such category of defendants in the post-World War II trials but—it is submitted—in today's world where religion is playing an increasing role in political violence,[83] the role of especially religious but also other social leaders in possible acts of aggression should not be underestimated. In about forty States, official ideologies are based upon religious sources,[84] and the partaking of (especially high-ranking) religious officials in national and international politics is a regular feature of those States' political realities. In some States, secular authorities are even subordinated to religious leaders by law, and are bound to coordinate their decisions with the ecclesiastic hierarchs.[85] As it cannot be excluded that the

[82] Cf. Werle 2009b, p. 414.

[83] See Sapronova 2007, p. 5.

[84] For an overview of such sources' influence upon legal and political processes in some theocratic Islamic States, see ibid., pp. 130–206.

[85] Cf., for example, Article 110 of the Constitution of the Islamic Republic of Iran, which regulates, *inter alia*, the functional relations between the country's spiritual Leader and President: "Following are the duties and powers of the Leadership: 1. Delineation of the general policies of the Islamic Republic of Iran after consultation with the Nation's Exigency Council; 2. Supervision over the proper execution of the general policies of the system; 3. Issuing decrees for national referenda; 4. Assuming supreme command of the armed forces; 5. Declaration of war and peace, and the mobilisation of the armed forces; 6. Appointment, dismissal, and acceptance of resignation of: 1. the fuqaha' on the Guardian Council; 2. the supreme judicial authority of the country; 3. the head of the radio and television network of the Islamic Republic of Iran; 4. the chief of the joint staff; 5. the chief commander of the Islamic Revolution Guards Corps; 6. the supreme commanders of the armed forces. 7. Resolving differences between the three wings of the armed forces and regulation of their relations; 8. Resolving the problems, which cannot be solved by conventional methods, through the Nation's Exigency Council; 9. Signing the decree formalising the election of the President of the Republic by the people. The suitability of candidates for the Presidency of the Republic, with respect to the qualifications specified in the Constitution, must be confirmed before elections take place by the Guardian Council; and, in the case of the first term [of the Presidency], by the Leadership; 10. Dismissal of the "President of the Republic, with due regard for the interests of the country, after the Supreme Court holds him guilty of the violation of his constitutional duties, or after a vote of the Islamic Consultative Assembly testifying to his incompetence on the basis of Article 89 of the Constitution; 11. Pardoning or reducing the sentences of convicts, within the framework of Islamic criteria, on a recommendation [to that effect] from the Head of judicial power. The Leader may delegate part of his duties and powers to another person". See http://www.iranonline.com/iran/iran-info/government/constitution-8.html (last accessed 15 November 2012).

religious element would play a key part in some international armed conflicts in the future (cf. supra 1.1.2.1), religious functionaries may be expected to play quite significant roles in initiating and directing those conflicts.

Also, especially in traditional societies, the role of other social leaders—such as community elders or tribal leaders whose authority over members of their respective tribes or clans may be virtually unlimited—may be important, for example, in mobilising human or other resources for the aggressive effort, or for disseminating propaganda for war (for a note on this crime, see infra 4.4).

4.3 The *corpus delicti* of the Crime of Aggression Under Customary International Law: Material Elements

Based on the analysis of national criminal laws[86] offered supra at 4.1, it will now be attempted to enunciate, in generalised terms, the material elements of the *corpus delicti* of the crime of aggression as a possible basis for the inference of customary international law on the matter.[87]

4.3.1 The Structure of the corpus delicti *of the Crime of Aggression*

The definition of a crime is closely related to its *corpus delicti*. While the definition reflects a criminal phenomenon in formal terms, the *corpus delicti* reveals the crime's interior construction and system-building elements and features. In the theory of criminal law, each *corpus delicti* is characterised by the following five elements: (1) it reflects the social danger and illegality of an act or omission; (2) it distinguishes a crime in question from other crimes; (3) it is codified in a source of criminal law or can be derived from it in the course of an official interpretation; (4) it is not derivative from other *corpus delicti*; and (5) it is characteristic of all crimes of a given kind.[88] In other words, a *corpus delicti* is a logical construction,

---

[86] On the relevance of national laws to the formation of customary international law in a given thematic area, see supra Chap. 2, note 56. See also Werle 2009a, pp. 31–32, 45–47, 356–357.

[87] According to Mike T. Molan, the material elements of an offence (*actus reus*) is "a term referring to the external elements of an offence, that is, those elements of the offence that have to be established by the prosecution, other than those that relate to the defendant's state of mind", see Molan 2008, p. 55. For a theoretical overview of the notion of *actus reus*, see idem., 54–71. Matthew R. Lippman's definition of *actus reus* is more detailed and involves three structural elements: "*Actus reus* generally involves three elements or components: (1) a voluntary act or failure to perform an act (2) that causes (3) a social harm condemned under a criminal statute", see analysis in Lippman 2010, pp. 84–112.

[88] See Kudryavtsev et al. 2005b, p. 98.

a legislator's vision of a specific crime, whereas its definition is a grammatical expression of this logical construction—and quite often an incomplete one, for more than a few elements of the definition of a specific crime are to be found in the General Part of a legislative act, or are quite simply implied.[89]

These elements do, by and large, apply to the *corpus delicti* of the crime of aggression as well. The social danger and illegality of the precursor of this crime—the crime of planning, preparing for, initiating or waging a war of aggression—was already recognised in the Charters and Judgments of the Nuremberg and Tokyo Tribunals and of the follow-up Nuremberg trials (see supra 1.2.2–1.2.4, 3.1.1–3.1.3, 4.1.1), in addition to war crimes and crimes against humanity, which had already possessed foundations of their own in international law. Subsequently, with the entry into force of the Charter of the United Nations, its relevant provisions—above all, Article 2(4) (see supra 2.1)—made up a more contemporary international legal framework for the use of military force in international relations. As was discussed above in this chapter, this progressive development of international law exercised an influence upon a number of national criminal justice systems, whereby aggression and other crimes against peace were codified in appropriate sources of national law in the framework of four predominant legislative models. As will be shown below, the *corpus delicti* of the crime of aggression covers the material elements of three legislative models under discussion, which derive from applicable international law (see supra 4.1.1–4.1.3).

It will also be shown that the crime of aggression can, in effect, be manifested in three distinct *corpus delicti*, depending on a specific stage of individual criminal conduct and on the range of perpetrators involved at the given stage. The succession of these *corpus delicti* includes the truncated, formal and material ones (see infra 4.3.1.1–4.3.1.3), and the criminality of a single act accordingly extends from the moment of its inception in the minds of its authors (see infra 4.5) until the "moment of aggression" (see infra 4.3.1.2).

4.3.1.1 Truncated *corpus delicti*

In criminal law theory, a truncated *corpus delicti* is one, in which the moment of completion of a crime is constituted at a stage preceding its actual commission.[90] The truncated *corpus delicti* apply to exceptionally grave crimes,[91] and it is therefore fully appropriate that aggression—the "supreme international crime"—is criminalised already at the planning and preparation stages. As will be seen below (at 4.3.1.1.1–4.3.1.1.2), the range of perpetrators is broader here than at the subsequent stages of the initiation and execution of the crime (for a general discussion on the range of possible perpetrators of the crime of aggression, see supra 4.2).

---

89 Ibid.

90 Ibid., p. 102.

91 Ibid.

4.3.1.1.1 Planning the Crime of Aggression

The mental element is fundamental to the commission of any crime.[92] Especially in the context of premeditated crimes, it lies at their very roots and guides all conscious developments related to their conceptualisation and commission. In the context of an individual crime of aggression, its direct intent[93]—the so-called *animus aggressionis* (see infra 4.5)—emerges before any objective action is embarked upon and accompanies the entirety of developments related to the commission of the crime.

In effect, the formation of an *animus aggressionis* in the minds of a group of individual civilian and/or military leaders of a State is the very first step in the process of planning the crime of aggression. The *animus aggressionis* is in place at the moment when one such leader first thinks of using force against another State, without that this planned use of force is manifestly consistent with the Purposes of the United Nations (cf. supra 2.1.1.1). Once the intent to use force against another State has been shared by its immediate initiator with the other individuals who are in a position effectively to exercise control over or to direct the political or military action of the State in question,[94] and generally agreed upon among them, the actual planning stage commences. At this stage, *inter alia*, one's own and the likely enemy State's military, economic, technical and human resources are assessed, strategic political aims of the prospective military campaign are defined, military plans are developed, and its ideological and (dis)informational foundations are laid. In other words, the planning stage includes joint conceptual work of top politicians who define goals at the other end of their policies, of high-ranking military officials who work out strategic military tools for the achievement of those goals, and of senior lawyers, diplomats and ideologists whose task it is to ensure, both nationally and internationally, the legality of the future campaign and a favourable disposition of the public opinion towards it (cf. infra 4.4). In

---

[92] See Kudryavtsev et al. 2005a, pp. 186–231.

[93] According to Antonio Cassese, the crime of aggression can also be committed with indirect intent: "[I]t must be shown that the perpetrator intended to participate in aggression and was aware of the scope, significance, and consequences of the action taken or, at the least, knowingly took the risk of bringing about the consequences of that action (*recklessness*)", quoted in Murphy 2006, p. 419. For a more detailed reflection, see infra 4.5.

[94] There is some disagreement in the criminal law theory with regard to whether the formation of a criminal intent itself constitutes a stage in a criminal enterprise. According to some authors, "unlike the preparation [for a crime], the formation of intent does not establish [...] preconditions for the commission of a crime; therefore, it cannot be regarded as a first stage in the commission of the crime". See *Kurs sovetskogo ugolovnogo prava* 1968, p. 545. While the formation of intent does not indeed constitute any objective preconditions for the commission of a crime, which are put in place at the subsequent stage of preparation, it does establish—in conjunction with planning, which follows, if the intent is generally endorsed—a mental framework, a conceptual model of the future act. It may therefore be suggested that whereas the formation of intent does not indeed constitute a separate stage in a criminal enterprise, it does establish a mental framework for the planning and is itself part of that first stage, i.e. of a truncated *corpus delicti* of the crime of aggression.

theocratic States, religious leaders (see supra 4.2.5) may also play a significant role already at the planning stage.

The criminality of planning the crime of aggression—as such and irrespective of whether an actual act of aggression (cf. infra 5.1.1.2) would have taken place—derives from the *animus aggressionis* of the planned act. It is this very element that turns military planning—a sovereign function of each State and a constitutional duty of supreme State officials—into an international crime. Therefore, in order for such military planning to be criminalised as one for aggression, its mental element (see infra 4.5) must be proved beyond reasonable doubt. Written documents with evidential value—such as (public and classified) minutes of official meetings, speeches and programmatic statements, interviews, books, publications in periodicals and other mass media, military maps and the like—would be particularly useful for this purpose.

If information about the planning of a potentially aggressive use of force comes to the attention of a prospective victim State, and the latter chooses to resort to armed force in self-defence, it would presumably invoke the doctrine of preventive self-defence (see supra 2.4.1.2) and bear the burden of proof of its preventive action's legality.

4.3.1.1.2 Preparation for the Crime of Aggression

The planning stage is followed by preparation for a crime. Whilst the borderline between them can, at times, be blurred, preparation means the taking of practical measures in fulfilment of the pre-arranged plans.[95] In other words, preparation is a conscious creation of an environment conducive to the commission of a crime in a formal (see infra 4.3.1.2) or material (see infra 4.3.1.3) sense of its *corpus delicti*.

The preparatory actions can be generally categorised under two major headings: (1) establishing material conditions for the commission of a crime, and (2) carrying out required organisational undertakings.[96] In the context of a crime of aggression, material preparations would include, for example, the acquisition, transportation and installation of weapons and munitions, the taking of measures for the organisation of a war economy, the removal of physical objects, which would inhibit the future movements of one's own troops, and the construction of appropriate defensive fortifications,[97] whilst organisational measures would consist in drafting and enacting necessary legislation, ordering and/or carrying out a general or partial mobilisation, organising the movement of troops and military equipment in accordance with military plans, evacuating the civilian population from certain areas, and networking with potential allies.

---

[95] See Radzinowicz 1966, p. 52.

[96] See Kudryavtsev et al. 2005b, p. 237.

[97] Ibid., p. 535.

As can be seen, the direct intent worked out at the planning stage (see supra 4.3.1.1.1) becomes, at the preparation stage, more express, concrete and precise. At this stage, a genuine feasibility of a State's aggressive use of armed force becomes discernible, which circumstance may prompt a potential victim State to have recourse to pre-emptive self-defence (see supra 2.4.1.3). A State so defending itself should be able to prove beyond all doubt the pre-existence of an *animus aggressionis* on the part of the State against which defensive measures would have been taken, otherwise a State claiming entitlement to pre-emptive self-defence could itself be accused of an unlawful—or even aggressive—use of force.

The range of subjects involved at the preparation stage is broader than that at the planning stage. It includes numerous individuals at lower administrative levels of a State's military and civilian hierarchies, and it would be important to assess the mental attitude of such subordinates among whom quite many would probably not have known of their superiors' aggressive intentions (cf. supra 3.1.3.2–3.1.3.3), or would almost surely claim the defence of superior orders (cf. infra 5.2.12), towards the crime, as well as the degree of their objective contribution to the overall aggressive effort of their State. It is suggested that an adequate test of the value of an individual contribution to that effort at the preparation stage is one of the *functional indispensability of a post to the aggressive effort*. This is to say that the degree of an individual's contribution to the preparation for the crime of aggression should be measured against the role of his or her post in the preparation mechanism. If the role of a specific post were so crucial that its function could not be successfully performed by, or easily transferred to, an individual occupying another post, and the individual occupying the post in question actually contributed to the aggressive effort of his or her State and thereby had a requisite state of mind, the criminal liability for the preparation for a crime of aggression should arise.

4.3.1.2 Formal *corpus delicti*: Initiation of the Crime of Aggression

The initiation of an act of aggression constitutes the crime of aggression's formal *corpus delicti*. The criminal law theory thus terms the *corpus delicti*, which do not require the onset of criminal consequences and are regarded as complete at the moment of the commission of a proscribed act.[98] The criminal consequences of the proscribed act are usually presumed. To the extent that such consequences of a crime of aggression consist in an aggressive war (in the sense of the "Nuremberg and Tokyo model", see supra 4.1.1), an assault against the territorial integrity or political independence of a State (in the sense of the legislative model of the same name, see supra 4.1.2), or in the occurrence of "hostile acts" or "hostilities" (in the sense of the "objective war model", see supra 4.1.3), it is suggested that its formal *corpus delicti* is constituted at the moment of the issuance of an order to use force against another State—which is usually issued by the Head of a State or a Government in his or her capacity of Commander-in-Chief of the State's armed

[98] Ibid., p. 102.

forces and approved, in due course, by other relevant State bodies (for example, the legislature).

At the moment of the issuance of such an order—which, for the purpose of this research, is termed *"the moment of aggression"*—the mental element of the crime is fulfilled, and all subsequent hostile actions, whereby the attainment of political goals set at the stage of planning (see supra 4.3.1.1.1) would be attempted through military means, would fall within the domain of the *jus in bello*, i.e. international humanitarian law for the regulation of the conduct of hostilities.[99] In this sense, as will be discussed below at 4.3.1.3, the subsequent conduct of hostilities should not itself be characterised as lawful or unlawful[100]—except for the purpose of preventing war crimes and prosecuting and punishing individuals for their commission—for it is not the legality or illegality of the resultant hostilities that matter in the context of the crime of aggression but the legality or illegality of the preceding decision to use force against another State. If the decision does not violate applicable international law (see supra 2.4), there is no crime of aggression. If, by contrast, it does, the crime of aggression is completed at the moment an order to use force is issued and approved. From the "moment of aggression" and until the occurrence of an actual armed attack, the target State already is entitled to exercise its right to interceptive self-defence (see supra 2.4.1.4).

The range of subjects involved in the issuance and approval of orders to use force is determined by applicable national procedures. In addition to supreme civilian and military policy-makers in the executive, it also usually includes members of the legislature who approve such decisions as matters of policy and finance.[101] Although they do not participate in the initiation of the crime at the very "moment of aggression", they are called upon to endorse the decision of the executive, and if they do so, they may be alleged to contribute to the initiation of aggression, provided that they share the requisite mental element of the crime (see infra 4.5). The mental element's significance would be particularly noticeable, for instance, in situations where decisions to use force would not meet with a unanimous parliamentary approval. Unanimity in approving the use of armed force might either mean the existence of a genuinely universal support for the decision (which is possible), or the impracticality of making a real political choice and the fact of voting under compulsion. By contrast, a division of opinions could testify to the practical possibility of voting against a decision to use force, which one might not share, and consequently, affirm the *animus aggressionis* of those who would vote in favour of an unlawful use of force.

---

[99] See generally Jessup 1954, pp. 98–103; McDougal 1955, pp. 63–68; Okimoto 2011, pp. 12–35; Orakhelashvili 2007, pp. 157–196.

[100] See Eagleton 1941, pp. 321–326.

[101] Cf., for example, para 11 of Section 8 of the Constitution for the United States of America: "The Congress shall have Power [...t]o declare War, grant Letters of Marque and Reprisal, and make Rules concerning Captures on Land and Water [...]". On the relationship between the war powers of US Congress and president, see Murphy 2006, pp. 213–214.

4.3.1.3 Material *corpus delicti*: Execution of the Crime of Aggression

A *corpus delicti* is referred to as material when it includes identifiable consequences of a crime in question.[102] The legislative models examined above at 4.1 reveal a variety of consequences of aggression and other crimes against peace—ranging from one-off acts of hostility to full-scale international armed conflicts amounting to internationally wrongful acts (cf. supra 2.2) against the victim States' territorial integrity or political independence. It is worth making a number of observations with regard to those criminal consequences, for they do have a bearing on the legal qualification of corresponding individual acts.

First, it is obvious that addressing the issue of criminal consequences of an alleged crime of aggression only makes sense in cases of *actual armed conflicts*, for if a State's aggressive effort is stopped (by the potential victim State(s), their allies, a regional security organisation or the United Nations) at the stages of planning, preparation or initiation, criminal liability for aggression would have effect only for the commission of the crime in its truncated (see supra 4.3.1.1) or formal (see supra 4.3.1.2) *corpus delicti*.

Second, it should be borne in mind that most of the acts that would be regarded as "hostile"—and, therefore, criminal—in the context of aggression would not automatically be viewed as unlawful in the light of applicable international humanitarian law, as long as they would not themselves amount to war crimes.[103] International humanitarian law applies from the beginning of an armed conflict, that is, from the moment a first "hostile act" is committed—and it would be a paradox, if the first act of a hostile nature were regarded as criminal (as one of aggression), and all subsequent acts of the same hostile nature, which would take place during the ensuing armed conflict, would be regarded as lawful, as long as they would not violate the applicable rules of humanitarian law. Consequently, it may be argued that the first hostile act is not by definition a crime under international law—because its (un)lawfulness should be measured by the standards of the *jus in bello*, not the *jus contra bellum*, and it may constitute a lawful act of warfare under the *jus in bello*—but it is rather a *moment signifying the transition* from the formal *corpus delicti* of the crime of aggression to the material one.

Third, and finally, if an international armed conflict actually occurs—and the material *corpus delicti* of the crime of aggression is thus constituted—its physical effects (in terms of numbers of the military personnel involved and equipment used, scale of spatial coverage and duration, etc.) should be used as indicators of the gravity of the crime of aggression and, correspondingly, as circumstances affecting the criminal liability of its authors. An aggression would still remain an aggression, even if a victim State were subjugated without a single shot—for an aggression is such by virtue of its mental element (see supra 4.1.1.3 and infra 4.5)—but its material consequences would matter for the purposes of assigning individual punishments and assessing the aggressor State's international responsibility more equitably.

---

[102] See Kudryavtsev et al. 2005b, p. 102.

[103] Cf. supra 4.1.3.

As it was argued above that a crime of aggression is formally accomplished at the "moment of aggression" (see supra 4.3.1.2), the issue of the range of subjects involved in the "execution" of the crime appears to be immaterial. Since an international armed conflict, which ensues from a given act of aggression, is—for the purpose of criminalisation—this act's "consequence", the range of to be indicted individuals should include those who would have previously contributed to the planning, preparation and initiation (see supra 4.3.1.1–4.3.1.2) of the act of aggression.

4.4 The Qualification of "Propaganda for War" as a Separate Crime

Michael G. Kearney, the author of an excellent monograph on the prohibition of the propaganda for war, qualified "propaganda for war" as a separate crime against peace,[104] despite the absence of a direct reference to the crime in the original sources of international law on the crimes against peace—the Charters of the Nuremberg and Tokyo Tribunals (see supra 1.2.2–1.2.3 and 3.1.1–3.1.2) and the Control Council Law № 10 (see supra 1.2.4 and 3.1.3). This crime's distinct nature lay in an offensive manipulation of the collective consciousness, for the purpose of "implanting in the minds of the "target" audience certain prejudices, beliefs or convictions aimed at persuading the latter to take certain action serving the interest of the communicator".[105] Through the intermediary of a 1933 treatise written by Frederick Lumley, Michael G. Kearney traced the etymological roots of the term "propaganda" back to Latin as follows:

> It is from *propagatus*, perfect participle of *propagare*, which had reference to the very specific act of fastening down slips or roots of plants in such a way as to cause them to multiply and spread; in other words it had reference to the gardener's work of forcing growth among plants or vegetables. It also had reference to the forced breeding of animals. Gradually, as with hosts of other words, it came to have an abstract meaning and to signify all of the processes involved in the propagation of anything from a bit of silly gossip to the majestic doctrine of transubstantiation.[106]

It is commonly agreed that the term "propaganda for war"—itself composed of two notions whose meaning for the purpose of international law is not undisputed[107]—is used to denote only wars in contravention of international law and

[104] Kearney 2007, pp. 36–40. See also Fenwick 1941, pp. 626–631; Preuss 1934, pp. 649–668; Van Dyke 1940, pp. 58–73; Whitton 1951, pp. 151–153; Wright 1948, pp. 128–136.

[105] Whitton 1974, at 239.

[106] Lumley FE (1933) *The Propaganda Menace*. New York, D. Appleton—Century Company, 56, quoted in Kearney 2007, p. 3.

[107] In this regard, Michael G. Kearney notes, rightly, as follows: "Neither is the word war itself frequently used in the context of international law, with aggression being the relevant term for the purposes of international criminal law and "armed conflict" or "use of force" employed by humanitarian lawyers". See Kearney 2007, p. 4.

does not cover lawful exceptions to Article 2(4) of the Charter of the United Nations (see supra 2.4). As is evident from examples of national provisions criminalising propaganda for war,[108] they cover a broad variety of individual activities aimed at encouraging a State's aggressive effort—especially, at the stages of its planning (see supra 4.3.1.1.1), preparation (see supra 4.3.1.1.2) or initiation (see supra 4.3.1.2)—and in this way reinforce the substantive prohibitions of aggression (see supra 4.1). The relevant norms are to be found in the Criminal Codes of a number of States Parties to the Rome Statute of the International Criminal Court and of non-Parties alike. The first group of States includes, for example, Estonia,[109] Finland,[110] Georgia,[111] Germany,[112] Hungary,[113]

---

[108] Again, according to Michael G. Kearney, the *travaux préparatoires* of Article 20(1) of the International Covenant on Civil and Political Rights, which requires that "propaganda for war" must be proscribed by law, suggest that penal sanctions for such propaganda would be more suitable than other forms of responsibility and perhaps the only effective means of giving effect to the obligation. See Kearney 2007, p. 134.

[109] Cf. the Criminal Code of Estonia, para 92 ("Propaganda for war"): "(1) Any incitement to war or other use of arms in violation of the generally recognised principles of international law is punishable by a pecuniary punishment or up to 3 years' imprisonment. (2) The same act, if committed by a legal person, is punishable by a pecuniary punishment".

[110] Cf. the Criminal Code of Finland, Chapter 2 ("Treasonable offences"), Section 2 ("Warmongering"): "If a person in Finland or a Finnish citizen outside of Finland, during an ongoing or imminent military crisis or international political crisis, for the purpose of causing Finland to be at war or the target of a military operation (1) publicly exhorts a foreign state to carry out an offensive against Finland or Finland to carry out an offensive against a foreign state; (2) publicly disseminates statements or other propaganda intended to turn the public opinion in favour of the carrying out of offensives; (3) systematically disseminates manifestly unfounded or misleading information on the Finnish defence or the military or security policy of Finland; or (4) unlawfully commits a violent act against a foreign state or the representative, territory or property of a foreign state so that the act evidently increases the danger of Finland being at war or the target of a military operation, that person shall be sentenced for *warmongering* to imprisonment for at least one and at most ten years".

[111] Cf. the Criminal Code of Georgia, Article 405 ("Calling for unleashing aggressive war"): "1. Calling the country for unleashing the war of aggression – shall be punishable by fine or by imprisonment for up to three years in length. 2. The same action perpetrated via media or by a person holding a State or political office – shall carry legal consequences of fine or imprisonment ranging from two to five years in length, be deprivation of the right to occupy a position or pursue a particular activity for the term not in excess of three years".

[112] Cf. the Criminal Code of Germany, Section 80a ("Incitement to a war of aggression"): "Whoever publicly incites to a war of aggression (Section 80) in a meeting or through the dissemination of writings (Section 11 subsection (3)) in the territorial area of application of this law shall be punished with imprisonment from three months to five years".

[113] Cf. the Criminal Code of Hungary, Section 153 ("Incitement to war"): "(1) The person who incites for war or otherwise displays war propaganda, commits a felony and shall be punishable with imprisonment from two years to eight years. (2) The punishment shall be imprisonment from five years to fifteen years, if the crime is committed before a great publicity. (3) The person who commits preparation for incitement for war, shall be punishable for a felony with imprisonment of up to three years".

Latvia,[114] and Tajikistan.[115] The second group is represented, especially, by a majority of member States of the Commonwealth of Independent States (CIS) as successors to the USSR, which actively promoted the subject of propaganda for war in the process of drafting Article 20(1) of the International Covenant on Civil and Political Rights,[116]—Armenia,[117] Azerbaijan,[118] Belarus,[119] Kazakhstan,[120]

[114] Cf. the Criminal Code of Latvia, Section 77 ("Incitement to a war of aggression"): "For a person who commits public incitement to a war of aggression or instigation to an armed conflict, the applicable sentence is deprivation of liberty for a term not exceeding eight years".

[115] Cf. the Criminal Code of Tajikistan, Article 396 ("Public appeals to unleashing an aggressive war"): "(1) Public appeals to unleashing an aggressive war is punishable by a fine of 500–1000 times the minimum monthly wage or imprisonment for a period of 2–5 years. (2) The same actions committed using mass media or by persons who hold state positions of the Republic of Tajikistan are punishable by imprisonment for a period of 7–10 years with deprivation of the right to hold certain positions or be engaged in certain activities for up to 5 years. *Note:* The list of persons who hold state positions is determined by the legislation of the Republic of Tajikistan".

[116] See Kearney 2007, p. 134.

[117] Cf. the Criminal Code of Armenia, Article 385 ("Public calls for aggressive war"): "1. Public calls for starting an aggressive war are punished with a fine of 100–200 minimal salaries, or with imprisonment for the term of up to 3 years. 2. The same actions which were implemented by mass media or by the highest state authority, are punished with a fine of 300–500 minimal salaries, or with imprisonment for the term of 2–5 years, by deprivation of the right to hold certain posts or practice certain activities for up to 3 years. 3. By the highest state authority referred to in this Article, we mean the President of the Republic of Armenia, the members of the Government of the Republic of Armenia, the members of the National Assembly of the Republic of Armenia".

[118] Cf. the Criminal Code of Azerbaijan, Article 101 ("Public appeals to implementation of aggressive war"): "1. Public appeals to implementation of aggressive war – shall be punished by restriction of freedom for the term up to three years or imprisonment on the same term. 2. The same acts accomplished with the use of mass media or official means – shall be punished by imprisonment for the term from two up to five years with deprivation of a right to hold a certain posts or to engage in the certain activities for the term up to three years or without it".

[119] Cf. the Criminal Code of Belarus, Article 123 ("Propaganda for war"): "1. The dissemination in any form of views, ideas or calls for the purpose of inspiring one country's aggression against another (propaganda for war)—shall be punished by a fine or by deprivation of liberty for a term not exceeding three years. 2. Propaganda for war by individuals occupying supreme official posts—shall be punished by deprivation of liberty for a term between two and five years with the deprivation of the right to occupy certain posts or to engage in certain activities without such a deprivation".

[120] Cf. the Criminal Code of Kazakhstan, Article 157 "("Propaganda and public calls for unleashing an aggressive war"): "1. Propaganda and public exhortations to unleash an aggressive war—shall be punished by a fine in an amount up to three thousand monthly assessment indices, or in an amount of wages of other income of a given convict for a period from three to nine months, or by imprisonment for a period up to three years. 2. The same acts committed with the use of the mass information media, or by an official holding a responsible position – shall be punished by a fine in an amount up to five thousand monthly assessment indices, or in an amount of wages of other income of a given convict for a period from six months up to one year, or by imprisonment for a period from two to five years with deprivation of the right to hold certain positions or to engage in certain types of activity for a period up to three years".

Moldova,[121] the Russian Federation,[122] Ukraine,[123] and Uzbekistan.[124] Notably, Turkmenistan—a permanently neutral State—did not enact a provision for the criminalisation of aggression but it has one proscribing the propaganda for war.[125] Thus, if a national trial on charges for a crime of aggression (or another crime against peace) should ever take place in the future (cf. infra 4.6.1), one may reasonably assume that this trial would also deal with charges of propaganda for war.

4.5 The *corpus delicti* of the Crime of Aggression Under Customary International Law: Mental Element

In the criminal law theory, the *mens rea*—or the mental element of a crime—is understood as a perpetrator's psychological attitude towards his or her crime as a whole, as well as towards its distinct objective elements (socially dangerous act or

[121] Cf. the Criminal Code of Moldova, Article 140 ("War propaganda"): "1. War propaganda, spreading of tendentious or invented news, of a nature to instigate to war, or any other activities oriented to unleashing a war, committed through speech, writing, radio, television, cinema or any other means,- Shall be punished by a fine in the amount of up to 500 conventional units or by imprisonment for a period of 3 to 8 years, in both cases with forfeiture of the right to hold certain positions or to engage in certain activities for an up to 5 year period. 2. Committing the acts set forth in paragraph (1) by a high official of public authority, Shall be punished by a fine in the amount of 500 to 1000 conventional units or by jail sentence of between 8 and 12 years, in both cases with forfeiture of the right to hold certain positions or to engage in certain activities for an up to 5 year period".

[122] Cf. the Criminal Code of the Russian Federation, Article 354 ("Public appeals to unleash an aggressive war"): "1. Public appeals to unleash an aggressive war—shall be punishable by a fine in the amount up to 300 thousand roubles, or in the amount of the wage or salary, or any other income of the convicted person for a period up to two years, or by deprivation of liberty for a term of up to three years. 2. The same acts, committed with the use of the mass media or by a person who holds a state post of the Russian Federation or a state post of a subject of the Russian Federation—shall be punishable by a fine in the amount of 100 thousand to 500 thousand roubles, or in the amount of the wage or salary, or any other income of the convicted person for a period of one to three years, or by deprivation of liberty for a term up to five years, with disqualification to hold specified offices or to engage in specified activities for a term of up to three years".

[123] Cf. the Criminal Code of the Ukraine, Article 436 ("Propaganda of war"): "Public calls to an aggressive war or an armed conflict, and also making of materials with calls to any such actions for distribution purposes or distribution of such materials—shall be punishable by correctional labour for a term up to two years, or arrest for a term up to six months, or imprisonment for a term up to three years".

[124] Cf. the Criminal Code of Uzbekistan, Article 150 ("Propaganda of war"): "Propaganda of war, that is, any form of dissemination of views, ideas or calls with the purpose of making aggression of one country against another one—shall be punished with imprisonment from five to ten years".

[125] Cf. the Criminal Code of Turkmenistan, Article 167 ("Propaganda for war"): "Propaganda for war, that is, the dissemination through the mass media or otherwise of calls for waging and aggressive war shall be punished with correctional labour for a term not exceeding two years or with deprivation of liberty for a term not exceeding five years".

omission, criminal consequences, causal link between the act or omission in question and its consequences, the crime's temporal and spatial circumstances, the tools and means for committing the crime, and other circumstances pertaining to the commission of the crime).[126] A composite phenomenon, the mental element incorporates a few interconnected social and psychological elements—such as guilt,[127] purpose and motive of a crime, as well as a perpetrator's emotional condition throughout the process of its commission (cf. supra 4.3)—in the context of applicable (national or international) criminal law. Since a use of armed force against another State is not an end in itself but a means for the attainment of political, economic, ideological or other goals (see supra 1.1.4), it will be useful to look especially at the purposes of the use of force, as it is those very purposes that normally attribute illegality to the use of force.

4.5.1 Occupation of Another State

It is an uneasy fact that the regime of military occupation is treated differently, on the one hand, in international (humanitarian) law and, on the other hand, in some national legal systems. In international law, military occupation is a recognised institution, whereby "[t]he authority of the legitimate power having in fact passed into the hands of the occupant, the latter [should] take all the measures in his power to restore, and ensure, as far as possible, public order and safety, while respecting, unless absolutely prevented, the laws in force in the country".[128] That is to say, occupation is regarded in international law as an admissible—although somewhat unfavourable—reality.[129] In the 1907 Hague Regulations, "occupation"

---

[126] See Kudryavtsev et al. 2005a, pp. 72–144, where the mental element (*mens rea*) of an offence is defined (at 72) as "the state of mind of the accused at the time of the commission of the *actus reus* of an offence. The traditional maxim is "*actus not facit reum nisi mens sit rea*": the act is not guilty unless the mind is also guilty". In turn, M. Lippman defines *mens rea* as "the "mental part" of crimes", see Lippman 2010, p. 114.

[127] In accordance with the psychological theory of criminal guilt, every socially dangerous act committed by a sane person is considered to be conscious and volitional—and hence, guilt is considered to include *intellectual* and *volitional* elements. Different forms of the *mens rea* (direct or indirect intent, negligence or *dolus eventualis*) result from various combinations of these elements. For the purpose of this research, the direct and indirect forms of intent are essential. The direct intent embraces three interrelated features: (1) a perpetrator's conscious attitude towards the social danger of his or her act (or omission, which is immaterial in the context of aggression); (2) prevision of the unavoidability or possibility of the act's socially dangerous consequences; and (3) desire for their onset. In turn, indirect intent too consists of three elements: (1) a perpetrator's conscious attitude towards the social danger of his or her act; (2) prevision of the possibility of the act's socially dangerous consequences; and (3) conscious allowance for their onset. See Kudryavtsev et al. 2005a, p. 193.

[128] See the 1907 Hague Regulations, Article 43.

[129] It is thereby understood that an Occupying Power must comply with the laws of war. See Freeman 1947, pp. 579–610; Tolochko 2009, pp. 180–188.

is defined as an actual placement of a territory "under the authority of the hostile army. The occupation extends only to the territory where such authority has been established and can be exercised".[130] By contrast, in some national laws, occupation is listed among unlawful consequences of individual acts whose authors should be held criminally liable. Article 271 of the Criminal Code of Romania (see supra 4.1.4.1, note 70) and Article 246(c) of the Criminal Code of Ethiopia (see supra 4.1.2.2, note 35) exemplify this. This inconsistency may be due to the origin of the national criminal prohibitions in international instruments, which themselves essentially contradict the Hague Regulations. Thus, Article 2(a) of the 1974 Definition of Aggression (see supra 2.3) qualifies as examples of acts of aggression "[t]he invasion or attack by the armed forces of a State of the territory of another State, or *any military occupation*, however temporary, resulting from such invasion or attack, or any annexation by the use of force of the territory of another State or part thereof" (emphasis added). This provision is reproduced verbatim in the Rome Statute's Article 8 bis 2(a) (see infra 5.1.1.3.1). Here, one is confronted with a normative collision whereby the same phenomenon is considered lawful under one legal regime—international humanitarian law—and is found illegal under some national criminal laws and international criminal law. In order to reconcile the contradiction, one has to turn to the rules of interpretation of treaties.[131]

It would be "manifestly absurd or unreasonable"—in the language of Article 32(b) of the 1969 Vienna Convention on the Law of Treaties—to suppose that the term "occupation" has different meanings in the 1907 Hague Regulations, the 1974 Definition of Aggression and the Rome Statute. As a technical legal term having a "special meaning" in the sense of Article 31(4) of the Vienna Convention, it must be interpreted in the light of "relevant rules of international law applicable in the relations between the parties"—in the given case, of Article 42 of the 1907 Hague Regulations where the term had been originally defined and described[132]—and the option of attributing two different meanings to the same term—under international humanitarian and criminal law—must be ruled out.

It would be equally unreasonable to suppose that what is legal under international humanitarian law becomes illegal under international criminal law (cf. supra 4.3.1.3). International criminal law defines war crimes—that is, particularly grave breaches of international humanitarian law[133]—but the establishment and exercise of the military occupation regime is not among them. Therefore, a possible explanation of the inconsistency in question is that criminalisation extends to one particular aspect of occupation—i.e. its conflict with the *jus cogens* prohibition of the threat or

---

[130] See the 1907 Hague Regulations, Article 42.

[131] In this context, Articles 31 ("General rule of interpretation") and 32 ("Supplementary means of interpretation") of the 1969 Vienna Convention on the Law of Treaties are particularly relevant.

[132] Another useful source for the interpretation of the military occupation regime is Section III of the Fourth Geneva Convention ("Occupied territories").

[133] For an overview of the law of war crimes, see Cassese 2008, pp. 81–97; Cryer et al. 2007, pp. 221–261; generally Meron 1998; Werle 2009a, pp. 344–473.

use of force against the territorial integrity of any state (which is violated by an occupation regime insofar as it means the placement of a national territory "under the authority of the hostile army"), which is reflected in Article 2(4) of the Charter of the United Nations (see supra 2.1). In other words, it is not occupation as an institution of international humanitarian law, which aims at the maintenance—to a practically possible extent—of law and order in the occupied territory, that is criminalised but the "invasion or attack by the armed forces" from which an occupation results, because such an invasion or attack would be aimed at violating the territorial integrity of the attacked State and/or at depriving the attacked territory from its political independence (cf. supra 4.1.2).[134] This specific intent of the authors of the crime of aggression would have to be supported by relevant evidence.

4.5.2 Annexation of Another State

A similar logic applies to the criminality of the annexation of another State, which is mentioned, for example, in Article 150 of the Criminal Code of Bosnia and Herzegovina (see supra 4.1.2.1, note 28), para 83 of the Criminal Code of Norway (see supra 4.1.2.1, note 32), Article 300 of the Criminal Code of Turkey (see supra 4.1.2.2, note 37), and Section 121A of the Criminal Code of Pakistan (see supra 4.1.3.2, note 56). The "annexation by the use of force of the territory of another State or part thereof" is an alternative criminal consequence of "invasion or attack" constituting aggression in the sense of the 1974 Definition of Aggression (see supra 2.3) or Article 8 bis 2(a) of the Rome Statute (see infra 5.1.1.3.1). Annexation appears to be a graver violation of international law than is military occupation, because the former represents a form of *unlawful acquisition of territorial sovereignty* by a State.[135] Whereas military occupation does not denote a form of sovereignty over a territory but only one of *temporary control*, annexation is a way for asserting permanent sovereign rights—hence, its illegality under international law and the criminal liability of its authors.

4.5.3 Subjugation of Another State

Quite a number of national criminal laws refer to the subjective orientation of the aggressive use of force against the political independence of the victim State.

---

[134] Cf. the first sentence of the 10th paragraph interpreting the prohibition of the threat or use of force in the 1970 Friendly Relations Declaration: "The territory of a State shall not be the object of military occupation resulting from the use of force in contravention of the provisions of the Charter".

[135] Cf. the second and third sentences of the 10th paragraph interpreting the prohibition of the threat or use of force in the 1970 Friendly Relations Declaration: "The territory of a State shall not be the object of acquisition by another State resulting from the threat or use of force. No territorial acquisition resulting from the threat or use of force shall be recognised as legal".

Relevant examples can be found in Article 215(1) of the Criminal Code of Argentina (see supra 4.1.2.1, note 27), Article 151 of the Criminal Code of Bosnia and Herzegovina (see supra 4.1.2.1, note 29), para 83 of the Criminal Code of Norway (see supra 4.1.2.1, note 32), Article 266(1) of the Criminal Code of Switzerland (see supra 4.1.2.1, note 33), Articles 246(a) and (b) of the Criminal Code of Ethiopia (see supra 4.1.2.2, note 35), Article 300 of the Criminal Code of Turkey (see supra 4.1.2.2, note 37), Section 1 of Chapter 19 of the Criminal Code of Sweden (see supra 4.1.4.1, note 69), Article 271 of the Criminal Code of Romania (see supra 4.1.4.1, note 70), and Article 102 of the Criminal Code of China (see supra 4.1.4.2, note 74). Along with the prohibition of the annexation of another State (see supra 4.5.2), these criminal proscriptions originate from Article 2(4) of the Charter of the United Nations—more specifically, from the part of the provision, which prohibits the threat or use of force against the "political independence of any state" (see supra 2.3). As does national territory, political independence constitutes an element of statehood.[136] Since depriving a State of its political independence would in effect mean the collapse of its very statehood, the legal qualification of military attacks against the political independence of States as aggression is absolutely appropriate.

4.5.4 Involving Another State in War

Another mental element, which is criminalised—mostly, in countries where the "objective war model" applies,—is a perpetrator's direct intent to commence an armed conflict against another State. Examples of relevant formulations are contained in Articles 211 and 212 of the Criminal Code of Albania (see supra 4.1.3.1, notes 42 and 43, respectively), Section 122 of the Criminal Code of India (see supra 4.1.3.2, note 53), Section 123 of the Criminal Code of Pakistan (see supra 4.1.3.2, note 57). In the framework of this legislative model, the prohibited acts consist in causing a State to engage in "hostilities" or "war", or else in causing an "armed intervention" against that State, and the crime's mental element accordingly consists in perpetrators' desire to attain those objective effects. The States protected by the "objective war model" seek to fully shield themselves against the crime of aggression (see supra 4.1.3.3), and hence they link its mental element to the actual use of force as such, without necessarily specifying the criminal consequences of the use of force.

4.5.5 Conspiracy

Another recognised form of criminal liability for aggression is conspiracy.[137] It found expression, for example, in Section 72 of the Criminal Code of Latvia (see

[136] See Lukashuk 2008, p. 25.

[137] Antonio Cassese notes that this form of liability originates from common law systems and is either unknown to, or accepted of a very limited extent by, civil law systems. See Cassese 2008, p. 227.

supra 4.1.1.1, note 11), Article 437 of the Criminal Code of Ukraine (see supra 4.1.1.2, note 21), Article 151 of the Criminal Code of Uzbekistan (see supra 4.1.1.2, note 24), Section 121A of the Criminal Code of India (see supra 4.1.3.2, note 52), Section 121A of the Criminal Code of Pakistan (see supra 4.1.3.2, note 56), Articles 92 and 101 of the Criminal Code of the Republic of Korea (see supra 4.1.3.2, notes 58 and 60, respectively), and Article 37(2) of the Criminal Code of Nigeria (see supra 4.1.4.1, note 73). Conspiracy consists in the agreement of two or more persons to commit a crime of aggression and is punishable even if the crime has not been completed.[138] That is, in States where the concept of conspiracy is recognised, liability for it would arise at the stages of planning and preparing for the commission of the crime of aggression (see supra 4.3.1.1.1–4.3.1.1.2), and at the stages of the initiation and commission of the crime (see supra 4.3.1.2–4.3.1.3) liability both for conspiracy and the completed crime would materialise.[139] The mental element of conspiracy required for each participant should include (1) the *knowledge* of the facts and circumstances pertaining to the intended crime, and (2) the *intent* to carry out the conspiracy, i.e. to perpetrate a substantive crime of aggression (cf. infra 5.2.9). Having said this, one should note that despite its fairly broad recognition, the concept of conspiracy is not impeccable, because—as Larry May cautions,—"the conspiracy theory makes good normative sense only if *mens rea* elements are not weakened. But then it will almost always make sense to charge the defendant with what he or she actually did and intended rather than with conspiracy. While useful for the prosecution, the conspiracy charge is not good for justice and the rule of law".[140]

4.6 Mechanisms of Enforcement

Given the relative normative wealth accumulated at the national level, criminal liability for the crime of aggression can be enforced indirectly (by national courts) and, in the future, hopefully, also directly (by the International Criminal Court).[141] In this respect, the International Law Commission opined in its official Commentary to Article 8 of the 1996 Draft Code of Crimes against the Peace and Security of Mankind (on the Draft Code itself, see supra 1.2.5.6 and 3.1.5) as follows:

> The second and third provisions of the article comprise a separate jurisdictional regime for the crime of aggression [...] This jurisdictional regime provides for the exclusive jurisdiction of an international criminal court for the crime of aggression with the singular exception of the national jurisdiction of the State which has committed aggression over its own nationals [...]

---

[138] Ibid.

[139] Ibid.

[140] May 2008, p. 251 and ff.

[141] See Reisinger Coracini 2009, p. 727. On the distinction between the indirect and direct enforcement of international criminal law, see also Safferling 2012, pp. 7–8.

> The second provision of the article establishes the principle of the exclusive jurisdiction of an international criminal court in determining the responsibility [...] of individuals [...] for the crime of aggression [...] subject to the singular exception recognised in the third provision of the article which is discussed below. This principle of exclusive jurisdiction is the result of the unique character of the crime of aggression [...] An individual cannot incur responsibility for this crime in the absence of aggression committed by a State. Thus, a court cannot determine the question of individual criminal responsibility for this crime without considering as a preliminary matter the question of aggression by a State. The determination by a national court of one State of the question of whether another State had committed aggression would be contrary to the fundamental principle of international law *par in parem imperium non habet.* Moreover, the exercise of jurisdiction by the national court of a State which entails consideration of the commission of aggression by another State would have serious implications for international relations and international peace and security [...]
>
> The third provision of the article recognises a singular national court jurisdiction exception to the otherwise exclusive jurisdiction of an international criminal court under the second jurisdictional regime for the crime of aggression. The only State that could try an individual for the crime of aggression in its national courts under this provision is the State referred to in article 16, namely the State whose leaders participated in the act of aggression. This is the only State which could determine the responsibility of such a leader for the crime of aggression without being required to also consider the question of aggression by another State. Thus, the national courts of such a State could determine the responsibility of an individual for the crime of aggression under the Code or under such relevant provisions of national criminal law as may be applicable [...T]he exercise of national jurisdiction by a State with respect to the responsibility of its nationals for aggression would not have the same negative consequences for international relations or international peace and security as the exercise of national jurisdiction in the same respect. In the event that the proceedings fail to meet the necessary standard of independence and impartiality, the national court proceedings would not preclude a subsequent trial by an international criminal court [...] Since the national court jurisdiction for the crime of aggression, as a limited exception to the otherwise exclusive jurisdiction of an international criminal court, is formulated in permissive rather than obligatory terms, there is no corresponding obligation for a State party to establish the jurisdiction of its national courts with respect to this crime under the article.[142]

This approach of the International Law Commission has been criticised—in the words of Astrid Reisinger Coracini, "rightly"—as "retrogressive" and "inconsistent with State practice".[143] She notes as follows with respect to the adjudication of an alleged crime of aggression by a foreign court:

> [I]t is not comprehensible why a national court deciding about the commission of an act of aggression would be perceived as substantially different from a national court judging the existence of a wide or systematic attack against a civilian population by a state, or the potential acknowledgement that genocide or war crimes were committed (in particular) as part of a state plan or policy [...] the crime of aggression is part of the same legal framework as all crimes under international law. Indirect enforcement of the crime of

---

[142] See Draft Code of Crimes against the Peace and Security of Mankind with commentaries 1996, p. 30.

[143] See Reisinger Coracini 2009, p. 731.

aggression faces the same difficulties and obstacles as the domestic prosecution of other crimes under international law.[144]

It is only possible to agree with this scholarly opinion. In a great majority of cases, crimes under international law would be inspired by the State and committed through its intermediary or with its support—and, in that sense, any qualification of a crime under international law by a foreign court might deteriorate its international relations with the State standing at the origin of the crime. Therefore, drawing a distinction between the crime of aggression and other crimes under international law, for that purpose, is quite unsubstantiated.

Further, the International Law Commission did not, indeed, appear to take account of relevant State practice with respect to the criminalisation of aggression, which had been developing since 1945 and resulted, over time, in a number of national criminal laws applicable to the crime. Many of these national laws (see supra 4.1) should apply to individual acts perpetrated by foreigners and leading to the commission of hostile acts by foreign States against "victim States" where the criminal prosecution were to be instituted. The main substantive and procedural features of these legal regimes will be considered below, at 4.6.1.

And, finally, with the adoption of a definition of the crime of aggression for the purpose of the Rome Statute of the International Criminal Court (Article 8 bis, see infra 5.1), States Parties to the Statute might—over time, as the new definition would be gaining recognition—be expected to take measures to implement it in their national penal laws (see supra 4.1.1.3, 4.1.2.3, 4.1.3.3).[145] This factor too is expected to contribute to strengthening the indirect enforcement regimes.

4.6.1 Indirect Enforcement (by National Courts)

There have been no prosecutions for the crime of aggression or other crimes against peace by national courts, despite the existence of substantive and

---

[144] Ibid.

[145] According to the Permanent Mission of the Principality of Liechtenstein, "government or parliamentary officials in at least the following States Parties are currently actively working on the ratification of the amendments on the crime of aggression: Argentina, Australia, Austria, Belgium, Brazil, Botswana, Chile, Costa Rica, Croatia, Cyprus, Dominican Republic, Ecuador, Estonia, Georgia, Germany, Italy, Latvia, Luxembourg, the Netherlands, Peru, Portugal, Romania, Slovenia, Switzerland, Trinidad and Tobago, and Uruguay. In the Czech Republic, Finland, Guatemala, Japan and Venezuela, the process is in its early stages" see document: "Status of Ratification and Implementation of the Kampala Amendments on the Crime of Aggression (information as of 9 October 2012)", 1 (document on file with the author). Further, "the following States Parties made concrete commitments to ratify the amendments on the crime of aggression: Austria, Argentina, Bolivia, Botswana, Estonia, Germany, Peru, South Africa, Spain, Switzerland, Trinidad and Tobago. In addition, the following countries made positive references to the amendments: Brazil, Burkina Faso, Canada, Croatia, Democratic Republic of the Congo, Denmark, Fiji, Finland, Ghana, Hungary, Japan, Jordan, Kenya, Lesotho, Mexico, Nigeria, Norway, Poland, Republic of Korea, Senegal, Serbia, Slovakia, Spain and the United Kingdom", see ibid., p. 2.

procedural rules for such prosecutions in States whose national criminal laws contain definitions of this crime (see supra 4.1). If such prosecutions were to occur in the future, national law enforcement authorities would be bound to observe the rules at all stages of the criminal procedure. In this section, we will consider these essential substantive and procedural rules and offer some concluding observations.

4.6.1.1 Substantive Rules

The application of national laws criminalising aggression and other related offences (see infra 4.1) is conditioned upon a number of material rules belonging to the general part of criminal law. We will omit here the provisions, which are treated elsewhere in this book—such as the principle of legality (see infra 5.2.1 and 5.2.2), non-retroactivity of criminal laws *ratione personae* (see infra 5.2.3), individual criminal responsibility (see infra 5.2.4), the minimum age for criminal prosecution (see infra 5.2.5), the responsibility of commanders and other superiors (see infra 5.2.7), non-applicability of statutes of limitations (see infra 5.2.8), the mental element (see supra 4.5 and infra 5.2.9), grounds for excluding criminal responsibility (see infra 5.2.10), mistake of fact or mistake of law (see infra 5.2.11), and superior orders and prescription of law (see infra 5.2.12). Instead, a brief observation on principles of establishing national jurisdiction with respect to such crimes will be useful.

The establishment of criminal jurisdiction by States with respect to their nationals is an internal matter of States.[146] It is subject to national laws regulating functional and personal immunities deriving from perpetrators' official capacities (see infra 4.6.1.2.1). Yet, trying its own nationals is any State's sovereign right, and hence, the active nationality principle is the primary ground for asserting national jurisdiction over the crime of aggression.[147] It is provided for in all criminal laws surveyed supra at 4.1.

As far as legal grounds for establishing jurisdiction over the crime of aggression committed by foreign nationals are concerned, the territoriality principle,[148] the passive personality principle[149] and the protective principle[150] are of particular relevance. The territoriality principle is reflected in all criminal laws surveyed supra at 4.1, whereas the passive personality and protective principles are included in most of them.

Thus, contrary to the International Law Commission's opinion (cf. supra 4.6), national criminal laws—and hence, customary international law—do provide for the criminal liability of foreign nationals for the crime of aggression. In practice,

---

146 See David 2009, p. 13.

147 Ibid., pp. 188–203.

148 Ibid., pp. 14–149.

149 Ibid., pp. 203–217.

150 Ibid., pp. 236–242.

it is likely that only victim States—if ever—might assert jurisdiction, and third States would refrain from doing so. At most, friendly third States might cooperate with victim States in apprehending potential defendants and handing them over to victim States for criminal prosecution (see infra 4.6.1.2.2). None of the national criminal laws surveyed supra at 4.1 (probably, with a relative exception of Romania, see supra 4.1.3.1, note 50) asserts universal jurisdiction over the crime of aggression.

4.6.1.2 Procedural Rules

National prosecutions for the crime of aggression would also be made conditional upon a number of procedural circumstances, among which potential defendants' official capacity, rules governing cooperation between States in criminal matters, and compliance with the recognised fair trial guarantees deserve a specific mention.

4.6.1.2.1 Official Capacity[151]

As the perpetrators of the crime of aggression and other related crimes would normally be very senior State officials, they would typically be protected by immunities under national and international law.

In international law, one commonly distinguishes between two types of immunities—personal and functional. Personal immunities are enjoyed by Heads of States, governments, Foreign Ministers and diplomats who are safeguarded against criminal prosecution for the duration of their terms of office. By contrast, functional immunities from prosecution for acts performed in an official capacity continue beyond the duration of an official's term of office, except with respect to prosecutions for the commission of crimes under international law.[152] This exception is explained in different ways. According to one view, crimes under international law

[151] On this issue, cf. also infra 5.2.6.

[152] The ICTY Appeals Chamber held in para 41 of its decision in *Prosecutor* v. *Blaškić* (29 October 1997) as follows: "The general rule under discussion [that the individual organ may not be held accountable for acts or transactions performed in its official capacity] is well established in international law [...] The few exceptions [...] arise from the norms of international criminal law prohibiting war crimes, crimes against humanity and genocide. Under these norms, those responsible for such crimes cannot invoke immunity from national or international jurisdiction even if they perpetrated such crimes while acting in their official capacity". For a similar opinion, see Cassese 2008, p. 305. It is submitted that the ICTY did not mention the crime of aggression among crimes under international law whose perpetrators may not invoke immunity because the ICTY had no jurisdiction with respect to crimes against peace, and not because it did not consider the rule in question to be inapplicable to such crimes. The practice of the Nuremberg and Tokyo tribunals discussed earlier in this chapter confirmed the *opinio juris* in this respect. See also Kemp 2010, pp. 179–181.

are regarded as "private acts", which are not covered by functional immunity.[153] This explanation seems to have one deficiency: many (if not most) individuals would not be capable of committing crimes under international law, if they had no support from States. This is especially true with respect to the crime of aggression: an individual would not be capable of committing it, if he or she did not occupy a high-ranking post within the State structure, or did not perform an important social function (see supra 4.2). In that sense, the crime of aggression is "the most official crime under international law", which a private individual is not capable of committing.

Another—and, in this author's view, more solid—way to explain the exception from the general protective rule establishing functional immunity is to accept that the commission of crimes under international law is not a normal function of a State,[154] and the perpetrators of such crimes must be prosecuted, because their acts would constitute severe and deliberate violations of international law (see supra 2.1–2.2) in excess of their regular professional functions. It seems that a national court, which might have to deal with an aggression case in the future, might rely—more successfully than not—upon this theory rather than upon the former one.

4.6.1.2.2 Cooperation Between States in Criminal Matters

With respect to bilateral cooperation between States in criminal matters[155] in conjunction with a crime of aggression, several typical scenarios are discernible. One may envisage cooperation (1) between States, which are parties to the Rome Statute of the International Criminal Court, (2) between States, one of which is party to the Statute, and another State is not, and (3) between States, which are not parties to the Statute. In each of these settings, it matters whether there is an extradition treaty providing for the crime of aggression in force between the States in question. In addition to this major legal factor, there would be additional considerations—chiefly, of a political nature—that would influence the quality of cooperation. Consequently, one may distinguish between the scenarios whose implications are outlined in Charts 4.1 and 4.2.

If there is no applicable extradition treaty in force between the States in question, no extradition shall, as a rule, be possible,[156] irrespective of whether the respective States' criminal laws contain compatible definitions of the crime in question. In such a case, though, a State may choose, exceptionally, another mode of surrendering a wanted individual to a friendly State, on an *ad hoc* basis[157]:

---

[153] Cf. Robertson 2002, p. 405.

[154] Ibid., p. 408.

[155] See generally Boytsov 2004; Cryer 2005, pp. 101–117; McDonald 2011, pp. 437–444; Nesterenko 2009, pp. 84–88; Nesterenko 2010, pp. 284–293.

[156] See Boytsov 2004, pp. 47–112.

[157] Ibid., pp. 357–399.

Chart 4.1 There is no extradition treaty in force between the states in question

State 1: requesting state	State 2: requested State		
	State party to the Rome Statute, which has recognised the Rome Statute's definition	State party to the Rome Statute, which has not recognised the Rome Statute's definition	State not party to the Rome Statute
State party to the Rome Statute, which has recognised the Rome Statute's definition	- As a rule, no formal extradition shall be possible; - Another mode of surrendering an individual may be agreed upon by the States in question, on an *ad hoc* basis.		
State party to the Rome Statute, which has not recognised the Rome Statute's definition			
State not party to the Rome Statute			

In turn, if there is an applicable extradition treaty in force between the States in question (see chart 4.2), the success of an extradition request would, in virtually all cases, depend on the compatibility of the respective national definitions of the crime of aggression, and on both States' formal compliance with the extradition treaty. If (especially) the requested State party to the Rome Statute would have also recognised the Rome Statute's definition of the crime of aggression (see infra 5.1), it would be bound to also take into account its content, when considering an extradition request.

For a detailed analysis of the predominant legislative approaches towards defining the crime of aggression at the national level, see supra 4.1.

4.6.1.2.3 Fair Trial Guarantees

The fair trial guarantees are another crucial factor in exercising national jurisdiction with respect to the crime of aggression. In fact, the prospect that a defendant's procedural rights can be violated in the requesting State may be regarded as a basis for refusing an extradition request.[158] It is submitted that in trials where charges are so heavy, and where the political element is of a decisive weight by definition, the fair trial guarantees must be offered to defendants with particular diligence,[159] so that, on the one hand, wrongful convictions for the "supreme crime" be excluded, and, on the other hand, the possibility of accusations of partiality be minimised. It is expected that, in ensuring defendants' procedural rights,

[158] See Boytsov 2004, pp. 767–777.

[159] See Sayapin 2004, pp. 158–159.

Chart 4.2 There is an extradition treaty in force between the States in question[160]

State 1: requesting State	State 2: requested State		
	State party to the Rome Statute, which has recognised the Rome Statute's definition	State party to the Rome Statute, which has not recognised the Rome Statute's definition	State not party to the Rome Statute
State party to the Rome Statute, which has recognised the Rome Statute's definition	Extradition should be effected in accordance with the applicable extradition treaty, on the assumption that both States' national definitions of the crime of aggression are compatible with each other and with its definition under international law.	Extradition shall be largely conditional upon the compatibility of national definitions of the crime of aggression.	Extradition shall be largely conditional upon the compatibility of national definitions of the crime of aggression.
State party to the Rome Statute, which has not recognised the Rome Statute's definition	Extradition shall be largely conditional upon the compatibility of national definitions of the crime of aggression, and of the requesting State's national definition with the definition under international law.	Extradition shall be largely conditional upon the compatibility of national definitions of the crime of aggression.	Extradition shall be largely conditional upon the compatibility of national definitions of the crime of aggression.
State not party to the Rome Statute	Extradition shall be largely conditional upon the compatibility of national definitions of the crime of aggression, and of the requesting State's national definition with the definition under international law.	Extradition shall be largely conditional upon the compatibility of national definitions of the crime of aggression.	Extradition shall be largely conditional upon the compatibility of national definitions of the crime of aggression.

[160] It is presumed that the general conditions essential to an extradition procedure shall be complied with:
- existence of an appropriate jurisdictional link between the requesting (victim) State and a specific crime of aggression;
- compatibility of the national definitions of the crime (of aggression);
- rule of specialty. See Nesterenko 2011, pp. 49–107.

national courts would have recourse to their respective national laws regulating criminal procedure as well as to appropriate sources of international law, such as the International Covenant on Civil and Political Rights[161] and applicable regional human rights instruments.[162]

4.6.1.3 Observations

Although no national system of criminal justice has yet exercised jurisdiction with respect to the crime of aggression, this prospect cannot be excluded in the future. True, aggression is currently criminalised in only a limited number of States (see supra 4.1), and these national mechanisms of criminalisation do have some limitations of both substantive and procedural nature but they *may* be triggered. There is a growing consensus within the international community that the "supreme international crime" must not go unpunished, and the indirect enforcement of criminal liability may be just as significant for preventing the crime and punishing individuals for its commission as the direct enforcement mechanism (see infra Chap. 5) is hoped to be. In fact, as the International Criminal Court shall not be completely free from the Security Council's influence in the exercise of jurisdiction over the crime of aggression (see infra 5.3.2.7, 5.3.2.8 and 5.3.3), the potential of the indirect enforcement mechanisms—as the primary elements in the International Criminal Court's complementarity system—should not be underestimated.

4.6.2 Direct Enforcement (by the International Criminal Court)

The key material and procedural aspects of direct enforcement of individual criminal liability for the crime of aggression by the International Criminal Court will be examined below in Chap. 5.[163]

---

[161] Cf. ICCPR, Articles 14 and 15.

[162] Cf. Article 6 ("Right to a fair trial") of the ECHR, Article 8 ("Right to a fair trial") of the ACHR, Article 7 of the ACHPR.

[163] For a detailed analysis of procedural rules for such possible future trials, see Safferling 2012, pp. 58–63 (regarding the relevance of human rights for the fair trial concept), 179–192 (regarding the right of defence), 286–291 (regarding the rights of the suspect), 378–419 (regarding the principles of the trial), 436–462 (regarding the structure of the trial), 463–515 (regarding evidence), 515–521 (regarding witnesses and victims protection), 522–527 (regarding rules for rendering judgments), 531–559 (regarding appeal and revision), 560–573 (regarding the contempt of Court).

References

Adilkariev HT (ed) (2003) Mejdunarodnoe pravo. [International Law], Tashkent

Barriga S (2011) The crime of aggression. In: Natarajan M (ed) International crime and justice. Cambridge University Press, Cambridge, pp 329–334

Bekyashev KA (1999) Mejdunarodnoe publichnoe pravo [Public International Law]. Prospect, Moscow

Boytsov AI (2004) Vydacha prestupnikov [The Rendition of Criminals]. Yuridicheskiy Centre, Moscow

Cassese A (2008) International criminal law, 2nd edn. Oxford University Press, Oxford

Cryer R (2005) Prosecuting international crimes: selectivity and the international criminal law regime. Cambridge University Press, Cambridge

Cryer R, Friman H, Robinson D and Wilmshurst E (2007) An introduction to international criminal law and procedure. Cambridge University Press, Cambridge

David É (2009) Éléments de droit pénal international et européen. Bruylant

Dinstein Y (2001) War, aggression and self-defence, 3rd edn. Cambridge University Press, Cambridge

Draft Code of crimes against the peace and security of mankind with commentaries (1996). In: Yearbook of the International Law Commission, volume II (Part Two), pp 17–56

Dubber MD (2007) Criminalizing complicity: a comparative analysis. JICJ 5:977–1001

Eagleton C (1938) The form and function of the declaration of war. AJIL 32:19–35

Eagleton C (1941) Acts of war. AJIL 35:321–326

Fenwick CG (1941) Intervention by way of propaganda. AJIL 35:626–631

Freeman AV (1947) War Crimes by enemy nationals administering justice in occupied territory. AJIL 41:579–610

Goldsmith JL, Posner EA (2005) The limits of international law. Oxford University Press, Oxford

Haumer S, Marschner L (2010) Der internationale Strafgerichtshof und das Verbrechen der Aggression nach Kampala—Zu den neuesten Ergänzungen im IStGH-Statut und ihren Auswirkungen auf das deutsche Strafrecht. HuV-I 23:188–196

Jessup PC (1954) Should international law recognize an intermediate status between peace and war? AJIL 48:98–103

Kalamkaryan A, Migachev YI (2005) Mejdunarodnoe pravo [International Law]. Eksmo Education, Moscow

Kearney MG (2007) The prohibition of the propaganda for war in international law. Oxford University Press, Oxford

Kemp G (2010) Individual criminal liability for the international crime of aggression. Intersentia

Kolosov YM, Kuzbetsov VI (eds) (1998) Mejdunarodnoe pravo [International Law]. Moscow

Kovalev AA, Chernichenko SV (eds) (2008) Mejdunarodnoe pravo [International Law]. Moscow, Omega-L

Kress C (2004) The german chief federal prosecutor's decision not to investigate the alleged crime of preparing aggression against Iraq. JICJ 2:245–264

Kudryavtsev VN, Luneev V, Naumov AV (eds) (2005a) Ugolovnoe pravo Rossii. Obshchaya chast [Russia's Criminal Law. General Part]. Moscow

Kudryavtsev VN, Luneev V, Naumov AV (eds) (2005b) Ugolovnoe pravo Rossii. Osobennaya chast. Russia's Criminal Law. Specific Part, Moscow

Kurs sovetskogo ugolovnogo prava [A Treatise in Soviet Criminal Law] (1968), volume 1. Moscow

Lauterpacht E (1968) The legal irrelevance of the "State of War". In: Proceedings of the American Society of International Law, vol 62, pp 58–68

Levin ID (2003) Suverenitet [Sovereignty]. Yuridicheskiy Centre Press, Moscow

Lippman MR (2010) Contemporary Criminal Law: Concepts, Cases and Controversies, 2nd edn. SAGE Publications, Inc

Lukashuk I (2008) Mejdunarodnoe pravo: Obshchaya chast [International Law: General Part], 3rd edn. Wolters Kluwer, Moscow
Luneev VV (2005) Prestupnost XX veka: mirovye, regionalnye i rossiyskie tendentsii [Criminality in the 20th Century: Trends in the World, Region and Russia]. Wolters Kluwer, Moscow
Lutz EL, Reiger C (2009) Introduction. In: Lutz EL, Reiger C (eds) Prosecuting Heads of State. Cambridge University Press, Cambridge, pp 1–24
Marchenko MN (ed) (2003) Politologiya: kurs lektsiy [Political Science: Lecture Course]. Moscow
Marochkin S (2006) International law in the courts of the Russian Federation: practice of application. Chinese JIL 5:329–344
May L (2008) Aggression and crimes against peace. Cambridge University Press, Cambridge
McDonald WF (2011) The longer arm of the law: the growth and limits of international law enforcement and criminal justice cooperation. In: Natarajan M (ed) International crime and justice. Cambridge University Press, Cambridge pp 437–444
McDougal MS (1955) Peace and war: factual continuum with multiple legal consequences. AJIL 49:63–68
Mégret F (2002) 'War'? Legal semantics and the move to violence. EJIL 13:361–399
Meron T (1998) War crimes law comes of age. Clarendon Press, Oxford
Molan MT (2008) Cases and materials on criminal law, 4th edn. Routledge-Cavendish
Murphy SD (2006) Principles of international law. Thomson & West
Nesterenko SS (2009) Mehanizm zashity prav cheloveka v mejdunarodnom ekstraditsionnom prave [The Human Rights Protection Mechanism in the International Extradition Law]. Almanach Int Law 1:84–88
Nesterenko SS (2010) Tendentsii razvitiya instituta okazaniya pravovoy pomoshchi po ugolovnym delam v XXI veke [The Development Trends of Mutual Assistance in Criminal Matters in the 21st Century]. Almanach Int Law 2:284–293
Nesterenko SS (2011) Mijnarodno-pravoviy zahist prav lyudini pri zdiysnenni ekstraditsii [The International Protection of Human Rights in Extradition Matters]. Odessa, Phoenix
O'Keefe R (2002) Customary international crimes in English courts. BYIL 73:293–335
Okimoto K (2011) The distinction and relationship between Jus ad Bellum and Jus in Bello. Hart Publishing, Oxford
Orakhelashvili A (2007) Overlap and convergence: the interaction between Jus ad Bellum and Jus in Bello. JCSL 12:157–196
Pictet JS (1952) Commentary of the first Geneva convention for the amelioration of the condition of the wounded and sick in armed forces in the field. ICRC, Geneva
Preuss L (1934) International responsibility for hostile propaganda against foreign states. AJIL 28:649–668
Radzinowicz L (1966) Ideology and crime. London
Reisinger Coracini A (2009) Evaluating domestic legislation on the customary crime of aggression under the Rome Statute's complementarity regime. In: Stahn C, Sluiter G (eds) The emerging practice of the International Criminal Court, Leiden, Boston, pp 725–754
Robertson G (2002) Crimes against humanity: struggle for global justice, 2nd edn. Penguin Books, London
Safferling C (2012) International criminal procedure. Oxford University Press, Oxford
Sapronova MA (2007) Vysshie organy gosudarstvennoy vlasti arabskih respublik [The Arab Republics' Supreme Bodies of State Authority]. Vostok–Zapad, Moscow
Sayapin S (2010a) Razvitie opredeleniya prestupleniya agressii v mejdunarodnom i natsionalnom ugolovnom prave [The Development of the Definition of the Crime of Aggression in International and National Criminal Law]. Almanach Int Law 2:294–316
Sayapin S (2010b) The compatibility of the Rome Statute's draft definition of the crime of aggression with national criminal justice systems. IRPL 81:165–187
Sayapin S (2004) The application of the fair trial guarantees to alleged terrorists in non-international armed conflicts. HuV-I 17:152–159

Strebel H (1976) Einwirkungen nationalen Rechts auf das Völkerrecht. ZaöRV 36:168–189
Tolochko ON (2009) Rejim voennoy okkupatsii v sovremennom mejdunarodnom gumanitarnom prave [The Regime of Military Occupation in the Contemporary International Humanitarian Law]. Almanach Int Law 1:180–188
Van Dyke V (1940) The responsibility of States for international propaganda. AJIL 34:58–73
Werle G (2009a) Principles of international criminal law, 2nd edn. T. M. C Asser Press, The Hague
Werle G (2009b) The crime of aggression between international and domestic criminal law. In: Manacorda S, Nieto A (eds), Criminal law between war and peace. Cuena, pp 405–421
Whitton JB (1974) Aggressive Propaganda. In: Bassiouni MC, Nanda VP (eds) International Criminal Law, Springfield, pp 238–272
Whitton JB (1951) Cold war propaganda. AJIL 45:151–153
Wildhaber L, Breitenmoser S (1988) The relationship between customary international law and municipal law in Western European countries. ZaöRV 48:163–207
Wright Q (1948) The crime of war-mongering. AJIL 42:128–136
Zelinskaya NA (2006) Mejdunarodnye prestupleniya i mejdunarodnaya prestupnost [International Crimes and International Criminality]. Yuridichna literatura

Chapter 5
The Crime of Aggression in the Rome Statute of the International Criminal Court

Abstract Articles 8 bis, 15 bis and 15 ter are novelties in the Rome Statute, and the Statute lays down a special regime for their prospective entry into force and application, after 1 January 2017. This chapter offers a detailed examination of the new substantive and procedural provisions, in the context of the general part of international criminal law, identifies consequential lacunae—especially, in Article 8 bis, and suggests that the effective power of the International Criminal Court to prosecute individuals for the crime of aggression might be significantly limited by realities of international politics. Although the Kampala amendments on the crime of aggression do have an appreciable potential for having a far-reaching impact upon the maintenance of international peace and security, this potential might, in fact, be limited by the Security Council's authority to defer an investigation or prosecution. The principle of complementarity—and, hence, a more effective criminalisation of aggression within national legal systems (for details, see Chap. 4)—should remain increasingly relevant.

Contents

S. Sayapin, *The Crime of Aggression in International Criminal Law*,
DOI: 10.1007/978-90-6704-927-6_5, © T.M.C. ASSER PRESS and the author 2014

The adoption of a definition of the crime of aggression for the purpose of the Rome Statute of the International Criminal Court and reaching an agreement with respect to the conditions under which the Court should be able to exercise its jurisdiction with respect to the crime[1] represent a milestone development in public international law and international criminal law in that they should hopefully be capable of resolving a long-lasting paradox in international law. For sixty-five years after the establishment of the United Nations (cf. supra 1.2.5), there existed no legally binding definition of a key concept of its Charter.[2] Now, it is expected, the success of having defined the crime of aggression for the purpose of the Statute would have, in fact, a more ambitious effect than just that of amending the Rome Statute.[3] It should also probably affect the subsequent practice of the UN Security Council, even if that indirect impact might, at least initially, be limited to the official attitudes of two permanent Security Council members (United Kingdom and France) and those non-permanent ones who are also Parties to the ICC Statute. This suggestion reasonably follows from the requirement that the new provisions be "consistent with the relevant provisions of the Charter of the United Nations"[4]: if they are consistent with the UN Charter, there is no reason why the States Parties to the Rome Statute should not also use its letter and spirit as an appropriate reference in their capacity of Security Council members. It would indeed be quite odd to assume that a State, having agreed in its capacity of a State Party to the Rome Statute that a specific act should be regarded as aggression, would advocate for a contrary view in the Security Council, or vice versa.[5]

[1] See ICC Statute, Articles 8 bis, 15 bis and 15 ter.

[2] On the legal significance of relevant preceding developments, see supra 1.2. See also Kemp 2010, pp. 73–101, 103–124; Petty 2008, pp. 1–24; Walzer 2007, pp. 635–643.

[3] See Amann and Sellers 2002, pp. 381–404; Bolton 2001, pp. 167–180; Brown 1999, pp. 855–891; Edlin 2006, pp. 1–22; Ferencz 2003, pp. 223–246; Fletcher and Ohlin 2006, pp. 428–433; Frank and Yuhan 2003, pp. 519–558; Latore 2002, pp. 159–176; Lietzau 2001, pp. 119–140; Mathias 2005, pp. 173–188; McNerney 2001, pp. 181–191; Schabas 2004, pp. 701–720; Scheffer 1999, pp. 12–22; Wegdwood 2001, pp. 193–214; Zolo 2007, pp. 799–807; Zwanenburg 1999, pp. 124–143.

[4] ICC Statute, Article 5(2): "The Court shall exercise jurisdiction over the crime of aggression once a provision is adopted in accordance with articles 121 and 123 defining the crime and setting out the conditions under which the Court shall exercise jurisdiction with respect to this crime. Such a provision shall be consistent with the relevant provisions of the Charter of the United Nations".

[5] See Sayapin 2008, at 335. See also Kemp 2010, pp. 189–190.

On the other hand, more time will be needed to bring the new provisions into force, so that they might become operational among the States Parties to the Rome Statute (see infra 5.1.2, 5.3.2.2 and 5.3.3). It was agreed at the Statute's First Review Conference (Kampala, 31 May–11 June 2010) that the International Criminal Court would not be able to exercise its jurisdiction with respect to the crime of aggression until, at least, 1 January 2017.[6] Accordingly, there exists a risk that during the remaining time before that date military force would be used, more than once, in international relations, with no prospect of individual criminal liability under the Statute. Hence, the national mechanisms for prosecuting individuals for aggression and related crimes against peace (see supra Chap. 4) should not be underestimated, both during this interim period and afterwards (see infra 5.3.1).

This chapter offers a detailed analysis of Articles 8 bis, 15 bis and 15 ter of the Rome Statute in the more general context of customary international law and of the Statute itself, and concludes with a note on the Elements of the crime of aggression.

5.1 The Definition of the Crime of Aggression for the Purpose of the Rome Statute (Article 8 bis)

The definition of the crime of aggression for the purpose of the International Criminal Court, as adopted by the First Review Conference, reads as follows[7]:

Article 8 bis
Crime of aggression

1. For the purpose of this Statute, "crime of aggression" means the planning, preparation, initiation or execution, by a person in a position effectively to exercise control over or to direct the political or military action of a State, of an act of aggression which, by its character, gravity and scale, constitutes a manifest violation of the Charter of the United Nations.
2. For the purpose of paragraph 1, "act of aggression" means the use of armed force by a State against the sovereignty, territorial integrity or political independence of another State, or in any other manner inconsistent with the Charter of the United Nations. Any of the following acts, regardless of a declaration of war, shall, in accordance with United Nations General Assembly resolution 3314 (XXIX) of 14 December 1974, qualify as an act of aggression:

   (a) The invasion or attack by the armed forces of a State of the territory of another State, or any military occupation, however temporary, resulting from such invasion or attack, or any annexation by the use of force of the territory of another State or part thereof;
   (b) Bombardment by the armed forces of a State against the territory of another State or the use of any weapons by a State against the territory of another State;
   (c) The blockade of the ports or coasts of a State by the armed forces of another State;

[6] See Safferling 2012, p. 83.

[7] Cf. document RC/Res. 6, Annex I, para 2.

(d) An attack by the armed forces of a State on the land, sea or air forces, or marine and air fleets of another State;
(e) The use of armed forces of one State which are within the territory of another State with the agreement of the receiving State, in contravention of the conditions provided for in the agreement or any extension of their presence in such territory beyond the termination of the agreement;
(f) The action of a State in allowing its territory, which it has placed at the disposal of another State, to be used by that other State for perpetrating an act of aggression against a third State;
(g) The sending by or on behalf of a State of armed bands, groups, irregulars or mercenaries, which carry out acts of armed force against another State of such gravity as to amount to the acts listed above, or its substantial involvement therein.

Hence, the draft definition of the crime presented to the Review Conference in the *Conference Room Paper on the Crime of Aggression* (document RC/WGCA/1/Rev. 2, see supra 1.2.6.3) was adopted *tel quel*, without any further modification. Recent as it is, the definition has already been confidently praised[8] and severely criticised.[9] Whereas advocates of the new definition view its adoption as a pioneering development, which is both reflective of earlier "best practices" and potentially capable of further containing the use of force in international relations, critics point to the imperfection of the new definition's chief legal foundations—the Nuremberg Charter (see supra 1.2.2) and the 1974 Definition of Aggression (see supra 2.3).[10] In turn, more moderate critics suggest "to submit the Kampala compromise to critical legal analysis and to elaborate a constructive, *bona fide* interpretation in order to mitigate, as far as possible, negative (and unintended) consequences".[11] It seems indeed that romanticising the provision would not add to its workability. By contrast, international legal scholars' and practitioners' critical awareness of the provision's strengths and weaknesses should reasonably contribute to its future efficacy—a consequence that would certainly be both positive and intended.

5.1.1 *Structure of the Rome Statute's Definition of the Crime of Aggression*

Article 8 bis of the Rome Statute has a three-level structure. In the first paragraph, the individual crime is defined, whereby the individual criminal acts are essentially linked to the commission of an act of aggression, which is defined in the

[8] See, for example, Ferencz 2009, at 281, where the author asserted that the crime had been "adequately defined".

[9] Thus, Matthias Schuster insists that the crime of aggression should be deleted from the Rome Statute, because a "legally sound" definition is impossible. See Schuster 2003, at 1, 2.

[10] See Glennon 2010, at 71, 74.

[11] Ambos 2010, at 481.

second paragraph, by a State.[12] Finally, a list of acts qualifying as aggression for the purpose of the Statute is provided in seven subparagraphs. All elements of this provision are interlinked and must be interpreted in each other's contexts. As Kai Ambos points out, "the existence of an (unlawful) act of aggression, as defined by Article 8 bis (2) on the basis of the GA Resolution 3314 does not automatically entail the individual criminal responsibility of the persons involved in this act".[13] In order for such a responsibility to arise, a number of conditions must be met. First, an alleged act of aggression must, "by its character, gravity and scale", constitute "a manifest violation of the Charter of the United Nations" (see infra 5.1.1.1.5). For the purpose of Article 8 bis of the Statute, a one-off border incident would not qualify as an act of aggression (cf. supra 4.1.3 and 4.3.1.3), neither would Article 8 bis cover—at least, in its present shape—legally contentious situations, such as humanitarian intervention (see supra 2.4.3.2 and infra 5.1.1.3).[14] Second, the range of potential subjects of the individual crime of aggression within the jurisdiction of the ICC would only be limited to persons "in a position effectively to exercise control over or to direct the political or military action of a State" (see infra 5.1.1.1.3). Consequently, the ICC would not be able to try lower ranking officials—such as the defendants in the follow-up Nuremberg trials (see supra 3.1.3)—allegedly involved in a crime of aggression, even if they were liable under the relevant national laws of the State(s) involved. Third, in order for an individual to be held liable for an alleged crime of aggression by the International Criminal Court, his or her personal contribution to the "planning, preparation, initiation or execution" of an act of aggression must be proved (see infra 5.1.1.1 and 5.2.4). The particulars of Article 8 bis are considered below.

5.1.1.1 Individual Crime of Aggression (Article 8 bis (1))

The first paragraph of Article 8 bis defines the individual crime of aggression for the purpose of the Rome Statute and provides as follows:

> 1. For the purpose of this Statute, "crime of aggression" means the planning, preparation, initiation or execution, by a person in a position effectively to exercise control over or to direct the political or military action of a State, of an act of aggression which, by its character, gravity and scale, constitutes a manifest violation of the Charter of the United Nations.

At first glance, this provision is merely a restatement of the pre-existing customary law on the subject: it starts with an allusion to the Nuremberg Charter ("planning,

---

[12] For an analysis of the relationship between collective and individual manifestations of aggression, respectively, at the "macro" and "micro" levels, see Ambos 2005, at 671–672; O'Connell and Niyazmatov 2012, pp. 189–207.

[13] See Ambos 2010, p. 482. In the context of the quoted passage, the existence of an act of aggression should presumably be determined in accordance with procedures established for the purpose of the ICC Statute.

[14] Ibid., p. 483.

preparation, initiation or execution"), confirms the Nuremberg and Tokyo Tribunals' findings with respect to the superior standing of potential defendants in their respective State structures ("person in a position effectively to exercise control over or to direct the political or military action of a State"), and concludes by reaffirming that only the most flagrant violations of the Charter of the United Nations ("which, by [their] character, gravity and scale, constitut[e ...] manifest violation[s]" of the UN Charter) may be regarded as acts of aggression for the purpose of the ICC. However, the drafters of the definition did, in fact, succeed in bringing about a progressive development in international law in that they went beyond merely restating the causal link between one or more individual criminal acts ("planning, preparation, initiation or execution") and the internationally wrongful act in question ("manifest violation of the Charter of the United Nations") and actually defined the individual crime of aggression *as an individual function in the mechanism of committing an act of aggression*, of which the State was previously recognised as a sole subject (see supra 2.2), *which is directly discharged by natural persons*. A grammatical interpretation of Article 8 bis (1)[15] implies that the planning, preparation, initiation or execution of *acts* of aggression is directly performed by identifiable natural persons, not by abstract State entities, and that such acts of aggression (grammatical object) would not occur without a direct participation (in either of the four criminalised modes of action) of specific natural persons (grammatical subjects). This is a novelty in comparison to some relevant pre-existing sources—such as the 1996 Draft Code of Crimes against the Peace and Security of Mankind whose Article 16 suggested that an act of aggression could only be committed by a State (see supra 3.1.5). Although Article 8 bis (2) of the Rome Statute contains a provision to a similar effect, the grammatical interpretation of its Article 8 bis (1) suggests that while natural persons are the subjects of an individual *crime* of aggression, they also are, at the same time, the *primary* subjects of an *act* of aggression, whereas the State at issue is that act's *secondary* subject (see infra 5.1.1.2 and 5.4).

5.1.1.1.1 "For the Purpose of this Statute"

Article 8 bis (1) starts with an important reservation to the effect that the definition of the crime of aggression shall apply "[f]or the purpose of [the Rome] Statute" only. This restrictive clause was a part of the compromise reached at the First Review Conference, in order to make the new definition workable and not to upset the interests of States, which are not Parties to the Statute. Professor Kai Ambos reports that the United States were preoccupied with making sure that the proposed amendment only affect the ICC Statute, without creating any legal effect beyond the material, personal and temporal fields of its application.[16] The Review

[15] See Lukashuk 2004, pp. 632–633.

[16] See Ambos 2010, p. 469.

Conference also adopted two understandings to this effect.[17] It must hence be concluded that the definition may not, at this stage, be regarded as claiming universal recognition, neither can it prevent the development, at the national or international levels, of alternative legal theories or rules pertaining to the crime of aggression, even after the entry into force of Article 8 bis (cf. infra 5.1.2).

5.1.1.1.2 "Planning, Preparation, Initiation or Execution" of an Act of Aggression

Article 8 bis (1) lists four modes of conduct, which are criminalised in connection with an act of aggression—planning, preparation, initiation and execution. These terms have (almost literally) been "borrowed" from the Nuremberg Charter and Judgment (see supra 1.2.2 and 3.1.1), with the exception of "execution", which replaced the original term "waging a war of aggression". The terminological meaning and legal significance of these modes of criminal conduct have been dealt with at some length above, at 4.2.1.1–4.2.1.3. As these may now be regarded as having a customary value, the reader is referred to those sections.

5.1.1.1.3 "Person in a Position Effectively to Exercise Control Over or to Direct the Political or Military Action of a State"

Since the Nuremberg, Tokyo and the follow-up trials under the Control Council Law № 10 (see supra 1.2.2–1.2.4 and 3.1.1–3.1.3), aggression is regarded as a "leadership crime" (see supra 4.2).[18] Lower ranking State agents who, in accordance with the laws and customary practices applicable in their States, are not able to exercise the requisite degree of influence are to be excluded from the range of potential subjects of the crime (see supra 4.2.1). Even where such individuals' criminal liability were not excluded in accordance with applicable national laws (for an overview, see supra 4.1), the ICC would, as a matter of principle, have no jurisdiction in their respect—Article 8 bis (1) states clearly that, for the purpose of the Statute's definition of the crime of aggression, the range of its subjects is limited to "person[s] in a position effectively to exercise control over or to direct the political or military action of a State". It is to be noted that this formula also

---

[17] Cf. document RC/Res. 6, Annex III: "4. It is understood that the amendments that address the definition of the act of aggression and the crime of aggression do so for the purpose of this Statute only. The amendments shall, in accordance with article 10 of the Rome Statute, not be interpreted as limiting or prejudicing in any way existing or developing rules of international law for purposes other than this Statute. 5. It is understood that the amendments shall not be interpreted as creating the right or obligation to exercise domestic jurisdiction with respect to an act of aggression committed by another State". On the legal value of the understandings on the crime of aggression, see Kreß et al. 2012, pp. 81–97. See also Heller 2012, pp. 229–248.

[18] See Barriga 2012, at 22–23; Kemp 2010, pp. 236–237.

encompasses leaders who would not officially occupy any posts in their States' hierarchies but would, as a matter of fact, exercise an important degree of influence upon those States' foreign policy or military affairs—as "spiritual leaders of the nation", "leaders of the revolution" and the like (see supra 4.2.5 and 4.3.1.1.2).

It is understood that Article 8 bis (1) does not cover (even large-scale instances of) autarkic use of armed force by non-State actors. Unlike some authors,[19] this writer does not believe that such cases must be covered by the Rome Statute's definition of the crime of aggression. Since its inception in the theory of international law, the concept of aggression was understood in its relationship with the State (see supra 2.2–2.3), and there is no obvious reason for changing this conceptual understanding. First, armed attacks by non-State actors would almost certainly be covered by other relevant rules of international law, including those of the Rome Statute (cf. Articles 6, 7 and 8). Second, such uses of force would be almost implausible without, at least, an implicit support or acquiescence from States harbouring the non-State actors perpetrating the attacks—a situation covered by Article 8 bis (2) (g) of the Rome Statute (for details, see infra 5.1.1.3.7). Subparagraph (g) refers to a State's "substantial involvement" in the "sending by or on behalf of a State of armed bands, groups, irregulars or mercenaries, which carry out acts of armed force against another State of such gravity as to amount to [acts of aggression]". It is submitted that allowing a non-State group to prepare for a large-scale armed attack against persons or property situated in another State should indeed be considered as the host State's "substantial involvement", because not taking determined measures for repressing such criminal activities would denote the host State's sharing those activities' aims or, at least, acquiescing to them. Displaying a similar tolerance towards a non-State actor's preparation for the commission of a crime under international law—genocide, crimes against humanity or war crimes—may be indicative of the existence of an aggressive *mens rea* on the part of leaders of the host State (see supra 4.5).

5.1.1.1.4 "Act of Aggression"

The notion of an act of aggression for the purpose of the ICC Statute (Article 8 bis (2)) will be considered below, at 5.1.1.2, in greater detail. It suffices to restate here (cf. supra 5.1.1.1) that an act of aggression should be regarded, in the context of Article 8 bis (1), as a *direct* result of perpetrators' criminal conduct, and not merely as its "by-product" delivered through the intermediary of a State. The potential perpetrators of the crime are described in Article 8 bis (1) as being *as such* capable of planning, preparing for, initiating or executing an act of aggression. In this logical structure, "the use of armed force by a State against the sovereignty, territorial integrity or political independence of another State, or in any other manner inconsistent with the Charter of the United Nations" referred to in Article 8 bis (2) results

[19] For a critical view, see Anderson 2010, pp. 411–451.

immediately from (an aggregate of) individual criminal acts, and "the State", which uses force against protected values listed in the provision becomes a "tool" in the perpetrators' hands—an indispensable one, given the nature of the crime at issue, but it still is a "mechanical" tool, not a subject capable of taking autonomous decisions to the contrary to the perpetrators' will, for they themselves embody the State's will. In other words, for the purpose of the ICC Statute, a "crime of aggression" consists in that "a person in a position effectively to exercise control over or to direct the political or military action of a State" participates in "planning, preparation, initiation or execution" of an internationally wrongful act involving "the use of armed force by a State against the sovereignty, territorial integrity or political independence of another State, or in any other manner inconsistent with the Charter of the United Nations", the "character, gravity and scale" of which would warrant the concern of the international community as a whole[20] (cf. infra 5.1.1.1.5).

5.1.1.1.5 "[W]hich, by its Character, Gravity and Scale, Constitutes a Manifest Violation of the Charter of the United Nations"

Article 8 bis (1) concludes with an essential provision to the effect that a use of force between States may be deemed to amount to an act of aggression for the purpose of the ICC Statute only if, "by its character, gravity and scale, [it] constitutes a manifest violation of the Charter of the United Nations".[21] In other words, in order to qualify as an act of aggression for the purpose of Article 8 bis (1), a State's use of force must be so unlawful, devastating and massive as to meet, respectively, the cumulative benchmarks of "character, gravity and scale" laid down in the "manifest standard".[22] This provision resulted from discussions within the Special Working Group on the Crime of Aggression (see supra 1.2.6.3) on the requisite intensity of armed force to be involved in an alleged State act of

[20] Cf. ICC Statute, 9th preambular paragraph: "Determined to these ends and for the sake of present and future generations, to establish an independent permanent International Criminal Court in relationship with the United Nations system, with jurisdiction over the most serious crimes of concern to the international community as a whole".

[21] See Barriga 2012, at 28–30; Kemp 2010, p. 234; Schüller 2008, pp. 73–81; Petty 2009, pp. 105–150; Werle 2009b, at 414.

[22] Cf. document RC/Res. 6, Annex III: "6. It is understood that aggression is the most serious and dangerous form of the illegal use of force; and that a determination whether an act of aggression has been committed requires consideration of all the circumstances of each particular case, including the gravity of the acts concerned and their consequences, in accordance with the Charter of the United Nations. 7. It is understood that in establishing whether an act of aggression constitutes a manifest violation of the Charter of the United Nations, the three components of character, gravity and scale must be sufficient to justify a "manifest" determination. No one component can be significant enough to satisfy the manifest standard by itself".

aggression,[23] in order for such act's authors to be held responsible by the ICC. As Stephan Barriga points out, an explicit aim of this clause is to exclude from the ICC jurisdiction "not only [...] minor border skirmishes and other small-scale incidents but also acts whose illegal character [would be] debatable rather than manifest",[24] and hence to limit the Court's jurisdiction to individual acts bringing about "the most serious" internationally wrongful uses of force (cf. supra 2.3) of "concern to the international community as a whole".[25] It is accordingly understood that inter-State confrontations involving the use of armed force[26] but not reaching the cumulative normative threshold articulated in Article 8 bis (1) should not be regarded as acts of aggression for the purpose of the ICC Statute, since, to borrow from S. Barriga's terminology, "border skirmishes and other small-scale incidents" would conspicuously not meet the "gravity" and "scale" requirements,[27] and, in turn, State acts whose illegality under applicable public international law were "debatable" (such as the forcible protection of nationals abroad or the *bona fide* "humanitarian intervention",[28] see supra 2.4.3.1–2.4.3.2) would not correspond to the "character" criterion—even if their gravity and/or scale were sufficient. It appears that the threshold was placed at such a high level—and appropriately so—on the one hand, with the purpose of limiting the ICC's future workload, and, on the other hand, with a view to reinforcing the link between a State act of aggression and a corresponding individual crime (see infra 5.3). Keith A. Petty explained such selectivity in the following manner:

> First, GA Resolution 3314 was adopted to guide the Security Council in making determinations of aggression. It was not adopted for the purpose of attaching individual criminal responsibility to a crime. Second, basing a definition of aggression on acts alone fails the *nullum crimen sine lege* requirement in criminal law. There must be a mental element—mens rea—to accompany criminal acts. Otherwise at least part of the definition is impermissibly ambiguous, failing to provide adequate notice to would-be violators. Finally, looking to acts alone without any reference to possible exceptions undermines the purpose of the threshold clause altogether—to remove borderline cases from the jurisdiction of the ICC.[29]

---

[23] Keith A. Petty pointed out, though, that the Special Working Group's opinion on this matter had not been unanimous, as some delegates had maintained that "any act of aggression [would] inherently [be] a manifest violation of the U.N. Charter", see Petty 2009, at 110. In the opinion of the "manifest standard" test's opponents, "[r]equiring an analysis of the magnitude of aggression [would add] an additional and unnecessary layer to the pre-trial determination—not to mention the elements that must be proven at trial. As such, the Prosecutor should consider only whether the listed acts of aggression contained in Article 3 of General Assembly Resolution 3314 [...] have occurred", see idem (footnotes omitted).

[24] See Barriga 2012, at 29.

[25] Cf. supra note 20.

[26] On the nature of modern warfare, see Smith 2005, pp. 267–370.

[27] Cf. also Petty 2009, at 108, confirming that "in order for criminal responsibility to attach, the State act in question must be more than a casual violation of the U.N. Charter".

[28] See Elshtain 2001, pp. 1–25; Leclerc-Gagné and Byers 2009, pp. 379–390.

[29] See Petty 2009, at 111 (footnotes omitted).

Although the final edition of Article 8 bis (1)—in contrast to some of its *travaux préparatoires*[30]—contains no examples of "manifest violation[s] of the Charter of the United Nations", it is understood that the provision indeed intends to cover acts akin to "a war of aggression or an act which has the object or result of establishing a military occupation of, or annexing, the territory of another State or part thereof",[31] and lesser uses of force would be beyond its scope. It is noticeable that whereas the "Nuremberg and Tokyo" (see supra 4.1.1) and the "territorial integrity or political independence" (see supra 4.1.2) models of criminalisation of the use of inter-State armed force are generally compatible with the high intensity standard set by Article 8 bis (1) of the Rome Statute, some situations of a less severe character, gravity and scale covered by the "objective war model" (see supra 4.1.3) may be less compatible with it and thus not be subject to the ICC jurisdiction. Nonetheless, individual criminal acts provoking the internationally wrongful uses of armed force in such situations shall still be subject to relevant national jurisdictions.

5.1.1.2 Act of Aggression (Article 8 bis (2))

The second paragraph of Article 8 bis defines an act of aggression for the purpose of the same Article's first paragraph:

> 2. For the purpose of paragraph 1, "act of aggression" means the use of armed force by a State against the sovereignty, territorial integrity or political independence of another State, or in any other manner inconsistent with the Charter of the United Nations. Any of the following acts, regardless of a declaration of war, shall, in accordance with United Nations General Assembly resolution 3314 (XXIX) of 14 December 1974, qualify as an act of aggression: [...]

The first sentence of the provision was almost literally borrowed from Article 1 of the 1974 Definition of Aggression,[32] and the latter's analysis offered above (see supra 2.3.1) applies to the provision "inherited" by Article 8 bis (2).

The provision's second sentence requires a few specific comments here. First, it is submitted that the reference to the declaration of war is superfluous.[33] Since the Second World War, such declarations have in practice been very rare and, besides, they lost their legal significance with the adoption of the 1949 Geneva Conventions.[34] The declaration of war must have been recalled in this context with

---

[30] See Barriga 2012, at 29–30, Petty 2009, at 108–109.

[31] See 2002 Coordinator's Paper (July), reprinted at Barriga and Kreß 2012, at 412 (Option 1).

[32] On implications of differences in the wording of Article 8 bis (2) of the ICC Statute and Article 1 of the 1974 Definition of Aggression, see Barriga 2012, at 25–28. See also Kemp 2010, pp. 218–222; Werle 2009b, at 413–414.

[33] See Sayapin 2008, p. 349.

[34] Article 2(1) common to all Geneva Conventions of 1949 reads: "[...] the present Convention shall apply to *all cases of declared war or of any other armed conflict* which may arise between two or more of the High Contracting Parties, *even if the state of war is not recognized by one of them*" (emphasis added).

a view to emphasising, once again, the important "threshold of gravity" of consequences an alleged act of aggression should entail (cf. supra 5.1.1.1.5)—that is to say, the level of violence of an international armed conflict. Even so, it would have been more accurate to refer to the non-recognition of a subsequent *state* of war by the States involved, and not to a prior or parallel *declaration* thereof, for such a declaration would not, in accordance with international humanitarian law, affect the legal qualification of the difference resulting from an alleged act of aggression as an international armed conflict, irrespective of the duration of that conflict.[35]

Next, the direct reference to the United Nations General Assembly resolution 3314 (XXIX) is certainly redundant, for at least two reasons.[36] First, all other crimes within the jurisdiction of the ICC (Articles 6–8) have been listed in the Statute as a matter of its own content, which reinforces the Court's *ratione materiae* competence. The definitions of those other crimes were either specifically formulated for the purpose of the Statute (crimes against humanity, Article 7), or classified for its purpose (war crimes, Article 8), or reproduced verbatim from a relevant international treaty (genocide, Article 6). It is uncertain why it was deemed necessary to quote a non-binding document—such as the General Assembly resolution 3314 (XXIX)—in Article 8 bis (2) while the other crimes within the jurisdiction of the Court had been formulated without references to other, even binding, sources of international law (with the exception of the 1949 Geneva Conventions in Article 8(2)(a) of the Statute and their Common Article 3 in Article 8(2)(c) of the Statute).

Third, as was noted above (see supra 2.3.2), the list of acts enumerated in Article 3 of the 1974 Definition of Aggression (which were reproduced in subparagraphs (a)–(g) of the ICC Statute's Article 8 bis (2)) does not yet enjoy universal recognition. It was reported that there had been no unanimity within the Special Working Group on the Crime of Aggression with respect to whether subparagraphs (a) to (g) of the 1974 Definition's Article 3 all represented current customary international law: some members of the Special Working Group "took the view that that was only true for subparagraph (g)", for its content had already been confirmed by the International Court of Justice (see supra 2.3.2).[37] Other experts noted that most of the acts listed in Article 3 had been "reflected in the practice of the Security Council", while for some acts there existed none.[38] This is unsurprising: the Security Council is a political body in whose action national interests of its members, especially of permanent members, prevail,[39] and the Council may not be expected to apply rules of international law in the same impartial way as a judicial

[35] According to the Commentary to the First Geneva Convention of 1949, "[a]ny difference arising between two States and leading to the intervention of armed forces is an armed conflict [...] even if one of the Parties denies the existence of a state of war [...]". See Pictet 1952, p. 32.

[36] See Sayapin 2008, pp. 346–347.

[37] See document ICC-ASP/6/SWGCA/INF.1 (25 July 2007), para 46.

[38] See ibid.

[39] Cf. Link 1998, p. 120; Chauprade 2003, p. 767.

body—such as, in the future, the International Criminal Court—should have to do. Be that as it may, Article 8 bis (2) could well have done without a direct reference to the General Assembly resolution 3314 (XXIX) but might have simply reproduced the relevant provisions of Article 3 of the 1974 Definition of Aggression as a matter of the Statute's own content. Such a verbatim integration of those provisions in the Rome Statute would have elevated them from the rank of "soft law" to the level of treaty law binding on the Statute's States Parties—certainly, pending the future entry into force of Article 8 bis (see infra 5.1.2)—and would have helped avoid scholarly critique similar to this author's.

5.1.1.3 Examples of Acts of Aggression

The generic definition of an act of aggression in Article 8 bis (2) is followed by seven specific examples (in subparagraphs (a)–(g)).[40] These examples are of a crucial significance, for they represent, for the purpose of the ICC Statute's definition of the crime of aggression, *prima facie* acts of aggression, about which the States Parties to the Statute agreed at the First Review Conference to the effect that "any" of such acts "*shall* [...] qualify as an act of aggression" (emphasis added)—of course, provided that they, by their character, gravity and scale, constitute manifest violations of the Charter of the United Nations (cf. supra 5.1.1.1.5). A brief analysis of subparagraphs (a)–(g) is offered below.

5.1.1.3.1 Invasion or Attack, Military Occupation, Annexation (Subparagraph (a))

Subparagraph (a) of Article 8 bis (2) reads as follows:

> a) The invasion or attack by the armed forces of a State of the territory of another State, or any military occupation, however temporary, resulting from such invasion or attack, or any annexation by the use of force of the territory of another State or part thereof;

This provision's keyword being "territory", it protects the territory of States against four modes of internationally wrongful military impact: invasion, attack, military occupation, annexation (cf. supra 4.5). From the point of view of international law, invasion and annexation are grave assaults against the territorial integrity of a State, whose manifest illegality derives from Article 2(4) of the Charter of the United Nations (see supra 2.1). It must be recalled that, since 1945, territorial acquisitions effected by military force in contravention of the Charter have usually been regarded as violations of international law (see supra 2.1.3). Likewise, "military occupation" means that restrictions are imposed upon the political

[40] Cf. Kemp 2010, pp. 235–236.

independence of a State,[41] and "invasion" implies that the armed forces of a State concerned trespass of another State's frontiers illegally, which constitutes a breach of the principle of the inviolability of frontiers.[42]

Yet, it may be recalled here that "attack"[43] and "military occupation" are not as such regarded as unlawful from the standpoint of international humanitarian law; it is submitted that the drafters of Article 8 bis (2) might well have omitted such debatable terms, in order to avoid a collision with other sources of international law applicable to situations of armed conflicts (cf. supra 4.3.1.3). Since the *corpus delicti* of the crime of aggression is accomplished at the "moment of aggression" (see supra 4.3.1.2), its extension to the circumstantial domain already governed by international humanitarian law—especially given the existing normative collision—may be regarded as superfluous.

It is understood that the term "the armed forces of a State" used in this subparagraph means that State's regular armed forces—as opposed to "armed bands, groups, irregulars or mercenaries" referred to in subparagraph (g) (see infra 5.1.1.3.7). The term may be interpreted in the sense of Article 43 of Protocol Additional to the Geneva Conventions of 12 August 1949, and relating to the Protection of Victims of International Armed Conflicts (Protocol I).[44]

---

[41] Cf. Article 42 of the 1907 Hague Regulations.

[42] On the principle, see Lukashuk 2008, pp. 314–316; Kolosov and Kuznetsov 1998, pp. 38–39.

[43] Additional Protocol I, Article 49 ("Definition of attacks and scope of application"): "1. "Attacks" means acts of violence against the adversary, whether in offence or in defence. 2. The provisions of this Protocol with respect to attacks apply to all attacks in whatever territory conducted, including the national territory belonging to a Party to the conflict but under the control of an adverse Party. 3. The provisions of this section apply to any land, air or sea warfare which may affect the civilian population, individual civilians or civilian objects on land. They further apply to all attacks from the sea or from the air against objectives on land but do not otherwise affect the rules of international law applicable in armed conflict at sea or in the air. 4. The provisions of this section are additional to the rules concerning humanitarian protection contained in the Fourth Convention, particularly in part II thereof, and in other international agreements binding upon the High Contracting Parties, as well as to other rules of international law relating to the protection of civilians and civilian objects on land, at sea or in the air against the effects of hostilities".

[44] Ibid., Article 43 ("Armed forces"): "1. The armed forces of a Party to a conflict consist of all organised armed forces, groups and units which are under a command responsible to that Party for the conduct of its subordinates, even if that Party is represented by a government or an authority not recognized by an adverse Party. Such armed forces shall be subject to an internal disciplinary system which, inter alia, shall enforce compliance with the rules of international law applicable in armed conflict. 2. Members of the armed forces of a Party to a conflict (other than medical personnel and chaplains covered by Article 33 of the Third Convention) are combatants, that is to say, they have the right to participate directly in hostilities. 3. Whenever a Party to a conflict incorporates a paramilitary or armed law enforcement agency into its armed forces it shall so notify the other Parties to the conflict".

5.1.1.3.2 Bombardment, Use of Weapons (Subparagraph (b))

Subparagraph (b) also seeks to protect States' territorial integrity, in accordance with Article 2(4) of the UN Charter (see supra 2.1), for it mentions "the territory of another State" twice:

> b) Bombardment by the armed forces of a State against the territory of another State or the use of any weapons by a State against the territory of another State;

Again, "bombardment" and "the use of any weapons" are actions permissible under international humanitarian law—certainly, with limitations deriving from the well-established principles of proportionality and distinction between combatants and civilians.[45] Likewise, any scholarly analysis of this provision should of necessity take into account the rules of international law applicable to the use of specific types of weapons—such as chemical, biological, nuclear and certain conventional weapons.[46] Yet, this provision is not about criminalising "bombardment" or "the use of [any] weapons" in the sense of international humanitarian law, for it does not cover unlawful attacks against enemy nationals or property—these are criminalised by Article 8 (war crimes) of the Rome Statute. Its *protected object* is different—a State's territory. The criminality of acts covered by subparagraph (b) of Article 8 bis (2) consists in that they are directed against a State's territory, which—along with population and public authorities—constitutes a State's very self.[47]

5.1.1.3.3 Blockade (Subparagraph (c))

The blockade of the ports or coasts of a State is criminalised in subparagraph (c) of Article 8 bis (2):

> c) The blockade of the ports or coasts of a State by the armed forces of another State;

The rationale for the criminalisation of blockade lies in the status of ports and coasts as parts of a coastal State's territory.[48] As in the context of the preceding paragraphs, the qualification of a violent ("by the armed forces of another State") restriction of the coastal State's sovereignty over its territory—including over its territorial

---

[45] See David 2011, pp. 268–350.

[46] Ibid., pp. 352–429.

[47] See Lukashuk 2008, p. 25.

[48] Cf. the 1982 United Nations Convention on the Law of the Sea, Article 11 ("Ports"): "For the purpose of delimiting the territorial sea, the outermost permanent harbour works which form an integral part of the harbour system are regarded as forming part of the coast. Off-shore installations and artificial islands shall not be considered as permanent harbour works".

sea[49]—as aggression is certainly warranted. Moreover, blockade can be used as a basis for attacks (see supra 5.1.1.3.1), bombardment or the use of weapons (see supra 5.1.1.3.2) against the coastal State, or for an attack on a State's armed forces (see infra 5.1.1.3.4), which in themselves qualify as acts of aggression.

5.1.1.3.4 Attack on a State's Armed Forces (Subparagraph (d))

Subparagraph (d) apparently criminalises the "first strike" (see supra 2.3.4) by the armed forces of a State against those of another State:

> d) An attack by the armed forces of a State on the land, sea or air forces, or marine and air fleets of another State;

It seems that this provision applies to the initial armed attack, because any response to such an attack—provided that it complies with applicable international law, in particular, in terms of proportionality—would be regarded as an individual or collective self-defence in the sense of Article 51 of the Charter of the United Nations (see supra 2.4.1.1–2.4.1.4). Although there is no mention of territory in this subparagraph, the reference to the "land, sea or air forces, or marine and air fleets" may be taken to imply that a State's territory, which includes its land and subsoil, territorial sea, internal waters,[50] and air space,[51] is the ultimate object of an armed attack hereby criminalised. As each of the constituents of territory is defended by a relevant combat branch, an aggressive attack against one of these should be regarded as (at least, an indirect) attack against the territorial object they defend. Hence, the qualification of such an armed attack as aggression does comply with the overall logic of Article 8 bis (2).

5.1.1.3.5 Internationally Wrongful Use of a State's Armed Forces Present Within the Territory of Another State (Subparagraph (e))

The case provided for in subparagraph (e) of Article 8 bis (2) is distinct in that it qualifies as an act of aggression the conduct of a State's armed forces, which had previously arrived in another State with the latter's consent (i.e., in accordance

---

[49] Cf. ibid., Article 2 ("Legal status of the territorial sea, of the air space over the territorial sea and of its bed and subsoil"): "1. The sovereignty of a coastal State extends, beyond its land territory and internal waters and, in the case of an archipelagic State, its archipelagic waters, to an adjacent belt of sea, described as the territorial sea. 2. This sovereignty extends to the air space over the territorial sea as well as to its bed and subsoil. 3. The sovereignty over the territorial sea is exercised subject to this Convention and to other rules of international law".

[50] Cf. ibid., Article 8(1) ("Internal waters"): "Except as provided in Part IV, waters on the landward side of the baseline of the territorial sea form part of the internal waters of the State".

[51] See Lukashuk 2008, p. 405.

with international law) but afterwards acted in a hostile manner either against the receiving State or against a third State:

> e) The use of armed forces of one State which are within the territory of another State with the agreement of the receiving State, in contravention of the conditions provided for in the agreement or any extension of their presence in such territory beyond the termination of the agreement;

In addition to dangers of a military character, which are implicit in this subparagraph and which might, in accordance with the other subparagraphs of the definition, themselves qualify as acts of aggression (see supra 5.1.1.3.1–5.1.1.3.4 and infra 5.1.1.3.6–5.1.1.3.7), the act in question would also violate the principle of fulfilment of obligations under international law in good faith.[52] As the material (*ratione materiae*) regulations for the presence of foreign armed forces in a State's territory are clearly determined in applicable treaties, and their temporal (*ratione temporis*) field of application is always determined (in the treaties themselves), the qualification of a grave (see supra 5.1.1.1.5) breach thereof as an act of aggression would duly conform to international law.

5.1.1.3.6 Allowing the Use of a State's Own Territory for the Commission of an Act of Aggression Against Another State (Subparagraph (f))

Subparagraph (f) of Article 8 bis (2), like the preceding one, also deals with the conduct of States, which accommodate foreign troops or armaments in their territories:

> f) The action of a State in allowing its territory, which it has placed at the disposal of another State, to be used by that other State for perpetrating an act of aggression against a third State;

In accordance with applicable international treaties, a State's territory may be placed at the disposal of another State for the stationing of armed forces, or the placement of armaments, or for both.[53] The responsibility of the host State would thereby consist in guaranteeing that the foreign armed forces or armaments would not be used for

---

[52] See UN Charter, Article 2(2): "All Members, in order to ensure to all of them the rights and benefits resulting from membership, shall fulfil in good faith the obligations assumed by them in accordance with the present Charter". The 1970 Friendly Relations Declaration elaborates upon this provision as follows: "Every State has the duty to fulfil in good faith the obligations assumed by it in accordance with the Charter of the United Nations. Every State has the duty to fulfil in good faith its obligations under the generally recognized principles and rules of international law. Every State has the duty to fulfil in good faith its obligations under international agreements valid under the generally recognized principles and rules of international law. Where obligations arising under international agreements are in conflict with the obligations of Members of the United Nations under the Charter of the United Nations, the obligations under the Charter shall prevail".

[53] See, for example, Svinarev 2000, at 194.

breaching international law.[54] In order to qualify as aggression, the allegedly unlawful acts actually perpetrated by the State whose armed forces are stationed, or whose armaments are placed, in the receiving State must be covered by any other substantive subparagraph of Article 8 bis (2). If the host State's relevant officials become aware of such unlawful acts, they must, without delay, resort to lawful—unilateral or multilateral—measures[55] available to their State to stop their occurrence, otherwise they may themselves become liable for facilitating or tolerating an act of aggression.

In this writer's view, the generic character of subparagraph (f) would have justified placing it at the bottom of the list in Article 8 bis (2), because its other subparagraphs articulate sufficiently specific types of conduct. In the current sequence, subparagraph (g)—which also enunciates a specific act of aggression—seems to be "detached" from the rest of the provision, and moving it upwards in the list would have been appropriate.

5.1.1.3.7 Sending Armed Bands, Groups, Irregulars or Mercenaries (Subparagraph (g))

The conduct referred to in subparagraph (g) of Article 8 bis (2) is the only example listed whose customary nature under international law has been corroborated by the International Court of Justice (see supra 2.3.2):

> g) The sending by or on behalf of a State of armed bands, groups, irregulars or mercenaries, which carry out acts of armed force against another State of such gravity as to amount to the acts listed above, or its substantial involvement therein.

While the phrase about carrying out "acts of armed force against another State of such gravity as to amount to the acts listed above" seems relatively clear in the light of the foregoing analysis, two supplementary observations ought to be made here. First, it is submitted that the phrase "armed bands, groups, irregulars or mercenaries" should especially cover, in the modern world, private military companies insofar as their staff engage in hostilities on behalf of the employer States or under their control, whereby private military companies may be dealt with under the heading of "armed groups".[56] The nature of such companies is perceptibly different from that of "armed bands" and "irregulars", nor would they normally meet either of the two "standard" international legal definitions of mercenaries,[57] so

[54] Ibid., pp. 195–196.

[55] Ibid., pp. 204–206.

[56] See Cameron 2006, pp. 573–598; Cockayne 2006, pp. 459–490; Cottier 2006, pp. 637–663; Gillard 2006, pp. 525–572; Mongelard 2006, pp. 665–691; Perrin 2006, pp. 613–635.

[57] Cf. Additional Protocol I, Article 47 ("Mercenaries"), and Article 1 of the International Convention against the Recruitment, Use, Financing and Training of Mercenaries, of 4 December 1989. It appears that the complex and cumulative character of these definitions would not allow to qualify almost anyone as a mercenary, cf. Best 1994, p. 350. See also Fallah 2006, pp. 599–611.

treating them, for the purpose of Article 8 bis (2), under the generic heading of "armed groups" is appropriate. Since international law for the regulation of private military companies' status is *in statu nascendi*, States may feel tempted to so frame the legal frameworks applicable to such private companies as to "outsource" to them some of their own tasks, and thus effectively to exempt themselves from a part of responsibility under international law. The outcomes of the so-called "Montreux process" remain to be seen.[58]

The second substantive comment pertains to the attribution of acts carried out by "armed bands, groups, irregulars or mercenaries" to the State on whose behalf they act. The rules of attributing such entities' conduct to a State are found, especially, in Articles 5,[59] 7[60] and 8[61] of the 2001 Articles on Responsibility of States for Internationally Wrongful Acts (cf. supra 2.2.1.2). The International Law Commission's official Commentary on Article 5 introduces the notion of "parastatal entities", which "exercise elements of governmental authority in place of State organs",[62] "provided that in each case the entity is empowered by the law of the State to exercise functions of a public character normally exercised by State organs, and the conduct of the entity relates to the exercise of the governmental authority concerned",[63] and directly mentions "private security firms" as an example of such parastatal entities.[64] In the opinion of the International Law Commission:

58 The so-called "Montreux Document"—jointly initiated by the Swiss Government and the ICRC—is devoted to promoting respect for IHL and human rights law in situations where private military and security companies operate in situations of armed conflicts. It deals, *inter alia*, with some aspects of such companies' legal status under applicable international law. For text, see: http://www.icrc.org/eng/resources/documents/publication/p0996.htm (last accessed 15 November 2012).

59 Cf. 2001 Articles on Responsibility of States for Internationally Wrongful Acts, Article 5 ("Conduct of persons or entities exercising elements of governmental authority"): "The conduct of a person or entity which is not an organ of the State under article 4 but which is empowered by the law of that State to exercise elements of the governmental authority shall be considered an act of the State under international law, provided the person or entity is acting in that capacity in the particular instance".

60 Ibid., Article 7 ("Excess of authority or contravention of instructions"): "The conduct of an organ of a State or of a person or entity empowered to exercise elements of the governmental authority shall be considered an act of the State under international law if the organ, person or entity acts in that capacity, even if it exceeds its authority or contravenes instructions".

61 Ibid., Article 8 ("Conduct directed or controlled by a State"): "The conduct of a person or group of persons shall be considered an act of a State under international law if the person or group of persons is in fact acting on the instructions of, or under the direction or control of, that State in carrying out the conduct".

62 See Draft articles on Responsibility of States for Internationally Wrongful Acts with commentaries 2001, p. 42.

63 Ibid., p. 43.

64 Ibid. It is known that private military and security companies are treated jointly for the purpose of the "Montreux process".

> The justification for attributing to the State under international law the conduct of "parastatal" entities lies in the fact that the internal law of the State has conferred on the entity in question the exercise of certain elements of the governmental authority [...] Article 5 does not attempt to identify precisely the scope of "governmental authority" for the purpose of attribution of the conduct of an entity to the State. Beyond a certain limit, what is regarded as "governmental" depends on the particular society, its history and traditions. Of particular importance will be not just the content of the powers, but the way they are conferred on an entity, the purposes for which they are to be exercised and the extent to which the entity is accountable to government for their exercise.[65]

Obviously, the exercise of military functions—a conventional State function—does fall within the area of "governmental authority", and the conduct—both lawful and unlawful—of staff members of private military companies and individuals belonging to other entities referred to in subparagraph (g) of Article 8 bis (2) of the ICC Statute must be attributed to the State, which hired and/or sent them. The hiring or sending State would always assert its disciplinary authority, in one way or another, over such entities so that they would act "on the instructions of, or under the direction or control" of that State, in the sense of Article 8 of the 2001 Articles of State Responsibility, for hiring them would make no sense, if they were not to comply with the State's instructions or would act contrary to its direction or control. Then again, in accordance with Article 7, their conduct would be attributable to the hiring State, even if they acted in excess or contravention of instructions. Consequently, the individual criminal responsibility for the crime of aggression connected with the employment of "parastatal entities" does have a foundation in international law and deserves inclusion in Article 8 bis (2) of the Rome Statute. As for the legal implications of the use of force by non-State actors on their own initiative, i.e. without that they are hired or sent by a State to do so, they are considered at some length above, at 5.1.1.1.3.

5.1.1.3.8 Exhaustive Character of the List

As a conventional provision of international criminal law, Article 8 bis (2) of the Rome Statute is exhaustive and must be interpreted restrictively (see infra 5.2.1).[66] For the sake of an effective enforcement of Article 8 bis, it will be important to bear in mind, in addition to what it covers, scenarios it does not cover. Among these, in addition to armed attacks perpetrated by non-State actors (see supra 5.1.1.1.3), the following may especially be singled out:

- The ICC would have no jurisdiction with respect to individual conduct bringing about a lawful employment of force by States as one not constituting aggression. The most obvious examples of such employment of force are exceptions to Article 2(4) of the Charter on the United Nations, which are explicitly indicated

[65] Ibid.

[66] On the "open", "closed" or "in-between" character of the list contained in Article 8 bis (2), see Barriga 2012, at 28, including relevant footnotes.

in the Charter (individual or collective self-defence (see supra 2.4.1.1), and enforcement measures sanctioned by the Security Council (see supra 2.4.1.5)), and the Charter-related exceptions ("Uniting for Peace" (see supra 2.4.2.1) and national liberation movements (see supra 2.4.2.2));

- Since the ICC would have jurisdiction with respect to individual conduct causing only "manifest violation[s] of the Charter of the United Nations" (see supra 5.1.1.1.5), more ambiguous situations such as extra-Charter exceptions to the prohibition of the use of force (protection of nationals abroad (see supra 2.4.3.1), "humanitarian intervention"[67] (see supra 2.4.3.2) and, somewhat less confidently, "pro-democratic intervention" (see supra 2.4.3.3)) would probably not be regarded as acts of aggression either;
- Article 8 bis (2) does not mention cyber-attacks among acts of aggression. Sure, this type of attacks was impracticable in 1974, when the General Assembly resolution 3314 (XXIX) was adopted, but ensuing technical developments made them possible, and military dangers posed by such attacks may be quite significant.[68] It may be argued that cyber-attacks could be criminalised under subparagraph (b) of Article 8 bis (2)—under the heading "use of any weapons" (see supra 5.1.1.3.2)—but first, computers do not as such meet the usual parameters of conventional "weapons", and second, cyber-attacks are carried out not "against the territory" of a State but against electronic systems, which are not covered by the accepted definitions of State territory;
- Equally, Article 8 bis (2) makes no reference to attacks on a State's spacecraft. It does mention, in subparagraph (d), "the armed forces of a State on the land, sea or air forces, or marine and air fleets of another State" but it does not mention objects launched into outer space. It is unclear whether subparagraph (b) might apply in the event of attack against a State's spacecraft, because the 1967 Treaty on Principles Governing the Activities of States in the Exploration and Use of Outer Space, including the Moon and Other Celestial Bodies, does not characterise spacecraft as belonging to the "territory" of the State on whose registry the object is carried. The Treaty stipulates in Article VIII that "[a] State Party to the Treaty on whose registry an object launched into outer space is carried shall retain *jurisdiction and control* over such object, and over any personnel thereof, while in outer space or on a celestial body. *Ownership* of objects launched into outer space, including objects landed or constructed on a celestial body, and of their component parts, is not affected by their presence in outer space or on a celestial body or by their return to the Earth" (emphasis added). However, references to "jurisdiction", "control" and "ownership" do not necessarily mean that objects launched into outer space constitute parts of the launching State's territory. Moreover, the same Treaty refers, in Articles V and VII, to "territory" in the term's accepted sense—which implies, again, that its drafters

---

[67] See Creegan 2012, pp. 59–82; Leclerc-Gagné and Byers 2009, pp. 379–390.

[68] See Adhami 2007, pp. 857–878; Lovely 2011, pp. 155–161; Schmitt 2002, pp. 365–399.

did not intend to incorporate spacecraft into the notion. Hence, an attack on a State's spacecraft would not constitute an act of aggression under Article 8 bis (2) of the Rome Statute.

It may thus be concluded that the ICC would exercise no jurisdiction with respect to individual conduct bringing about the commission of acts of aggression beyond the scope of Article 8 bis (2).[69] Even if the Security Council determines that an act committed by a State does constitute aggression (cf. supra 2.3.3) but this act is not listed in Article 8 bis (2), the ICC shall not be able to exercise jurisdiction with respect to the authors of this act, in accordance with the *nullum crimen sine lege* principle (see infra 5.2.1). In such situations, alternative (first of all, national, see supra 4.6.1) mechanisms of bringing responsible individuals to justice should be sought.

5.1.2 Conditions for the Entry into Force of Article 8 bis

Now that the crime of aggression has been defined for the purpose of the Rome Statute, it will be important to bring Article 8 bis and the pertinent provisions on jurisdiction (see infra 5.3.2 and 5.3.3) into force. The First Review Conference confirmed the determination of the States Parties to the Statute "to activate the Court's jurisdiction over the crime of aggression as early as possible",[70] and decided in this matter as follows:

> [T]o adopt, in accordance with article 5, paragraph 2, of the Rome Statute of the International Criminal Court (hereinafter: "the Statute") the amendments to the Statute contained in annex I of the present resolution, which are subject to ratification or acceptance and shall enter into force in accordance with article 121, paragraph 5 [...][71]

Article 121(5) of the Rome Statute provides that:

> [a]ny amendment to articles 5, 6, 7 and 8 of this Statute shall enter into force for those States Parties which have accepted the amendment one year after the deposit of their instruments of ratification or acceptance. In respect of a State Party which has not accepted the amendment, the Court shall not exercise its jurisdiction regarding a crime covered by the amendment when committed by that State Party's nationals or on its territory.[72]

Accordingly, "[t]he Court may exercise jurisdiction only with respect to crimes of aggression committed one year after the ratification or acceptance of the amendments by thirty States Parties".[73] As a matter of fact, this norm must be read to mean "no earlier than one year after the ratification or acceptance of the amendments by

[69] For a critical view, see Drumbl 2009, pp. 291–319.

[70] Cf. document RC/Res. 6, 6th preambular paragraph.

[71] Ibid., para 1. See also Clark 2009, pp. 413–427.

[72] Cf. Barriga 2012, at 39–41.

[73] Cf. ICC Statute, Articles 15 bis (2), 15 ter (2).

thirty States Parties", since Articles 15 bis and ter also contain additional provisions regulating the exercise of the Court's jurisdiction over the crime of aggression (see infra 5.3.2 and 5.3.3, respectively). As of 26 September 2013, instruments of ratification (or acceptance, in the case of Andorra) with respect to Article 8 bis were only deposited by Liechtenstein (on 8 May 2012), Samoa (on 25 September 2012), Trinidad and Tobago (on 13 November 2012), Luxembourg (on 15 January 2013), Estonia (on 27 March 2013), Germany (on 3 June 2013), Botswana (on 4 June 2013), Cyprus(on 25 September 2013), Slovenia (on 25 September 2013), Andorra (on 26 September 2013), and Uruguay (on 26 September 2013).[74]

At first glance, the relevant provisions have been so devised as to bring Article 8 bis into force relatively quickly. While the Rome Statute itself entered into force on 1 July 2002, "following the date of the deposit of the 60th instrument of ratification, acceptance, approval or accession with the Secretary-General of the United Nations",[75] Article 8 bis has to be ratified or accepted by thirty—twice as few—States, in order to enter into force. At the same time, States Parties have a possibility to lodge a declaration with the ICC Registrar to the effect that they do not accept the Court's jurisdiction with respect to the crime of aggression; such a declaration may be withdrawn at any time, and this withdrawal should be considered by the State Party in question within three years (cf. infra 5.3.2.4).[76] It is to be hoped now that Article 8 bis would be ratified or accepted by the required number of States within a foreseeable period; given that the First Review Conference adopted Article 8 bis by consensus, such hopes presumably are not unjustified.

5.2 The Crime of Aggression in the Context of the "General Part" of International Criminal Law

As it may now be hypothesised that the International Criminal Court might, at some point in the future, exercise jurisdiction with respect to the crime of aggression,[77] it will be useful to scrutinise the application of the "general part" of international criminal law to prospective defendants.[78] The relevant principles will be

---

[74] See UNTC, Chapter XVIII ("Penal matters", section 10.b ("Amendments on the crime of aggression to the Rome Statute of the International Criminal Court"), available at: http://treaties.un.org/pages/ViewDetails.aspx?src=TREATY&mtdsg_no=XVIII-10-b&chapter=18&lang=en (last accessed 26 September 2013).

[75] Cf. ICC Statute, Article 126(1).

[76] ICC Statute, Article 15 bis (4).

[77] C. Safferling singled out six general purposes of international criminal prosecutions, which, it appears, would also be relevant in the context of trials with respect to alleged crimes of aggression: unfolding the truth about the crimes; identifying and punishing the persons responsible for these crimes; preventing future crimes; reinstating the dignity of victims; rehabilitating and compensating the victims; promoting reconciliation. See Safferling 2012, p. 77.

[78] See generally Ambos 2006, pp. 660–673; Bogush 2009, pp. 78–94.

analysed in this section in the context of the Rome Statute itself, with due regard to customary international law on the subject.

5.2.1 Nullum Crimen Sine Lege

This principle emerged as a matter of international criminal law after the Second World War, as trials were held to prosecute and punish the perpetrators of crimes related to the war, and in the meantime was integrated in the most important universal and regional human rights treaties.[79] Along with its sentencing counterpart *nulla poena sine lege* (see infra 5.2.2), it means that an individual may be held criminally liable only for conduct, which was explicitly criminal in accordance with applicable (national or international) criminal law in force at the time the conduct occurred, and must be sentenced in accordance with that law.[80] The *nullum crimen sine lege* principle consists of four key elements: (1) the reflection of a crime in written (national or international) law; (2) the value of legal certainty; (3) the prohibition of analogy; and (4) non-retroactivity (for the latter element, see an additional note below, at 5.2.3).[81] Although the degree of importance ascribed to these elements in civil and common law systems varies,[82] the principle as such may now be said to represent a well-established norm of customary international law. Accordingly, there existed a general agreement at the 1998 Rome Conference about the relevance of Article 22 of the Rome Statute, as finally adopted:

1. A person shall not be criminally responsible under this Statute unless the conduct in question constitutes, at the time it takes place, a crime within the jurisdiction of the Court.
2. The definition of a crime shall be strictly construed and shall not be extended by analogy. In case of ambiguity, the definition shall be interpreted in favour of the person being investigated, prosecuted or convicted.
3. This article shall not affect the characterization of any conduct as criminal under international law independently of this Statute.

---

[79] See ICCPR, Article 15(1), first sentence: "No one shall be held guilty of any criminal offence on account of any act or omission which did not constitute a criminal offence, under national or international law, at the time when it was committed"; ECHR, Article 7(1): "No one shall be held guilty of any criminal offence on account of any act or omission which did not constitute a criminal offence under national or international law at the time when it was committed"; ACHR, Article 9, first sentence: "No one shall be convicted of any act or omission that did not constitute a criminal offense, under the applicable law, at the time it was committed"; ACHPR, Article 7(2), first sentence: "No one may be condemned for an act or omission which did not constitute a legally punishable offence at the time it was committed".

[80] See Hauck 2008, pp. 58–65; Kibalnik 2003, pp. 91–110; Kielsgard 2012, pp. 119–136; Lamb 2002, at 733–734; Milanovic 2012, pp. 165–187; Safferling 2012, p. 83; Von Feuerbach 2007, pp. 1005–1008.

[81] See Lamb 2002, at 734.

[82] Ibid., at 740.

If applied specifically to the crime of aggression, Article 22 lets one usefully highlight a few key points. It follows from Article 22(1) that "a person [...] criminally responsible under [the] Statute" for a "crime [of aggression] within the jurisdiction of the Court" shall be, in the language of Article 8 bis (1), one "in a position effectively to exercise control over or to direct the political or military action of a State" (see supra 5.1.1.1.3). All other individuals "shall not be criminally responsible under [the] Statute" for the crime of aggression as a matter of principle; they may, however, be held liable "independently of [the] Statute" (cf. supra 4.6.1), in the language of Article 22(3).

In accordance with Article 22(2), the definition of the crime of aggression should be strictly construed and should not be extended by analogy. As was discussed above (see supra 5.1.1.1.2, 5.1.1.1.4, 5.1.1.1.5, 5.1.1.3), the substantive crime should consist in the planning, preparation, initiation or execution of an act of aggression, which, by its character, gravity and scale, would constitute a manifest violation of the UN Charter. The prohibition of extending the definition of the crime by analogy suggests that crimes whose commission may, in some cases, lead or be otherwise related to an international war or armed conflict—such as treason (see supra 4.1.4)—are not covered by Article 8 bis (cf., however, infra 5.2.4.3 for an observation on propaganda for war). Neither would the Court have jurisdiction with respect to individual acts leading to the use of force by a State Party to the Rome Statute, which, by its character, gravity and scale, would not reach the threshold of "a manifest violation" of the UN Charter (see supra 5.1.1.1.5). In turn, the strict construction of the definition of the crime of aggression means that individual acts leading to the use of force by a State in other forms than ones listed in subparagraphs (a)–(g) of Article 8 bis (2) would not be covered by Article 8 bis (see supra 5.1.1.3.8). Lastly, in accordance with the second sentence of Article 22(2), any ambiguity of fact or law should be interpreted in favour of the person(s) being investigated, prosecuted or convicted (for a note on mistakes of fact or law, see infra 5.2.11).

5.2.2 *Nulla Poena Sine Lege*

A substantive counterpart of the foregoing principle, *nulla poena sine lege* has been embodied in all major universal and regional human rights treaties,[83] and is

[83] See ICCPR, Article 15(1), second and third sentences: "Nor shall a heavier penalty be imposed than the one that was applicable at the time when the criminal offence was committed. If, subsequent to the commission of the offence, provision is made by law for the imposition of the lighter penalty, the offender shall benefit thereby"; ECHR, Article 7(1), second sentence: "Nor shall a heavier penalty be imposed than the one that was applicable at the time the criminal offence was committed"; ACHR, Article 9, second and third sentences: "A heavier penalty shall not be imposed than the one that was applicable at the time the criminal offense was committed. If subsequent to the commission of the offense the law provides for the imposition of a lighter punishment, the guilty person shall benefit therefrom"; ACHPR, Article 7(2), second sentence: "No penalty may be inflicted for an offence for which no provision was made at the time it was committed".

part of the "hard core of human rights".[84] The principle means that no heavier criminal sanction may be imposed upon a convicted person than the one in force at the time the offence was committed.[85] The second and third sentences of Article 15(1) of the International Covenant on Civil and Political Rights, for example, phrase the principle as follows (emphasis added):

> No one shall be held guilty of any criminal offence on account of any act or omission which did not constitute a criminal offence, under national or international law, at the time when it was committed. *Nor shall a heavier penalty be imposed than the one that was applicable at the time when the criminal offence was committed. If, subsequent to the commission of the offence, provision is made by law for the imposition of the lighter penalty, the offender shall benefit thereby.*

As the International Criminal Court represents a self-contained system of international criminal justice, its Statute accordingly provides for an autonomous mechanism of criminal sanctions; the autonomy of the Court's sanctioning mechanism is underscored in Article 80 of the ICC Statute.[86] Three Articles of the ICC Statute are particularly relevant to the *nulla poena sine lege* principle. Article 23 provides generally:

> A person convicted by the Court may be punished only in accordance with this Statute.

The detailed rules on the imposition and enforcement of sanctions are included, respectively, in Part VII ("Penalties") and Part X ("Enforcement") of the Statute. Article 77 ("Applicable penalties") lists the entirety of criminal sanctions, which may be applied by the Court:

> 1. Subject to article 110, the Court may impose one of the following penalties on a person convicted of a crime referred to in Article 5 of this Statute:
>
>   (a) Imprisonment for a specified number of years, which may not exceed a maximum of 30 years;
>
>   or
>
>   (b) A term of life imprisonment when justified by the extreme gravity of the crime and the individual circumstances of the convicted person.

[84] See ICCPR, Article 4(2); ECHR, Article 15(2); ACHR, Article 27(2). The African Charter on Human and Peoples' Rights does not contain any provisions with respect to derogation.

[85] See Lamb 2002, at 756. See also Schabas 2000, pp. 521–539.

[86] See ICC Statute, Article 80 ("Non-prejudice to national application of penalties and national laws"): "Nothing in this Part affects the application by States of penalties prescribed by their national law, nor the law of States which do not provide for penalties prescribed in this Part". See also Carcano 2002, pp. 583–609; Henham 2003, pp. 81–114; Rosenfeld 2012, pp. 249–265.

2. In addition to imprisonment, the Court may order:

   (a) A fine under the criteria provided for in the Rules of Procedure and Evidence[87];
   (b) A forfeiture of proceeds, property and assets derived directly or indirectly from that crime, without prejudice to the rights of bona fide third parties.

Article 110 ("Review by the Court concerning reduction of sentence") provides additionally:

1. The State of enforcement shall not release the person before expiry of the sentence pronounced by the Court.
2. The Court alone shall have the right to decide any reduction of sentence, and shall rule on the matter after having heard the person.
3. When the person has served two-thirds of the sentence, or 25 years in the case of life imprisonment, the Court shall review the sentence to determine whether it should be reduced. Such a review shall not be conducted before that time.

---

[87] See ICC Rules of Procedure and Evidence, document ICC-ASP/1/3, Rule 146 ("Imposition of fines under article 77"): "1. In determining whether to order a fine under article 77, paragraph 2 (a), and in fixing the amount of the fine, the Court shall determine whether imprisonment is a sufficient penalty. The Court shall give due consideration to the financial capacity of the convicted person, including any orders for forfeiture in accordance with article 77, paragraph 2 (b), and, as appropriate, any orders for reparation in accordance with article 75. The Court shall take into account, in addition to the factors referred to in rule 145, whether and to what degree the crime was motivated by personal financial gain. 2. A fine imposed under article 77, paragraph 2 (a), shall be set at an appropriate level. To this end, the Court shall, in addition to the factors referred to above, in particular take into consideration the damage and injuries caused as well as the proportionate gains derived from the crime by the perpetrator. Under no circumstances may the total amount exceed 75 per cent of the value of the convicted person's identifiable assets, liquid or realizable, and property, after deduction of an appropriate amount that would satisfy the financial needs of the convicted person and his or her dependants. 3. In imposing a fine, the Court shall allow the convicted person a reasonable period in which to pay the fine. The Court may provide for payment of a lump sum or by way of instalments during that period. 4. In imposing a fine, the Court may, as an option, calculate it according to a system of daily fines. In such cases, the minimum duration shall be 30 days and the maximum duration five years. The Court shall decide the total amount in accordance with sub-rules 1 and 2. It shall determine the amount of daily payment in the light of the individual circumstances of the convicted person, including the financial needs of his or her dependants. 5. If the convicted person does not pay the fine imposed in accordance with the conditions set above, appropriate measures may be taken by the Court pursuant to rules 217–222 and in accordance with article 109. Where, in cases of continued wilful non-payment, the Presidency, on its own motion or at the request of the Prosecutor, is satisfied that all available enforcement measures have been exhausted, it may as a last resort extend the term of imprisonment for a period not to exceed a quarter of such term or five years, whichever is less. In the determination of such period of extension, the Presidency shall take into account the amount of the fine, imposed and paid. Any such extension shall not apply in the case of life imprisonment. The extension may not lead to a total period of imprisonment in excess of 30 years. 6. In order to determine whether to order an extension and the period involved, the Presidency shall sit in camera for the purpose of obtaining the views of the sentenced person and the Prosecutor. The sentenced person shall have the right to be assisted by counsel. 7. In imposing a fine, the Court shall warn the convicted person that failure to pay the fine in accordance with the conditions set out above may result in an extension of the period of imprisonment as described in this rule".

4. In its review under paragraph 3, the Court may reduce the sentence if it finds that one or more of the following factors are present:
   (a) The early and continuing willingness of the person to cooperate with the Court in its investigations and prosecutions;
   (b) The voluntary assistance of the person in enabling the enforcement of the judgements and orders of the Court in other cases, and in particular providing assistance in locating assets subject to orders of fine, forfeiture or reparation which may be used for the benefit of victims; or
   (c) Other factors establishing a clear and significant change of circumstances sufficient to justify the reduction of sentence, as provided in the Rules of Procedure and Evidence.
5. If the Court determines in its initial review under paragraph 3 that it is not appropriate to reduce the sentence, it shall thereafter review the question of reduction of sentence at such intervals and applying such criteria as provided for in the Rules of Procedure and Evidence.[88]

Thus, unlike as a result of the Nuremberg (see supra 3.1.1) and Tokyo (see supra 3.1.2) trials, in accordance with the Rome Statute, no person convicted of the crime of aggression might, in the future, be sentenced to death. In the system of international criminal justice, he or she would be immune from the death penalty, even if a national law applicable to the case provided to the effect, if the person were to be tried by a competent national court of law (cf. supra 4.6.1). The specific duration of imprisonment—and the amount of a fine—to be imposed upon a person convicted under Article 8 bis would depend on his or per individual role in the criminal mechanism. It is now difficult to say whether the ICC Judges would, in the future assignment of sanctions under Article 8 bis, follow the example of the Nuremberg Tribunal,[89] or whether they would opt for assigning more severe sanctions, given "the extreme gravity of the crime" (cf. Article 77(1)(b)). It is understood that the Judges would have a margin of appreciation in assigning terms of imprisonment and fines, whereas the "proceeds, property and assets derived directly or indirectly" from the commission of a crime of aggression should be forfeited in full, with due regard to the rights of bona fide third parties (cf. Article 77(2)(b)), for no criminal acquisition of property should be recognised as legitimate.

[88] Ibid., Rule 223 ("Criteria for review concerning reduction of sentence"): "In reviewing the question of reduction of sentence pursuant to article 110, paragraphs 3 and 5, the three judges of the Appeals Chamber shall take into account the criteria listed in article 110, paragraph 4 (a) and (b), and the following criteria: (a) The conduct of the sentenced person while in detention, which shows a genuine dissociation from his or her crime; (b) The prospect of the resocialization and successful resettlement of the sentenced person; (c) Whether the early release of the sentenced person would give rise to significant social instability; (d) Any significant action taken by the sentenced person for the benefit of the victims as well as any impact on the victims and their families as a result of the early release; (e) Individual circumstances of the sentenced person, including a worsening state of physical or mental health or advanced age".

[89] Notably, defendants Schacht and Von Papen who had been charged by the Nuremberg Tribunal with crimes against peace but not also with other crimes within the Tribunal's jurisdiction were acquitted. See International Military Tribunal (Nuremberg), Judgment of 1 October 1946, pp. 504–507 and 517–519.

5.2.3 *Non-Retroactivity Ratione Personae*

The principle of legality delineated in Articles 22 and 23 of the Rome Statute is completed by Article 24 ("Non-retroactivity *ratione personae*"):

1. No person shall be criminally responsible under this Statute for conduct prior to the entry into force of the Statute.
2. In the event of a change in the law applicable to a given case prior to a final judgement, the law more favourable to the person being investigated, prosecuted or convicted shall apply.

In accordance with Article 24(1), no person should be held criminally responsible under Article 8 bis until it would have entered into force, at some point in the future, i.e. at least until one year after the ratification or acceptance of the amendments by thirty States Parties (see supra 5.1.2), and subject to the specific provisions of Articles 15 bis and 15 ter (see infra 5.3.2 and 5.3.3, respectively). In turn, Article 24(2) implies, first of all, that possible future amendments to the Rome Statute (or other law applicable to an individual case[90]) might improve the legal standing of persons being investigated, prosecuted or convicted under Article 8 bis, if such subsequent law excluded (fully or in part) the criminality of aggression for the purpose of the Rome Statute.[91] It is clear that the possible addition of new elements either to the definition of the individual crime of aggression (Article 8 bis(1), see supra 5.1.1.1) or to that of an act of aggression (Article 8 bis (2), see supra 5.1.1.2–5.1.1.3) would not affect situations, which would have occurred prior to the amendments' entry into force. As for criminal sanctions applicable to persons to be convicted of the crime of aggression, such possible developments in the law of the ICC might apply retrospectively, if the terms of imprisonment (cf. Article 77(1)) were to be decreased, or an additional sanction (fine or forfeiture of proceeds, property and assets, cf. Article 77(2)), or an element thereof, were to be deleted from the Rome Statute. The introduction of new or graver criminal sanctions would only have a prospective effect, i.e. such sanctions would only apply to the crimes of aggression within the jurisdiction of the ICC, which would have been committed after the entry into force of relevant amendments to Article 77.

5.2.4 *Individual Criminal Responsibility*

Article 25 of the Rome Statute lays down the principle of individual criminal responsibility for the commission of international crimes within the jurisdiction of

[90] See also Degan 2005, pp. 45–83; Zimmermann 2012, pp. 209–227.

[91] See Juratowitch 2005, pp. 337–362; Kibalnik 2003, pp. 135–151; Safferling 2012, pp. 83–84; Zelinskaya and Dryomina-Volok 2010, pp. 189–209.

the ICC, including with respect to the crime of aggression. However incomplete this article may purportedly be,[92] it appears to be indicative of a progressive development of international criminal law in comparison with earlier sources on the subject (in the first place, the ICTY[93] and ICTR[94] Statutes) and is among the fundamental provisions of the Rome Statute.[95] As Albin Eser points out, Article 25 may be said to comprise a general framework of the individual criminal responsibility regime for the purpose of the International Criminal Court, while some specific elements thereof are scattered throughout the rest of Part III of the Rome Statute ("General principles of international criminal law")[96] (see supra 5.2.1–5.2.3 and infra 5.2.5–5.2.12).

---

[92] See Cryer 2001, pp. 3–31; Eser 2002, at 768; Kibalnik 2003, pp. 65–91; Posner and Sykes 2007, pp. 1–63; Spinedi 2002, pp. 895–899; Werle 2007, pp. 953–975; Wilmshurst 2004, pp. 93–96.

[93] Cf. the ICTY Statute, Article 6 ("Personal jurisdiction"): "The International Tribunal shall have jurisdiction over natural persons pursuant to the provisions of the present Statute", and Article 7 ("Individual criminal responsibility"): "1. A person who planned, instigated, ordered, committed or otherwise aided and abetted in the planning, preparation or execution of a crime referred to in articles 2 to 5 of the present Statute, shall be individually responsible for the crime. 2. The official position of any accused person, whether as Head of State or Government or as a responsible Government official, shall not relieve such person of criminal responsibility nor mitigate punishment. 3. The fact that any of the acts referred to in articles 2 to 5 of the present Statute was committed by a subordinate does not relieve his superior of criminal responsibility if he knew or had reason to know that the subordinate was about to commit such acts or had done so and the superior failed to take the necessary and reasonable measures to prevent such acts or to punish the perpetrators thereof. 4. The fact that an accused person acted pursuant to an order of a Government or of a superior shall not relieve him of criminal responsibility, but may be considered in mitigation of punishment if the International Tribunal determines that justice so requires".

[94] Cf. the ICTR Statute, Article 5 ("Personal jurisdiction"): "The International Tribunal for Rwanda shall have jurisdiction over natural persons pursuant to the provisions of the present Statute", and Article 6 ("Individual Criminal Responsibility"): "1. A person who planned, instigated, ordered, committed or otherwise aided and abetted in the planning, preparation or execution of a crime referred to in Articles 2 to 4 of the present Statute, shall be individually responsible for the crime. 2. The official position of any accused person, whether as Head of state or government or as a responsible government official, shall not relieve such person of criminal responsibility nor mitigate punishment. 3. The fact that any of the acts referred to in Articles 2–4 of the present Statute was committed by a subordinate does not relieve his or her superior of criminal responsibility if he or she knew or had reason to know that the subordinate was about to commit such acts or had done so and the superior failed to take the necessary and reasonable measures to prevent such acts or to punish the perpetrators thereof. 4. The fact that an accused person acted pursuant to an order of a government or of a superior shall not relieve him or her of criminal responsibility, but may be considered in mitigation of punishment if the International Tribunal for Rwanda determines that justice so requires".

[95] See Werle 2009a, pp. 165–185.

[96] See Eser 2002, at 769–770.

5.2.4.1 ICC Jurisdiction Over Natural Persons

In accordance with Article 25(1), the ICC shall have jurisdiction with respect to the crime of aggression only over natural persons but not over collective entities as such (even if the crime of aggression is typically committed in organisational or institutional frameworks) or States:

1. The Court shall have jurisdiction over natural persons pursuant to this Statute.

This provision is evocative of a rule of international law, which emerged after the Second World War, to the effect that individuals may be held accountable directly under international law for criminal violations thereof they would have perpetrated (see supra 1.2.2–1.2.3). The Statute's drafters decided to limit the Court's jurisdiction to natural persons, because the contentious issue of the criminal responsibility of subjects other than individuals is not yet settled in customary international law.[97] Besides, they apparently wished to avoid the employment of the arguable concept of "joint criminal enterprise"; therefore, the Court would have to take account, when determining the guilt of individual perpetrators "pursuant to [the] Statute", of their specific roles in shaping the criminal plan and all relevant circumstances of its execution (for details, see infra 5.2.4.2 and other relevant paragraphs of this chapter).

5.2.4.2 Individual Responsibility and Liability for Punishment

Until the adoption of the Rome Statute in July 1998 (cf. supra 1.2.6.1), the concept of so-called "joint criminal enterprise" was prevalent in the international criminal law doctrine, despite some criticism.[98] At first glance, this theory might suit well the mechanism of the crime of aggression: it takes into account the existence of a design to commit the crime, the collective nature of the criminal mechanism, the perpetrators' awareness of the common plan, and the impact of their positions of authority. However, the theory was certainly more suitable in the framework of the post-World War II trials, which favoured expedited proceedings and less stringent standards of evidence,[99] and would be less well-placed in the context of

---

[97] See Chouliaras 2010, pp. 191–214; Engelhart 2010, pp. 175–190; Van den Herik 2010, pp. 155–173.

[98] See Ambos 2007, pp. 159–183; Ohlin 2007, Van der Wilt 2007, pp. 91–108; Werle 2009a, pp. 174–175.

[99] Cf. Article 19 of the Charter of the Nuremberg Tribunal: "The Tribunal shall not be bound by technical rules of evidence. It shall adopt and apply to the greatest possible extent expeditious and nontechnical procedure, and shall admit any evidence which it deems to be of probative value", and Article 13(a) of the Charter of the Tokyo Tribunal: "[…] The Tribunal shall not be bound by technical rules of evidence. It shall adopt and apply to the greatest possible extent expeditious and non-technical procedure, and shall admit any evidence which it deems to have probative value. All purported admissions or statements of the accused are admissible".

proceedings before an international criminal court, which claims to comply with all fundamental procedural standards accepted in modern international law (see supra 4.6.1.2.3). Given that the identification of perpetrators' individual roles in the criminal mechanism of aggression (cf. supra 4.3) should in no way conflict with the ICC's foreseeable task of analysing the inherently systemic character of alleged crimes of aggression, which the ICC might have to adjudicate in the future (cf. infra 5.3), Article 25(2) of the Rome Statute is generally to be regarded as an apposite and contemporary legal basis for asserting individual criminal responsibility (emphasis added)[100]:

> 2. A person who commits a crime within the jurisdiction of the Court shall be *individually* responsible and liable for punishment in accordance with this Statute.

Naturally, the precise degree of responsibility and punishment (see supra 5.2.2) should depend on co-perpetrators' specific political, military or other individual roles in the planning, preparation, initiation or execution of an alleged crime of aggression (cf. supra 5.1.1.1.2), and the ICC would have to be as impartial and meticulous as it possibly could in determining and assessing those individual roles (see infra 5.2.4.3).

5.2.4.3 Perpetration and Participation

Article 25(3) of the Rome Statute spells out, in an inclusive manner, the notions of perpetration and participation for the purpose of the Statute.[101] As there exists extensive scholarly literature on Article 25(3),[102] various modes of criminal conduct listed therein are only briefly considered in this section in the specific context of the crime of aggression. In accordance with Article 25(3) bis[103]—by which

[100] On individual criminal responsibility, see, for example, Militello 2007, pp. 941–952.

[101] Cf. ICC Statute, Article 25(3): "3. In accordance with this Statute, a person shall be criminally responsible and liable for punishment for a crime within the jurisdiction of the Court if that person: (a) Commits such a crime, whether as an individual, jointly with another or through another person, regardless of whether that other person is criminally responsible; (b) Orders, solicits or induces the commission of such a crime which in fact occurs or is attempted; (c) For the purpose of facilitating the commission of such a crime, aids, abets or otherwise assists in its commission or its attempted commission, including providing the means for its commission; (d) In any other way contributes to the commission or attempted commission of such a crime by a group of persons acting with a common purpose. Such contribution shall be intentional and shall either: (i) Be made with the aim of furthering the criminal activity or criminal purpose of the group, where such activity or purpose involves the commission of a crime within the jurisdiction of the Court; or (ii) Be made in the knowledge of the intention of the group to commit the crime [...]".

[102] See Barriga 2012, at 20–22; Burghardt 2010, pp. 81–94; Cassese 2008, pp. 214–232; Eser 2002, pp. 781–807; Werle 2009a, pp. 176–185.

[103] Cf. ICC Statute, Article 25(3) bis: "In respect of the crime of aggression, the provisions of this article shall apply only to persons in a position effectively to exercise control over or to direct the political or military action of a State", see document RC/Res.6, Annex I, para 5.

Article 25(3) was amended at the Statute's First Review Conference with respect to the crime of aggression—all subjects (co-perpetrators) of a crime of aggression for the purpose of the ICC must be "persons in a position effectively to exercise control over or to direct the political or military action of a State" (see supra 4.2 and 5.1.1.1.3), and the Court may not hold lower-ranking State officials responsible for the crime of aggression. An analogous provision was also included in the Elements of crimes for the crime of aggression (see infra 5.4, especially footnote 177). The fact that the other crimes within the jurisdiction of the ICC—genocide, crimes against humanity or war crimes—are not subject to such a restrictive clause is due to the nature of the crime of aggression, which lower ranking officials are simply not able to commit (cf. supra 4.2.1). In order to bring about a massive use of force by his or her own State against another State (cf. supra 5.1.1.1.5 for an observation on the requisite level of military violence), an individual must have access to the most powerful political and military leverages, which are inherent to the State machinery; obviously, these criteria can only be met by the most senior political, military, economic, religious and social leaders of a State (cf. supra 4.2.2–4.2.5) possessing a requisite state of mind (cf. supra 4.5 and infra 5.2.9). Likewise, it is widely agreed that a crime of aggression—unlike genocide, crimes against humanity or war crimes, which can also be perpetrated individually—can by its very nature only be committed by a group of persons,[104] and Article 25(3) of the ICC Statute therefore remains fully applicable to the criminal mechanism of aggression, subject to the provision of Article 25(3) bis.

In the strict sense of the term, the *commission* of a crime of aggression, in the sense of subparagraph (a), "whether as an individual, jointly with another or through another person, regardless of whether that other person is criminally responsible" means the "initiation or execution" of an act of aggression in the sense of Article 8 bis (1) of the Rome Statute (see supra 5.1.1.1.2; for an observation on the formal *corpus delicti* of the crime of aggression, see supra 4.3.1.2; for an observation on the material *corpus delicti* of the crime of aggression, see supra 4.3.1.3). One may contend that, in fact, a crime of aggression is always committed—i.e. an order to commit an act of aggression is always issued to and executed by—a State's armed forces, and therefore, through their intermediary, "through another person". However, in accordance with customary international law embodied in Article 25(3) bis, members of a State's armed forces outside their very top echelons cannot themselves be held responsible for the crime of aggression in the sense of Article 25(3)(a) bis, as they are not "in a position effectively to exercise control over or to direct the political or military action of [their] State". It goes without saying, though, that such members of the armed forces (of both the aggressor and victim States) may be held responsible for the other crimes within the jurisdiction of the International Criminal Court—genocide, crimes against humanity or war crimes—if they occur in the international armed conflict arising from an act of aggression in question.

[104] See Anggadi et al. 2012, at 67. See also footnote 178 below.

It is also understood that the range of individuals over whom the International Criminal Court might exercise jurisdiction for their involvement in facilitating the commission of a crime of aggression, aiding, abetting or otherwise assisting in its commission or its attempted commission in the sense of subparagraph (c), or in contributing to the commission or attempted commission of such a crime in the sense of subparagraph (d) of Article 25(3) should include only the most senior officials or influential personalities (see supra 4.2 and 5.1.1.1.3).[105] Lower ranking officials should be exempted from the ICC jurisdiction, even if they were to be held criminally responsible in accordance with applicable national laws. Importantly, here one needs to reconcile the provisions of subparagraphs (c) and (d) of Article 25(3) with Article 8 bis (1) of the Statute ("*planning, preparation*, initiation or execution" of an act of aggression (emphasis added), see supra 5.1.1.1.2)). The problem is that criminal responsibility under subparagraphs (c) and (d) arises *only if a crime within the jurisdiction of the ICC in fact occurs or is attempted*; they do not provide for a criminal responsibility for the planning of or preparation for a crime before its successful or attempted commission, whereas Article 8 bis (1) does criminalise these preliminary stages in a criminal mechanism of aggression as well. A possible interpretative way of reconciling these seemingly conflicting rules is that individuals should be held responsible under Article 25(3) (a) of the Rome Statute for the initiation or execution of an act of aggression, whereas planning and preparation as such would be covered by Articles 25(3)(c) or 25(3)(d), depending on the specific role of an individual in the criminal mechanism (for an observation on the truncated *corpus delicti* of the crime of aggression, see supra 4.3.1.1).[106] Of course, an act of aggression would need to occur or be attempted, in order for its planning or preparation for it to be criminalised under Articles 25(3)(c) or (d). However, for the purpose of the ICC, even the initiation or execution of an act of aggression would only be justiciable, if it occurred in fact or were attempted, because an individual crime would need to have led to an act of aggression in the sense of Article 8 bis (2) (see supra 5.1.1.2). In other words, an act of aggression would need to have occurred or, at least, have been attempted, in order for the ICC to exercise jurisdiction with respect to the initiation or execution of an associated individual crime of aggression (under Article 25(3)(a)), or with respect to its planning or preparation (under 25(3)(c) or (d)). See also infra 5.2.4.5 for an observation on the (decriminalised) abandonment of the effort to commit the crime of aggression.

Finally, Article 25(3)(b) criminalises ordering, soliciting or inducing the commission of a crime within the jurisdiction of the ICC, which in fact occurs or is

[105] See Anggadi et al. 2012, at 67.

[106] It is understood accordingly that individuals who would initiate or execute a crime of aggression would almost certainly also be responsible for its planning or preparation; however, not all individuals participating at the planning and preparation stages would also be involved in the initiation or execution of the crime. See supra 4.3.

attempted, including the crime of aggression. A typical example of soliciting or inducing the commission of a crime of aggression would be propaganda for war (cf. supra 4.4 and 5.2.1). As both soliciting and inducing are only criminalised, if the crime in question occurs or is attempted (but not before the occurrence or attempt), one may conclude that the ICC also possesses a limited jurisdiction with respect to propaganda for war, and such an interpretation should not be regarded as a violation of the *nullum crimen sine lege* principle (see supra 5.2.1). The problem of ordering the commission of a crime of aggression will be considered below, at 5.2.7 and 5.2.12.

5.2.4.4 Attempt to Commit a Crime of Aggression

In accordance with customary international law,[107] the first sentence of Article 25(3)(f) of the Rome Statute criminalises attempts to commit international crimes within the jurisdiction of the International Criminal Court, including the crime of aggression:

> (f) Attempts to commit such a crime by taking action that commences its execution by means of a substantial step, but the crime does not occur because of circumstances independent of the person's intentions [...]

In the context of the definition of the crime of aggression for the purpose of the Rome Statute,[108] "taking action that commences [the] execution [of the crime of aggression] by means of a substantial step" is the initiation of the crime (see supra 4.3.1.2) at the "moment of aggression"—the instant of issuing an order (see infra 5.2.7 and 5.2.12) to commit an act of aggression (in the sense of Article 8 bis (2) of the Rome Statute) against another State (see supra 5.1.1.2). In such a case, the possible "circumstances independent of the person's [aggressive] intentions" (cf. supra 4.5) causing the non-occurrence of the act of aggression might include, in theory, a considerable change of weather (provided that particular weather conditions would have been essential to the success of the attack), an unexpected failure of weapons or other required equipment, or an unforeseen lack of preparedness on the part of the potential aggressor State's armed forces to comply with the order. Another possible situation covered by Article 25(3)(f) is the exercise by the potential victim State of its right to pre-emptive or interceptive self-defence (see supra 2.4.1.3 and 2.4.1.4). In any such event, the criminal liability of person(s) issuing the order to carry out an armed attack in violation of Article 8 bis of the Rome Statute should arise, since their aggressive intent would be at hand.

---

[107] On attempt, see Ambos 1999, at 488–489; Werle 2009a, pp. 230–231 (including bibliographical references).

[108] On individual attempt specifically in the context of the crime of aggression, see Barriga 2012, at 23–24.

5.2.4.5 The Abandonment of the Effort to Commit a Crime of Aggression

In accordance with the second sentence of Article 25(3)(f), the abandonment of the effort to commit a crime of aggression is decriminalised:

> (f) [...] However, a person who abandons the effort to commit the crime or otherwise prevents the completion of the crime shall not be liable for punishment under this Statute for the attempt to commit that crime if that person completely and voluntarily gave up the criminal purpose.

This provision lists three (two alternative objective and one required subjective) conditions for the decriminalisation of the conduct of a person who had previously participated in the criminal mechanism of aggression but then decided to abandon the effort. The required condition for decriminalisation is the person's giving up, completely and voluntarily, the criminal purpose, so that the *animus aggressions* required by the definition of the crime (see supra 4.5 and infra 5.2.9) ceases to exist. The complete and voluntary change in the individual's mental attitude towards the crime should presumably be expressed in his or her ensuing (physical and verbal) conduct. In turn, the alternative objective conditions require that the person either "abandons the effort to commit the crime" (passive condition), i.e. he or she stops contributing to the planning of or preparation for an aggression (for example, by leaving the post essential to the aggressive effort and thus technically distancing himself or herself from the crime, cf. supra 4.3.1.1.2 for the "functional indispensability test"), or that the person "otherwise prevents the completion of the crime" (active condition)—that is, he or she takes conscious and proactive measures for the prevention of the crime (for example, through improper fulfilment of his or her professional duties or anti-war propaganda). In either case, the required Elements for the crime of aggression would not be fulfilled (cf. infra 5.4), and the person in question should not be held criminally responsible.

5.2.5 Exclusion of Jurisdiction Over Persons Under Eighteen

Article 26 of the Rome Statute stipulates that "[t]he Court shall have no jurisdiction over any person who was under the age of 18 at the time of the alleged commission of a crime".[109] This rule is compatible with the United Nations Convention on the Rights of the Child[110] and has a distinct practical significance in the context of the crime of aggression. It is highly unlikely that a person aged below eighteen would be "in a position effectively to exercise control over or to

109 See Safferling 2012, p. 84.

110 See the UN Convention on the Rights of the Child, Article 1: "For the purposes of the present Convention, a child means every human being below the age of eighteen years unless under the law applicable to the child, majority is attained earlier".

direct the political or military action of a State" and thus would be able to commit a crime of aggression in the sense of Article 8 bis (1) of the Rome Statute (see supra 5.1.1.1.3). Whereas the other core crimes within the jurisdiction of the ICC—genocide, crimes against humanity and war crimes—can, as a matter of fact, be committed by persons aged below eighteen but the Court would have no jurisdiction over such persons in accordance with Article 26 of the Statute, in the case of the crime of aggression, the ICC would have no jurisdiction because no person aged below eighteen would practically be capable of committing the crime.

5.2.6 Irrelevance of Official Capacity

Similarly, Article 27 of the Rome Statute relates specifically to potential subjects of the crime of aggression in the sense of Article 8 bis:

1. This Statute shall apply equally to all persons without any distinction based on official capacity. In particular, official capacity as a Head of State or Government, a member of a Government or parliament, an elected representative or a government official shall in no case exempt a person from criminal responsibility under this Statute, nor shall it, in and of itself, constitute a ground for reduction of sentence.
2. Immunities or special procedural rules which may attach to the official capacity of a person, whether under national or international law, shall not bar the Court from exercising its jurisdiction over such a person.

Obviously, Article 27(1) lists a number of official capacities ("a Head of State or Government, a member of a Government or parliament, an elected representative or a government official") the holders of which are "in a position effectively to exercise control over or to direct the political or military action of a State" in the sense of Article 8 bis (1) of the Statute (see supra 5.1.1.1.3), and thus are capable of committing (cf. supra 5.2.4.3 and 5.2.4.4) a crime of aggression. This implies, as a matter of fact, that (almost) all such individuals normally enjoy, in accordance with applicable (international and/or national) law (cf. supra 4.6.1.2.1), one or more immunities, which Article 27 of the Statute seeks to render relatively irrelevant[111] for the purpose of the ICC jurisdiction.

An important issue about the Rome Statute's definition of the crime of aggression in the context of functional and/or personal immunities applicable under customary international law is its qualification as a perpetrator's private or official act. Clearly, it cannot credibly be characterised as a private act committed in violation of international

[111] The reservation "*relatively* irrelevant" relates to Article 98(1) of the ICC Statute ("Cooperation with respect to waiver of immunity and consent to surrender") limiting the field of application of Article 27, which otherwise would have been quite absolute for the purpose of the Statute: "The Court may not proceed with a request for surrender or assistance which would require the requested State to act inconsistently with its obligations under international law with respect to the *State or diplomatic immunity* of a person or property of a third State, unless the Court can first obtain the cooperation of that third State for the waiver of the immunity" (emphasis added).

law,[112] because no private individual is able to commit a crime of aggression in the sense of Article 8 bis of the Statute: it states plainly that the crime of aggression is an act perpetrated in one's professional capacity (by a person "in a position effectively to exercise control over or to direct the political or military action of a State"), in "manifest violation of the Charter of the United Nations". Yet, within the normative framework of the Rome Statute, not even the functional immunity might be invoked as a reason for shielding a subject of the crime of aggression from criminal prosecution: presumably, it is the peremptory (*jus cogens*) nature of the norms of international law, which are violated by the crime of aggression—i.e., above all, of Article 2(4) of the UN Charter (see supra 2.1.3)—that takes precedence over a defendant's functional immunity, which would otherwise be available to him or her outside the Rome Statute's normative framework, and justifies its waiver in line with Article 27 of the Statute. It is by virtue of the *jus cogens* character of Article 2(4) of the Charter of the United Nations that, in the future, neither the potential defendants themselves nor their defence lawyers would be entitled to invoke any type of immunity, whether under national or international law, as a defence argument at any stage of proceedings before any organ of the ICC, and the Court would be entitled to discard any such argument, except if it is introduced in concurrence with other relevant circumstances as a ground for the reduction of sentence (cf. the second sentence of Article 27(1)).

However, it may be assumed that the issue of immunities would be more significant *before* the start of proceedings in the ICC, i.e. at the stage of processing the Court's requests for arrest and surrender (see Articles 87 and ff. of the ICC Statute). As was noted above (cf. supra note 111), it follows from Article 98(1)) of the Rome Statute that the State receiving such a request may not be required to process it in violation of its existing obligations under international law, including with respect to the State or diplomatic immunity of agents of third States. Neither may the ICC proceed, in accordance with Article 98(2), "with a request for surrender which would require the requested State to act inconsistently with its obligations under international agreements pursuant to which the consent of a sending State is required to surrender a person of that State to the Court, unless the Court can first obtain the cooperation of the sending State for the giving of consent for the surrender". The ICC should therefore be prepared to provide suitable arguments already at the pre-trial stages, in order to get hold of the accused individuals in the first place.

5.2.7 Responsibility of Commanders and Other Superiors[113]

The crime of aggression is, by definition (see supra 5.1.1.1.3), one that cannot be perpetrated without a direct and active involvement of the most senior officials of

[112] See David 2009, p. 676.

[113] On the criminal responsibility of commanders and other superiors, see Arnold 2002, pp. 191–231; Bantekas 1999, pp. 573–595; Bing 2004, pp. 1–42; Bonafé 2007, pp. 599–618; Martinez 2007, pp. 638–664; Meloni 2007, pp. 619–637; Nerlich 2007, pp. 665–682; Weigend 2010, pp. 67–80.

a State—that is, of those in charge, at the supreme levels in the chain of authority, of a State's executive branch of power, including of its armed forces.[114] As the commission of the crime of aggression would involve both a political and a military effort on the part of a State, the dual role of the Heads of States and/or governments—whoever would constitutionally possess the highest executive authority in a State—as Commanders-in-Chief of the armed forces and supreme civilian officials, in the criminal mechanism of aggression should be assessed in the light of Article 28 of the Rome Statute.[115] Article 28 would not formally apply to situations where the Head of a State and/or government would himself or herself direct the effort of a criminal mechanism of aggression; in such situations, his or her criminal responsibility would arise in accordance with Article 25 of the Rome Statute (see supra 5.2.4.1–5.2.4.5). It is possible, though, that an *animus aggressions* (see supra 4.3.1.1.1 and 4.5) originates at a lower organisational level, and the Head of the State and/or government in question only subsequently become(s) aware that his or her subordinates were "about to commit [the crime of aggression in the sense of Article 8 bis]" (cf. Articles 28(a)(i) and 28(b)(i)). In such circumstances, he or she would be obliged, in accordance with Articles 28(a)(ii) or 28(b)(iii), "to take all necessary and reasonable measures within his or her power to prevent or repress [the] commission [of the crime] or to submit the matter to the competent authorities for investigation and prosecution". Since the planning of or preparation for the crime of aggression by subordinate officials would clearly concern "activities [...] within the effective responsibility and control" (cf. Article 28(b)(ii)) of the Head of the State and/or government, the failure to prevent or repress the criminal activities of his or her subordinates would constitute a ground for criminal responsibility under Article 28 of the Rome Statute. Given the dual

[114] On the criminal responsibility of commanders and other superiors specifically in the context of the crime of aggression, see Barriga 2012, at 19–20.

[115] See ICC Statute, Article 28: "In addition to other grounds of criminal responsibility under this Statute for crimes within the jurisdiction of the Court: (a) A military commander or person effectively acting as a military commander shall be criminally responsible for crimes within the jurisdiction of the Court committed by forces under his or her effective command and control, or effective authority and control as the case may be, as a result of his or her failure to exercise control properly over such forces, where: (i) That military commander or person either knew or, owing to the circumstances at the time, should have known that the forces were committing or about to commit such crimes; and (ii) That military commander or person failed to take all necessary and reasonable measures within his or her power to prevent or repress their commission or to submit the matter to the competent authorities for investigation and prosecution. (b) With respect to superior and subordinate relationships not described in paragraph (a), a superior shall be criminally responsible for crimes within the jurisdiction of the Court committed by subordinates under his or her effective authority and control, as a result of his or her failure to exercise control properly over such subordinates, where: (i) The superior either knew, or consciously disregarded information which clearly indicated, that the subordinates were committing or about to commit such crimes; (ii) The crimes concerned activities that were within the effective responsibility and control of the superior; and (iii) The superior failed to take all necessary and reasonable measures within his or her power to prevent or repress their commission or to submit the matter to the competent authorities for investigation and prosecution".

role of the Heads of States and/or governments referred to above, their criminal responsibility would arise under paragraph (a) of Article 28 for the military component of their subordinates' criminal effort, and under paragraph (b) of the same Article—for its civilian component.

5.2.8 *Non-Applicability of Statute of Limitations*

Article 29 of the Rome Statute states straightforwardly:

> The crimes within the jurisdiction of the Court shall not be subject to any statute of limitations.

Whereas genocide, crimes against humanity and war crimes have already for some time been exempted from statutes of limitation as a matter of international law,[116] the application of an analogous exemption to the crime of aggression is a novelty. For practicable reasons, neither the Charters of the Nuremberg or Tokyo Tribunals (see supra 1.2.2–1.2.3), nor the Control Council Law № 10 (see supra 1.2.4), nor the 1996 Draft Code of Crimes against the Peace and Security of Mankind (see supra 1.2.5.6 and 3.1.5) contained any provisions to the effect.[117] It must be noted that the non-applicability of statutes of limitations to the crime of aggression in the sense of Article 29 of the Rome Statute would only have a prospective effect, i.e. after the entry into force of Articles 8 bis (see supra 5.1.2), 15 bis (see infra 5.3.2.2–5.3.2.3) and 15 ter (see infra 5.3.3) of the Statute. The statute of limitations would not apply retrospectively, i.e. the Court would have no jurisdiction with respect to the crimes of aggression, which could be committed on the territory of States Parties to the Rome Statute or by their nationals (cf. Article 12(2)[118]) before the date of the entry into force of those Articles.

---

116 See generally Kok 2007. See also Miller 1971, pp. 476–501.

117 Notably, quite many national criminal laws contain provisions on the non-applicability of statutes of limitation to the crime of aggression, which might be evident of the existence of a customary rule of international law to the effect. See, for example, the Criminal Codes of Armenia (Article 75(6)), Azerbaijan (Article 80(4)), Bosnia and Herzegovina (Article 20), Georgia (Article 76(4)), Kazakhstan (Article 69(6)), Macedonia (Article 112), Mongolia (Article 70(6)), Romania (Article 146(2)), the Russian Federation (Article 78(5)), Tajikistan (Article 75(6)), Turkey (Article 66(7)), Ukraine (Article 49(5)), and Uzbekistan (Article 64(7)).

118 See ICC Statute, Article 12(2) ("Preconditions to the exercise of jurisdiction"): "In the case of article 13, paragraph (a) or (c), the Court may exercise its jurisdiction if one or more of the following States are Parties to this Statute or have accepted the jurisdiction of the Court in accordance with paragraph 3: (a) The State on the territory of which the conduct in question occurred or, if the crime was committed on board a vessel or aircraft, the State of registration of that vessel or aircraft; (b) The State of which the person accused of the crime is a national".

5.2.9 *Mental Element*

Article 30 of the Rome Statute is fundamental in that it lays down a framework for the mental element of crimes within the jurisdiction of the International Criminal Court[119]:

1. Unless otherwise provided, a person shall be criminally responsible and liable for punishment for a crime within the jurisdiction of the Court only if the material elements are committed with intent and knowledge.
2. For the purposes of this article, a person has intent where:
   (a) In relation to conduct, that person means to engage in the conduct;
   (b) In relation to a consequence, that person means to cause that consequence or is aware that it will occur in the ordinary course of events.
3. For the purposes of this article, 'knowledge' means awareness that a circumstance exists or a consequence will occur in the ordinary course of events. 'Know' and 'knowingly' shall be construed accordingly.

Since Article 8 bis and the corresponding Elements of crimes (see infra 5.4) do not provide to the contrary, it is understood that the *mens rea* of the crime of aggression within the jurisdiction of the ICC should be assessed in accordance with the rules of Article 30. By and large, these rules are reflective of customary international law on the subject (see supra 4.5), whereby the direct intent ("that person means to cause that consequence" in the sense of Article 30(2)(b), and "awareness that a circumstance exists" in the sense of the first sentence of Article 30(3)) is recognised as the "primary" or "standard" mental element of the crime of aggression since the Nuremberg and Tokyo trials (see supra 3.1.1–3.1.2), and the indirect intent ("that person [...] is aware that [a consequence] will occur in the ordinary course of events" in the sense of Article 30(2)(b) and the first sentence of Article 30(3)) is regarded as a reasonable alternative. Hence, in conjunction with Article 8 bis of the Statute, the criminalised "conduct" should be understood as an intentional "planning, preparation, initiation or execution" of an act of aggression (see supra 5.1.1.1.2, 5.2.4.3, 5.2.4.4), and the occurrence of one or more sub-types of an act of aggression listed in subparagraphs (a)–(g) of Article 8 bis (2) (see supra 5.1.1.3.1–5.1.1.3.7) would be a certain or reasonably foreseeable "consequence" of the conduct.

5.2.10 *Grounds for Excluding Criminal Responsibility*

It appears that, in practice, subjects of a crime of aggression within the jurisdiction of the ICC (see supra 4.2.2–4.2.5 and 5.1.1.1.3) would be able only to partially benefit from Article 31 of the Rome Statute ("Grounds for excluding criminal

[119] On the mental element, see Kemp 2010, p. 235; Piragoff 1999, pp. 527–535; Werle 2009a, pp. 146–165 (including bibliographical references).

responsibility").[120] The established existence on the part of a defendant, at the time of conduct (see supra 5.1.1.1.2 and 5.2.4.3–5.2.4.4) of a mental disease or defect in the sense of Article 31(1)(a) would indeed constitute a well-founded ground for excluding his or her criminal responsibility[121]; its validity has been confirmed by relevant jurisprudence (see supra 3.1.2.1). Also, the existence of a sound threat of an impending armed attack by another State might warrant the application of Article 31(1)(c) ("[t]he person acts reasonably to defend himself or herself or another person[122] [...] against an imminent and unlawful use of force in a manner proportionate to the degree of danger to the person or the other person [...] protected"),[123] or of Article 31(1)(d) ("[t]he conduct [...] has been caused by duress resulting from a threat of imminent death or of continuing or imminent serious bodily harm against that person or another person, and the person acts necessarily and reasonably to avoid this threat, provided that the person does not intend to

[120] See ICC Statute, Article 31: "1. In addition to other grounds for excluding criminal responsibility provided for in this Statute, a person shall not be criminally responsible if, at the time of that person's conduct: (a) The person suffers from a mental disease or defect that destroys that person's capacity to appreciate the unlawfulness or nature of his or her conduct, or capacity to control his or her conduct to conform to the requirements of law; (b) The person is in a state of intoxication that destroys that person's capacity to appreciate the unlawfulness or nature of his or her conduct, or capacity to control his or her conduct to conform to the requirements of law, unless the person has become voluntarily intoxicated under such circumstances that the person knew, or disregarded the risk, that, as a result of the intoxication, he or she was likely to engage in conduct constituting a crime within the jurisdiction of the Court; (c) The person acts reasonably to defend himself or herself or another person or, in the case of war crimes, property which is essential for the survival of the person or another person or property which is essential for accomplishing a military mission, against an imminent and unlawful use of force in a manner proportionate to the degree of danger to the person or the other person or property protected. The fact that the person was involved in a defensive operation conducted by forces shall not in itself constitute a ground for excluding criminal responsibility under this subparagraph; (d) The conduct which is alleged to constitute a crime within the jurisdiction of the Court has been caused by duress resulting from a threat of imminent death or of continuing or imminent serious bodily harm against that person or another person, and the person acts necessarily and reasonably to avoid this threat, provided that the person does not intend to cause a greater harm than the one sought to be avoided. Such a threat may either be: (i) Made by other persons; or (ii) Constituted by other circumstances beyond that person's control. 2. The Court shall determine the applicability of the grounds for excluding criminal responsibility provided for in this Statute to the case before it. 3. At trial, the Court may consider a ground for excluding criminal responsibility other than those referred to in paragraph 1 where such a ground is derived from applicable law as set forth in article 21. The procedures relating to the consideration of such a ground shall be provided for in the Rules of Procedure and Evidence". See Creegan 2012, pp. 59–82; O'Donovan 2007, pp. 507–530.

[121] On mental disease or defect, see Krug 2000, pp. 317–335.

[122] In this context, the words "another person" may be taken to denote the civilian population of a State defending itself against an "imminent and unlawful" armed attack by another State (cf. supra 2.4.1.1). See also DeNicola 2008, pp. 641–689.

[123] On self-defence or defence of others, see Eser 1999, at 548–550; Werle 2009a, pp. 199–203 (including bibliographical references).

cause a greater harm than the one sought to be avoided").[124] Such a duress would both be "[m]ade by other persons" (Article 31(1)(d)(i)) and be "[c]onstituted by other circumstances beyond [a defendant's] control" (Article 31(1)(d)(ii)). In either case, the reactive use of armed force on the initiative of a defendant should be assessed against the background of the magnitude of the imminent threat in question and the proportionality of the military response offered (see also infra 5.2.11).

In turn, the defence of intoxication in the sense of Article 31(1)(b)[125] might only have a limited validity (for example, in the case of an "instant aggression" such as an excessive use of force in the exercise of interceptive self-defence (see supra 2.4.1.4), or (more unlikely) if in existence at the "moment of aggression" (see supra 4.3.1.2)), for it is virtually impracticable for a person to be intoxicated during a protracted period, which is normally required for "planning, preparation, initiation or execution" of an act of aggression (see supra 5.1.1.1.2), and still participate in the criminal mechanism of aggression.

Finally, it is understood that the list of grounds for excluding criminal responsibility provided in Article 31(1) is not exhaustive, and "the Court may consider a ground for excluding criminal responsibility other than those referred to in paragraph 1", in accordance with Article 31(3).[126] The relevant rules are found in the Rules of Procedure and Evidence.[127]

5.2.11 Mistake of Fact or Mistake of Law[128]

Article 32 of the Rome Statute does not have an autonomous value (because it is associated with the Statute's provisions on the mental element, see supra 5.2.9) but, in and of itself, is generally reflective of customary international law:

1. A mistake of fact shall be a ground for excluding criminal responsibility only if it negates the mental element required by the crime.
2. A mistake of law as to whether a particular type of conduct is a crime within the jurisdiction of the Court shall not be a ground for excluding criminal responsibility. A mistake of law may, however, be a ground for excluding criminal responsibility if it negates the mental element required by such a crime, or as provided for in article 33.

---

[124] On duress, see Eser 1999, at 550–552; Werle 2009a, pp. 203–209 (including bibliographical references).

[125] On intoxication, see Eser 1999, at 546–548; Werle 2009a, pp. 221–224 (including bibliographical references).

[126] On other grounds for excluding criminal responsibility, see Eser 1999, at 553–554; Inogamova-Hegay 2003, pp. 160–165; Werle 2009a, pp. 224–227 (including bibliographical references); Yee 2004, pp. 87–134.

[127] ICC Rules of Procedure and Evidence, supra note 87, see in particular Rules 121(9) ("Proceedings before the confirmation hearing") and 145(2)(a)(i) ("Determination of sentence").

[128] On mistakes of fact and law, see Werle 2009a, pp. 209–213 (including bibliographical references).

As the "mental element" is referred to in both paragraphs of Article 32, it must correspondingly be interpreted in conjunction with Article 30 (see supra 5.2.9). With regard to a mistake of fact, "[a] requirement for exclusion of responsibility [...] is, first of all, that the perpetrator's mistaken perception refer to the facts underlying the material elements of the crime".[129] In other words, a mistake of fact exists when a person subjectively and faithfully presumes the existence of a factual circumstance, which prompts him to bring about the material elements of a crime, not knowing that the objective nature of the factual circumstance is different (for example, less dangerous or grave), and the individual would probably refrain from performing the conduct, if he or she knew the true nature of the presumed factual circumstance. In conjunction with Article 8 bis of the Rome Statute, possible examples of mistakes of fact might include a comprehensive use of armed force by a State in response to training manoeuvres in another State—whereby the manoeuvres are misperceived for genuine military preparations for an attack, and the attacking State's own use of armed force is perceived as interceptive self-defence (see supra 2.4.1.4),—or shooting down a foreign civilian aircraft, which is misperceived for a military one, as it enters a State's airspace and does not identify itself to ground services because of equipment breakdown. In such cases, criminal responsibility for the crime of aggression in the sense of Article 8 bis of the ICC Statute should be excluded, because there probably would have existed no *animus aggressionis* at the time of the conduct, if the true nature of the circumstances in question had been known.

It must be noted, though, that the conduct actually perpetrated might contain the elements of other crimes under international or national law, and criminal responsibility might nonetheless arise—but not for a crime of aggression in the sense of Article 8 bis of the Rome Statute. Yet, if the consequence(s) of an individual conduct were not objectively covered by Article 8 bis (2) of the ICC Statute (see supra 5.1.1.3.8), no criminal responsibility should arise, even if the mental element required by Article 30 did exist.

As far as mistakes of law are concerned, "ignorance of the law is not, in principle, a ground for excluding criminal responsibility; nor is a perpetrator's mistaken assumption that his or her act does not fall under the jurisdiction of the International Criminal Court. In these cases, only mitigation of punishment is possible".[130] Thus, if a perpetrator were genuinely not aware of an aggressive nature of his act(s) or mistakenly believed that the act or acts would be outside the ambit of Article 8 bis of the Rome Statute, the ICC might only assign one a lighter punishment (cf. supra 5.2.2) but not exclude his or her criminal responsibility altogether.

[129] Ibid., p. 211.

[130] Ibid., p. 212 (footnotes omitted).

5.2.12 *Superior Orders and Prescription of Law*[131]

It appears from Article 33 of the Rome Statute that the defence of superior orders might have a limited validity in the context of the crime of aggression in the sense of Article 8 bis. Article 33 lists a number of conditions, which must be met cumulatively, so that a person could be relieved of criminal responsibility, and such circumstantial combinations would not seem impracticable in the context of a crime as idiosyncratic as that of aggression:

1. The fact that a crime within the jurisdiction of the Court has been committed by a person pursuant to an order of a Government or of a superior, whether military or civilian, shall not relieve that person of criminal responsibility unless:
   (a) The person was under a legal obligation to obey orders of the Government or the superior in question;
   (b) The person did not know that the order was unlawful; and
   (c) The order was not manifestly unlawful.
2. For the purposes of this article, orders to commit genocide or crimes against humanity are manifestly unlawful.

Obviously, an order to participate in the planning, preparation, initiation or execution (see supra 4.3, 5.1.1.1.2, 5.2.4.3 and 5.2.4.4) of an act, which might qualify as one of aggression, is, in accordance with Article 33(2), not manifestly unlawful, and correctly so. The use of force by a State is lawful, if it is consistent with Article 2(4) of the Charter of the United Nations, its other related provisions and other applicable rules of international law (see supra Chap. 2), and the degree of this consistency should be assessed on a case-by-case basis. As is stipulated in Article 33(1)(b), a person partaking in an organisational mechanism, which afterwards is to be qualified as one of aggression, might not know, at the time of participating in the mechanism, that the orders he or she follows are unlawful.[132] The fact that officials in the highest echelons of civilian and military authority—i.e. "potential" subjects of the crime of aggression—would usually be "under a legal obligation to obey orders of the Government or the superior in question" (i.e. of the Head of a State and/or government, see supra 5.2.7) in the sense of Article 33(1)(a) adds to the presumption that, unlike in the context of genocide or crimes against humanity (cf. Article 33(2) of the ICC Statute), the defence of superior orders might, in at least some cases, be objectively valid in the context of the crime of aggression. However, in order to lessen the manipulation of this defence in the course of would-be trials on charges deriving from Article 8 bis (see supra 5.1), the ICC would have to analyse carefully all relevant evidence before it and establish the degree of defendants' individual guilt (see supra 5.2.4) with an appropriate flexibility.

---

[131] On superior orders and prescription of law, see Gaeta 1999, pp. 172–191; generally Green 1976.

[132] On superior orders and prescription of law specifically in the context of the crime of aggression see Barriga 2012, at 19–20.

5.3 Exercise of Jurisdiction Over the Crime of Aggression

As a self-contained system of international criminal justice, the ICC has a set of own rules for the direct enforcement of criminal liability for the crime of aggression as defined in Article 8 bis of the Rome Statute (on distinction between indirect and direct enforcement, see supra 4.6). With due regard to the basic principle of complementarity (see infra 5.3.1), these rules should regulate the interaction between various organs of the Court—as well as between the Court and States and other international institutions or organs, such as the United Nations Security Council—in the process of asserting jurisdiction with respect to the crime of aggression and initiating related investigations and criminal prosecutions.[133] This section critically examines relevant procedural provisions—Articles 15 bis and ter of the Rome Statute, as adopted at the First Review Conference (see infra 5.3.2 and 5.3.3)—in a more general context of the Statute itself and other applicable international law.

5.3.1 Continued Relevance of the Principle of Complementarity[134]

The principle of complementarity[135] applies to the crime of aggression as much as it does to the other international crimes within the jurisdiction of the ICC. As fundamental as it is in the context of the ICC Statute, the principle of complementarity was reaffirmed at the First Review Conference in June 2010 as follows[136]:

> The Review Conference [...]
>
> 1. *Recognizes* the primary responsibility of States to investigate and prosecute the most serious crimes of international concern;
> 2. *Emphasizes* the principle of complementarity as laid down in the Rome Statute and *stresses* the obligations of States Parties flowing from the Rome Statute;
> 3. *Recognizes* the need for additional measures at the national level as required and for the enhancement of international assistance to effectively prosecute perpetrators of the most serious crimes of concern to the international community;

---

[133] It is understood that the actual investigations and prosecutions as well as the enforcement of sentences should be carried out in accordance with relevant provisions of the Rome Statute, see especially Parts V–X of the Statute.

[134] On the principle of complementarity, see Kemp 2010, pp. 187–188; Lijun 2005, pp. 121–132; Safferling 2012, pp. 95–108; Van Schaak 2012, pp. 133–164.

[135] Cf. ICC Statute, Article 1 ("The Court"): "An International Criminal Court ('the Court') is hereby established. It [...] shall be complementary to national criminal jurisdictions [...]".

[136] See document Resolution RC/Res.1 (8 June 2010).

4. *Notes* the importance of States Parties taking effective domestic measures to implement the Rome Statute;
5. *Recognizes* the desirability for States to assist each other in strengthening domestic capacity to ensure that investigations and prosecutions of serious crimes of international concern can take place at the national level;

[...]

7. *Welcomes* the fruitful discussions on the issue of complementarity held during the Review Conference;
8. *Encourages* the Court, States Parties and other stakeholders, including international organizations and civil society to further explore ways in which to enhance the capacity of national jurisdictions to investigate and prosecute serious crimes of international concern [...]

The First Review Conference thus restated that Article 17[137] of the ICC Statute should continue to apply uniformly to all crimes within the jurisdiction of the Court—including to the crime of aggression. Hence, in view of the continued primacy of national jurisdictions (in the language of para 1 of Resolution RC/Res. 1, "the primary responsibility of States to investigate and prosecute the most serious crimes of international concern"), the ICC would normally exercise jurisdiction with respect to the crime of aggression as defined in Article 8 bis of the Statute (see supra 5.1) where the State(s) in question were unwilling or unable genuinely to carry out the relevant investigation or prosecution in the sense of Article 17 of the Rome Statute. A typical example of unwillingness to investigate or prosecute a crime of aggression in the sense of Article 17(2) would be where an aggressor State refused to take steps to enforce the provisions of its national law(s)

[137] Cf. ICC Statute, Article 17 ("Issues of admissibility"): "1. Having regard to paragraph 10 of the Preamble and article 1, the Court shall determine that a case is inadmissible where: (a) The case is being investigated or prosecuted by a State which has jurisdiction over it, unless the State is unwilling or unable genuinely to carry out the investigation or prosecution; (b) The case has been investigated by a State which has jurisdiction over it and the State has decided not to prosecute the person concerned, unless the decision resulted from the unwillingness or inability of the State genuinely to prosecute; (c) The person concerned has already been tried for conduct which is the subject of the complaint, and a trial by the Court is not permitted under article 20, paragraph 3; (d) The case is not of sufficient gravity to justify further action by the Court. 2. In order to determine unwillingness in a particular case, the Court shall consider, having regard to the principles of due process recognized by international law, whether one or more of the following exist, as applicable: (a) The proceedings were or are being undertaken or the national decision was made for the purpose of shielding the person concerned from criminal responsibility for crimes within the jurisdiction of the Court referred to in article 5; (b) There has been an unjustified delay in the proceedings which in the circumstances is inconsistent with an intent to bring the person concerned to justice; (c) The proceedings were not or are not being conducted independently or impartially, and they were or are being conducted in a manner which, in the circumstances, is inconsistent with an intent to bring the person concerned to justice. 3. In order to determine inability in a particular case, the Court shall consider whether, due to a total or substantial collapse or unavailability of its national judicial system, the State is unable to obtain the accused or the necessary evidence and testimony or otherwise unable to carry out its proceedings".

criminalising aggression (see supra 4.1), whereas a victim State's institutional inability to investigate or prosecute such a crime in the sense of Article 17(3) might be a direct consequence of an act of aggression (see supra 5.1.1.2) committed against it.

In pursuance of paras 3–5 of the First Review Conference's Resolution RC/Res.1, States Parties to the ICC Statute, which would have ratified the amendments to the Statute pertaining to the crime of aggression (see supra 5.1.2 and infra 5.3.2.2–5.3.2.3, 5.3.3), may be expected to enact, in a foreseeable future, further national (material and procedural) provisions. Likewise, civil society—in particular, pro-ICC NGOs and academic circles—should continue contributing to the progressive development of the international legal doctrine on the crime of aggression, in the sense of paragraph 8 of the same Resolution.[138]

5.3.2 State Referral, proprio motu *(Article 15 bis)*

Article 15 bis of the Rome Statute ("Exercise of jurisdiction over the crime of aggression (State referral, *proprio motu*)") lays down, in ten paragraphs, special procedural rules for the initiation of an individual prosecution on charges under Article 8 bis of the Statute (for a comprehensive examination of that article's material provisions, see supra 5.1) on the basis of a State referral or *proprio motu* by the Prosecutor.[139] An analysis of specific provisions of Article 15 bis is offered below.

5.3.2.1 Lex specialis

In accordance with para 1, Article 15 bis develops and adapts the provisions of Article 13, paragraphs (a) and (c),[140] to the context of the crime of aggression:

1. The Court may exercise jurisdiction over the crime of aggression in accordance with article 13, paragraphs (a) and (c), subject to the provisions of this article.

---

[138] Cf. supra note 116.

[139] On mechanisms triggering the ICC jurisdiction with respect to the crime of aggression, see Barriga 2012, at 31–32. Specifically on the role of the ICC Prosecutor, see generally Safferling 2012, pp. 147–157, 251–285, 350–357.

[140] ICC Statute, Article 13 ("Exercise of jurisdiction"): "The Court may exercise its jurisdiction with respect to a crime referred to in article 5 in accordance with the provisions of this Statute if: (a) A situation in which one or more of such crimes appears to have been committed is referred to the Prosecutor by a State Party in accordance with article 14; [...] or (c) The Prosecutor has initiated an investigation in respect of such a crime in accordance with article 15".

It follows from this opening paragraph that the ICC Statute's relevant jurisdictional provisions—including but not limited to Articles 14[141] and 15[142] referred to, respectively, in paragraphs (a) and (c) of Article 13—shall continue to apply in the context of a crime of aggression, insofar as they are not fine-tuned by more specific rules of Article 15 bis.[143] The substantive modifications introduced by Article 15 bis are essentially threefold: (1) special rules as regards the Court's jurisdiction *ratione temporis* with respect to the crime of aggression (paras 2 and 3, see infra 5.3.2.2 and 5.3.2.3, respectively); (2) opportunity for a State Party to the Rome Statute to lodge an opt-out declaration with the Registrar (see infra 5.3.2.4); and (3) additional procedural rules for the Prosecutor to initiate and proceed with an investigation with respect of a crime of aggression (paras 6–8, see infra 5.3.2.6–5.3.2.8). The rule contained in para 5 of Article 15 bis (see infra 5.3.2.5) partially modifies a pre-existing provision of the Statute, while paras 9 and 10 (see infra 5.3.2.9 and 5.3.2.10, respectively) complete the International Criminal Court's autonomous jurisdictional regime with respect to the crime of aggression.

[141] Ibid., Article 14 ("Referral of a situation by a State Party"): "1. A State Party may refer to the Prosecutor a situation in which one or more crimes within the jurisdiction of the Court appear to have been committed requesting the Prosecutor to investigate the situation for the purpose of determining whether one or more specific persons should be charged with the commission of such crimes. 2. As far as possible, a referral shall specify the relevant circumstances and be accompanied by such supporting documentation as is available to the State referring the situation". On Article 14, see Kirsch and Robynson 2002a, b, pp. 619–625.

[142] ICC Statute, Article 15 ("Prosecutor"): "1. The Prosecutor may initiate investigations *proprio motu* on the basis of information on crimes within the jurisdiction of the Court. 2. The Prosecutor shall analyse the seriousness of the information received. For this purpose, he or she may seek additional information from States, organs of the United Nations, intergovernmental or non-governmental organizations, or other reliable sources that he or she deems appropriate, and may receive written or oral testimony at the seat of the Court. 3. If the Prosecutor concludes that there is a reasonable basis to proceed with an investigation, he or she shall submit to the Pre-Trial Chamber a request for authorization of an investigation, together with any supporting material collected. Victims may make representations to the Pre-Trial Chamber, in accordance with the Rules of Procedure and Evidence. 4. If the Pre-Trial Chamber, upon examination of the request and the supporting material, considers that there is a reasonable basis to proceed with an investigation, and that the case appears to fall within the jurisdiction of the Court, it shall authorise the commencement of the investigation, without prejudice to subsequent determinations by the Court with regard to the jurisdiction and admissibility of a case. 5. The refusal of the Pre-Trial Chamber to authorise the investigation shall not preclude the presentation of a subsequent request by the Prosecutor based on new facts or evidence regarding the same situation. 6. If, after the preliminary examination referred to in paragraphs 1 and 2, the Prosecutor concludes that the information provided does not constitute a reasonable basis for an investigation, he or she shall inform those who provided the information. This shall not preclude the Prosecutor from considering further information submitted to him or her regarding the same situation in the light of new facts or evidence". On Article 15, see Kirsch and Robinson 2002b, pp. 657–664.

[143] On the general rules for triggering the ICC jurisdiction, see Safferling 2012, pp. 86–91.

5.3.2.2 Ratification or Acceptance by Thirty States Parties

The commencement of the ICC's jurisdiction with respect to the crime of aggression has been made conditional upon two cumulative circumstances.[144] First, in accordance with Article 15 bis (2), which mirrors Article 121(5) of the Rome Statute, the Court "may exercise jurisdiction only with respect to crimes of aggression committed one year after the ratification or acceptance of the amendments by thirty States Parties".[145] This future date remains, for now, undetermined. Although the amendments are intended to attain thirty ratifications relatively quickly—possibly even quicker than the Rome Statute itself had attained, in April 2002, sixty ratifications required for its entry into force (cf. supra 5.1.2 and infra 5.3.3), the Court's jurisdiction over the crime of aggression would commence no earlier than one year after their ratification or acceptance by the thirtieth State Party to the Rome Statute, and even then, in accordance with Article 121(5) of the Statute, "[i]n respect of a State Party which has not accepted the amendment, the Court shall not exercise its jurisdiction regarding a crime covered by the amendment when committed by that State Party's nationals or on its territory".[146] As of 26 September 2013, instruments of ratification (or acceptance, in the case of Andorra) with respect to Article 15 bis were only deposited by Liechtenstein (on 8 May 2012), Samoa (on 25 September 2012), Trinidad and Tobago (on 13 November 2012), Luxembourg (on 15 January 2013), Estonia (on 27 March 2013), Germany (on 3 June 2013), and Botswana (on 4 June 2013), Cyprus (on 25 September 2013), Slovenia (on 25 September 2013), Andorra (on 26 September 2013), and Uruguay (on 26 September 2013).[147] The second mandatory condition for the commencement of the ICC's jurisdiction over the crime of aggression is considered below, at 5.3.2.3.

---

[144] Cf. document RC/Res. 6, Annex III: "3. It is understood that in case of article 13, paragraph (a) or (c), the Court may exercise its jurisdiction only with respect to crimes of aggression committed after a decision in accordance with article 15 bis, paragraph 3, is taken, *and* one year after the ratification or acceptance of the amendments by thirty States Parties, *whichever is later*" (emphasis added).

[145] In accordance with para 1 of Resolution 6 adopted by the First Review Conference, the States Parties to the Rome Statute are meant to ratify or accept the amendments to the Rome Statute contained in Articles 8 bis, 15 bis and 15 ter as a package (cf. supra note 71). The material (Article 8 bis) and procedural (Articles 15 bis and 15 ter) amendments to the Statute would thus become binding upon such State Parties simultaneously.

[146] This rule would not apply to Security Council referrals in accordance with Article 13 (b) and subject to the provisions of Article 15 ter of the Statute. See infra 5.3.3. See Akande 2003, pp. 618–650.

[147] See UNTC, Chapter XVIII ("Penal matters", section 10.b ("Amendments on the crime of aggression to the Rome Statute of the International Criminal Court"), available at: http://treaties.un.org/pages/ViewDetails.aspx?src=TREATY&mtdsg_no=XVIII-10-b&chapter=18&lang=en (last accessed 26 September 2013).

5.3.2.3 Role of the Assembly of States Parties

The second condition for the commencement of the ICC's jurisdiction with respect to the crime of aggression has been laid down in Article 15 bis (3):

> 3. The Court shall exercise jurisdiction over the crime of aggression in accordance with this article, subject to a decision to be taken after 1 January 2017 by the same majority of States Parties as is required for the adoption of an amendment to the Statute.

It follows from this provision that the ICC would not be able to exercise its jurisdiction over the crime of aggression before 1 January 2017, even if Articles 8 bis and 15 bis (as well as Article 15 ter, see infra 5.3.3) were ratified or accepted by thirty States Parties to the ICC Statute before 1 January 2016 (which, hopefully, would be the case, see supra 5.1.2 and 5.3.2.2)—i.e. one year before the earliest scheduled date of consideration of the issue by the Assembly of States Parties, to make possible the amendments' entry into force by 1 January 2017 in accordance with Article 121(5) of the Statute. If the required number of instruments of ratification or acceptance is not reached by 1 January 2016, the Assembly of States Parties may still decide upon the issue at its earliest convenience after 1 January 2017 and activate the Court's jurisdiction with respect to the crime of aggression on the condition that it may be exercised one year after the thirtieth instrument of ratification or acceptance has been deposited (cf. supra note 145). Pursuant to Article 121 (3) of the Rome Statute,[148] the adoption of a decision under Article 15 bis (3) shall require a two-thirds majority of States Parties.

5.3.2.4 Opt-Out Declaration

Any State Party not willing to accept the International Criminal Court's jurisdiction with respect to the crime of aggression under Article 15 bis may lodge a declaration to the effect[149]:

> 4. The Court may, in accordance with article 12, exercise jurisdiction over a crime of aggression, arising from an act of aggression committed by a State Party, unless that State Party has previously declared that it does not accept such jurisdiction by lodging a declaration with the Registrar. The withdrawal of such a declaration may be effected at any time and shall be considered by the State Party within three years.

---

[148] ICC Statute, Article 121(3) ("Amendments"): "The adoption of an amendment at a meeting of the Assembly of States Parties or at a Review Conference on which consensus cannot be reached shall require a two-thirds majority of States Parties". On Article 121(3), see Clark 1999, at 1268.

[149] Cf. Safferling 2012, p. 91.

The opt-out effect of Article 15 bis (4) potentially goes even further than that of Article 124,[150] which allows a State Party to temporarily—for a period of seven years after the entry into force of the Rome Statute for the State concerned—exempt itself from the Court's jurisdiction with respect to war crimes,[151] for it theoretically creates an opportunity for an open-ended exemption from the Court's jurisdiction with respect to the crime of aggression.[152] Yet, the proliferation of States Parties to the Rome Statute, which would not accept the ICC's jurisdiction with respect to the crime of aggression, certainly is not a desired development, for it would render Article 8 bis (see supra 5.1) futile. The second sentence of Article 15 bis (4) therefore calls upon States to withdraw declarations lodged under the first sentence of the same article, and stipulates that, in any event, such withdrawals should be considered "within three years"—it appears, within three years of lodging respective opt-out declarations with the ICC Registrar. In general, a withdrawal may be effected "at any time"—hence, also with immediate effect, if a respective State Party so desires, or starting from a specific date to be determined by that State Party.

5.3.2.5 States, Which are not Parties to the Statute

In line with a more general provision of the Statute,[153] Article 15 bis (5) provides as follows:

---

[150] Ibid., Article 124 ("Transitional provision"): "Notwithstanding article 12, paragraphs 1 and 2, a State, on becoming a party to this Statute, may declare that, for a period of seven years after the entry into force of this Statute for the State concerned, it does not accept the jurisdiction of the Court with respect to the category of crimes referred to in article 8 when a crime is alleged to have been committed by its nationals or on its territory. A declaration under this article may be withdrawn at any time. The provisions of this article shall be reviewed at the Review Conference convened in accordance with article 123, paragraph 1". On Article 124, see Zimmermann 1999, pp. 1281–1285.

[151] The First Review Conference decided "to retain article 124 in its current form". See paragraph 6 of document RC/Res. 4 (10 June 2010). This decision is provisional and should, in accordance with paragraph 7 of the same Resolution, be revised at the fourteenth session of the Assembly of States Parties to the Rome Statute.

[152] This would not apply to Security Council referrals in accordance with Article 13 (b) and subject to the provisions of Article 15 ter of the Statute. See infra 5.3.3.

[153] ICC Statute, Article 12 ("Preconditions to the exercise of jurisdiction"): "1. A State which becomes a Party to this Statute thereby accepts the jurisdiction of the Court with respect to the crimes referred to in article 5. 2. In the case of article 13, paragraph (a) or (c), the Court may exercise its jurisdiction if one or more of the following States are Parties to this Statute or have accepted the jurisdiction of the Court in accordance with paragraph 3: (a) The State on the territory of which the conduct in question occurred or, if the crime was committed on board a vessel or aircraft, the State of registration of that vessel or aircraft; (b) The State of which the person accused of the crime is a national. 3. If the acceptance of a State which is not a Party to this Statute is required under paragraph 2, that State may, by declaration lodged with the Registrar, accept the exercise of jurisdiction by the Court with respect to the crime in question. The accepting State shall cooperate with the Court without any delay or exception in accordance with Part 9".

5. In respect of a State that is not a party to this Statute, the Court shall not exercise its jurisdiction over the crime of aggression when committed by that State's nationals or on its territory.[154]

This rule constitutes a partial modification of the more general provision contained in Article 12 of the Statute.[155] Whereas Article 12 would normally authorise States, which are not Parties to the Statute, to accept the jurisdiction of the ICC with respect to the crimes referred to in Articles 6, 7 and 8 of the Statute on an *ad hoc* basis, by means of lodging corresponding declarations with the ICC Registrar, the absence of a similar clause in Article 15 bis (5) should be presumed to mean that no such *ad hoc* measure would be possible in the context of State referral or *proprio motu* action by the Prosecutor with respect to a crime of aggression.

However, the absence of jurisdiction under Article 15 bis (5) does not mean that nationals of a State that is not a Party to the Rome Statute are entirely immune from prosecution by the ICC for a crime of aggression. The Court would have jurisdiction, if a situation in which the crime would appear to have been committed were referred to the Prosecutor by the Security Council acting under Chapter VII of the Charter of the United Nations, in accordance with Article 13 (b) of the Statute and subject to the rules of Article 15 ter (see infra 5.3.3). Likewise, prosecutions initiated in accordance with Article 13 (b) and subject to the provisions of Article 15 ter would be feasible with respect to nationals of States Parties to the Rome Statute, which would not have ratified or accepted the amendments (see supra 5.3.2.2, especially note 146) or would have lodged opt-out declarations with the ICC Registrar (see supra 5.3.2.4, especially note 152).

5.3.2.6 Notification of the Secretary-General of the United Nations by the ICC Prosecutor

In accordance with pre-existing international law, the determination of the existence of a State's act of aggression by the UN Security Council was regarded as a condition *sine qua non* for the possible prosecution for the corresponding individual crime (see supra 3.1.5). With due regard to this pre-existing rule, para 6 of Article 15 bis stipulates that the ICC Prosecutor,[156] before proceeding with an investigation in respect of a crime of aggression, must notify the Secretary-General of the United Nations of the situation before the Court:

6. Where the Prosecutor concludes that there is a reasonable basis to proceed with an investigation in respect of a crime of aggression, he or she shall first ascertain whether the Security Council has made a determination of an act of aggression committed by the

[154] Cf. Safferling 2012, p. 92.

[155] See generally Akande 2003, pp. 618–650; Deen-Racsmany 2001, Van Syumey 2009, pp. 511–521.

[156] See Danner 2003, pp. 510–552; Safferling 2012, pp. 219–228.

> State concerned. The Prosecutor shall notify the Secretary-General of the United Nations of the situation before the Court, including any relevant information and documents.[157]

This provision adds to the rules of Articles 14 (see supra note 141) and 15 (see supra note 142) of the Rome Statute and must be read in conjunction with those articles. The most important procedural alteration it introduces consists in the requirement for the Prosecutor to notify the Secretary-General *before* submitting a request for authorisation of an investigation to the Pre-Trial Chamber[158] pursuant to Article 15(3), and then to act in accordance either with para 7 or para 8 (see infra 5.3.2.7 and 5.3.2.8) of Article 15 bis, depending on the attitude of the Security Council. Otherwise, para 6 reproduces the relevant pre-existing rules of the Statute: the phrase "reasonable basis to proceed with an investigation" has been borrowed from Article 15(3), and the "situation before the Court" referred to in the second sentence of the same paragraph should be understood in the sense of Article 14(1) (see supra note 141). In turn, "any relevant information and documents", which the Prosecutor must submit to the Secretary-General of the United Nations together with the notification, must include the "supporting documentation as is available to the State referring the situation" (if the situation is referred to the Prosecutor by a State Party) in the sense of Article 14(2), as well as "additional information [received] from States, organs of the United Nations, intergovernmental or non-governmental organizations, or other reliable sources that [the Prosecutor] deems appropriate, and […] written or oral testimony [received by the Prosecutor] at the seat of the Court" in the sense of Article 15(2). It seems that the notification should be accompanied not by all information on the subject in possession of the Prosecutor but only by "*any relevant* information and documents" (emphasis added), which might prompt the Security Council to react to the Prosecutor's notification in either of the ways suggested in paras 7 or 8 of Article 15 bis, within six months after the date of notification (cf. infra 5.3.2.8).

5.3.2.7 Positive Determination by the Security Council

Paragraph 7 of Article 15 bis authorises the Prosecutor to proceed with the investigation without delay where the Security Council of the United Nations has already—*prior* to the Prosecutor's notification (see supra 5.3.2.6)—made a positive determination of the existence of an act of aggression committed by a State Party to the Rome Statute (cf. supra 5.1.1.2)[159]:

> 7. Where the Security Council has made such a determination, the Prosecutor may proceed with the investigation in respect of a crime of aggression.

The conclusion that the Prosecutor would not require any formal authorisation from the Security Council in such a situation derives from the first sentence of paragraph

---

[157] Cf. Safferling 2012, p. 92.

[158] On the role of the Pre-Trial Chamber, see Safferling 2012, pp. 137–142, 236–239.

[159] See Barriga 2012, at 32–33; Blokker 2007, pp. 867–894; Escarameia 2004, pp. 133–143; Gaja 2004, pp. 121–124; Kemp 2010, pp. 225–227; Lehto 2004, pp. 145–149; Stein 2005, pp. 1–36; Yengejeh 2004, pp. 125–132.

6: the Prosecutor is well able to himself or herself "ascertain whether the Security Council has [already] made a determination of an act of aggression committed by the State concerned", given that such a determination can be found in the Security Council's appropriate resolution.[160] In such a situation, the Prosecutor's notification addressed to the Secretary-General in accordance with para 6 would appear to be a simple formality, for the positive pre-condition for an investigation would be fulfilled (although the Security Council would still have the power to defer the investigation or prosecution in accordance with Article 16, see infra 5.3.2.8).

Alternatively, the Security Council can make a positive determination *subsequently*, within six months of addressing the Prosecutor's notification to the Secretary-General; in such a case, the Prosecutor might also proceed with an investigation without any further delay. However, once a notification has been made, the Prosecutor would seem to be compelled to wait for the Security Council's explicit or implicit reaction for a maximum of 6 months (see infra 5.3.2.8).

Importantly, para 7 of Article 15 bis suggests that where the Security Council has made a positive determination of the existence of an act of aggression, the Prosecutor would not need an authorisation from the Pre-Trial Chamber to proceed with an investigation, in the sense of paras 3 and 4 of Article 15. There are two arguments in favour of this conclusion: first, para 7 of Article 15 bis reads unambiguously that the Prosecutor "may proceed" with the investigation, without detailing this provision any further[161]; secondly, para 8 of the same article

[160] Cf. Safferling 2012, p. 92.

[161] It is supposed that relevant details are to be found in Article 53 ("Initiation of an investigation") of the Rome Statute: "1. The Prosecutor shall, having evaluated the information made available to him or her, initiate an investigation unless he or she determines that there is no reasonable basis to proceed under this Statute. In deciding whether to initiate an investigation, the Prosecutor shall consider whether: (a) The information available to the Prosecutor provides a reasonable basis to believe that a crime within the jurisdiction of the Court has been or is being committed; (b) The case is or would be admissible under article 17; and (c) Taking into account the gravity of the crime and the interests of victims, there are nonetheless substantial reasons to believe that an investigation would not serve the interests of justice. If the Prosecutor determines that there is no reasonable basis to proceed and his or her determination is based solely on subparagraph (c) above, he or she shall inform the Pre-Trial Chamber. 2. If, upon investigation, the Prosecutor concludes that there is not a sufficient basis for a prosecution because: (a) There is not a sufficient legal or factual basis to seek a warrant or summons under article 58; (b) The case is inadmissible under article 17; or (c) A prosecution is not in the interests of justice, taking into account all the circumstances, including the gravity of the crime, the interests of victims and the age or infirmity of the alleged perpetrator, and his or her role in the alleged crime; the Prosecutor shall inform the Pre-Trial Chamber and the State making a referral under article 14 or the Security Council in a case under article 13, paragraph (b), of his or her conclusion and the reasons for the conclusion. 3. (a) At the request of the State making a referral under article 14 or the Security Council under article 13, paragraph (b), the Pre-Trial Chamber may review a decision of the Prosecutor under paragraph 1 or 2 not to proceed and may request the Prosecutor to reconsider that decision. (b) In addition, the Pre-Trial Chamber may, on its own initiative, review a decision of the Prosecutor not to proceed if it is based solely on paragraph 1 (c) or 2 (c). In such a case, the decision of the Prosecutor shall be effective only if confirmed by the Pre-Trial Chamber. 4. The Prosecutor may, at any time, reconsider a decision whether to initiate an investigation or prosecution based on new facts or information". On Article 53, see Bergsmo and Kruger 1999, pp. 701–714.

provides that the Prosecutor must obtain the Pre-Trial Division's authorisation in the absence of a determination by the Security Council in accordance with Article 15—and thereby indirectly confirms that no such authorisation is required where there exists a positive determination by the Security Council of the existence of an act of aggression, whether prior to or following the Prosecutor's notification addressed to the Secretary-General of the United Nations.

In turn, an inverse interpretation of Article 15 bis (7) suggests that the Prosecutor should, as a matter of practicality, not proceed with an investigation where the Security Council determines that no act of aggression has been committed by the State concerned. Although a determination of an act of aggression by an organ outside the Court—including, theoretically, by the Security Council—is, in accordance with para 9 of Article 15 bis, without prejudice to the Court's own findings under the Statute (see infra 5.3.2.9), the Prosecutor's decision to proceed with an investigation despite the Security Council's negative determination regarding the existence of an act of aggression would almost surely prompt the Security Council to defer the investigation in accordance with Article 16 (see infra 5.3.2.8).

5.3.2.8 Implicit Consent by the Security Council to an Investigation in Respect of an Alleged Crime of Aggression

Given that the Security Council has, in the past, only rarely determined the existence of acts of aggression (see supra 1.2.5.2), it is not impossible that the Council would continue refraining from making such public determinations, as a matter of policy. In order to increase the degree of the ICC's relative (cf. infra 5.3.2.9) independence from the Security Council as far as the exercise of the Court's jurisdiction with respect to the crime of aggression is concerned, the following provision was adopted as para 8 of Article 15 bis:

> 8. Where no such determination is made within six months after the date of notification, the Prosecutor may proceed with the investigation in respect of a crime of aggression, provided that the Pre-Trial Division has authorized the commencement of the investigation in respect of a crime of aggression in accordance with the procedure contained in article 15, and the Security Council has not decided otherwise in accordance with article 16.[162]

Article 15 bis (8) allows for a six-month period to let the Security Council assess the information and documents attached to the Prosecutor's notification addressed to the Secretary-General of the United Nations (see supra 5.3.2.6) and react to that notification by adopting a corresponding resolution. It follows from this provision that the Prosecutor must be prepared to wait for such a resolution for a maximum of six months after the date of notification, after which he or she might proceed—in the absence of a negative determination by the

[162] Cf. Safferling 2012, p. 92. See also Kemp 2010, pp. 227–231.

Security Council—with the investigation in respect of a crime of aggression on the basis of available evidence (which he or she might certainly continue collecting while expecting the Security Council's reaction). As the Security Council bears the primary responsibility for the maintenance of international peace and security, to which an alleged act of aggression would constitute the most important threat (see supra 1.2.5.2), the Council should not normally fail to react to the Prosecutor's notification and provide a response within six months. It is submitted that the absence of a negative determination by the Security Council within six-month period should be presumed to constitute an implicit approval of the Prosecutor's assessment of the situation in question by the Security Council and a tacit authorisation to proceed with an investigation in respect of the alleged crime of aggression in accordance with the procedure contained in Article 15. The Prosecutor would still have to obtain the Pre-Trial Division's (in the language of Article 15—the Pre-Trial Chamber's) authorisation to commence the investigation, because of the *tacit* nature of the Security Council's approval—if the Security Council reacted to the Prosecutor's notification by a positive determination of the existence of an act of aggression, the Prosecutor might proceed with an investigation in accordance with the benign procedure laid down in Article 15 bis (7) (see supra 5.3.2.7).

5.3.2.9 The ICC's Relative Autonomy in Determining the Existence of an Act of Aggression

Paragraph 9 of Article 15 bis lays down the International Criminal Court's relative autonomy in determining the existence of an act of aggression[163]:

> 9. A determination of an act of aggression by an organ outside the Court shall be without prejudice to the Court's own findings under this Statute.

It appears that this provision refers both to international organs and national authorities. As was discussed above (see supra 1.2.5.2–1.2.5.4), the Security Council is not the only international organ, which may determine the existence of an act of aggression, although it is the Security Council's *primary* responsibility to do so. Among the organs of the United Nations, especially the General Assembly and the International Court of Justice may, in certain circumstances, determine the existence of an act of aggression. Some international organisations—such as the North Atlantic Treaty Organisation (NATO) or the Collective Security Treaty Organisation (CSTO)—may, as well, be expected to officially pronounce themselves to the effect. It is clear that such statements should be regarded as expressions of official positions of the relevant organisations' Member States and may not necessarily be shared

[163] See Barriga 2012, at 30–31. However, as was discussed above at 5.3.2.6–5.3.2.8, the Security Council is capable of exercising both direct and indirect influence upon the ICC proceedings relating to the crime of aggression, and hence the ICC's autonomy must be regarded as relative.

by other—intergovernmental or non-governmental—international actors. As far as national organs authorised to express official positions of States with respect to the use of force, including alleged acts of aggression, are concerned, these include, first of all, Heads of States and governments, Ministers of Defence and Foreign Affairs, as well as national judicial authorities involved in adjudicating criminal cases on charges of aggression or other crimes against peace. The ICC organs might take such opinions into consideration but none of them would be bound to accept any such opinions as binding. It appears that the autonomy of the ICC's assessment derives from the Statute's rules on complementarity (see supra 5.3.1).

5.3.2.10 Exercise of Jurisdiction with Respect to Other Crimes Within the ICC Jurisdiction

Finally, paragraph 10 of Article 15 bis stipulates that the special rules contained in that article shall only apply to the exercise of the ICC's jurisdiction with respect to the crime of aggression, and shall not affect the general jurisdictional regime applicable to other crimes referred to in Article 5 of the Rome Statute[164]:

> 10. This article is without prejudice to the provisions relating to the exercise of jurisdiction with respect to other crimes referred to in article 5.

At least, two important conclusions are to be drawn from Article 15 bis (10). First, the States Parties to the Rome Statute agree that the entry into force of the jurisdictional regime applicable to the crime of aggression is a matter of the future (see supra 5.3.2.2–5.3.2.3), and this process should not prevent the ICC from continuing to normally exercise jurisdiction with respect to the crime of genocide, crimes against humanity and war crimes. This means, *inter alia*, that if an international armed conflict occurs with the involvement of one or more States Parties to the Rome Statute before the entry into force of Articles 8 bis and 15 bis (and 15 ter, see infra 5.3.3), the ICC might assert its jurisdiction with respect to those three types of crimes, with due regard to the principle of complementarity, and the absence of jurisdiction with respect to the crime of aggression should not affect that capacity of the Court. Second, once Articles 8 bis, 15 bis and 15 ter enter into force, the procedure for asserting the International Criminal Court's jurisdiction with respect to the crimes referred to in Articles 6, 7 and 8 shall be distinct from that applicable to the crime laid down in Article 8 bis. More precisely, the Prosecutor would be able to proceed with investigations with respect to alleged crimes of genocide, crimes against humanity or war crimes in accordance with general rules laid down in the Rome Statute, whereas with respect to an alleged crime of aggression the Prosecutor should first have to ascertain whether the Security Council has made a determination of the existence an act of aggression, notify the Secretary-General of the situation before the Court, and proceed with due regard to the Security Council's reaction (cf. supra 5.3.2.6–5.3.2.8).

---

[164] See Barriga 2012, at 33.

5.3.3 Security Council Referral (Article 15 ter)

The First Review Conference also adopted Article 15 ter, which relates to the Security Council referral as a ground for the exercise of the ICC's jurisdiction over the crime of aggression.[165] This provision constitutes a *lex specialis* with respect to Article 13(b) of the Rome Statute,[166] and restates some of the provisions of Article 15 bis:

1. The Court may exercise jurisdiction over the crime of aggression in accordance with article 13, paragraph (b), subject to the provisions of this article.
2. The Court may exercise jurisdiction only with respect to crimes of aggression committed one year after the ratification or acceptance of the amendments by thirty States Parties.
3. The Court shall exercise jurisdiction over the crime of aggression in accordance with this article, subject to a decision to be taken after 1 January 2017 by the same majority of States Parties as is required for the adoption of an amendment to the Statute.
4. A determination of an act of aggression by an organ outside the Court shall be without prejudice to the Court's own findings under this Statute.
5. This article is without prejudice to the provisions relating to the exercise of jurisdiction with respect to other crimes referred to in article 5.[167]

As concise as Article 15 ter is, it establishes a *sui generis* jurisdictional *modus operandi*, which may be expected to be more practicable than that laid down in Article 15 bis (see infra 5.3.2). The *ratione temporis* rules of Article 15 ter (paras 2 and 3) are identical to those of Article 15 bis (see supra 5.3.2.2 and 5.3.2.3). Likewise, Article 15 ter confirms the International Criminal Court's autonomy of normative assessment of alleged acts of aggression (para 4, cf. supra 5.3.2.9) and separate jurisdictional treatment of related individual crimes (para 5, cf. supra 5.3.2.10). However, the jurisdictional *modus operandi* under Article 15 ter does differ from that established by Article 15 bis, by virtue of the absence in Article 15 ter of several procedural provisions, which are present in Article 15 bis. The most obvious differences are: (1) the irrelevance of the non-recognition of amendments to the Rome Statute contained in Articles 8 bis (cf. supra 5.1.2), 15 bis (cf. supra 5.3.2.2) and 15 ter by States Parties; (2) the irrelevance of opt-out declarations made by States Parties under Article 15 bis (4) (cf. supra 5.3.2.4); (3) the irrelevance of a State's non-participation in the Statute (cf. supra 5.3.2.5)[168]; and (4) a different procedure to be followed by the Prosecutor (cf. supra 5.3.2.6–5.3.2.8). In

---

[165] Cf. supra note 145 for a note on the entry of Article 15 ter into force.

[166] See ICC Statute, Article 13 ("Exercise of jurisdiction"): "The Court may exercise its jurisdiction with respect to a crime referred to in article 5 in accordance with the provisions of this Statute if: [...](b) A situation in which one or more of such crimes appears to have been committed is referred to the Prosecutor by the Security Council acting under Chapter VII of the Charter of the United Nations; [...]" On Article 13(b), see Safferling 2012, pp. 88–90; Williams 1999, at 350.

[167] On this "less complicated procedure" of triggering the ICC jurisdiction with respect to the crime of aggression, cf. Safferling 2012, p. 92.

[168] Cf. document RC/Res. 6, Annex III: "2. It is understood that the Court shall exercise jurisdiction over the crime of aggression on the basis of a Security Council referral in accordance with article 13, paragraph (b), of the Statute irrespective of whether the State concerned has accepted the Court's jurisdiction in this regard".

other words, in the case of a Security Council referral, the ICC *would* have jurisdiction with respect to an alleged crime of aggression irrespective of the circumstances referred to in the first three points, by virtue of the Council's acting under Chapter VII of the Charter of the United Nations, and the States concerned would have to comply with the Security Council's referral as Members of the United Nations.[169] As far as the applicable procedure is concerned, clearly, no notification of the Secretary-General of the situation before the Court (cf. supra 5.3.2.6) and no authorisation on the part of the Pre-Trial Chamber (cf. supra 5.3.2.8) would be required, and the Prosecutor would have to proceed in accordance with Article 53 of the Statute (cf. supra note 161).

5.4 The Elements of Crimes for the Crime of Aggression

The amendments to the Elements of crimes pertaining to the crime of aggression for the purpose of the ICC are contained in Annex II to Resolution 6 adopted by the First Review Conference.[170] In accordance with Article 9(1) of the Rome Statute,[171] the Elements of crimes should assist the organs of the ICC in the interpretation and application of, *inter alia*, Article 8 bis, and, pursuant to para 3 of of the same Article, the Elements of crimes and amendments thereto—including those made at the First Review Conference—must be consistent with the ICC Statute. Like the Elements of the other crimes within the jurisdiction of the Court,[172] the Elements of the crime of aggression consist of an Introduction and the Elements proper:

---

[169] Cf. Article 24(1) of the UN Charter: "In order to ensure prompt and effective action by the United Nations, its Members confer on the Security Council primary responsibility for the maintenance of international peace and security, *and agree that in carrying out its duties under this responsibility the Security Council acts on their behalf*" (emphasis added).

[170] On the Elements of the crime of aggression, see Anggadi et al. 2012, pp. 58–80. Since it was theoretically possible that the ICC jurisdiction with respect to the crime of aggression might have been activated right after the adoption of relevant amendments to the Rome Statute, having Elements of the crime of aggression adopted together with those amendments was considered useful. See Anggadi et al. 2012, at 59.

[171] ICC Statute, Article 9 ("Elements of crimes"), as amended by para 6 of Resolution 6 of the First Review Conference: "1. Elements of Crimes shall assist the Court in the interpretation and application of articles 6, 7, 8 and 8 bis. They shall be adopted by a two-thirds majority of the members of the Assembly of States Parties. 2. Amendments to the Elements of Crimes may be proposed by: (a) Any State Party; (b) The judges acting by an absolute majority; (c) The Prosecutor. Such amendments shall be adopted by a two-thirds majority of the members of the Assembly of States Parties. 3. The Elements of Crimes and amendments thereto shall be consistent with this Statute". On the Elements of crimes, see Pellet 2002, at 1059–1062.

[172] The text of the Elements of crimes is available at: http://www.icc-cpi.int/Menus/ICC/Legal+Texts+and+Tools/Official+Journal/Elements+of+Crimes.htm (last accessed 15 November 2012).

Introduction[173]

1. It is understood that any of the acts referred to in article 8 bis, paragraph 2, qualify as an act of aggression.[174]
2. There is no requirement to prove that the perpetrator has made a legal evaluation as to whether the use of armed force was inconsistent with the Charter of the United Nations.
3. The term "manifest" is an objective qualification.
4. There is no requirement to prove that the perpetrator has made a legal evaluation as to the "manifest" nature of the violation of the Charter of the United Nations.

Elements

1. The perpetrator planned, prepared, initiated or executed an act of aggression.[175]
2. The perpetrator was a person[176] in a position effectively to exercise control over or to direct the political or military action of the State which committed the act of aggression.[177]
3. The act of aggression—the use of armed force by a State against the sovereignty, territorial integrity or political independence of another State, or in any other manner inconsistent with the Charter of the United Nations—was committed.
4. The perpetrator was aware of the factual circumstances that established that such a use of armed force was inconsistent with the Charter of the United Nations.[178]
5. The act of aggression, by its character, gravity and scale, constituted a manifest violation of the Charter of the United Nations.[179]
6. The perpetrator was aware of the factual circumstances that established such a manifest violation of the Charter of the United Nations.

It is submitted that the Elements of the crime of aggression, as they are, might require a number of improvements. First, it appears that it would have been more appropriate to entirely devote the Introduction to the State act of aggression in the sense of Article 8 bis (2) (see supra 5.1.1.2–5.1.1.3), i.e. to the objective "context of organised violence" of an alleged individual crime of aggression in the sense of Article 8 bis (1) (see supra 5.1.1.1),[180] and to provide the details of such an individual crime as well as of the rapport between an act of aggression and the crime,

---

173 On the Introduction to the Elements of the crime of aggression, see Anggadi et al. 2012, at 77–79.

174 On the reflection of a State act of aggression in the Elements of a crime of aggression, see Anggadi et al. 2012, at 68–71.

175 On the reflection of individual conduct in the Elements of the crime of aggression, see Anggadi et al. 2012, at 64–66.

176 A footnote to this paragraph reads as follows: "With respect to an act of aggression, more than one person may be in a position that meets these criteria".

177 On the leadership requirement in the Elements of the crime of aggression, see Anggadi et al. 2012, at 66–68. See also Werle 2009b, at 414.

178 On the reflection of the mental element in the Elements of the crime of aggression, see Anggadi et al. 2012, at 71–75.

179 On the material and mental elements of the threshold requirement, see Anggadi et al. 2012, at 75–77. See also Kemp 2010, p. 237.

180 On the context of organised violence, see Werle 2009a, p. 141.

in the Elements. The current edition of the text, whereby distinct constituents of a State act of aggression are contained both in the Introduction and the Elements, appears to be somewhat incoherent, and grouping them together in the Introduction would have been more articulate.

Second, the Elements repeat, in paras 1 and 2, the logical ambiguity contained in Article 8 bis with respect to the subject(s) capable of committing an act of aggression, whereby para 1 names "the perpetrator", i.e. a *natural person*, as such a (grammatical and legal) subject, and para 2 indicates that the act of aggression is committed by a *State*. It is unclear how the ICC organs would interpret this ambiguity in their future practice, and to which extent it would have a practical relevance, but viewing natural persons—the subjects of the individual crime—also as the primary subjects of an act of aggression and the respective State as the secondary one could be a possible solution (see supra 5.1.1.1).

At the same time, it is noted with approval that the Elements do not require the perpetrator to have made a legal evaluation as to whether the allegedly aggressive use of armed force was inconsistent with the Charter of the United Nations (Introduction, para 2), as well as to the "manifest" nature of such a violation of the Charter (Introduction, para 4), but only require the perpetrator to be aware of the factual circumstances that established the inconsistency of the use of force with the Charter (Elements, para 4) and the manifest nature of the alleged violation of the Charter (Elements, para 6). In other words, the perpetrator is not required or presumed to have any professional knowledge of the Charter of the United Nations (cf. supra Chap. 2), so as to assess his or her conduct against the background of its provisions, and his or her individual conscience must only embrace (cf. supra 4.5) the objective qualifications of circumstances surrounding an alleged act of aggression (cf. supra 5.1.1.2–5.1.1.3), whereas appropriate legal evaluations are to be made by the organs of the International Criminal Court in the course of (trial) proceedings. It is believed that this emphasis upon objective qualifications of an alleged act of aggression (see supra 5.1.1.2), and the absence of more specific regulations of the related crime's mental element deviating from Article 30 of the Rome Statute (cf. supra 4.5 and 5.2.9), should serve the purpose of prosecuting defendants more fairly, especially when dealing with various defences of a subjective nature (see supra 5.2.10–5.2.12).

References

Adhami W (2007) The strategic importance of the Internet for armed insurgent groups in modern warfare. IRRC 89:857–878

Akande D (2003) The jurisdiction of the International Criminal Court over nationals of non-parties: legal basis and limits. JICJ 1:618–650

Amann DM, Sellers MNS (2002) The United States of America and the International Criminal Court. AJCL 50:381–404

Ambos K (1999) Article 25: Individual criminal responsibility. In: Triffterer O (ed.) Commentary on the Rome statute of the International Criminal Court: observers' notes, article by article, Nomos Verlagsgesellschaft, pp 475–492

Ambos K (2005) Strafrecht und Krieg: strafbare Beteiligung der Bundesregierung am Irak-Krieg? In: Arnold J et al. (eds.) Menschengerechtes Strafrecht: Festschrift für Albin Eser, pp 671-690
Ambos K (2006) Remarks on the general part of international criminal law. JICJ 4:660–673
Ambos K (2007) Joint criminal enterprise and command responsibility. JICJ 5:159–183
Ambos K (2010) The crime of aggression after Kampala. German YIL 53:463–509
Anderson M (2010) Reconceptualizing aggression. Duke LJ 60:411–451
Anggadi F, French G, Potter J (2012) Negotiating the elements of the crime of aggression. In: Barriga S, Kreß C (eds.) The travaux préparatoires of the crime of aggression, Cambridge University Press, Cambridge, pp 58–80
Arnold R (2002) Command responsibility: a case study of alleged violations of the laws of war at Khiam detention centre. JCSL 7:191–231
Bantekas I (1999) The contemporary law of superior responsibility. AJIL 93:573–595
Barriga S (2012) Negotiating the amendments on the crime of aggression. In: Barriga S, Kreß C (eds.) The travaux préparatoires of the crime of aggression, Cambridge University Press, Cambridge, pp 3–80
Bergsmo M, Kruger P (1999) Article 53: Initiation of an investigation. In: Triffterer O (ed.) Commentary on the Rome Statute of the International Criminal Court: observers' Notes, Article by Article, Nomos Verlagsgesellschaft, pp 701–714
Best G (1994) War and law since 1945. Clarendon Press, Oxford
Bing JB (2004) The doctrine of command responsibility revisited. Chinese JIL 3:1–42
Blokker N (2007) The crime of aggression and the United Nations Security council. Leiden JIL 20:867–894
Bogush GI (2009) Obshchie printsipy ugolovnogo prava v Rimskom statute Mejdunarodnogo ugolovnogo suda. ["The General Principles of Criminal Law in the Rome Statute of the International Criminal Court"]. In: Bogush GI, Trikoz EN (eds.) Mejdunarodnoe ugolovnoe pravosudie: sovremennye problemy [International Criminal Justice: Contemporary Issues], Moscow, pp 78–94
Bolton JR (2001) The risks and weaknesses of the International Criminal Court from America's perspective. LCP 64:167–180
Bonafé BE (2007) Finding a proper role for command responsibility. JICJ 5:599–618
Brown BS (1999) U.S. objections to the statute of the International Criminal Court: a brief response. ILP 31:855–891
Burghardt B (2010) Modes of participation and their role in a general concept of crimes under international law. In: Burchard C, Triffterer O, Vogel J (eds.) The review conference and the future of the International Criminal Court: proceedings of the First AIDP symposium for young penalists in Tübingen, Germany, co-organized by the AIDP YP Committee, Wolters Kluwer Law & Business, Carl Heymanns Verlag, pp 81–94
Cameron L (2006) Private military companies: their status under international humanitarian law and its impact on their regulation. IRRC 88:573–598
Carcano A (2002) Sentencing and the gravity of the offence in international criminal law. ICLQ 51:583–609
Cassese A (2008) International criminal law, 2nd edn. Oxford University Press, Oxford
Chauprade A (2003) Géopolitique: constantes et changements dans l'histoire. Ellipses, Paris
Chouliaras A (2010) State Crime and individual criminal responsibility: theoretical inquiries and practical consequences. In: Burchard C, Triffterer O, Vogel J (eds.) The review conference and the future of the International Criminal Court: proceedings of the First AIDP symposium for young penalists in Tübingen, Germany, co-organized by the AIDP YP Committee, Wolters Kluwer Law & Business, Carl Heymanns Verlag, pp 191–214
Clark RS (1999) "Article 121: Amendments". In: Triffterer O (ed.) Commentary on the Rome Statute of the International Criminal Court: observers' notes, article by article, Nomos Verlagsgesellschaft, pp 1265–1271
Clark RS (2009) Ambiguities in articles 5(2), 121 and 123 of the Rome Statute. Case Western Res JIL 41:413–427

Cockayne J (2006) The global reorganization of legitimate violence: military entrepreneurs and the private face of international humanitarian law. IRRC 88:459–490
Cottier M (2006) Elements for contracting and regulating private security and military companies. IRRC 88:637–663
Creegan E (2012) Justified uses of force and the crime of aggression. JICJ 10:59–82
Cryer R (2001) The boundaries of liability in international criminal law, or 'selectivity by stealth'. JCSL 6:3–31
Danner AM (2003) Enhancing the legitimacy and accountability of prosecutorial discretion at the International Criminal Court. AJIL 97:510–552
David É (2009) Éléments de droit pénal international et européen. Bruylant
David E (2011) Printsipy prava voorujennyh konfliktov [Principles of the Law of Armed Conflicts], 2nd edn. Moscow, ICRC
Degan VD (2005) On the sources of international criminal law. Chinese JIL 4:45–83
Deen-Racsmany Z (2001) The nationality of the offender and the jurisdiction of the International Criminal Court. AJIL 9:606–623
DeNicola CP (2008) A shield for the "Knights of Humanity": the ICC should adopt a humanitarian necessity defence to the crime of aggression. UPJIL 30:641–689
Draft articles on Responsibility of States for Internationally Wrongful Acts with commentaries (2001) Yearbook of the International Law Commission, vol II (Part Two)
Drumbl MA (2009) A push to criminalize aggression: something lost amid the gains? Case Western Reserve JIL 41:291–319
Edlin DE (2006) The anxiety of sovereignty: Britain, the United States and the International Criminal Court. BCICLR 29:1–22
Elshtain JB (2001) The third annual Grotius lecture: just war and humanitarian intervention. Am Univ Int Law Rev 17:1–25
Engelhart M (2010) International criminal responsibility of corporations. In: Burchard C, Triffterer O, Vogel J (eds.) The review conference and the future of the International Criminal Court: Proceedings of the First AIDP symposium for young penalists in Tübingen, Germany, co-organized by the AIDP YP Committee, Wolters Kluwer Law & Business, Carl Heymanns Verlag, pp 175–190
Escarameia P (2004) The ICC and the Security Council on aggression: overlapping competencies? In: Politi M, Nesi G (eds.) The International Criminal Court and the crime of aggression. Ashgate Publishing Limited, pp 133–143
Eser A (1999) Article 31: grounds for excluding criminal responsibility. In: Triffterer O (ed.) Commentary on the Rome statute of the International Criminal Court: Observers' Notes, article by Article, Nomos Verlagsgesellschaft, pp 537–554
Eser A (2002) Individual criminal responsibility. In: Cassese A, Gaeta P, Jones JRWD (eds.) The Rome statute of the International Criminal Court: a commentary. Oxford University Press, Oxford vol I, pp 767–822
Fallah K (2006) Corporate actors: the legal status of mercenaries in armed conflict. IRRC 88:599–611
Ferencz BB (2003) Misguided fears about the International Criminal Court. Pace ILR 15:223–246
Ferencz BB (2009) Ending impunity for the crime of aggression. Case Western Reserve JIL 41:379–390
Fletcher GP, Ohlin JD (2006) The ICC—two courts in one? JICJ 4:428–433
Frank TM, Yuhan SH (2003) The United States and the International Criminal Court: unilateralism Rampant. ILP 35:519–558
Gaeta P (1999) The defence of superior orders: the statute of the International Criminal Court *vs* customary international law. EJIL 10:172–191
Gaja G (2004) The respective roles of the ICC and the Security Council in determining the existence of aggression. In: Politi M, Nesi G (eds.) The International Criminal Court and the crime of aggression, Ashgate Publishing Limited, pp225–227
Gillard EC (2006) Business goes to war: private military/security companies and international humanitarian law. IRRC 88:525–572

Glennon M (2010) The blank-prose crime of aggression. Yale JIL 35:71–114
Green LC (1976) Superior orders in national and international law. A. W. Sijthoff International Publishing Company, Leiden
Hauck P (2008) The challenge of customary international crimes to the principle of *Nullum Crimen Sine Lege*. HuV-I 21:58–65
Heller KJ (2012) The uncertain legal status of the aggression understandings. JICJ 10:229–248
Henham R (2003) Some issues for sentencing in the International Criminal Court. The ICLQ 52:81–114
Inogamova-Hegay LV (2003) Mejdunarodnoe ugolovnoe pravo [International Criminal Law]. Yuridicheskiy Centre, Moscow
International Military Tribunal (Nuremberg), Judgment of 1 October 1946. In: The trial of German major war criminals. In: Proceedings of the International Military Tribunal sitting at nuremberg, Germany, Part 22 (22nd August, 1946 to 1st October, 1946)
Juratowitch B (2005) Retroactive criminal liability and international human rights law. BYIL 76:337–362
Kemp G (2010) Individual criminal liability for the international crime of aggression. Intersentia
Kibalnik AG (2003) Sovremennoe mejdunarodnoe ugolovnoe pravo: ponyatie, zadachi i printsipy [The Contemporary International Criminal Law: Notion, Objectives and Principles]. Yuridicheskiy Centre, Moscow
Kielsgard MD (2012) The legality principle in sentencing at the ECCC: Making up law as it goes along? Asian JIL 2:119–136
Kirsch P, Robynson D (2002a) Referral by States Parties. In: Cassese A, Gaeta P, Jones JRWD (eds.) The Rome Statute of the International Criminal Court: a Commentary. Oxford University Press, Oxford, vol I, pp 619–625
Kirsch P, Robynson D (2002b) Initiation of proceedings by the prosecutor. In: Cassese A, Gaeta P, Jones JRWD (eds.) The Rome Statute of the International Criminal Court: a Commentary. Oxford University Press, Oxford, vol I, pp 657–664
Kok RA (2007) Statutory limitations in international criminal law. T.M.C Asser Press, The Hague
Kolosov YM, Kuzbetsov VI (eds.) (1998) Mejdunarodnoe pravo [International Law]. Moscow
Kreß C, Barriga S, Groover L, Von Holtzendorff L (2012) Negotiating the Understandings on the crime of aggression. In: Barriga S, Kreß C (eds.) The travaux préparatoires of the crime of aggression. Cambridge University Press, Cambridge pp 81–97
Krug P (2000) The emerging mental incapacity defense in international criminal law: some initial questions of implementation. AJIL 94:317–335
Lamb S (2002) Nullum crimen, nulla poena sine lege in international criminal law. In: Cassese A, Gaeta P, Jones JRWD (eds.) The Rome Statute of The International Criminal Court: a commentary. Oxford University Press, Oxford, vol I, pp 733–766
Latore RM (2002) Escape out the back door or charge in the front door: U.S. reactions to the International Criminal Court. BCICLR 25:159–176
Leclerc-Gagné E, Byers M (2009) A Question of intent: the crime of aggression and unilateral humanitarian intervention. Case Western Res JIL 41:379–390
Lehto M (2004) The ICC and the Security Council: about the argument of politicization. In: Politi M, Nesi G (eds.) The International Criminal Court and the crime of aggression, Ashgate Publishing Limited, pp 145–149
Lietzau WK (2001) International criminal law after Rome: concerns from a U.S. military perspective. LCP 64:119–140
Lijun Y (2005) On the principle of complementarity in the Rome statute of the International Criminal Court. Chinese JIL 4:121–132
Link W (1998) Die neuordnung der Weltpolitik an der Schwelle zum 21. Verlag C. H Beck OHG, Jahrhundert
Lovely R (2011) Cybercrime. In: Natarajan M (ed.) International crime and justice. Cambridge University Press, Cambridge, pp 155–161
Lukashuk II (2004) Sovremennoe pravo mejdunarodnyh dogovorov [The Contemporary Law of Treaties], vol I. Wolters Kluwer

Lukashuk II (2008) Mejdunarodnoe pravo: Obshchaya chast [International Law: General Part], 3rd edn. Wolters Kluwer

Martinez JS (2007) Understanding mens rea in command responsibility: from *Yamashita* to *Blaškić* and beyond. JICJ 5:638–664

Mathias S (2005) The United States and the Security Council. In: Blokker N, Schrijver N (eds.) The Security Council and the use of force: theory and reality—a need for change? Martinus Nijhoff Publishers, pp 173–188

McNerney P (2001) The International Criminal Court: issues for consideration by the United States senate. LCP 64:181–191

Meloni C (2007) Command responsibility: mode of liability for the crimes of subordinates or separate offence of the superior? JICJ 5:619–637

Milanovic M (2012) Aggression and legality: custom in Kampala. JICJ 10:165–187

Militello V (2007) The personal nature of individual criminal responsibility and the ICC statute. JICJ 5:941–952

Miller RH (1971) The Convention on the non-applicability of statutory limitations to war crimes and crimes against humanity. AJIL 65:476–501

Mongelard E (2006) Corporate civil liability for violations of international humanitarian law. IRRC 88:665–691

Nerlich V (2007) Superior responsibility under Article 28 ICC Statute: For what exactly is the superior held responsible? JICJ 5:665–682

O'Connell ME, Niyazmatov M (2012) What is aggression?: comparing the *Jus ad Bellum* and the ICC Statute. JICJ 10:189–207

O'Donovan M (2007) Criminalizing war: towards a justifiable crime of aggression. BCICLR 30:507–530

Ohlin JD (2007) Three conceptual problems with the doctrine of joint criminal enterprise. JICJ 5:69–90

Pellet A (2002) Applicable Law. In: Cassese A, Gaeta P, Jones JRWD (eds.) The Rome Statute of the International Criminal Court: a commentary, vol II. Oxford University Press, Oxford, pp 1051–1084

Perrin B (2006) Promoting compliance of private security and military companies with international humanitarian law. IRRC 88:613–635

Petty KA (2008) Sixty years in the making: the definition of aggression for the international criminal court. Hastings ICLR 31:1–24

Petty KA (2009) Criminalizing force: resolving the threshold question for the crime of aggression in the context of modern conflict. SULR 33:105–150

Pictet JS (1952) Commentary of the first Geneva convention for the amelioration of the condition of the wounded and sick in armed forces in the field. ICRC, Geneva

Piragoff DK (1999) Article 30: Mental element. In: Triffterer O (ed.) Commentary on the Rome Statute of the International Criminal Court: observers' notes, article by article, Nomos Verlagsgesellschaft, pp 527–535

Posner EA, Sykes AO (2007) An Economic analysis of state and individual responsibility under international law. ALER 9:1–63

Rosenfeld F (2012) Individual civil responsibility for the crime of aggression. JICJ 10:249–265

Safferling C (2012) International criminal procedure. Oxford University Press, Oxford

Sayapin S (2008) The definition of the crime of aggression for the purpose of the Rome Statute of the International Criminal Court: problems and perspectives. JCSL 13:333–352

Schabas WA (2000) Perverse effects of the *Nulla Poena* principle: national practice and the *Ad Hoc* Tribunals. EJIL 11:521–539

Schabas WA (2004) United States hostility to the International Criminal Court: it's all about the Security Council. EJIL 15:701–720

Scheffer DJ (1999) The United States and the International Criminal Court. AJIL 93:12–22

Schmitt MN (2002) Wired warfare: computer network attack and jus in bello. IRRC 84:365–399

Schüller A (2008) 'Gravity' under the Rome Statute: procedural filter or instrument of shaping criminal policy? HuV-I 21:73–81

Schuster M (2003) The Rome Statute of the ICC and the crime of aggression: a gordian knot in search of a sword. CLF 14:1–57

Smith R (2005) The utility of force: the art of war in the modern world. Allen Lane, London

Spinedi M (2002) State responsibility v. individual responsibility for international crimes: *Tertium Non Datur*? EJIL 13:895–899

Stein MS (2005) The Security Council, the International Criminal Court, and the crime of aggression: how exclusive is the Security Council's power to determine aggression? Indiana ICLR 16:1–36

Svinarev VV (2000) Pravovoe polojenie rossiyskih voennyh baz za rubejom ["The Legal Status of Russian Legal Bases Abroad"]. Moscow J Int Law 40:194–210

Van den Herik L (2010) Subjecting corporations to the ICC regime: analyzing the legal counter-arguments. In: Burchard C, Triffterer O, Vogel J (eds.) The review conference and the future of the International Criminal Court: proceedings of the First AIDP symposium for young penalists in Tübingen, Germany, co-organized by the AIDP YP Committee, Wolters Kluwer Law & Business, Carl Heymanns Verlag, pp 155–173

Van der Wilt H (2007) Joint criminal enterprise: possibilities and limitations. JICJ 5:91–108

Van Schaak B (2012) Par in Parem Imperium Non Habet: Complementarity and the crime of aggression. JICJ 10:133–164

Van S (2009) O vliyanii yurisdiktsii Mejdunarodnogo ugulovnogo suda na neuchastvuyushie gosudarstva ["On the Impact of the Jurisdiction of the International Criminal Court upon Non-State Parties"]. In: Bogush GI, Trikoz EN (eds.) Mejdunarodnoe ugolovnoe pravosudie: sovremennye problemy [International Criminal Justice: Contemporary Issues], Moscow, pp 511–521

Von Feuerbach PJA (2007) The foundations of criminal law and the *Nullum Crimen* principle. Reprinted in JICJ 5:1005–1008

Walzer M (2007) The crime of aggressive war. WUGSLR 6:635–643

Wegdwood R (2001) The irresolution of rome. LCP 64:193–214

Weigend T (2010) Superior responsibility: complicity, omission or over-extension of the criminal law? In: Burchard C, Triffterer O, Vogel J (eds.) The review conference and the future of the International Criminal Court: proceedings of the first AIDP symposium for young penalists in Tübingen, Germany, co-organized by the AIDP YP Committee, Wolters Kluwer Law & Business, Carl Heymanns Verlag, pp 67–80

Werle G (2007) Individual criminal responsibility in Article 25 ICC statute. JICJ 5:953–975

Werle G (2009a) Principles of international criminal law, 2nd edn. T. M. C Asser Press, The Hague

Werle G (2009b) The crime of aggression between international and domestic criminal law. In: Manacorda S, Nieto A (eds.) Criminal law between war and peace. Cuena, pp 405–421

Williams SA (1999) Exercise of jurisdiction. In: Triffterer O (ed.) Commentary on the Rome Statute of the International Criminal Court: observers' notes, article by article, Nomos Verlagsgesellschaft, pp 343–351

Wilmshurst E (2004) Definition of the crime of aggression: state responsibility or individual criminal responsibility? In: Politi M, Nesi G (eds.) The International Criminal Court and the crime of aggression. Ashgate Publishing Limited, pp 93–96

Yee S (2004) The *Tu Quoque* argument as a defence to international crimes, prosecution or punishment. Chinese JIL 3:87–134

Yengejeh SM (2004) Reflections on the role of the Security Council in determining an act of aggression. In: Politi M, Nesi G (eds.) The International Criminal Court and the crime of aggression. Ashgate Publishing Limited, pp 125–132

Zelinskaya NA, Dryomina-Volok NV (2010) Kontseptsiya prestupleniy po obshchemu mejdunarodnomu pravu v kontekste problemy retroaktivnogo primeneniya norm mejdunarodnogo ugolovnogo prava ["The Concept of Crimes under General International Law in the Context of the Problem of Retroactive Application of Norms of International Criminal Law"]. Almanach Int Law 2:189–209

Zimmermann A (1999) Article 124: transitional provision. In: Triffterer O (ed.) Commentary on the Rome Statute of the International Criminal Court: observers' notes, article by article, Nomos Verlagsgesellschaft, pp 1281–1285

Zimmermann A (2012) Amending the amendment provisions of the Rome Statute: the Kampala compromise on the crime of aggression and the law of treaties. JICJ 10:209–227

Zolo D (2007) Who is afraid of punishing aggressors? On the double-track approach to international criminal justice. JICJ 5:799–807

Zwanenburg M (1999) The statute for an international criminal court and the United States: peacekeepers under fire? EJIL 10:124–143

Chapter 6
Conclusion

Abstract This concise chapter summarizes, in twenty items, the main conclusions and recommendations of the book. Generally, it calls upon a further development of international—both conventional and customary—criminal law, with a view to a more effective prevention and, as the case may be in the future, repression of the crime of aggression.

Content

As a matter of the international and national law enforcement practice, the crime of aggression has been a "sleeping beauty" for more than 60 years now. After the successful—although somewhat imperfect—completion of the Nuremberg (see supra 3.1.1), Tokyo (see supra 3.1.2) and the Nuremberg follow-up trials (see supra 3.1.3), no one was prosecuted on these charges. The adoption of the Rome Statute of the International Criminal Court, on 17 July 1998, whereby the crime of aggression was included among the crimes within the jurisdiction of the ICC[1] (see supra 1.2.6.1), was an important development but its potential should not be exaggerated, because the ICC is—and would, in a foreseeable future, continue to be—functioning in the UN Charter-based system of international relations where States' power politics would, more than just occasionally, prevent individual prosecutions for crimes as politically coloured as the international crime of aggression

[1] ICC Statute, Article 5 ("Crimes within the jurisdiction of the Court"): "1. The jurisdiction of the Court shall be limited to the most serious crimes of concern to the international community as a whole. The Court has jurisdiction in accordance with this Statute with respect to the following crimes: (a) The crime of genocide; (b) Crimes against humanity; (c) War crimes; (d) The crime of aggression. 2. The Court shall exercise jurisdiction over the crime of aggression once a provision is adopted in accordance with articles 121 and 123 defining the crime and setting out the conditions under which the Court shall exercise jurisdiction with respect to this crime. Such a provision shall be consistent with the relevant provisions of the Charter of the United Nations".

S. Sayapin, *The Crime of Aggression in International Criminal Law*,
DOI: 10.1007/978-90-6704-927-6_6,

is. By way of summarizing the foregoing chapters' conclusions, the following observations and submissions are offered to readers' attention:

(1) The Nuremberg and Tokyo trials as well as the Nuremberg follow-up trials have been landmark developments in international law, among other things, with respect to the criminalization of aggression and other crimes against peace. They affected the development of customary international law on the subject and constitute the entirety of the case law on the subject to date. Yet, international law relating to the legality of the use of force continued developing after the Second World War, and its modern sources encompass, first of all, Article 2(4) of the UN Charter (see supra 2.1), other relevant provisions of the Charter (see supra 2.4.2) and other relevant international law (see supra 2.4.3). The provisions of international and national criminal law pertaining to the individual criminalization of internationally wrongful uses of force should therefore derive from these sources, if they are to be of a contemporary and workable nature.

(2) Article 2(4) of the Charter of the United Nations remains a rule of reference with respect to the use of force in international relations, owing to its *jus cogens* nature (see supra 2.1.3). The use of force should be a measure of last resort to be used in conformity with the Charter and other relevant sources of international law, and manifestly aggressive violations of Article 2(4) should entail legal consequences provided for violations of peremptory norms of general international law (see supra 2.1.3).

(3) In any event, States using force, first of all, in offence but also in defence must be prepared to judicially substantiate the use of force as a matter of applicable international and their national law (see supra 2.4.1.1.3–2.4.1.1.4). The role of, especially, the International Court of Justice could be instrumental in this regard (see supra 1.2.5.4). The role of the International Criminal Court would also become more prominent (see supra Chap. 5), once the relevant provisions of its Statute enter into force.

(4) Even though the theories of anticipatory self-defence (see supra 2.4.1.2–2.4.1.3) do represent certain dangers related to the unilateral and subjective appraisal by a State of the existence and gravity of a threat to its security, it would seem irrational for a State to always wait until an armed attack occurs to invoke the right to individual or collective self-defence in the sense of Article 51 of the UN Charter. In the aftermath of 11 September 2001 (see supra 2.1.1.2.1 for some discussion), it appears that some States would favor more flexible interpretations of Article 51, in order for them to be able to better defend themselves and their nationals against military and physical dangers, including ones emanating from non-State actors.[2] It appears that at least some of these views are not entirely unfounded as a matter of international law. However, anticipatory

[2] See Franck 2002.

actions in self-defence should conform to the "just war" principles in their contemporary sense (see supra 1.1.2.3).

(5) Some more time would elapse until sufficiently comprehensive rules for the regulation of "extra-Charter" exceptions to the general prohibition of the use of force are produced. Among these, especially "humanitarian intervention" (see supra 2.4.3.2) should be placed in a clearer legal framework (probably, in the shape of an international treaty), so as to enable prompt and effective international military responses when such are required to defend civilian populations against massive violations of human rights. It is understood that such actions' only purpose must consist in the protection of civilian human groups against mass abuses—comparable in terms of gravity, scale, and nature to crimes against humanity—if their (exceptional) legitimacy is to be recognized.

(6) Likewise, States' claim to the entitlement to use military force to protect their nationals in the face of massive and discriminatory dangers abroad, if a host State is unable or unwilling to protect them, and there is a likelihood of success on the part of the State whose nationality the individuals requiring protection possess (see supra 2.4.3.1), requires a more inclusive regulation. It is submitted that such operations too may be regarded as exceptionally legitimate, as a measure of last resort, and that a State intervening in another State for this purpose must immediately withdraw, together with its rescued nationals, once an operation in question is over, in order not to forfeit this exceptional legitimacy.

(7) By contrast, the so-called "pro-democratic intervention" aimed at changing the political regime in a target State (see supra 2.4.3.3) may not be regarded as legitimate, as it violates the principle of nonintervention in the matters of States, which essentially are within their domestic jurisdiction.[3] Besides, it is not obvious that such interventions would reliably comply with the principle of equal rights and self-determination of peoples (see supra 2.1.1.1, 2.1.3.2, 2.2), despite their declared aims.

(8) Any deliberate and comprehensive use of force by a State that would not constitute a lawful exception to the prohibition of the use of force in international relations might potentially qualify as an act of aggression. In accordance with applicable international and national law, the planning, preparation, initiation, or execution of an act of aggression should entail its authors' individual criminal responsibility.

(9) The next important developments in international law with respect to the criminalization of aggression should be (in either order) the entry into force of Articles 8 bis (see supra 5.1, 5.1.2), 15 bis (see supra 5.3.2, 5.3.2.2) and 15 ter (see supra 5.3.3) of the Rome Statute, and the activation of the International Criminal Court's jurisdiction with respect to the crime

[3] UN Charter, Article 2(7): "Nothing contained in the present Charter shall authorize the United Nations to intervene in matters which are essentially within the domestic jurisdiction of any state or shall require the Members to submit such matters to settlement under the present Charter; but this principle shall not prejudice the application of enforcement measures under Chapter VII".

of aggression by a decision of the Assembly of States Parties to the Rome Statute (see supra 5.3.2.3). Once these measures have been taken, a provision of international criminal law, which was dormant since 1949, would be revived as a matter of law. It is not clear, however, to which extent it will be revived as a matter of practice.

(10) The International Criminal Court will not be able to exercise jurisdiction with respect to the crime of aggression, at least, until 1 January 2017 (see supra 5.3.2.3). During this period, international armed conflicts might occur, whose authors would not be subject to the International Criminal Court's jurisdiction. Not even the UN Security Council would be able to refer relevant situations to the ICC (see supra 5.3.3).

(11) Given the past practice of the ICC, the normative relationship between the Rome Statute and the Charter of the United Nations, and the functional relationship between the ICC and the UN Security Council (see supra 5.3.2.9), it is likely that prosecutions for the crime of aggression in the ICC—once the measures referred to above at p. 9 have been taken—would be limited to leaders of relatively weak States with no consistent or traditional allies among the permanent Members of the UN Security Council. No prosecutions at all would be possible against the leaders of the permanent Members and their allies, due to their veto power and the Security Council's right to defer an investigation or prosecution (see supra 5.3.2.8).

(12) As the International Criminal Court is a self-contained system of international criminal justice, it should be guided, in the administration of justice with respect to authors of alleged crimes of aggression, by its own material and procedural rules laid down in the Rome Statute and other relevant sources of international and national law.[4]

(13) Since the adoption, in June 2010, of a definition of the crime of aggression and of related procedural provisions for the purpose of the International Criminal Court should not preclude other, alternative, developments in international criminal law pertaining to the same subject (see supra Chap. 5, footnote 17), the International Law Commission and other relevant expert bodies and institutions—as well as individual experts representing all major legal

---

[4] ICC Statute, Article 21 ("Applicable law"): "1. The Court shall apply: (a) In the first place, this Statute, Elements of Crimes and its Rules of Procedure and Evidence; (b) In the second place, where appropriate, applicable treaties and the principles and rules of international law, including the established principles of the international law of armed conflict; (c) Failing that, general principles of law derived by the Court from national laws of legal systems of the world including, as appropriate, the national laws of States that would normally exercise jurisdiction over the crime, provided that those principles are not inconsistent with this Statute and with international law and internationally recognized norms and standards. 2. The Court may apply principles and rules of law as interpreted in its previous decisions. 3. The application and interpretation of law pursuant to this article must be consistent with internationally recognized human rights, and be without any adverse distinction founded on grounds such as gender as defined in article 7, paragraph 3, age, race, colour, language, religion or belief, political or other opinion, national, ethnic or social origin, wealth, birth or other status".

systems[5]—should be encouraged to continue researching the matter and publishing their findings.

(14) The role of the national criminal justice systems with respect to repressing the crime of aggression (see supra 4.1) should be continuously strengthened. States—both Parties to the ICC Statute and non-Parties—should remain seized of the matter, with a view to introducing and developing (existing) apposite regimes for criminalizing aggression.

(15) National laws criminalizing aggressive uses of force should be defined as clearly as possible, in accordance with the principle of legality (see supra 5.2.1). At the same time, the "threshold of violence" to be criminalized (acts of war vs. acts short of war) may vary from one State to another. Among the current legislative models of criminalizing aggression at the national level, the "objective war model" (see supra 4.1.3) appears to be the most comprehensive, and States should be encouraged to progressively adopt (further) national legislative acts for the criminalization of aggression and other crimes against peace, with due regard to their legal traditions and systems, with a view to restraining other States' potentially aggressive efforts.

(16) With due regard to social developments since the completion of the Nuremberg, Tokyo, and the follow-up trials, the range of individual subjects of a crime of aggression should not be limited to States' political and military leaders only (see supra 4.2.2–4.2.3). It may include, where appropriate, economic (see supra 4.2.4), religious and other social (see supra 4.2.5) leaders having genuine capacity to influence their State's political or military effort.

(17) It must be noted, though, that the possibility of prosecuting natural persons for the crime of aggression at the national level shall be limited by a number of factors. The alleged offenders' functional and personal immunities shall be the prime factor (see supra 4.6.1.2.1). The formalities of inter-State cooperation in judicial matters shall be another factor (see supra 4.6.1.2.2). Therefore, national trials on charges of aggression, where alleged offenders would be got hold of, are most likely to occur either as an immediate result of prospective defendants' capture by the winning side in an international armed conflict, or else later in the course of time after such an armed conflict, if an alleged offender is apprehended in a friendly State and, probably, handed over to a requesting State.

(18) Among the principles of establishing jurisdiction (at the national level) over an alleged crime of aggression, the territoriality, active and passive personality principles as well as the protective principle shall be of particular relevance (see supra 4.6.1.1).

(19) As concerns the other applicable provisions of the general part of national criminal law (e.g., the age of criminal responsibility, statutory limitations,

[5] The role of experts on Islamic law would be particularly pertinent, given the obvious underrepresentation of Islamic States in the Assembly of States Parties to the Rome Statute of the International Criminal Court. On elements of Islamic (international criminal) law in the Rome Statute, see Malekian 2011, pp. 341–408.

applicable penalties, etc.), the crime of aggression is subject to those, within applicable national legal frameworks, with due regard to specific regulations, which apply, *inter alia*, to crimes against the peace and security of mankind (see supra 4.6.1.1).

(20) Last but not least, the viability of the Rome Statute's new provisions on the crime of aggression would manifest itself in the course of time. At the present stage, it is indeed too early to remove them from the Statute.[6] Ultimately, the efficiency of existing and emerging rules of international and national criminal law pertaining to the crime of aggression shall express itself at two qualitative levels: (1) such rules must deter States' leaders from causing their States to use military force against other States in violation of international law, instead of using, as exhaustively as possible, means for the pacific settlement of international disputes and (2) they must serve as yardsticks for measuring the degree of such leaders' guilt, if these do contribute to the planning, preparation, initiation or execution of actual acts of aggression. In the first case, an indicator of relevant rules' efficiency would be the uninterrupted absence of an international armed conflict between given States, and in the second one, it would consist in the institution of appropriate investigations or prosecutions with regard to respective individuals.

References

1. Franck TM (2002) Recourse to force: state action against threats and armed attacks. Cambridge University Press, Cambridge
2. Haskos SN (2011) An argument for the deletion of the crime of aggression from the Rome statute of the international criminal court. Pace Int Law Rev 23:249–268
3. Malekian F (2011) Principles of Islamic international criminal law: a comparative study, 2nd edn. Brill

[6] Cf. Haskos 2011, 249–268.

Index

S. Sayapin, *The Crime of Aggression in International Criminal Law*,
DOI: 10.1007/978-90-6704-927-6, © T.M.C. ASSER PRESS and the author 2014

MIX
Papier aus verantwortungsvollen Quellen
Paper from responsible sources
FSC® C105338

If you have any concerns about our products,
you can contact us on
ProductSafety@springernature.com

In case Publisher is established outside the EU,
the EU authorized representative is:
Springer Nature Customer Service Center GmbH
Europaplatz 3, 69115 Heidelberg, Germany

Printed by Libri Plureos GmbH
in Hamburg, Germany